Financial Mathematics, Volatility and Covariance Modelling

This book provides an up-to-date series of advanced chapters on applied financial econometric techniques pertaining to the various fields of commodities finance, mathematics and stochastics, international macroeconomics, and financial econometrics.

Financial Mathematics, Volatility and Covariance Modelling: Volume 2 provides a key repository on the current state of knowledge, the latest debates, and recent literature on financial mathematics, volatility, and covariance modeling. Part 1 is devoted to mathematical finance, stochastic modeling, and control optimization. Chapters explore the recent financial crisis, the increase of uncertainty and volatility, and propose an alternative approach to deal with these issues. Part 3 covers financial volatility and covariance modeling and explores proposals for dealing with recent developments in financial econometrics.

This book will be useful to students and researchers in applied econometrics: academics and students seeking convenient access to an unfamiliar area. It will also be of great interest established researchers seeking a single repository on the current state of knowledge, current debates and relevant literature.

Julien Chevallier is Full Professor of Economics at the University Paris 8 (LED), France. He undertakes research and lectures on empirical finance, applied time-series econometrics, and commodity markets. He has published articles in leading refereed journals.

Stéphane Goutte is a Maître de Conférences-HDR of Financial Mathematics at University Paris 8, France and Senior Lecturer in Mathematics at University of Luxembourg. He is also a researcher at the Chair European Electricity Markets of Paris Dauphine PSL University.

David Guerreiro is an Assistant Professor of Economics at the University Paris 8 (LED), France. His fields of research are international macroeconomics, monetary economics, and meta-analysis, and he has published in numerous peer-reviewed journals.

Sophie Saglio is an Assistant Professor of Economics at the University Paris 8 (LED), France. Her research focuses on international economics and finance, and she has published in various peer-reviewed journals.

Bilel Sanhaji is an Assistant Professor of Economics at the University Paris 8 (LED), France. His main research focuses on nonlinear time series econometrics and modeling volatility. He has published theoretical and applied research papers in various peer-reviewed journals.

Routledge Advances in Applied Financial Econometrics
Julien Chevallier
University Paris 8, France

The Routledge Advances in Applied Financial Econometrics series brings together the latest research on econometric techniques and empirical cases in the fields of commodities finance, mathematics and stochastics, international macroeconomics and financial econometrics. It provides a single repository on the current state of knowledge, the latest debates and recent literature in the field.

International Financial Markets
Volume 1
*Edited by Julien Chevallier, Stéphane Goutte, David Guerreiro,
Sophie Saglio and Bilel Sanhaji*

Financial Mathematics, Volatility and Covariance Modelling
Volume 2
*Edited by Julien Chevallier, Stéphane Goutte, David Guerreiro,
Sophie Saglio and Bilel Sanhaji*

For more information about this series, please visit: www.routledge.com/Routledge-Advances-in-Applied-Financial-Econometrics/book-series/RAAFE

Financial Mathematics, Volatility and Covariance Modelling

Volume 2

Edited by Julien Chevallier, Stéphane Goutte, David Guerreiro, Sophie Saglio and Bilel Sanhaji

Routledge
Taylor & Francis Group

LONDON AND NEW YORK

First published 2019
by Routledge
2 Park Square, Milton Park, Abingdon, Oxon OX14 4RN

and by Routledge
605 Third Avenue, New York, NY 10017

First issued in paperback 2021

Routledge is an imprint of the Taylor & Francis Group, an informa business

British Library Cataloguing-in-Publication Data
A catalogue record for this book is available from the British Library

Library of Congress Cataloging-in-Publication Data
Names: Chevallier, Julien, editor.
Title: Financial mathematics, volatility and covariance modelling / edited by
   Julien Chevallier [and four others].
Description: Abingdon, Oxon ; New York, NY : Routledge, 2019. | Series:
   Routledge advances in applied financial econometrics ; Volume 2 | Includes
   bibliographical references and index.
Identifiers: LCCN 2019009498 (print) | LCCN 2019011684 (ebook) |
   ISBN 9781315162737 (Ebook) | ISBN 9781138060944 (hardback :
   alk. paper)
Subjects: LCSH: Finance—Mathematical models.
Classification: LCC HG106 (ebook) | LCC HG106 .F566 2019 (print) |
   DDC 332.01/5195—dc23
LC record available at https://lccn.loc.gov/2019009498

ISBN 13: 978-0-367-78558-1 (pbk)
ISBN 13: 978-1-138-06094-4 (hbk)

Typeset in Times New Roman
by Apex CoVantage, LLC

Contents

About the editors

Julien Chevallier is Full Professor of Economics at the University Paris 8 (LED). He undertakes research and lectures on empirical finance, applied time-series econometrics, and commodity markets. He has published articles in leading refereed journals, including the *Journal of Empirical Finance; International Review of Financial Analysis; Quantitative Finance; Journal of Forecasting; Journal of International Financial Markets, Institutions & Money*; and *Annals of Operations Research*.

Stéphane Goutte holds a Ph.D. in Mathematics. He is a Maître de Conférences-HDR of Financial Mathematics at University Paris 8 and Senior Lecturer in Mathematics at University of Luxembourg. He is also a researcher at the Chair European Electricity Markets of Paris Dauphine PSL University. He has several publications in peer-reviewed academic journals in the field of mathematical finance, theoretical probability, and energy economics.

David Guerreiro is an Assistant Professor of Economics at the University Paris 8 (LED). His fields of research are international macroeconomics, monetary economics, and meta-analysis. He has published in peer-reviewed journals such as *World Development, Journal of Macroeconomics, Economic Modelling, Journal of Economic Integration*, and the *Journal of International Trade and Economic Development*.

Sophie Saglio is an Assistant Professor of Economics at the University Paris 8 (LED). Her research focuses on international economics and finance. She has published in peer-reviewed journals including *Review of International Economics*, and *Oxford Bulletin of Economics and Statistics*.

Bilel Sanhaji is an Assistant Professor of Economics at the University Paris 8 (LED). His main research focuses on nonlinear time series econometrics and modeling volatility. He has published theoretical and applied research papers in peer-reviewed journals such as *Annals of Economics and Statistics* and *Applied Economics*.

Contributors

René Aïd
Université Paris-Dauphine, PSL Research University, LEDa.

Cristina Amado
University of Minho and NIPE, CREATES and Aarhus University. camado@eeg.uminho.pt

Denisa Banulescu-Radu
LEO, University of Orléans, CNRS, 45067 Orléans, France. denisa.banulescu-radu@univ-orleans.fr

Luciano Campi
Statistics Department, London School of Economics. Postal address: Statistics Department, Columbia House, London School of Economics and Political Science, 10 Houghton Street, London WC2A2AE. Email: l.campi@lse.ac.uk

Jonathan Chavez-Casillas
The University of Calgary, Canada.

Steven J. Cochran
Associate Professor of Finance, Department of Finance, Villanova School of Business, Villanova University, Villanova, PA, USA

Antonio Cosma
CREA, University of Luxembourg, Luxembourg

Gianluca Cubadda
Universita' di Roma "Tor Vergata", Dipartimento di Economia e Finanza, Via Columbia 2, 00133 Roma, Italy. Email: gianluca.cubadda@uniroma2.it

Elena Dumitrescu
EconomiX, UPL, Univ. Paris Nanterre, CNRS, F92000. Nanterre, France. elena.dumitrescu@parisnanterre.fr

Robert Elliott
University of Calgary, Canada, University of South Australia, Australia.

Fausto Galli
DISES and CELPE, University of Salerno. Corresponding author. Address: Dipartimento di Scienze Economiche e Statistiche (DISES), Campus di Fisciano,

Universita degli Studi di Salerno, Via Giovanni Paolo II 132, 84084 Fisciano (SA), Italy. Email: fgalli@unisa.it, Phone: +39 089 96 8154.

Alain Hecq
Maastricht University, Department of Quantitative Economics, P.O.Box 616, 6200 MD Maastricht, The Netherlands. Email: a.hecq@maastrichtuniversity.nl

Menelaos Karanasos
Brunel University, London, UK

Yuta Koike
Graduate School of Mathematical Sciences, University of Tokyo: 3-8-1 Komaba, Meguro-ku, Tokyo 153-8914, Japan. CREST, Japan Science and Technology Agency. e-mail: kyuta@ms.u-tokyo.ac.jp

Panagiotis Koutroumpis
Queen Mary University, London, UK

Konstantin Kuck
University of Hohenheim, Germany
E-mail address: konstantin.kuck@uni-hohenheim.de (K. Kuck).

Delphine Lautier
Université Paris Dauphine, PSL Research University, DRM UMR CNRS 7088, and FiME Lab - Laboratoire de Finance des Marchés d'Energie.

Robert Maderitsch
Daimler AG, Germany

Iqbal Mansur
Professor of Finance, School of Business Administration, Widener University, Chester, PA, USA

Zannis Margaronis
RGZ Ltd., UK

Iuliana Matei
Economics Department, IESEG-Paris and University Paris 1 Panthéon-Sorbonne, France. Emails: i.matei@ieseg.fr and iuliana.matei@malix.univ-paris1.fr

Rajat Nath
RGZ Ltd., UK

Babatunde Odusami
School of Business Administration, Widener University, USA

Bruno Remillard
HEC Montréal, Québec, Canada.

Antonio Riccardo
ICE Data Services Italy, Via Cristoforo Colombo, 149, 00147 Rome, Italy. Email: a.riccardo90@gmail.com

Annastiina Silvennoinen
School of Economics and Finance, Queensland University of Technology. silvennoinen@qut.edu.au

Genaro Sucarrat
Department of Economics, BI Norwegian Business School, Nydalsveien 37, 0484 Oslo, Norway. Email: genaro.sucarrat@bi.no, phone +47+46410779, fax +47+23264788. Webpage: http://www.sucarrat.net/

Anatoliy Swishchuk
University of Calgary, Canada.

Timo Teräsvirta
CREATES and Aarhus University, C.A.S.E., Humboldt-Universität zu Berlin. tterasvirta@econ.au.dk

Zijia Wang
University of Calgary, Canada

Nakahiro Yoshida
Graduate School of Mathematical Sciences, University of Tokyo: 3-8-1 Komaba, Meguro-ku, Tokyo 153-8914, Japan. CREST, Japan Science and Technology Agency. e-mail: nakahiro@ms.u-tokyo.ac.jp

Introduction

Summary

The Routledge Advances in Applied Financial Econometrics series provides an up-to-date series of advanced chapters on applied financial econometric techniques pertaining the various fields of commodities finance, mathematics and stochastics, international macroeconomics, and financial econometrics. Applied econometrics being a booming academic discipline, with its well-established academic journals and associations, we hope that the contents of this series will be useful to students and researchers in applied econometrics; academics and students seeking convenient access to an unfamiliar area; as well as established researchers seeking a single repository on the current state of knowledge, current debates, and relevant literature.

Structure of volume II

Volume II is titled *Financial Mathematics, Volatility and Covariance Modelling*. It contains 13 chapters organized in three parts.

Part 1 deals with specific characteristics of commodity markets, such as storage costs and the convenience yields. The chapters cover more especially the importance of rollover in commodity returns, long memory and asymmetry in commodity returns and finally the non-linearities and asymmetries in the dependence on short-, mid-, and long-term volatilities. Taken together, these contributions highlight the increasing linkages between commodities and financial econometrics tools.

Part 2 is devoted to the recent financial crisis, the increasing of uncertainty, and volatility or jumps in financial markets that lead the researchers to propose an alternative approach to deal with these issues.

Part 3 gives an overview of the financial volatility modeling in the univariate and multivariate framework. Recent developments in financial econometrics are proposed through surveys or empirical analyses using conditional and stochastic volatility.

A brief outline of the contribution of each chapter in the three parts of the volume follows.

Chapter contributions

Chapter 1, by Cochran, Mansur, and Odusami, develops a double threshold fractionally integrated GARCH $(1,\delta,1)$, model in order to investigate the threshold effects of commodity returns and return volatility. Using the term spread as the threshold variable, the authors examine whether commodity returns and both short-term and long-term volatility persistence exhibit asymmetric patterns. The term spread is used as the threshold variable since it plays an important role in asset valuation and is a robust indicator of future economic activity. The use of a threshold variable extends the current literature in that it can capture important asymmetries in both commodity returns and their volatilities. Their results show that commodity returns and their volatilities possess distinct patterns of non-linearity which are adequately modeled by a DT-FIGARCH$(1,\delta,1)$ specification. The null hypothesis of symmetric coefficient sensitivity above and below the threshold level is rejected in virtually all cases. The long-memory parameters are found to be regime dependent and exhibit greater persistence in volatility during high term-spread (high inflationary) periods than during low term-spread (low inflationary) periods.

Chapter 2, by Kuck and Maderitsch, provides a comprehensive view on volatility dynamics in precious metals and crude oil markets. Using high-frequency futures data, the authors construct realized volatilities and estimate (quantile) heterogeneous autoregressive models for the daily volatility of gold, silver, and crude oil futures. They model realized volatility as a linear function of lagged realized volatility, measured over different time resolutions to explicitly account for the potentially heterogeneous impact of market participants with different trading motives and investment horizons. Using quantile regression allows them to identify potential non-linearities and asymmetries in the dependence on short-, mid-, and long-term volatilities with respect to different levels of current volatility. They document considerable changes in the relative importance of short-, mid-, and long-term volatility components under varying market conditions. The identified patterns are remarkably similar across the three assets. Specifically, past daily and monthly volatility have a strong positive impact on today's volatility, when current volatility is low (lower quantiles of the volatility distribution). The effect of past weekly volatility, however, increases distinctly from intermediate to higher quantiles of the conditional volatility distribution.

Chapter 3, by Karanasos, Koutroumpis, Margaronis, and Nath, considers daily commodity data for use in practical trading systems. The authors assess that mapping that accounts for rollover at contract expiry is required to modify the data. This is because the individual contract data that constitute a conventional time series do not account for contract expiry and the roll that is inherent in it. Both mapped and unmapped data series for certain key commodities are investigated using econometric PARCH models. The analysis is carried out over a range of commodities in different sectors in order to capture the significance of rollover in each. The metals results show how copper prices and platinum prices have a small rollover, therefore mapping the data does not significantly change its behavior. The model which best fits the data, therefore, remains very similar for mapped and unmapped data. Energies' results showed that the roll does, in fact, have a significant impact on the data. The authors find that the significance of such an approach is that the creation of time series that account for roll will allow more accurate back-testing of any algorithmic trading system.

* * *

Part 2 covers broad areas in financial mathematics and stochastics. **Chapter 4**, by Swishchuk and Wang, proposes to study variance and volatility swaps and futures pricing for stochastic volatility models. In this chapter, the authors consider a volatility swap, variance swap, and VIX future pricing under different stochastic volatility models and jump-diffusion models which are commonly used in the financial market. They use convexity correction approximation technique and Laplace transform method to evaluate volatility strikes and estimate VIX future prices. In an empirical study, they use Markov chain Monte Carlo algorithm for model calibration based on S&P 500 historical data, evaluate the effect of adding jumps into asset price processes on volatility derivatives pricing, and compare the performance of different pricing approaches.

Chapter 5, by Cosma and Galli, aims to analyze the Autocorrelated Conditional Duration (ACD) process applied to durations between financial events. The authors propose a fully nonparametric approach. They use a recursive algorithm to estimate the nonparametric specification. In a Monte Carlo experiment, the authors analyze its forecasting performance and compare it with a correct and a misspecified parametric estimator. On a real dataset, the nonparametric estimator seems to mildly overperform in terms of predictive power. The nonparametric analysis can also provide guidance on the choice between alternative parametric specifications. In particular, once intraday seasonality is directly modeled in the conditional duration function, the nonparametric approach provides insights into the time-varying nature of the dynamics in the model that the standard procedures of deseasonalization may lead one to overlook.

Chapter 6, by Matei, investigates the issue of the sovereign debt crisis and economic growth. The author proposes a new evidence for the specific euro area. Indeed, the recent euro area financial crisis has revived the debates on the macroeconomic impact of sovereign debts. After the 2009 Greek announcement of untenable budget deficits, interest rates on sovereign debt increased in a number of EU member states requiring constant interventions and bailouts by international monetary institutions (IMF, ECB, and European Commission). Although the conventional wisdom tells us that debt crisis produces harmful effects on economic growth and that huge increases in public debt have frequently led to sovereign defaults, there is still no consensus regarding the magnitude of the output losses and the timing of the recovery after debt episodes. This current chapter investigates – from an empirical perspective – the short and the long-run impact of the debt crisis on GDP in the case of 18 euro area (EA) countries over the period 1995–2014. Recent dynamic panel heterogeneity models introduced by Pesaran, Shin, and Smith (1999) are employed to disentangle both the long- and short-term effects of the debt crisis on economic growth. The results suggest that the sovereign debt crisis produces significant long-lasting output losses, particularly in the case of EA countries that received financial help from international monetary institutions.

Chapter 7, by Aïd, Campi, and Lautier, aims to study the spot-futures no-arbitrage relations in commodity markets. In commodity markets, the convergence of futures towards spot prices, at the expiration of the contract, is usually justified by no-arbitrage arguments. In this chapter, the authors propose an alternative approach that relies on the expected profit maximization problem of an agent, producing and storing a commodity while trading in the associated futures contracts. In this framework, the relation between the spot and the futures prices holds through the well-posedness of the maximization problem. It is shown that the futures price can still be seen as the risk-neutral expectation of the spot price at maturity and the authors propose an explicit formula for the forward volatility. Moreover, they provide a heuristic analysis of the optimal solution for the production/storage/trading problem, in a Markovian setting. This approach is particularly interesting in the case of energy commodities, like electricity: this framework indeed remains suitable for commodities characterized by storability constraints, when standard no-arbitrage arguments cannot be safely applied.

Chapter 8, by Swishchuk, Remillard, Elliott, and Chavez-Casillas, investigates an innovative modeling of limit order books to manage the fluctuations of the volatility of the financial market. The authors introduce two new Hawkes processes, namely, compound and regime-switching compound Hawkes processes, to model the price processes in limit order books. They prove law of large numbers and functional central limit theorems (FCLT) for both processes. The two FCLTs are applied to limit order books where they use these asymptotic methods to study the link between price volatility and order flow in our two models by using the diffusion limits of these price processes. The volatilities of price changes are expressed in terms of parameters describing the arrival rates and price changes. The authors also present some numerical examples to illustrate the results.

* * *

Part 3 begins in **Chapter 9** with an extensive survey by Amado, Silvennoinen, and Teräsvirta that covers second conditional moments modeling with multiplicative decomposition. The conditional variances, covariances, and correlations are expressed with a multiplicative short- and long-run components. The long-term component can be either deterministic or stochastic. This modeling deals with nonstationary time series and may explain variations in volatility by economic variables. Several univariate and multivariate models are discussed, and misspecification tests are introduced in both frameworks. This survey sheds light on univariate models with a deterministic long-run component where the latter can be parametric, nonparametric, spline-based or use flexible Fourier form. Models with stochastic multiplicative decomposition are also presented including nonparametric, exogenous random variable, or splines component. Extensions of the well-known BEKK and DCC, as well as multivariate time-varying GARCH models, are also considered. More models are included making this survey the main reference in this strand of literature.

Chapter 10 investigates the potential advantages from using ex-post high-frequency measures of volatility and correlations in conditional covariance forecasting. Banulescu-Radu and Dumitrescu use the realized GARCH modeling with time-varying conditional copulas and compare their forecasting abilities with well-established competing models. More precisely, the forecasting abilities of six competing models are examined with the model confidence set approach with robust loss functions. The empirical illustration considers high-frequency data from three pairs of blue-chip stocks from 2009 to 2016. The authors use the same methodology as used in Chapter 3 to clean the dataset. The key findings indicate that including copulas improves the accuracy of the forecasts. The specifications proposed in this chapter contains useful information in covariance forecasting that is preferred to usual multivariate GARCH modeling. From an applied-user perspective, this chapter gives the technical details and the necessary references on different conditional covariance models. Moreover, the results of the forecast methodology presented here should help to determine the appropriate model to use. Thus, this ex-post analysis prevents misspecification modeling issues often encountered in time series econometrics.

Cubadda, Hecq, and Riccardo perform in **Chapter 11** an empirical analysis of the US banking sector. Considering both univariate and multivariate models for realized volatilities series, the authors compare the forecasting performances. In this chapter, intra-day data of the 13 major US banks are analyzed over the period 2006–2014. This sector is known to be interdependent and it is important to use the right modeling to obtain the best forecasting performances. The authors give a detailed procedure to clean the data and introduce the vector heterogeneous autoregressive model and its extension. The main findings are that univariate methods outperform the multivariate ones and imposing common component in the VHAR does not significantly increase the forecasting accuracy. Exploring the co-movements in volatility of asset returns matters for portfolio and fund managers who want to diversify their risks. Since that can be performed by a large system of univariate models or directly by a multivariate setup, such empirical illustration is necessary. The dataset is replaceable and such analysis can be easily realized following the details are given in this chapter.

In **Chapter 12**, Koike and Yoshida propose a survey on covariance estimation and quasi-likelihood analysis. High-frequency data is more and more available and research on statistical inference has increased. This chapter deals with the nonparametric estimation of realized covariance. Estimation details are recalled since high-frequency data encounters many issues such that jumps, irregular sampling, nonsynchronous observations, and microstructure noise. To treat the latter one, univariate and multivariate approaches of synchronization and denoising procedures are given. Parametric inference for stochastic processes based on quasi-likelihood analysis is discussed, including the method itself, the ergodic and jump-diffusion processes, and the parametric estimation of volatility. Applied econometricians can find in this chapter the necessary theoretical background for a concrete use of such stochastic modeling in the high-frequency domain. All the references included in this chapter give to the reader the motivation for using such models.

In **Chapter 13**, Sucarrat proposes an overview of the log-GARCH model and its ARMA representations. For any applied econometrician, this model has many advantages such that the positivity of the volatility or the robustness to outliers, among others. The ARMA representations of this model lead to easy estimation and result interpretations. The author presents an asymmetric specification of the log-GARCH and its ARMA representation before adding stochastic conditioning covariates. The estimation of the coefficient covariance matrix is detailed and empirical examples are given. As in the previous chapter, the multivariate part is not omitted. The equation-by-equation estimation is preferred here to break the curse of dimensionality commonly encountered in multivariate conditional heteroskedastic modeling. In this chapter, stationary and non-stationary cases are considered. Moreover, solutions to handle zeros in practice are reviewed.

Part I
Commodities finance

1 Long memory and asymmetry in commodity returns and risk

The role of term spread

Steven J. Cochran, Iqbal Mansur, and Babatunde Odusami

1. Introduction

There is considerable evidence that commodity and, in particular, metal return, volatility exhibits long-term temporal dependence (see, e.g., Crato and Ray (2000), Jin and Frechette (2004), Baillie et al. (2007), Figuerola-Ferretti and Gilbert (2008), and Cochran et al. (2012)). However, these studies, as well as others, assume that the volatility generating process follows a single regime. The single regime assumption is an important limitation since a significant amount of research has shown that financial time series often exhibit strong non-linearities and that the single regime Generalized Autoregressive Conditional Heteroskedastic (GARCH) family of models are unable to capture the full extent of the non-linear behavior (see, e.g., Hsieh (1991)). For example, if structural breaks exist, financial time series may appear to be piecewise linear but are, in fact, jointly non-linear. Lamoureux and Lastrapes (1990) have shown that structural breaks in the variance, which may result from factors such as changes in Federal Reserve monetary policy, economic outlook, and inflationary expectations, may produce spuriously high persistence in volatility in a GARCH model. If the variance is high and remains so for a period and then low and remains so for a period, persistence of such piecewise homoskedastic periods results in volatility persistence. A GARCH model that cannot adequately capture the persistence of such periods may not only produce volatility persistence that is·spurious but parameter estimates that are unstable.

The objective of this study is to address the issues of period-wise linearity and overall non-linearity by introducing a threshold effect in commodity returns and in their conditional volatilities for four major commodity groups, namely, industrial metals, precious metals, and agricultural and energy commodities. A double threshold fractionally integrated GARCH, (DT)-FIGARCH$(1,\delta,1)$, model is developed in order to examine the threshold effect and, based on the findings of Jin and Frechette (2004), Baillie et al. (2007), and Cochran et al. (2012), will be employed to incorporate the long-memory process of commodity return volatility. Using the term spread as a proxy for inflationary expectations, the endogenously determined threshold employed in this study permits the determination of whether commodity returns and both short-term and long-term volatility persistence exhibit asymmetric patterns, which are ordinarily assumed away under a single regime specification.

The four commodity groups studied here are vital to global economic activity and include industrial metals (aluminum, copper, tin, and zinc), precious metals (gold, silver, and platinum), agricultural commodities (corn and soybeans), and energy commodities (oil, heating oil, and natural gas). This broad sample of commodities permits an investigation as to whether commodities constitute a homogenous asset class with regard to their relationships with the stock market and whether these relationships are regime dependent. Given the economic importance of these commodities, investors, traders, portfolio managers, and central bank and other government officials should be interested in understanding their return and volatility dynamics and how these dynamics are affected by threshold regime changes. Although the price of each commodity is affected by the fundamental demand-supply dynamics and speculative forces in its own market,[1] commodity prices are, in general, highly correlated. For example, the correlation coefficients between oil prices and the prices of the agricultural commodities, precious metals, and industrial metals used in this study are in the range of 0.80.[2] For the energy commodities, the correlation coefficient between oil and heating oil is also approximately 0.80 but that between oil and natural gas prices is the weakest (0.24) among all commodities. Natural gas prices are also negatively correlated with gold, silver, tin, soybean, and corn prices. Although a substitute for oil in various circumstances, the demand-supply forces in the natural gas market appear to differ substantially from those in the other energy markets (oil and heating oil). The relationship between oil and natural gas prices is indirect and is based on the competition between natural gas and residual fuel oil (see Hartley et al. (2008)). Although a long-term relationship exists between crude oil and natural gas prices, the short-run dynamics can result in considerable variation in the relative prices of these two energy commodities (see Brown and Yücel (2008)). Additionally, factors such as inventories and weather, as well as other seasonal events and factors, have significantly more impact on the short-run dynamics of natural gas prices than on those of other non-agricultural prices.

During mid-2008, led by crude oil, commodity prices reached virtually unbelievable highs and then subsequently declined very quickly. Persistent decreases in commodity prices continued over the 2010–2015 period. Since 2010, commodity prices have fallen by 40% while growth in emerging and developing economies has slowed from 7.1% in 2010 to 3.3% in 2015 (Commodity Market Outlook (January 2016)). Although the issue is largely unsettled, financialization in the form of speculative buying by index funds in the commodity futures and over-the-counter (OTC) derivatives markets is often considered to be a contributing factor in the creation of speculative bubbles that result in commodity prices, and crude oil prices in particular, to far exceed their fundamental values at their peaks (see Gheit (2008)). Additionally, recent studies have argued that global investors consider commodities as alternative investment instruments and, therefore, are subject to speculative behavior. As oil and precious metals are priced in US dollars, these commodities can be used as hedges by investors and speculators. In terms of portfolio diversification, Hammoudeh et al. (2009) recommend the inclusion of gold and silver in a portfolio that already holds oil and copper. Similarly, Sari et al. (2010) find that investors may reduce portfolio risk by diversifying across assets such as precious metals and oil. Monetary policy implications have been drawn from movements in commodity prices. Hammoudeh et al. (2009) argue that changes in the prices of oil and silver and in the exchange rate can provide signals concerning the actions of monetary policy authorities and the future direction of the short-term rate of interest (defined by the US T-bill rate). Hammoudeh et al. (2009) conclude that a concurrent rise in oil and silver prices and an appreciation of the US dollar against major foreign currencies is a signal for tighter monetary policy which may lead to an increase in the short-term interest rate.

The remainder of this paper is organized as follows. Section 2 discusses the importance of investigating long-memory in commodity return volatility within a threshold framework. In Section 3, the methodology employed, data definitions and descriptive statistics are presented. Section 4 contains the empirical results, and conclusions are given in Section 5.

2. Threshold, term spread, and asymmetry

2.1. Why use threshold models?

The single regime GARCH class of models is widely used in modeling financial market volatility. There are, however, two major limitations associated with the single regime GARCH family of models that call into question the accuracy of the estimates from these models. These limitations are their inability to capture all of the observed non-linearity in the series being examined due to structural discontinuity and the fact that the persistence of shocks decays at a relatively fast geometric rate.

To address the issue of non-linearity in return, a new set of models, the self-exciting threshold autoregressive (SETAR) family of models, were introduced by, among others, Tong (1983, 1990) and Tsay (1989). In a SETAR model, it is assumed that the dynamic behavior of a time series variable follows a linear autoregressive process where the regime that is operative at time t depends on the observable past history of the series itself with a delayed effect (d). The SETAR model has been extended by Tong (1990) to capture asymmetry in returns and changing volatility by using a threshold ARCH model. Li and Li (1996) extended the model in order to capture asymmetry in the mean and volatility by developing a double threshold ARCH (DT-ARCH) model. Brooks (2001) further generalized this approach to a double threshold GARCH (DT-GARCH) specification. Li and Li (1996) compared the results of the DT-ARCH model with those of the SETAR and threshold ARCH (T-ARCH) models and found that the DT-ARCH model captures the changes in the mean and variance structures better than the other two models. Similarly, Brooks

(2001) reports that the out-of-sample forecasts for exchange rate volatility are improved when both regime shifts are considered.

One of the major weaknesses of both the DT-ARCH model of Li and Li (1996) and the DT-GARCH model of Brooks (2001) is that the threshold values are subjectively fixed.[3] The working assumption of the SETAR models that commodity returns undergo regime shifts as determined only by their own past values appears to be too restrictive. Various methodologies have been employed to determine threshold values. Threshold models, which encompass regime switching models, have been found to be successful in modeling metal and commodity returns (see, e.g., Choi and Hammoudeh (2010) and Bhar and Malliaris (2011)). Compared to the most commonly used Markov switching models where regimes are driven by unobservable Markov chains, threshold models utilize observable state variables which permit certain asymmetric features of the data to be related to observable financial and economic factors. Chen and So (2006) develop a threshold GARCH model where the threshold variable is defined by a weighted average of auxiliary variables. These auxiliary variables are highly relevant to regime switching, can take the form of exogenous variables, and may be affected by the dynamic structure of the return series. In this study, the term spread is used as the threshold variable and is estimated using the Tsay (1998) methodology. A detailed discussion follows in Section 2.2.

The issue of asymmetry in the conditional volatility of commodity returns is important for a number of reasons as it has implications for macroeconomic policy, accuracy in the measurement of underlying risks, and for forecast accuracy. Concerning macroeconomic policy, variability in commodity prices greatly affects the export revenues of commodity-dependent countries. Policymakers in economies that rely heavily on commodity exports should be cautious when implementing policies intended to ameliorate the effects of commodity price shocks on the domestic economy. The effectiveness of policy initiatives is greatly influenced by the nature of shock persistence and long memory. Thus, it is crucial to understand the potential macroeconomic policy implications of asymmetric volatility shocks for these economies. For example, if return sensitivity to macroeconomic drivers is heightened or adversely affected during periods of high inflation (regime I in this study) or if volatility shocks persist longer during this regime, it may become necessary for the government to implement macroeconomic stabilization measures in a more effective and expedient manner in order to counteract any adverse effects of such asymmetry.

Asymmetry in commodity returns and return volatility has important implications in the valuation of options and in volatility forecasting. As pointed out by Engle (2004), the presence of asymmetric volatility in equity returns, if unaccounted for, will lead to an underestimation of the Value-at-Risk. A better understanding of the factors that contribute to volatility asymmetry would permit economists to refine existing volatility models by incorporating variables that adequately account for the asymmetry. Finally, the DT-FIGARCH $(1,\delta,1)$ approach offers a unified framework in which one can test for general regime switching dynamics in commodity returns and return volatility. Additionally, the methodology permits the statistical significance of specific asymmetries in returns and in return volatility to be determined. The various asymmetry hypotheses to be tested in this study are presented in Section 3.3.

2.2. The term spread as the threshold variable

The term spread, defined as the difference in yield between 10-year Treasury bonds and 90-day Treasury bills, is specified as the threshold variable and the threshold values are endogenously determined by using the Tsay (1998) methodology.[4] According to the expectations hypothesis of the term structure, current long-term yields are simply the geometric average of current and expected short-term yields and the difference between long-term and short-term yields, defined as the term spread, is the additional compensation (positive or negative) investors require to hold long-term bonds. Since it is assumed that both the long-term and short-term government bonds used here are free of risk, changes in the term spread are brought about by changes in inflationary expectations.

The term spread possesses a number of unique characteristics that makes it appealing for use as the threshold variable.[5] First, research has shown that the term spread systematically affects the asset market return and, thus, it plays an important role in asset valuation (see, e.g., Chen et al. (1986)). Second, the slope of the term structure (i.e., term spread) has been proposed as an indicator of monetary policy because, in principle, the term structure should change in response to changes in expected inflation (see Fuhrer (1993)). As the expectation of long-term inflation increases, investors in long-term bonds will require an additional inflation premium as compensation for the loss in the real value of bonds. The result is not only an increase in the yield on long-term bonds but a steeper slope of the term structure. On the other hand, decreases in long-term inflationary expectations will have the opposite effect, resulting in a yield curve that becomes flatter or inverted. Fama and French (1989) found that an increase in today's spread is associated with a future increase in the inflation premium and a future decrease in the real rate of interest. Additionally, empirical findings suggest that the term spread is a robust indicator of future economic activity (see, e.g., Estrella and Hardouvelis (1991), Estrella and Mishkin (1996), and Paya et al. (2005)). Third, the slope of the yield curve has predictive power in addition to that of other macroeconomic variables and can predict cumulative changes in real output for up to four years (see Estrella and Hardouvelis (1991)). Current empirical literature strongly supports the notion that a steeper (flatter) slope of the yield curve tends to imply a faster (slower) rate of future economic growth. Finally, the term spread variable defined here possesses a continuous set of data that meets the Tsay (1998) specification of an arranged regression. Since the term spread can be positive or negative, this precludes the arbitrary assignment of a value for the grid search process.[6] In this study, the threshold value for each commodity return, presented in Table 1.1, is estimated after controlling for market effects (MSCI world index and VIX) and macroeconomic variables (exchange rate and term spread).

Table 1.1 Data diagnostics daily
Data from January 4, 1999 to December 31, 2013

	Industrial Metals				Precious Metals			Agricultural		Energy		
	RALU	RCOP	RTIN	RZINC	RGOL	RSIL	RPLA	RCORN	RSOY	ROIL	RHOIL	RNGAS
Mean (%)	0.01	0.04	0.04	0.02	0.04	0.04	0.03	0.02	0.02	0.05	0.06	0.01
Std. Dev (%)	1.38	1.81	1.57	1.94	1.15	1.94	1.47	2.00	1.75	2.42	2.60	5.79
Min (%)	-9.95	-18.64	-11.40	-24.45	-8.88	-12.98	-12.40	-11.02	-11.13	-17.09	-47.01	-54.59
Max (%)	10.41	16.00	13.62	27.44	10.39	12.77	9.58	12.20	7.41	16.41	22.95	59.24
Skewness	-0.09	-0.14	-0.15	-0.08	-1.47	-0.64	-0.59	0.02	-0.73	-0.21	-1.73	0.03
Kurtosis	4.42	8.30	7.01	18.85	6.41	6.17	6.03	2.94	4.82	4.73	43.95	13.96
J-B (p Value)	0.00	0.00	0.00	0.00	0.00	0.00	0.00	0.00	0.00	0.00	0.00	0.00
Q(5)	2.55	4.27	7.05	1.45	5.46	0.90	3.32	3.34	9.94	10.95	39.96	212.35
Q(20)	20.75	12.05	21.11	18.37	30.09	20.38	29.77	32.52	41.76	35.46	64.42	792.92
Q²(5)	12.32	7.20	19.24	38.13	6.57	5.42	2.55	14.64	4.61	39.06	988.95	123.61
Q²(20)	22.19	19.53	93.33	48.74	79.63	36.86	20.75	30.90	45.42	156.56	1197.90	327.98
ADF (4)	-27.35	-28.54	-27.94	-27.58	-26.79	-27.99	-27.74	-28.46	-26.57	-28.80	-40.18	-29.99
ADF (4,t)	-27.36	-28.54	-27.94	-27.58	-26.79	-27.99	-27.76	-28.46	-26.56	-28.81	-40.18	-26.98
PP(0)	-62.85	-67.73	-58.28	-66.32	-61.75	-62.25	-59.65	-63.23	-64.27	-63.30	-101.63	-62.46
PP(4)	-62.85	-67.76	-58.32	-66.35	-61.75	-62.25	-59.60	-63.23	-64.24	-63.31	-125.89	-69.48
R/S-Return	1.15	1.14	1.20	1.38	1.66	1.47	1.08	1.08	0.93	1.13	1.26	1.07
R/S-Sq. Return	2.61	1.83	2.26	2.36	1.61	2.04	1.40	2.04	1.69	1.45	1.09	1.53
Threshold (in %)	2.73	2.70	2.82	3.14	3.21	3.21	3.00	2.97	2.98	2.85	2.83	3.02
Delay (in Days)	5	6	4	7	5	7	5	7	2	5	2	6

Total number of observations, N = 3,881. The critical values of Q(5) and Q(20) (Q²(5) and Q²(20)) at the 5% level are 15.08 and 31.41, respectively. The critical values at the 1% level for ADF(4) and ADF(4,t) are −3.43 and −3.96, respectively. The critical values for PP(0) and PP(4) are −3.43. The critical value for the R/S test statistics at the 5% level is 1.74.

The economic significance of the term spread threshold is that it is the level of the term spread beyond which the effects on commodity returns and return volatility are clearly different from those of the previous regime. In this framework, the term spread must cross a specific threshold value for a given commodity return series such that a regime shift occurs that alters the underlying relationships driving the return and volatility generating processes. While applications of the threshold model are no longer uncommon, it should be mentioned that the magnitudes of estimated threshold values are not explained in any economic sense in the literature (see, e.g., Meyer and von Cramon-Taubadel (2004)). Instead, the values are interpreted as the minimum incentives required of economic agents to elicit price or return adjustments (see, e.g., Meyer and von Cramon-Taubadel (2004)).

The major findings of this study are as follows. First, commodity returns and their volatilities possess distinct patterns of non-linearity which are adequately captured by a DT-FIGARCH $(1,\delta,1)$ model. Second, using the term spread as the threshold variable, the null hypothesis of symmetric economic sensitivity above (regime I – high inflationary expectations) and below (regime II – low inflationary expectations) the threshold is rejected in virtually all cases. Third, all long-memory parameters are determined to be statistically significant and, with the exception of tin, zinc, platinum, and natural gas, exhibit greater persistence in volatility in regime I than in regime II. Finally, the short-memory component of the volatility process (the GARCH coefficient) is statistically significant in all cases but fails to display asymmetric sensitivity for copper, platinum, and silver returns.

3. Methodology and data

The double threshold (DT)-FIGARCH $(1,\delta,1)$ model used in this study is developed by combining the FIGARCH $(1,\delta,1)$ volatility specification of Baillie et al. (1996) with a four factor generalization of the threshold model in Tsay (1998). The approach employed in estimating the DT-FIGARCH $(1,\delta,1)$ model, which follows a two-step process, is similar to that used in Elyasiani et al. (2013). In the first step, a Tsay (1998) type methodology is employed in estimating the threshold and delay parameter values associated with each commodity. In the subsequent step, the estimated values are used to permit the conditional variance of the FIGARCH $(1,\delta,1)$ process to be drawn from two different regimes.

3.1. The commodity return model

In order to determine the appropriate return generating model, the presence of long-memory in commodity returns is tested for using the modified R/S test (see Lo (1991)) and by examining the autocorrelation of returns over a 900-day window. Using the R/S test (results presented in Table 1.1), the null hypothesis of no long-memory cannot be rejected for any of the commodity return series.[7] The presence of long-memory can also be determined by examining the persistence of the autocorrelations for each series. The autocorrelations of a long-memory process decline at a hyperbolic rate to zero, a much slower rate of decay than the exponential decay of the ARMA process. Figure 1.1, Panels A, B, C and D, presents the autocorrelation plots over 900 lags for industrial metals, precious metals, agricultural commodities, and energy commodities, respectively. The autocorrelation plot for each commodity return series shows a clear

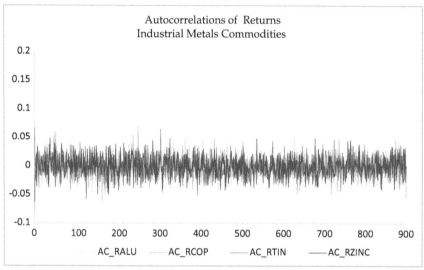

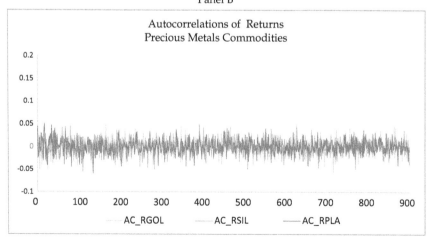

Figure 1.1 Autocorrelation of returns

Panel C

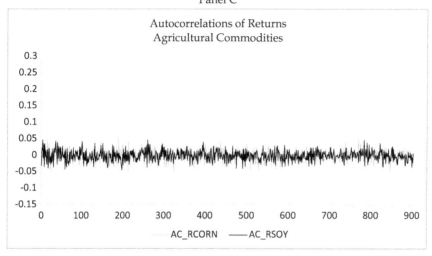

Panel D

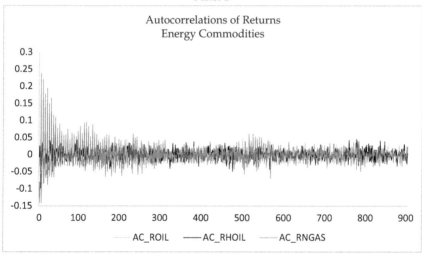

Figure 1.1 (Continued)

lack of dependence. All commodity return series fail to exhibit a clear pattern of hyperbolic decay and, thus, do not possess long memory. These results provide support for those obtained from the modified R/S test. The finding of an absence of long-memory in commodity returns is consistent with Crato and Ray (2000), Jin and Frechette (2004), and Cochran et al. (2012), among others. As a result, rather than attempting to model the return series as autoregressive fractionally integrated moving average processes, each series is modeled as an extended CAPM model. The single-index CAPM has been used extensively in modeling commodity returns with varying levels of success (see, e.g., Dusak (1973), Carter et al. (1983), and Chang et al. (1990)). Building on and extending these previous studies, a multi-index CAPM is employed here in the modeling of commodity returns. This return specification, which takes into account regime shifts that occur due to threshold effects, is presented below:

$$R_{i,t} = \sum_{j=1}^{J=2} I_t^{(j)} (b_0^{(j)} + b_1^{(j)} RM_t + b_2^{(j)} REXR_t + b_3^{(j)} VIX_t + b_4^{(j)} TERM_{t-d} + \varepsilon_t) \tag{1}$$

$$\varepsilon_t | \Omega_{t-1} \tilde{N}(0, \sigma_t^2)$$

$$j = 1 \ when \ TERM_{t-d} \geq r, \ and \ j = 2 \ when \ TERM_{t-d} < r$$

where $R_{i,t}$ is the return on commodity i ($i = 1,2, \ldots,12$) calculated as $\log(p_t/p_{t-1})$ where p is the daily closing spot price, $I_t^{(j)}$ is the indicator function where $j = 1$ (above threshold) and $j = 2$ (below threshold), and RM_t is defined as the market index and is calculated as the log difference in the daily closing prices of the Morgan Stanley Capital International (MSCI) world index.[8] $REXR_t$, the exchange rate variable, is calculated as the log difference in the daily values of the FRB trade-weighted index, implied volatility in the equity market is defined by the VIX_t index of the Chicago Board Options Exchange, and $TERM_t$ is the term spread as defined previously, and d is the delay parameter.[9] The error term is given by $\varepsilon_t | \Omega_{t-1} \sim N(0, \sigma_t^2)$ where $N(\cdot)$ represents the conditional normal density function with mean zero and variance (σ_t^2) contingent on the information set Ω at time $t - 1$.[10]

3.1.1. Theoretical justification for the macroeconomic variables

Not only have the economic variables used in this study been shown to have forecasting power in the equity and bond markets, a number of these variables (with the exception of the VIX index) have been widely employed in various combinations in the modeling of commodity returns. For example, Jaffe (1989), Bessembinder and Chan (1992), Bjornson and Carter (1997), and Akram (2009) collectively provide evidence on the effects of a broad range of economic variables on commodity returns. Recent movements in commodity prices and the changes in macroeconomic drivers that often determine such price movements seem to indicate that various forces are acting in a very complex way, including demand-supply fundamentals, speculative market forces, and geopolitical concerns, in determining commodity prices. Although there is no consensus at this moment on which factors are the primary determinants of the movements in commodity prices, a brief review of the theory of commodity price formation may be helpful in understanding why commodity prices respond to macroeconomic forces.

Under the assumptions that commodity prices are flexible and commodities are traded in efficient markets, commodity systematic risk is defined by the relationship between commodity returns and market returns. If commodity returns positively co-vary with those of the market, systematic risk is positive while systematic risk is negative if the covariance between commodity and market returns is negative. A negative systematic risk coefficient (negative coefficient on the market return) for a commodity will significantly enhance its ability to diversify portfolio risk. Choi and Hammoudeh (2010) find that commodity traders concurrently look at both stock and commodity market fluctuations to infer the trend of each market. Comparing the dynamic volatility of commodity and equity prices provides useful information about possible substitution strategies between these two asset classes.

Since commodity prices are denominated in US dollars in this study, the law of one price for tradable goods dictates a negative relationship between the value of the dollar and the dollar price of commodities. For the law of one price to hold, a decline in the value of the dollar must be compensated for by an increase in the dollar price of commodities or by a commensurate fall in foreign currency prices in order to ensure the same commodity price when measured in dollars. Thus, the relationship between a change in the exchange rate and commodity returns is expected to be negative.

The term spread not only systematically affects the asset market return but also is closely related to economic activity. As stated previously, a steeper (flatter) slope of the yield curve tends to imply a faster (slower) rate of future economic growth and consequently higher (lower) demand for commodities. It should be noted however, that shifts in the slope of the yield curve may be brought about by a large number of factors, including changes in long-term inflationary expectations, expectations of significant short-term interest rate changes, and changes in the relative risk preference between long-term and short-term instruments. Given the various factors which may have an effect, the direction and significance of the coefficient on the term spread is largely an empirical issue.

We adopt the approach taken by Cochran et al. (2012, 2015) where the VIX index is used as a proxy for the financialization of commodity returns. While Cochran et al. (2012) is limited in that the investigation is performed under a single regime, Cochran et al. (2015) expand the model by using VIX as the threshold variable and examine whether the significant increase in investor demand for commodities has affected the dynamics of information flow between the commodity market and the equity market.

When the VIX index increases, the volatility of the market is expected to increase in the near future and investors may exhibit "flight-to-safety" behavior. The direction of the coefficient sign on VIX is largely an empirical issue. If a commodity is perceived as a "flight-to-safety" asset, the contemporaneous return on this commodity should be positively related to an increase in implied volatility. On the other hand, if the commodity serves as an inflation proxy or the global demand for the commodity decreases due to an increased level of risk, the relationship between VIX and the commodity return is expected to be negative. It may be useful for a number of reasons to examine whether the underlying relationships between a large group of commodity returns and changes in VIX are regime dependent when the regimes are currently defined by the magnitude of the term spread. First, a reevaluation of investment portfolios may result from increased volatility in the stock market and, due to the "flight to quality" nature of some commodities, additional investment may be directed in favor of commodities. Second, understanding whether the factors that contribute to commodity volatility are regime dependent can assist regulatory bodies and investment advisors in establishing better rules and policies regarding investment in commodities.

3.2. The FIGARCH (1,δ,1) volatility process

Baillie et al. (1996) and Ding and Granger (1996) show that the volatilities of financial asset returns decay more slowly than those of standard GARCH processes, suggesting that they may be characterized as fractionally integrated processes. Evidence obtained here using R/S test statistics (presented in Table 1.1) support the Baillie et al. (1996) and Ding and Granger (1996) findings.[11] In addition, autocorrelation plots of squared returns over a 900-day window are consistent with these results. Figure 1.2, Panels A, B, C and D, presents the autocorrelation plots for squared returns for industrial metals, precious metals, agricultural commodities, and energy commodities, respectively. Unlike the

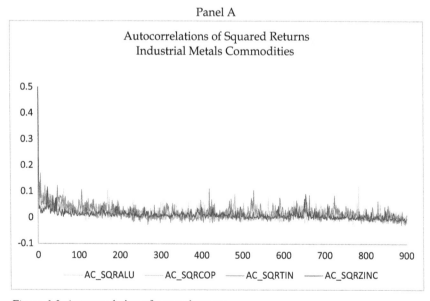

Figure 1.2 Autocorrelation of squared returns

Panel B

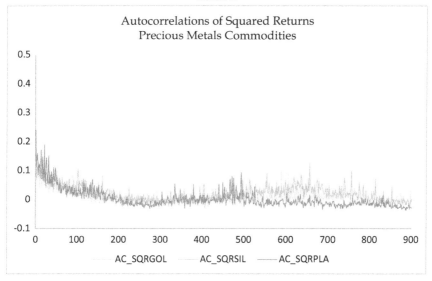

Panel C

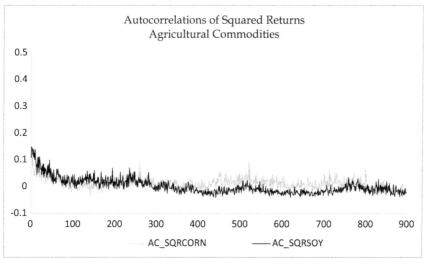

Figure 1.2 (Continued)

Panel D

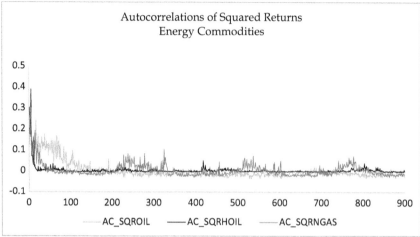

Figure 1.2 (Continued)

autocorrelation functions of returns, the autocorrelation functions of squared returns possess hyperbolic decay. The autocorrelation functions show a high degree of persistence at the beginning but decline rapidly in magnitude over a few lags. The rate of decay slows for subsequent lags but the length of decay remains strong for a large number of time periods. The FIGARCH (p, δ, q) model proposed by Baillie et al. (1996), which captures the hyperbolic decay in the volatility process for a single regime, is modified to represent a two regime threshold specification and is presented below:

$$\sigma_t^2 = \sum_{j=1}^{j=2} I_t^{(j)} \omega^{(j)} [1 - \beta^{(j)}(1)]^{-1} + \{1 - [1 - \beta^{(j)}(L)]^{-1} \phi^{(j)}(L)(1 - L)^{\delta^{(j)}}\} \varepsilon_t^2 \quad (2)$$

$$j = 1 \ when \ TERM_{t-d} \geq r, \ and \ j = 2 \ when \ TERM_{t-d} < r$$

where ε_t, σ^2, $I_t^{(j)}$ are as previously defined, ω^j is a constant, $\phi^{(j)} \equiv [1 - \alpha^{(j)}(L) - \beta^{(j)}(L)](1 - L)^{-1}$ is the moving average component of the short-term volatility dynamics where $\alpha^{(j)}$ and $\beta^{(j)}$ are the ARCH and GARCH parameters, respectively, L denotes the lag operator and, finally, $\delta^{(j)}$ is the fractional order of differencing $0 < \delta < 1$, which accounts for long-term persistence in the FIGARCH specification.[12]

The conditional mean, given in equation (1), and the conditional variance, given in equation (2), are defined for each regime in equations (3) and (4), respectively, and are presented below:

$$
R_{i,t} = \begin{cases} b_0^1 + b_1^1 RM_t + b_2^1 REXR_t + b_3^1 VIX_t + b_4^1 TERM_{t-d} + \varepsilon_t & \text{if } TERM_{t-d} \geq r \\ b_0^2 + b_1^2 RM + b_2^2 REXR_t + b_3^2 VIX_3 + b_4^2 TERM_{t-d} + \varepsilon_t & \text{if } TERM_{t-d} < r \end{cases}
$$

$$(3)$$

$$
\sigma_{i,t}^2 = \begin{cases} \omega^1 + \beta^1 \sigma_{t-1}^2 + [1 - \beta^1(L) - (1 - \phi^1(L))(1 - (L))^{\delta^1}]\varepsilon_t^2 & \text{if } TERM_{t-d} \geq r \\ \omega^2 + \beta^2 \sigma_{t-1}^2 + [1 - \beta^2(L) - (1 - \phi^2(L))(1 - (L))^{\delta^2}]\varepsilon_t^2 & \text{if } TERM_{t-d} < r. \end{cases}
$$

$$(4)$$

Equations (3) and (4) are estimated using maximum likelihood methods, which entails searching for the parameter space Θ that maximizes the log-likelihood function $L(.)$ represented by equation (5):

$$
L(\Theta; R_{i,t}, ...R_{i,T}) = \sum_{t=2}^{T} \ln[f(R_{i,t}|\Omega_{t-1})]
$$

$$(5)$$

$$
f(R_{i,t}|\Omega_{t-1}) = \frac{1}{\sqrt{2\pi(\sigma_t^2)}} \exp\left(-\frac{(R_{i,t} - \hat{R}_{i,t})^2}{2(\sigma_t^2)}\right).
$$

The parameter space Θ contains $(b_k^j, \omega^j, \beta^j, \phi^j, \text{and } \delta^j)$ where $k = 0, 1, 2, ...12$, $j = 1, 2$, t represents time ($t = 1, 2, . . . , T$), and where the regime coefficients are estimated simultaneously.

3.3. Testable hypotheses regarding asymmetry

The DT-FIGARCH $(1,\delta,1)$ specification is appropriate in the testing of hypotheses regarding (1) important asymmetries associated with both returns and their volatilities, and (2) the appropriate model specification. Hypotheses concerning the symmetry of shocks above and below the threshold are presented below:

- H_1: Market return sensitivity is symmetric – $H_0 : b_1^1 = b_1^2$
- H_2: Exchange rate sensitivity is symmetric – $H_0 : b_2^1 = b_2^2$
- H_3: VIX sensitivity is symmetric – $H_0 : b_3^1 = b_3^2$
- H_4: Term spread sensitivity is symmetric – $H_0 : b_4^1 = b_4^2$
- H_5: GARCH effect is symmetric – $H_0 : \beta^1 = \beta^2$
- H_6: Long-memory process is symmetric – $H_0 : \delta^1 = \delta^2$.

Hypotheses regarding model specifications are as follows:

- H_7: The proper model specification is GARCH(1,1) – $H_0 : \delta^1 = \delta^2 = 0$
- H_8: The proper model specification is IGARCH – $H_0 : \delta^1 = \delta^2 = 1$.

3.4. Descriptive statistics

Summary statistics for the commodity returns for the period January 4, 1999, to December 31, 2013, are presented in Table 1.1. The results reveal that as a group (the exception being natural gas), the energy commodities performed best, with crude oil and heating oil exhibiting 0.05% and 0.06% average daily returns, respectively. The performance of the energy commodities is followed by those of the precious metals (gold, silver, and platinum displaying average daily returns of 0.04%, 0.04%, and 0.03%, respectively) and industrial metals (aluminum, copper, tin, and zinc exhibiting average daily returns of 0.01%, 0.04%, 0.04%, and 0.02%, respectively). Agricultural commodities performed the poorest with corn and soy both displaying average daily returns of 0.02%. Precious metals on average exhibit the lowest unconditional volatility, as represented by the standard deviation of return (1.15%, 1.94%, and 1.47% for gold, silver, and platinum, respectively), followed by the industrial metals (1.38%, 1.81%, 1.57%, and 1.94% for aluminum, copper, tin, and zinc, respectively), and the agricultural commodities (2.00% and 1.75% for corn and soy, respectively). Energy commodities exhibit the highest standard deviations of returns (2.42%, 2.60%, and 5.79% for crude oil, heating oil, and natural gas, respectively). Precious metals, which display the second highest average daily returns and lowest standard deviations, dominate all other commodities in terms of reward-to-unconditional risk.

Ten of the 12 commodity return series are negatively skewed (the exceptions are corn and natural gas), with the precious metals displaying the largest values of negative skewness. A negative (positive) skewness indicates a distribution where extreme negative (positive) returns have a greater probability of occurring than extreme positive (negative) returns. All commodity returns series (with the exception of corn) are found to be leptokurtic, a result similar to that obtained by Figuerola-Ferretti and Gilbert (2008). In general, energy commodity returns exhibit the highest level of excess kurtosis, with heating oil possessing the highest level (43.95). Agricultural commodity returns display the lowest values of excess kurtosis, with corn having the lowest value at 2.94. A leptokurtic distribution, also known as a fat-tailed distribution, has a higher-than-normal probability of generating large movements in returns. Additionally, based on the sample skewness and kurtosis measures, the Jarque-Bera test statistic rejects the null hypothesis of joint normality for each return series. The Ljung-Box $Q(20)$ statistic shows evidence of serial correlation in the returns of the agricultural and energy commodities, but not in the returns of the industrial and precious metals. The $Q^2(20)$ statistic indicates the presence of ARCH effects in the returns of all energy commodities, as well as for tin, zinc, gold, silver, and soy. The existence of asymmetry, along with the presence of ARCH effects in the return distribution, suggests that an asymmetric-ARCH specification is best suited for modeling the return dynamics of the commodity series.[13]

4. Empirical results

4.1. Threshold effects in conditional returns

The DT-FIGARCH $(1, \delta, 1)$ estimation results are presented in Table 1.2. For each variable, two coefficients, one pertaining to regime I, the high term spread (HTS) regime (b_i^1), and the other to regime II, the low term spread (LTS) regime (b_i^2), are presented.[14] Within the context of DT-FIGARCH model, when the term spread is greater than or equal to the estimated threshold value, the underlying relationship follows regime I. This defines a period where a higher than expected term spread leads to a structural change in the underlying relationship between commodity returns and other market variables. Similarly, the underlying relationship follows regime II when the term spread is less than the estimated threshold value, denoting a market where a lower than expected term spread prevails. In a more general sense, changes in the term spread are caused by changes in inflationary expectation.

In Table 1.2, the coefficients obtained from the estimations of the threshold FIGARCH models of commodity returns are reported. The market return coefficients (b_1^1 and b_1^2) are statistically significant and positive for all commodities with the exception of b_1^2 being negative for gold and silver. On the whole, the market betas obtained for regime I are greater than those for regime II. This finding suggests the existence of an asymmetry in the sensitivity of commodity returns to the broad market return. In the HTS periods, the b_1^1 values vary widely, from 0.11 for aluminum to 0.86 for crude oil. In the LTP periods, the b_1^2 values vary less widely, with the exception of gold and silver which have negative b_1^2 values. In the single regime scenario, gold returns have been found to possess a very low correlation with stock returns (see, e.g., Jaffe (1989) and Cochran et al. (2012)). The low correlation is often considered as the reason investment in gold helps to diversify portfolio risk. However, the threshold results suggest that the true relationship between the returns on precious metals (gold and silver) and the market return is negative during the low term spread periods. These findings indicate that conclusions drawn from a single regime study will underestimate the diversification benefits of precious metals during low term spread periods and call into question the accuracy of the market betas estimated under the single regime scenario. The test of symmetry concerning the threshold coefficients on the market return, presented in Table 1.3, strongly rejects the null hypothesis of symmetry in favor of an asymmetric market beta for each commodity with the exception of natural gas. Thus, the relationship between the returns on each commodity and the market return differs significantly depending on the magnitude of the term spread (i.e., in HTS regime or LTS regime).

All exchange rate coefficients (b_2^1 and b_2^2) are negative and significant, as expected. The finding of a negative relationship between commodity returns and exchange rate movements is consistent with those in the literature obtained under a single regime (see, e.g., Sherman (1983), Tulley and Lucey (2007) and

Table 1.2 DT-FIGARCH estimation results
Daily Data from January 4, 1999 to December 31, 2013

Variable	Coefficient	Industrial Metals				Precious Metals			Agricultural		Energy		
		RALU	RCOP	RTIN	RZINC	RGOL	RSIL	RPLA	RCORN	RSOY	ROIL	RHOIL	RNGAS
$CONS^1$	b_0^1	0.25	−0.08	0.42	−0.16	0.18	−0.41	0.44	0.35	−0.03	1.69	0.72	−0.70
		60.00	*−8.54*	*64.14*	*−7.83*	*17.25*	*−4.43*	*36.90*	*39.64*	*−0.19*	*5.24*	*45.99*	*−1.40*
$CONS^2$	b_0^2	0.13	0.23	−0.02	0.40	0.05	0.12	−0.02	−0.01	0.08	0.14	0.22	0.24
		49.95	*80.00*	*−9.06*	*173.54*	*32.80*	*17.01*	*−5.32*	*−1.82*	*2.45*	*3.91*	*25.40*	*3.64*
RM^1	b_1^1	0.11	0.41	0.22	0.51	0.15	0.41	0.32	0.33	0.43	0.86	0.57	0.15
		21.15	*45.54*	*46.60*	*23.27*	*31.73*	*17.38*	*25.49*	*23.55*	*18.72*	*50.75*	*39.01*	*2.47*
RM^2	b_1^2	0.10	0.08	0.12	0.13	−0.13	−0.02	0.03	0.07	0.06	0.09	0.10	0.12
		29.35	*27.05*	*50.42*	*60.23*	*−86.70*	*−5.02*	*7.68*	*13.49*	*7.33*	*8.15*	*11.66*	*5.05*
$REXR^1$	b_2^1	−0.51	−1.77	−1.02	−0.67	−1.33	−2.59	−1.02	−1.10	−0.38	−0.81	−0.85	−1.34
		−73.26	*−66.52*	*−46.37*	*−13.91*	*−60.19*	*−34.70*	*−29.90*	*−31.76*	*−6.24*	*−17.74*	*−30.69*	*−9.53*
$REXR^2$	b_2^2	−0.86	−1.12	−0.96	−1.34	−1.47	−2.78	−1.02	−0.86	−0.56	−1.74	−1.27	−0.38
		−75.62	*−87.33*	*−111.57*	*−121.08*	*−241.30*	*−108.36*	*−87.83*	*−90.91*	*−16.67*	*−41.64*	*−39.03*	*−4.29*
VIX^1	b_3^1	−0.02	−0.01	−0.02	0.01	−0.01	0.02	−0.01	−3.7E-03	−0.01	−0.02	−0.01	0.02
		−123.75	*−31.11*	*−84.34*	*14.09*	*−12.08*	*5.62*	*−16.87*	*−10.44*	*−1.55*	*−6.69*	*−8.79*	*2.91*
VIX^2	b_3^2	−0.004	−0.010	0.003	−0.017	1.7E-04	−0.003	0.006	0.005	−0.002	−0.001	−0.009	−0.005
		−32.97	*−72.23*	*42.24*	*−149.61*	*2.73*	*−20.45*	*33.40*	*28.84*	*−1.19*	*−0.49*	*−21.73*	*−1.64*
$TERM^1$	b_4^1	0.10	0.10	0.04	−0.02	0.01	0.01	−0.05	−0.11	0.05	−0.37	−0.14	0.11
		81.34	*32.93*	*18.12*	*−2.38*	*1.60*	*0.76*	*−13.65*	*−39.95*	*1.56*	*−3.82*	*−28.55*	*0.75*
$TERM^2$	b_4^2	−0.02	0.03	−0.02	−3.20E-03	−0.02	−5.4E-04	−0.04	−0.05	0.01	−0.01	0.01	−0.09
		−9.86	*22.88*	*−15.98*	*−2.09*	*−25.96*	*−0.14*	*−16.11*	*−23.77*	*1.01*	*−1.37*	*1.55*	*−4.83*
Const. Vol^1	ω^1	2.0E-09	5.3E-02	5.1E-02	7.0E-09	−4.0E-09	7.7E-02	−1.0E-09	−1.3E-07	1.5E-02	−2.6E-08	0.0E+00	−2.0E-09
		0.00	*2.33*	*5.86*	*0.00*	*0.00*	*1.50*	*0.00*	*0.00*	*1.10*	*−0.01*	*0.00*	*0.00*
Const. Vol^2	ω^2	1.8E-03	2.3E-02	8.0E-09	4.0E-09	1.6E-06	1.0E-09	2.0E-02	8.8E-06	5.3E-08	1.6E-03	3.0E-09	0.0E+00
		0.12	*1.64*	*0.00*	*0.00*	*0.00*	*0.00*	*−4.05*	*0.00*	*0.00*	*0.24*	*0.00*	*0.00*
$GARCH^1$	β^1	0.74	0.62	0.78	0.73	0.70	0.79	0.25	0.62	0.95	0.98	0.72	0.69
		82.05	*47.78*	*71.98*	*31.25*	*36.17*	*9.69*	*8.53*	*39.75*	*62.18*	*170.71*	*32.52*	*11.37*
$GARCH^2$	β^2	0.40	0.57	0.78	0.74	0.57	0.81	0.78	0.13	0.61	0.96	−0.55	0.88
		27.45	*55.71*	*159.50*	*103.47*	*77.83*	*28.41*	*99.36*	*10.61*	*7.82*	*75.97*	*−49.81*	*48.29*

	1	2	3	4	5	6	7	8	9	10	11	12
PHI¹ ϕ^1	0.39	0.23	0.91	0.44	0.39	0.20	0.00	0.34	0.00	1.00	0.36	0.18
	25.15	*16.11*	*107.94*	*14.35*	*12.23*	*3.32*	*0.00*	*17.43*	*0.02*	*415.12*	*10.54*	*2.60*
PHI² ϕ^2	0.32	0.30	0.51	0.39	0.29	0.57	0.37	0.00	0.31	0.99	0.22	0.03
	20.38	*24.44*	*62.79*	*38.24*	*35.12*	*11.37*	*26.98*	*0.00*	*4.54*	*198.83*	*16.27*	*1.51*
DECAY¹ δ^1	0.37	0.51	0.16	0.38	0.41	0.72	0.33	0.30	0.98	0.13	0.49	0.73
	33.10	*38.96*	*9.96*	*15.96*	*17.92*	*8.57*	*15.22*	*21.08*	*33.85*	*4.37*	*23.15*	*11.63*
DECAY² δ^2	0.22	0.37	0.41	0.45	0.38	0.42	0.60	0.22	0.35	0.10	0.46	0.95
	22.76	*40.27*	*66.68*	*58.79*	*60.84*	*18.65*	*53.94*	*28.21*	*7.02*	*4.94*	*46.85*	*90.08*
LL Value	*-6387.95*	*-7137.58*	*-6653.78*	*-7339.87*	*-5303.90*	*-7115.19*	*-6386.71*	*-7921.43*	*-7335.66*	*-8263.39*	*-8271.02*	*-11204.62*

Model Diagnostic Statistics

Based on ($\varepsilon/\sqrt{h}$)

	1	2	3	4	5	6	7	8	9	10	11	12
Skewness	-0.01	-0.01	-0.02	-0.15	-0.02	-0.15	-0.03	0.01	-0.12	-0.03	-0.01	0.08
Kurtosis	3.05	2.62	4.27	3.63	3.43	2.45	1.78	2.59	2.38	1.50	1.09	2.63
J-B*	0.00	0.00	0.00	0.00	0.00	0.00	0.00	0.00	0.00	0.00	0.00	0.00
Q(20)	21.67	42.83	18.32	23.88	25.90	21.05	10.87	28.24	36.96	16.95	13.54	508.30

Based on ($\varepsilon/\sqrt{h}$)²

	1	2	3	4	5	6	7	8	9	10	11	12
Skewness	8.50	8.12	6.96	17.51	8.50	6.76	5.78	6.32	5.83	5.32	5.44	10.14
Kurtosis	123.70	121.92	71.40	582.75	112.46	72.57	66.46	64.20	51.81	43.70	56.48	236.05
J-B*	0.00	0.00	0.00	0.00	0.00	0.00	0.00	0.00	0.00	0.00	0.00	0.00
Q(20)	11.92	9.93	7.32	15.64	13.38	10.15	34.68	18.17	12.63	14.54	25.20	51.14

*t-values are presented below each coefficient. The critical t-values at the 1%, 5%, and 10% levels are 1.65, 1.97, and 2.60, respectively. The critical value of Q(20) (Q²(20)) at the 5% level is 31.41. *J-B values pertain to the level of significance.*

Table 1.3 DT-FIGARCH models hypotheses tests results

Hypotheses	Null Hypothesis	Test Statisitc	Industrial Metals				Precious Metals			Agricultural		Energy		
			RALU	RCOP	RTIN	RZINC	RGOL	RSIL	RPLA	RCORN	RSOY	ROIL	RHOIL	RNGAS
Symmetry Hypotheses														
Symmetry of Market Return Sensitivity	H_1: $b_1^1 = b_1^2$	$\chi^2(1)$	0.06	0.00	0.00	0.00	0.00	0.00	0.00	0.00	0.00	0.00	0.00	0.68
Symmetry of Exchange Rate Sesitivity	H_2: $b_2^1 = b_2^2$	$\chi^2(1)$	0.00	0.00	0.00	0.00	0.00	0.01	0.91	0.00	0.01	0.00	0.00	0.00
Symmetry of VIX Sensitivity	H_3: $b_3^1 = b_3^2$	$\chi^2(1)$	0.00	0.00	0.00	0.00	0.00	0.00	0.00	0.00	0.34	0.00	0.01	0.00
Symmetry of Term Spread Sensitivity	H_4: $b_4^1 = b_4^2$	$\chi^2(1)$	0.00	0.00	0.00	0.06	0.00	0.47	0.11	0.00	0.24	0.00	0.00	0.18
Symmetry of GARH Effect	H_6: $\beta^1 = \beta^2$	$\chi^2(1)$	0.00	0.00	0.96	0.72	0.00	0.81	0.00	0.00	0.00	0.22	0.00	0.00
Symmetry of Long-Memory	H_7: $\delta^1 = \delta^2$	$\chi^2(1)$	0.00	0.00	0.00	0.00	0.26	0.00	0.00	0.00	0.00	0.22	0.14	0.00
Model Specification Hypotheses														
Model Specification is GARCH (1,1)	H_8: $\delta^1 - \delta^2 = 0$	$\chi^2(2)$	0.00	0.00	0.00	0.00	0.00	0.00	0.00	0.00	0.00	0.00	0.00	0.00
Model Specification is IGARCH (1,1)	H_9: $\delta^1 - \delta^2 = 1$	$\chi^2(2)$	0.00	0.00	0.00	0.00	0.00	0.00	0.00	0.00	0.00	0.00	0.00	0.00

Symmetry hypotheses are tested using a $\chi^2(1)$ test and the model specification hypotheses are tested using a $\chi^2(2)$ test. The *p*-values pertaining to $\chi^2(1)$ and $\chi^2(2)$ are presented in the table.

Cochran et al. (2012)). The sensitivity of commodity returns to exchange rate movements is very pronounced ($|b_2| > 1.0$) for all precious metals, and with silver in particular, during both the HTS and LTS periods. Other commodities with pronounced sensitivity are copper, tin, corn, and natural gas in the HTS period and copper, zinc, crude oil, and heating oil in the LTS period. In terms of commodity groupings, gold and silver have greater sensitivity to exchange rate changes in the LTS period than in the HTS period. Similar results are evident for aluminum, zinc, soy, crude oil, and heating oil. Additional evidence of this asymmetry is presented in Table 1.3 where the null hypothesis of a symmetric exchange rate beta is strongly rejected for all commodities with the exception of platinum.

The coefficients pertaining to VIX (b_3^1 and b_3^2), are statistically significant in both the HTS and LTS regimes and for all commodities, with the exception of soy in both regimes and crude oil in the LTS periods. The sign on the VIX beta (b_3^1) in the HTP regime is negative for all commodities, with the exception of zinc, silver, and natural gas. In the LTS regime, the VIX coefficient (b_3^2) is positive for tin, two precious metals, gold and platinum, and corn. In the equity return literature, there is substantial evidence that, under a single regime scenario, the contemporaneous correlation between changes in VIX and S&P 100 returns is negative (see, e.g., Fleming et al. (1995) and Banerjee et al. (2007)). Christie (1982) attributes the inverse relationship between stock returns and changes in future volatility to the leverage effect.[15] The results obtained here suggest an overwhelmingly negative relationship between VIX and commodity returns and is similar to that which exists between VIX and equity returns. This, in turn, provides additional evidence for the financialization of the commodity markets. Although natural gas is part of the energy sector, the underlying relationship between the returns on this commodity and VIX is positive rather than negative. Finally, the test of asymmetry of VIX sensitivity, presented in Table 1.3, rejects the null hypothesis of symmetry for all commodities, with the exception of soy.

The results presented in Table 1.2 show significant term spread effects in both the HTS and LTS regimes. The coefficients (b_4^1 and b_4^2) pertaining to the term spread are positive and significant for all industrial metals in the HTS regime. For aluminum, copper, and tin the effect is positive while for zinc, it is negative. The remaining significant negative coefficients are associated with platinum, corn, crude oil, and heating oil. In the LTS regime, the term spread betas are negative and significant for all commodities with the exception of copper, soy, and heating oil. In the single regime case, Roache (2008) finds significant positive relationships between the term spread and copper and platinum returns and insignificant relationships between the term spread and gold and silver returns. Additionally, Cochran et al. (2012) find significant positive relationships between the term spread and all metals studied with the exception of gold, where the coefficient was found to be negative and significant.

Within the context of this study, investment in commodities may offer an effective hedge against inflation under either of two conditions. First, commodity returns would tend to be high when expected inflation is relatively high (HTS regime). Conversely, when expected inflation is relatively low (LTS regime), commodity returns would tend to be low. Statistically, these conditions may be interpreted as implying a positive relationship between commodity returns and the term spread. The results from Table 1.2 suggest that the industrial metals aluminum, copper, and tin serve as hedges against inflation since their term spread coefficients are positive in the HTS regime while investment in zinc, platinum, corn, crude oil, and heating oil may not offer a hedge against inflation. In LTS regime, gold and platinum appear not to serve as a hedge against inflation. Additionally, all other significant coefficients (aluminum, tin, zinc, corn, and natural gas) are negative, with the exception of copper which is positive. Finally, the test of asymmetry in Table 1.3 reveals that, with the exception of silver, platinum, soy, and natural gas, the null hypothesis of coefficient symmetry is rejected for each metal.

4.2. Threshold effects in conditional volatility

The results presented in Table 1.2 strongly support previous studies which have concluded that the FIGARCH $(1,\delta,1)$ specification appropriately describes commodity return volatility. Consistent with those studies, all long-memory parameters (δ) are found to be statistically significant. Additionally, this study extends the literature by determining whether the long memory parameters (δ) are regime dependent. In the HTS regime, the long-memory parameters range between 0.13 (crude oil) and 0.98 (soy) and, in the LTS regime, the parameters range between 0.10 (crude oil) and 0.95 (natural gas). With the exception of tin, zinc, platinum, and natural gas, the parameter is larger during the HTS as compared to the LTS regime, a finding which suggests that, in general, volatility persistence is greater during periods of high inflationary expectations. Thus, it is during periods of heightened risk that shocks to the volatility processes of commodities persist for longer periods of time.[16] The long-memory parameters obtained in this study differ considerably from those obtained using a single regime scenario. This is particularly the case for gold where Baillie et al. (2007) and Cochran et al. (2012), using daily data, report the magnitude of (δ) as 0.29 and 0.55, respectively, compared to the values of 0.41 (HTS regime) and 0.38 (LTS regime) presented in Table 1.2 of this study. On the other hand, the magnitudes of (δ) obtained for platinum in this study, 0.33 and 0.60 for the HTS and LTS regimes, respectively, are substantially smaller than that obtained (0.70) by Cochran et al. (2012). Table 1.3 shows that the null hypothesis of coefficient symmetry is rejected for all commodities, with the exception of gold, crude oil, and heating oil, thereby establishing differential rates of decay in long memory in the two regimes.

   Two hypotheses regarding model specification are tested and the results are presented in Table 1.3. The null hypotheses regarding GARCH (H_8), $\delta^1 = \delta^2 = 0$, and integrated GARCH (H_9), $\delta^1 = \delta^2 = 1$, are rejected for each metal, indicating that neither specification is appropriate. Using daily data and a single regime scenario, Baillie et al. (2007) and Cochran et al. (2102) obtained similar results regarding model specification. Long-memory in commodity return volatility appears to be a characteristic feature of daily commodity returns and must be modeled as such.

From Table 1.2, the GARCH parameters (β^1, β^2) for each commodity and for both regimes are positive (with the exception of heating oil), less than unity, and are highly statistically significant. The GARCH parameters range between 0.25 (platinum) and 0.98 (crude oil) in the HTS regime and between 0.13 (corn) and 0.96 (crude oil) in the LTS regime. It appears that in a single regime setting the true underlying magnitudes of short-term and long-term temporal dependence in return volatility cannot be determined due to the aggregation of data over the different phases of inflationary expectations. Similar to the case with long-memory, the results in Table 1.3 show that the null hypothesis of coefficient symmetry in short-term volatility can be rejected for all commodities except tin, zinc, silver, and crude oil.[17]

With the exception of silver and zinc, the standardized residuals from the DT-FIGARCH models given in Table 1.2 show that skewness is statistically insignificant for each commodity. Although kurtosis remains significant in all cases, the magnitudes are considerably below the unconditional levels. The reduction in kurtosis is especially significant for zinc, heating oil, and natural gas. The Q(20) statistic rejects the null of no autocorrelation in the standardized residuals for copper, soy, and natural gas, while the $Q^2(20)$ statistic rejects the null of no higher order autocorrelation (no ARCH effects) for platinum and natural gas. These results are very similar to those reported by Baillie et al. (2007) and Cochran et al. (2012) who also found that the standardized residuals from FIGARCH estimations continued to exhibit features of non-normality.

4.3. Robustness tests of the DT-FIGARCH (1, δ, 1) model

In evaluating the suitability of the double threshold FIGARCH model used in this study, it is determined whether this methodology provides more information concerning the true data generating processes for the commodity series than the single regime FIGARCH or the threshold mean model. In examining this issue, two hypotheses are tested, where restrictions are placed on various parameter estimates. First, tests of asymmetry are performed on the coefficients from the double threshold model for the HTS and LTS regimes. Absence of asymmetry implies that the true data generating process is linear and, thus, the double threshold methodology provides no more information than the single regime FIGARCH model. The results resented in Table 1.3 largely support the presence of asymmetry in the coefficients from the two regimes and, thus, provide evidence in favor of the double threshold model. In addition, the joint test of coefficients, presented in equation (6), rejects the null hypothesis in favor of the double threshold specification:

$$H_0 : b_0^1 = b_0^2; ...; b_4^1 = b_4^2; \omega^1 = \omega^2; \alpha^1 = \alpha^2; \beta^1 = \beta^2; \phi^1 = \phi^2; \delta^1 = \delta^2. \quad (6)$$

In the second test, the coefficients in the volatility equation of the double threshold model are restricted to zero. The null hypothesis for this joint test is:

$$H_0 : \omega^1 = 0; \omega^2 = 0; \beta^1 = 0; \beta^2 = 0; \phi^1 = 0; \phi^2 = 0; \delta^1 = 0; \delta^2 = 0. \quad (7)$$

This joint test permits a determination of whether the double threshold approach provides more information than the single threshold framework. The test is asymptotically $\chi^2(n)$ with $n = 8$ degrees of freedom. The results provide strong evidence in the support of the double threshold model. The p-value associated with the joint test for each commodity, with the exception of corn, is 0.00. Taken together, both sets of tests indicate that the double threshold model is an improvement over the widely used single regime specifications in terms of explaining the dynamics of commodity returns.

5. Conclusions

In this study, the threshold effects of the term spread in metal returns and return volatilities are examined within a double threshold FIGARCH(1,δ,1) approach. The term spread is used as the threshold variable since it plays an important role in asset valuation and is a robust indicator of future economic activity. The use of a threshold variable extends the current literature in that it can capture important asymmetries in both commodity returns and their volatilities. These asymmetries are ordinarily assumed away under a single regime specification.

The results show that the commodity returns and their volatilities possess distinct patterns of non-linearity which are adequately modeled by a DT-FIGARCH (1,δ,1) specification. Null hypotheses regarding GARCH, $\delta^1 = \delta^2 = 0$, and integrated GARCH, $\delta^1 = \delta^2 = 1$, are consistently rejected for all commodities. These findings are consistent with those of Baillie et al. (2007) and Cochran et al. (2012) who reach similar conclusions about model specification under a single regime scenario. In the conditional mean equation, almost all coefficients (108 of 120) pertaining to the economic variables are found to be statistically significant in both regimes. More importantly, the coefficients are found to be threshold dependent. The null hypothesis of symmetric coefficient sensitivity above and below the threshold level is rejected in virtually all cases. Finally, one of the key findings of this study is that the long-memory parameters are regime dependent and exhibit greater persistence in volatility during high inflationary periods than during low inflationary periods. The results of this study suggest that long-term temporal dependence is strongly affected by threshold regime changes and that failure to account for such threshold effects will yield misleading conclusions. Future research should focus on improving the modeling of the volatility process by combining long-range volatility dependence, power transformation of the conditional variance, and the asymmetric response of volatility to positive and negative shocks in a multivariate framework along the lines of an asymmetric power FIGARCH specification.

Notes

1 A recent World Bank study (see Baffes et al. (2015)) decomposed oil price movements into demand and supply factors and suggests that since mid-2014, the decline in oil prices has been predominantly (about 65%) driven by supply forces while softening demand in both developed and emerging economies contributed the rest.

2 Values are calculated by the authors and are available upon request.

3 Both Li and Li (1996) and Brooks (2001) used SETAR models to determine threshold values. In the Li and Li (1996) model, the change in regime is triggered by a positive and negative value of the return series. Brooks (2001) did not estimate the threshold values for the estimations. Instead, Brooks (2001) utilized the exchange rate threshold values obtained by Chappell et al. (1996).

4 Appendix A presents a brief explanation of the estimation process for the threshold and delay parameters.

5 There is an extensive literature on the role of the term spread in asset valuation. For a discussion, see Avramov (2004).

6 As discussed in Section 3, a double threshold (DT)-FIGARCH $(1,\delta,1)$ model is employed in the estimation. In the first step of a two-step estimation procedure, a Tsay (1998) type methodology is used and the threshold value and the delay parameter are estimated using a process that transforms the threshold model into a change point problem. This is done by arranging the regression according to the increasing order of the threshold variable, which assumes both positive and negative values. If a short-term or long-term rate of interest, which can only be positive, were employed as the threshold variable, an artificial positive value would have to be provided for the grid search process. This would, in essence, compromise the true magnitude of the threshold variable.

7 The R/S test statistics (critical value is 1.74 at the 5% level) are 1.15 for aluminum (RALU), 1.14 for copper (RCOP), 1.20 for tin (RTIN), 1.38 for zinc (RZINC), 1.66 for gold (RGOL), 1.47 for silver (RSIL), 1.08 for platinum (RPLA), 1.08 for corn (RCORN), 0.93 for soybeans (RSOY), 1.13 for oil (ROIL), 1.26 heating oil (RHOIL), and 1.07 for natural gas (RNGAS).

8 The subscript i denotes R_1, R_2, ..., R_{12} where 1=RALU (aluminum), 2=RCOP (copper), 3=RTIN (tin), 4=RZINC(zinc), 5=RGOL (gold), 6=RSIL (silver), 7=RPLA (platinum), 8=RCORN (corn), 9=RSOY (soybeans), 10=ROIL (oil), 11=RHOIL (heating oil) and 12=RNGAS (natural gas).

9 The daily closing commodity spot prices and the MSCI world index data are from www.Globalfinancialdata.com. The FRB trade-weighted exchange rate index and the 90-day Treasury bill and 10-year Treasury bond yields are obtained from FRED® at the St. Louis Federal Reserve Bank web site. The VIX index is obtained from financeyahoo.com. The MSCI world index is a free float-adjusted market capitalization index that measures developed market equity performance throughout the world. The index is comprised of companies that are representative of the structures of 23 developed markets in North America, Europe, and the Asia/Pacific region. The FRB trade-weighted index is very broad in scope and the weights are derived from US export shares and from US and foreign import shares. Any changes to these values over time reflect the current trade balance. VIX is the ticker symbol of the Chicago

Board Options Exchange volatility index, which is a measure of the implied volatility of S&P500 index options. A high value of VIX is associated with greater volatility while a low value is consistent with greater stability in the market.

10 To avoid repetition and improve clarity, the subscript i is not included on the coefficients.

11 The autocorrelation plots of the squared commodity return series clearly display a pattern of hyperbolic decay. The R/S test statistics for the squared commodity return series (critical value is 1.74 at the 5% level) are 2.61 for aluminum, 1.83 for copper, 2.26 for tin, 2.36 for zinc, 1.61 for gold, 2.04 for silver, 1.40 for platinum, 2.04 for corn, 1.69 for soybeans, 1.45 for oil, 1.09 for heating oil, and 1.53 for natural gas, respectively.

12 Meeting the non-negativity constraint of conditional variance in the FIGARCH (p, δ, q) model is substantially more difficult than the GARCH(1,1) model. As pointed out by Conrad and Haag (2006), it is possible that the conditional variance can become negative, although all the parameters are positive. Additionally, they point out that even if all parameters (with the exception of δ) are negative, the conditional variance can be non-negative. As a result, they suggest that independent of the sign of the estimated parameters, the non-negativity conditions should be further verified.

13 Tests of stationarity are performed for all commodity return series using the augmented Dickey and Fuller (1979, 1981) test with four lags (ADF(4)) and four lags and a trend (ADF(4, t)), and using the Phillips and Perron (1988) test with zero lags (PP(0)) and four lags (PP(4)). In all cases, the null of stationarity cannot be rejected. Tests of long memory in the commodity returns and squared returns are performed using the R/S test statistic. Drawing from the results, we fail to reject the null in all cases for the returns, and about half of the cases for the squared returns.

14 In our sample, the lowest value of the term spread (2.73%) obtained for regime I is in the 69th percentile of spreads. However, it should be noted that the definitions of high and low term spread periods used in this study are not necessarily the same as those used by market participants but are, instead, employed for the purpose of exposition here.

15 This inverse relationship is primarily due to the fact that, when stock prices fall relative to bond prices, leverage increases which, in turn, causes expected volatility to increase

16 Although not examined in this study, it is widely held that changes in the economic environment can have significant effects on business, default, and credit risk. See, e.g., Bhansali et al. (2008), Bachmann et al. (2010), and Roldan-Pena (2012) for discussions related to credit, business, and default risk, respectively. Additionally, the growth rate in gross domestic product has been found to be negatively correlated with default risk (see, e.g., Altman et al. (2005)).

17 See Hyung et al. (2008) for a discussion of various long-memory (break, components, regime switching, and FIGARCH) and short-memory (GARCH and GJR-GARCH) models.

18 See Tsay (1998) for a detailed discussion of the methodology.

Bibliography

Altman, E., Brady, B., Resti, A., and Sironi, A. 2005. The link between default and recovery rates: Theory, empirical evidence and implications. *Journal of Business*, 78, 2203–2227.

Akram, Q. 2009. Commodity prices, interest rates and the dollar. *Energy Economics, 31*, 838–851.

Avramov, D. 2004. Stock return predictability and asset pricing models. *Review of Financial Studies*, 17, 699–738.

Bachmann, R., Elstner, S., and Sims, E. 2010. Uncertainty and economic activity: Evidence from business survey data. NBER Working Paper (16143).

Baffes, J., Kose, M., Ohnsorge, F., and Stocker, M. 2015. The great plunge in oil prices: Causes, consequences, and policy responses. Policy Research Note 1, World Bank, Washington DC.

Bhansali, V., Gingrich, R., and Longstaff, F. 2008. Systemic credit risk: What is the market telling us? *Financial Analysts Journal*, 64, 16–24.

Bhar, R., and Malliaris, A. 2011. Oil prices and the impact of the financial crisis of 2007–2009. *Energy Economics*, 33, 1049–1054.

Banerjee, P., Doran, J., and Peterson, D. 2007. Implied volatility and future portfolio returns. *Journal of Banking and Finance*, 31, 3183–3199.

Baillie, R., Bollerslev, T., and Mikkelsen, H. 1996. Fractionally integrated generalized autoregressive conditional heteroskedasticity. *Journal of Econometrics*, 74, 3–30.

Baillie, R., Han, Y.-W., Myers, R., and Song, J. 2007. Long memory models for daily and high frequency commodity futures returns. *Journal of Futures Markets*, 27, 643–668.

Bessembinder, H., and Chan, K. 1992. Time-varying risk premia and forecastable returns in futures markets. *Journal of Financial Economics*, 32, 169–193.

Bjornson, B., and Carter, C. 1997. New evidence on agricultural commodity return performance under time-varying risk. *American Journal of Agricultural Economics*, 79, 918–930.

Brooks, C. 2001. A double threshold GARCH model for the French franc/Deutschmark exchange rate. *Journal of Forecasting*, 20, 135–143.

Brown, S., and Yücel, M. 2008. What drives natural gas prices? *Energy Journal*, 29, 45–60.

Carter, C., Rausser, G., and Schmitz, A. 1983. Efficient asset portfolio and the theory of normal backwardation. *Journal of Political Economy*, 91, 319–331.

Chang, E., Chen, C., and Chen, S. 1990. Risk and return in copper, platinum, and silver futures. *Journal of Futures Markets*, 10, 29–39.

Chappell, D., Padmore, J., Mistry, P., and Ellis, C. 1996. A threshold model for the French franc/Deutschmark exchange rate. *Journal of Forecasting*, 15, 155–164.

Chen, C., and So, M. 2006. On a threshold heteroscedastic model. *International Journal of Forecasting*, 22, 73–89.

Chen, N.-F., Roll, R., and Ross, S. 1986. Economic forces and the stock market. *Journal of Business*, 59, 383–403.

Choi, K., and Hammoudeh, S. 2010. Volatility behavior of oil, industrial commodity and stock markets in a regime-switching environment. *Energy Policy*, 38, 4388–4399.

Christie, A. 1982. The stochastic behavior of common stock variances: Value, leverage, and interest rate effects. *Journal of Financial Economics*, 10, 407–432.

Cochran, S., Mansur, I., and Odusami, B. 2012. Volatility persistence in metal returns: A FIGARCH approach. *Journal of Economics and Business*, 64, 287–305.

Cochran, S., Mansur, I., and Odusami, B. 2015. Equity market implied volatility and energy prices: A double threshold GARCH approach. *Energy Economics*, 50, 264–272.

Conrad, C., and Haag, B. 2006. Inequality constraints in the fractionally integrated GARCH model. *Journal of Financial Econometrics*, 4, 413–449.

Crato, N., and Ray, B. 2000. Memory in returns and volatilities of futures' contracts. *Journal of Futures Markets*, 20, 525–544.

Dickey, D., and Fuller, W. 1979. Distribution of the estimators for autoregressive time series with a unit root. *Journal of the American Statistical Association*, 74, 427–431.

Dickey, D., and Fuller, W. 1981. Likelihood ratio statistics for autoregressive time series with a unit root. *Econometrica*, 49, 1057–1072.

Ding, Z., and Granger, C. 1996. Modeling volatility persistence of speculative returns. *Journal of Econometrics*, 73, 185–215.

Dusak, K. 1973. Futures trading and investor returns: An investigation of commodity market risk premiums. *Journal of Political Economy*, 81, 1387–1406.

Elyasiani, E., Mansur, I., and Odusami, B. 2013. Sectoral stock return sensitivity to oil price changes: A double threshold FIGARCH model. *Quantitative Finance*, 13, 593–612.

Engle, R. 2004. Risk and volatility: Econometric models and financial practice. *American Economic Review*, 94, 405–420.

Estrella, A., and Hardouvelis, G. 1991. The term structure as a predictor of real economic activity. *Journal of Finance*, 46, 555–576.

Estrella, A., and Mishkin, F. 1996. The yield curve as a predictor of U.S. recessions. *Federal Reserve Bank of New York Current Issues in Economics and Finance*, 2, 1–6.

Fama, E., and French, K. 1989. Business conditions and expected returns on stocks and bonds. *Journal of Financial Economics*, 25, 23–49.

Figuerola-Ferretti, I., and Gilbert, C. 2008. Commonality in the LME aluminum and copper volatility processes through a FIGARCH lens. *Journal of Futures Markets*, 28, 935–962.

Fleming, J., Ostdiek, B., and Whaley, R. 1995. Predicting stock market volatility: A new measure. *Journal of Futures Markets (1986–1998)*, 15, 265–302.

Fuhrer, J. 1993. Commodity prices, the term structure of interest rates, and exchange rates: Useful indicators for monetary policy? *New England Economic Review*, (November), 18–32.

Gheit, F. Testimony before the Subcommittee on Oversight and Investigations of the Committee on Energy and Commerce, U.S. House of Representatives. Internet Site: http://energycommerce.house.gov/cmte_mtgs/110-oi-hrg.062308.Gheit-testimony.pdf (Accessed June 23, 2008).

Hammoudeh, S., Sari, R., and Ewing, B. 2009. Relationships among strategic commodities and with financial variables: A new look. *Contemporary Economic Policy*, 27, 251–264.

Hartley, P., Medlock III, K., and Rosthal, J. 2008. The relationship of natural gas to oil prices. *Energy Journal*, 29, 47–65.

Hsieh, D. 1991. Chaos and nonlinear dynamics: Application to financial markets. *Journal of Finance*, 46, 1839–1877.

Hyung, N., Poon, S.-H., and Granger, C. 2008. Chap. 9 in *Forecasting in the Presence of Structural Breaks and Model Uncertainty*, 329–380. D. Rapach and M. Wohar (eds.). In *Frontiers of Economics and Globalization* (vol. 3). Bingley, West Yorkshire, England: Emerald Group Publishing Limited.

Jaffe, J. 1989. Gold and gold stocks as investments for institutional portfolios. *Financial Analysts Journal*, 45, 53–59.

Jin, H., and Frechette, D. 2004. Fractional integration in agricultural future price volatilities. *American Journal of Agricultural Economics*, 86, 432–443.

Lamoureux, C., and Lastrapes, W. 1990. Persistence in variance, structural change, and the GARCH model. *Journal of Business and Economic Statistics*, 8, 225–234.

Li, C., and Li, W. 1996. On a double threshold autoregressive heteroscedastic time series model. *Journal of Applied Econometrics*, 11, 253–274.

Lo, A. 1991. Long-term memory in stock market prices. *Econometrica*, 59, 1279–1313.

Meyers, J., and von Cramon-Taubadel, S. 2004. Asymmetric price transmission: A Survey. *Journal of Agricultural Economics*, 55, 581–611.

Paya, I., Matthews, K., and Peel, D. 2005. The term spread and real economic activity in the US inter-war period. *Journal of Macroeconomics*, 27, 331–343.

Phillips, P., and Perron, P. 1988. Testing for a unit root in time series regression. *Biometrika*, 75, 335–346.

Roache, S. 2008. Commodities and the market price of risk. IMF Working Paper (WP/08/221), 1–23.

Roldan-Pena, J. 2012. Default risk and economic activity: A Small open economy model with sovereign debt and default. Banco de Mexico Working Paper (No. 2012–16).

Sari, R., Hammoudeh, S., and Soytas, U. 2010. Dynamics of oil price, precious metal prices, and exchange rate. *Energy Economics*, 32, 351–362.

Sherman, E. 1983. A gold pricing model. *Journal of Portfolio Management*, 9, 68–70.

Tong, H. 1983. Threshold models in non-linear time series analysis. In *Vol. 21 of Lecture Notes in Statistics*. New York: Springer-Verlag.

Tong, H. 1990. *Nonlinear time series: A dynamical system approach*. Oxford: Oxford University Press.

Tsay, R. 1989. Testing and modeling threshold autoregressive process. *Journal of the American Statistical Association*, 84, 231–240.

Tsay, R. 1998. Testing and modeling multivariate threshold models. *Journal of the American Statistical Association*, 93, 1188–1202.

Tulley, E., and Lucey, B. 2007. A power GARCH examination of the gold market. *Research in International Business and Finance*, 21, 316–325

Appendix A

Estimation of the threshold and delay parameters

Consider the following return generating process

$$R_t = \begin{cases} f_1(X_t'; \varepsilon_t) & \text{if } z_{t-d} \geq r \\ f_2(X_t'; \varepsilon_t) & \text{if } z_{t-d} < r \end{cases} \tag{A1}$$

$$\text{where } X_t = \{1, F_{1t}', ..., F_{kt}', z_{t-d}'\}.$$

In the above specification, R_t is the $n \times 1$ vector of commodity returns, X_t is an $n \times (k+1)$ matrix of exogenous regressors that contains the economic variables $(F_{1,t}, ..., F_{k,t})$, ε_t is the error term, lagged z_t is the threshold variable, d is the delay parameter, r is a real number, and t represents time. This model implies that the trajectory of R_t is governed by $k + 1$ exogenous factors and the threshold variable z_{t-d}. More specifically, equation (A1) specifies a two-regime model where the behavior of R_t is determined by X_t and the information variable z_{t-d} at time t with a d-period delay. When $z_{t-d} \geq r$, R_t follows a piecewise linear path defined by regime $j = 1$ and when $z_{t-d} < r$, R_t follows a different linear trajectory defined by regime $j = 2$, where $j = 1$, 2 represents the number of regimes in R_t.

The mean equation of the empirical model employed in this study follows the generalization of Tsay (1998) and is presented above in equation (A1). This model allows for an exogenous threshold variable, defined here as the term spread ($z_{t-d} = TERM_{t-d}$), and the simultaneous estimation of the delay parameter d and the threshold value of r. This is done by transforming the mean equation into a change point problem, in which the change point is determined in an arranged regression. To identify the change point, a recursive least squares regression is performed with (d), set at 1, 2, ..., 7, and the order statistics of z_{t-d}. The regression produces a grid $C(d)$ that contains the values of d, r, and the selection criterion of the Akaike Information Criterion (AIC). For each commodity, the optimal values of the threshold r^* and delay d^* are simultaneously determined by selecting the set (r^*, d^*) that minimizes the AIC.[18] The results pertaining to the term spread thresholds and the delay parameters are reported in the last two rows of Table 1.1.

2 The quantile-heterogeneous autoregressive model of realized volatility

New evidence from commodity markets

Konstantin Kuck and Robert Maderitsch

1. Introduction

This chapter presents new insights into the dynamics of gold, silver, and crude oil market volatility. Specifically, we start by using a heterogeneous autoregressive model of realized volatility (HAR-RV) to obtain insights into the temporal dependence of today's volatility with respect to past daily, weekly, and monthly volatility aggregates. This allows us to explicitly capture the possibly different contributions of market participants with diverse trading motives and investment horizons. The interaction of heterogeneous traders seems particularly evident in commodity markets. On the one hand there are producers and commercial traders that aim to hedge against (future) price changes (long-term horizon). On the other hand, there are investors that have no 'real' interest in the underlying asset but consider the future itself as a financial asset (short- and medium-term horizon). The resulting linear description of the average volatility dynamics and relative importance of past volatility components might, however, provide an incomplete view if the volatility process, in fact, is non-linear (i.e., depends on the level of volatility itself).

Therefore, we additionally consider a so-called quantile-heterogeneous autoregressive model of realized volatility (Q-HAR-RV).[1] This model is particularly well suited in this context since it allows to capture time-varying volatility dynamics and hence to explicitly consider different 'states' of the financial markets. Upper quantiles of the realized volatility indicate high-volatility days. These days are particularly interesting from a risk management perspective as they are typically associated with increased uncertainty and high trading intensity in a market. Intermediate (and lower) quantiles of the volatility distribution, by contrast, represent medium- and low-volatility days that are typically related to phases of calm market conditions and relatively low trading volumes.

Interest in commodity market volatility has increased steadily over the last years. Particularly through index investment, commodity futures have become part of more and more investment portfolios due to expected diversification benefits (Tang and Xiong, 2012). An increasing share of investors thus regards commodity futures as assets (Adams and Glück, 2015). Typically, trading commodity futures is now also embedded into complex risk management processes ('dynamic risk management'), while the perceived complexity of commodity futures markets seems to have increased for commodity producers and consumers alike (see, e.g., Aepli et al., 2017).[2]

The remainder of this chapter is structured as follows: we start with a brief introduction into realized volatility estimation. Then, we describe the heterogeneous autoregressive model of realized volatility (HAR-RV) which provides the basis for the quantile-heterogeneous autoregressive model of realized volatility that we present in the subsequent section. We discuss basic econometric features of this new model. Also, we explain why we consider this model particularly interesting for the analysis of commodity market volatility and how it contributes to answering commodity market-specific economic questions. To illustrate our theoretical considerations (different traders, trading motives), we present an empirical application for selected commodity futures (gold, silver, and crude oil) together with a detailed economic interpretation. We conclude with a short summary and outlook.

2. Realized volatility and quantile regression

2.1. Realized volatility

Return volatility is typically perceived as the *risk* associated with a particular asset. Alternatively, it is (often) interpreted as a measure for *information flow* in financial markets. It is central in finance, both in theory and practice. Option pricing and asset allocation, portfolio selection and re-balancing are only some applications to which *volatility* is a highly important input parameter. Various popular risk measurement and risk management approaches such as Value-at-Risk rely on it either. Volatility estimation hence is an important topic. As most of these applications are typically embedded in a dynamic context, understanding the behavior of volatility over time is clearly of great relevance as well.

A fundamental problem with volatility is the fact that real world financial time series are observable at certain points in time (frequencies) only while the true underlying *price processes* are continuous. Therefore, volatility, in fact, is latent and needs to be estimated from data, often observed at lower frequencies. The literature proposes various different solutions. For example, historical volatility, range-based volatility, implied volatility, and the popular ARCH and GARCH models belong to the methods widely used to estimate volatility from daily, weekly, and monthly return data. Recently, the use of *realized volatilities* has become more and more popular. On the one hand, this can be explained by the increasing availability of high-frequency data; on the other hand this may be due to the realized volatility's attractive empirical features.

The theoretical foundation for the realized volatility relies on the assumption of a continuous (stochastic) price process and the theory of quadratic variation. Andersen et al. (2001a) have shown that the volatility of the latent price process can be obtained consistently, if the sampling frequency tends to an infinitesimal time interval. The daily volatility, for instance, can then simply be estimated from the square root of the sum of squared intra-day returns observed at ultra-high frequencies.[3] The resulting quantities can then be treated as observed realizations of daily volatility, which means that they can directly be used in conventional econometric models.

In practice, however, an important problem with high-frequency financial data is the presence of so-called market microstructure noise. While the theory suggests to sample at the finest time intervals possible, in reality, price observations at ultra-high frequencies are typically characterized by various distorting effects such as discreteness, jumps, bid-ask bouncing (occurring when transactions are priced between the bid and ask prices), or non-synchronous trading. Presence of either of these microstructure effects leads to a bias in the resulting volatility estimates. The benefits of frequent sampling are thus traded off against the issues caused by cumulating noise.

Empirical applications typically avoid these problems by using a sampling frequency that balances the trade-off between bias and variance. There are various different tools that can help to pick the optimal sampling frequency. For example, volatility signature plots, proposed by Andersen and Bollerslev (1998), help in visualizing this bias-frequency relationship and hence can provide guidance in finding the appropriate sampling frequency.[4] Typically, the findings suggest to sample at moderate intra-daily frequencies such as every 5, 10, or 30 minutes and to discard the information from within those time intervals. Overall, however, the 5-minute frequency has become most common in the literature. It has been shown to be most adequate in solving the trade-off between bias and variance in the realized volatility estimator (Andersen et al., 2010, Liu et al., 2015). Alternatively, bias correction techniques or market microstructure robust volatility estimators can be used for data sampled at ultra-high frequencies instead. Andersen et al. (2001a), for instance, propose a moving-average filter for raw high-frequency returns. Martens and van Dijk (2007) propose the realized range estimator, which is robust to bid-ask bounce, while Andersen et al. (2012) suggest the jump-robust median realized volatility.

Compared to traditional volatility proxies such as squared daily returns, realized volatilities are characterized by a much higher precision since they incorporate more information about the price process (see Andersen and Bollerslev, 1998). Additionally, and in contrast to volatilities estimated from the popular ARCH and GARCH models, realized volatilities are *model-free ex-post* estimates of the underlying asset return volatilities in the sense that they do not rely on the assumption(s) of a parametric model. That is, no potentially restrictive assumptions on the dynamics of the underlying conditional distribution are necessary.

Until recently, studies on realized volatilities focused on the stock and foreign exchange markets (see, for example, Andersen et al., 2001a, b, 2003; Corsi, 2009; Bubák et al., 2011). With a growing interest in commodity markets (index investment, risk management) and an increasing availability of commodity market high-frequency data, however, some authors started to consider these markets as well (see, e.g., Martens and Zein, 2004; Wang et al., 2008; Souček and Todorova, 2013; Todorova et al., 2014; Todorova, 2015).

2.2. *The heterogeneous autoregressive model of realized volatility (HAR-RV)*

One model for the daily realized volatility that has attracted considerable attention in the literature recently is the heterogeneous autoregressive model of realized volatility (HAR-RV), initially proposed by Corsi (2009). In essence, this model is an autoregressive-type cascade model for volatility components aggregated over different time horizons (daily, weekly, monthly). From a theoretical point of view, the HAR-RV model builds upon the considerations of the heterogeneous market hypothesis according to Müller et al. (1997). It basically assumes that volatilities measured over different time resolutions reflect the perceptions and activities of market agents with heterogeneous investment time horizons. The HAR-RV model identifies three main time resolutions: (1) *daily* to capture the activities of short-term traders with a daily or even higher trading frequency, (2) *weekly* for medium-term investors typically re-balancing their positions about once per week, and (3) *monthly* for longer-term traders with a time horizon of one month or more. This choice corresponds also broadly to behavior observed in real financial markets (Corsi, 2009).

The popularity of the HAR-RV model can be explained mainly by its remarkable empirical performance. Despite its simplicity, it is well suited to reproduce the pronounced volatility persistence as well as many of the other features of financial data. Put differently, it captures the persistence and summarizes the dynamics in the mean of realized volatility with only a few parameters. Further, the parameters in the HAR-RV model have a clear economic interpretation which is a considerable advantage compared to many other approaches that are often characterized by a lack of economic intuition (see Corsi, 2009, and the literature mentioned therein).

Following Corsi (2009) in the first step of our analysis, we consider a basic univariate specification of the HAR-RV model for each of our different markets. More precisely, we express the conditional mean of the realized volatility of today as a linear function of past realized volatilities measured over daily, weekly and monthly time horizons:

$$RV_t^{(d)} = \alpha + \beta^{(d)}RV_{t-1}^{(d)} + \beta^{(w)}RV_{t-1}^{(w)} + \beta^{(m)}RV_{t-1}^{(m)} + \varepsilon_t, \tag{1}$$

with $RV_{t-1}^{(d)}$, $RV_{t-1}^{(w)}$ and $RV_{t-1}^{(m)}$ corresponding to the above-mentioned daily, weekly and monthly volatility aggregates and ε_t being a serially uncorrelated zero mean innovation term. Specifically, $RV_{t-1}^{(d)}$ corresponds to the lagged daily realized volatility, whereas the weekly and monthly volatility components, $RV_{t-1}^{(w)}$ and $RV_{t-1}^{(m)}$, are averages over the past 5 and 22 trading days, computed as $(1/5) \times (RV_{t-1}^{(d)} +$

$RV_{t-2}^{(d)} + ... + RV_{t-5}^{(d)})$ and $(1/22) \times (RV_{t-1}^{(d)} + RV_{t-2}^{(d)} + ... + RV_{t-22}^{(d)})$, respectively. This specification corresponds to a parsimonious autoregressive-type model for the realized volatility, just like an AR(22) process with restrictions.

Using conventional ordinary least squares (OLS) regression techniques, Corsi (2009) estimates the conditional mean of the (daily) realized volatility, given the three right-hand-side volatility components, realized over different time horizons. The estimated dependence parameters allow to obtain insights with respect to the relative importance of past volatilities on the daily volatility. For the S&P 500 Index Future, for example, Corsi (2009) finds a decreasing dependence from the daily, to the weekly, to the monthly volatility component (i.e., $\beta^{(d)} > \beta^{(w)} > \beta^{(m)}$). Differences between dependencies across different volatility aggregates might indicate an asymmetric information flow between short-, medium-, and long-term traders and different proportions of such traders being present in the markets.

2.3. The quantile-heterogeneous autoregressive model of realized volatility (Q-HAR-RV)

Being confined to the analysis of the conditional mean of realized volatility, however, the HAR-RV model according to Corsi (2009) is not able to capture any details about state dependence in the volatility dynamics. Put differently, the HAR-RV model cannot describe the potentially time-varying relative importance of past volatility components. Since volatility is typically used in dynamic contexts, it would be very interesting to obtain insights into the temporal dependence with respect to different volatility levels.

Inspired by the work of Baur (2013) and Žikeš and Baruník (2016), we therefore extend the basic HAR-RV model by using the quantile (auto-)regression framework according to Koenker and Xiao (2006). Conventional OLS based autoregressive models focus on the effects of a variable's own lags on its conditional mean. Quantile autoregression instead can be used to estimate the dependence of specific conditional quantiles of the dependent variable on its own lags. That is, the analysis is not confined to study location shifts, but allows to obtain a detailed description of the tails of the dependent variable's conditional distribution. Quantile regression basically allows to describe the complete conditional distribution of the dependent variable. Further, it is robust to conditional heteroskedasticity, skewness, and leptokurtosis which are common features of realized volatility as reflected also in the descriptive statistics of our realized volatility time series (see Table 2.1). Using quantile regressions, we thus essentially relax the assumption of a (constant) linear impact of the different volatility aggregates onto the conditional volatility. More specifically, we can uncover non-linearities and asymmetries in the temporal dependence across specific conditional quantiles of the realized volatility, given the volatility components, measured over different time horizons. Compared to other non-linear models such as the threshold autoregressive models (Tong, 1983) and Markov-switching models

Table 2.1 Descriptive statistics for the daily realized volatilities

	Mean	SD	Skew	Kurt	Min	Max	Obs
Gold RV	1.2334	0.8187	1.90	7.67	0.0971	6.0314	2648
log(Gold RV)	0.0182	0.6323	−0.28	3.58	−2.3324	1.7970	2648
Silver RV	2.1122	1.3131	1.62	6.64	0.1458	10.9597	2410
log(Silver RV)	0.5622	0.6394	−0.56	3.87	−1.9253	2.3942	2410
WTI RV	1.6759	1.1194	2.11	9.89	0.1165	10.0306	2714
log(WTI RV)	0.3157	0.6606	−0.48	3.62	−2.1500	2.3056	2714
S&P500 RV	1.0480	0.6755	2.96	18.03	0.1030	8.1343	3807
log(S&P500 RV)	−0.1027	0.5306	0.27	3.68	−2.2731	2.0961	3087

(Hamilton, 1989; 1994), quantile regression is flexible in the sense that also complex non-linear dynamics can be captured accurately with a few a priori restrictions. Particularly, it is not necessary to predetermine the number of 'states' or thresholds.

Until now, there are various general applications of quantile regression in empirical finance (e.g., Koenker and Zhao, 1996; Chernozhukov and Umantsev, 2001; Engle and Manganelli, 2004). An application in the context of the HAR-RV model, however, has to the best of our knowledge, so far, only been considered by Bonaccolto and Caporin (2014) and Žikeš and Baruník (2016). Similarly to us, Žikeš and Baruník (2016) employ quantile regression techniques to estimate the dependence parameters for univariate specifications of the HAR-RV model. Their focus, however, is on forecasting specific quantiles of the conditional distribution of daily realized volatility. Our aim, by contrast, is to provide a detailed description of the volatility dynamics with respect to different states of the financial markets. Further, their motivation is rather of a pure econometric nature, whilst our goal is to draw concrete economic conclusions which seem to be absent in this particular literature so far. Apart from that, we apply our Q-HAR-RV in order to study commodity futures markets which is to the best of our knowledge a unique feature as well.

Based on the flexible semi-parametric quantile regression framework, Equation (1) now takes the following form of a quantile-heterogeneous autoregressive model of realized volatility (Q-HAR-RV):

$$Q_{RV_t^{(d)}}(\tau \mid \mathcal{F}_{t-1}) = \alpha(\tau) + \beta^{(d)}(\tau)RV_{t-1}^{(d)} + \beta^{(w)}(\tau)RV_{t-1}^{(w)} + \beta^{(m)}(\tau)RV_{t-1}^{(m)}, \quad (2)$$

where $\mathcal{F}_{t-1}$ denotes the information available at day $t-1$ and $Q_{RV_t^{(d)}}(\tau \mid \mathcal{F}_{t-1})$ is τth quantile of the realized volatility, conditional on $\mathcal{F}_{t-1}$. Hence, $\beta^{(d)}(\tau)$, $\beta^{(w)}(\tau)$ and $\beta^{(m)}(\tau)$ are the quantile-specific volatility-dependence parameters which are of central interest to us. We interpret them as quantile-specific daily, weekly, and monthly persistence parameters. Estimating Equation (2) over the range of all quantiles $\tau \in [.01, .02, \ldots, .99]$ allows us to characterize volatility persistence and dynamics with respect to different states of the commodity markets.

Primarily, we are interested in comparing high and low volatility, i.e., upper and lower quantiles of the volatility distribution. Medium volatility around the central quantiles might be of interest as well. According to Baur (2013), the sequence of temporal dependence parameters across all quantiles describes the *structure of dependence*, in our case, however, with respect to the level of today's volatility. In the presentation of our results, we contrast these quantile sequences to the corresponding coefficient estimates from OLS regressions as a benchmark and measure for the *degree* of dependence.

Besides the graphical presentation of the results, we perform a Kolmogorov-Smirnov-type test as well as a Wald-type test to formally test for non-linearities and assess the presence of asymmetries in the temporal dependence across low- and high-volatility days. First, to test for the presence of overall quantile effects with respect to the corresponding (linear) dependence parameter (estimated by OLS), we use a Kolmogorov-Smirnov type test according to Bera et al. (2014). This test allows us to check the general presence of quantile-specific dependencies that differ from the OLS benchmark. In particular, we produce a sequence of Wald statistics $(W(\tau = L), \ldots, W(\tau = U))$ out of individual Wald tests for specific ranges of quantiles $(\mathcal{T} = [L, U])$. The null hypothesis for the presence of an overall quantile effect is then H_0: $\beta(\tau = j) = \beta^{OLS}$ for all $j \in \mathcal{T}$. We evaluate the supremum of the sequence of Wald statistics:

$$W_n := \sup_{\tau \in \mathcal{T}} W(\tau), \tag{3}$$

where W_n does not follow a standard χ_p^2-distribution. According to Bera et al. (2014), we approximate the p-values by using an upper boundary, taking the form

$$\Pr(W_n > u) \le \Pr(\chi_p^2 > u) + \frac{u^{\frac{p-1}{2}}}{2^{\frac{p}{2}} \exp(u/2)\Gamma(p/2)} \int_{\mathcal{T}} E\left| \frac{\partial W_n^{\frac{1}{2}}(\tau)}{\partial \tau} \right| d\tau. \tag{4}$$

We estimate $\int_{\mathcal{T}} E\left|\frac{\partial W_n^{\frac{1}{2}}(\tau)}{\partial \tau}\right| d\tau$ from the total variation $V = |W_n^{\frac{1}{2}}(\tau_1) - W_n^{\frac{1}{2}}(\tau_L)| + |W_n^{\frac{1}{2}}(\tau_2) - W_n^{\frac{1}{2}}(\tau_1)| + \cdots + |W_n^{\frac{1}{2}}(\tau_U) - W_n^{\frac{1}{2}}(\tau_k)|$, where $\tau_1, \tau_2, \ldots, \tau_k$ are the turning points of $W_n^{\frac{1}{2}}(\tau)$ and L and U are the lower and upper bounds of τ.

Further, to test for the presence of differences in the volatility dynamics with respect to different volatility levels prevailing, we use Wald tests again. The null hypothesis to compare a range of dependence coefficients across quantiles is H_0: $\beta(\tau = .01) + \ldots + \beta(\tau = d) = \beta(\tau = u) + \ldots + \beta(\tau = .99)$, where the Wald statistic takes the form

$$W_{d,u} = (\mathbf{R}\boldsymbol{\beta}(\tau) - r)'(\mathbf{R}\hat{\Omega}_B\mathbf{R}')^{-1}(\mathbf{R}\boldsymbol{\beta}(\tau) - r), \tag{5}$$

with $\mathbf{R} = (1, \ldots, 1, -1, \ldots, -1)$, $\boldsymbol{\beta}(\tau) = (\beta(\tau = .01), \ldots, \beta(\tau = d), \beta(\tau = u), \ldots, \beta(\tau = .99))'$, $r = 0$ and $\hat{\Omega}_B$ as the covariance matrix.[5] For one linear restriction, as in our case, the Wald statistic is approximately χ^2-distributed with one degree of freedom.

The model described in Equation (2) is linear in parameters (for a given quantile, τ) and all parameters can be estimated according to the standard optimization routine presented in Koenker and Bassett (1978) and implemented, for example, in R. Further, we estimate asymptotic standard errors based on bootstrap methods.

While quantile regression is not well-suited for (multiple step ahead) forecasting applications (since future quantiles are unknown in advance), it can be used to obtain a precise description of the volatility dynamics. In essence, the Q-HAR-RV model allows us to broaden the perspective and to study differences and changes in the volatility dynamics along two dimensions: first, motivated by economic theory and like the pure HAR-RV model, it captures the relative importance of volatility measured over different time resolutions which we assume to reflect the activities of heterogeneous market participants. Second, the use of quantile regression allows us to capture the changing relative importance of volatility components, depending on the state of the volatility or put differently, the respective quantile of the (conditional) volatility distribution.

3. Motivation for an application to commodity markets

3.1. Volatility persistence and differences across markets: HAR-RV

The heterogeneous market hypothesis proposed by Müller et al. (1997) states that volatility measured over different time resolutions reflects the perceptions and activities of market agents characterized by heterogeneous investment horizons. While traders may differ along several dimensions, a distinction between different types of traders with respect to their investment time horizon seems economically plausible and useful (see, e.g., Müller et al., 1997; Corsi, 2009; Pennings and Garcia, 2010).

In our point of view, the interplay between market agents with different trading motives and time horizons might be particularly evident in commodity markets. On the one hand, there are producers and commercial traders, having a 'real' and rather longer term interest behind their transactions. These traders will typically trade infrequently. Often, the primary objective behind their transactions is to transfer their exposure to future price movements to speculators taking the corresponding long and short positions. On the other hand, there is a large fraction of speculators who have no interest in the delivery of the underlying commodity but consider the futures contract itself a (financial) asset. Among them, there are index investors and participants trading a lot among each other and executing transactions also at very high frequencies, constantly monitoring and re-evaluating the markets. Obviously, these short-term traders might react quickly to changes in short-term volatility. Short-term traders, and thus the short-term (daily) volatility, however, may also be affected by medium- and long-term volatility. By contrast, for investors with rather long time horizons, the short-term volatility might be relatively unimportant. Their decisions can be assumed to be mostly impacted by long-term volatility and 'fundamentals' (Müller et al., 1997, p. 217).

In addition, volatility dynamics may vary across commodity markets (agriculture, energy, precious metals, rare-earth elements) due to differences in certain characteristics of the underlying commodities. Precious metals, such as gold and silver, are durable and provide a store of value. Hence, precious metals are used as *investment asset.*[6] For gold, this might be particularly true. It is widely used for portfolio diversification and is kept as a reserve by virtually every central bank in the world. By the nature of silver and gold, we would hence expect a large share of speculative investment traders to be active in these markets. Since they are used as investment assets they might in many respects behave very similar to financial assets, like for example, equities. Beyond that, precious metals are also used in industry (Schweikert, 2018). For instance, gold is used in restorative dentistry and for high-quality electrical connectors. Silver is the most reflective metal and is used in photography, optics, and the solar energy industry. By contrast, other commodities have industrial use only, are non-durable and hence share the properties of a *consumption asset.* Crude oil, for instance, is primarily used for transportation and heating fuel. It is also utilized for electricity generation and as an input for the production of asphalt and road oil as well as the making of chemicals, plastics, and synthetic materials. Crude oil hence is an important economic input factor. This may also manifest in the presence of a more pronounced 'real' delivery aspect. The cost of carry, the lease rate (compensation for lending) and the convenience yield are more important than in case of silver and gold. Moreover, the price of crude oil reacts more sensitively to the supply side, since the stockpile of crude oil is substantially less than the annual extraction. In contrast, the prices of precious metals are rather driven by the demand-side since they are durable assets and stockpile outweighs annual production.

We believe that the above-mentioned considerations can provide valuable economic intuition for the interpretation of our estimation results. We translate the above considerations into two summarizing statements on commodity market realized volatility dynamics:

1. Measured volatility dependence might differ across (commodity) markets. The dependence patterns identified might provide valuable indications about investors' time horizons and the proportion between short- and long-term traders being active in the markets.
2. For non-durable assets (*consumption assets*) like crude oil, the volatility of today might depend more strongly on the long-term and less strongly on the short-term volatility component in comparison to *investment assets* such as silver and gold.

3.2. State-dependent volatility dynamics: Q-HAR-RV

The use of the Q-HAR-RV model is mainly motivated by the potential presence of state dependence in the volatility dynamics. Traders' heterogeneity in time horizons might not only result in heterogeneous reactions to price fluctuations captured over different time intervals, but also in different reactions or attention shifts depending on high, moderate and low volatility, and thus state dependence. For financial returns, for example, it is a well-known phenomenon that temporal dependencies can be characterized by asymmetries under certain circumstances (see, e.g., Barberis et al., 1998; Veronesi, 1999; Zhang, 2006; Baur et al., 2012; Kuck et al., 2015).

Theoretically, asymmetries in realized volatility dependence might be explained by shifts in traders' attention or by changes in the shares of certain types of traders being active in the markets. In presence of very high volatility (today), for instance, uncertainty prevails and speculators might react more strongly to past volatility than in the presence of moderate volatility. If prices fluctuate strongly (in the short run), the potential for short-term gains is high. Traders might therefore open and close their positions more quickly than during episodes of moderate volatility due to an increased attractiveness of short-term speculation. This might even be self-reinforcing, by first increasing the share of speculators and second, causing further increases in volatility on high volatility days. At the same time, episodes of uncertainty and crises are typically characterized by extreme negative returns. The need to close out positions in order to avoid losses or meet margin calls might be stronger then. That is, tensions on the financial markets and commodity markets, might also force traders to react and rebalance their portfolios more quickly. This effect might be reflected in a particularly pronounced increase in the dependence on the past short-term volatility component.

Finally, drawing attention to the differences between consumption and investment assets, we would again expect the share of short-term speculators to be particularly high in investment markets which might result in stronger differences in volatility patterns between high and low volatility days in these markets. By contrast, for consumption assets, state dependence of the volatility dynamics could be less pronounced due to a smaller share of short-term speculators and a tendency of market participants to focus on the long term.

In essence, there are various different reasons to assume that volatility dependence might be characterized by asymmetry. They translate into the following summarizing statements:

3. Realized volatility dependence might differ statistically significantly across the high and low volatility state.
4. The asymmetries in dependence across the high and low volatility state might be more pronounced in case of investment assets (gold, silver, S&P 500) than in case of consumption assets (crude oil).

4. Empirical evidence from major commodity markets

4.1. Data

The data that we use for the empirical illustrations consists of WTI light sweet crude oil, gold and silver futures bid and ask quotes from the Thomson Reuters TickHistory database. The sample covers the period from January 2007 to

September 2014 for gold and silver and from January 2000 to September 2014 in case of WTI light sweet crude oil.

While multiple futures contract maturities are traded simultaneously, it is convention to consider only the price of the next-to-maturity contract (front contract). To get a continuous series of futures prices over an extended period it is thus necessary to 'switch' from the front contract to the next one (the second next-to-maturity) at some point. Here, the expiry date of the front contract is chosen as the so-called *rollover* date, that is, the point at which we switch from one contract to another.[7] Assuming that gold, silver, and WTI futures contracts are traded actively, i.e., are liquid, the choice of the rollover date should not affect the resulting time series in any systematic way. Carchano and Pardo (2009), for example, are not able find any evidence for a significant impact of the choice of the rollover date on the return series.

For the construction of intra-day returns underlying our realized measures, we follow Scharth and Medeiros (2009), Giot et al. (2010), Andersen et al. (2012) and others and use the midpoint of the bid and ask quotes as a price indication. An appealing feature of proceeding this way is that we can rule out the presence of bid-ask bounce effects which might distort volatility estimation when transaction prices are used instead.[8]

As common in the literature, we sample our intra-day returns at the 5 minutes interval. Then we compute the daily realized volatilities by

$$RV_t^{(d)} = \sqrt{\sum_{j=1}^{M} r_{t,j}^2},$$

where $r_{t,j}$ is the jth 5-minute return on day t and M is the number of intra-day returns. That is, we construct the daily realized volatilities for each of our markets by summing up the squared intra-daily log-returns ($r_{t,j}^2$) for each single trading day in the sample. Following e.g., Bubák et al. (2011), we define a trading day to last from 21:00 GMT to 20:59 GMT the following day. We delete weekends as well as public holidays such as Christmas Eve and New Year in order to avoid periods of low trading volume. For model estimation, we log-transform the realized volatilities, in order to improve the statistical properties of the time series.

The (daily) mid-prices and the corresponding realized volatilities of our three futures are depicted in Figure 2.1. All series show typical characteristics of financial time series. Whereas the mid-prices resemble non-stationary random series, the realized volatilities appear stationary and show volatility clustering (strong persistence).

4.2. Estimation results

HAR-RV Results

The estimation results for the pure HAR-RV model for the three commodities are reported in Table 2.2. In order to compare the magnitude of the estimated

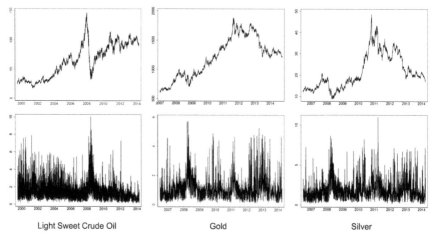

Light Sweet Crude Oil   Gold   Silver

Figure 2.1 Time series of prices and realized volatilities

Notes: Daily mid-prices are depicted in the upper panel. The lower panel shows daily realized volatilities.

coefficients, all variables have been standardized before estimation (Verbeek, 2017). To put our findings into perspective, we include also the estimation results for a HAR-RV model for the S&P 500 futures.[9] First, the temporal dependence coefficients for the past daily, weekly and monthly volatility components are, generally, statistically significant across all four series, indicating long memory, i.e., persistence in the volatility series. The only exceptions exist for gold and silver where the coefficient for the past weekly realized volatility components are not statistically significantly different from zero. Regarding the magnitudes of the coefficients, gold and silver appear to be very similar. Substantial differences are, however, evident between precious metals and both crude oil and the equity market.

Following Corsi (2009), temporal dependence on past realized volatilities aggregated over different time scales might represent the activities of market participants with different time horizons. The coefficients on the volatility aggregates might hence provide an indication if a market is composed rather by homogeneous or heterogeneous market participants. The differences across coefficients that are evident in Table 2.2, indeed support the presence of heterogeneous traders across the four markets (Statement 1). As a general pattern, we find the coefficients for the monthly component to be (slightly) more pronounced than the daily and weekly components in case of commodities. This might indicate the relative importance of market participants with long-term time horizons in the commodities markets, particularly in the crude oil market.[10]

Comparing now in detail gold, silver, crude oil, and S&P 500 volatility dynamics, it is apparent that the coefficient on monthly volatility for precious metals is similar in magnitude to that of the S&P 500's monthly component.[11]

Table 2.2 HAR-RV estimation results

	Gold	Silver	WTI Crude Oil	S&P500
Constant	0.0012	0.0026	−0.0017	−0.0016
	(.07)	(.14)	(−.13)	(−.18)
Daily	0.2265***	0.1886***	0.0918***	0.2725***
	(10.40)	(8.14)	(5.58)	(14.03)
Weekly	0.0238	0.0414	−0.1830***	0.3965***
	(.78)	(1.29)	(−6.81)	(13.80)
Monthly	0.2464***	0.2476***	0.5339***	0.1949***
	(8.90)	(8.51)	(21.06)	(8.69)

Notes: *t*-statistics in parentheses.
***(**, *) denotes significance at a 1% (5%, 10%) significance level.

In contrast to precious metals, the dependence on past weekly volatility appears to be relatively more important than both the daily and monthly volatility component for equity. Like for equities (S&P 500), the volatilities of precious metals exhibit marked dependence on past daily volatility, although somewhat less pronounced. This result supports our idea that precious metals are also used similar to traditional investment assets. In case of crude oil, by contrast, we find a strikingly low dependence on the daily volatility component, while the dependence on the monthly volatility component is rather strong (in absolute terms), also relative to that of the other assets.[12] Moreover, we find a negative relation between past weekly volatility and daily realized volatility in case of crude oil futures. This may indicate some form of cyclicality.

Overall and in line with Statement 2, the impact of long-term volatility is strongest for crude oil while we find it to be substantially weaker for gold, silver and S&P 500 (in absolute terms). This supports the idea that the crude oil futures market might be characterized by a comparably larger share of traders with a long-term investment horizon whereas the gold and silver futures markets appear to be composed of both short-term and long-term oriented traders. This might also reflect that precious metals, particularly gold, are investment assets but also have industrial use, while crude oil is of industrial use only.

Q-HAR-RV results

For ease of understanding, we present the estimation results of the Q-HAR-RV models graphically.[13] For each market, Figure 2.2 shows the sequence of the estimated $\hat{\beta}(\tau)$s over all percentiles τ (black solid curve) together with the corresponding 99% confidence band (gray-shaded area). In addition, we show the benchmark OLS coefficient with its 99% confidence interval (dashed line). The lower and upper bounds of the confidence bands for the quantile regression coefficients are based on bootstrapping techniques.

On the one hand, as evident in Figure 2.2, there are substantial differences in the volatility dependence parameters across quantiles for commodities, indicating that the volatility dynamics are time-varying. For the S&P 500, by contrast, the

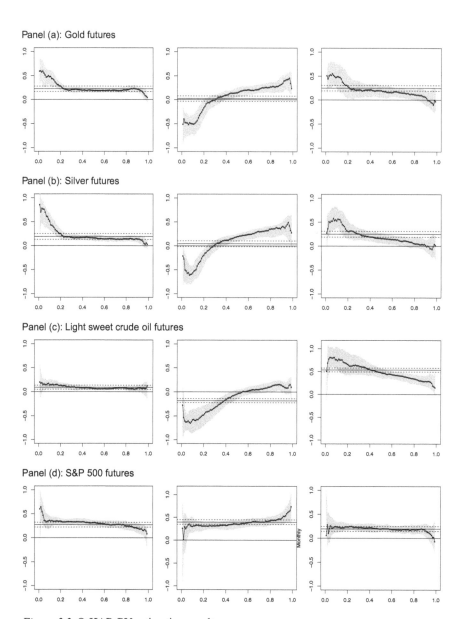

Figure 2.2 Q-HAR-RV estimation results

Notes: Dependence on past daily (left), weekly (middle), and monthly (right) volatility. Solid horizontal line: OLS coefficient; dashed horizontal lines: corresponding 99% confidence bands. Solid curve: quantile-specific coefficients; Gray-shaded: area within the corresponding 99% confidence band; Confidence bands are based on standard errors estimated via bootstrapping techniques.

quantile specific coefficients are very close to their OLS benchmark. Though the asymmetry is not very pronounced for the S&P 500, the overall pattern in the temporal dependence structure, in particular with respect to past daily and weekly volatility, appears similar to that of silver and gold. On the other hand, there are also some general patterns and similarities in dependencies across our commodity futures: first, the dependence tends to be stable (the quantile-specific dependence parameters evolve relatively horizontal) across quantiles for the daily volatility component, except for very extreme quantiles. Second, the impact of the weekly volatility component is significantly negative for lower and positive for upper (conditional) quantiles of the daily realized volatility. Moreover, the dependence on past weekly volatility seems to become more important when today's volatility increases from moderate to high levels. Third, in contrast, the temporal dependence tends to decrease from lower to upper quantiles for the monthly volatility aggregate. More specifically, the dependence on the monthly volatility component becomes insignificant for extreme upper quantiles. In essence, this suggests that information generated over the medium term (five days) gains relative importance in phases of increased uncertainty. To sum up, the estimated impact of past realized volatility is significantly positive across quantiles except for extreme quantiles. Only for the weekly volatility component in the commodities markets we find a significant negative impact on today's volatility at lower quantiles.

Specifically, our results indicate that the daily volatility component tends to be a stronger volatility driver (or amplifier) on low volatility days. On high volatility days, however, it tends to have a relatively weaker (positive) impact. The weekly component, by contrast, tends to have a dampening impact on low volatility days and a positive, amplifying effect on high volatility days. For the monthly volatility component, our findings suggest the presence of an amplifying impact that tends to be particularly strong when today's volatility is low. By contrast, when volatility is high, the dependence on past monthly volatility becomes insignificant. In sum, volatility on low volatility days tends to be driven strongly by past daily and monthly volatility, whereas volatility on high volatility days tends to be driven strongly by the weekly volatility component.

From an economic perspective, these findings suggest the following conclusions: first, when volatility is low (moderate) it seems to be mainly caused by the activities of traders with short- and long-term investment horizon. Second, high volatility is driven particularly by the activities of traders with medium-term time horizon. Moreover, the observed negative dependence on past weekly volatility in commodity markets when volatility is low might be related to some sort of cyclicality. It seems that for the weekly component, a change in traders' composition might be apparent. Alternatively, traders might tend to focus more strongly on ex-post volatility measured over the medium-term in case of high (extreme) volatility days. Simultaneously, their attention to the long-run volatility component tends to decrease.

Finally, we use Wald-type tests according to Bera et al. (2014) in order to formally assess the statistical significance of the non-linearities in the volatility

Table 2.3 Tests for non-linearities and asymmetries between low and high volatility

	Daily	*Weekly*	*Monthly*
Panel (a): Tests for non-linearities (quantile effects)			
Gold	30.06	84.30	18.46
	(0.00)	(0.00)	(0.00)
Silver	66.31	144.00	49.71
	(0.00)	(0.00)	(0.00)
Oil	11.51	63.57	22.73
	(0.03)	(0.00)	(0.00)
S&P 500	21.48	14.21	6.65
	(0.00)	(0.01)	(0.34)
Panel (b): Tests for asymmetries			
Gold	24.72	77.47	25.24
	(0.00)	(0.00)	(0.00)
Silver	71.27	92.96	31.37
	(0.00)	(0.00)	(0.00)
Oil	2.92	46.93	22.57
	(0.09)	(0.00)	(0.00)
S&P 500	14.97	8.70	1.71
	(0.00)	(0.00)	(0.21)

Note: p-values in parentheses.

dynamics. First, a sup-Wald test is used to study the presence of significant overall non-linearities (quantile effects). Second, we apply a Wald test to investigate the significance of potential asymmetries in dependencies for different levels of the daily realized volatility. Specifically, we test the presence of differences in the temporal dependence on past volatilities across the 1%–10% and the 90%–99% quantiles (see Statement 3). The sup-Wald tests confirm the presence of non-linearities in the temporal dependence on past volatilities aggregated over daily, weekly and monthly time horizons, see Table 2.3, Panel (a). Only in case of crude oil and S&P 500, the null hypothesis of linear temporal dependencies cannot be generally rejected at conventional significance levels. Specifically, the dependence on past daily volatility is not characterized by non-linearities in case of crude oil. For the S&P 500, the dependence on past weekly and monthly volatilities seems to be linear. Likewise, the tests confirm the presence of asymmetric dependence particularly between low and high volatility, see Table 2.3, Panel (b). Only for past daily and past monthly volatility the null hypothesis of symmetric temporal dependence across quantiles cannot be rejected in case of crude oil and S&P 500, respectively.

5. Summary and outlook

This chapter revisited the HAR-RV and Q-HAR-RV models and demonstrated their usefulness to obtain interesting new insights into volatility dynamics of commodity markets. Specifically, we studied the temporal dependencies of gold, silver and crude oil futures volatility in detail.

First, the differences across the dependence on the daily, weekly, and monthly volatility components that we find are theoretically consistent with the presence of traders with heterogeneous time horizons. Specifically, the impact of long-term volatility appears to be more dominant in our analyzed commodity markets than in the equity market. In addition, the differences across different commodity markets that we find might indicate different proportions between short-term and long-term traders across investment and consumption asset markets. In the case of crude oil as a consumption asset, we find the dependence on the longer term (monthly) volatility component to be substantially stronger than in case of the investment assets gold, silver, and the S&P 500.

Second, using the Q-HAR-RV model, we find volatility dynamics in the markets for precious metals and crude oil to be characterized by substantial state dependence. The non-linear dependence patterns that we reveal appear to be theoretically consistent with the idea of shifts in investor attention or changes in investor composition depending on the level of current volatility. Interestingly, we find strong similarities in the dependence patterns across our commodity futures. Specifically, for the weekly and monthly volatility component there are substantial differences in the dependence on past volatility aggregates between low- and high-volatility states. In presence of high volatility, the dependence on the long-term (monthly) volatility component tends to decrease generally while the dependence on the medium-term (weekly) volatility aggregate tends to increase notably.

It will be of interest in future work to compare these findings based on a small selection of commodity markets with a broader set of commodities as well as other financial markets (e.g., foreign exchange). Further studies could also investigate the dependence structure across indexed and non-indexed commodities.

Acknowledgments

We are indebted to Robert Jung, Dirk G. Baur, Karsten Schweikert, František Čech, the editor Julien Chevallier, and an anonymous referee for valuable comments and suggestions on earlier versions of the manuscript. We further thank seminar participants at the University of Hohenheim and the attendees of the International Conference on Computational and Financial Econometrics, held in London, in 2015 and 2017. Access to Thomson Reuters TickHistory (SIRCA) provided by the Hohenheim Datalab is gratefully acknowledged.

Notes

1 Similar models have been used in slightly different forms by Bonaccolto and Caporin (2014) and by Žikeš and Baruník (2016).
2 Moreover, speculative trading with commodities, particularly with agricultural commodities, is perceived controversially in both media and academia. See for example

Gilbert (2010) and the literature mentioned therein on the heated discussions about the drivers of agricultural futures prices.

3 See also Andersen and Bollerslev (1998), Andersen et al. (2001a), Andersen et al. (2001b), and Barndorff-Nielsen and Shephard (2002) for fundamental literature.

4 If microstructure noise is present, it will distort the average realized volatility if the sampling frequency is increased. Plotting the average realized volatility against the return frequency hence may help to find the appropriate sampling frequency, i.e., where the average realized volatility stabilizes.

5 Note that we estimate the variance-covariance matrix Ω for the quantile-dependent autoregressive coefficients by using bootstrap techniques.

6 Note that in addition to bars and coins, jewelry provides a store of value and may be purchased for the purpose of portfolio diversification as well.

7 In our case this results in 12 rollover dates each year due to monthly expiry cycle.

8 As argued in Hansen and Lunde (2006), using mid-quotes instead of transaction data reduces the spurious serial correlation in the high-frequency returns due to bid-ask bounce and non-synchronous trading effects.

9 Specifically, we consider the E-mini S&P 500 Futures contracts.

10 If investors have limited attention and short-term traders care about short-, medium-, and long-term volatility whereas long-term traders only care about long-term volatility, then this should be reflected in a stronger dependence on the long-term volatility component than the short-term (medium-term) component.

11 Considering the coefficient's dimensions and their precision (large t-statistics) allows to uncover differences in the parameters across different models. Approximately, if the confidence intervals of two coefficients do not overlap this points to their statistical diversity. Note that it is not possible to formally test parameter equality across equations (different models) using conventional Wald-type tests.

12 Given the high precision of the estimates, it can well be assumed that the confidence intervals on the coefficient of the monthly component of crude oil do not overlap with that of gold and silver, respectively.

13 Again, we standardize the dependent and independent variables before estimation in order to be able to compare the magnitudes of coefficients.

Bibliography

Adams, Z., Glück, T., 2015. Financialization in commodity markets: A passing trend or the new normal? *Journal of Banking and Finance* 60(Supplement C), 93–111.

Aepli, M. D., Füss, R., Henriksen, T. E. S., Paraschiv, F., 2017. Modeling the multivariate dynamic dependence structure of commodity futures portfolios. *Journal of Commodity Markets* 6, 66–87.

Andersen, T. G., Bollerslev, T., 1998. Answering the skeptics: Yes, standard volatility models do provide accurate forecasts. *International Economic Review* 39(4), 885–905.

Andersen, T. G., Bollerslev, T., Diebold, F. X., Ebens, H., 2001a. The distribution of realized stock return volatility. *Journal of Financial Economics* 61(1), 43–76.

Andersen, T. G., Bollerslev, T., Diebold, F. X., Labys, P., 2001b. The distribution of realized exchange rate volatility. *Journal of the American Statistical Association* 96(453), 42–55.

Andersen, T. G., Bollerslev, T., Frederiksen, F., Nielsen, M. O., 2010. Continuous-time models, realized volatilities, and testable distributional implications for daily stock returns. *Journal of Applied Econometrics* 25(2), 233–261.

Andersen, T. G., Bollerslev, T., Labys, F. X. D. P., 2003. Modeling and forecasting realized volatility. *Econometrica* 71, 579–625.

Andersen, T. G., Dobrev, D., Schaumburg, E., 2012. Jump-robust volatility estimation using nearest neighbor truncation. *Journal of Econometrics* 169(1), 75–93.

Barberis, N., Shleifer, A., Vishny, R., 1998. A model of investor sentiment. *Journal of Financial Economics* 49(3), 307–343.

Barndorff-Nielsen, O. E., Shephard, N., 2002. Estimating quadratic variation using realized variance. *Journal of Applied Econometrics* 17, 457–477.

Baur, D., 2013. The structure and degree of dependence: A quantile regression approach. *Journal of Banking & Finance* 37(3), 786–798.

Baur, D., Dimpfl, T., Jung, R., 2012. Stock return autocorrelations revisited: A quantile regression approach. *Journal of Empirical Finance* 19(2), 254–265.

Bera, A. K., Galvao, A. F., Wang, L., 2014. On testing the equality of mean and quantile effects. *Journal of Econometric Methods* 3(1), 47–62.

Bonaccolto, G., Caporin, M., 2014. Modelling and forecasting the realized range conditional quantiles. Available at SSRN.

Bubák, V., Kočenda, E., Žikeš, F., 2011. Volatility transmission in emerging european foreign exchange markets. *Journal of Banking & Finance* 35(11), 2829–2841.

Carchano, O., Pardo, A., 2009. Rolling over stock index futures contracts. *Journal of Futures Markets* 29(7), 684–694.

Chernozhukov, V., Umantsev, L., 2001. Conditional Value-at-Risk: Aspects of modeling and estimation. *Empirical Economics* 26(1), 271–292.

Corsi, F., 2009. A simple approximate long-memory model of realized volatility. *Journal of Financial Econometrics* 7, 174–196.

Engle, R., Manganelli, S., 2004. CAViaR: conditional autoregressive value at risk by regression quantiles. *Journal of Business & Economic Statistics* 22, 367–381.

Gilbert, C. L., 2010. How to understand high food prices. *Journal of Agricultural Economics* 61(2), 398–425.

Giot, P., Laurent, S., Petitjean, M., 2010. Trading activity, realized volatility and jumps. *Journal of Empirical Finance* 17(1), 168–175.

Hamilton, J. D., 1989. A new approach to the economic analysis of nonstationary time series and the business cycle. *Econometrica* 57(2), 357–384.

Hamilton, J. D., 1994. *Time series analysis*. Princeton, NJ: Princeton University Press.

Hansen, P. R., Lunde, A., 2006. Consistent ranking of volatility models. *Journal of Econometrics* 131(12), 97–121.

Koenker, R., Bassett, G., 1978. Regression quantiles. *Econometrica* 46(1), 33–50.

Koenker, R., Xiao, Z., 2006. Quantile autoregression. *Journal of the American Statistical Association* 101(475), 980–990.

Koenker, R., Zhao, Q., 1996. Conditional quantile estimation and inference for ARCH models. *Econometric Theory* 12(5), 793–813.

Kuck, K., Maderitsch, R., Schweikert, K., 2015. Asymmetric over- and undershooting of major exchange rates: Evidence from quantile regressions. *Economics Letters* 126(C), 114–118.

Liu, L. Y., Patton, A. J., Sheppard, K., 2015. Does anything beat 5-minute RV? A comparison of realized measures across multiple asset classes. *Journal of Econometrics* 187(1), 293–311.

Martens, M., van Dijk, D., 2007. Measuring volatility with the realized range. *Journal of Econometrics* 138(1), 181–207.

Martens, M., Zein, J., 2004. Predicting financial volatility: High-frequency time-series forecasts vis-á-vis implied volatility. *Journal of Futures Markets* 24(11), 1005–1028.

Müller, U. A., Dacorogna, M. M., Davé, R. D., Olsen, R. B., Pictet, O. V., von Weiz-säacker, J. E., 1997. Volatilities of different time resolutions analyzing the dynamics of market components. *Journal of Empirical Finance* 4(23), 213–239.

Pennings, J. M. E., Garcia, P., 2010. Risk and hedging behavior: The role and determinants of latent heterogeneity. *Journal of Financial Research* 33(4), 373–401.

Scharth, M., Medeiros, M. C., 2009. Asymmetric effects and long memory in the volatility of Dow Jones stocks. *International Journal of Forecasting* 25(2), 304–327.

Schweikert, K., 2018. Are gold and silver cointegrated? New evidence from quantile cointegrating regressions. *Journal of Banking & Finance* 88, 44–51.

Souček, M., Todorova, N., 2013. Realized volatility transmission between crude oil and equity futures markets: A multivariate HAR approach. *Energy Economics* 40(C), 586–597.

Tang, K., Xiong, W., 2012. Index investment and the financialization of commodities. *Financial Analysts Journal* 68(6), 54–74.

Todorova, N., 2015. The course of realized volatility in the LME non-ferrous metal market. *Economic Modelling* 51(Supplement C), 1–12.

Todorova, N., Worthington, A., Souček, M., 2014. Realized volatility spillovers in the non-ferrous metal futures market. *Resources Policy* 39(Supplement C), 21–31.

Tong, H., 1983. *Threshold models in nonlinear time series analysis.* Springer, New York.

Verbeek, M., 2017. *A guide to modern econometrics*, 5th Edition. John Wiley & Sons, West Sussex, England.

Veronesi, P., 1999. Stock market overreaction to bad news in good times: A rational expectations equilibrium model. *Review of Financial Studies* 12(5), 975–1007.

Wang, T., Wu, J., Yang, J., 2008. Realized volatility and correlation in energy futures markets. *Journal of Futures Markets* 28(10), 993–1011.

Zhang, X. F., 2006. Information uncertainty and stock returns. *Journal of Finance* 61(1), 105–137.

Žikeš, F., Baruník, J., 2016. Semi-parametric conditional quantile models for financial returns and realized volatility. *Journal of Financial Econometrics* 14(1), 185–226.

3 The importance of rollover in commodity returns using PARCH models

Menelaos Karanasos, Panagiotis Koutroumpis, Zannis Margaronis, and Rajat Nath

1. Introduction

The most important aspect of any algorithmic system is to ensure the data with which the system is back-tested is correct and completely agrees with the data of the platform which is then used to trade. Generally most studies in econometrics do not specify which type of data is used, whether futures or spot, or at which time the data is taken. The application of any of the theoretical models to real-life trading situations is rare. Finding the correct prices for back-testing is more difficult than was initially thought. It is therefore not straightforward to obtain the data required to back-test. Such data is normally obtained from two places: Bloomberg and Thomson Reuters Datastream. In order for a real time series to be created, it is necessary to search and download the prices available for each individual active (front month) contract for the given security. The data obtained then needs to be mapped if futures contracts are being considered since these expire on a regular basis. Carrying out an analysis on any data that is not mapped makes it inapplicable to real-life trading systems, for these are based on continuous data sets. The aim of this study is to show how the unmapped and mapped data differ econometrically. Showing this will confirm that any analysis carried out for the purposes of real-life trading requires mapped data to be used because the differences between the mapped and unmapped data can be significant.

The data section describes the data and degrees of homoskedasticity. The main issue with such data sets is that for a trading algorithm to be applied, the data itself must be continuous and contemporaneous for security spreads, if considered. Due to the existence of monthly contracts, expiry of the front month contract means the second month contract then becomes the new front month contract, and since these prices differ, a rollover or basis exists. If this roll is not taken into account, any trading system will misestimate the profits generated. The value and significance of the roll differs greatly from instrument to instrument. It has been found to be significant for most instruments, greatest of all in energies and least of all in metals, considered as a percentage of price.

This chapter will analyze the differences, econometrically, between data that has been mapped and data that is unmapped. This is significant for algorithmic trading because the roll that exists can significantly change a data set. When a model is optimized based on the data, it is clear how having incorrect data with respect to real-life trading situations can lead to a very erroneous and wrong optimized algorithm parameters. The significance of the rollover will be compared econometrically by running PARCH (power autoregressive conditional homoskedasticity) models and the various coefficients within the models will be analyzed across securities. If coefficients change significantly between a single time series, one that has been mapped and one that is unmapped, then it will be concluded that the impact of roll is large.

2. Literature review

As pointed out by Karanasos et al. (2018), modeling the stochastic properties of commodity and financial returns has attracted wide attention to the fields of energy and financial economics, given their important practical implications for investors. For instance, interpreting the stochastic properties of returns may assist investors in terms of forecasting market movements, while strong relationships between commodity and/or financial returns would indicate limited portfolio diversification opportunities for them. Even though there is a considerable amount of literature that has examined the returns properties of international financial markets such as those of equity, foreign exchange, and bond, and their cross-shock and volatility spillovers (see, e.g., Aloui et al., 2011; Bubák et al., 2011; Coudert et al., 2011; Philippas and Siriopoulos, 2013; Caporale et al., 2014; among others), many studies have also been investigating the returns characteristics of commodity markets.

From the aforementioned rapidly expanding literature, many studies have analyzed the stochastic properties of commodity returns, including those of metals (see O'Connor et al., 2015 and Vigne et al., 2017 for recent surveys on precious metals). For instance, Watkins and McAleer (2008) claim that the conditional volatility of aluminium and copper returns have been time-varying when analyzed over a long horizon using a rolling AR(1)-GARCH(1,1) model. Choi and Hammoudeh (2010) instead run a Markov-switching model and argue that spot commodity returns (i.e., Brent oil, WTI oil, copper, gold, and silver) display disparate volatility persistence in response to financial and geopolitical crises. Vivian and Wohar (2012) in their analysis support that the volatility persistence of spot commodity returns, including those of precious metals, remains on high levels even when structural breaks are considered.

Sensoy (2013) further affirm that the volatility of palladium and platinum, unlike that of gold and silver, displayed some inflationary dynamics during the turbulent year 2008 using spot price data over the period January 1999 to April 2013. Arouri et al. (2012), on the other hand, by employing parametric and semiparametric methods provided solid proof of long-range dependence in the conditional returns and volatility processes for the daily precious metals (i.e., gold, silver, platinum, and palladium), whereas Demiralay and Ulusoy (2014) have examined short and long trading positions and demonstrated that long memory volatility specifications under student-t distribution perform well in forecasting a one-day-ahead VaR for both positions.

Some other studies have also examined the links across commodity prices and their returns and volatility. Ciner (2001) cites that gold and silver futures contracts traded in Japan are not cointegrated, using daily data from 1992 to 1998. In addition, Erb and Harvey (2006) support that commodity futures returns have been mostly uncorrelated with one another, particularly across the different sectors. Nevertheless, by employing daily data of gold, platinum, and silver futures contracts traded in both the US and Japanese markets, Xu and Fung (2005) documented strong volatility feedback between these precious metals across both markets. Choi and Hammoudeh (2010), running a dynamic conditional correlation model, also report growing correlations among all the considered spot commodity returns (i.e., Brent oil, WTI oil, copper, gold, and silver) over recent years.

Several studies have further explored the dynamic relationships across both financial and commodity markets. In particular, Choi and Hammoudeh (2010) discovered signs of declining correlations between spot commodity returns (i.e., Brent oil, WTI oil, copper, gold, and silver) and the US S&P 500 stock market returns over recent years. On the other hand, Mensi et al. (2013), using a VAR GARCH model, found that there are significant spillovers in terms of volatility and shock between the S&P 500 stock returns and spot commodity market returns. More specifically, their estimation outputs showed that past shock and volatility of such stock returns significantly affect oil and gold market returns. Cochran et al. (2012), on the other hand, support that the VIX index is a crucial role in the determination of metal returns and their volatility, employing spot price data on copper, gold, platinum, and silver from January 1999 to March 2009.

As pointed out by Karanasos et al. (2018) the effect of the macroeconomic performance on commodity prices and their returns and volatility has also attracted much of attention. Tulley and Lucey (2007) corroborate that the US dollar is the main macroeconomic variable that influences gold. Sari et al. (2010) find that spot metal prices (i.e., gold, silver, platinum, and palladium) display a strong relationship with the dollar-euro exchange rate. Hammoudeh et al. (2010) argue that of major precious metals (i.e., gold, silver, platinum, and palladium), silver volatility demonstrates a very strong reaction to that of the dollar-euro exchange rate. By contrast, Hammoudeh and Yuan (2008), provide evidence that rising interest rates dampen precious metals futures volatilities. Furthermore, Batten et al. (2010) have explored the macroeconomic determinants of four different precious metals (i.e., gold, silver, platinum, and palladium) and find that the gold price is highly influenced by monetary variables (with the exception of the silver price). Their findings provide supporting evidence of volatility feedback between the precious metals as well. Finally, a recent study by Andreasson et al. (2016) found indications of nonlinear causal linkages of commodity futures returns with stock market returns and implied volatility.

Tansuchat et al. (2009) have carried out an impressive analysis modeling long memory volatility in a number of agricultural futures returns and they have found that the FIGARCH $(1,d,1)$ and FIEGARCH $(1,d,1)$ models outperform the conventional GARCH $(1,1)$ and EGARCH $(1,1)$ models. This is an in-depth analysis looking into many agriculturals, but mapping was not considered at any point throughout the analysis and by looking at the results of this chapter, it will be made clear that the model which best fits a time series can significantly change when rollover is accounted for and mapped data is introduced. Of course this analysis appears to be concentrating more on the theoretical side of the science rather than the more practical trading aspects considered in this paper.

Chatrath et al. (2002) showed that commodity prices are chaotic to a certain degree. This chapter only considers the prices of four agricultural commodities that tend to 'spike' more often since they are less liquid markets. They use ARCH processes to explain the non-linearity in data, but given the stability of trading algorithms in terms of their returns, the extra volatility obtained in certain seasons exists but is not significant for a trading system which trades at a low frequency. This is because the optimization of the algorithm takes into account any extra volatility obtained, even if it is seasonal.

Vivian and Wohar (2012) noted that the increased volatility exhibited by commodities in the recent financial crisis was not significant and that there are no resulting volatility breaks. This is not true for other financial crises, however, where the volatility breaks are more obvious. For this chapter the recent financial crisis is more of interest as the optimizations are carried out over 5 years of data. The fact that their findings show no real evidence of volatility breaks, despite the financial crisis, is important. This is because the profits obtained from the trading algorithms also show no structural breaks in volatility, even during the financial crisis. This was confirmed from the homoskedastic nature of the profit profiles obtained.

Ji and Fan (2012) have argued that the impacts of the oil market spill over into other commodity markets. This may indeed be true in terms of price, but it is clear that after applying a trading strategy to many instruments, the way in which the algorithm trades and is optimized for different securities varies. It is important to remember the significance of diversification along with the idea of trading spreads, which reduces the exposure to any single commodity. This is linked to the analysis of correlation between securities where the prices and daily returns may be correlated, but the returns of the algorithms are not by virtue of the important fact that algorithms will not predict securities to be in the same buy/sell positions. Margaronis et al. (2011) have already demonstrated the fundamental effect of correlation dilution of a diversified trading system which uses securities that are highly correlated, especially intra-sector.

Cheung and Miu (2010) agree that diversification benefits can be gained by investing in commodities and also that the diversification benefit of commodities is far more complex than is generally understood in finance. The fact that commodities regimes are constantly changing is also interesting as we see a significant amount of heteroskedasticity throughout our analysis. However, diversifying into portfolios with commodities yielding a positive risk-return relationship compared to international equities is in line with what the authors believe, given that commodities' low volatility leads to lower returns. The RGZ algorithms (2010a and 2010b) have proved, however, that being diversified correctly can lead to a superior portfolio performance even in times of a bearish commodity environment. This is due to the inclusion of security spreads, single securities in different sectors and asset classes in the portfolio, as well as dilution effect on the daily return correlations mentioned earlier, which generate a profit profile that is truly diversified and offers a superior return-risk characteristic.

Based on the past literature suggestions, unlike copper, empirical evidence in relation to gold has attracted much of the interest along with silver and some other metals. In addition, a few studies have examined the effect of the recent crisis on the stochastic properties of metal returns; however, they only consider spot price data.

The aim of this paper is to analyze the impact of the recent crisis on the volatility dynamics of various futures returns, namely copper, platinum, RBOB, heating oil, WTI, and natural gas and by using different econometric techniques and data compared to the wide existing literature. More specifically, we will employ the APGARCH model (it is sufficiently flexible and allows for asymmetric power modeling of volatility) on two types of data: mapped and unmapped (see also Karanasos et al., 2018).

3. Data

This particular study is based on trading the front month contract based on daily prices at 2100 hrs GMT (for most instruments) or at the close of business for each respective instrument. All data was obtained from Thomson Reuters Datastream and Bloomberg and the prices are daily for the front month futures contract at that particular time. For example, on May 5, 2008, the active contract that was trading on that particular date needs to be obtained so that backtesting for that time is carried out on correct data. This will require knowledge of the correct ticker corresponding to that month. Tickers are defined by the security, month and year, so a three-part code is required for every contract search. This results in a large number of contracts required to generate a time series. Given the hours of trading of certain securities, the time to trade algorithmically varies. The data was selected with respect to the structural breaks that exist. For most time series the sample size is from January 2007, for five years.

3.1. Mapping procedure

Karanasos et al. (2018) argued that various procedures have been used to construct continuous futures series (see Ma et al., 1992). For example, Coakley et al. (2011) and Gutierrez (2013) roll contracts over to the next ones on the first business day of the contract month in analyzing a wide range of futures.

Martikainen and Puttonen (1996) roll the contract over to the next a week before the contract expires in analyzing the Finnish stock index futures market. Hou and Li (2016) roll contracts over to the next ones ten working days before maturity in analyzing both the S&P 500 and the CSI 300 stock index futures markets.

Moreover, our findings have implications for the literature on rolling over futures contracts and/or the so-called expiration effect in futures markets, pointed out by Samuelson (1965). Since our estimations on the time-varying volatility persistence are generally the same in relation to the use of mapped or unmapped data, they are consistent with previous related studies on the limited support for the expiration effect in commodity futures (e.g., Daal et al., 2006; Duong and Kalev, 2008; Carchano and Pardo, 2009).

Given that, this paper provides comprehensive evidence on the effect of mapping in relation to the metal futures, future research could focus attention on analyzing such an impact on the time series properties of other commodity futures (e.g., energy, grains, softs, etc.) traded in the US and outside the US, including emerging countries (e.g., China), thereby providing further light on this issue to the academic community as well as practitioners.

Finally, unlike most relevant research studies on the linkages among commodity futures, prices which do not take into account the abnormal volatility in the last weeks of life of the futures contracts, pointed out by Samuelson (1965) (see, e.g., Hammoudeh and Yuan, 2008; Bhar and Lee, 2011; Ewing and Malik, 2013; Beckmann and Czudaj, 2014; Sadorsky, 2014; among others), the present paper sheds light on the volatility dynamics of the considered metal and energy futures and their interactions using two types of data: unmapped and mapped.

Rollover, or roll, occurs when the current contract of a commodity instrument expires and the next month contract then becomes the new front month contract. As this happens, the price of the instrument may jump since the front month contract and next month contract do not have the same price at the time of rollover (for more details, see Samuelson, 1965). In this first analysis, therefore, the data have not been mapped to account for the rollover values. It has been discovered that taking into account the roll can significantly change the time series since these roll values can be significant in the commodities considered (Margaronis, 2015).

The mapping procedure involves the use of a program. The input for the program is the entire set of front month contracts obtained as explained earlier in order in a series (front month contract from January 2007, 5 years of daily settlement data). The program then takes the last price of each contract, being the price on expiry of the contract, and lines it up by date to the price of the second month contract. The program uses a counter for both the price series and the date series. When the counters match on the day of expiry, mapping occurs. The front and second month prices on that date are then lined up and their difference gives the basis or rollover for that contract. This is done consistently throughout the entire data set and each roll value or basis value is stored and accumulated in order for a calculation of the cumulative roll or basis to be made [(see Figure 3.1a below)]. Mapping data can have a huge impact on a price

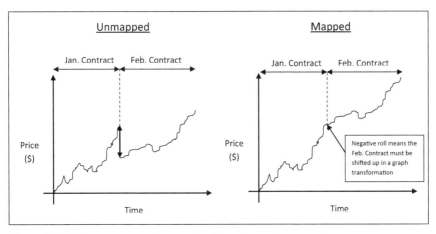

Figure 3.1a Diagram representing mechanism of mapping procedure

series if the roll value or basis value is significant. It is less significant in instruments which do not exhibit large rolls. However, given that the cumulative roll is required, especially when a trading algorithm is applied, even if the roll values are not significant the fact that it accumulates over time makes the mapping procedure imperative no matter the magnitude of the roll or basis.

3.2 Metals

In this paper, we explore the effect of the recent financial crisis on two metals futures' volatility dynamics: copper and platinum. These metal futures are under consideration due to their sheer daily volumes. Copper is the main industrial metal, with various applications in electronics, mainly in wiring. It is far more abundant in comparison to other metals, and hence it is a useful candidate metal to be considered for this analysis.

It is quite clear that while the two metals have, very different applications, when an important world event takes place influencing foreign exchange, volatility tends to be induced in most financial securities. Sensoy (2013) argues that precious metals are used in times of financial turmoil to hedge and diversify portfolios and as alternative investment vehicles.

Figure 3.1b shows the price of copper for the past five years. Generally there is a degree of homoskedasticity. The copper price seems to possess homoskedasticity throughout the time series. From the plot it is clear that there is a slight difference between the mapped and unmapped prices. The differences can also be seen in Figure 3.1b below where the logarithmic returns for unmapped and mapped copper prices are shown. These graphs demonstrate that the inclusion of rollover in any time series can have an impact on the data, and as predicted earlier, given the smaller level of roll in metals, the effect of mapping is not as significant for the time series. This will be further investigated in the analysis

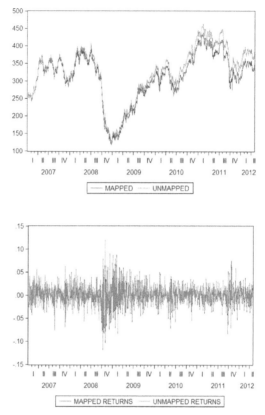

Figure 3.1b Mapped and unmapped prices and returns for copper

section. Platinum is also shown in Figure 3.1c, where the less significant roll in metals can again be seen despite differences in heteroskedasticity.

3.3. Energies

The level of roll for energies such as heating oil is generally very significant. Energies' futures cannot be traded algorithmically unless some kind of data manipulation is carried out. The graph of Figure 3.1d shows how significant the impact of mapping for the price and the returns of heating oil is (mapped and unmapped). Generally, the entire time series seems to be very homoskedastic over the five-year period. There seems to be far more irregularity in the returns of this particular commodity since a greater proportion of the unmapped returns plot can be seen to be larger than the corresponding mapped returns. This means that there is an artificial return in the data due to the roll. Very similar behaviour can be seen in the plot of RBOB[1] in Figure 3.1e. The energy commodities seem to have increased volatility in similar periods while also having quite a

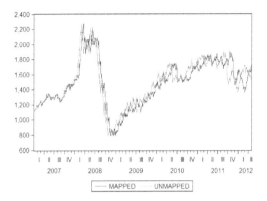

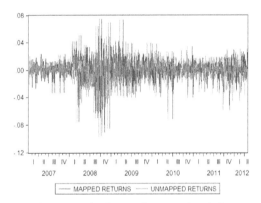

Figure 3.1c Mapped and unmapped prices and returns for platinum

significant roll. Heating oil returns seem to be slightly more volatile, but the level of heteroskedasticity for both instruments is similar, with both experiencing more volatile returns around the end of 2007 and the beginning of 2008. In the case of WTI it is clear there is a significant difference between the mapped and unmapped prices, as can be seen in Figure 3.1f. Despite the very large decline in prices between the end of 2008 and the beginning of 2009, the data is quite homoskedastic throughout the sample period, except during the decline. The crisis in 2008 caused a volatility in the oil price, which is evident. However, the price resumed its original behaviour by 2009. In the case of the returns, there is evidence that the mapping procedure has created a series that is different to the original due to the rolls that have now been accounted for. These observations are generally quite consistent with what was seen earlier in Figures 3.1d and 3.1e. In Figure 3.1g there is a very large inconsistency between the mapped and unmapped data sets for natural gas. Unfortunately, it is not possible to understand these differences between mapped and unmapped data sets until the analysis in concluded. By the end of

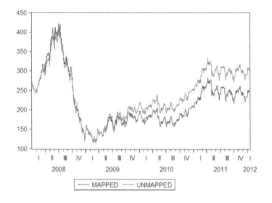

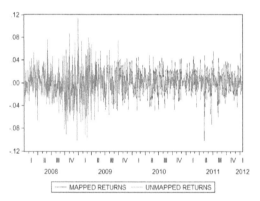

Figure 3.1d Mapped and unmapped prices and returns for heating oil

2009 and the beginning of 2010, there is a three quarter period of increased volatility. The reason for the very large differences between mapped and unmapped prices in this case may be due to the significant and sudden loss of homoskedasticity. Generally, however, the time series is consistent with the presumption that the energy sector of commodities yields significantly different series after being mapped.

4. PARCH model

In this section, for the different commodity returns, we will estimate AR-PARCH models. Since PARCH models require stationary data to be run, the returns of each of the instruments will be considered. The data was summarized briefly in the data summary section. For each instrument, the mapped and unmapped returns will be analyzed. The data itself is run through different PARCH models within the Eviews and RATS software. This is because a pre-analysis showed that a PARCH model was far more suited to the data than GARCH

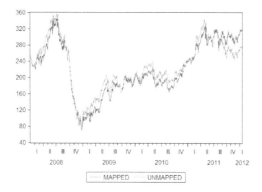

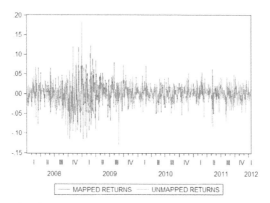

Figure 3.1e Mapped and unmapped prices and returns for RBOB

models, the reason being that the PARCH model allows estimation of the power or an a priori specification of a power. In a GARCH model this power is, of course, fixed at a value of 2. The pre-analysis also confirmed that the heteroskedasticity consistent covariance (Bollerslev-Wooldridge) option for coefficient covariance was used for robust standard errors. This is due to the nature of the returns, as seen earlier in the data summary section. The optimization algorithm selected was the default Marquardt, and the method was chosen to favor accuracy over speed since computational time was not of particular significance.

After running the data for a number of combinations of models, some very interesting findings were made. The mapped and unmapped data, as predicted, differed in terms of coefficients and sometimes even in terms of the model specification which suited the data best. Throughout the analysis the errors were assumed to be of Gaussian distribution.

Overall, the Akaike Information Criterion (AIC) was used to measure the relative goodness of fit of each model, and this was the final criterion by which each model for each data set was selected. Throughout the analysis, a level of significance of 0.10 was chosen for the significance of coefficients.

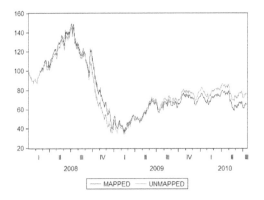

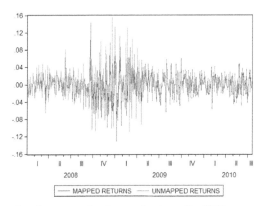

Figure 3.1f Mapped and unmapped prices and returns for WTI

Let commodity returns be denoted by $y_t = (logp_t - logp_{t-1}) \times 100$, where p_t is the commodity futures price at time t, and define its mean equation as:

$$y_t = \varphi_0 + \varphi_1 y_{t-1} + \zeta \sigma_t^\delta + \varepsilon_t$$

where $\varepsilon_t|\Omega_{t-1} \sim N(0, \sigma_t^2)$ is the innovation, which is conditionally (as of time $t - 1$) normally distributed with zero mean and conditional variance σ_t^2. In addition it is specified as a PARCH(1,1) process[2] (a model developed by Ding et al., 1993; see also Karanasos and Kim, 2006).

Variance equation:

$$\sigma_t^\delta = \omega + \alpha(|\varepsilon_{t-1}| - y\varepsilon_{t-1})^\delta + \beta\sigma_{t-1}^\delta,$$

where α and β denote the ARCH and GARCH parameters, and δ is the power term. The 'persistence' in the conditional variance, in the absence of breaks, is given by $c = \alpha k + \beta$, where $k = \frac{2^{\frac{\delta}{2}}}{\sqrt{\pi}} \Gamma\left(\frac{\delta+1}{2}\right)$ under normality (see Karanasos and Kim, 2006).

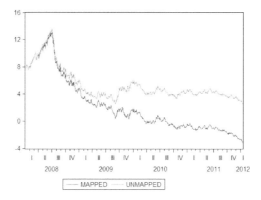

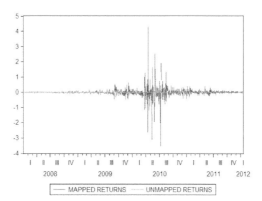

Figure 3.1g Mapped and unmapped prices and returns for natural gas

The results of both the Augmented Dickey-Fuller and Phillips–Perron unit-root tests (not reported) imply that we can treat all the series (namely the copper, platinum, RBOB, heating oil, WTI, and natural gas) as stationary processes. The summary statistics (not reported) indicate that the distribution of all the series deviates from normality.

Next, we examine the sample autocorrelations of the power transformed absolute future returns $|y|^{\delta}$ for various positive values of δ. Figures 3.2a to 3.2f show the autocorrelogram of $|y|^{\delta}$ from lag 1 to 40 for $\delta = 0.7$, 1.0, 1.2, 1.5 and 2.0. The horizontal lines represent the $\pm 1.96/\sqrt{T}$ confidence interval (CI) for the estimated sample autocorrelations if the process y_t is *i.i.d.*

The empirical justification of the PARCH process is based on the examination of the sample autocorrelations of the power transformed absolute future returns in the aforementioned Figures (3.2a to 3.2f). In particular our estimates show (in all cases but one; that of copper) that for $1 < \delta < 2$ the $|y|^{\delta}$ displays the strongest and slowest decaying autocorrelation at every lag up to at least 40 lags. This result is in line with previous work on inflation (see Karanasos and Schurer,

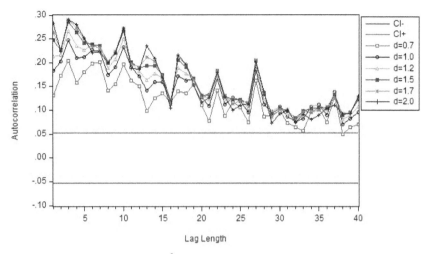

Figure 3.2a Autocorrelation of $|y|^\delta$ from high to low – copper

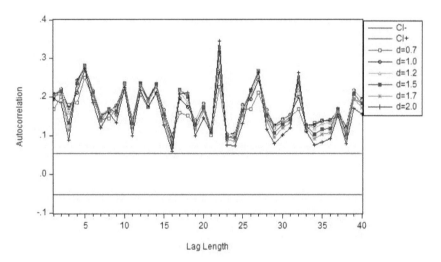

Figure 3.2b Autocorrelation of $|y|^\delta$ from high to low – platinum

2008), growth (see Karanasos and Schurer, 2005) and stock returns (see Karanasos and Kim, 2006, and Karanasos et al., 2011, 2016). Furthermore, the power transformations of absolute future returns when $\delta = 0.7$ (copper), $\delta = 1.5$ (platinum), and $\delta = 1$ (RBOB, WTI, heating oil) have significant positive autocorrelations at least up to lag 40.

To explore further the choice of the PARCH process, we calculate the sample autocorrelations of the absolute value of future returns $\rho_\tau(\delta)$ as a function of δ

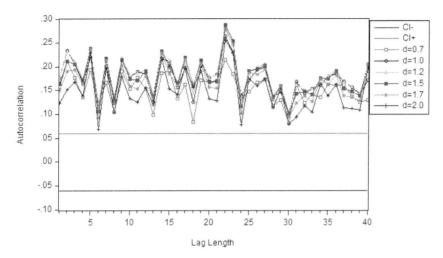

Figure 3.2c Autocorrelation of $|y|^\delta$ from high to low – RBOB

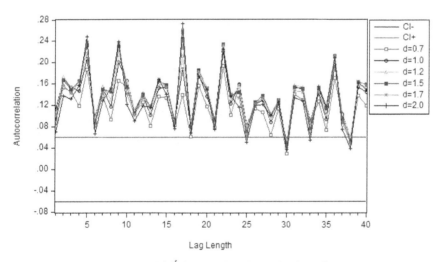

Figure 3.2d Autocorrelation of $|y|^\delta$ from high to low – heating oil

for lags $\tau = 1, 5, \ldots, 30$ and taking $\delta = 0.125, 0.25, \ldots, 4.0$. Figures 3.3a to 3.3f below provide the plots of the calculated $\rho_\tau(\delta)$. For example, for lag 30, there is a unique point δ^* equal to 0.7 and 1.2 for copper and WTI respectively, such that $\rho_{30}(\delta)$ reaches its maximum at this point: $\rho_{30}(\delta^*) > \rho_{30}(\delta)$ for $\delta \neq \delta^*$. For the case of platinum and RBOB the autocorrelation for lag 20, reaches its maximum at δ^* equal to 1.0 and 1.20 accordingly, whereas for heating oil and natural gas

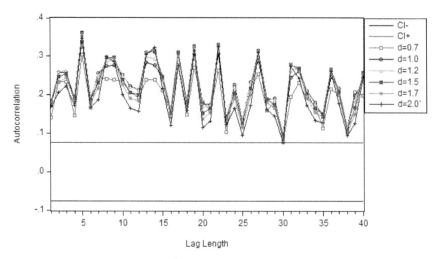

Figure 3.2e Autocorrelation of $|y|^\delta$ from high to low – WTI

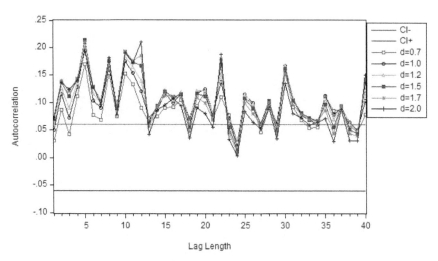

Figure 3.2f Autocorrelation of $|y|^\delta$ from high to low – natural gas

the sample autocorrelograms show maximum ρ for lag 1 and δ equal to 1.0 and 2.0 correspondingly.

All the instruments considered will follow this model, but some will differ due to symmetry, meaning the asymmetry term (γ) will not exist in that particular model. The coefficients of each individual series (mapped and unmapped) are shown later.

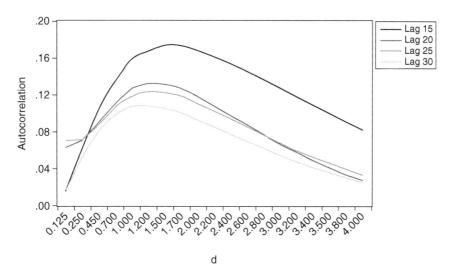

Figure 3.3a Autocorrelation of $|y|^{\delta}$ at lag 15, 20, 25, and 30 – copper

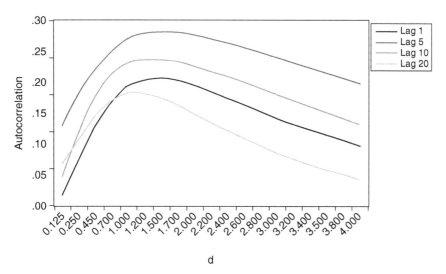

Figure 3.3b Autocorrelation of $|y|^{\delta}$ at lag 1, 5, 10, and 20 – platinum

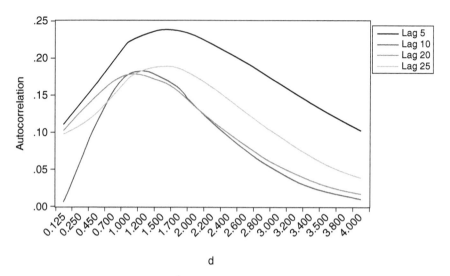

Figure 3.3c Autocorrelation of $|y|^{\delta}$ at lag 5, 10, 20, and 25 – RBOB

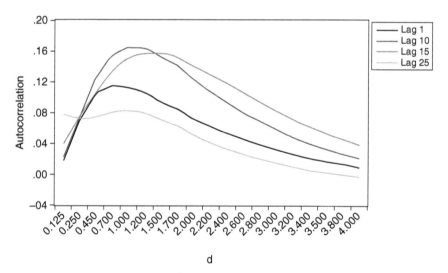

Figure 3.3d Autocorrelation of $|y|^{\delta}$ at lag 1, 10, 15, and 25 – heating oil

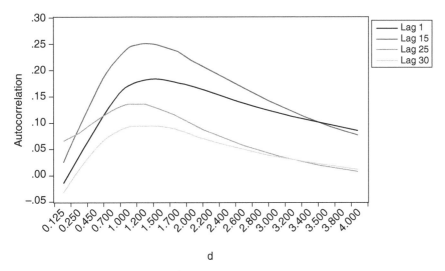

Figure 3.3e Autocorrelation of $|y|^\delta$ at lag 1, 15, 25, and 30 – WTI

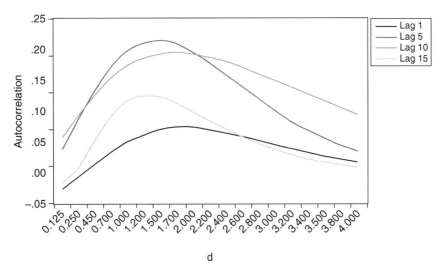

Figure 3.3f Autocorrelation of $|y|^\delta$ at lag 1, 5, 10, and 15 – natural gas

5. Empirical analysis

Let it be noted that throughout the analysis the AIC was minimized for each instrument by running different versions of the models.

5.1. Metals

Copper returns

The mapped and unmapped copper returns fitted almost identical models with only the power favored being slightly different. Both favored asymmetric (P)ARCH models with very similar fixed powers (0.72 for the mapped and 0.71 for the unmapped, see Table 3.1a).

Platinum returns

In the case of the platinum returns the models were actually identical with both mapped and unmapped sets of returns, favoring symmetric (P)ARCH models and a fixed power of 1.60.

From the results it is clear that the metals' roll is not significant. The mapped and unmapped data yield very similar results and have an almost identical model. Further, the coefficients are almost exactly the same. This supports the suggestion made earlier that the rollover on metals is less significant. The impact on the results of mapping the data is not crucial in this case. A trading algorithm optimized on unmapped data may therefore not be erroneous in reality with respect to the trades it makes.

In this case the roll is not significant, hence the models throughout for each instrument, even if mapping has been carried out, are similar. Since the roll is not large, the data is not transformed as much, so similar models should result, as expected. The results clearly show this with a maximum percentage

Table 3.1a Table of results showing coefficients for unmapped and mapped data and their percentage changes for metals

Metals	Copper			Platinum		
	Unmapped	Mapped	% change	Unmapped	Mapped	% change
α	0.055*	0.057*	−2.96%	0.088*	0.088*	0.08%
	(0.011)	(0.012)		(0.021)	(0.021)	
β	0.941*	0.937*	0.37%	0.906*	0.906*	−0.03%
	(0.013)	(0.014)		(0.023)	(0.022)	
γ	0.806*	0.802*	0.54%			
	(0.167)	(0.167)				
δ	0.720	0.710	1.39%	1.600	1.600	0.00%
ϕ_1	−0.055*	−0.053*	3.35%	0.108*	0.108*	−0.27%
	(0.026)	(0.026)		(0.030)	(0.030)	

$$y_t = \varphi_0 + \varphi_1 y_{t-1} + \zeta \sigma_t^\delta + \varepsilon_t$$
$$\sigma_t^\delta = \omega + \alpha(|\varepsilon_{t-1}| - \gamma \varepsilon_{t-1})^\delta + \beta \sigma_{t-1}^\delta,$$

All figures are to 3 d.p.
Standard errors are shown in brackets.
*Coefficient is significant at a 5% level.

change being in α for copper at 2.96%, which is far less than the 30% change tolerance set.

5.2. Energies

RBOB returns

In the case of energy commodities such as RBOB and heating oil, the rollover is considered to be larger than in most other sectors, so the differences in model between the mapped and unmapped data are expected to be quite substantial.

The mapped and unmapped returns for RBOB also have quite a significant roll, which explains why the models for the RBOB mapped and unmapped returns differed so much (see Table 3.1b). In the case of the unmapped returns, an asymmetric (P)ARCH model was favored with a fixed power at 1.10. However, for the mapped returns a GARCH model (that is with a fixed power of 2.00) was favored.

Table 3.1b Table of results showing coefficients for unmapped and mapped data and their percentage changes for energies

Energies RBOB				Heating Oil		
	Unmapped	Mapped	% change	Unmapped	Mapped	% change
α	0.061*	0.059*	2.60%	0.042*	0.040*	5.38%
	(0.021)	(0.017)		(0.013)	(0.011)	
β	0.931*	0.927*	0.40%	0.958*	0.958*	−0.03%
	(0.023)	(0.020)		(0.013)	(0.013)	
γ	0.520*			0.642*		
	(0.250)			(0.243)		
δ	1.100	2.000	**−81.82%**	0.920	1.550	**−68.48%**
Energies WTI				Natural Gas		
	Unmapped	Mapped	% change	Unmapped	Mapped	% change
α	0.047	0.049	−4.26%	0.065*	0.204*	**−214%**
	(0.026)	(0.028)		(0.017)	(0.037)	
β	0.946*	0.939*	0.74%	0.918*	0.852*	7.19%
	(0.021)	(0.021)		(0.018)	(0.023)	
γ	0.887	0.685	22.77%			
	(0.594)	(0.462)				
δ	1.180	1.420	−20.34%	2.000	1.300	**35%**
ϕ_1				−0.072*		
				(0.032)		

$$y_t = \varphi_0 + \varphi_1 y_{t-1} + \zeta \sigma_t^\delta + \varepsilon_t$$
$$h_t^{\frac{\delta}{2}} = \omega + \alpha(|\varepsilon_{t-1}| - y\varepsilon_{t-1})^\delta + \beta h_{t-1}^{\frac{\delta}{2}}$$

All figures are to 3 d.p.
Results in bold signify percentage change greater than 30%.
Standard errors are shown in brackets.
*Coefficient is significant at a 5% level.

Heating oil returns

For heating oil the values of the roll were quite significant, which explains why the models for the mapped and unmapped returns differed so much. The unmapped heating oil returns favored an asymmetric (P)ARCH model with a power fixed at 0.92. On the other hand, the mapped returns favored a symmetric (P)ARCH model and the power was fixed at 1.55. Thus, the models were very different due to the power values and the presence of asymmetries in the unmapped data (see Table 3.1b).

WTI returns

The mapped and unmapped returns for WTI also favored models that differed. In the case of the unmapped returns, an asymmetric (P)ARCH model was favored with power fixed at 1.18. In the case of the mapped returns, however, the same model specifications were favored, with the significant difference that the power was fixed at 1.42.

Natural gas

Similar to RBOB, the returns for natural gas favored very different models for unmapped and mapped returns. The unmapped returns favored a symmetric GARCH model (power being 2.00). On the other hand, the mapped returns favored a symmetric (P)ARCH model where the power was fixed at 1.3 (see Table 3.1b).

From the results it can be concluded that the roll does in fact have a significant impact on the data in the case of energies. This can be clearly seen from the data, as the unmapped data favors a model of asymmetry in three cases, whereas mapped data favors a model of symmetry in two out of the four cases (that is RBOB and heating oil). This suggests that in this particular case, not accounting for roll introduces an asymmetric component to the behavior of the data over time. There is also a significant change in the value of the power parameter, which impacts the model greatly. Interestingly, however, the values of the other coefficients are not very different (see Table 3.1b).

The reason why the RBOB and natural gas changes are slightly larger may be connected with the storage implications in reality. This means there can be very large spikes in prices, which can have an impact on the roll if the spike occurs at rollover. This may also be due to larger errors in the data for the same reasons. The results for WTI showed that of all the energies it is the least sensitive to mapping, with none of its parameter percentage changes exceeding the tolerance set. On the other hand, the natural gas returns yielded results that show the mapped and unmapped data is significantly different, primarily because the model is different. Generally, however, there is a significant difference between mapped and unmapped data for energies and the results confirm this.

5.3. Results allowing the conditional means and variances to switch across the breakpoints

Karanasos et al. (2018) stated that the financial crisis of 2007–2008 and the European sovereign-debt crisis that occurred afterwards affected seriously the financial and commodity markets around the world. Given the negative macro-economic environment and the widespread fear of an international systemic financial collapse, an interesting issue is whether the main stochastic properties of the underlying financial time series of these markets have been affected by the crisis. In another paper Karanasos et al. (2014) do indeed find time-varying characteristics in the persistence of the volatility of stock market returns during that period. Surprisingly, the effect mentioned above in relation to the commodity futures markets has drawn little attention. To the best of our knowledge, the studies by Vivian and Wohar (2012) and Sensoy (2013) are the only ones to date to have examined the impact of the recent crisis on the volatility of commodity returns, even though they consider spot price data.

This paper contributes to the existing literature in the following ways. First, we employ several modern econometric approaches for univariate time series modeling, among which we consider the possibility of breaks taking place in the volatility dynamics of these metal futures returns to capture the different stages of the recent financial crisis. In particular, we employ a Bai-Perron test to identify the number and estimate the timing of breaks, both in the mean and volatility dynamics. Then, we use these breaks in the univariate context, by adopting a (P)ARCH model, to determine changes in the volatility persistence. Based on Karanasos et al. (2018) knowledge of the time-varying volatility persistence and the spillovers mechanism adopted in this paper could be of high importance to investors since they could give rise to time-varying trading strategies, thereby minimizing the risk exposure and maximizing the returns.

Second, our estimation outputs affect other related research areas in the empirical finance and economics literature. We achieve this by providing consistent empirical findings to the extensive literature on volatility persistence in financial and/or commodity returns, which emphasizes that these volatility structures exhibit a time-varying pattern (see, e.g., Watkins and McAleer, 2008; Choi and Hammoudeh, 2010; Karanasos et al., 2014; Adesina, 2017; Andriosopoulos et al., 2017; to name a few) driven by structural changes in volatility induced in the financial system. Our results show that the considered metal futures are not exceptions.

This section reports the baseline results provided by the conditional maximum likelihood estimates of the (P)ARCH model allowing the conditional means and variances to switch across the breakpoints identified by the Bai and Perron (2003) procedure, see Tables 3.2 and 3.3 respectively. First we present the breakpoints that we obtained from Bai-Perron and discuss the potential major economic events that are associated with them. Then we focus our analysis based on these breaks to discuss the findings produced by our univariate models in Table 3.4.

Estimated breakpoints

An analysis of breakpoints was conducted for each series of returns (Table 3.2) and squared returns (Table 3.3), where a dummy variable was utilized in order to determine the precise dates, at which the data's behavior changed. The breakpoints are detailed in the two tables shown (Tables 3.2 and 3.3) and, using the dates of past events, the reasons behind the breaks will be explained where possible. Table 3.2 reports breaks in the mean equation, while Table 3.3 reports the variance breaks. The dates in bold indicate break dates for which at least one dummy variable is significant in either mean or variance equation of each commodity series (for instance for platinum 20/08/2008 (see Table 3.3) breakpoint β^2 is significant). In the following breakpoint analysis we will focus on the significant break dates.

By applying the Bai and Perron (2003) breakpoint estimation procedure on commodity and squared commodity returns we identify five breaks during the sample period. Furthermore, there are several cases where the breaks are either identical or very close to one another, which clearly show the significant impact that some economic events had on the commodities returns under consideration. The main finding supports the suggestion that the financial crisis of 2007–2008 and the European sovereign-debt crisis that followed are reflected in all commodity returns and squared returns series (see Tables 3.2 and 3.3). However, despite the sharp downturn in prices during 2008 and early 2009 in most of the series, prices began to rise again from late 2009 to mid-2010 (a resounding exception is the case of natural gas, where prices are still falling after 2008, causing significant problems in exporting countries such as Russia).

Table 3.2 The break points (commodity returns)

	1st Break	*2nd Break*	*3rd Break*	*4th Break*	*5th Break*
Metals Platinum	03/09/2007	05/03/2008	24/07/2008	12/12/2008	12/05/2009
Energies Natural Gas	22/05/2008	09/10/2008	26/02/2009	16/07/2009	03/12/2009

Table 3.3 The break points (squared commodity returns)

	1st Break	*2nd Break*	*3rd Break*	*4th Break*	*5th Break*
Metals Platinum	06/02/2008	**20/08/2008**	**07/01/2009**	12/07/2010	10/11/2011
Energies Natural Gas	22/05/2008	**09/10/2008**	**26/02/2009**	16/07/2009	03/12/2009

Notes: The dates in bold indicate breakdates for which, at least one dummy variable is significant in the variance equation of each commodity series (for instance for platinum 20/08/2008 breakpoint β^2 is significant).

Platinum

The platinum time series saw no significant breaks in the mean equation through-out the period (see Table 3.2). Metals are non-consumable and recyclable and in the case of precious metals, they can be considered as reserve currencies. These are probably the reasons why the metals time series saw no significant breaks in their time series. In the case of breaks in the variance (Table 3.3), where the squared returns are utilized, the platinum series experiences two significant breaks. One occurred in August 2008 and shortly before the Fannie Mae, Freddie Mac, and Ginnie Mae takeover by the Federal Reserve Bank (FRB) and the other in January 2009, when the FRB began purchasing mortgage backed securities guaranteed by the same companies. This may be explained by the use of precious metals in times of financial turmoil as reserve currencies, where a sudden surge in demand for them is manifested as confidence in other securities falls.

Natural gas

The natural gas time series saw no significant breaks in the mean equation throughout the period (see Table 3.2). In the case of breaks in the variance, there are two significant break dates: one on 9 October 2008 and one on 26 February 2009 (Table 3.3). The first break occurred during the worst week for the stock market in 75 years, meaning economic confidence and stability were at a historically low level, hence affecting demand for consumables such as natural gas. Another factor that might explain the break in October of 2008 could be the start of the winter months in Europe, where natural gas is used for household heating. The second break (26 February 2009) took place when the Federal Deposit Insurance Corporation (FDIC) announced its list of 'problem banks', as well as huge losses being announced by Fannie Mae. Once more the economic confidence must have been affected by these two events. Furthermore, the end of February marks the end of the harsh winter in many parts of Europe, where natural gas is used to heat households, adding a reason that might explain the displayed break.

4. PARCH models with breaks

In this section, for the different commodity returns we will estimate AR power ARCH models with structural breaks (for applications of GARCH models with structural breaks, see Karanasos et al., 2014 and the references therein).

Let commodity returns be denoted by $y_t = (logp_t - logp_{t-1}) \times 100$, where p_t is the commodity futures price at time t, and its mean equation be defined as:

$$y_t = \phi_0 + \varphi_1 y_{t-1} + \varphi_1^3 D_t^3 y_{t-1} + \varepsilon_t \tag{1}$$

where $e_t|\Omega_{t-1} \sim N(0, \sigma_t^2)$ is the innovation, which is conditionally (as of time $t-1$) normally distributed with zero mean and conditional variance σ_t^2. D^τ are dummy variables defined as 0 in the period before each break and 1 after the break. The breakpoints $\tau = 1, 2, \ldots, 5$ are given in Tables 3.2 and 3.3. In addition σ_t^δ is specified as a PARCH(1,1) process:

$$\sigma_t^\delta = \omega + \alpha(|\,\varepsilon_{t-1}| + \gamma\varepsilon_{t-1})^\delta + \sum_{\tau=1}^{3} \alpha^\tau D_t^\tau \varepsilon_{t-1}^\delta + (\beta + \sum_{\tau=1}^{3} \beta^\tau D_t^\tau)\sigma_{t-1}^\delta, \qquad (2)$$

where α and β denote the ARCH and GARCH parameters, and δ is the power term. The 'persistence' in the conditional variance, in the absence of breaks, is given by $c = \alpha k + \beta$, where $k = \frac{2^{\frac{\delta}{2}}}{\sqrt{\pi}} \Gamma(\frac{\delta+1}{2})$ under normality.

Table 3.4 below reports the baseline results provided by the conditional quasi maximum likelihood (QML) estimates of the (P)ARCH(1,1) model allowing the

Table 3.4 The estimated univariate (P)ARCH(1,1) allowing tor breaks in the mean and in the variance

	Platinum	Natural Gas
Mean Equation		
φ_0	0.001***	−0.002
	(2.62)	(−1.05)
φ_1	0.11***	–
	(3.75)	
Variance Equation		
ω	0.0001***	0 004***
	(3.58)	(3.77)
α	0.17***	0.18***
	(3.68)	(5.22)
β	0.83***	0.50***
	(22.07)	(4.74)
α^2	−0.09**	
	(−1.97)	
β^2	0.10***	0.15**
	(2.77)	(2.84)
β^3	−0.03***	0.16**
	(−2.83)	(2.70)
δ	1.60	1.30
LB(1)	0.09	2.40
	[0.765]	[0.12]
MCL(1)	0.83	3.31
	[0.36]	[0.07]

Notes: Table 3.4 reports parameter estimates for the following model:

$$y_t = \phi_0 + \phi_1 y_{t-1} + \varepsilon_t$$

$$\sigma_t^\delta = \omega + \alpha(|\varepsilon_{t-1}| + \gamma\varepsilon_{t-1})^\delta + \sum_{\tau=1}^{3} \alpha^\tau D_t^\tau \varepsilon_{t-1}^\delta + (\beta + \sum_{\tau=1}^{3} \beta^\tau D_t^\tau)\sigma_{t-1}^\delta$$

The number in parentheses represent t-statistics. LB and MCL represent Ljung-Box and McLeod-Li tests for serial correlations of one lag on the standardized and squared standardized residuals, respectively (*p*-values reported in brackets).
***, **, *, indicates significance at the 1%, 5%, 10% levels, respectively.

conditional means and variances to switch across the breakpoints [see Eq. (1) and (2) above] identified by the Bai and Perron (2003) procedure. The tests for remaining serial correlation suggest that all the models seem to be well-specified since there is no remaining autocorrelation in either the standardized residuals or squared standardized residuals at the 5% statistical significance level. In the case of the two constants (φ_0, ω) as well as the autoregressive coefficients the effects of breaks are insignificant in all of the cases. As far as the conditional variance is concerned, the ARCH parameter (α) shows time-varying behavior with one break in the case of platinum. The GARCH parameter (β) shows two significant breaks in the cases of platinum and natural gas. As far as the power parameter is concerned, it is fixed and equal to 1.60 and 1.30 for platinum and natural gas, respectively (different from either zero or unity).

Forecasting using spectral techniques

In this section we employ spectral techniques in order to forecast the commodity prices, namely platinum and natural gas (to the best of our knowledge, this is the first time that forecasting using spectral techniques has been employed in commodity prices data). In particular we implement an algorithm suggested by Geweke and Porter-Hudak (1983). The basis of the method is the moving average representation:

$$y_t = c(L)\varepsilon_t, \text{ where } c(0) = 1 \text{ and } \varepsilon \text{ is fundamental for Y}$$

Spectral techniques permit us to compute an estimate of the Fourier transform of c, which in turn can be employed to compute forecasts. In this study we will attempt to forecast the prices of platinum from 30 April 2012 (end of our original dataset) to 29 June 2012 or for 45 steps ahead. In the case of natural gas we will forecast the price for 117 steps ahead since the end of our original dataset is 18 January 2012. The reason behind the choice of that period (end of June 2012) lies in the fact that during the first quarter of 2012 United Kingdom (UK) announced a negative growth rate for a second consecutive time, formally entering a recession, while the euro zone showed negative growth rates for three consecutive quarters (2011Q4 to 2012Q2) after the recession of 2009. It would be only some months later that the euro zone would experience a double dip recession. Hence it would be interesting to investigate whether or not the forecasting technique was able to capture the effects of this negative economic atmosphere (on the commodity prices) that dominated the European economy.

During the period under consideration (daily data covering a period from January 2007 to April 2012) the commodity prices went through many variations due to the financial and the EU sovereign debt crisis of 2007–2008 and 2009–present, respectively. Hence, employment of forecasting methods that are not sensitive to dynamic variations such as the aforementioned is a vital stage of the estimation procedure. Therefore, taking into consideration the properties of the spectral forecasting method, could be considered as an appropriate technique for the forecasting of the commodity prices.

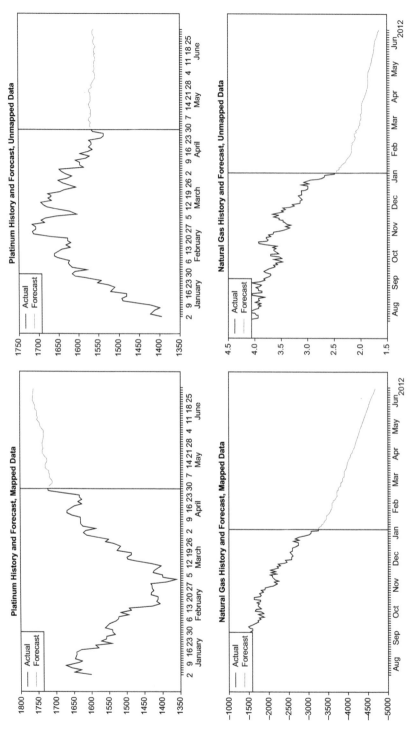

Figure 3.4 Forecasting under spectral analysis

Figure 3.4 displays the history and the forecast for each of both the mapped and unmapped commodity prices.[3] First, notice that regardless of whether the data for each commodity are mapped or unmapped the trend is roughly the same. Specifying the results, in the case of platinum the forecasting algorithm predicts that the prices overall will slightly increase in the period from 30 April 2012 to 29 June 2012. In contrast, the predicted prices of natural gas show a clear declining trend. To check the validity of our results and the accuracy of the forecasting algorithm we compared the predicted prices (for the unmapped data) with that of the actual prices during the period under examination and we found that the way they behave (both predicted and actual series) is very similar.[4] Hence spectral methods could be a reliable tool for predicting the future prices of commodities.

6. Conclusion

From the results presented it can be concluded that some data sets are more sensitive than others when it comes to data mapping. The analysis was carried out over a range of commodities in different sectors in order to capture the significance of rollover in each. The metals results showed how copper prices and platinum prices have a small rollover, therefore mapping the data does not significantly change its behavior. The model which best fits the data therefore remains very similar for mapped and unmapped data. On the other hand, the energies' results showed that the roll does in fact have a significant impact on the data.

The impact of the roll may not seem substantial; however, in the world of real life trading, where the front month contract of any instrument is the active contract, the inclusion of roll into prices used to back-test could be the difference between a trading strategy being successful or not. Therefore, it must be concluded that data mapping should be an essential pre-analysis carried out before back-testing any trading system. Just as a PARCH model's coefficients differ as data is mapped or unmapped, so may the parameters of a trading algorithm differ too. The more significant the roll for a given commodity, the larger was the observed difference in model coefficients and general specification. The significance of the current approach is that the creation of time series that account for roll will allow more accurate back-testing of any algorithmic trading system that is proposed including those of RGZ Ltd.

Acknowledgment

The authors would like to thank RGZ Ltd. for the use of their Reagan–class mapping algorithm and its output.

Notes

1 RBOB stands for Reformulated Blendstock for Oxygenate Blending.

2 In order to distinguish the general PARCH from a version in which δ is fixed (but not necessarily equal to 2) we refer to the latter as (P)ARCH.
3 For platinum the forecasting period is 30/04/2012 to 29/06/2012, whereas for natural gas it is 18/01/2012 to 29/06/2012.
4 Actual data during the first two quarters of 2012 for the commodities under investigation are not plotted graphically, graphs upon request.

Bibliography

Adesina, T., 2017. Estimating volatility persistence under a Brexit-vote structural break. *Finance Research Letters* 23, pp. 65–68.

Aloui, R., Aïssa, M. S. B., & Nguyen, D. K., 2011. Global financial crisis, extreme interdependences, and contagion effects: The role of economic structure? *Journal of Banking & Finance* 35(1), pp. 130–141.

Andreasson, P., Bekiros, S., Nguyen, D. K., & Salah Uddin, G., 2016. Impact of speculation and economic uncertainty on commodity markets. *International Review of Financial Analysis* 43, pp. 115–127.

Andriosopoulos, K., Galariotis, E., & Spyrou, S., 2017. Contagion, volatility persistence and volatility spillovers: The case of energy markets during the European financial crisis. *Energy Economics* 66, pp. 217–227.

Arouri, M., Hammoudeh, S., Lahiani, A., & Nguyen, D. K., 2012. Long memory and structural breaks in modeling the return and volatility dynamics of precious metals. *The Quarterly Review of Economics and Finance* 52(2), pp. 207–218.

Bai, J., & Perron, P., 2003. Computation and analysis of multiple structural change models. *Journal of Applied Econometrics* 18(1), pp.1–22.

Batten, J. A., Ciner, C., & Lucey, B. M., 2010. The macroeconomic determinants of volatility in precious metals markets. *Resources Policy* 35(2), pp. 65–71.

Beckmann, J., & Czudaj, R., 2014. Volatility transmission in agricultural futures markets. *Economic Modelling* 36, pp. 541–546.

Bhar, R., & Lee, D., 2011. Time-varying market price of risk in the crude oil futures market. *Journal of Futures Markets* 31(8), pp. 779–807.

Bubák, V., Kocenda, E., & Zikes, F., 2011. Volatility transmission in emerging European foreign exchange markets. *Journal of Banking and Finance* 35(11), pp. 2829–2841.

Caporale, G. M., Hunter, J., & Menla Ali, F., 2014. On the linkages between stock prices and exchange rates: Evidence from the banking crisis of 2007–2010. *International Review of Financial Analysis* 33, pp. 87–103.

Carchano, Ó., & Pardo, Á., 2009. Rolling over stock index futures contracts. *The Journal of Futures Markets* 29(7), pp. 684–694.

Chatrath, A., Adrangi, B., & Dhanda, K.K., 2002. Are commodity prices chaotic? *Agricultural Economics* 27(2), pp.123–137.

Cheung, C. S., & Miu, P., 2010. Diversification benefits of commodity futures. *Journal of International Financial Markets, Institutions and Money* 20(5), pp. 451–474.

Choi, K., & Hammoudeh, S., 2010. Volatility behavior of oil, industrial commodity and stock markets in a regime-switching environment. *Energy Policy* 38(8), pp. 4388–4399.

Ciner, C., 2001. On the long run relationship between gold and silver prices: A note. *Global Finance Journal* 12(2), pp. 299–303.

Coakley, J., Dollery, J., & Kellard, N., 2011. Long memory and structural breaks in commodity futures markets. *Journal of Futures Markets* 31(11), pp. 1076–1113.

Cochran, S. J., Mansur, I., & Odusami, B., 2012. Volatility persistence in metal returns: A FIGARCH approach. *Journal of Economics and Business* 64(4), pp. 287–305.

Coudert, V., Couharde, C., & Mignon, V., 2011. Exchange rate volatility across financial crises. *Journal of Banking and Finance* 35(11), pp. 3010–3018.

Daal, E., Farhat, J., & Wei, P. P., 2006. Does futures exhibit maturity effect? New evidence from an extensive set of US and foreign futures contracts. *Review of Financial Economics* 15(2), pp. 113–128.

Demiralay, S., & Ulusoy, V., 2014. Non-linear volatility dynamics and risk management of precious metals. *The North American Journal of Economics and Finance* 30, pp. 183–202.

Ding, Z., Granger, C. W., & Engle, R. F., 1993. A long memory property of stock market returns and a new model. *Journal of Empirical Finance* 1(1), pp. 83–106.

Duong, H. N., & Kalev, P. S., 2008. The Samuelson hypothesis in futures markets: An analysis using intraday data. *The Journal of Banking and Finance* 32(4), pp. 489–500.

Erb, C. B., & Harvey, C. R., 2006. The strategic and tactical value of commodity futures. *Financial Analysts Journal* 62(2), pp. 69–97.

Ewing, B. T., & Malik, F., 2013. Volatility transmission between gold and oil futures under structural breaks. *International Review of Economics & Finance* 25, pp. 113–121.

Geweke, J., & Porter-Hudak, S., 1983. The estimation and application of long memory time series models. *Journal of Time Series Analysis* 4(4), pp. 221–238.

Gutierrez, L., 2013. Speculative bubbles in agricultural commodity markets. *European Review of Agricultural Economics* 40(2), pp. 217–238.

Hammoudeh, S., & Yuan, Y., 2008. Metal volatility in presence of oil and interest rate shocks. *Energy Economics* 30(2), pp. 606–626.

Hou, Y., & Li, S., 2016. Information transmission between U.S. and China index futures markets: An asymmetric DCC GARCH approach. *Economic Modelling* 52, pp. 884–897.

Ji, Q., & Fan, Y., 2012. How does oil price volatility affect non-energy commodity markets? *Applied Energy* 89(1), pp. 273–280.

Karanasos, M., Conrad, C., & Zeng, N., 2011. Multivariate fractionally integrated APARCH modelling of stock market volatility: a multi country study. *Journal of Empirical Finance* 18, pp. 147–159.

Karanasos, M., & Kim, J., 2006. A re-examination of the asymmetric power ARCH model. *Journal of Empirical Finance* 13(1), pp.113–128.

Karanasos, M., Menla Ali, F., Margaronis, Z., & Nath, R., 2018. Modelling time varying volatility spillovers and conditional correlations across commodity metal futures. *International Review of Financial Analysis*, forthcoming.

Karanasos, M., Paraskevopoulos, A. G., Menla Ali, F., Karoglou, M., & Yfanti, S., 2014. Modelling stock volatilities during financial crises: A time varying coefficient approach. *Journal of Empirical Finance* 29, pp.113–128.

Karanasos, M., & Schurer, S., 2005. Is the reduction in output growth related to the increase in its uncertainty? The case of Italy. *WSEAS Transactions on Business and Economics* 2(3), pp. 116–122.

Karanasos, M., & Schurer, S., 2008. Is the relationship between inflation and its uncertainty linear? *German Economic Review* 9(3), pp. 265–286.

Karanasos, M., Yfanti, S., & Karoglou, M., 2016. Multivariate FIAPARCH modelling of financial markets with dynamic correlations in times of crisis. *International Review of Financial Analysis* 45, pp. 332–349.

Ma, C. K., Mercer, J. M., & Walker, M. A., 1992. Rolling over futures contracts: A note. *The Journal of Futures Markets* 12(2), pp. 203–217

Margaronis, Z. P., 2015. *The Significance of mapping data sets when considering commodity time series and their use in algorithmically-traded portfolios.* Unpublished paper, Brunel University, London.

Margaronis, Z. P., Nath, R. B., Karanasos, M., & Koutroumpis, P., 2011. *The significance of rollover in commodity returns: A PARCH approach.* Unpublished paper, Brunel University London.

Martikainen, T., & Puttonen, V., 1996. Sequential information arrival in the Finnish stock index derivatives markets. *The European Journal of Finance* 2(2), pp. 207–217.

Mensi, W., Beljid, M., Boubaker, A., & Managi, S., 2013. Correlations and volatility spillovers across commodity and stock markets: Linking energies, food, and gold. *Economic Modelling* 32, pp. 15–22.

O.Connor, F. A., Lucey, B. M., Batten, J. A., & Baur, D. G., 2015. The financial economics of gold: A survey. *International Review of Financial Analysis* 41, pp. 186–205.

Philippas, D., & Siriopoulos, C., 2013. Putting the "C" into crisis: Contagion, correlations and copulas on EMU bond markets. *Journal o International Financial Markets, Institutions and Money* 27, pp. 161–176.

RGZ Research, 2010a. Econometric analysis of precious metals and crude oils commodity pairs, internal document, RGZ Ltd.

RGZ Research, 2010b. Mapping crude oil futures contract data for use in algorithmic processing, internal document, RGZ Ltd.

Sadorsky, P., 2014. Modelling volatility and correlations between emerging market stock prices and the prices of copper, oil and wheat. *Energy Economics* 43, pp. 72–81.

Samuelson, P., 1965. Proof that properly anticipated prices fluctuate randomly. *Industrial Management Review* 6(2), pp. 41–49.

Sari, R., Hammoudeh, S., & Soytas, U., 2010. Dynamics of oil price, precious metal prices, and exchange rate. *Energy Economics* 32, pp. 351–362.

Sensoy, A., 2013. Dynamic relationship between precious metals. *Resources Policy* 38(4), pp. 504–511.

Tansuchat, R., Chang, C. L., & McAleer, M., 2009. Modelling long memory volatility in agricultural commodity futures returns. *Annals of Financial Economics* 7(2), p. 1250010.

Tulley, E., & Lucey, B. M., 2007. A power GARCH examination of the gold market. *Research in International Business and Finance* 21(2), pp. 316–325.

Vigne, S. A., Lucey, B. M., O.Connor, F. A., & Yarovaya, L., 2017. The financial economics of white precious metals: A survey. *International Review of Financial Analysis* 52, pp. 292–308.

Vivian, A., & Wohar, M. E., 2012. Commodity volatility breaks. *Journal of International Financial Markets, Institutions and Money* 22(2), pp. 395–422.

Watkins, C., & McAleer, M., 2008. How has the volatility in metals markets changed? *Mathematics and Computers in Simulation* 78(2–3), pp. 237–249.

Xu, X. E., & Fung, H. G., 2005. Cross-market linkages between U.S. and Japanese precious metals futures trading. *Journal of International Financial Markets, Institutions and Money* 15(2), pp. 107–124.

Appendix

Metals results summary

Copper

	Unmapped	Mapped
PARCH	√	√
Power	0.72	0.71
Asymmetry	√	√
ARCH-M	x	x
AR(1) ($\varphi1$)	√	√

Platinum

	Unmapped	Mapped
PARCH	√	√
Power	1.6	1.6
Asymmetry	x	x
ARCH-M	x	x
AR(1) ($\varphi1$)	x	x

Energies results summary

Heating oil

	Unmapped	Mapped
PARCH	√	√
Power	0.92	1.55
Asymmetry	√	x
ARCH-M	x	x
AR(1) ($\varphi1$)	x	x

RBOB

	Unmapped	Mapped
PARCH	√	x
Power	1.1	2
Asymmetry	√	x
ARCH-M	x	x
AR(1) ($\varphi1$)	x	x

WTI

	Unmapped	*Mapped*
PARCH	√	√
Power	1.18	1.42
Asymmetry	√	√
ARCH-M	x	x
AR(1) ($\varphi 1$)	x	x

Natural gas

	Unmapped	*Mapped*
PARCH	x	√
Power	2	1.3
Asymmetry	x	x
ARCH-M	x	x
AR(1) ($\varphi 1$)	√	x

Part 2

Mathematical stochastical finance

4 Variance and volatility swaps and futures pricing for stochastic volatility models

Anatoliy Swishchuk and Zijia Wang

1. Variance and volatility swaps for stochastic volatility models

In this chapter, we will focus on the variance and volatility swap pricing under stochastic volatility models and stochastic volatility models with jumps. The continuous variance strike under these models can be found through definition. However, the non-linearity property of square root function requires us to apply some techniques when evaluating the continuous volatility strike. In the following sections, we will use the convexity correction formula to approximate volatility strikes, and the closed-form solutions developed in Broadie and Jain (2008) will also be presented, for the sake of completeness of the presentation.

1.1. Heston stochastic volatility model

We assume all the price dynamics are modeled under risk neutral measure. Now we present an analysis of variance and volatility swaps under Heston stochastic volatility model. The Heston model (1993) is given by

$$
\begin{aligned}
dS_t &= rS_t dt + \sqrt{V_t} S_t dW_t^1 \\
dV_t &= \kappa(\theta - V_t)dt + \sigma\sqrt{V_t} dW_t^2,
\end{aligned}
\tag{1}
$$

the first equation in (1) gives the dynamics of the stock price S_t, r is the spot interest rate, $\sqrt{V_t}$ is the volatility of stock price and the variance V_t is a C-I-R process. κ represents the speed of mean reversion, θ is the long run average of variance and σ is the volatility of variance. W_t^1 and W_t^2 are two standard Brownian motion with correlation ρ.

Instead of finding the explicit solution for Heston model, we will derive the mean and variance of V_t. To do so, we let

$$
V_t = e^{-\kappa t} Z_t \text{ with } Z_0 = V_0,
$$

then

$$
dV_t = -\kappa e^{-\kappa t} Z_t dt + e^{-\kappa t} dZ_t = -\kappa V_t dt + e^{-\kappa t} dZ_t,
$$

and

$$dZ_t = \kappa\theta e^{\kappa t}dt + \sigma e^{\kappa t}\sqrt{V_t}dW_t^2,$$

Take the integration and substitute initial value we have that

$$Z_t = \theta(e^{\kappa t} - 1) + \sigma\int_0^t e^{\kappa s}\sqrt{V_s}dW_s^2 + V_0$$

and therefore

$$V_t = e^{-\kappa t}Z_t = \theta + (V_0 - \theta)e^{-\kappa t} + \sigma e^{-\kappa t}\int_0^t e^{\kappa s}\sqrt{V_s}dW_s^2. \tag{2}$$

Notice that expectation of Itô integral is zero, we have that

$$E(V_t) = e^{-\kappa t}Z_t = \theta + (V_0 - \theta)e^{-\kappa t}. \tag{3}$$

By using Itô isometry property we obtain following formula for variance of V_t

$$Var(V_t) = \sigma^2 e^{-2\kappa t}Var\left(\int_0^t e^{\kappa s}\sqrt{V_s}dW_s^2\right)$$

$$= \sigma^2 e^{-2\kappa t}E\left(\int_0^t e^{2\kappa s}V_s ds\right)$$

$$= \sigma^2 e^{-2\kappa t}\int_0^t e^{2\kappa s}(\theta + (V_0 - \theta)e^{-\kappa s})ds \tag{4}$$

$$= \frac{\theta\sigma^2}{2\kappa}(1 - e^{-2\kappa t}) + \frac{(V_0 - \theta)\sigma^2}{\kappa}(e^{-\kappa t} - e^{-2\kappa t}).$$

1.1.1. Variance swap for the Heston's model

In the case of Heston stochastic volatility model, continuous realized variance is given by

$$RV_c(0, T) = \frac{1}{T}\int_0^T V_t dt \tag{5}$$

and the fair continuous variance strike is given by

$$K_{var}^* = E(\frac{1}{T}\int_0^T V_t dt) = \theta + \frac{V_0 - \theta}{\kappa T}(1 - e^{-\kappa T}). \tag{6}$$

1.1.2. Volatility swap for the Heston's model (convexity correction method)

The realized volatility is commonly calculated by using the square root of the realized variance define in (5), and the fair continuous volatility strike K_{vol}^* for

Heston's model is given by

$$K^*_{vol} = E\left(\sqrt{RV_c(0,T)}\right) = E\left(\sqrt{\frac{1}{T}\int_0^T V_t dt}\right).$$ (7)

For fair continuous volatility strike K^*_{vol}, we have following theorem.

Theorem 1. *The fair continuous volatility strike under Heston's model can be approximated as following*

$$K^*_{vol} \approx \sqrt{\theta + \frac{V_0 - \theta}{\kappa T}(1 - e^{-\kappa T})} - \frac{\frac{\sigma^2 e^{-2\kappa T}}{2\kappa^3 T^2}[(V_0 - \theta),(2e^{2\kappa T} - 4e^{\kappa T}\kappa T - 2)]}{8\left(\theta + \frac{V_0 - \theta}{\kappa T}(1 - e^{-\kappa T})\right)^{\frac{3}{2}}}$$

$$- \frac{\frac{\sigma^2 e^{-2\kappa T}}{2\kappa^3 T^2}[\theta(2e^{\kappa T}\kappa T - 3e^{2\kappa T} + 4e^{\kappa T} - 1)]}{8\left(\theta + \frac{V_0 - \theta}{\kappa T}(1 - e^{-\kappa T})\right)^{\frac{3}{2}}}$$ (8)

Proof. To evaluate the fair discrete volatility strike under Heston's model, we need to find the risk neutral expectation of the square root of realized variance. Brockhaus and Long (2002) show that the fair volatility strike K^*_{vol} can be approximated by using Taylor's expansion of $\sqrt{RV_c(0,T)}$ around $E(RV_c(0,T))$ as following

$$\sqrt{RV_c(0,T)} \approx \sqrt{E(RV_c(0,T))} + \frac{RV_c(0,T) - E(RV_c(0,T))}{2\sqrt{E(RV_c(0,T))}}$$

$$- \frac{(RV_c(0,T) - E(RV_c(0,T)))^2}{8\sqrt{(E(RV_c(0,T)))^3}}.$$ (9)

Taking expectations under the risk-neutral measure on both sides of (9) gives

$$K^*_{vol} = E\left(\sqrt{RV_c(0,T)}\right) \approx \sqrt{E(RV_c(0,T))} - \frac{Var(RV_c(0,T))}{8(E(RV_c(0,T)))^{\frac{3}{2}}}.$$ (10)

Thus, the fair volatility strike can be approximated by the convexity correction formula (10), which only requires to find expectation and variance of realized variance.

Specifically, for the Heston's model, the expectation of realized variance is given by (6) while the variance can be found through the following steps.

Since

$$E\left(\int_0^t e^{\kappa x}\sqrt{V_x}dW_x^2 \cdot \int_0^s e^{\kappa x}\sqrt{V_x}dW_x^2\right)$$

$$= \int_0^{t\wedge s} E(e^{2\kappa x}V_x)dx \tag{11}$$

$$= \frac{\theta}{2\kappa}e^{2\kappa(t\wedge s)} + \frac{V_0-\theta}{\kappa}e^{\kappa(t\wedge s)} - \frac{\theta}{2\kappa} - \frac{V_0-\theta}{\kappa},$$

and from (2) we have that

$$E(V_tV_s) = (V_0^2+\theta^2)e^{-\kappa(t+s)} - 2V_0\theta e^{-\kappa(t+s)} + (V_0\theta-\theta^2)(e^{-\kappa t}+e^{-\kappa s}) + \theta^2$$

$$+ \sigma^2 e^{-\kappa(t+s)}E\left(\int_0^t e^{\kappa x}\sqrt{V_x}dW_x^2 \cdot \int_0^s e^{\kappa x}\sqrt{V_x}dW_x^2\right)$$

$$= (V_0-\theta)^2 e^{-\kappa(t+s)} + (V_0\theta-\theta^2)(e^{-\kappa t}+e^{-\kappa s}) + \theta^2 + \sigma^2 e^{-\kappa(t+s)} \tag{12}$$

$$\frac{\theta}{2\kappa}e^{2\kappa(t\wedge s)} + \sigma^2 e^{-\kappa(t+s)}\frac{V_0-\theta}{\kappa}e^{\kappa(t\wedge s)} + \frac{\sigma^2 e^{-\kappa(t+s)}(\theta-2V_0)}{2\kappa},$$

and,

$$Var\left(\frac{1}{T}\int_0^T V_t dt\right) = E\left(\left(\frac{1}{T}\int_0^T V_t dt\right)^2\right) - E^2\left(\frac{1}{T}\int_0^T V_t dt\right)$$

$$= \frac{1}{T^2}\int_0^T\int_0^T E(V_tV_s)dsdt - E^2\left(\frac{1}{T}\int_0^T V_t dt\right). \tag{13}$$

substitutes (6) and (12) into (13) we have

$$Var\left(\frac{1}{T}\int_0^T V_t dt\right) = \frac{\sigma^2 e^{-2\kappa T}}{2\kappa^3 T^2}[(V_0-\theta)(2e^{2\kappa T}-4e^{\kappa T}\kappa T-2)$$

$$+\theta(2e^{\kappa T}\kappa T-3e^{2\kappa T}+4e^{\kappa T}-1)]. \tag{14}$$

From the convexity correction formula (10) we have

$$K_{vol}^* \approx \sqrt{E(RV_c(0,T))} - \frac{Var(RV_c(0,T))}{8(E(RV_c(0,T)))^{\frac{3}{2}}}$$

$$= \sqrt{\theta + \frac{V_0-\theta}{\kappa T}(1-e^{-\kappa T})} - \frac{\frac{\sigma^2 e^{-2\kappa T}}{2\kappa^3 T^2}((V_0-\theta)(2e^{2\kappa T}-4e^{\kappa T}\kappa T-2))}{8(\theta + \frac{V_0-\theta}{\kappa T}(1-e^{-\kappa T}))^{\frac{3}{2}}} \tag{15}$$

$$- \frac{\frac{\sigma^2 e^{-2\kappa T}}{2\kappa^3 T^2}(\theta(2e^{\kappa T}\kappa T-3e^{2\kappa T}+4e^{\kappa T}-1))}{8(\theta + \frac{V_0-\theta}{\kappa T}(1-e^{-\kappa T}))^{\frac{3}{2}}}.$$

1.1.3. Volatility swap for the Heston's model (Laplace transform method)

It is convenient to use convexity correction formula to approximate the fair volatility strike, but the realized variance is required to be in the radius of convergence to make the first three terms in the Taylor expansion be a good approximation of square root function. Broadie and Jain (2008) claim that the fourth order terms in Taylor expansion of square root function are not small enough in the Heston stochastic volatility model, and hence the convexity correction formula will not provide a good estimate of the fair volatility strike. Instead of using Taylor expansion, they consider following formula for square root function

$$\sqrt{x} = \frac{1}{2\sqrt{\pi}} \int_0^\infty \frac{1 - e^{-sx}}{s^{\frac{3}{2}}} ds, \qquad (16)$$

and by taking expectation on both sides of (16) and using Fubini's theorem we have that

$$E(\sqrt{x}) = \frac{1}{2\sqrt{\pi}} \int_0^\infty \frac{1 - E(e^{-sx})}{s^{\frac{3}{2}}} ds. \qquad (17)$$

Theorem 2. *For the Heston stochastic volatility model, the fair continuous volatility strike is given by*

$$K_{vol}^* = E(\sqrt{RV_c(0,T)}) = \frac{1}{2\sqrt{\pi}} \int_0^\infty \frac{1 - E(e^{-sRV_c(0,T)})}{s^{\frac{3}{2}}} ds, \qquad (18)$$

where

$$E(e^{-sRV_c(0,T)}) = \exp(A(T,s) - B(T,s)V_0), \qquad (19)$$

$$A(T,s) = \frac{2\kappa\theta}{\sigma^2} \log\left(\frac{2\gamma(s)e^{\frac{T(\gamma(s)+\kappa)}{2}}}{(\gamma(s)+\kappa)(e^{T\gamma(s)}-1)+2\gamma(s)}\right),$$

$$B(T,s) = \frac{2s(e^{T\gamma(s)}-1)}{T(\gamma(s)+\kappa)(e^{T\gamma(s)}-1)+2T\gamma(s)},$$

$$\gamma(s) = \sqrt{\kappa^2 + \frac{2\sigma^2 s}{T}}.$$

See Broadie and Jain (2008, Prop. 3.1, page 774) for more details. The above formula for the Laplace transform of the continuous realized variance can be justified by using Feynman-Kac formula (Cairns, 2004).

1.1.4. Numerical example for the Heston's model

For a better understanding of swaps pricing under the Heston's model, we provide following numerical example.

Table 4.1 Means and standard deviation of estimated parameters

Parameters	Heston	Bates
r	−0.0018	−0.0044
	(0.0794)	(0.0824)
κ	0.8519	0.8269
	(0.7590)	(0.7239)
θ	0.1574	0.1793
	(0.2939)	(0.2959)
σ	0.2403	0.2916
	(0.0768)	(0.0384)
ρ	−0.8740	−0.8734
	(0.0478)	(0.0439)
λ		0.0038
		(0.0027)
a		−0.0001
		(0.9985)
b^2		0.0500
		(0.0294)

We choose the value evaluated in the empirical study in section 2.2, see Table 4.1, for the Heston's model parameters, which are evaluated through Markov chain Monte Carlo algorithm based on historical data of the S&P 500 index over the period from January 13, 2015 to January 13, 2017 (One can refer to section 2.2.1 for details). The estimation of parameters in Heston's model are

$$r = -0.0018, \kappa = 0.8519, \theta = 0.1574, \sigma = 0.2403, \rho = -0.8740, V_0 = 0.0093.$$

Therefore, the fair continuous variance strike of a S&P 500 variance swap with one year maturity is

$$
\begin{aligned}
K^*_{var} &= \theta + \frac{V_0 - \theta}{\kappa T}(1 - e^{-\kappa T}) \\
&= 0.1574 + \frac{0.0093 - 0.1574}{0.8519 \cdot 1}(1 - e^{-0.8519 \cdot 1}) \\
&\approx 0.0577,
\end{aligned}
\tag{20}
$$

the related fair continuous volatility strike derived from the convexity correction formula is

$$
\begin{aligned}
K^*_{vol} \approx \sqrt{0.0577} &- \frac{\dfrac{0.2403^2 e^{-2 \cdot 0.8519}}{2 \cdot 0.8519^3}[(0.0093 - 0.1574),(2e^{2 \cdot 0.8519} - 4e^{0.8519} \cdot 0.8519 - 2)]}{8(0,,0577)^{\frac{3}{2}}} \\
&- \frac{\dfrac{0.2403^2 e^{-2 \cdot 0.8519}}{2 \cdot 0.8519^3}[0.1574(2e^{0.8519} \cdot 0.8519 - 3e^{2 \cdot 0.8519} + 4e^{0.8519} - 1)]}{8(0.0577)^{\frac{3}{2}}} \\
&\approx 0.3012.
\end{aligned}
\tag{21}
$$

Now we use the second approach—the closed-form solution developed from Laplace transform to evaluate the related continuous volatility strike. From Theorem 2, we have that

$$\gamma(s) = \sqrt{\kappa^2 + \frac{2\sigma^2 s}{T}} = \sqrt{0.8519^2 + 2 \cdot 0.2403^2 s},$$

$$A(T,s) = \frac{2\kappa\theta}{\sigma^2} \log \left(\frac{2\gamma(s)e^{\frac{T(\gamma(s)+\kappa)}{2}}}{(\gamma(s)+\kappa)(e^{T\gamma(s)}-1)+2\gamma(s)} \right)$$

$$= \frac{2 \cdot 0.8519 \cdot 0.1574}{0.2403^2} \log \left(\frac{2\gamma(s)e^{\frac{\gamma(s)+0.8519}{2}}}{(\gamma(s)+0.8519)(e^{\gamma(s)}-1)+2\gamma(s)} \right),$$

$$B(T,s) = \frac{2s(e^{T\gamma(s)}-1)}{T(\gamma(s)+\kappa)(e^{T\gamma(s)}-1)+2T\gamma(s)}$$

$$= \frac{2s(e^{\gamma(s)}-1)}{(\gamma(s)+0.8519)(e^{\gamma(s)}-1)+2\gamma(s)},$$

$$E(e^{-sRV_c(0,T)}) = \exp(A(T,s)-B(T,s)V_0)$$

$$= \exp\left(A(T,s)-B(T,s)\cdot 0.0093\right),$$

thus the fair continuous volatility strike evaluated through the Laplace transform method is

$$K_{vol}^* = \frac{1}{2\sqrt{\pi}} \int_0^\infty \frac{1-E(e^{-sRV_c(0,T)})}{s^{\frac{3}{2}}}\,ds$$

$$\approx 0.1202.$$

1.2. Merton jump diffusion model

In this section we consider the dynamic of underlying asset prices follow the Merton jump-diffusion model

$$\frac{dS_t}{S_t^-} = (r-\lambda m)dt + \sigma dW_t + dJ_t \tag{22}$$

where $J_t = \sum_{i=1}^{N_t}(Y_i-1)$ is a compound Poisson process with intensity λ. $Y_i \sim Log-Normal(a, b^2)$ represent the jump size of price, and $E(Y_i-1) = m$ while the parameters are related by the equation $e^{a+\frac{1}{2}b^2} = m+1$. Moreover, when the jumps occur at time τ_i, we have $S(\tau_i^+) = S(\tau_i^-)Y_i$.

For an asset which can be modeled by (22), the variance of price comes from two parts: the diffusion of price process and jumps in price. Thus the continuous realized variance over $[0, T]$ in Merton jump diffusion model can be expressed as

$$RV_c(0, T) = \frac{1}{T} \int_0^T \sigma^2 dt + \frac{1}{T} \left(\sum_{i=1}^{N(T)} (ln(Y_i))^2 \right), \tag{23}$$

and the fair continuous variance strike is

$$K_{var}^* = E(R_*V_c(0, T)) = \frac{1}{T} \int_0^T \sigma^2 dt + \frac{1}{T} E \left(\sum_{i=1}^{N(T)} (ln(Y_i))^2 \right) = \sigma^2 + \lambda(a^2 + b^2), \tag{24}$$

which depends on the volatility parameter σ as well as the distribution of jump size.

To evaluate the continuous volatility strike in the Merton jump diffusion model, we can either use convexity correction method or Laplace transform.

Theorem 3. *From the convexity correction formula (10) we have following approximation for fair continuous volatility strike in Merton jump diffusion model*

$$K_{vol}^* \approx \sqrt{\sigma^2 + \lambda(a^2 + b^2)} - \frac{\lambda(a^4 + 6a^2b^2 + 3b^4)}{8T(\sigma^2 + \lambda(a^2 + b^2))^{\frac{3}{2}}}. \tag{25}$$

Proof. Since

$$\begin{aligned}
Var(RV_c(0, T)) &= Var\left(\frac{1}{T} \int_0^T \sigma^2 dt + \frac{1}{T}(\sum_{i=1}^{N(T)} (ln(Y_i))^2) \right) \\
&= Var\left(\frac{1}{T}(\sum_{i=1}^{N(T)} (ln(Y_i))^2) \right) \\
&= \frac{1}{T^2} \cdot \lambda T \cdot E((ln(Y_i))^4) \\
&= \frac{\lambda(a^4 + 6a^2b^2 + 3b^4)}{T},
\end{aligned} \tag{26}$$

substitute (24) and (26) into convexity correction formula, we have that

$$\begin{aligned}
K_{vol}^* &\approx \sqrt{E(RV_c(0, T))} - \frac{Var(RV_c(0, T))}{8(E(RV_c(0, T)))^{\frac{3}{2}}} \\
&= \sqrt{\sigma^2 + \lambda(a^2 + b^2)} - \frac{\lambda(a^4 + 6a^2b^2 + 3b^4)}{8T(\sigma^2 + \lambda(a^2 + b^2))^{\frac{3}{2}}}.
\end{aligned} \tag{27}$$

Theorem 4. *By applying Laplace transform method, we have following evaluation for the fair continuous volatility strike in Merton jump diffusion model*

$$K_{vol}^* = E(\sqrt{RV_c(0, T)}) = \frac{1}{2\sqrt{\pi}} \int_0^\infty \frac{1 - E(e^{-sRV_c(0,T)})}{s^{\frac{3}{2}}} ds, \tag{28}$$

where

$$E(e^{-sRV_c(0,T)}) = \exp\left(-s\sigma^2 + \lambda T\left(\frac{\exp\left(\frac{-sa^2}{T+2sb^2}\right)}{\sqrt{1+\frac{2sb^2}{T}}} - 1\right)\right).$$

Proof. Since

$$RV_c(0,T) = \sigma^2 + \frac{1}{T}\left(\sum_{i=1}^{N(T)} (ln(Y_i))^2\right),$$

and

$$\ln(Y_i) \sim N(a,b^2),$$

we have that

$$E\left(\exp\left(-s\left(\sigma^2 + \frac{1}{T}\sum_{i=1}^{N(T)}(ln(Y_i))^2\right)\right)\right)$$

$$= e^{-s\sigma^2} E\left(E\left(\exp\left\{-\frac{s}{T}\sum_{i=1}^{N(T)}(\ln(Y_i))^2\right\}\Big|N(T)=n\right)\right)$$

$$= e^{-s\sigma^2}\sum_{n=1}^{\infty}\frac{(\lambda T)^n e^{-\lambda T}}{n!} E\left(\exp\left\{-\frac{s}{T}\sum_{i=1}^{N(T)}(\ln(Y_i))^2\right\}\right)$$

$$= \exp\left(-s\sigma^2 + \lambda T\left(\frac{\exp\left(\frac{-sa^2}{T+2sb^2}\right)}{\sqrt{1+\frac{2sb^2}{T}}} - 1\right)\right).$$

See Broadie and Jain (2008, Prop. 3.1, page 771 and Prop. 5.1, page 774) for more details.

1.2.1. Numerical example for the Merton's model

Now we provide a numerical example for Merton's model. The parameters are evaluated through MCMC algorithm based on historical data of the S&P 500 index over the period from January 13, 2015 to January 13, 2017. Let

$$\lambda = 0.0038, a = -0.0001, b^2 = 0.05, r = -0.0044, \sigma = 0.1.$$

Then, the fair continuous variance strike for a variance swap with maturity of one year is

$$K_{var}^* = \sigma^2 + \lambda(a^2 + b^2) \approx 0.0102.$$

Using Theorem 3, we have following evaluation for fair continuous volatility strike

$$K_{vol}^* \approx \sqrt{\sigma^2 + \lambda(a^2 + b^2)} - \frac{\lambda(a^4 + 6a^2b^2 + 3b^4)}{8T(\sigma^2 + \lambda(a^2 + b^2))^{\frac{3}{2}}} \approx 0.097,$$

and the volatility strike evaluated from Laplace transform method is

$$K_{vol}^* = E(\sqrt{RV_c(0, T)}) = \frac{1}{2\sqrt{\pi}} \int_0^\infty \frac{1 - E(e^{-sRV_c(0,T)})}{s^{\frac{3}{2}}} ds$$

$$= \frac{1}{2\sqrt{\pi}} \int_0^\infty \frac{1 - \exp\left(-s\sigma^2 + \lambda T \left(\frac{\exp\left(\frac{-sa^2}{T + 2sb^2}\right)}{\sqrt{1 + \frac{2sb^2}{T}}} - 1\right)\right)}{s^{\frac{3}{2}}} ds \approx 0.0246.$$

1.3. Bates jump diffusion model

Heston's and Merton's models are combined by Bates (1996) in 1996, who proposed the stochastic volatility with jumps model as following

$$\frac{dS_t}{S_t^-} = (r - \lambda m)dt + \sqrt{V_t}dW_t^1 + dJ_t,$$

$$dV_t = \kappa(\theta - V_t)dt + \sigma\sqrt{V_t}dW_t^2, \tag{29}$$

where the meanings of parameters are same as in Heston's stochastic volatility model (1) and J_t is a compound Poisson process with the same properties as in Merton jump diffusion model (22). Moreover, we assume that the jump process and Brownian motions are independent.

Similar to the Merton's jump diffusion model (22), the variance of price comes from the diffusion of price process and jumps in price. Thus the continuous realized variance over $[0, T]$ in Bates jump diffusion model is

$$RV_c(0, T) = \frac{1}{T} \int_0^T V_t dt + \frac{1}{T} \left(\sum_{i=1}^{N(T)} (ln(Y_i))^2\right), \tag{30}$$

and the fair continuous variance strike is

$$K_{var}^* = E(RV_c(0, T)) = E\left(\frac{1}{T} \int_0^T V_t dt\right) + \frac{1}{T} E\left(\sum_{i=1}^{N(T)} (ln(Y_i))^2\right) \tag{31}$$

$$= \theta + \frac{V_0 - \theta}{\kappa T}(1 - e^{-\kappa T}) + \lambda(a^2 + b^2).$$

Now we use both the convexity correction method and the Laplace transform method to evaluate the continuous volatility strike in the Bates jump diffusion model.

Theorem 5. *From the convexity correction formula (10) we have following approximation for fair continuous volatility strike under Bates jump diffusion model*

$$K_{vol}^* \approx \sqrt{E(RV_c(0,T))} - \frac{Var\left(\frac{1}{T}\int_0^T V_t dt\right)}{8(E(RV_c(0,T)))^{\frac{3}{2}}} - \frac{Var\left(\frac{1}{T}\left(\sum_{i=1}^{N(T)}(ln(Y_i))^2\right)\right)}{8(E(RV_c(0,T)))^{\frac{3}{2}}}.$$

(32)

where $E(RV_c(0,T))$ and $Var\left(\frac{1}{T}\int_0^T V_t dt\right)$ are given by (31) and (14), respectively, and

$$Var\left(\frac{1}{T}\left(\sum_{i=1}^{N(T)}(ln(Y_i))^2\right)\right) = \frac{\lambda}{T}\cdot(a^4 + 6a^2b^2 + 3b^4).$$

Proof. Since

$$RV_c(0,T) = \frac{1}{T}\int_0^T V_t dt + \frac{1}{T}\left(\sum_{i=1}^{N(T)}(ln(Y_i))^2\right),$$

by using the convexity correction formula, we have that

$$K_{vol}^* \approx \sqrt{E(RV_c(0,T))} - \frac{Var(RV_c(0,T))}{8(E(RV_c(0,T)))^{\frac{3}{2}}}$$

$$= \sqrt{E(RV_c(0,T))} - \frac{Var\left(\frac{1}{T}\int_0^T V_t dt\right)}{8(E(RV_c(0,T)))^{\frac{3}{2}}} - \frac{Var\left(\frac{1}{T}\left(\sum_{i=1}^{N(T)}(ln(Y_i))^2\right)\right)}{8(E(RV_c(0,T)))^{\frac{3}{2}}},$$

and

$$Var\left(\frac{1}{T}\left(\sum_{i=1}^{N(T)}(ln(Y_i))^2\right)\right) = \frac{1}{T^2}\cdot\lambda T\cdot E((ln(Y_i))^4)$$

$$= \frac{\lambda(a^4 + 6a^2b^2 + 3b^4)}{T}.$$

Theorem 6. *By applying Laplace transform method, we have following evaluation for the fair continuous volatility strike of Bates jump diffusion model*

$$K_{vol}^* = E(\sqrt{RV_c(0,T)}) = \frac{1}{2\sqrt{\pi}}\int_0^\infty \frac{1 - E(e^{-sRV_c(0,T)})}{s^{\frac{3}{2}}}ds,$$

(33)

where

$$E(e^{-sRV_c(0,T)}) = E\left(e^{-\frac{s}{T}\int_0^T V_t dt}\right) \cdot E\left(e^{-\frac{s}{T}\sum_{i=1}^{N(T)} (lnY_i)^2}\right)$$

$$= \exp\left(A(T,s) - B(T,s)V_0 + \lambda T\left(\frac{\exp\left(\frac{-sa^2}{T+2sb^2}\right)}{\sqrt{1+\frac{2sb^2}{T}}} - 1\right)\right).$$

$A(T, s)$ ans $B(T, s)$ are given by (19).

See Broadie and Jain, (2008, Prop. 5.1, page 774) for more details.

1.3.1. Numerical example for the Bates' model

Now we provide a numerical example for Bates' model. The parameters are evaluated through MCMC algorithm based on historical data of the S&P 500 index over the period from January 13, 2015 to January 13, 2017. Let $r = -0.0044$, $\kappa = 0.8269$, $\theta = 0.1793$, $\sigma = 0.2916$, $\rho = -0.8734$, $\lambda = 0.0038$, $a = -0.0001$, $b^2 = 0.05$, $V_0 = 0.0103$. Then, the fair continuous variance strike for a variance swap with maturity of one year is

$$K_{var}^* = \theta + \frac{V_0 - \theta}{\kappa T}(1 - e^{-\kappa T}) + \lambda(a^2 + b^2) \approx 0.0645.$$

The fair volatility strike evaluated from convexity correction formula is

$$K_{vol}^* = \sqrt{E(RV_c(0,T))} - \frac{Var\left(\frac{1}{T}\int_0^T V_t dt\right)}{8(E(RV_c(0,T)))^{\frac{3}{2}}} - \frac{Var\left(\frac{1}{T}\left(\sum_{i=1}^{N(T)}(ln(Y_i))^2\right)\right)}{8(E(RV_c(0,T)))^{\frac{3}{2}}}$$

$$\approx \sqrt{0.0645} - \frac{-0.0119}{8(0.0645)^{\frac{3}{2}}} - \frac{0.00003}{8(0.0645)^{\frac{3}{2}}} \approx 0.3445.$$

The fair volatility strike evaluated from Laplace transform method given in Theorem 9 is

$$K_{vol}^* = \frac{1}{2\sqrt{\pi}}\int_0^\infty \frac{1 - E(e^{-sRV_c(0,T)})}{s^{\frac{3}{2}}} ds$$

$$= \frac{1}{2\sqrt{\pi}}\int_0^\infty \frac{1 - \exp\left(A(T,s) - B(T,s)V_0 + \lambda T\left(\frac{\exp\left(\frac{-sa^2}{T+2sb^2}\right)}{\sqrt{1+\frac{2sb^2}{T}}} - 1\right)\right)}{s^{\frac{3}{2}}} ds$$

$$\approx 0.1312.$$

1.4. Lévy-based Heston model

1.4.1. α-stable distributions and Lévy processes

In probability theory, a distribution is said to be stable if a linear combination of two independent copies of a random sample has the same distribution, up to location and scale parameters. Specifically, the characteristic function of symmetric α-stable distributed random variables has following form

$$\varphi(u) = e^{i\delta u - \sigma|u|^{\alpha}},$$

where $\alpha \in (0, 2]$ is the characteristic exponent(stability parameter) which determines the shape of the distribution, $\delta \in (-\infty, \infty)$ is the location parameter and $\sigma \in (0, \infty)$ is the dispersion, which measures the width of distribution. For $0 < \alpha \leq 1$, δ is the median, while for $1 < \alpha \leq 2$, δ is the mean. A symmetric α-stable distribution is called standard if $\delta = 0$ and $\sigma = 1$. For more details about symmetric α-stable distribution, one can refer to Swishchuk (2009).

However, there is no closed form expression exists for general α-stable distribution other than the Lévy ($\alpha = 1/2$), the Cauchy ($\alpha = 1$) and the Gaussian ($\alpha = 2$) distributions. Also, only moments of order less than α exist for the non-Gaussian family of α-stable distribution. The fractional lower order moments with $\delta = 0$ are given by

$$E|X|^p = D(p, \alpha)\sigma^{p/\alpha} \ \text{ for } 0 < p < \alpha$$

where

$$D(p, \alpha) = \frac{2^p \Gamma\left(\frac{p+1}{2}\right) \Gamma\left(1 - \frac{p}{\alpha}\right)}{\alpha \sqrt{\pi} \Gamma\left(1 - \frac{p}{2}\right)}$$

and $\Gamma(\cdot)$ is the Gamma distribution.

One important characteristic of symmetrical α-stable distribution is that the smaller α is, the heavier the tails of the α-stable density. The heavy tail characteristic makes the distribution appropriate for modeling noise which is impulsive in nature, for example, electricity prices or volatility (see Swishchuk, 2009).

Definition 2.1.2 Let $\alpha \in (0, 2]$, an α-stable Lévy process L_t is a process such that L_1 has a strictly α-stable distribution (i.e., $L_1 \equiv S_\alpha(\sigma, \beta, \delta)$ for some $\alpha \in (0, 2]\backslash\{1\}, \sigma \in \mathbb{R}_+, \beta \in [-1, 1], \delta = 0$ or $\alpha = 1, \sigma \in \mathbb{R}_+, \beta = 0, \delta \in \mathbb{R}$). We call L_t is a symmetric α-stable Lévy process if the distribution of L_1 is symmetric α-stable (i.e., $L_1 \equiv S_\alpha(\sigma, 0, 0)$ for some $\alpha \in (0, 2], \sigma \in \mathbb{R}_+$). L_t is $(T_t)_{t \in \mathbb{R}_+}$-adapted if L_t is a constant on $[T_{t-}, T_{t+}]$ for any $t \in \mathbb{R}_+$.

The α-stable Lévy processes are the only self-similar Lévy processes such that $L(at) =^{\text{Law}} a^{1/\alpha}L(t), a \geq 0$. They are either Brownian motion or pure jump. For $1 < \alpha < 2$, we have $E(L_t) = \delta t$ where δ is the location parameter of the α-stable distribution. For more details about properties of α-stable Lévy processes, one can refer to Swishchuk (2009).

1.4.2. Change of time method for the stochastic differential equations driven by Lévy processes

Let $L^\alpha_{a.s.}$ denotes the family of all real measurable $\mathcal{F}_t$-adapted processes $a(t, \omega)$ on $\Omega \times [0, +\infty)$, such that for every $T > 0$,

$$\int_0^T |a(t, \omega)|^\alpha dt < +\infty \ \ a.s.$$

Now we consider stochastic differential equations that have following form

$$dX(t) = a(t, X(t-))dL(t),$$

where $L(t)$ is an α-stable Lévy process.

Theorem 7. *Let $a \in L^\alpha_{a.s.}$ such that $T(u) := \int_0^u |a|^\alpha dt \to +\infty$ a.s. as $u \to +\infty$. If $\hat{T}(t) := inf\{u : T(u) > t\}$ and $\hat{\mathcal{F}}_t = \mathcal{F}_{\hat{T}(t)}$, then the time-changed stochastic integral $\hat{L}(t) = \int_0^{\hat{T}(t)} adL(t)$ is an $\hat{\mathcal{F}}_t$ α-stable Lévy process, where $L(t)$ is $\mathcal{F}_t$-adapted α-stable Lévy process. Consequently, for each $t > 0$, $\int_0^t adL = \hat{L}(T(t))$ a.s., i.e., the stochastic integral with respect to a α-stable Lévy process is nothing but another α-stable Lévy process with randomly changed time scale.*

See Rosinski and Woyczinski (1986) for more details.

1.4.3. Variance swaps for the Lévy-based Heston model

Assume the price and variance of underlying asset satisfy following model

$$dS_t = rS_t dt + \sqrt{V_t} S_t dW_t$$
$$dV_t = \kappa(\theta - V_t)dt + \sigma\sqrt{V_t} dL_t, \tag{34}$$

where parameters have same meanings as in (1) while W_t and L_t are independent Brownian motion and α-stable Lévy process with $\alpha \in (0, 2]$. By using the same method as in Section 5.1 and the change of time method (Swishchuk, 2009), we have following solution for the second SDE

$$V_t = \theta + e^{-\kappa t}(V_0 - \theta + \hat{L}(\hat{T}_t)) \tag{35}$$

where

$$\hat{L}(\hat{T}_t) = \int_0^t \sigma e^{\kappa s} \sqrt{V_s} dL_s$$

and

$$\hat{T}_t = \sigma^\alpha \int_0^t [e^{\kappa \hat{T}_s}(V_0 - \theta + \hat{L}(\hat{T}_s)) + \theta e^{2\kappa \hat{T}_s}]^{\alpha/2} ds.$$

Thus the fair continuous variance strike $K_{var}^* = E(RV_c(0,T))$ is given by

$$K_{var}^* = E\left(\frac{1}{T}\int_0^T V_t dt\right) = E\left(\frac{1}{T}\int_0^T \theta + e^{-\kappa t}(V_0 - \theta + \hat{L}(\hat{T}_t))dt\right)$$

$$(Fubini's\ Theorem) = \frac{1}{T}\int_0^T \theta + e^{-\kappa t}(V_0 - \theta + E(\hat{L}(\hat{T}_t)))dt \qquad (36)$$

$$= \theta + \frac{(1 - e^{-\kappa T})(\kappa V_0 - \kappa\theta + \delta)}{\kappa^2 T} - \frac{\delta e^{-\kappa T}}{\kappa}.$$

However, only moments of order less than α exist for the non-Gaussian family of α-stable distribution, which means we are not able to evaluate the variance of the realized variance $RV_c(0, T)$. Therefore, the convexity correction method are not able to be used to find the continuous volatility strike under the Lévy-based Heston model.

1.4.4. Numerical example for the Lévy-based Heston model

Assume the dynamics of an asset price can be modeled as in (34), where the driven Lévy process is symmetric α-stable (i.e., $\beta = \delta = 0$), $\mu = -0.0018$, $\kappa = 0.8519$, $\theta = 0.1574$, $\sigma = 0.2403$, $\rho = -0.8740$, and $V_0 = 0.0093$. Then, the fair continuous variance strike of a variance swap with maturity of one year is given by

$$K_{var}^* = \theta + \frac{(1 - e^{-\kappa T})(\kappa V_0 - \kappa\theta + \delta)}{\kappa^2 T} - \frac{\delta e^{-\kappa T}}{\kappa}$$

$$= 0.1574 + \frac{(1 - e^{-0.8519})(0.8519 \cdot 0.0093 - 0.8519 \cdot 0.1574)}{0.8519^2}$$

$$\approx 0.0577,$$

which is same as the variance strike in numerical example of Heston's model in section 1.1.4.

2. VIX futures pricing

In this section, we will consider a highly traded volatility derivative—the VIX future. We will price the VIX future under Heston's and Bates' models, and evaluate the pricing performance of different models with different approaches by comparing the estimated future prices with the market future prices.

2.1. VIX futures

The Volatility Index (VIX) introduced by the Chicago Board Options Exchange (CBOE) in 1993 has been considered as a key measure of the stock market volatility. The original CBOE Volatility Index was designed to measure the market's expectation of 30-day implied volatility by at-the-money S&P 100 Index option prices. In 2003, CBOE together with Goldman Sachs updated the VIX to reflect a new way to measure expected volatility, which is based on the S&P 500 Index (SPX) and estimates expected volatility by averaging the weighted prices of SPX puts and calls over a wide range of strike prices. CBOE introduced the first exchange-traded VIX futures contract on March 24, 2004 and launched VIX options after two years. The trading in VIX options and futures are very active and has grown to over 800,000 contracts per day in just 10 years since the launch. See CBOE (2014).

As described in the CBOE white paper (CBOE, 2014), the generalized formula used in the VIX calculation is

$$\text{VIX}_t^2 = \left(\frac{2}{\tau} \sum_i \frac{\Delta K_i}{K_i^2} e^{r\tau} Q(K_i) - \frac{1}{\tau} \left(\frac{F}{K_0} - 1 \right)^2 \right) \times 100^2, \tag{37}$$

where $\tau = \frac{30}{365}$, K_i is the strike price of the ith out-of-money option in the calculation, F is the forward index level at time t, $Q(K_i)$ denotes the mid-quote price of the out-of-money options at strike K_i at time t, K_0 is the first strike below the forward index level, and r is the risk-free rate with maturity τ. Mathematically, (2.1) can be recognized as a simple discretization of the forward integral over $[t, t + \tau]$ (Lin, 2007), i.e.,

$$\text{VIX}_t^2 = \left(\frac{\xi_1}{\tau} E_t \left(\int_t^{t+\tau} V_s ds \right) + \xi_2 \right) \times 100^2, \tag{38}$$

where V_t is the instantaneous variance, $E(X)$ is the expectation under the risk-neutral probability measure and $E_t(X) := E(X|\mathcal{F}_t)$, ξ_1 and ξ_2 are coefficients determined by the price dynamics (See Appendix A in Lin (2007) for more details about the coefficient).

The expression of the VIX squared can also be given in terms of risk-neutral expectation of the log contract (Zhu and Lian, 2011):

$$\text{VIX}_t^2 = -\frac{2}{\tau} E_t \left(ln \left(\frac{S_{t+\tau}}{S_t e^{r\tau}} \right) \right) \times 100^2. \tag{39}$$

Carr and Wu (2006) showed that the price of a VIX future is a martingale under the risk-neutral measure, and the value of a VIX future contract with

$$\text{VIX}_T).\tag{40}$$

2.1.1. VIX futures pricing under the Heston's model

Assume the dynamics of S&P 500 Index can be approximated by Heston's stochastic volatility model as in (1), in which we have that $\xi_1 = 1$ and $\xi_2 = 0$. Thus the VIX squared in this case is

$$\begin{aligned}
\text{VIX}_t^2 &= \frac{100^2}{\tau} E_t \left(\int_t^{t+\tau} V_s ds \right) \\
&= 100^2 \times \left(\theta + \frac{V_t - \theta}{\kappa\tau} (1 - e^{-\kappa\tau}) \right),
\end{aligned}\tag{41}$$

and the present value of a VIX future contract with maturity T is

$$\begin{aligned}
F(T) &= E(\text{VIX}_T) \\
&= 100 \times E \left(\sqrt{\theta + \frac{V_T - \theta}{\kappa\tau} (1 - e^{-\kappa\tau})} \right).
\end{aligned}\tag{42}$$

Now we use convexity correction formula and Laplace transform method to evaluate $F(T)$ separately.

Theorem 8. *Applying the convexity correction formula (10) to (42), we have the following approximation for the value of VIX future contract,*

$$\begin{aligned}
F(T) &\approx 100 \times (\sqrt{\theta - \frac{\theta(1 - e^{-\kappa\tau})}{\kappa\tau} + \frac{1 - e^{-\kappa\tau}}{\kappa\tau} \cdot E(V_T)} \\
&\quad - \frac{(1 - e^{-\kappa\tau})^2 Var(V_T)}{8\kappa^2\tau^2 \left(\theta - \frac{\theta(1 - e^{-\kappa\tau})}{\kappa\tau} + \frac{1 - e^{-\kappa\tau}}{\kappa\tau} \cdot E(V_T) \right)^{3/2}}),
\end{aligned}\tag{43}$$

where

$$E(V_T) = \theta + (V_0 - \theta)e^{-\kappa T}$$

and

$$Var(V_T) = \frac{\theta\sigma^2}{2\kappa}(1 - e^{-2\kappa T}) + \frac{(V_0 - \theta)\sigma^2}{\kappa}(e^{-\kappa T} - e^{-2\kappa T}).\tag{44}$$

Proof. By applying convexity correction formula, we have that

$$F(T) = 100 \times E\left(\sqrt{\theta + \frac{V_T - \theta}{\kappa\tau}(1 - e^{-\kappa\tau})} \right)$$

$$\approx 100 \times \left(\sqrt{E\left(\theta + \frac{V_T - \theta}{\kappa\tau}(1 - e^{-\kappa\tau})\right)} - \frac{Var\left(\theta + \frac{V_T-\theta}{\kappa\tau}(1 - e^{-\kappa\tau})\right)}{8\left(E\left(\theta + \frac{V_T-\theta}{\kappa\tau}(1 - e^{-\kappa\tau})\right)\right)^{\frac{3}{2}}} \right)$$

$$= 100 \times \left(\sqrt{\theta - \frac{\theta(1 - e^{-\kappa\tau})}{\kappa\tau} + \frac{1 - e^{-\kappa\tau}}{\kappa\tau} \cdot E(V_T)} \right.$$

$$\left. - \frac{(1 - e^{-\kappa\tau})^2 Var(V_T)}{8\kappa^2\tau^2\left(\theta - \frac{\theta(1-e^{-\kappa\tau})}{\kappa\tau} + \frac{1-e^{-\kappa\tau}}{\kappa\tau} \cdot E(V_T)\right)^{3/2}} \right).$$

Zhu and Lian (2011) consider a general model for the S&P 500 which incorporates stochastic volatility and simultaneous jumps in both the asset price and the volatility process. They found the closed-form pricing formula for the exact price of a VIX future by solving a backward partial integro-differential equation (PIDE). Now we give following closed-form pricing formula for the Heston stochastic volatility model by modifying the result in Zhu and Lain (2011).

Theorem 9. *Assume the dynamics of S&P 500 Index is given by the Heston stochastic volatility model (1), the price of a VIX future with maturity This then*

$$F(T, V_0) = \frac{1}{2\sqrt{\pi}} \int_0^\infty \frac{1 - e^{-100^2 sB}f(-100^2 sA; T, V_0)}{s^{3/2}} ds, \tag{45}$$

where

$$A = \frac{1 - e^{-\kappa\tau}}{\kappa\tau}, \quad B = \theta\left(1 - \frac{1 - e^{-\kappa\tau}}{\kappa\tau}\right),$$

and $f(\phi;T, V_0)$ is the moment generating function of the stochastic variable V_T, given by

$$f(\phi; T, V_0) = e^{C(\phi,T)+D(\phi,T)V_0}$$

with

$$C(\phi, T) = \frac{-2\kappa\theta}{\sigma^2} \cdot \ln\left(1 + \frac{\sigma^2\phi}{2\kappa}(e^{-\kappa T} - 1)\right)$$

and

$$D(\phi, T) = \frac{2\kappa\phi}{\sigma^2\phi + (2\kappa - \sigma^2\phi)e^{\kappa T}}.$$

See Zhu and Lian (2011) for more details.

2.1.2. VIX futures pricing under the Bates model

In this section we derive the present value of VIX futures in Bates' model (29), where $\xi_1 = 1$ and $\xi_2 = 2\lambda(m-a)$. By the definition of VIX squared (38), we have that

$$
\begin{aligned}
\text{VIX}_t^2 &= \left(\frac{1}{\tau}E_t(\int_t^{t+\tau} V_s ds) + 2\lambda(m - a)\right) \times 100^2 \\
&= 100^2 \times \left(\theta + \frac{V_t - \theta}{\kappa\tau}(1 - e^{-\kappa\tau}) + 2\lambda(m - a)\right),
\end{aligned}
\tag{46}
$$

and the present value of a VIX future contract with maturity T is

$$
\begin{aligned}
F(T) &= E(\text{VIX}_T) \\
&= 100 \times E\left(\sqrt{\theta + \frac{V_T - \theta}{\kappa\tau}(1 - e^{-\kappa\tau}) + 2\lambda(m - a)}\right).
\end{aligned}
\tag{47}
$$

Once again, we use convexity correction formula and Laplace transform method to evaluate $F(T)$ in (47).

Theorem 10. *By using the convexity correction formula (10), we have following approximation for the value of VIX future contract in Bates' model,*

$$
\begin{aligned}
F(T) \quad &\approx 100 \times (\sqrt{\theta - \frac{\theta(1 - e^{-\kappa\tau})}{\kappa\tau} + \frac{1 - e^{-\kappa\tau}}{\kappa\tau} \cdot E(V_T) + 2\lambda(m - a)} \\
&- \frac{(1 - e^{-\kappa\tau})^2 Var(V_T)}{8\kappa^2\tau^2\left(\theta - \frac{\theta(1 - e^{-\kappa\tau})}{\kappa\tau} + \frac{1 - e^{-\kappa\tau}}{\kappa\tau} \cdot E(V_T) + 2\lambda(m - a)\right)^{3/2}}),
\end{aligned}
\tag{48}
$$

where $E(V_T)$ and $Var(V_T)$ are same as in (44).

Proof. By using convexity correction formula, we have that

$$F(T) = 100 \times E\left(\sqrt{\theta + \frac{V_T - \theta}{\kappa\tau}(1 - e^{-\kappa\tau}) + 2\lambda(m - a)}\right)$$

$$\approx 100 \times \left(\sqrt{E(\theta + \frac{V_T - \theta}{\kappa\tau}(1 - e^{-\kappa\tau}) + 2\lambda(m - a))}\right.$$

$$\left. - \frac{Var\left(\theta + \frac{V_T - \theta}{K\tau}(1 - e^{-\kappa\tau}) + 2\lambda(m - a)\right)}{8\left(E\left(\theta + \frac{V_T - \theta}{\kappa\tau}(1 - e^{-\kappa\tau})\right) + 2\lambda(m - a)\right)^{\frac{3}{2}}}\right)$$

$$= 100 \times \left(\sqrt{\theta - \frac{\theta(1 - e^{-\kappa\tau})}{\kappa\tau} + \frac{1 - e^{-\kappa\tau}}{\kappa\tau} \cdot E(V_T) + 2\lambda(m - a)}\right.$$

$$\left. - \frac{(1 - e^{-\kappa\tau})^2 Var(V_T)}{8\kappa^2\tau^2\left(\theta - \frac{\theta(1 - e^{-\kappa\tau})}{\kappa\tau} + \frac{1 - e^{-\kappa\tau}}{\kappa\tau} \cdot E(V_T) + 2\lambda(m - a)\right)^{3/2}}\right).$$

$$(49)$$

Theorem 11. *Assume the dynamics of S&P 500 Index is given by the Bates jump model, then the price of a VIX future with maturity T is given by*

$$F(T, V_0) = \frac{1}{2\sqrt{\pi}} \int_0^\infty \frac{1 - e^{-100^2 sB} f(-100^2 sA; T, V_0)}{s^{3/2}} ds, \qquad (50)$$

where

$$A = \frac{1 - e^{-\kappa\tau}}{\kappa\tau}, \quad B = \theta\left(1 - \frac{1 - e^{-\kappa\tau}}{\kappa\tau}\right) + 2\lambda(m - a),$$

and $f(\phi;T, V_0)$ is the moment generating function of the stochastic variable V_T, given by

$$f(\phi; T, V_0) = e^{C(\phi,T) + D(\phi,T)V_0}$$

with

$$C(\phi, T) = \frac{-2\kappa\theta}{\sigma^2} \cdot \ln\left(1 + \frac{\sigma^2\phi}{2\kappa}(e^{-\kappa T} - 1)\right)$$

and

$$D(\phi, T) = \frac{2\kappa\phi}{\sigma^2\phi + (2\kappa - \sigma^2\phi)e^{\kappa T}}.$$

See Zhu and Lain (2011) for more details.

2.2. Empirical studies

In this section we will use historical data of the S&P 500 index and the pricing formulas derived in the above section to price the VIX futures, and evaluate the pricing performance by comparing the estimated prices with market prices of VIX futures.

2.2.1. Calibration

It has been shown that the Markov chain Monte Carlo (MCMC) algorithm outperforms some other calibration methods in many ways. Its' advantages such as stability, computational efficiency, the ability of detecting jumps (Cape et al., 2015) make it suitable for parameters estimation in our cases. In this section, we use MCMC algorithm to estimate the model parameters from the historical data of the S&P 500 index over the period from January 13, 2015 to January 13, 2017.

In our study, we use the method provided in (Cape et al., 2015) and (Johannes and Polson, 2006), which use Gibbs sampler for parameter estimation and Metropolis-Hasting algorithm for simulating the variance process V_t. We implement the MCMC calibration by using the R package provided by the authors in (Cape et al., 2015). The calibration procedure was applied to Heston's and Bates' models respectively. The following were chosen as the prior distribution parameters,

$$r \sim N(0, 1),$$

$$\kappa \sim N(0, 1),$$

$$\theta \sim N(0, 1),$$

$$\psi := \rho\sigma \sim N\left(0, \frac{\Omega}{2}\right),$$

$$\Omega := \sigma^2(1 - \rho^2) \sim IG\left(2, \frac{1}{200}\right),$$

$$\lambda \sim Beta(2, 40),$$

$$\text{lem } a \sim N(0, 1),$$

$$b^2 \sim IG(5.0, 0.2).$$

Initial values for the MCMC algorithm were chosen based off the observed data when possible or a random assignment when more educated estimates were not possible (see Cape et al., 2015). As a result, the following initials were chosen:

$$r^{(0)} = 0.1,$$

$$\kappa^{(0)} = 5,$$

$$\theta^{(0)} = 0.0225,$$

$$\Omega = 0.02,$$

$$\psi^{(0)} \sim N\left(0, \frac{\Omega^{(0)}}{2}\right),$$

$$\lambda^{(0)} \sim \text{Beta}(2, 40),$$

$$a^{(0)} = 0,$$

$$b^{2(0)} = 0.1.$$

After our simulations, we discarded the first 3,000 runs as 'burn-in' period and used the last 8,000 iterations to estimate model parameters. Means of the draws from the posterior distributions of each parameter are reported as well as the standard deviation of the draws for the distribution. The algorithm was run 10 times, recording the parameter values after each run after which the means were calculated from the ten runs. Each run took about 20 minutes and was done completely in the statistical language of R, utilizing pre-defined routines for random number generation. Table 4.1 provides a summary of the results obtained from the MCMC simulations.

Like other published results (e.g., Cape et al., 2015, Zhu and Lian, 2011), there is a strong negative correlation between the instantaneous volatility and returns, and the correlation is even stronger than others that have been observed. The estimation of λ indicate that the jump happens very infrequently, with roughly one jump observed per year. Although Cape et al. (2015) point out that the MCMC algorithm we used has the difficulty in detecting jumps during times of high volatility such as the late 2008, the S&P 500 index is relatively stable during the period we choose.

2.2.2. Comparative studies in VIX future pricing performance

In this section, we use VIX futures market prices as the benchmark, and compare the pricing performance of Heston's and Bates' models under convexity correction approximation and closed-form solution pricing formula. By following the studies in Habtemicael et al. (2016), we employ following measures of "goodness of fit" of the estimated VIX future prices: the absolute percentage error (APE), the average absolute error (AAE), the average relative percentage error (ARPE), the root-mean-square error (RMSE), and the residual standard error (RSE), which are given by

$$\text{APE} = \frac{1}{\text{mean price}} \sum_{\text{data points}} \frac{|\text{market price} - \text{model price}|}{\text{data points}},$$

$$\text{AAE} = \sum_{\text{data points}} \frac{|\text{market price} - \text{model price}|}{\text{data points}},$$

$$\text{ARPE} = \frac{1}{\text{data points}} \sum_{\text{data points}} \frac{|\text{market price} - \text{model price}|}{\text{data points}},$$

$$\text{RMSE} = \sqrt{\sum_{\text{data points}} \frac{|\text{market price} - \text{model price}|}{\text{data points}}}, \quad \text{RSE} = \sqrt{\frac{SSE}{n-k}},$$

where SSE is the sum of square error, n is the number of observations and k is the number of parameters to be estimated. By using the estimated parameters reported in Table 4.1, we compute the VIX futures prices with different maturities on January 13, 2017. The values of APE, AAE, ARPE, RMSE, and RSE are tabulated in Table 4.2.

From the Table 4.2, we can draw some conclusions about the pricing performance. All these five different measures of pricing performance show that the

Table 4.2 The test of pricing performance

Pricing Errors	Models and Pricing Methods	All Futures	$T < 30$	$30 < T < 90$	$90 < T$
APE	Heston (Convex)	0.1928	0.0497	0.1022	0.3114
	Heston (Closed-form)	0.0774	0.0737	0.0473	0.0959
	Bates (Convex)	0.1811	0.1143	0.0472	0.2873
	Bates (Closed-form)	0.0820	0.0258	0.0291	0.1383
AAE	Heston (Convex)	3.0759	0.6531	1.5556	5.7046
	Heston (Closed-form)	1.2353	0.9679	0.7201	1.7569
	Bates (Convex)	2.8896	0.4289	0.7183	5.2627
	Bates (Closed-form)	1.3087	0.3384	0.4431	2.5326
ARPE	Heston (Convex)	0.2197	0.1633	0.3889	0.9508
	Heston (Closed-form)	0.0882	0.2420	0.1800	0.2928
	Bates (Convex)	0.2064	0.3753	0.1796	0.8771
	Bates (Closed-form)	0.0935	0.0846	0.1108	0.4221
RMSE	Heston (Convex)	1.7538	0.8081	1.2472	2.3884
	Heston (Closed-form)	1.1114	0.9838	0.8486	1.3255
	Bates (Convex)	1.6999	0.6549	0.8475	2.2941
	Bates (Closed-form)	1.1440	0.5817	0.6657	1.5914
RSE	Heston (Convex)	6.0902	0.5559	1.3931	5.9026
	Heston (Closed-form)	2.2036	0.7935	0.6515	1.9498
	Bates (Convex)	5.7498	1.2680	0.7135	5.5626
	Bates (Closed-form)	2.7307	0.2866	0.4435	2.6792

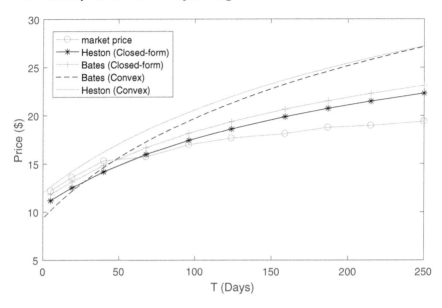

Figure 4.1 Comparison of VIX futures market price with estimated price

Source: CBOE (2014). The CBOE Volatility Index – VIX. White Paper. (http://www.cboe.com/micro/vix/vixwhite.pdf)

VIX futures prices estimated from closed-form solutions are more accurate than those estimated from convexity correction approximation for both Heston's and Bates' models, generally. However, the convex correction method outperforms the closed-form solution method for the short-term futures in the Heston's model. Also, for short-term and medium-term futures, Bates' model with closed-form solution performs better than the other cases.

To illustrate the pricing performance more clearly, we plot the market prices of VIX futures and estimated prices on the same graph in Figure 4.1. It can be observed that the Heston model with convexity correction approximation always overvalue the futures; for the short-term VIX futures, the Bates model with closed-form solution provides the best estimation; for the VIX futures with medium- to long-term maturities, all of the pricing methods will over-price the futures.

However, we think the trading volumes of VIX futures is a main reason for the poor pricing performance for long-term VIX futures. From Table 4.3 we can see that the trading of short-term VIX future (within one month) are very active, and the total trading volume decreases significantly as the time-to-expire increases. The data we downloaded from CBOE website shows that there is no VIX future with maturity longer than 250 days had been traded in the market. To some degree, this explain the deviation of the estimated price and the market price of long-term futures as in Figure 4.1. The prices of long-term VIX futures with low trading volume are model-free and thus cannot reflect the market expectation on the underlying asset.

Table 4.3 Total trading volumes of VIX futures with different maturities on January 13, 2017

Time to expire (days)	Total volume (contracts)
5	110184
33	113493
68	34580
96	12146
124	7351
159	5007
187	1815
215	343
250	0

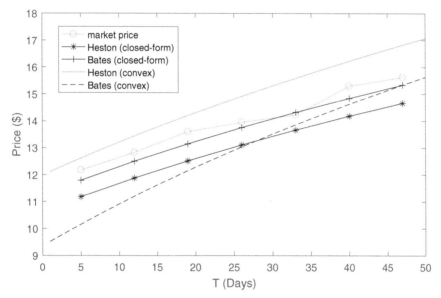

Figure 4.2 Comparison of short-term VIX futures market price with estimated price

For better comparison of pricing performance for short-term VIX futures, we pick more short-term VIX futures and repeat the procedure, and we get the pricing result as in Figure 4.2, which shows that Bates (closed-form) can provide relatively reliable estimation of the market price, and it is even more accurate when the time to expire is between 25 to 35 days. We want to point out that the conclusion would be more convincing if we took VIX futures on different date into account instead of only considering the pricing performance on January 13, 2017. One possible way to do that is collect the market data, sort all the observed futures pricing according to expiration, group these futures by every 30 days to expiration, and then compute the average prices of each group Zhu et al. (2011). Due to the computational complexity, in this thesis we just use the data on a specific date to provide an intuitively understanding, although the conclusions coincide with those in Zhu et al. (2011).

3. Conclusion

In this paper, we considered variance and volatility swaps pricing for different stochastic volatility models, such as Heston, Bates, Merton and Lévy-based Heston models, and presented numerical results based on historical data of the *S&P* 500 Index, January 13, 2005 to January 13, 2017. We also studied VIX futures pricing for the Heston and the Bates models, presented empirical studies for them, based on the above-mentioned data, and performed comparative studies.

Acknowledgments

The authors wish to thank NSERC for continuing support.

Bibliography

Bates, D. (1996). Jump and Stochastic Volatility: Exchange Rate Processes Implicit in Deutsche Mark in Options, *Review of Financial Studies*, 9, pp. 69–107.

Broadie, M. and Jain, A. (2008). The Effect of Jumps and Discrete Sampling on Volatility and Variance Swaps, *International Journal of Theoretical and Applied Finance*, 11(8), pp. 761–797.

Brockhaus, O. and Long, D. (2002). Volatility Swaps Made Simple, *Risk*, 19(1), pp. 92–95.

Cairns, A. (2004). *Interest Rate Models: An Introduction*. (Princeton University Press, Princeton, USA).

Cape, J., Dearden, W., Gamber, W., Liebner, J., Lu, Q. and Nguyenu, M. (2015). Estimating Heston's and Bates' Models Parameters Using Markov Chain Monte Carlo Simulation, *Journal of Statistical Computation and Simulation*, 85(11).

Carr, P. and Wu, L. (2006). A Tale of Two Indices, *The Journal of Derivatives*, 13(3).

CBOE (2014). The CBOE Volatility Index – VIX. *White Paper*. (http://www.cboe.com/micro/vix/vixwhite.pdf)

Habtemicael, S. and SenGupta, I. (2016). Pricing Variance and Volatility Swaps for Barndorff-Nielsen and Shephard Process Driven Financial Markets, *International Journal of Financial Engineering*, 3(4).

Heston, S. (1993). A Closed-Form Solution for Options with Stochastic Volatility with Applications to Bond and Currency Options, *The Review of Financial Studies*, 6(2), pp. 327–343.

Johannes, M. and Polson, N. (2006). MCMC Methods for Continuous-Time Financial Econometrics. In: *Handbook in Financial Econometrics*, Vol. 2, Chapter 13, pp. 1–72. (Ed. Y. Ait-Sahalia and L. P. Hansen).

Lin, Y. (2007). Pricing VIX Futures: Evidence from Integrated Physical and Risk-neutral Probability Measures, *Journal of Futures Markets*, 27(12), pp. 1175–1217.

Rosinski, J and Woyczinski, W. (1986). On Ito Stochastic Integration with Respect to p-Stable Motion: Inner Clock, Integrability of Sample Paths, Double and Multiple Integrals, *Annals of Probability*, 14, pp. 271–286.

Swishchuk, A. (2009). Multi-Factor Lévy Models for Pricing Financial and Energy Derivatives, *Canadian Applied Mathematics Quarterly*, 17(4), Winter.

Zhu, S. and Lian, G. (2011). An Analytical Formula for VIX Futures and Its Applications, *Journal of Futures Markets*, 32(2), pp. 166–190.

5 A nonparametric ACD model

Antonio Cosma and Fausto Galli

1. Introduction

Waiting times between particular financial events, such as trades, quote updates, or volume accumulation, are an important object of analysis in the econometrics of financial market microstructure. The statistical inspection of the durations between these events reveals the presence of a series of stylized facts (for instance, clustering and overdispersion) that are rather common features in financial data. For instance, they can be compared with the clustering and fat tails displayed by the time-varying conditional variance of financial returns. The traditional econometric approach to duration analysis therefore needs to be extended to be able to fit and reproduce these peculiarities.

To this end, the autoregressive conditional duration (ACD) model, originally introduced by Engle Russell (1998), combines elements from the ARCH literature and of duration analysis. The main structure of this model is composed of a random variable (the so-called baseline duration), the distribution of which follows a law characterized by a positive support (such as an exponential or a Weibull), multiplied by a deterministic conditional duration, which in the seminal specification was a linear function of lagged values of the observations and of the conditional duration itself.

A rich family of parametric extensions followed this first specification of the ACD model. These contributions develop along two main lines: the functional form of the time-varying conditional duration mean and the distribution of the innovations of the conditional duration. Among the first line of extensions (which abound in the literature), consider the log-ACD proposed by Bauwens and Giot (2000), where the conditional mean function takes an exponential form, the asymmetric ACD, by Bauwens and Giot (2003), characterized by the presence of a threshold in the conditional mean, and the Box-Cox transformation proposed by Fernandes and Grammig (2006). Other interesting extensions are those of Ghysels et al. (2004) and Bauwens and Veredas (2004) who introduce an element of randomness in the conditional mean, which in the previous specifications was deterministically modeled. For a review of several of these model variants, see Pacurar (2008) or Hautsch (2011).

The second line of extensions addresses the modeling of the distribution of the conditional duration, suggesting laws characterized by higher degrees of parametrization and generality. Among the most commonly adopted densities are the Weibull, the gamma, the lognormal, the Burr (encompassing the Weibull), the generalized gamma (encompassing the Weibull and the Gamma) and the generalized F (encompassing the Burr). Combinations of distributions have also been advanced (see De Luca and Zuccolotto (2006) or Luca and Gallo (2008)).

In the ACD literature, this variety of parametric specifications for the conditional mean and distribution has only partially been matched by attempts to provide semiparametric expressions for the conditional mean, which have the advantage of being robust to misspecification. A number of semiparametric point process specifications have been proposed; see, for instance, Saart et al. (2015), Brownlees et al. (2012) or Gerhard and Hautsch (2007).

The aim of this work is to introduce an even more general, fully nonparametric form of the ACD family model, where the conditional mean is expressed as a generic function of the lagged observation and of its own past and is nonparametrically estimated. Bauwens et al. (2004) note that more complex specifications of the distribution of the innovations do not seem to provide substantial improvements in the goodness of fit, and thus we believe that a more flexible definition of the conditional mean function could provide improvements in fitting the data.

The main difficulty of estimating ACD models in a fully nonparametric way resides in the unobservability of one or some regressors. To overcome this difficulty, various solutions have been proposed in the literature on GARCH models, which share many commonalities with ACD models. Hafner (1998), proposes replacing the unobservable regressor with a function of several lagged values of the observations. We can understand this approach as an approximation of a GARCH(p,q) by an ARCH(∞) model. This approach is straightforward to implement, but because of the large number of regressors, it is computationally heavy and suffers severely from the curse of dimensionality. Another interesting solution comes from Franke and Muller (2002) and Franke et al. (2003), who employ a deconvolution kernel estimator, which relies heavily on the normality of the innovations (meaning that this approach would hardly be extendable to an ACD framework) and has a rather slow rate of convergence. The iterative scheme proposed by Bühlmann McNeil (2002) is an approach that naturally adapts to ACD models. Under a central, and albeit rather restrictive, contraction hypothesis, the authors of the latter work show that the estimator is consistent and has a rate of convergence equal to that of a usual bivariate nonparametric regression technique. We thus expect this estimator to perform better than the deconvolution kernel.

The advantages of the Bühlmann and McNeil (2002) approach are, in principle, rather significant. As do all nonparametric methods, it only imposes very mild assumptions on the function to be estimated, almost entirely eliminating the risk of incorrect specification. However, its main cost is that the exact role played by an independent variable in the model cannot be summarized in a single vector of parameters, and this limits the scope for inference. The main finding of this paper is that the nonparametric ACD estimator improves, albeit not dramatically, on the forecasting precision of the linear specification.

More interestingly, close inspection of the conditional mean surfaces that we obtain from the nonparametric analysis can provide valuable information on the possibly nonlinear structure of the conditional mean function and on how to take into account the seasonality in the data introduced by the time-of-the-day variable.

The outline of this work is as follows: Section 2 introduces the nonparametric estimator for financial duration. In Section 3, a Monte Carlo experiment compares the performance of the nonparametric estimator and of the maximum likelihood parametric estimator. In Section 4, we estimate on a financial dataset that is commonly used in the ACD literature and perform some forecast accuracy comparisons. Section 4 also presents an evaluation of the shock impact curve calculated on the basis of a nonparametric estimation and the results of joint estimation of the conditional duration and of the seasonality effects. Section 5 concludes.

2. The theoretical framework

2.1. The model

We introduce in this section the ACD model in the form that can be usually found in the literature and then rewrite it in a way that allows us to estimate it nonparametrically. Let $\{X_t\}$ be a nonnegative stationary process adapted to the filtration $\{\mathcal{F}_t, t \in \mathbb{Z}\}$, with $\mathcal{F}_t = \sigma(\{X_s; s \leq t\})$, such that

$$X_t = \psi_t \epsilon_t,$$

$$\psi_t = f(X_{t-1}, \cdots, X_{t-p}, \psi_{t-1}, \cdots, \psi_{t-q}), \tag{1}$$

where $p, q \geq 0$ and $\{\epsilon_t\}$ is an *iid* nonnegative process with mean 1 and a finite second moment. We assume $f(\cdot)$ to be a strictly positive function. Since $f(\cdot)$ is $\mathcal{F}_{t-1}$-measurable, we have that $E(X_t \mid \mathcal{F}_{t-1}) = \psi_t$, i.e., ψ_t is the time-varying conditional mean of the process. We focus on the case in which $p = q = 1$, this restriction being widely justified by empirical works. Several parameterizations of (1) have been introduced, the first being the linear specification:

$$\psi_t = \omega + \alpha \psi_{t-1} + \beta X_{t-1}. \tag{2}$$

More complex specifications followed (2), allowing for nonlinearity in the response of the conditional mean to the realizations of X_t or in the autoregressive part. In our setup, $f(\cdot)$ is allowed to be any function of the past realizations X_{t-1} and of the lagged conditional mean ψ_{t-1}. Moreover, parametric specifications of the ACD family often make use of highly parameterized functions for the distributions of the innovations ϵ_t, while here we only require the mean of the ϵ_t to be one and the variance to be finite. We expect our estimation to outperform parametric models in the case in which the 'real' f shows some accentuated nonlinearity as in the *threshold* models:

$$\psi_t = h(X_{t-1}) + \sum_i \beta_i \mathbb{I}_{[X_{t-1} \in B_i]} \psi_{t-1},$$

where B_i are disjoint subsets of $\mathbb{R}_+$ and $h(x)$ is again a strictly positive function. To estimate f, we rewrite (1) in the additive form:

$$X_t = f(X_{t-1}, \psi_{t-1}) + \eta_t, \tag{3}$$

$$\eta_t = f(X_{t-1}, \psi_{t-1})(\epsilon_t - 1).$$

The process $\{\eta_t\}$ is a white noise, as $E(\eta_t) = E(\eta_t|\mathcal{F}_{t-1}) = 0$ and $E(\eta_s \eta_t) = E[E(\eta_s \eta_t|\mathcal{F}_{t-1})] = 0$ for $s < t$. The conditional variance of X_t is $\mathrm{Var}(X_t|\mathcal{F}_{t-1}) = f^2(X_{t-1}, \psi_{t-1})(E(\epsilon_t^2) - 1)$. Thus, formally, $f(X_{t-1}, \psi_{t-1})$ could be estimated by regressing X_t on $f(X_{t-1}, \psi_{t-1})$. In practice, the ψ_t are unobserved variables. To overcome this problem, we adapt the recursive algorithm suggested by Bühlmann and McNeil (2002).

2.2. The estimation procedure

The algorithm is built as follows. Let $\{x_t; 1 \leq t \leq n\}$ be realizations[1] of the process (1), with $p = q = 1$. The steps of the algorithm are indexed by j.

Step 1. Choose the starting values for the vector of the n conditional means. Index these values by 0: $\{\psi_{t,0}\}$. Set $j = 1$.

Step 2. Regress nonparametrically $\{x_t; 2 \leq t \leq n\}$ on $\{x_{t-1}; 2 \leq t \leq n\}$ and on the conditional means computed in the previous step: $\{\psi_{t-1, j-1}; 2 \leq t \leq n\}$, to obtain an estimate $\hat{f}_j$ of f.

Step 3. Compute $\{\hat{\psi}_{t,j} = \hat{f}_j(x_{t-1}, \hat{\psi}_{t-1,j}); 2 \leq t \leq n\}$; remember to choose some sensible value for $\hat{\psi}_{1,j}$, which cannot be computed recursively.

Step 4. Increment j, and return to step two to run a new regression using the $\{\psi_t\}$ computed in Step 3.

Averaging the estimates of the last steps of the algorithm, when it becomes more stable, further improves the estimation procedure.

We refer to Bühlmann and McNeil (2002) for a justification and theoretical discussion of the algorithm. We state here from the main theorem of that paper, which provides the convergence rates of the estimates delivered by the algorithm. We first need some notation. Henceforth, $\|Y\|$ denotes the $\mathcal{L}_2$ norm of Y: $\|Y\|^2 = \mathbb{E}(Y^2)$. Let

$$\tilde{f}_{t,j}(x, \psi) = E(X_t|X_{t-1} = x, \hat{\psi}_{t-1,j-1} = \psi),$$

$$\tilde{\psi}_{t,j} = \tilde{f}_{t,j}(x_{t-1}, \hat{\psi}_{t-1,j-1});$$

That is, $\tilde{\psi}_{t,j}$ is the true conditional expectation of X_t given the value of $\hat{\psi}_{t-1,j-1}$ estimated at the previous step of the algorithm. Thus, the quantity

$$\Delta_{t,j,n} \equiv \tilde{\psi}_{t,j} - \hat{\psi}_{t,j}, \; j = 1, 2, \cdots, t = j+2, \cdots, n,$$

gives us the estimation error introduced at the j-th step solely due to the estimation of f. In nonparametric language, $\|\Delta\|$ is the stochastic component of the risk of the estimator $\hat{\psi}_{t,j}$ of $E(X_t|X_{t-1}, \psi_{t-1, j-1})$.

Theorem 1 (Theorems 1 and 2 in Bühlmann and McNeil (2002)) *Assume that*

1   $\sup_{x \in \mathbb{R}}|f(x, \psi) - f(x, \varphi)| \leq D|\psi - \varphi|$ *for some* $0 < D < 1$, $\forall \psi, \; \varphi \in \mathbb{R}_+$.
2   $E|\psi_t|^2 \leq C_1, \; E|\psi_{t,0}|^2 \leq C_2, \; \max_{2 \leq t \leq n} E|\hat{\psi}_{t,0}|^2 \leq C_3, \; C_{1,2,3} < \infty$,
    $\|\psi_j - \psi_{j,0}\| < \infty, \; \|\hat{\psi}_{j,0} - \psi_{j,0}\| < \infty \; \forall j$.
3   $E(\{\tilde{\psi}_{t,j} - \psi_{t,j}\}^2) \leq G^2 E(\{\hat{\psi}_{t-1,j-1} - \psi_{t-1,j-1}\}^2)$ *for some* $0 < G < 1$, *for* $t = j+2, j+3, \dots$ *and* $j = 1, 2, \dots$
4   $\Delta_n \doteq \sup_{j \geq 1} \max_{j+2 \leq t \leq n} \|\Delta_{t,j,n}\| \to 0$, *as* $n \to \infty$ *for* $j = 1, 2, \dots, t = j+2, \dots, n$.

Then, if $\{X_t\}_{t \in \mathbb{N}}$ *is as in* (1) *with* $p = q = 1$ *and choosing* $m_n = C\{-\log \Delta_n\}$,

$$\max_{m_n+2 \leq t \leq n} \|\hat{\psi}_{t,m_n} - \psi_t\| = O(\Delta_n), \; \text{as } n \to \infty.$$

The theorem tells us that if all the assumptions hold, then the upper bound on the quadratic risk of the estimates of the $\{\psi_t\}$ is of the same order as Δ_n, that is, the error of a one-step nonparametric regression to estimate $\psi_{t,j}$ from (x_{t-1}, ψ_{t-1}). That is, in a bivariate nonparametric regression with an appropriate choice of the kernel function and of the smoothing parameter and assuming, for instance, that $f(x, \psi)$ is twice continuously differentiable, the convergence rates are $O(n^{-1/3})$. The authors suggest as a practical rule $m_n \sim 3 \log(n)$.

We briefly discuss the assumptions of the theorem. For further insights, refer to Bühlmann and McNeil (2002). First, let us write

$$\|\hat{\psi}_{t,j} - \psi_t\| \leq \leq \|\hat{\psi}_{t,j} - \tilde{\psi}_{t,j}\| + \|\tilde{\psi}_{t,j} - \psi_{t,j}\| + \|\psi_{t,j} - \psi_t\|. \tag{4}$$

The first two components of the risk (4) are the usual quadratic risk of an estimator $\hat{\psi}_{t,j}$ of $\psi_{t,j}$. The additional component $\|\psi_{t,j} - \psi_t\|$ is included because we do not observe ψ_t. Assumption 1 controls this last part of the risk. If there were no estimation error in passing from one step of the algorithm to the next, Assumption 1 combined with the recursive form of the algorithm would be sufficient to ensure the convergence of $\psi_{t,m}$ to the true value ψ_t. Assumption 2 is technical and needed to give an upper bound to the estimation error of the first step of the algorithm. Assumption 3 is used to control the second component of (4).

It can be written in the following way: $\|\tilde{\psi}_{t,j} - \psi_{t,j}\| = \|E(X_t|X_{t-1}, \hat{\psi}_{t-1,j-1}) - E(X_t|X_{t-1}, \psi_{t-1,j-1})\|$ so Assumption 3 is a contraction property of the conditional expectation with respect to $\|\hat{\psi}_{t-1,m-1} - \psi_{t-1,j-1}\|$. It is again a technical property that Bühlmann and McNeil are obliged to impose on the process to prove the consistency of the estimates delivered by the algorithm. Assumption 4 bounds the first term of (4). It gives an upper bound to the one-pass regression of X_t on X_{t-1} and $\psi_{t-1, j-1}$.

2.3. The practical implementation

In our application to simulated and real data, we use the following settings. For the initial values of the $\{\psi_t\}$ to use in the first step of the algorithm, we choose a vector of random draws from an exponential distribution with expectation equal to the unconditional mean of the data series $\{x_t\}$. Bühlmann and McNeil (2002) suggest using a parametric estimate, which is to be improved in the following steps of the algorithm. Since our goal is to compare parametric with nonparametric estimates, we believe that challenging the nonparametric procedure by providing dull initial values would make the competition fairer and the results more reliable. Moreover, we noticed that the algorithm yields essentially the same outcome in both cases, that is, when providing the random draws or the parametric estimate as starting values. We can say that the algorithm is quite insensitive to changes in the choice of the initial values, provided that these are sensible.

As far as the choice of the nonparametric technique is concerned, we use the locally weighted smoother (LOESS)[2], developed by Cleveland 1979. Hastie and Tibshirani 1990 provide a good introduction to this nonparametric technique. The main idea is to perform a local polynomial least squares fit in the neighbourhood of a point x_0. The design points entering the local regression are chosen as in the k-nearest neighbour method, and the value of the function at each design point is weighted with a tri-cube kernel. The degree of smoothing is determined by the percentage of the data points (also called the *span*) entering the local regression. Following the suggestion of Cleveland, we fit a local polynomial of order 1.

The reliance on nearest neighbours as an alternative to a symmetric, area-based (as in the case of standard kernel smoothing) criterion as a method of selecting of the neighbourhood of interest seems to be particularly useful given the particular features of our data. In our application, the predictors are the lagged durations X_{t-1} and the conditional means at the j-th step of the algorithm $\psi_{t-1,j}$. As Figure 5.1 shows, the predictor variables form a non-uniform random design in the $x\psi$ plane and are visibly more dense in the region next to the axes, drawing in the $x\psi$ plane a "falling star" pattern. We therefore need a method that is capable of adapting, in the neighbourhood of interest, to the local density of the predictors. Moreover, the bias of the local linear estimator does not depend on the marginal density of the predictors, thereby addressing the boundary in the domain of the regression function (both regressors are

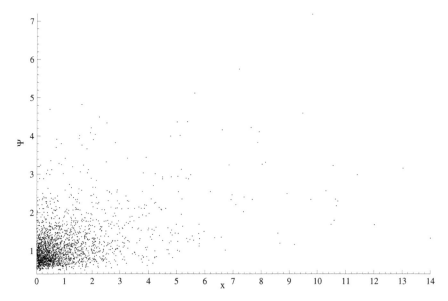

Figure 5.1 Scatterplot of a typical $x\psi$ domain

nonnegative). Following Hastie and Tibshirani (1990), we use a generalized cross validation (GCV) criterion to choose the span parameter. It can be proved that minimizing GCV is asymptotically equivalent to minimizing the mean square error of the regression. At each loop (and in the final averaged smoothing), we therefore use the span that minimizes the quantity

$$GCV = \frac{n - \sum_{t=1}^{n} (x_t - \hat{\psi}_{t,j})^2}{(n - trL)^2},$$ (5)

where n is the sample size, $\hat{\psi}_{t,j}$ is the predictor of x_t corresponding to the loop j, and L is the smoother matrix, that is, the matrix that premultiplied to the vector of observed values $\{x_t\}$ yields the estimates. The quantity trL, the trace of the matrix L, plays a role analogous to the number of degrees of freedom in a standard linear regression.

Finally, the error appearing in Equation (3) is heteroskedastic, thus calling for a weighted fit. Obviously, the true weights would depend on the values ψ_t that we are estimating. We therefore replace them in each loop with the estimates of the conditional durations that were computed in the previous iteration.

3. Estimation of simulated processes

In this section, we assess the performance of the nonparametric specification via a comparison with the estimates of a linear ACD model on different simulated series. The first simulated series is characterized by an asymmetry in the conditional mean equation, which has the following form:

$$f(x_{t-1}, \psi_{t-1}) = 0.2 + 0.1x_{t-1} + (0.3\mathbb{I}_{[x_{t-1} \leq 0.5]} + 0.85\mathbb{I}_{[x_{t-1} > 0.5]})\psi_{t-1}, \qquad (6)$$

and the conditional duration is Weibull distributed, with the scale parameter such that its mean is equal to one. The sizes of the generated samples are 1,000, 5,000, and 10,000 observations. We simulate 50 series from model (6). The simulated series are estimated by ML with a linear ACD(1,1) specification and by the nonparametric smoother described in Section 2.2 with 10 basic iterations, and we perform a final smoothing based on the arithmetic mean of the last $K = 4$ iterations. The performance of the parametric and nonparametric estimators is compared by computing two widely used measures of estimation errors. The first one is the mean square error (MSE) based on a quadratic loss function:

$$MSE = \frac{1}{nM} \sum_{l=1}^{M} \sum_{i=1}^{n} (\hat{\psi}_{il} - \psi_{il})^2, \qquad (7)$$

where $i = 1, \ldots, n$ denotes the i-th estimated conditional mean within the series, and $l = 1, \ldots, M = 50$ labels the 50 series simulated from Equation (6).

The second measure is the mean absolute error (MAE):

$$MAE = \frac{1}{nM} \sum_{l=1}^{M} \sum_{i=1}^{n} |\hat{\psi}_{il} - \psi_{il}|. \qquad (8)$$

We perform the same type of analysis on series simulated from a standard ACD(1,1) model with no asymmetric component in the specification of the conditional mean equation. The functional form is of the conditional mean is

$$f(x_{t-1}, \psi_{t-1}) = 0.1 + 0.1x_{t-1} + 0.75\psi_{t-1}, \qquad (9)$$

and the conditional distribution and the sample size are the same as in the first group of simulated series. The settings of the parametric and nonparametric estimators do not change from the first example. In particular, we estimate a parametric ACD(1,1) model, which is now correctly specified.

Figure 5.2 displays in a 200 data window an example of the evolution of the simulated ψ_t (hence the true dgp), and of those estimated parametrically and nonparametrically. Note that the parametric estimator seems to overreact and it yields too large estimates for a small number of points. Figure 5.3 shows the surfaces $f(x_{t-1}, \psi_{t-1})$ generated from the nonlinear model in Equation (6) in their simulated version and in that estimated nonparametrically. The abrupt change in the slope of $f = \hat{\psi}_t(x_{t-1}, \psi_{t-1})$ as a function of ψ_{t-1} for $x \leq 0.5$ and $x > 0.5$ is quite visible in the bottom part of the estimated surface (near the origin), where the data are very dense and the bandwidth is rather small. Farther from the origin, observations in the support become more sparse, and the result is somewhat more smoothed. In any case, it is clear that the slope increases as x

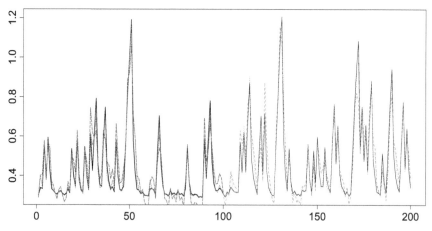

Figure 5.2 Nonlinear ACD, simulated conditional mean (solid), parametric estimate (dashed) and nonparametric estimate (dotted)

increases. To complete the analysis on this group of simulations, we give in Table 5.1 an example of how the span parameter minimizing the generalized cross-validation criterion evolves with the steps of the algorithm. It is clear that the main loop converges quite early to a stable value. Since the value of the span depends on the distribution of the predictors, a stable value of this parameter indicates that there are no major changes in the distribution of the $\{\psi_t\}$, suggesting that the algorithm has converged.

Table 5.2 compares the performance of the nonparametric and parametric estimators in terms of MSE and MAE. In the case of the nonlinear model, both statistics show that the the nonparametric estimator outperforms the parametric estimator. Both MSE and MAE decrease at each loop and decline further after the final averaging. When instead the series is simulated starting from the linear ACD model, the parametric estimator is correctly specified and, unsurprisingly, obtains the lowest MSE and MAE. The nonparametric estimator selects a large span. This means that almost all data points enter the local linear regression, making the LOESS smoother behave more like a standard linear regression. We do not show the charts of the reconstructed surfaces in this case, as they appear to be rather uninformative and flat.

4. Estimation on a financial data set

In this section, we evaluate the performance of the nonparametric specification of the ACD model on a financial dataset. The estimated series consists in a set of trade, volume and price durations of the following stocks traded in 1997 on the New York Stock Exchange: Boeing, Disney, and IBM.

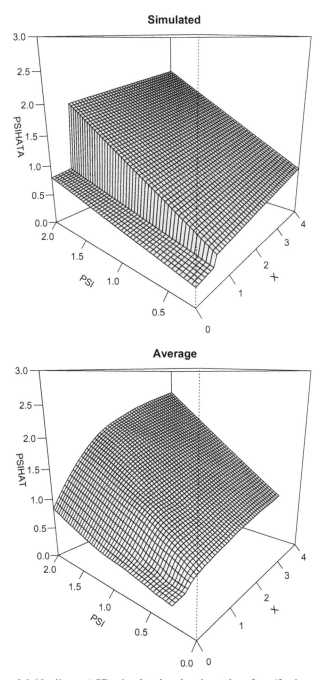

Figure 5.3 Nonlinear ACD, simulated and estimated surface (final average).

Table 5.1 Evolution of the GCV-selected bandwidth in an estimation of a series of 5000 observations simulated from a nonlinear and linear ACD specification

Loop	Nonlinear	Linear
1	0.831	0.999
2	0.206	0.999
3	0.708	0.999
4	0.597	0.999
5	0.612	0.999
6	0.736	0.999
7	0.612	0.999
8	0.623	0.999
9	0.622	0.999
10	0.622	0.999
Average	0.621	0.999

4.1. Evidence on deseasonalized data

As noted in the seminal paper by Engle and Russell (1998), there is a strong intraday seasonality in tick-by-tick data, as durations have a tendency to be shorter on average at the beginning and close of trading sessions. It is therefore common to remove the seasonal pattern by means of a nonparametric regression of raw durations on the time of the day and to fit the adjusted data. In this round of estimations, we employ the simplified deseasonalization technique used both in Engle and Russell (1998) and Bauwens and Giot (2000). In a first step, one estimates the cyclical component. This is done by averaging the durations over 30-minute intervals for each day in our sample. The average value for each of the thirteen 30-minute bins (from 9h30 to 16h) is the value of the cyclical component at the mid point of each interval. We obtain the value of the cyclical component as a smooth function of the time-of-day variable by interpolating the 30 points using a cubic spline. Figures 5.5 and 5.6 present the surfaces estimated nonparametrically with 10 loops and a final average of the last 4. The visual analysis suggests some conclusions. First, some nonlinearity is present in almost all surfaces, although it never reaches the extreme features of the discontinuity as in the data simulated in the previous section. Second, for some datasets, notably Disney volume and, to a lesser degree, Boeing price and IBM trade durations, the surface is almost linear. This is also supported by the very high values of the spans minimizing the generalized cross-validation (0.999, 0.995, and 0.981, respectively) criterion. In other datasets, the nonlinearities appear more marked. Third, in these cases, the real data-generating process in the conditional mean equation seems to place a low weight on the lagged observation X_{t-1}, and the dependence of ψ_t on ψ_{t-1} appears to diminish as X grows. This is a reasonable feature. Let us consider a regime-switching model, which is dependent on whether the market speeds up or slows down. When the market speeds up (short durations), we are more likely to observe bunching in the data, that is, there is a larger autocorrelation component in the conditional mean equation

Table 5.2 Evolution of MSE and MAE for 50 series of 1,000, 5,000, and 10,000 observations simulated from a nonlinear and linear simulated ACD specification.

	1000 obs				5000 obs				10000 obs			
	Nonlinear		Linear		Nonlinear		Linear		Nonlinear		Linear	
Loop	MSE	MAE	MSE	MAE	MSE	MAE	MSE	MAE	MSE	MAE	MSE	MAE
1	0.060	0.120	0.0025	0.033	0.044	0.099	0.00054	0.015	0.042	0.098	0.00036	0.013
2	0.058	0.115	0.0028	0.036	0.037	0.088	0.00063	0.016	0.034	0.084	0.00039	0.013
3	0.057	0.114	0.0032	0.038	0.034	0.084	0.00072	0.017	0.030	0.078	0.00040	0.013
4	0.056	0.113	0.0036	0.040	0.032	0.082	0.00074	0.018	0.028	0.076	0.00042	0.014
5	0.056	0.113	0.0035	0.040	0.031	0.081	0.00074	0.017	0.027	0.074	0.00046	0.014
6	0.055	0.112	0.0035	0.040	0.031	0.081	0.00077	0.018	0.026	0.073	0.00045	0.014
7	0.057	0.113	0.0036	0.040	0.030	0.080	0.00078	0.018	0.026	0.073	0.00044	0.014
8	0.055	0.112	0.0036	0.040	0.030	0.080	0.00074	0.017	0.026	0.074	0.00044	0.014
9	0.056	0.113	0.0037	0.041	0.030	0.080	0.00077	0.018	0.026	0.073	0.00046	0.014
10	0.057	0.114	0.0038	0.040	0.030	0.080	0.00079	0.018	0.026	0.073	0.00049	0.014
avg	0.054	0.112	0.0033	0.038	0.030	0.080	0.00074	0.017	0.026	0.072	0.00045	0.014
par	0.086	0.143	0.0012	0.025	0.077	0.138	0.00024	0.011	0.074	0.135	0.00016	0.009

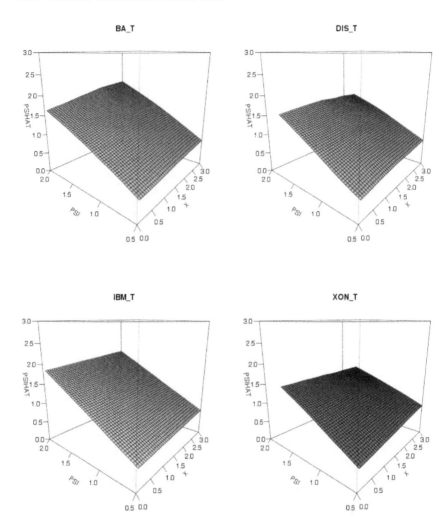

Figure 5.4 Estimated surfaces (final average) for trade durations of Boeing, Disney, IBM, and Exxon stocks

and hence a stronger dependence of ψ_t on ψ_{t-1}. When the market cools down, we observe less clustering in the duration data, and the conditional duration in the conditional mean is weaker.

We now proceed to compare the forecasting performance of the nonparametric and parametric estimators with an in-sample forecasting experiment. Using the result of the estimation, we use the conditional duration mean for time t estimated both parametrically and nonparametrically as a forecast for the duration observed at time $t + 1$. We display the averages of the squared (MSE) and absolute (MAE) forecast errors in Table 5.3, along with the percentage gains obtained by nonparametric estimation. We also test for the significance of differences in

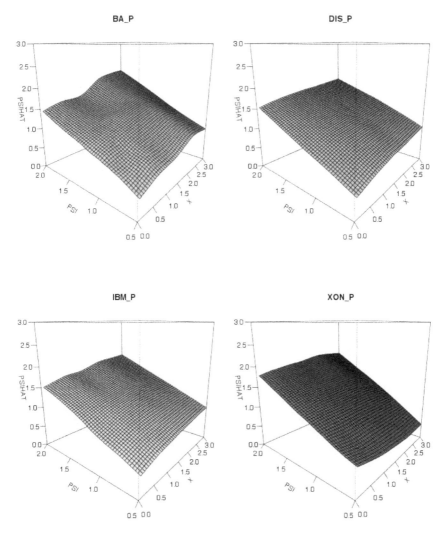

Figure 5.5 Estimated surfaces (final average) for price durations of Boeing, Disney, IBM, and Exxon stocks

forecast accuracy by performing a Diebold and Mariano (2002) test with an absolute loss function for MAE and a squared one fore MSE. In the table, percentage gains between parentheses are not significant at the 5% level.

The nonparametric estimator seems to yield an improvement in the one-step-ahead forecast accuracy in almost all cases, although only a few of them appear to be significant. Overall, the differences tend to be small in magnitude, but whenever there is a statistically significant difference, it is in favor of the non-parametric forecast.

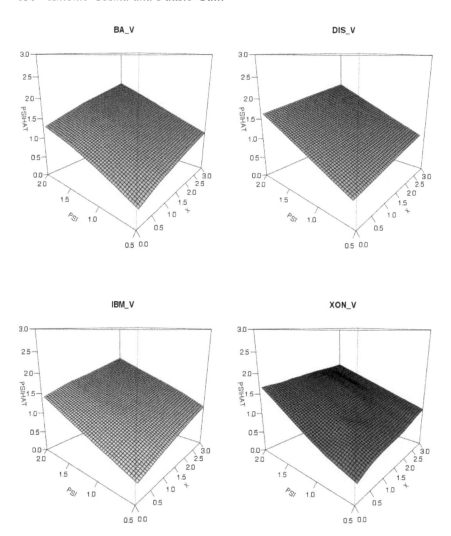

Figure 5.6 Estimated surfaces (final average) for trade durations of Boeing, Disney, IBM, and Exxon stocks

4.2. Empirical application: evaluation of the shock impact curve

Engle and Russell (1998) note that the ACD model has the tendency to overpredict after very long or very short durations. This would make a model with a concave shock impact function (that in the ACD is linear) better suited as a forecasting tool. The desirability of this feature has been explicitly acknowledged in the subsequent literature, and the Box-Cox transformation-based ACD family of specifications proposed by Fernandes and Grammig (2006) indeed shows concavity in the shape of the curve. The model proposed in this paper does not

Table 5.3 In-sample MSE, MAE and percentage gain of the nonparametric estimator on a set of trade, price and volume durations, the intraday seasonality of which was removed and the average of which was normalized to one. Percentage gains are in parentheses if the forecasts are not significantly different for the 5%-sized corresponding Diebold-Mariano test.

Type	Obs	Stock	MSE			MAE		
			Par	Nonpar	%	Par	Nonpar	%
Trade	75435	**Boeing**	1.417	1.416	*(0.02)*	0.772	0.768	*0.41*
	61630	**Disney**	1.426	1.425	*(0.06)*	0.818	0.816	*(0.10)*
	136020	**Ibm**	1.240	1.240	*(0.02)*	0.742	0.741	*0.17*
	74170	**Exxon**	1.275	1.274	*(0.08)*	0.771	0.771	*(0.02)*
Price	8682	**Boeing**	1.750	1.738	*(0.58)*	0.821	0.806	*1.86*
	5985	**Disney**	1.362	1.360	*(0.11)*	0.765	0.761	*(0.50)*
	18878	**Ibm**	1.305	1.301	*(0.21)*	0.754	0.749	*(0.59)*
	12974	**Exxon**	2.243	2.107	*6.44*	0.849	0.831	*2.04*
Volume	4261	**Boeing**	0.415	0.409	*1.31*	0.483	0.478	*1.01*
	3450	**Disney**	0.355	0.356	*(-0.42)*	0.465	0.465	*(-0.09)*
	9684	**Ibm**	0.413	0.379	*(0.18)*	0.457	0.457	*(0.46)*
	5597	**Exxon**	0.413	0.412	*(0.29)*	0.488	0.485	*(0.56)*

have an a priori form for the shock impact curve because, depending on the resulting estimated surface, the response of the expected conditional duration to a shock in the baseline duration can vary. As an experiment, we estimate our model with the same data (quote durations for the IBM stock) used in Fernandes and Grammig (2006) and compute the resulting shock impact curve by fixing ψ_{i-1} at 1 and letting ϵ_{t-1} vary to evaluate its impact on the value of the expected conditional duration ψ_t.

Figure 5.7 displays the curve resulting from the nonparametric estimation along with that resulting from the estimation of a parametric ACD model. The result seems to confirm the hypothesis of Engle and Russell (1998). The nonparametric estimator in fact seems to benefit from its greater flexibility and to produce a slightly concave response curve. We can also notice that the concavity resulting from our estimator seems less pronounced than that observed in the estimations of the modes proposed by Fernandes and Grammig (2006), at least on the basis of a simple visual evaluation.

4.3. Inclusion of the time of the day as a covariate

Maximum likelihood estimation of linear ACD models on deseasonalized data can be seen as a de facto semiparametric two-step procedure, where a first nonparametric deseasonalization is followed by the fully parametric estimation of the actual ACD model proper.[3] Yet, this standard practice does not take into account a possible time-dependence of the ACD parameters. The risk of this approach is the possibility of missing some of the information contained in the data and therefore providing suboptimal fit and forecasts if the seasonality-affected observations are the actual object of the analysis.

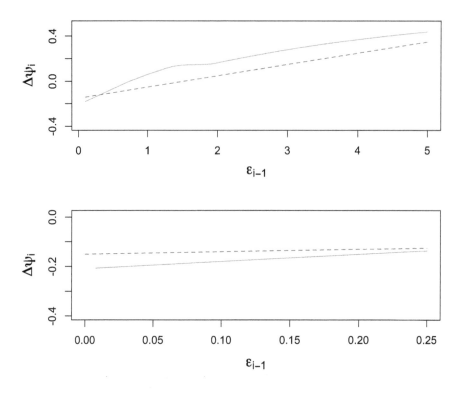

Figure 5.7 Empirical shock impact curves of a parametric (dashed) ACD estimation and a nonparametric (solid) estimation. Wider (above) and smaller (below) intervals for ϵ_t

In this subsection, we exploit the flexibility of the nonparametric ACD estimator and include in the formula for the conditional duration the time of the day as an explanatory variable. In this setup, Equation (3) becomes

$$D_t = f(D_{t-1}, \psi_{t-1}, \tau_t) + \eta_t, \tag{10}$$

with

$$\eta_t = f(D_{t-1}, \psi_{t-1}, \tau_t)(\epsilon_t - 1),$$

where τ_t is the time of the day corresponding to the t-th observation, expressed in seconds from the beginning of the trading session, and D_t is the t-th undeseasonalized duration.

The estimation of the nonparametric ACD as described in Section 2 does not require major changes in the recursive procedure, as τ_t is fully observable and can be treated as an exogenous covariate. The practical implementation is also

Table 5.4 In-sample MSE, MAE and percentage gain of the nonparametric estimator on a set of trade, price and volume durations with time of the day entered as a regressor. Percentage gains are in parentheses if the forecasts are not significantly different for the 5%-sized corresponding Diebold-Mariano test.

Type	Stats				MSE			MAE		
	Obs	Mean	Stdev	Stock	Par	Nonpar	%	Par	Nonpar	%
trade	75435	32	42	**Boeing**	1584	1581	*(0.22)*	25	25	*0.33*
	61630	39	50	**Disney**	2351	2351	*(0.01)*	32	32	*(0.12)*
	136020	18	22	**Ibm**	438	437	*0.22*	13	13	*0.42*
	74170	33	40	**Exxon**	1487	1485	*0.17*	25	23	*(0.06)*
price	8682	274	434	**Boeing**	160962	163029	*(−1.28)*	226	224	*(0.82)*
	5985	396	555	**Disney**	273336	263796	*3.49*	309	308	*0.44*
	18878	127	172	**Ibm**	24133	25915	*0.83*	98	97	*0.74*
	12974	184	307	**Exxon**	85822	86463	*(−0.75)*	158	161	*(−1.68)*
volume	4261	560	463	**Boeing**	147635	150132	*(−1.69)*	275	275	*(−0.22)*
	3450	690	499	**Disney**	190170	192158	*(−1.04)*	325	324	*(0.30)*
	9684	249	207	**Ibm**	28009	27879	*(0.46)*	116	115	*(0.66)*
	5597	428	343	**Exxon**	86696	87806	*(−1.28)*	212	211	*(0.34)*

straightforward since the LOESS function in R can accommodate a set of three explanatory variables instead of the two used with deseasonalized data. To make the forecasts comparable, we multiply the parametric ACD one-step-ahead predictions by the same values of the estimated time-of-the-day effect used to deseasonalize the raw data before estimation.

Table 5.4 reports a comparison between forecast absolute and quadratic errors of the parametric and nonparametric estimators. As in the case of deseasonalized data, many differences in forecasting accuracy do not seem significant at the 5% level for price and volume durations. By comparing Tables 5.3 and 5.4, we can see that the performance of the nonparametric estimator improves for the figures related to the trade duration. In the case of IBM trade durations, the percentage decreases in both MSE and MAE are statistically significant, according to the Diebold-Mariano test. Although the absolute differences remain small, the general picture is in favor of better performance by the nonparametric estimator. As in the deseasonalized dataset, whenever the forecasting difference is statistically significant at the 5% level, it is the nonparametric estimator that is more accurate.

A visual account of the evolution of the nonparametrically estimated surface is provided by Figures 5.8, 5.9, and 5.10, which display contour plots of the estimated surface of Boeing price, volume and trade durations computed at 30-minute intervals from 9:30 am to 4:00 pm. The shape of the estimated conditional duration clearly varies during the day. Moreover, the contour lines seemingly tend to shift gradually from one time period to the following period, suggesting a clear pattern of time dependency of the parameters of the model. Analogous time patterns of the estimated surface are present for all other durations of all stocks. This evidence clearly suggests that the standard practice of separating the estimations of the seasonality component and the conditional

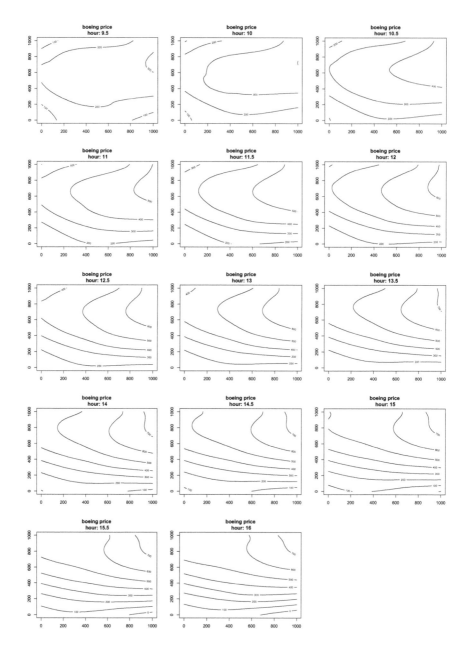

Figure 5.8 Contour plots of the estimated surface for Boeing price durations computed at 30-minute intervals

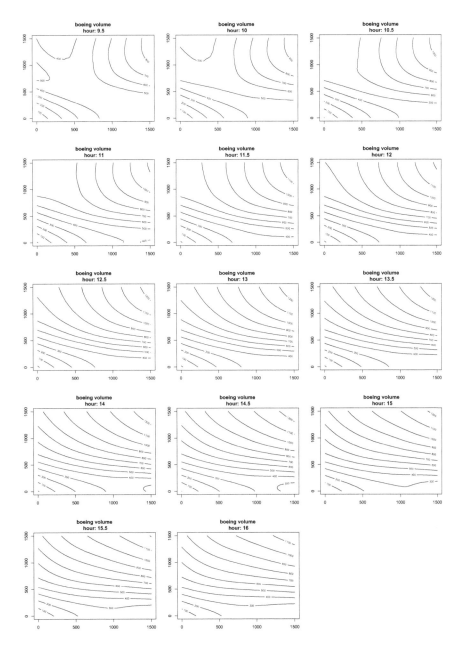

Figure 5.9 Contour plots of the estimated surface for Boeing volume durations computed at 30-minute intervals

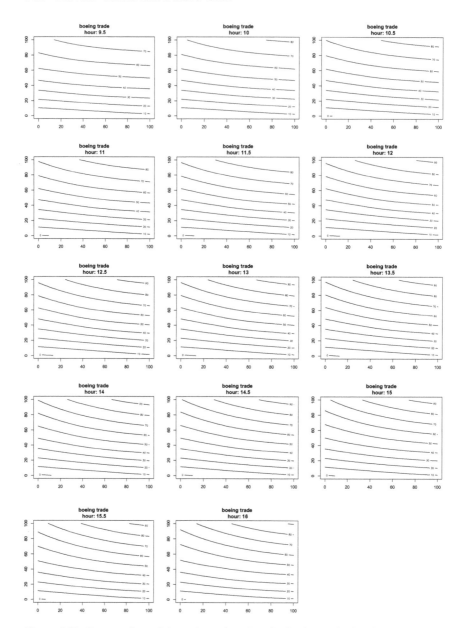

Figure 5.10 Contour plots of the estimated surface for Boeing trade durations computed at 30-minute intervals

duration function risks missing the opportunity to exploit significant information present in the data. Even in a fully parametric specification, it may be therefore beneficial to include some form of interaction between time of the day and the other model parameters.

5. Conclusion

The nonparametric specification of the ACD model encompasses most of the parametric forms thus far introduced to study high-frequency transaction data, the only exception being constituted by models with two stochastic components, such as the SCD. The model can easily be estimated by standard nonparametric techniques, although a recursive approach is necessary to address the fact that some regressors are not directly observable. The simulated examples show that in the presence of asymmetry in the specification of the conditional mean equation, the nonparametric estimator easily outperforms the symmetric parametric estimator. An estimation on a financial data set shows a marginally better performance of the nonparametric model in terms of forecasting power. When we include in the model time-of-the-day seasonality and estimate it jointly with the conditional duration surface, the gain in forecast accuracy from using the nonparametric estimator marginally improves for some stocks. Nevertheless, although not providing a specification test for parametric models, the nonparametric analysis can be useful as a benchmark in choosing the right parametric specification. The graphical study of the dependence of the conditional mean on its lags can provide valuable information on which type of parametric specification to choose. Including the time-of-the-day variable in the nonparametric analysis can provide valuable information on which deseasonalization procedure to use or suggest a possible time variation of the parameters of the parametric specification.

Finally, we discuss what could be a further use of this estimation strategy in empirical analysis. We believe that it could be beneficial to include in the regression of market microstructure variables, such as volume, prices, bid-ask spread or, when available, dummies for the arrival of news in the market. These variables have often been used in ACD estimations, but their impact on the frequency of trading is not always clear, and they could be easily the subject of a nonparametric or, eventually, a semiparametric analysis. We leave this development for further research.

Notes

1 We differentiate the population random variables X_t from the actual realizations x_t.
2 We use the R implementation of LOESS.
3 The literature offers some exceptions to this practice: Rodríguez-Poo et al. (2008), Brownlees and Gallo (2011) and Bortoluzzo et al. (2010).

Bibliography

Bauwens, L. and Giot, P. (2000). The logarithmic ACD model: An application to the bidask quote process of three nyse stocks. *Annales d'Economie et de Statistique*, 60(Special Issue, "Financial Market Microstructure"):117–149.

Bauwens, L. and Giot, P. (2003). Asymmetric ACD models: Introducing price information in acd models with a two state transition model. *Empirical Economics*, 28(4):709–731.

Bauwens, L., Grammig, J., Giot, P., and Veredas, D. (2004). A comparison of financial duration models with density forecasts. *International Journal of Forecasting*, 20:589–609.

Bauwens, L. and Veredas, D. (2004). The stochastic conditional duration model: A latent factor model for the analysis of financial durations. *Journal of Econometrics*, 119(2): 381–412.

Bortoluzzo, A. B., Morettin, P. A., and Toloi, C. M. (2010). Time-varying autoregressive conditional duration model. *Journal of Applied Statistics*, 37(5):847–864.

Brownlees, C. T., Cipollini, F., and Gallo, G. M. (2012). Multiplicative error models. *Handbook of volatility models and their applications*. NJ: Wiley.

Brownlees, C. T. and Gallo, G. M. (2011). Shrinkage estimation of semiparametric multiplicative error models. *International Journal of Forecasting*, 27(2):365–378.

Bühlmann, P. and McNeil, A. J. (2002). An algorithm for nonparametric GARCH modelling. *Computational Statistics and Data Analysis*, 40:665–683.

Cleveland, W. (1979). Robust locally weighted regresson and smoothing scatterplots. *Journal of the American Statistical Association*, 74(368):829–836.

De Luca, G. and Zuccolotto, P. (2006). Regime-switching Pareto distributions for acd models. *Computational Statistics & Data Analysis*, 51(4):2179–2191.

Diebold, F. X. and Mariano, R. S. (2002). Comparing predictive accuracy. *Journal of Business & Economic Statistics*, 20(1).

Engle, R. and Russell, J. R. (1998). Autoregressive conditional duration: A new approach for irregularly spaced transaction data. *Econometrica*, 66:1127–1162.

Fernandes, M. and Grammig, J. (2006). A family of autoregressive conditional duration models. *Journal of Econometrics*, 130(1):1–23.

Franke, J., Hardle, W., and Kreiss, J. (2003). Non parametric estimation in a stochastic volatility model. *Recent advances and trends in Nonparametric Statistics*. Elsevier.

Franke, J. H. and Muller, M. (2002). Nonparametric estimation of GARCH processes. *Applied Quantitative Finance*, 367–383.

Gerhard, F. and Hautsch, N. (2007). A dynamic semiparametric proportional hazard model. *Studies in Nonlinear Dynamics & Econometrics*, 11(2).

Ghysels, E., Gouriéroux, C., and Jasiak, J. (2004). Stochastic volatility durations. *Journal of Econometrics*, 119(2):413–433.

Hafner, C. M. (1998). Estimating high-frequency foreign exchange rate volatility with non-parametric arch models. *Journal of Statistical Planning and Inference*, 68(2):247–269.

Hastie, T. and Tibshirani, R. (1990). *Generalized additive models*. Chapman and Hall.

Hautsch, N. (2011). *Econometrics of financial high-frequency data*. Springer.

Luca, G. D. and Gallo, G. M. (2008). Time-varying mixing weights in mixture autoregressive conditional duration models. *Econometric Reviews*, 28(1–3):102–120.

Pacurar, M. (2008). Autoregressive conditional duration (ACD) models in finance: A survey of the theoretical and empirical literature. *Journal of Economic Surveys*, 22(4):711–751.

Rodríguez-Poo, J. M., Veredas, D., and Espasa, A. (2008). Semiparametric estimation for financial durations. In *High frequency financial econometrics*, 225–251. Springer.

Saart, P. W., Gao, J., and Allen, D. E. (2015). Semiparametric autoregressive conditional duration model: Theory and practice. *Econometric Reviews*, 34(6–10):849–881.

6   Sovereign debt crisis and economic growth

New evidence for the euro area

Iuliana Matei

1. Introduction

The recent economic and financial crisis in Europe and the institutional changes in reaction to the crisis have considerably renewed the debates on the detrimental impact of debt crisis on economic activity. After the 2009 Greek government announcement relying on untenable budget deficits, several euro area (EA) economies faced market concerns of sharp increases in fiscal deficit and government debt. Indeed, public debts strongly increased in some peripheral European countries and this movement became quickly a problem for the entire region sharing the euro currency because of beliefs that high public debts would hurt their economic growth rates (Figure 6.1).

But, how did Greece get first to this point? One of the causes of Greek dramatic situation is the decline in competitiveness of its economy until the beginning of the Great Recession of 2008. This implies that the political system has in some way failed to develop institutions that sustain economic growth by improving education, by declining unit labor costs and by doing major investments in research and infrastructure (Papaioannou, 2011). Another explanation to the crisis is that Greek authorities took advantage of historically low interest rates following the introduction of the euro in order to borrow for funding transfer payments, pensions and an overstaffed public sector (Ioannides, 2012). But, other peripheral EA countries have followed this trend as well and took advantage of low interest rates until 2008, as Figure 6.2 shows. However, some EA countries, Greece among them, seem to have redirected more borrowed money by public and private consumption than by investment.

Figure 6.3 explores the above hypothesis by studying the relationship between the private and public consumption (as a share of GDP) and the current account deficit (as a share of GDP) from 1995 to 2014. It clearly appears that the larger is the average, over 1995–2014, of total consumption relative to GDP, the bigger is the current account deficit ratio to GDP. The outcomes show that countries such as Greece, Latvia, Lithuania, Cyprus, and Portugal are somewhat "bad outliers" while Ireland economy (who also received financial assistance from monetary international institutions) is a "good outlier". If one would search for a plausible explanation of this interesting result, one would observe that the net national

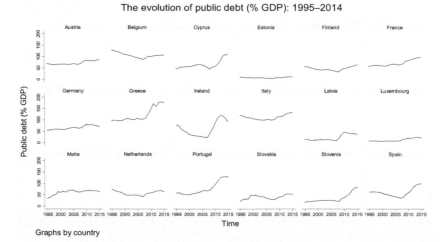

Figure 6.1 The evolution of public debt (% GDP) for EA countries: 1995–2014

Note: Data come from AMECO database. Author's computation.

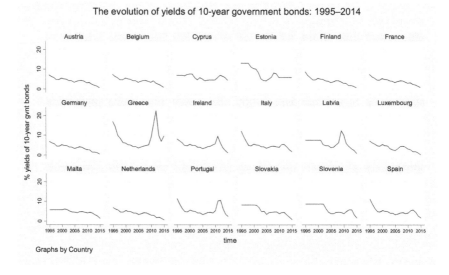

Figure 6.2 The evolution of yields of 10-year government bonds in EA countries: 1995–2014

Note: Data come from AMECO database. Author's computation.

savings (as a share of GDP) is positive for Ireland, and for almost all EA countries, of course, with different magnitudes. On the other hand, countries like Greece, Portugal, and Latvia have not improved their saving performance starting with 1995. Overall, what emerges from these developments is that the North

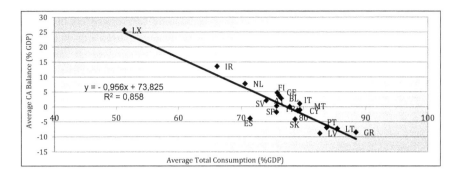

Figure 6.3 Relationship between consumption and CA balance: 1995–2014

Note: BL, GE, ES, IR, GR, SP, FR, IT, CY, LV, LT, LX, MT, NL, AT, PT, SV, SK and FI means Belgium, Germany, Estonia, Ireland, Greece, Spain, France, Italy, Cyprus, Latvia, Luxembourg, Malta, Netherlands, Austria, Portugal, Slovenia, Slovakia and Finland. Data come from AMECO database. Author's computation. Estimations with variables in logs are qualitatively similar.

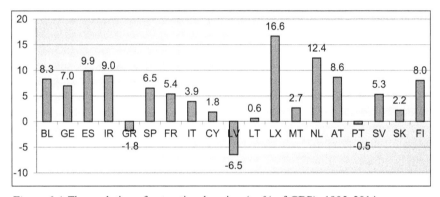

Figure 6.4 The evolution of net national saving (as % of GDP): 1995–2014

Note: BL, GE, ES, IR, GR, SP, FR, IT, CY, LV, LT, LX, MT, NL, AT, PT, SV, SK and FI means Belgium, Germany, Estonia, Ireland, Greece, Spain, France, Italy, Cyprus, Latvia, Luxembourg, Malta, Netherlands, Austria, Portugal, Slovenia, Slovakia and Finland. Data come from AMECO database.

EA countries have a better savings performance (more than 7%) than the South EA countries. Furthermore, the Ireland crisis seems to be different from that of Greece in the sense that it would be caused by an overinvestment than by an overconsumption situation given the low interest rates until 2008.

A second motivation for studying the harmful effects of debt crisis on economic growth, although the possible reverse causality problem between them, is that the current sovereign debt crisis provides an unique opportunity to investigate this topic in a currency union context. Furthermore, defining debt crisis only as simple sovereign defaults has been considered too strictly by the empirical literature for the reason that the development of international capital markets (notably, the development of bond markets for emerging market sovereign issuers) has been to some extent neglected since 1990s. Therefore, as the standard empirical[1] definition of debt crisis has become less consistent with the notion of debt-servicing difficulties, recent research has proposed a more reliable indicator for debt crisis which takes into account turbulences in emerging or advanced bond markets (see, for example, Beim and Calomiris, 2001; Detragiache and Spilimbergo, 2001; Manasse, Roubini and Schimmelpfennig, (2003), et al., Sy, 2004; Pescatori and Amadou, 2007 for a review on this). Finally, as there is still no consensus on an unique definition on debt crisis, and on its impact on economic growth, I believe that follow-up studies investigating this topic are welcome.

Two related strands of the literature explore the relationship between financial crisis and economic growth. The first strand of the literature focuses on the hurting effects of debt crisis on economic growth and tries to appraise them. Even if the traditional wisdom tells us that debt crisis produces harmful effects on GDP growth and that huge increases in public debt have frequently led to sovereign defaults, only few studies have tested the effect of debt crisis on the output and the timing of the recovery after debt episodes (see, e.g., Cerra and Saxena, 2008; Panizza and Presbitero, 2012; Furceri and Zdzienicka, 2012; Checherita and Rother, 2010; Baum et al., 2013). With cross-section and panel data, Sturzenegger (2004) highlights that debt defaults are associated with a reduction in output growth of about 0.6–2.2 percentage points. In the same vein, Borensztein and Panizza (2009) found that defaults have involved a decrease in growth of 1.2 percentage points per year. Using an unbalanced panel of 154 countries from 1970 to 2008, Furceri and Zdzienicka (2012) showed that debt crisis generates output losses by about 10% after 8 years, and that debt crisis are more harmful than banking and currency crisis. The Levy-Yeyati and Panizza (2011) results contrast with those obtained by the previous studies in the sense that they found evidence that economic growth recovers in the quarters immediately after the occurrence of a debt crisis.

The second strand of the literature investigates effectively the link between the debt and economic growth. A seminal contribution that emphasizes this relationship is that of Reinhart and Rogoff (2010, 2012). The authors pointed out a strong negative correlation between high public debt and economic growth. They found that above 90%, median growth rates fall by 1% while average growth decline substantially more. Conversely, Herndon et al. (2013) results highlight that growth did not decline sharply above the threshold of 90% of GDP. Their finding contrasts with the argument, frequently presented, that high public debt thresholds decline inevitably growth. Most recently, Egert (2015) uses historical data from 1946 to 2009, and by employing nonlinear threshold models, finds evidence for a negative nonlinear relationship between the public debt-to-GDP ratio and economic growth. However, results appear extremely sensitive to model choices and data coverage. This paper is a contribution to the first strand of this empirical literature.

From all these existing studies, the use of different countries, time periods, modeling techniques and different proxy variables during the financial crisis produces mixed results which suggest that the paper's topic is still new and stimulating.

The paper contributes to this burgeoning dynamic area of research – from an empirical perspective – by analyzing the short and the long-term impact of debt crisis on economic activity in the case of euro area countries in the following ways. First, the paper employs the recent dynamic panel heterogeneity analysis introduced by Pesaran et al. (1999) which, in my opinion, fits better the data and produces consistent results than the traditional generalized method of moments (GMM) estimator, most frequently used by previous studies under the Arellano and Bond (1991) form. The last method requires a large number of cross-sectional observations and a small number of time-series observations, and usually relies on a combination of fixed effects estimators and instrumental-variables estimators to avoid endogeneity and omitted variable biases. Although the GMM estimator takes into account the dynamic dimension of the data, and uses the lags of dependent and explanatory variables to instrument the contemporaneous crisis effects on economic growth, it only provides a short-run analysis, and disregards the non-stationarity problems. This is an aspect explicitly exploited by the Pooled Mean Group (PMG) model of Pesaran et al. (1999) given the increase of temporal observations. Furthermore, the PMG estimator allows that the intercept, the short-run coefficients and error variances be different across economies, but, constrains the long-run coefficients to be the same across them (which are pieces ignored by the GMM). An additional point is that the full set of euro area countries allows studying the detrimental effects of sovereign debt crisis on economic activity in the particular context of a currency union. Third, the paper distinguishes between the whole euro area countries and the countries receiving bailouts from the Troika institutions (the ECB, the IMF and the European Commission) when analyzing the debt impact on GDP growth. Finally, for robustness checks, additional panel models are conducted, e.g., the panel threshold models by Hansen (2000). These models capture the short-run dynamics across countries and do not consider explicitly the country-specific heterogeneity (as would the PMG estimator). The results suggest that debt crisis produces significant long-lasting GDP losses particularly for EA countries that received financial assistance by international monetary institutions during the recent crisis.

The rest of the paper is organized as follows. Section 2 presents a brief review of the literature regarding the different impacts of debt crisis on economic growth. Section 3 describes the employed methodology and presents the data. The estimation results are displayed and discussed in Section 3. Section 4 provides some robustness checks for our results. Section 5 contains the main conclusions.

2. Brief review of the literature

The current euro area sovereign debt crisis has revived the academic debates around the economic effects of debt crisis. The current section provides a brief overview on the most recent empirical studies analyzing this topic. Going through the current empirical research, there are two related strands that examine the persistent output losses from financial crises.

The first strand focuses on the harmful effects of debt crisis on the economic growth and on the timing of recovery after debt episodes and attempts to quantify these effects. In this sense, one of these contributions by Cerra and Saxena (2008) documents the behavior of output after financial (currency, banking and twin) and political crises for a set of 190 countries over the period 1960–2001. Their impulse response functions indicate that less than 1 percentage point of the deepest output loss is regained by the end of ten years following a currency crisis, banking crisis, deterioration in political governance, twin financial crises, or twin political crises. Their results also show that the magnitude of persistent output loss ranges from around 4% to 16% for different shocks and report partial rebounds in output only for civil wars. From their point of view, while temporary output losses are exposed by the capacity utilization or other elements of business cycle models, explaining permanent effects becomes a really puzzle. Another contribution is that of Furceri and Zdzienicka (2012) who assess the short- and medium-term effects of debt crises on GDP. Using an unbalanced panel of 154 countries from 1970 to 2008, the paper finds that debt crises produce significant and long-lasting output losses, reducing output by about 10% after eight years. However, the authors recognize that their results should be interpreted with some cautions because the empirical research may suffer from two main biases. First, sovereign debt crises may be considered as endogenous to output declines. In these sense, many authors (such as Borensztein and Panizza (2009)) show that many of episodes of debt defaults have occurred in period of strong output contractions. For example, Chiang and Coronado (2005) and Borensztein and Panizza (2009) investigate this issue by using a two-step approach, in which the probability of sovereign defaults is estimated in the first stage regression, and then used in the second stage in the growth regression. However, it should be noted that this approach does not fully deal with endogeneity given the impossibility to find strongly exogenous instruments for debt crises. In addition, the results of the second stage show that the model is very sensitive to the model that estimates the crisis probabilities. The second bias comes from the quasi-impossibility to distinguish different links that exists between currency, banking and debt crises. This is particularly the case for emerging economies that have been frequently hit by the simultaneous occurrence of banking, currency, and debt crises. The simultaneous occurrence of these forms of financial crises is often attributed to the so called "original sin" syndrome (Eichengreen et al., 2003), occurring when most of the private and public debt is short-term denominated in foreign currency. In this particular case, large domestic exchange rate depreciations associated with currency crises, public debt (when mostly foreign denominated) can increase considerably and lead to defaults. Reinhart and Rogoff (2010a, b) suggest the following causality regarding this aspect: private sector defaults precede banking sector crises that may coincide or precede public debt defaults. At the same time, the opposite scenario may also occur: public debt defaults may generate banking crises. This thing typically happens when banks are the main holders of government debt. Another possible scenario is when banking and debt crises lead to currency crises. For instance, third generation crises theory (Krugman, 1999) underlines the role of maturity mismatches and currency disequilibria in private (mostly banking sector) balance sheets as the main reason for the onset of currency crises.

Overall, Furceri and Zdzienicka (2012) results suggest that debt crises tend to be more detrimental than banking and currency crises. The authors note that the significance of the results is robust to different specifications, identification and endogeneity checks, and datasets. In the same veine, Sturzenegger (2004), by employing cross-country and panel specifications, finds that debt defaults are associated with a reduction in output growth of about 0.6–2.2 percentage points. Similarly, Borensztein and Panizza (2009) find that defaults are associated with a decrease in growth of 1.2 percentage points per year. De Paoli et al. (2009), comparing output growth five years before and after the occurrence of a debt crisis, find that debt crises are associated with large output losses of at least 5% per year. Panizza, Sturzenegger and Zettelmeyer (2009) purpose a survey of the recent literature on sovereign debt and relate it to the evolution of the legal principles underlying the sovereign debt market, the experience of the most recent debt crises and sovereign defaults. Their research finds more support for explanations highlighting the role of domestic costs of default than for theories supporting the feasibility of sovereign debt based on either external sanctions or exclusion from the international capital markets. The authors emphasize the importance that institutions must have in reducing the costs of defaults and recognize that the design of such institutions is not an easy task. By employing an instrumental variable approach, Panizza and Presbitero (2012) investigate whether public debt has a causal effect on economic growth in the case of OECD countries. The empirical analysis covers the 1980–2006 period and shows evidence in favor of a negative correlation between debt and growth. The empirical estimates indicate also that once the debt variable is instrumented with a variable capturing the interaction between foreign currency debt and exchange rate volatility, the link between public debt and economic growth disappears. The battery of robustness checks indicates that their findings are not affected by weak instruments problems. Another recent contribution is that of Levy-Yeyati and Panizza (2011). By analyzing quarterly data, the authors find that economic growth recovers in the quarters immediately after the occurrence of a debt crisis. In the same veine, Levy-Yeyati and Panizza (2006) used quarterly data for emerging countries to asses the impact of sovereign default on economic growth. Their empirical estimates show that output contractions precede sovereign defaults. Moreover, contrary to conventional wisdom (defaults are followed by output contractions), the authors show that when the contraction coincides with the quarter of default, and that output starts to increase after that, estimates suggest that default episode seems to indicate the beginning of the economic recovery rather than a further decline. In other words, independently from the negative effects a default may have on economic growth, those effects result from anticipation of a default rather than the default itself which is not a trivial finding. Thus, from a policy point of view, their outcome has key policy implications for both debt management policies and for debt sustainability. It does not imply that economic policies that involved a default have no costs; but, that the large GDP decline that generally precedes a sovereign default may reflect in part the anticipation of the default decision. It could be observed that, from a methodological point of view, the most part of these current researches focused on traditional dynamic and static panel data models such as generalized method of moments (GMM), vectorial autoregressive models (VAR models) or instrumental approaches.

The second strand of the empirical literature investigates effectively the relationship between economic growth and public debt, especially in the particular context of the 2008–2009 crisis which has put considerable tension on the public finances in the euro area, in particular on government debt. In these sense, Checherita and Rother (2010) investigate the non-linear effect of public debt-to-GDP ratio on the economic growth rates of 12 euro area countries in the period 1970–2011. Their findings show a non-linear impact of debt on growth with a turning point – beyond which the government debt-to-GDP ratio has a harmful impact on long-term growth – at about 90%–100% of GDP. Furthermore, the confidence intervals of their empirical estimates regarding the debt turning point suggest that the negative impact of public debt on economic growth begin from levels of about 70%–80% of GDP. From a policy perspective, this result is an indication for prudent indebtedness policies, especially for the euro area economies with high risk with regard to fiscal sustainability. By employing a dynamic threshold panel methodology, Baum et al. (2013) analyze the non-linear effect of public debt on GDP growth for 12 euro area countries on the period 1990–2010. Their empirical results indicate that the short-run effect of public debt on economic growth is positive and statistically significant, but decreases to around zero and loses significance beyond public debt-to-GDP ratios of about 67%. This result is robust throughout most of their empirical estimations, in the dynamic and non-dynamic threshold models alike. For debt-to-GDP ratios more than 95%, they find that additional debt levels have a negative effect on economic activity. The authors also observe that high debt-to-GDP ratio (above 70%) has put considerable pressures on the long-term interest rate, which broadly supports the previous findings. In "Growth in Time of Debt," Reinhart and Rogoff (2010a, b) propose to analyze the relationship between public debt and GDP growth by using non-parametric methods. The authors categorize country-years in four groups by public debt/GDP ratios (0–30%, 30–60%, 60–90%, and greater than 90%) and compare average real GDP growth rates across the debt/GDP groups. The non-parametric results highlight a nonlinear relationship, with various impacts corresponding at levels of public debt around 90% of GDP. By assuming that the implied direction of causation runs from public debt to GDP growth, the authors reveal interesting results, at least, from a policy point of view. First, when the linkage between economic growth and debt are relatively week, which happens at 'normal' debt levels, "median growth rates for countries with public debt over roughly 90 percent of GDP are about one percent lower than otherwise; (mean) growth rates are several percent lower" (Reinhart and Rogoff 2010a p. 573). From a policy perspective, a negative effect of public debt on economic growth strengthens the arguments for ambitious debt reduction by means of fiscal consolidation plans. The research by Herndon et al. (2013), tries to replicate the Reinhart and Rogoff (2010a, b) framework, and show evidence that "coding errors, selective exclusion of available data, and unconventional weighting of summary statistics lead to serious errors that inaccurately represent the relationship between public debt and GDP growth among 20 advanced economies in the post-war period". Their main result is different from that obtained by Reinhart and Rogoff (2010a, b). More precisely, the authors show that the average real GDP growth rate for countries carrying a public-debt-to-GDP ratio of over 90% is actually 2.2% not −0.1% as found by Reinhart and Rogoff (2010a, b). In other words, contrary to Reinhart and Rogoff (2010a, b), the average GDP growth at public debt/GDP ratios over 90% is not considerably different than when debt/GDP ratios are lower. The authors also show evidence that the linkage between public debt and GDP growth differs significantly by time period and country. However, their results should not be an indication for neglecting the arguments for ambitious debt reduction through fiscal consolidation. Most recently, Egert (2015) uses historical data from 1946 to 2009, and by employing nonlinear threshold models, finds evidence for a negative nonlinear relationship between the public debt-to-GDP ratio and economic growth. However, results appear extremely sensitive to model choices and data coverage. This paper is to a certain extent a contribution to the first strand of this empirical literature. In conclusion, the literature, in particular the empirical research on the relationship between government debt and economic growth produced relatively mixed results that still stimulates the research on this field.

3. Methodology and data

Methodology

The paper estimates the depressing effects of debt crisis on economic growth by using the pooled mean group model (PMG) for dynamic heterogeneous panels by Pesaran, Shin and Smith (1999). Most studies have focused on the generalized methods of moments (GMM – developed by Arellano and Bond, 1991 – e.g., Furceri and Zdzienicka, 2012) to analyze the long-run relationship between the debt, banking, and currency crisis and GDP growth or on the panel threshold models to better capture the short-run dynamics (e.g., Baum et al., 2013). Even if the GMM method allows estimating country-specific intercepts, the PMG method imposes the long-run homogeneity without making the hypothesis of identical short-run dynamics in each country. Furthermore, it is widely accepted that when the time dimension is larger than the number of cross-sectional units, the PMG model offers better estimation results (e.g., Samargandi et al., 2014). A larger time span of data implies a larger number of instruments which is likely to affect the validity of the Sargan test of over-identification restriction, and thus, the null of exogeneity of instruments (see Roodman, 2006). Also, by imposing the homogeneity of slope coefficients of lagged dependent variables, the GMM results are likely to be biased (as emphasized by Pesaran et al. (1999), and Pesaran and Shin (1995)) because this implies that economies exhibit the same common dynamics in the short-run.

(i) Pooled mean group (PMG) model

The empirical literature (e.g., Johansen (1995)) highlights the need to have consistent and efficient estimates of the long-run parameters which implies that variables require the same order of integration. Pesaran et al. (1999) detail an autoregressive distributed lag (ARDL) model in an original cointegration form and show that their model can be applied even with variables with different orders or integration (i.e., I(0) or I(1) or a mixture of two). This is a key benefit of ARDL panel models because it does not require the test for unit roots and cointegration necessary. Furthermore, the ARDL model provides consistent estimates although the presence of possible endogeneity because it includes lags of dependent and independent variables.

By using the autoregressive distributed lag (ARDL) model for time periods $t = 1, 2, ..., T$ and groups $i = 1, 2, ..., N$, the model can be written as follows:

$$gdp_{it} = \mu_i + \sum_{j=1}^{p} \lambda_{ij} gdp_{i,t-j} + \beta_i D_{i,t}^{D} + \sum_{j=0}^{q} \gamma'_{ij} Z_{i,t-j} + \varepsilon_{it} \qquad (1)$$

where gdp_{it} is the dependent variable (the logarithm of real GDP per capita), $D_{i,t}^{D}$ is a dummy variable that takes the value 1 if a debt crisis happened in country i at time t and zero otherwise, μ_i denotes country-specific effects accounting for different growth trends among countries, Z_{it} is the k × 1 vector of explanatory variables for country i that affects economic growth, λ_{ij} are scalar coefficients of the lagged dependent variables, *and* γ_{ij} are k × 1 coefficient vectors. The choice of explanatory variables is inspired by the recent empirical literature on the determinants of growth (e.g., Sala-i-Martin, 1997, Sala-i-Martin et al., 2004). The control variable's vector will include the log of trade openness (defined as the sum of exports and imports in terms of GDP), the population growth, the domestic credit growth, the real exchange rate growth, the initial lagged level of GDP and the logarithm fixed brut capital formation (as a proxy for investment and measured as percentage of GDP) and an interaction term between the quality of euro area member and a second crisis dummy which relies on the 2008 financial crisis. By re-parameterizing Equation (1), the following panel vector error correction form is obtained:

$$\Delta gdp_{it} = \varphi_i [gdp_{i,t-1} + \mu'_i + \theta'_i Z_{i,t-1}] + \sum_{j=1}^{p-1} \lambda^*_{ij} \Delta gdp_{i,t-j}$$
$$+ \sum_{j=0}^{q-1} \gamma^{*'}_{ij} \Delta Z_{i,t-j} + u_{it} \tag{2}$$

where u_{it} are independently distributed across i and t, with zero means and variances $\sigma_i^2 > 0$ and: $\varphi_i = -(1 - \sum_{j=1}^p \lambda_{ij})$; $\theta_i = \sum_{j=0}^q \gamma_{ij} / (1 - \sum_k \lambda_{ik})$; $\lambda^*_{ij} = - \sum_{m=j+1}^p \lambda_{im}$ with j=1,2, ...,p −1 and $\gamma^*_{ij} = - \sum_{m=j+1}^q \gamma_{im}$ with j = 1, 2, ..., q − 1 and i = 1,2, ..., N.

The PMG model allows assessing two types of impacts by employing a maximum likelihood method to estimate the parameters: a short-run impact by testing the significance of the coefficients of the lagged differences of economic variables (λ^*_{ij} *and respectively,* γ^*_{ij}) and a long-run impact by using the speed of adjustment coefficient (φ_i) that needs to be negative for telling that variables exhibit a long-run equilibrium. A high value of φ_i implies a stronger response of the variable to the deviation from long-run equilibrium; a low value indicates that any deviation from long-run equilibrium of the GDP growth needs much longer time to force the variables back to the long-run equilibrium. Note also that there are good reasons to believe in common long-run coefficients for euro area countries, given that these countries are likely to have access to common technologies and enjoy reciprocally from intra-trade and foreign direct investments which contribute to obtain quite similar production function parameters. Furthermore, long-run homogeneity assumption allows the identification of the long-run parameters that affect the steady state path of GDP per capita.

(ii) Robustness check through panel threshold model

To check for the robustness of the results, the panel threshold model by Hansen (2000) for balanced panels is applied. This model permits to search for the presence of non-linearities in the debt-growth nexus by dividing the observations into two or more regimes depending on whether each observation is above or below the threshold level. The panel threshold model can be written as follows:

$$y_{it} = \mu_{it} + \sum_{k=0}^{K-1} \beta_{k+1} x_{it} I(\gamma_k < q_{it} \leq \gamma_{k+1}) + \beta_{K+1} x_{it} I(\gamma_K < q_{it} \leq \gamma_{K+1}) + \varepsilon_{it} \tag{3}$$

where subscript i stands for the cross-sections with $(1 \leq i \leq N)$ and t is the time $(1 \leq t \leq T)$, μ_{it} is the country-specific fixed effect and the error term ε_{it} is assumed to be independently and identically distributed with mean zero and finite variance σ_ε^2. $I(.)$ is a function indicating the regimes defined by the threshold variable, q_{it}, and the threshold parameter γ. y_{it} is the dependent variable and x_{it} is the vector of explanatory variables. Equation (3) stands for K thresholds values and therefore, (K + 1) regimes. In each regime, the marginal effect of x_{it} (e.g., β_k) on y_{it} may be different. The benchmark model is presented in Equation (4):

$$
\begin{aligned}
gdpg_{it} = {} & \mu_{it} + \beta_1\, debt_{it}\, I(debt_K < \gamma_{k1}) + \beta_2\, debt_{it}\, I(\gamma_{k1} \le debt_K \\
& < \gamma_{k2}) + \beta_3\, debt_{it}\, I(debt_K \\
& \ge \gamma_{k2}) + \alpha_1\, Inv_{it} + \alpha_2\, TO_{it} + \alpha_3\, Popg_{it} + \alpha_4\, REER_{it} + \alpha_5\, Cred_{it} \\
& + \alpha_6\, dc_{it} + u_{it} + \varepsilon_{it}
\end{aligned}
$$

$$(4)$$

where subscript $i = 1, \ldots, N$ corresponds to the country, $t = 1, \ldots, T$ represents the time, μ_i captures the fixed effects, $I(.)$ is a function indicating the regimes defined by the threshold variable γ_k and β_k are regression slopes for the threshold variables, α_i (with $i = 1, .., 6$) are the regression slopes for the explanatory variables included in the model and ε_{ij}'s is the error term independently distributed across i and t, with zero means and variances $\sigma_i^2 > 0$. In Equation (4), the dependent variable is the real GDP growth per capita ($gdpg_{it}$) and the independent variables are government debt ($debt_{it}$), investment (Inv_{it}), economic openness (TO_{it}), population growth ($Popg_{it}$), real effective exchange rate ($REER_{it}$), domestic credit to private sector ($Cred_{it}$) and a debt crisis dummy (dc_{it}).

Variables and data

To study the relationship between output growth and debt crisis, both time and cross-country variation in the data are considered. The data sample covers 18 euro area countries and the period from 1995 until 2014. This time period also accounts quite accurately for the recent global financial crisis that strongly affected the economic growth in euro area. For the dependent variable measuring the economic growth, I employ yearly data on real per capita GDP. The vector of independent variables includes yearly data on the initial real GDP per capita (to capture the tendency for economic growth rates to converge across countries over time), gross fixed capital formation (to measure the investment in physical capital), trade openness to GDP (to account for the impact of the international factors on economic growth), population growth (as a proxy for the growth of labor force), real effective exchange rate with 42 partners (to measure the trade competitiveness with 42 partners), domestic credit growth (to assess the financial development), central government debt and government expenditure as a share of GDP (to capture the various effects of public spending and taxation).

Data are provided by World Bank database and Eurostat (for the last two variables). Due to data availability, the period of estimation is from 1995 to 2014. I use data on 18 euro area countries: Austria, Belgium, Cyprus, Estonia, Finland, France, Greece, Germany, Ireland, Italy, Latvia, Luxembourg, Malta, Netherlands,

Portugal, Slovakia, Slovenia, and Spain. I also estimate the models using variables transformed in natural logarithms (except the dummy variables). Accordingly, each estimated coefficient should be interpreted as a constant elasticity of the dependent variable with respect to the independent variable.

To identify a sovereign debt crisis episode (SDC) or alternatively a credit event, the paper relies on a number of definitions found in the recent empirical literature. Strictly speaking, a sovereign debt crisis is defined as a "technical default" which triggers a renegotiation process of debt or as ratings downgrades that increase the probability of a default. Recently, Pescatori and Sy (2004) structured the existing SDC definitions in four dimensions: (1) debt crisis as sovereign defaults; (2) debt crisis as large arrears; (3) debt crisis as large IMF loans; and (4) debt crisis as distress episodes. Table 6.1 presents briefly the corresponding definitions.

The paper relies on the last two definitions. A country faces a debt crisis (1) if it is considered in default by Standard and Poor's and it receives substantial IMF assistance or (2) if bond spreads are trading at 1,000 basis points (bp) or more above German bonds. Table 6.2 details the number of debt crisis that encompasses the years 1995–2014 according to each dataset.

Table 6.1 Debt crisis definitions

Debt crisis dimensions	SDC definition	Some references
SDC as sovereign defaults	"When scheduled debt service is not paid on the due date or an exchange offer of new debt contains less favourable terms than the original issue"	Moody's, Standard & Poor's
SDC as large arrears	- If there are arrears of principal or interest on external obligations towards commercial creditors (banks or bondholders) of more than 5% of total commercial outstanding; + - If there is debt restructuring agreement or a rescheduling with commercial creditors as scheduled by the World Bank's Global Development Finance	Detragiache and Spilimbergo (2001)
SDC as large IMF loans	- If the country is considered in default by Standard and Poor's + - If the country receives a large non-concessional IMF loan defined as access in excess of 100% of quota.	Manasse et al. (2003)
SDC as distress episodes	A debt crisis is reflected by sovereign distressed events: (i) when bond spreads are trading 1,000 bp or more above US treasuries and (ii) the 1,000 bp mark is a "psychological barrier" by market participants.	Sy (2003)

Note: the debt crisis definitions are based on Pescatori and Sy (2004) research.

Table 6.2 Debt crisis episodes

Country	MRS	SY
Greece	1995, 2010–2014	1995, 2010–2013
Cyprus	2011–2014	–
Ireland	2010–2013	–
Portugal	2011–2014	2011–2012
Spain	2011–2013	–
Italy	–	–

Note: MRS – Manasse, Roubini & Schimmelpfenning (2003); SY- Sy (2003) with yield spreads > 1,000 bp; – means no default.

Table 6.3 Main descriptive statistics over the period 1995–2014

Country	GDP per cap	Trade openness	Pop growth	REER	Credit	Investment
Mean	28731.83	112.00	0.413017	98.65	22.68	88.54
Median	27594.03	101.75	0.351763	99.41	22.27	85.40
Maximum	87772.69	374.15	2.890960	133.36	37.09	311.99
Minimum	3568.407	37.11	−2.081305	64.67	10.82	1.13
Std. deviation	16380.78	61.12	0.766107	8.916	4.06	48.81
No obs	360	360	360	360	360	360

Note: descriptive statistics are provided for euro area countries as a whole.

Table 6.3 gives some descriptive statistics for the variables included in the models. The highest average of real GDP per capita in EA countries equals 87,772 dollars while the lowest level equals 3,580 dollars. The lowest level of EA trade openness equals 37% and the highest level is 374%. The highest level of population growth is 2.9%, and its lowest level is −2.08%. The smallest level of domestic credit to private sector (as a share of GDP) is 10.8% and the highest level equals 37.1%. Furthermore, the maximum level of investment to GDP is 312% while its smallest level is 1.13%. Regarding the REER (an increase in real effective exchange rate implies a loss in country trade competitiveness with its 42 partners), the upper level equals 133 while its lower level equals 65.

Table 6.4 displays the matrix correlation of explanatory variables. It shows that only the population growth is positively and moderately correlated with domestic credit to private sector. Therefore, I decide to keep this variable in the vector of the independent variables.

4. Estimation results and discussion

This section studies the short-run and long (or medium)-run effects of debt crisis episodes on economic growth for two samples: (1) for 18 EA countries and

Table 6.4 Matrix correlation

	Ln TO	Ln POPG	Ln REER	MRS_crisis	Ln DCD	SY_crisis	Ln Inv
Ln TO	1						
Ln POPG	0.21	1					
Ln REER	0.02	−0.08	1				
MRS_crisis	−0.01	−0.05	0.14	1			
Ln DCR	−0.10	0.44	−0.03	0.13	1		
SY_crisis	−0.03	−0.01	0.03	0.44	−0.02	1	
Ln Inv	0.00	−0.10	−0.11	−0.21	−0.33	0.04	1

Note: TO – trade openness, POPG – population growth, REER – real effective exchange rate, MRS_crisis – dummy crisis based on MRS (2003) definition, DCR – domestic credit, SY-crisis – dummy crisis based on Sy (2003) definition, Inv – fixed brut capital formation.

(2) for EA countries that have received bailouts from Troika Institutions during the recent financial crisis episodes.

(i) *Pooled mean group (PMG) results*

Table 6.8 presents the results of Equation (2) which includes the long-run parameter estimates of each explanatory variable and the averaged short-run parameters. The second column details the results based on the first dataset of debt crisis according to the Sy (2003) definition. The third column shows an alternative specification (for robustness checks) by including the investment in physical capital as an important driver of economic growth. The fourth column reports the results based on the second dataset of debt crisis constructed by following the debt crisis definition of Manasse, Roubini and Schimmelpfenning (2003). The last column includes the investment in physical capital in the model for robustness checks.

Estimates reported in Table 6.8 suggest that debt crisis significantly reduces the output growth by around of 0.31 to 0.63 percentage points in the long-run. The significance of the results is robust across the four specifications. The magnitude of the debt defaults is in line with the outcomes obtained, e.g., by Sturzenegger (2004) and Borensztein and Panizza (2009) that highlight a decline in output growth of about 0.6–2.2 percentage points per year. Interestingly, the short-run dynamics suggests a significant (positive) averaged effect of debt crisis on GDP growth by around of 0.02–0.03 percentage points. The estimated parameters can be interpreted as temporary effects on economic growth involved by temporary deviations from the steady-state path of real output per capita.

Tables 6.6 and 6.7 report the estimation results of Equation (2) relating to the role of explanatory variables in the short-run by allowing parameters to vary across countries. These tables list practically the country-specific short-run coefficients being just an exhaustive report of the estimation of Equation (2). It should be recalled that all augmented models include investment (in physical capital) as an additional explanatory variable. The results suggest that debt crisis has a statistically significant (negative) short-run impact for France, Italy, Portugal and Spain by around of 0.01–0.02 percentage points according

Table 6.5 PMG model: long-run and short-run estimates with the dep. var., GDP growth for the whole euro area (columns from 1 to 4)

Sample	M – SY	R – SY	M – MRS	R – MRS
Long-run coefficients				
Openness	−0.030 (0.037)	0.712*** (0.059)	0.175*** (0.052)	0.201** (0.089)
Population growth	−0.071*** (0.028)	−0.036 (0.029)	−0.043* (0.025)	−0.253*** (0.046)
REER	0.926*** (0.036)	1.098*** (0.124)	0.736*** (0.046)	1.023*** (0.096)
Debt crisis	−0.318*** (0.028)	−0.527*** (0.076)	−0.312*** (0.044)	−0.626*** (0.106)
Credit to private sector	−0.032*** (0.002)	−0.017 (0.016)	−0.032*** (0.006)	−0.076*** (0.019)
Investment	–	1.396** (0.111)	–	0.738*** (0.097)
Error correction term (ECT)	−0.142*** (0.027)	−0.069** (0.017)	−0.137** (0.023)	−0.075*** (0.010)
Short-run coefficients				
Δ lagged GDP growth$_{i,t-1}$	0.259*** (0.076)	–	0.236*** (0.058)	–
Δ lagged GDP growth$_{i,t-2}$	0.089** (0.046)	–	–	–
Δ Openness	0.186*** (0.038)	0.100*** (0.034)	0.156*** (0.043)	0.071 (0.054)
Δ Population growth$_{i,t}$	0.032 (0.293)	0.047** (0.024)	0.044** (0.022)	0.062** (0.08)
Δ REER growth$_{i,t}$	−0.014 (0.081)	−0.008 (0.075)	−0.023 (0.087)	−0.042 (0.095)
Δ Debt crisis$_{i,t}$	0.035*** (0.007)	0.023*** (0.006)	0.032*** (0.007)	0.033*** (0.007)
Δ Credit growth$_{i,t}$	−0.033 (0.032)	−0.020 (0.023)	−0.000 (0.026)	−0.017 (0.016)
Δ Investment growth	–	0.130*** (0.039)	–	0.117*** (0.025)
Constant	0.873*** (0.153)	−0.170** (0.049)	0.829*** (0.121)	0.212*** (0.025)
No. obs.	306	342	323	341
No. groups	18	18	18	18

Note: ECT – the speed of adjustment coefficient, *p < 0.10, **p < 0.05, p < 0.01; M-SY model is an ARDL (3,1,1,1,1,1); R-SY model is an ARDL (1,1,1,1,1,1); M-MRS model is an ARDL (2,1,1,1,1); R-MRS model is an ARDL (1,1,1,1,1,1,1); REER is the real effective exchange rate, Investment is proxied by the fixed brut capital formation to GDP while the variable credit refers to domestic credit to private sector as a share of GDP. Estimates are done by using Eviews; M-SY and M-MRS are the baseline specifications while R-SY and R-MRS are the alternative specifications (for robustness checks).

Table 6.6 PMG model: Short-run parameters by country for EA_18

Countries/Variables	ECT	ΔOpenness	ΔPopg$_{i,t}$	ΔREER$_{i,t}$	ΔDebt crisis	ΔCredit	ΔInvestment
SY (2003) definition							
Austria	−0.06*** (0.00)	0.14*** (0.00)	−0.05*** (0.00)	0.05** (0.02)	0.03*** (0.00)	−0.04*** (0.00)	−0.01* (0.005)
Belgium*	0.01* (0.00)	0.06*** (0.01)	0.05*** (0.02)	−0.15** (0.02)	0.01*** (0.00)	0.13*** (0.01)	0.10*** (0.01)
Cyprus	−0.05*** (0.00)	0.26*** (0.01)	0.32*** (0.00)	0.40*** (0.02)	0.02*** (0.00)	0.03*** (0.00)	0.06*** (0.00)
Estonia	−0.20*** (0.00)	−0.00 (0.00)	−0.01*** (0.00)	−0.91*** (0.01-	0.07*** (0.00)	0.01*** (0.00)	0.04*** (0.00)
Finland	−0.21*** (0.00)	0.18*** (0.00)	0.13*** (0.01)	0.21*** (0.01)	0.06*** (0.00)	−0.13*** (0.01)	−0.12*** (0.01)
France*	0.02*** (0.00)	0.17*** (0.00)	−0.01*** (0.00)	0.10*** (0.01)	**−0.02*** (0.00)**	−0.22*** (0.00)	0.48*** (0.01)
Germany	−0.11*** (0.00)	0.04*** (0.00)	−0.00*** (0.00)	−0.03*** (0.00)	0.05*** (0.00)	−0.20*** (0.02)	−0.06*** (0.00)
Greece	−0.02*** (0.00)	−0.14*** (0.01)	0.07*** (0.01)	−0.18* (0.07)	0.01*** (0.00)	0.14*** (0.00)	0.31*** (0.01)
Italy*	0.02*** (0.00)	0.24*** (0.00)	0.00*** (0.01)	0.25*** (0.00)	**−0.01*** (0.00)**	0.04*** (0.01)	0.48*** (0.00)
Latvia	−0.10*** (0.00)	−0.10** (0.02)	0.16*** (0.00)	−0.32*** (0.04)	0.05*** (0.00)	0.09*** (0.00)	0.10*** (0.01)
Malta	−0.05*** (0.00)	0.23*** (0.01)	0.07*** (0.00)	−0.19*** (0.04)	0.02*** (0.00)	−0.01*** (0.00)	−0.01*** (0.00)
Netherlands	−0.13*** (0.00)	0.09*** (0.00)	0.06*** (0.00)	0.06*** (0.00)	0.04*** (0.00)	−0.05*** (0.00)	0.14*** (0.00)
Portugal	−0.03*** (0.00)	0.12*** (0.00)	0.04*** (0.00)	0.16*** (0.00)	**−0.01*** (0.00)**	−0.04*** (0.00)	0.26*** (0.00)
Slovakia	−0.04*** (0.00)	0.02*** (0.00)	−0.05*** (0.00)	−0.05*** (0.00)	0.02*** (0.00)	−0.01*** (0.00)	0.17*** (0.00)
Slovenia	−0.15*** (0.00)	0.09*** (0.00)	−0.01*** (0.00)	0.05* (0.01)	0.06*** (0.00)	−0.07*** (0.00)	−0.01 (0.01)
Spain*	0.02*** (0.00)	0.02*** (0.00)	0.04*** (0.00)	−0.13*** (0.00)	**−0.01*** (0.00)**	0.04*** (0.00)	0.28*** (0.00)
Ireland	−0.06*** (0.00)	−0.05 (0.02)	0.13*** (0.00)	−0.27** (0.06)	0.02*** (0.00)	−0.08*** (0.00)	−0.05*** (0.01)
Luxembourg	−0.12*** (0.01)	0.44*** (0.02)	−0.20*** (0.01)	0.49** (0.10)	0.01*** (0.00)	−0.00 (0.00)	−0.04*** (0.01)

Note: The debt crisis dummy takes also into account the 2008 financial crisis. *The ECT is positive (variables no exhibit a long run equilibrium).

Table 6.7 PMG model: Short-run parameters by country for EA_18

Countries/Variables	ECT	ΔOpenness	ΔPopg$_{i,t}$	ΔREER$_{i,t}$	ΔDebt crisis	ΔCredit	ΔInvestment
MRS (2003) def.							
Austria	−0.05*** (0.00)	0.16*** (0.00)	−0.04*** (0.00)	0.11*** (0.02)	0.03*** (0.00)	−0.03*** (0.00)	0.01 (0.01)
Belgium	−0.06* (0.00)	0.06*** (0.01)	0.05*** (0.02)	−0.02 (0.01)	0.02*** (0.00)	0.02*** (0.00)	0.08*** (0.00)
Cyprus	−0.05*** (0.00)	0.33*** (0.01)	0.39*** (0.03)	0.36*** (0.02)	0.02*** (0.00)	0.03*** (0.00)	0.07*** (0.00)
Estonia	−0.17*** (0.00)	−0.10 (0.00)	0.00*** (0.00)	−0.80*** (0.02)	0.10*** (0.00)	0.01*** (0.00)	0.19*** (0.00)
Finland	−0.11*** (0.00)	0.25*** (0.00)	0.22*** (0.01)	0.20*** (0.02)	0.04*** (0.00)	−0.14*** (0.01)	0.08*** (0.01)
France	−0.05*** (0.00)	0.10*** (0.00)	0.08*** (0.00)	0.09*** (0.01)	0.02*** (0.00)	−0.00 (0.01)	0.20*** (0.02)
Germany	−0.07*** (0.00)	0.05*** (0.00)	0.00*** (0.00)	−0.06*** (0.00)	0.04*** (0.00)	−0.20*** (0.01)	−0.18*** (0.00)
Greece	**−0.09*** (0.00)**	**−0.15*** (0.01)**	**−0.03*** (0.01)**	**−0.21* (0.02)**	**−0.01*** (0.00)**	**0.06*** (0.00)**	**0.13*** (0.00)**
Italy	−0.05*** (0.00)	0.13*** (0.00)	0.00*** (0.01)	0.13*** (0.01)	0.02*** (0.00)	−0.04*** (0.00)	0.37*** (0.00)
Latvia	−0.02*** (0.00)	−0.34** (0.02)	0.11*** (0.00)	−0.57*** (0.03)	0.05*** (0.00)	0.10*** (0.00)	0.26*** (0.01)
Malta	−0.07*** (0.00)	0.23*** (0.01)	0.07*** (0.00)	−0.17*** (0.05)	0.03*** (0.00)	−0.01*** (0.00)	−0.01*** (0.00)
Netherlands	−0.13*** (0.00)	0.15*** (0.00)	0.13*** (0.00)	0.17*** (0.00)	0.04*** (0.00)	−0.05*** (0.00)	0.11*** (0.00)
Portugal*	0.003*** (0.00)	0.10*** (0.00)	0.09*** (0.00)	0.27*** (0.01)	0.01*** (0.00)	−0.02*** (0.00)	0.26*** (0.00)
Slovakia	−016*** (0.00)	0.03*** (0.00)	0.04*** (0.00)	−0.02* (0.01)	0.08*** (0.00)	0.01*** (0.00)	0.05*** (0.00)
Slovenia	−0.07*** (0.00)	0.17*** (0.00)	0.03*** (0.00)	0.12*** (0.02)	0.06*** (0.00)	0.03*** (0.00)	0.06*** (0.01)
Spain	−0.04*** (0.00)	0.10*** (0.00)	0.04*** (0.00)	−0.04*** (0.00)	0.01*** (0.00)	0.03*** (0.00)	0.11*** (0.00)
Ireland	−0.11*** (0.00)	−0.48*** (0.02)	0.09*** (0.00)	−0.997*** (0.04)	0.03*** (0.00)	−0.07*** (0.00)	−0.02*** (0.00)
Luxembourg	−0.07*** (0.00)	0.48*** (0.02)	−0.17*** (0.01)	0.67*** (0.08)	0.01*** (0.00)	−0.005 (0.003)	0.005 (0.005)

Note: The debt crisis dummy takes also into account the 2008 financial crisis (except for EA economies that received bailouts from Troika).

Table 6.8 PMG model: long-run and short-run estimates with the dep. var., GDP growth, for EA_5 receiving bailouts (columns from 1 to 4)

Sample	M – SY	R1 – SY	M – MRS	R1 – MRS	R2 – MRS
Long-run coefficients					
Openness	0.47*** (0.13)	0.68*** (0.08)	0.39*** (0.06)	0.70*** (0.11)	0.94*** (0.12)
Population growth	0.10*** (0.03)	−0.01 (0.03)	0.05*** (0.02)	−0.28*** (0.09)	0.13*** (0.04)
REER	0.47*** (0.22)	0.25** (0.11)	−0.12*** (0.10)	−0.20 (0.21)	0.33 (0.21)
Debt crisis	**−0.13*** (0.03)**	**−0.09*** (0.01)**	**−0.11*** (0.02)**	**−0.24*** (0.05)**	**−0.19*** (0.04)**
Credit to private sector	−0.02 (0.06)	−0.08 (0.03)	0.07*** (0.02)	1.04*** (0.32)	0.11 (0.06)
Investment	—	0.42*** (0.11)	—	1.04*** (0.32)	−0.02 (0.12)
EMU*2008 crisis	—	—	—	—	**−0.67*** (0.09**
Error correction term (ECT)	−0.22*** (0.03)	−0.22** (0.08)	−0.38** (0.10)	−0.08*** (0.01)	−0.06 (0.06)
Short-run coefficients					
Δ lagged GDP growth$_{i,t-1}$	0.10 (0.17)	−0.02 (0.16)	0.13 (0.18)	—	—
Δ lagged GDP growth$_{i,t-2}$	0.05 (0.14)	0.01 (0.14)	−0.05 (0.21)	—	—
Δ Openness	0.04 (0.06)	0.02 (0.08)	0.12 (0.07)	0.02 (0.11)	−0.07 (0.14)
Δ Population growth	−0.03 (0.10)	0.02 (0.03)	−0.06 (0.10)	0.11** (0.05)	0.02 (0.04)
Δ REER growth$_{i,t}$	0.05 (0.05)	0.09 (0.08)	0.20*** (0.07)	−0.002 (0.00)	−0.09 (0.20)
Δ Debt crisis$_{i,t}$	**0.02*** (0.00)**	**0.01** (0.01)**	**0.04* (0.02)**	**0.01 (0.01)**	**−0.017* (0.01)**
Δ Credit growth$_{i,t}$	−0.03 (0.03)	−0.01 (0.01)	−0.11 (0.13)	−0.02 (0.02)	0.09* (0.05)
Δ Investment growth	—	0.09* (0.05)	—	0.09* (0.05)	0.15** (0.07)
EMU*2008 crisis	—	—	—	—	**0.03 (0.03)**
Constant	1.33*** (0.20)	0.96*** (0.36)	3.29*** (0.85)	0.41*** (0.09)	0.41*** (0.09)
No. obs.	85	85	80	95	95
No. groups	5	5	5	5	5

Note: ECT – the speed of adjustment coefficient, *p < 0.10, p < 0.05, ***p < 0.01; M-SY model is an ARDL (3,1,1,1,1,1); R1-SY model is an ARDL (3,1,1,1,1,1); M-MRS model is an ARDL (4,1,1,1,1); R1-MRS and R2-MRS models are ARDL (1,1,1,1,1,1); M-SY and M-MRS are the baseline specifications whilst R1-SY, R1-MRS and R2-MRS are the alternative specifications (for robustness checks). REER is the real effective exchange rate, Investment is proxied by the fixed brut capital formation to GDP and credit refers to the domestic credit to private sector to GDP. Estimates are done by using Eviews. The estimation of the last model (last column) is not possible by using the Sy (2003) definition.

Table 6.9 PMG model: Short-run parameters by country for EA_5 that have received bailouts

Countries/Variables	ECT	ΔOpenness	ΔPopg$_{i,t}$	ΔREER$_{i,t}$	ΔDebtcrisis	ΔCredit	ΔInvestment	Δemu * crisis
Sy (2003)								
Cyprus	-0.12*** (0.00)	0.33*** (0.01)	-0.08*** (0.01)	0.28*** (0.01)	0.01*** (0.00)	0.02*** (0.00)	-0.00 (0.00)	—
Greece	-0.16*** (0.00)	-0.07*** (0.01)	-0.01* (0.00)	0.00 (0.04)	0.01*** (0.00)	0.00 (0.01)	0.16*** (0.00)	—
Portugal	-0.40*** (0.00)	-0.12*** (0.01)	0.07*** (0.03)	-0.006 (0.00)	0.02*** (0.00)	-0.04*** (0.00)	0.06*** (0.00)	—
Spain*	-0.002 (0.01)	0.05 (0.00)	0.00*** (0.00)	-0.11*** (0.01)	-0.002*** (0.00)	-0.01*** (0.00)	0.26*** (0.00)	—
Ireland	-0.42*** (0.00)	-0.07*** (0.00)	0.10*** (0.01)	0.28*** (0.03)	0.03*** (0.00)	-0.014*** (0.00)	-0.02*** (0.00)	—
MRS (2003)								
Cyprus	-0.05*** (0.00)	0.33*** (0.00)	0.31* (0.04)	0.46*** (0.02)	-0.016** (0.00)	0.04*** (0.00)	0.08*** (0.00)	—
Greece	-0.08*** (0.00)	-0.04** (0.01)	0.04*** (0.00)	-0.01*** (0.06)	0.00*** (0.00)	0.02*** (0.01)	0.19*** (0.00)	—
Portugal	-0.03*** (0.00)	0.11*** (0.00)	0.07*** (0.00)	0.17*** (0.01)	-0.00*** (0.00)	-0.03*** (0.00)	0.19*** (0.00)	—
Spain	-0.09*** (0.00)	0.06*** (0.00)	0.02*** (0.00)	0.09*** (0.01)	0.01*** (0.00)	0.04*** (0.00)	0.08*** (0.00)	—
Ireland	-0.13*** (0.00)	-0.34*** (0.02)	0.12*** (0.00)	-0.57*** (0.05)	0.00*** (0.00)	-0.02*** (0.00)	-0.08*** (0.00)	—
MRS (2003)								
Cyprus	-0.07*** (0.00)	0.09*** (0.02)	-0.12* (0.05)	0.26*** (0.02)	-0.01** (0.00)	-0.004*** (0.00)	0.08*** (0.01)	0.03*** (0.00)
Greece	-0.06*** (0.00)	-0.30*** (0.01)	0.05*** (0.00)	-0.30*** (0.06)	-0.012*** (0.00)	0.26*** (0.01)	0.32*** (0.00)	0.05*** (0.00)
Portugal	-0.07*** (0.00)	0.01*** (0.00)	0.04*** (0.00)	0.07*** (0.01)	0.01*** (0.00)	-0.02*** (0.00)	0.24*** (0.00)	0.02*** (0.00)
Spain*	0.14*** (0.00)	0.33*** (0.00)	0.10*** (0.00)	0.25*** (0.01)	-0.04*** (0.00)	0.14*** (0.00)	0.26*** (0.00)	-0.07*** (0.00)
Ireland	-0.24*** (0.00)	-0.45*** (0.00)	0.01*** (0.00)	-0.73*** (0.01)	-0.04*** (0.00)	0.06*** (0.00)	-0.09*** (0.00)	0.11*** (0.00)

Note: The parameters estimates are given for the model R1-Sy (2003) and the model R2-MRS (2003). *ECT is positive (meaning that variables do not exhibit a long-run equilibrium).

to the Sy (2003) definition of debt crisis. However, the speed of adjustment coefficient is negative only for Portugal, meaning that variables reach a long-run equilibrium only in this case. Based on the MRS (2003) definition, results suggest also a negative and significant (but, low) short-run impact of debt crisis in the case of Greece by around of 0.01 percentage point.

Table 6.8 analyzes the impact of debt crisis episodes in the case of EA countries that received financial assistance from the international monetary institutions (ECB, IMF, and European Commission) during the selected period. The baseline specifications (i.e., the models presents in columns from 2 to 5) include only one type of crisis: the debt crisis according to the Sy (2003) and MRS (2003) definitions. But, the closed connection, often impossible to differentiate, between banking, currency and debt crisis that have occurred during the studied period makes not easy to isolate the impact of debt crisis on economic growth. The literature emphasizes two main reasons explaining the concurrent occurrence of these types of financial crisis. The first one is attributed to the "original sign" pattern (Eichengreen et al., 2003) that emerges when most part of the private or public debt is short-term denominated in foreign currency. In this case, huge domestic exchange rate depreciations involve currency crisis which increases public debt and lead to defaults. The second one, was explained by the seminal contribution of Reinhart and Rogoff (2010) that suggest different causalities between these three types of financial crisis: (1) private sector defaults trigger banking crisis that coincide or precede public debt crisis, (2) public defaults may lead to banking crisis when banks are the main holders of government debt; (3) banking and debt crisis may also generates currency crisis and finally, (4) these crisis could also occurs simultaneously which corresponds to twin financial crisis. For example, in the case where a banking crisis generates a debt crisis, the estimated effect of debt crisis on contemporaneous GDP growth could be understood as the lagged effect of banking (or currency) crisis. To overcome this technical difficulty, I include alternatively in the last column specification, for each of the above factors, an interaction term between the EA membership and the 2008 banking crisis dummies (Reinhart and Rogoff, 2010; Furceri and Zdzienicka, 2012). The estimated parameters are able to assess the 2008 financial crisis effect on economic growth for euro area countries or as a country that integrates the euro area. However, the estimated coefficients should be interpreted with some caution, independently of the debt crisis definition I have used. Estimates from the last column allow us to differentiate the debt and banking crisis impact in decreasing the economic growth and the importance of this factor for the euro area members. Results are in line with theoretical predictions highlighting that defaults and banking crisis produces harmful effect on economic growth. The estimated share of the debt and banking crisis for EA members is quite large in these estimations (0.19 percentage point per year for debt crisis and 0.67 percentage points for the banking crisis for euro area members). All the other alternative specifications suggest that output growth decreases by about 0.9–0.24 percentage points in the long (or medium) run. Results show also that the debt crisis effect is lower (in

absolute value) than the 2008 banking crisis effect. Comparing the two definitions of debt crisis episodes, the MRS (2003) definition produces more hurting
effects on output growth.

Furthermore, in all specifications where trade openness, population growth,
real effective exchange rate, investment in physical capital and financial development variables are included, the long-run coefficients have the expected
sign and are globally significant.

When regarding the short-run dynamics to capture cross-country differences
in Table 6.9, we find a low (negative) and significant impact of debt crisis episodes on output growth by about 0.01 to 0.04 percentage points for Cyprus,
Greece, Spain, and Ireland based on the MRS (2003) definition. This values contrasts with (many) previous studies that found greater effects of debt crisis episodes on economic growth. However, these effects should be interpreted merely
as temporary effects of debt crisis on GDP growth.

(ii) *Panel Threshold Regression (PTR) results*

To make sure that results are robust in the PMG model, I estimate an additional
panel model which divides the observations into two or more regimes depending
on whether each observation is above or below a threshold level of public debt.
This general specification was suggested by Hansen (1999, 2000). The estimated
panel threshold specifications are given by the following equations:

Model 1:

$$gdpg_{it} = \mu_{it} + \beta_1 \, debt_{it} \, I(debt_K < \gamma_{k1}) + \beta_2 \, debt_{it} \, I(debt_K \\ \geq \gamma_{k2}) + \alpha_1 \, Inv_{it} + \alpha_2 \, TO_{it} + \alpha_3 \, Popg_{it} + \alpha_4 \, REER_{it} + \alpha_5 \, Cred_{it} \\ + \alpha_6 \, dc_{it} + \varepsilon_{it}$$

(5)

and

Model 2:

$$gdpg_{it} = \mu_{it} + \beta_1 \, debt_{it} \, I(debt_K < \gamma_{k1}) + \beta_2 \, debt_{it} \, I(debt_K \\ \geq \gamma_{k2}) + \alpha_1 \, Inv_{it} + \alpha_2 \, TO_{it} + \alpha_3 \, Popg_{it} + \alpha_4 \, REER_{it} + \alpha_5 \, Cred_{it} \\ + \alpha_6 \, dc_{it} + \alpha_7 \, emu * crisis_{it} + u_{it} + \varepsilon_{it}$$

(6)

where the dependent variable is the real GDP growth per capita ($gdpg_{it}$) and the
independent variables (in logs) are the central government debt ($debt_{it}$), the
investment (Inv_{it}), the economic openness of countries (TO_{it}), the population
growth ($Popg_{it}$), the real effective exchange rate ($REER_{it}$), the domestic credit
to private sector ($Cred_{it}$), a debt crisis dummy (dc_{it}) and an interaction term
between the debt crisis dummy and the EA membership ($emu * crisis_{it}$) for the last
equation.

Table 6.10 Identification of the PSTR models: nonlinearities in GDP growth-debt crisis nexus

Debt crisis definition	Nb. of thresholds tested	First transition function (F-test)	Threshold value (log)	Threshold Interval (log)
Sy – Model 1	1 threshold – F test (p-value)	11.59 (0.35)	4.2725	[4.244, 4.277]
Sy – Model 2	1 threshold – F test (p-value)	11.53 (0.383)	4.2725	[4.242, 4.277]
MRS-Model 1	1 threshold – F test (p-value)	10.88 (0.463)	4.2655	[4.241, 4.273]
MRS-Model 2	1 threshold – F test (p-value)	10.78 (0.417)	4.2725	[4.242, 4.277]

Note: Bootstrap p-values are given in brackets; ***, **, * – the null of no threshold is rejected at 1, 5, and 10%.

According to Reinhart and Rogoff (2010), public debt is found to reduce economic growth above the 90% threshold by 1% while this relation seems to be less evident below the 90% level. Because it is difficult to assume a clear-cut shape of the public debt-economic growth link, and particularly regarding the presence or the absence of nonlinearities, I start by testing for the presence of a single-threshold model by means of F-test with the null of no threshold. The results detailed in Table 6.10 show that the number of thresholds has to be blocked to zero in these transition functions. Indeed, the F-statistic is not significant in any of the models considered. Obviously, the single-threshold models are accepted with a probability equal to 0.35–0.46. The results do not suggest the existence of robust non-linearities regarding the effect of debt crisis on economic growth when the threshold variable is the central government debt. This is why, the PMG linear models estimated previously can be considered as a right choice.

5.   Conclusions

The paper investigates the impact of debt crisis on economic growth in 18 euro area economies. The analysis is performed over the period 1995–2014 and uses dynamic panel estimation models, including the Pooled Mean Group estimator (Pesaran et al., 1999) and Panel Threshold estimator (Hansen, 1999). The results suggest that debt crisis produces harmful effects on GDP growth in the euro area countries, particularly in the case of euro area economies that received financial assistance from international monetary Institutions (IMF, ECB, and European Commission) like Greece, Ireland, Portugal, Cyprus, and Spain. The outcomes suggest also that additional variables such as trade openness, population growth, real effective exchange rate, financial development and investment in physical capital affect significantly and quite coherently the economic activity, particularly in the long run.

Note

1 Strictly speaking, a sovereign debt crisis is defined as a "technical default" which implies a renegotiation process of debt or as ratings downgrades that increase the probability of a default.

Bibliography

Arellano, M. and S. Bond (1991), "Some Tests of Specification for Panel Data: Monte Carlo Evidence and an Application to Employment Equations", *Review of Economic Studies*, Vol. 58(2), 277–297.

Baum, A., C. Checherita and P. Rother (2013), "Debt and Growth: New Evidence from the Euro Area", *Journal of International Money and Finance*, Vol. 32, 809–821.

Beim, David O., Charles W. Calomiris (2001), *Emerging Financial Markets*. Published by McGraw-Hill/Irwin.

Borensztein, E. and U. Panizza (2009), "The Costs of Sovereign Default", *International Monetary Fund Staff Papers*, Vol. 56(4), 683–741.

Cerra,V., S. Saxena (2008), "Growth Dynamics: The Myth of Economic Recovery", *American Economic Review*, Vol. 98, 439–457.

Checherita, C., P. Rother (2010), "The impact of High and Growing government debt on economic growth: An empirical investigation for the euro area", ECB WP no. 1237, August.

Chiang, G., J. Coronado (2005), "A Two Step Approach to Assess the Cost of Default for Latin America", www.urrutiaelejalde.org/SummerSchool/2005/papers/coronadochiang. pdf.

De Paoli, B., G. Hoggarth, V. Saporta (2009), "Output Costs of Sovereign Crises: Some Empirical Estimates", Bank of England Working Paper No. 362.

Detragiache, E., A. Spilimbergo (2001), "Crises and Liquidity: Evidence and Interpretation", IMF Working Paper No. 01/2, (Washington: International Monetary Fund).

Egert, B. (2015), "Public Debt, Economic Growth and Nonlinear Effects: Myth or Reality?", *Journal of Macroeconomics*, Vol. 43(C), 226–238.

Eichengreen, B., R Hausmann, U. Panizza (2003), "Currency Mismatches, Debt Intolerance, and Original Sin: Why They Are Not the Same and Why It Matters", NBER Working Paper No. 10036 (Cambridge, MA: National Bureau of Economic Research).

Furceri, D., A. Zdzienicka (2012), *Journal of International Money and Finance*, Vol. 31, 726–742.

Hansen, Bruce E. (2000), "Sample splitting and threshold estimation", *Econometrica*, Vol. 68(3): 575–603.

Herndon, T., A. Michael, R. Pollin (2013), "Does High Public Debt Consistently Stifle Economic Growth? A Critique of Reinhart and Rogoff", Political Economy Research Institute Working Paper No. 322.

Ioannides, Y. (2012), "Greece, the Eurozone, and the Debt Crisis", Paper for Conference Talk, "A World of Crisis and Shifting Geopolitics"-http://greekeconomistsforreform. com/wp-content/uploads/Ioannides-Presentation-Fletcher-Oct-28-11-Text+Figs3.pdf

Johansen, S. (1995) "Likelihood-Based Inference in Cointegrated Vector Autoregressive Models". Oxford University Press, Oxford.

Krugman, P. (1999), "Balance Sheets, the Transfer Problem, and Financial Crises", *International Tax and Public Finance*, Springer, Vol. 6(4), 459–472.

Levy Yeyati, E. (2006), "The Elusive Costs of Sovereign Defaults", Washington, DC, United States: Inter-American Development Bank, Research Department Working paper No. 581, Mimeographed document.

Levy-Yeyati, E., Panizza, U. (2011), "The Elusive Costs of Sovereign Defaults", *Journal of Development Economics*, Vol. 94(1), 95–105.

Manasse, Paolo, Nouriel Roubini, and Axel Schimmelpfennig. 2003. "Predicting Sovereign Debt Crises." International Monetary Fund Working Paper 03/221.

Moody's Investors Service (2003), "Sovereign Bond Defaults, Rating Transitions, and Recoveries (1985–2002)" Special comments (February), pp. 2–52.

Panizza, U., A. F. Presbitero (2012), "Public Debt and Economic Growth: Is There a Causal Effect?", MoFiR Working Paper No. 65.

Panizza, U., F. Sturzenegger, J. Zettelmeyer (2009), "The Economics and Law of Sovereign Debt and Default", *Journal of Economic Literature*, Vol. 47(3), 1–47.

Papaioannou, E. (2011). "The Injustice of the justice System". http://greekeconomistsfor reform.com/wp-content/uploads/injustice Papaioannou.pdf

Pesaran, M. H., Y. Shin, and R. P. Smith (1999), "Pooled Mean Group Estimation of Dynamic Heterogeneous Panels", *Journal of the American Statistical Association*, Vol. 94(446), 621–634.

Pesaran, M. H. and Y. Shin (1995). "An Autoregressive Distributed Lag Modelling Approach to Cointegration Analysis," Cambridge Working Papers in Economics 9514, Faculty of Economics, University of Cambridge.

Pescatori, Andrea and Amadou N. R. Sy (2004), "Debt Crises and the Development of International Capital Markets", IMF Working Paper, WP/04/44.

Pescatori, Andrea, and Amadou N. R. Sy (2007). "Are Debt Crises Adequately Defined?" IMF Staff Papers, 54(2): 306–37.

Reinhart, Carmen M., and Kenneth S. Rogoff (2010), "Growth in a Time of Debt", *American Economic Review: Papers & Proceedings*, Vol. 100(2): 573–78.

Reinhart, Carmen M, Vincent R. Reinhart, and Kenneth S. Rogoff (2012), "Public Debt Overhangs: Advanced-Economy Episodes since 1800", *Journal of Economic Perspectives*, Vol. 26(3), 69–86.

Reinhart, Carmen M., and Kenneth S. Rogoff. (2010a), "Growth in a Time of Debt" *American Economic Review* 100(2): 573–78.

Reinhart, Carmen M., and Kenneth S. Rogoff (2010b), "Debt and Growth Revisited." Vox EU, August 11.

Roodman, D. (2006), "How to Do xtabond2: An Introduction to Difference and System GMM in Stata", Center for Global Development Working Paper No. 103.

Sala-i-Martin, X. (1997), "I Just Ran Two Million Regressions", *American Economic Review*, Vol. 87(2), 178–83.

Sala-i-Martin, X., G. Doppelhofer, R. I. Miller (2004), "Determinants of Long-Term Growth: A Bayesian Averaging of Classical Estimates (BACE) Approach", *American Economic Review*, American Economic Association, Vol. 94(4), 813–835.

Samargandi, N., J. Fidrmuc, S. Ghosh. (2014), "Financial Development and Economic Growth in an Oil-Rich Economy: The Case of Saudi Arabia", *Economic Modelling*, 43, 267–278.

Standard and Poor's (2002), "Sovereign Defaults: Moving Higher Again in 2003?" September 24, 2002. Reprinted for Ratings Direct.

Sturzenegger, F. (2004), "Toolkit for the Analysis of Debt Problems", *Journal of Restructuration Finance*, Vol. 1(1), 201–203.

Sy, Amadou N. R. (2004), "Rating the Rating Agencies: Anticipating Currency Crises or Debt Crises?", *Journal of Banking and Finance*, Vol. 28 (November): 2845–2867.

7 On the spot-futures no-arbitrage relations in commodity markets*

René Aïd, Luciano Campi,
and Delphine Lautier

1. Introduction

In this article we aim at explaining, through a parsimonious model, the relation between the spot and the futures prices of a commodity. The prices relation derives from the well-posedness of the optimization problem of an operator involved in the production and (when possible) the storage of a commodity. This producer also trades in the futures market. Such an approach is different from the classical no-arbitrage reasoning usually employed to explain the temporal basis in commodity markets. Interestingly, it remains relevant for non storable commodities, when standard no-arbitrage arguments cannot be safely applied.[1]

The traditional no-arbitrage relation, initially developed for investment assets like stocks and bonds, states that the futures price $F(t, T)$ of a contract written on the investment asset, observed at date t for a delivery at T, is the spot price S_t capitalized at the interest rate r between t and T: $F(t, T) = S_t e^{r(T-t)}$. The cost of carrying commodities, however, can not be reduced to the interest rate. One need to take into consideration warehousing and/or depreciation costs (see, among others, Fama and French, 1987 or, more recently, Eydeland, 2002, Chap. 4, pp. 140–143).

Introducing storage costs in the analysis is not even sufficient to depict the behavior of the prices spread in commodity markets: in addition, there is a need to explain negative spreads[2] and the simultaneous presence of positive inventories and backwardated prices (see among others, Working, 1933). The no-arbitrage relation can only be preserved by the introduction of an extra variable: the convenience yield (see Kaldor, 1940 or more recently, Lautier, 2009). The latter represents an implicit revenue. The presence of such a yield, which is associated with the holding of the physical commodity but not with the futures contract, explains that the operators maintain their inventories even in the presence of negative spreads. With the introduction of this variable, the no arbitrage relation is extended to: $F(t, T) = S_t e^{(r-y)(T-t)}$, where y is the convenience yield net of storage costs.

Financial models explicitly designed for the pricing of commodity derivatives and relying on the concept of convenience yield have been quite extensively built in the literature (see Lautier, 2005 for a review). These models perform well, especially the two-factor model proposed by Schwartz (1997), where the convenience yield is mean reverting and plays the role of a dividend yield in the drift of the spot price. In this setting, however, the relation between the spot and the futures prices relies on the hypothesis that arbitrage operations are perfect. Consequently, there exists a unique risk-neutral measure, that can be calibrated thanks to market data. Moreover the spot price, in such analysis, is exogenous.

An effort has been undertaken in the economic and financial literature in order to propose structural models that rely on endogenous spot prices to explain the interaction between the spot and futures prices. In such cases, the spot price derives from production, consumption and storage of the commodity. In this setting, the spot price is the result of an equilibrium between production and consumption. The futures price is defined as the expectation of the spot price.

Within this literature, our model is close to those of Brennan (1958) and Routledge et al. (2000). In these works, the authors develop production-storage models that connect the spot and the futures prices. Nevertheless, the models are mainly developed in order to allow for comparative statics and little information on the conditions under which no-arbitrage holds is given (this is especially true for the model of Routledge et al. (2000).

The development of electricity markets in the last 30 years has introduced new challenges in the literature on commodity prices. More precisely, the idea that the futures price of a commodity is linked to its spot price by a convenience yield has been highly debated, as electricity cannot be stored. Many authors have argued that the convenience yield may not apply in the case of electricity. Still, futures prices of electricity exhibit both contango and backwardation situations (Benth et al., 2013). Others have also stressed that the no-arbitrage method used in mathematical finance to obtain a risk-neutral measure should be reconsidered (Benth et al., 2003). Finally, due to the particular nature of the futures contracts negotiated in these markets (which are basically swaps, see Frestad, 2010), even the convergence of the futures price to the spot price has become an issue (Viehmann, 2011).

Since in the case of electricity the pricing of derivatives cannot rely on the concept of a convenience yield – at least in its restricted initial definition, where the yield comes from the holding of inventories – this non-storable commodity has fostered research on how to restore a relation between the spot and the futures prices. The first approaches relied on two-date equilibrium models (Anderson and Hu, 2008; Bessembinder and Lemmon, 2002; Aid et al., 2011), where the risk-neutral measure was extracted from the risk aversion parameters of the agents. A more complex approach consists in the extension of the market beyond the underlying asset, to include or production factors (Aïd et al., 2009, 2013), production constraints (Bouchard and Nguyen Huu, 2013) or gas storage levels (Douglas and Popova, 2008).

In this article, we propose an analysis where the futures prices can be related to the spot price by arbitrage arguments, independently of the storability properties of the underlying asset. This does not mean, however, that the model is especially designed for non-storable commodities, as done, for example, in Benth et al. (2007, 2008), Meyers-Brandis and Tankov (2008), and Hess (2013), among others.

Our framework could be applied to any commodity, would it be storable or not. This can be useful for a large range of industrial companies operating in commodity futures markets, such as energy utilities, airline companies, producers and processors of metals or of agricultural products. The profit maximization of such companies relies on the spot prices as well as on the futures prices. Within our framework, once a spot price model and the market price of demand risk are chosen, there is only one futures price model that would be consistent with their optimization process.

The remaining of the article is organized as follows. First, we first propose a simple model of production, storage and trading, where an operator maximizes his expected utility. This operator has no impact on the spot price. The storage costs and the production function are supposed to be convex. The storage capacity is bounded. The same is true for the instantaneous storage and withdrawal. Moreover, the operator has access to a derivative market where a futures written on the commodity is traded. The contract is negociated on one maturity only and the liquidity of the futures market is supposed to be unlimited. Naturally, the operator has no impact on the futures price.

Second, we show that the existence of a risk-neutral measure is the consequence of the finiteness of the operator's value function. This result is linked with previous results established in, e.g., Rogers (1994) and Ankirchner and Imkeller (2005) for a pure trader. This result means that if there were no risk-neutral measures, the operator could take advantage of his production capacity or storage facilities to get an infinite utility. In the same section, we also prove that the futures price always converges to the spot price, regardless of the storability properties of the commodity. This result is important, especially for the analysis of electricity markets. It has been indeed pointed out that the electricity futures prices predict realized spot prices rather poorly (Prevot et al., 2004). This study was however done on monthly contracts while the convergence issue concerns only maturities close to zero. For instance, day-ahead futures contracts quoted on the German electricity market exhibit lower discrepancy with the realized spot prices (see Viehmann, 2011).

We finally discuss the trading-production problem faced by the operator, with a specification of the demand dynamics. We obtain an explicit formula for the volatility of the futures contract and we relate it to the volatility of the underlying conditional demand for the commodity. Moreover we argue that, in a Markovian setting and for an agent having a power type utility function, the optimal command for the management of storage is of a bang-bang type. Not surprisingly, the decision to store or to withdraw the commodity is based on the comparison between the spot price and the ratio between the marginal utility of one unit of storage and the marginal utility of the wealth of the operator. Lastly, in this setting the optimal trading strategy on the futures market is such that the operator holds a long position when the futures prices exhibit a positive trend.

2. The model for the individual producer

In this section we provide the full description of a simple model of production, storage and trading. This model will be used and investigated throughout the whole article. For the sake of readability, the proofs are all gathered in the Appendix.

Let $(\Omega, (\mathcal{F}_t)_{t\in[0,T]}, \mathbb{P})$ be a filtered probability space satisfying the usual conditions, i.e., $(\mathcal{F}_t)$ is a $\mathbb{P}$-completed and right-continuous filtration. Moreover, for mathematical convenience, we assume that $\mathcal{F}_{T-} = \mathcal{F}_T$. This property is satisfied, e.g., when $(\mathcal{F}_t)$ is the natural filtration generated by a multivariate Brownian motion. All processes considered in this article are assumed to be defined in this space and adapted to this filtration.

Our agent is the producer of a commodity. He also trades in the associated derivative market. This producer is a price taker. On the physical market, he has the possibility to sell the whole quantity he produced at a specific date, or less (he then stores a part of the production), or more (he then reduces his stocks). On the derivative market, he has the possibility to buy or to sell a certain amount of a unique futures contract. His choices depend on the price conditions he faces, both on the physical and on the derivative markets. In what follows, we will first focus on the physical market. Then we will expose the trading activity on the derivative market.

2.1. The profit on the physical market

On the physical market, the agent has the possibility to decide how much he produces and to manage his stocks dynamically. His instantaneous profit π_t can be written as follows:

$$\pi_t = (q_t - u_t)S_t - c(q_t) - k(X_t) \tag{2.1}$$

where:

- q_t is the production of the agent,
- u_t is the amount stored ($u_t > 0$) or withdrawn ($u_t < 0$),
- S_t is the spot price of the commodity,
- $c : \mathbb{R}_+ \to \mathbb{R}$ is the production function, with $c(0) = 0$,
- $k : \mathbb{R}_+ \to \mathbb{R}$ is the storage function, with $k(0) = 0$,
- X_t is the storage level at time t.

Assumption 1. *We assume that both functions* c *and* k *are differentiable, strictly increasing, strictly convex and nonnegative.*

Moreover, we will always work under the following assumption on the dynamics of the spot price:

Assumption 2. *Let* (S_t) *be a bounded continuous process.*

The producer faces several constraints on the physical market. They can be summarized as follows:

- the agent's production cannot exceed his capacity $\bar{q}$: $q_t \in [0, \bar{q}]$ for some $\bar{q} > 0$;

- instantaneous storage and withdrawal are bounded, with $u_t \in [\underline{u}, \bar{u}]$ for given thresholds $\underline{u} < 0 < \bar{u}$;
- the storage capacity itself is bounded by some $\bar{X} \geq 0$, so that adding the positivity constraint on the inventories we have $X_t \in [0, \bar{X}]$ a.s. for all $t \in [0, T]$;
- the storage dynamics is: $dX_t = u_t dt$, with $X_0 = u_0 > 0$.

To simplify, we assume that there is no uncertainty on the production of the commodity. The only source of uncertainty comes from the demand side, which is reasonable for a large number of commodities.

2.2. The trading activity on the derivative market

On the derivative market there is only one futures contract available, for a given maturity $T > 0$. The price of this contract at t is $F_t = F(t, T)$. We assume that the futures price process (F_t) is a continuous semi-martingale, adapted to the filtration $(\mathcal{F}_t)$, and that the interest rate is zero. The value of the trading portfolio on this contract is given by:

$$V_T^\theta = \int_0^T \theta_t dF_t \tag{2.2}$$

where θ is any real-valued predictable (F_t)-integrable process such that $\theta_{T-} := \lim_{t \uparrow T} \theta_t$ exists a.s. We consider that the futures market is liquid, which is standard in this context. On the empirical point of view, this is the case for a very large spectrum of commodities, especially on the short-term maturities. This is however less obvious, at least up to now, for electricity markets (Aïd, 2015, Chap. 2, Sect. 2.2.3).

2.3. The production-trading problem

As a commodity producer, the agent acts so as to maximize the expected utility of his terminal wealth. His utility function $U : \mathbb{R}_+ \to [-\infty, \infty[$ satisfies Inada conditions and is such that $U(x) \to \infty$ whenever $x \to \infty$. Moreover, we assume Reasonable Asymptotic Elasticity (RAE: see Kramkov and Schachermayer, 1999):

$$AE(U) := \limsup_{x \to \infty} \frac{xU'(x)}{U(x)} < 1$$

In this setting, we propose the following production-trading problem:

$$v(r_0) := \sup_{u, q, \theta} \mathbb{E}\left[U\left(r_0 + \int_0^T \pi_t dt + V_T^\theta + \theta_{T-}(F_T - S_T) \right) \right] \tag{2.3}$$

where:

- $r_0 > 0$ is the initial wealth of the operator,

- π_t is the instantaneous profit on the physical market, expressed as a function of the quantities produced and stored, given by Equation (2.1),
- V_T^θ is the value of the trading portfolio in the futures market as given by Equation (2.2),
- the term $\theta_{T-}(F_T - S_T)$ can be explained by the delivery conditions of the futures contract at expiration (see the heuristic discussion for the discrete time case, which follows).

The controls (u, q, θ) have to satisfy the following additional constraints:

- constraint on the wealth of the agent to prevent infinite borrowing:

$$R_t^{r_0,u,q,\theta} := r_0 + \int_0^t \pi_s ds + V_t^\theta + \theta_{T-}(F_T - S_T)1_{(t=T)} \geq -a, \quad t \in [0, T], \quad (2.4)$$

for some threshold $a > 0$,
- the production-storage controls $(u_t, q_t)_{t \in [0, T]}$ are predictable processes with respect to the filtration $(\mathcal{F}_t)$ and they satisfy the constraints previously described in Paragraph 2.1.

Discrete-time heuristics. Let us now provide some heuristics in discrete-time, in order to better explain the form of the continuous-time problem (2.3). The terminal total wealth for a trader-producer who produces, e.g., energy from fuels, and trades in futures contracts on energy over the finite time grid $\{0, 1, \ldots, T\}$ with $T \in \mathbb{N}$ can be written as follows:

$$R_T = \sum_{t=0}^{T-1} [(q_t - u_t)S_t - c(q_t) - k(X_t)] + \sum_{t=0}^{T-1} \theta_t(F_{t+1} - F_t)$$
$$+ \theta_{T-1}F_{T-1} - h_T S_T - c(q_T) - k(X_T)$$

where h_T is the quantity bought or sold at terminal date in order to fulfill the commitment taken on the futures market at the expiration of the contract, i.e., h_T is such that:

$$\theta_{T-1} = h_T + q_T - u_T$$

so that the terminal total wealth becomes:

$$R_T = \sum_{t=0}^{T} [(q_t - u_t)S_t - c(q_t) - k(X_t)] + \sum_{t=0}^{T-2} \theta_t(F_{t+1} - F_t) + \theta_{T-1}(F_T - S_T)$$
$$= \sum_{t=0}^{T} [(q_t - u_t)S_t - c(q_t) - k(X_t)] + \sum_{t=0}^{T-1} \theta_t(F_{t+1} - F_t) + \theta_{T-1}(F_{T-1} - S_T)$$

$$(2.5)$$

which constitutes the discrete-time analogue of the total wealth appearing inside the utility function in Equation (2.3). Notice that we assumed that F is continuous in time, so that in particular $F_{T-} = F_T$ a.s.

In what follows, we prove that a necessary condition for the problem (2.3) to be well-posed is the equality $F_T = S_T$, so that the third summand vanishes in Equation (2.4). Our first objective is to deduce, from the well-posedness of the problem described by Equation (2.3), the no-arbitrage condition that would link spot and futures prices, i.e., to prove that there exists some equivalent probability measure Q such that

$$F_t = \mathbb{E}_Q[S_T|\mathcal{F}_t], \quad t \in [0, T]$$

and to compute this futures price explicitly.

3. Existence of the optimum and spot-futures no-arbitrage relations

In this section we derive the existence and the uniqueness of an optimal solution (q^*, u^*, θ^*) for the optimization problem (2.3). Meanwhile, we obtain no-arbitrage relations between the spot and futures prices, as well as the convergence of the futures prices to the spot prices when the time-to-maturity goes to zero. Moreover, we show that the optimal production q^* can be computed explicitly even in this general framework. For expository reasons, the explicit expressions for the other optimal quantities (storage and trading activity (u^*, θ^*)) will be given in the next section. We remind the reader that all the proofs can be found in the appendix.

Assumption 3. *Let $v(r_0) < \infty$ for some initial wealth $r_0 > 0$.*

Convergence of the futures to the spot prices and no-arbitrage relation. Our first result states that, as long as our optimization problem is well-posed, one must have a convergence of the futures price towards the spot price when the time-to-maturity tends to zero. This is true even when the underlying commodity of the contract is non storable.

Proposition 4. *Under Assumption 3, we have $F_T = S_T$.*

Before proving the existence of a solution to our optimization problem, we deduce the no-arbitrage property for the futures contracts from the finiteness of $v(r_0)$. This is the content of the next proposition, which adapts arguments from Proposition 1.2 in Ankirchner and Imkeller (2005), where No Free Lunch with Vanishing Risk (henceforth NFLVR) for simple trading strategies is deduced from the well-posedness of an optimal pure investment problem. We refer to Delbaen and Schachermayer's article (1994) for the definition of NFLVR as well as the proof of their celebrated version of the fundamental theorem of asset pricing. In this article, we deduce something stronger, namely a variant of NFLVR not only for (simple) trading portfolios but also for production and storage. To be more precise, let us redefine the NFLVR condition for our setting. We recall that a simple trading strategy θ is any linear combination of strategies of the form $\alpha 1_{]\tau_1,\tau_2]}$ where α is a bounded $\mathcal{F}_{\tau_1}$-measurable random variable and τ_1 and τ_2 are $[0, T]$-valued stopping times for the filtration $(\mathcal{F}_t)$.

Definition 5. A Free Lunch with Vanishing Risk with simple trading strategies, production and storage *is a sequence of admissible plans* $(q_t^n, u_t^n, \theta_t^n)$, $n \geq 1$, *such that*:

(i)   *each* θ^n *is a simple trading strategy*,
(ii) $R_T^{0,n} := R_T^{0,q^n,u^n,\theta^n}$ *converges a.s. towards some nonnegative r.v.* R_T^0 *satisfying* $\mathbb{P}(R_T^0 > 0) > 0$ *and*
(iii) $\| (R_T^n)^- \|_\infty \to 0$ *as* $n \to \infty$.

We will say that NFLVR with simple trading strategies, production and storage is satisfied if there are no such admissible plans in the model.

Notice that since the production and storage controls are bounded, there exists a constant $M > 0$ such that $| \int_0^T \pi_t dt | \leq M$ for any admissible (q, u) giving the instantaneous profit π_t. This fact will be used in the proof of the following result.

Proposition 6 Under Assumptions 1, 2, 3 and for all $r_0 > M$ we have that $v(r_0) < \infty$ implies NFLVR with simple trading strategies, production and storage. In particular, NFLVR with simple trading strategies and for futures prices (F_t) also holds.

Notice that the previous result does not necessarily imply the existence of a (local) martingale measure Q for the futures prices (F_t) and hence the well-known formula $F_t = \mathbb{E}_Q[S_T \mid \mathcal{F}_t]$. Indeed to have the existence of such a measure, our model should satisfy the classical No-Arbitrage (NA) condition[3] too (see, e.g., Theorem 9.7.6 in [20]). This is something that would need to be imposed later in this paper.

Existence and separation principle. An immediate consequence of the previous convergence result is the following separation principle, stating that solving our optimization problem is equivalent to maximize first with respect to the production control q and then with respect to the storage and trading controls (u, θ). On the other hand, maximizing the production can also be performed in two steps. Let us denote:

$$v(r_0) = \sup_{u,q,\theta} \mathbb{E}\left[U(r_0 + Y_T^q + Z_T^u + V_T^\theta) \right]$$

where we set

$$Y_T^q := \int_0^T (q_t S_t - c(q_t)) dt, \quad Z_T^u := -\int_0^T (u_t S_t + k(X_t)) dt$$

We can solve our problem in two separate steps. First we solve $v(r_0)$ with respect to the production control q (for given u, θ); second, we solve with respect to the controls (u, θ). Let us start from the production side.

Proposition 7. *Under Assumptions 1, 2, 3, for any given admissible investment strategy θ and storage policy u, the optimal production control $q*$ is given by*

$$q_t^* = (c')^{-1}(S_t) \vee \bar{q}, \quad t \in [0, T] \tag{3.1}$$

Let us denote

$$Y_T^* := Y_T^{q^*} = \int_0^T (q_t^* S_t - c(q_t^*)) dt$$

where q_t^* is given by (3.1). Now, let us consider the optimal storage/trading problem

$$v(r_0) := \sup_{u,\theta} \mathbb{E}\left[U(r_0 + Y_T^* + Z_T^u + V_T^\theta)\right] \tag{3.2}$$

The next result establishes existence of a unique optimal storage/trading policy $(u*, \theta*)$.

Proposition 8. *Under Assumptions 1, 2 and 3, there exists a unique solution $(u*, \theta*)$ to the problem (3.2).*

The fact that the trading-production problem above can be solved in successive steps does not mean that the optimal controls are independent. Only the production control q can be deduced independently from u and θ. Indeed, since the producer has no impact on the spot price, his optimal strategy is simply to equal his marginal cost of production with the spot price. Thus, no matter whether there exists a futures market or not, one would observe the same production level q. This is not the case for the optimal storage policy u and the optimal trading strategy θ: they are not independent. This fact has two consequences. First, the introduction of a futures market modifies the way storage capacities are managed. This point may be of interest for the econometric analysis of the relations between the level of the inventories and the prices. Second, as soon as the industrial process includes storage activities, the trading cannot be separated from the storage without a loss of value. This should be taken into account for the organization of the trading activities in industrial companies.

4. The optimal production-trading problem

In this section we illustrate, in a simple setting, how the approach developed in the previous sections can lead to a consistent model for futures prices.

We discuss the trading-production problem faced by the operator with a specification of the demand dynamics. Then we determine the volatility of the futures contract and we relate it to the volatility of the underlying conditional demand.

4.1. *The dynamics of the demand for the commodity*

In order to illustrate the previous approach, we use a simple dynamics for the demand. In particular, since our goal is not to propose a model that would match all stylized facts, we do not include features such as seasonality and jumps.

In commodity markets, the spot price S_t results from the availability of the raw material on the physical market. In our model, this availability is measured through the confrontation of the total capacities of the market and the demand for the commodity, in the following way:

$$S_t = b \cdot g(\bar{C} - D_t) \cdot f(D_t) \tag{4.1}$$

with b a constant of normalization for dimension purposes, $\bar{C} > 0$ the maximum available production and storage capacities of the market (supposed constant), D_t the total exogenous demand for the commodity (which is an $(\mathcal{F}_t)$-adapted continuous process) and $f(D)$ the marginal cost of production and storage for a demand level D. As there is a non negativity constraint on inventories, the spot price can jump to very high levels when the total capacities are not sufficient to fully satisfy the demand. This behavior is captured by the scarcity function g:

$$g(x) = \mathbf{1}_{x>0} \cdot \min(1/x, 1/\epsilon) + \mathbf{1}_{x<0} 1/\epsilon$$

The effect of scarcity on commodity prices is clearly illustrated for the case of oil in Buyukşahin et al. (2008 p. 56, fig. 10). The specific form of g above has been successfully implemented in the case of electricity spot prices in Aïd et al. (2013).

Since the production optimization problem has been solved in Proposition ([7]), it remains to treat:

$$v(x) = \sup_{u,\theta} \mathbb{E}[U(x + Y_T^* + Z_T^u + V_T^\theta)]$$

where

$$Y_T^* = \int_0^T (q_t^* S_t - c(q_t^*))dt, \qquad t \in [0, T].$$

with q_t^* as in (3.1). We recall that $Z_T^u = u_0 + \int_0^T u_t dt$ is the cumulated storage and that $V_T^\theta = \int_0^T \theta_t dF_t$ is the portfolio traded over the period $[0, T]$.

We assume that the futures price process (F_t) is an Itô process. More precisely:

Assumption 9.

1. *Let the demand for energy D_t be mean reverting, with a long-run mean set to zero:*

$$dD_t = aD_t dt + \sigma dW_t \tag{4.2}$$

where a, σ are constants and W is a standard Brownian motion. We denote by $(\mathcal{F}_t)$ the natural filtration generated by W and completed with the $\mathbb{P}$-null sets.

2. Assume that the futures price F is an Itô process fulfilling

$$dF_t = \alpha_t dt + \beta_t dW_t$$

where α, β are some $(\mathcal{F}_t)$-predictable real-valued processes such that a.s.

$$\int_0^T |\alpha_t| dt + \mathbb{E}\left[\int_0^T \beta_t^2 dt\right] < \infty$$

The integrability assumption on the volatility is here only to have the (true) martingale property of F_t and consequently the very useful formula $F_t = \mathbb{E}^Q[S_T \mid \mathcal{F}_t]$.

4.2. Equivalent martingale measures and forward volatility

First of all, we notice that Assumption 9 together with $F_T = S_T$ (ref. Proposition 4) implies that

$$F_t = \mathbb{E}^Q[S_T \mid \mathcal{F}_t], \quad t \in [0, T]$$

where Q is an equivalent martingale measure for the futures process (F_t), which means that Q must satisfy:

$$L_t^\lambda := \frac{dQ}{d\mathbb{P}}|_{\mathcal{F}_t} = \exp\left\{-\int_0^t \lambda_s dW_s - \frac{1}{2}\int_0^t \lambda_s^2 ds\right\}$$

where λ is a $(\mathcal{F}_t)$-adapted process (viewed as "market price of demand risk") such that

- $\alpha_t - \lambda_t \beta_t = 0$ a.e. $d\mathbb{P} \otimes dt$,
- $\int_0^T \lambda_s^2 ds < \infty$,
- $\mathbb{E}[L_T^\lambda] = 1$.

At this point, in order to specify completely the dynamics of the futures price under $\mathbb{P}$, we need to assume a particular and tractable form for the market price of demand risk λ_t.

Assumption 10. *Let us assume that* $\lambda_t = \lambda_0(t) + \lambda_1(t)D_t$, $t \in [0, T]$, *where* $\lambda_0, \lambda_1 : [0, T] \to \mathbb{R}$ *are deterministic functions such that the last three properties above are satisfied.*

A consequence of this assumption is that the drift α_t of the futures price takes the form $\alpha_t = (\lambda_0(t) + \lambda_1(t)D_t)\beta_t$, which is completely determined up to the volatility β_t.

We will see in what follows that the special form of the production function defining the spot price S_T in (4.1) implies a particular functional form for the volatility of the futures price process (F_t).

Let Q be the equivalent martingale measure corresponding to the market price of demand risk λ_t as in Assumption 10. Under such a measure, the demand has a dynamics characterized as follows:

$$dD_t = ((a + \lambda_1(t)\sigma)D_t + \lambda_0(t)\sigma)dt + \sigma dW_t^Q$$

where W^Q is a standard Q-BM. Thus, the conditional distribution of D_T given D_t under Q is Gaussian with conditional mean $m_{t,T}^Q$ and variance $\Sigma_{t,T}^2$ given by

$$m_{t,T}^Q = e^{\int_t^T (a+\lambda_1(s)\sigma)ds} \left(D_t + \int_t^T e^{-\int_0^s (a+\lambda_1(u)\sigma)du} \lambda_0(s) \sigma ds \right), \tag{4.3}$$

$$\Sigma_{t,T}^2 = \sigma^2 \int_t^T e^{-2\int_t^s (a+\lambda_1(u)\sigma)du} ds. \tag{4.4}$$

To complete the description of our model, we set a specific shape for the marginal cost of production.

Assumption 11. *Let the marginal cost of production f be equal to*

$$f(d) = d^\alpha \mathbf{1}_{(0 \le d \le M)} + M^\alpha \mathbf{1}_{(d \ge M)}, \quad d \in \mathbb{R}$$

for some exponent $\alpha \in (0, 1)$ and some upper bound $M > 0$ such that our conditions on f are fulfilled. Moreover, let $M \ge \bar{C} - \epsilon$.

Under all these assumptions, we can express the spot price S_t as a function of the demand $S_t = \psi(D_t)$, where the function ψ is given as follows:

$$\psi(d) = b \cdot \left(\frac{d^\alpha}{\epsilon} \mathbf{1}_{(0 \le d < \bar{C} - \epsilon)} + \frac{d^\alpha}{\bar{C} - d} \mathbf{1}_{(\bar{C} - \epsilon \le d < M)} + \frac{M}{\bar{C} - d} \mathbf{1}_{(d \ge M)} \right) \tag{4.5}$$

Notice that the spot price S_t is always nonnegative.

The futures price at time t computed under the above measure Q is given by

$$F_t = E_t^Q[\psi(D_T)], \quad t \in [0, T]$$

where E_t^Q denotes the conditional Q-expectation given $\mathcal{F}_t = \mathcal{F}_t^D$. We denote by $h_{T,D_t}(y)$ the conditional density of D_T given D_t, that is:

$$h_{T,D_t}(y) = \frac{1}{\Sigma_{t,T}\sqrt{2\pi}} \exp\left(-\frac{(y - m_{t,T}^Q)^2}{2\Sigma_{t,T}^2} \right)$$

where the mean $m_{t,T}^Q$ and the variance $\Sigma_{t,T}^2$ are given in, respectively, (4.3) and (4.4). We recall that the variance does not depend on D_t.

We can express the futures price F_t as a function of the demand at time t, D_t, as:

$$F_t = \varphi(t, D_t) = \int_{\mathbb{R}} \psi(y) h_{T,D_t}(y) dy$$

A simple application of Itô's formula together with the martingale property of the futures price F_t under Q gives that the volatility of the futures price, $\beta(t, D_t)$, is given by:

$$\beta_t = \beta_t^T = \sigma \frac{\partial \varphi}{\partial d}(t, D_t)$$

If we compute explicitly the first and second derivatives of the futures price, $\varphi(t, D_t)$, with respect to the demand, we obtain the following result giving a complete specification of the parameters of the forward dynamics.

Proposition 12. *Under Assumptions 9, 10 and 11, the well-posedness of the optimal production-trading problem (2.3) implies that*

$$dF_t = a_t dt + \beta_t dW_t$$

where

$$a_t = \tilde{a}(t, D_t) = (\lambda_0(t) + \lambda_1(t)D_t)\beta_t$$

$$\beta_t = \tilde{\beta}(t, D_t) = \sigma \int_{\mathbb{R}} \psi(y) \frac{y - m_{t,T}^Q}{\Sigma_{t,T}^2} e^{\int_t^T (a + \lambda_1(u)\sigma) du} h_{T,D_t}(y) dy$$

for all $t \in [0, T]$. Moreover, the forward volatility $\tilde{\beta}(t, D_t)$ is increasing in the demand.

4.3. The production-trading optimization problem in a Markovian setting

Let us now provide, for the sake of completeness, an informal discussion of the optimal solutions within the Markovian model determined in the previous proposition. Let us assume that the preferences of the agent are of power type, i.e., $U(x) = x^\gamma$, $x > 0$, where $\gamma \in (0, 1)$. Recall that the problem we want to solve is the following:

$$v(x) := \sup_{(u,q,\theta) \in \mathcal{A}} \mathbb{E}\left[\left(r_0 + \int_0^T \pi_t dt + V_T^\theta\right)^\gamma\right] \tag{4.6}$$

where $r_0 > 0$ is the initial wealth. Recall that π_t is the profit rate given by:

$$\pi_t = (q_t - u_t)S_t - c(q_t) - k(X_t), \quad X_t = u_0 + \int_0^t u_s ds$$

while $V_T^\theta = \int_0^T \theta_t dF_t$ is the gain from the self-financing portfolio traded on the futures market. $\mathcal{A}$ denotes the set of all admissible controls (u, q, θ). More precisely, we will say that a triplet (u, q, θ) is an admissible control if:

- $q = (q_t)_{t \in [0, T]}$ and $u = (u_t)_{t \in [0, T]}$ are adapted processes with values, respectively, in $[0, \bar{q}]$ and $[\underline{u}, \bar{u}]$;
- $\theta = (\theta_t)_{t \in [0,T]}$ is any predictable real-valued F-integrable process such that the resulting wealth is a.s. nonnegative at any time, i.e.,

$$r_0 + \int_0^t \pi_s ds + V_t^\theta \geq 0, \quad t \in [0, T]$$

The relevant state variable of the problem is $Z = (R, X, D)$ where R is the wealth of the agent, i.e.,

$$R_t = r_0 + \int_0^t \pi_s ds + V_t^\theta, \quad t \in [0, T]$$

The dynamics of the state variable is given by:

$$dR_t = ((q_t - u_t)\psi(D_t) - c(q_t) - k(X_t) + \alpha(t, D_t)\theta_t)dt + \beta(t, D_t)\theta_t dW_t$$

$$dX_t = u_t dt$$

$$dD_t = aD_t dt + \sigma dW_t$$

Let us introduce the value function of the optimization problem as

$$v(t, r, x, d) = \sup_{(u,q,\theta) \in \mathcal{A}_t} \mathbb{E}((R_T)^\gamma | Z_t = (r, x, d))$$

where $\mathcal{A}_t$ denotes the set of all admissible controls starting at time t. The corresponding Hamilton-Jacobi-Bellman equation (HJB equation) is given by

$$-v_t - \sup_{(u,q,\theta) \in A} \mathcal{L}v = 0, \quad \text{with } A := [\underline{u}, \bar{u}] \times [0, \bar{q}] \times \mathbb{R} \tag{4.7}$$

with terminal condition

$$v(T, r, x, d) = r^\gamma \tag{4.8}$$

and where

$$\mathcal{L}v = uv_x + adv_d + ((q - u)\psi(d) - c(q) - k(x) + \alpha(t, d)\theta)v_r + \frac{1}{2}\sigma^2 v_{dd}$$
$$+ \frac{1}{2}\beta(t, d)^2 \theta^2 v_{rr}$$

The HJB equation may be rewritten as

$$0 = - v_t - adv_d + k(x)v_r - \frac{1}{2}\sigma^2 v_{dd}$$
$$- \sup_{(u,q,\theta) \in A} \left\{ uv_x + ((q - u)\psi(d) - c(q) + \alpha(t, d)\theta)v_r + \frac{1}{2}\beta(t, d)^2 \theta^2 v_{rr} \right\}$$

Rearranging the terms gives

$$0 = - v_t - adv_d + k(x)v_r - \frac{1}{2}\sigma^2 v_{dd}$$

$$- \sup_{(u,q,\theta)\in A} \left\{ (v_x - \psi(d)v_r)u - (c(q) - q\psi(d))v_r + \alpha(t,d)\theta v_r + \frac{1}{2}\beta(t,d)^2\theta^2 v_{rr} \right\} \tag{4.9}$$

We notice immediately from the above HJB equation that the optimal candidate rule for the storage management is

$$u_t^* = \underline{u}\,\mathbf{1}_{(\psi(D_t)v_r > v_x)} + \bar{u}\,\mathbf{1}_{(\psi(D_t)v_r \le v_x)} \tag{4.10}$$

where, to simplify the notation, we dropped the arguments (t, R_t, X_t, D_t) from the derivatives of the value functions v_r and v_x. Depending on the ratio $\eta = v_x/\psi(d)$ between the marginal utility of one unit of storage and the spot price, it is optimal either to buy and store at maximum capacity or to withdraw and sell at maximum capacity. One may have thought that this ratio should simply be compared to one. This is not the case as it has to be compared to the marginal utility of one unit of wealth, v_r. As pointed at the end of the preceding section, we see that the storage control depends on the wealth and hence on the trading activities.

Furthermore, the heuristic computation above confirms the fact that the optimal control for production is to produce until the marginal cost of production equals the spot price, i.e., Equation (3.1).

Finally, solving the maximization problem in (4.9) gives the optimal control for the trading portfolio as

$$\theta_t^* = -\frac{\alpha(t,D_t)}{\beta(t,D_t)^2}\frac{v_r}{v_{rr}}(t, R_t, X_t, D_t) \tag{4.11}$$

Since it is likely that v_{rr} is negative because U is concave, one recovers the expected result that the agent holds a long position if futures prices are exhibiting a positive trend. Moreover, θ^* is similar to the Sharpe ratio, a tradeoff between the expected trend of the futures prices compared to their volatility.

Notice that, to rigorously solve the optimization problem, one should prove that the Cauchy problem (4.7, 4.8) admits a unique solution with the required regularity together with a verification theorem. This could be achieved using the techniques developed in, e.g., Pham (2002 [33]) for quite a large class of multidimensional stochastic volatility models. Adapting such a method to our setting would however go far beyond the scope of the present article.

5. Conclusion

In this article, we develop a parsimonious structural model of commodity prices that can explain the relation between the spot and the futures prices by arbitrage arguments. This result is obtained for every underlying asset, would it be storable or not. We show that the existence of a risk-neutral measure is the consequence of the finiteness of the operator's value function, and that the futures price converges to the spot price, regardless of the storability properties of the commodity. Finally, we discuss the solution of the trading-production problem faced by the agent, with a specification of the demand dynamics. We show how the different controls can be separated. In particular, the optimal storage policy is impacted by the possibility of trading on the futures market.

Notes

* This study was supported by the Finance and Sustainable Development Chair sponsored by EDF and CACIB, and hosted by Ecole Polytechnique, Université Paris-Dauphine, PSL Research University and CREST.
1 This does not mean, however, that our framework is relevant only to non-storable commodities, like electricity, nor that it is focused on commodities with storable inputs (Aïd et al., 2009, 2013).
2 A positive spread (a contango) arises when at date t, the futures price $F(t, T)$ is higher than the spot price S_t. A negative spread (a backwardation) is a situation where $F(t, T) < S_t$.
3 See Definition 9.2.8 in [20].

Bibliography

Aïd, R., *Electricity Derivatives*, 2015 (SpringerBriefs in Quantitative Finance).
Aïd, R., Campi, L. and Langrené, N., A structural risk neutral model for pricing and hedging power derivatives. *Mathematical Finance*, 2013, 23(3), 387–438.
Aïd, R., Campi, L., Nguyen Huu, A. and Touzi, N., A structural risk neutral model of electricity prices. *Int. Jour. of Theoretical and Applied Finance*, 2009, 12(7), 925–947.
Aïd, R., Chemla, G., Porchet, A. and Touzi, N., Hedging and vertical integration in electricity markets. *Management Science*, 2011, 57(8), 1438–1452.
Anderson, E. J. and Hu, X., Forward contracts and market power in an electricity market. *Int. J. of Industrial Organization*, 2008, 26, 679–694.
Ankirchner, S. and P. Imkeller, P., Finite utility on financial markets with asymmetric information and structure properties of the price dynamics. *Annals of Henri Poincaré Institute*, 2005, 41, 479–503.
Benth, F. E., Ekeland, L., Hauge, R. and Nielsen B. F., A note on arbitrage-free pricing of forward contracts in energy markets. *Applied Mathematical Finance*, 2003, 10(4), 325–336.
Benth, F. E., Kallsen, J., Meyer-Brandis, T., A non-Gaussian Ornstein-Uhlenbeck process for electricity spot price modeling and derivative pricing. *Applied Mathematical Finance*, 2007, 14(2), 153–169.
Benth, F. E., Biegler-König, R. and Kiesel R., An empirical study of the information premium on electricity markets. *Energy Economics*, 2013, 36, 55–77.
Benth, F. E., Saltyte-Benth, J., Koekebakker, S., *Stochastic Modeling of Electricity and Related Markets*, 2008 (World Scientific).
Bessembinder, H. and Lemmon, M. L., Equilibrium pricing and optimal hedging in electricity forward markets. *Journal of Finance*, 2002, 23, 1347–82.

Bouchard, B. and Nguyen Huu, A., No marginal arbitrage of the second kind for high production regimes in discrete time production-investment models with proportional transaction costs. *Mathematical Finance*, 2013, 23(2), 366–386.

Brennan M. J., The supply of storage. *The American Economic Review*, 1958, 48(1), 50–72.

Buyukşahin, B., Haigh, M. S., Harris, J. H., Overdahl, J. A. and Robe, M. A., Fundamentals, trader activity and derivative pricing, 2008, available at SSRN: http://ssrn.com/abstract=966692.

Chambers, M. J. and Bailey, R. E., A theory of commodity price fluctuations. *Journal of Political Economy*, 1996, 104(5), 924–957.

Danthine, J. P., Martingale, market efficiency and commodity prices. *European Economic Review*, 1977, 10(1), 1–17.

Deaton, A. and Laroque, G., On the behaviour of commodity prices. *Review of Economic Studies*, 1992, 59(1), 1–23.

Deaton, A. and Laroque, G., Competitive storage and commodity price dynamics. *Journal of Political Economy*, 1996, 104(5), 896–923.

Delbaen, F. and Schachermayer, W., A general version of the fundamental theorem of asset pricing. *Mathematische Annalen*, 1994, 300(1), 463–520.

Delbaen, F. and Schachermayer, W., *The Mathematics of Arbitrage*, 2006 (Springer Science & Business Media).

Douglas, S. and Popova, J., Storage and the electricity forward premium. *Energy Economics*, 2008, 30(4), 1712–1727.

Eydeland, A. and Wolyniec, K., *Energy and Power Risk Management: New Developments in Modeling, Pricing and Hedging*, 2002 (Wiley).

Fama, E. and French, K., Commodity futures prices: Some evidence on forecast power, premiums, and the theory of storage. *Journal of Business*, 1987, 60(1), 55–73.

Frestad, D., Benth, F. E. and Koekebakker S., Modeling term structure dynamics in the Nordic electricity swap market. *The Energy Journal*, 2010, 31(2), 53–86.

Hess, M., Pricing Electricity Derivatives under Future Information. *Working Paper*, 2013.

Kabanov, Y., and Safarian, M., *Markets with Transaction Costs: Mathematical Theory*, 2009 (Springer).

Kaldor, N., A note on the theory of the forward market. *Review of Economic Studies*, 1940, 7(3), 196–201.

Kramkov, D. and Schachermayer, W., The asymptotic elasticity of utility functions and optimal investment in incomplete markets. *Annals of Applied Probability*, 1999, 904–950.

Lautier, D., Term structure models of commodity prices: A review, *The Journal of Alternative Investments*, 2005, 42–64.

Lautier, D., Convenience yield and commodity markets. *Bankers, Markets and Investors*, 2009, 102, 59–66.

Liu, P. and Tang, K., No-arbitrage conditions for storable commodities and the modeling of futures term structures. *Journal of Banking & Finance*, 2010, 34(7), 1675–1687.

Meyer-Brandis, T. and Tankov, P., Multi-factor jump-diffusion models of electricity prices. *International Journal of Theoretical and Applied Finance*, 2008, 11(5), 503–528.

Pham, H., Smooth solutions to optimal investment models with stochastic volatilities and portfolio constraints. *Applied Mathematics and Optimization*, 2002, 46(1), 55–78.

Pham, H., *Continuous-Time Stochastic Control and Optimization with Financial Applications*, 2009, Vol. 1 (Berlin: Springer).

Prevot, H., de Juvigny, B., Lehmann, F., Louvot, M. and Izart, C., Rapport d'enquête sur les prix de l'électricité, 2004, *Document, French Ministry of Economy, Finance and Industry, October.*

Protter, P. E., *Stochastic Integration and Differential Equations: Version 2.1*, 2004, Vol. 21 (Springer).

Rogers, L. C. G., Equivalent martingale measures and no-arbitrage. *Stochastics: An International Journal of Probability and Stochastic Processes*, 1994, 51.1–2, 41–49.

Routledge, B. R., Seppi, D. J. and Spatt, C. S., Equilibrium forward curves for commodities. *Journal of Finance*, 2000, 55(3), 1297–1338.

Scheinkman, J. A. and Schechtman, J., A simple competitive model with production and storage. *Review of Economic Studies*, 1983, 50(162), 427.

Schwartz, E., The stochastic behavior of commodity prices: Implications for valuation and hedging. *Journal of Finance*, 1997, 52(3), 923–973.

Viehmann, J., Risk premiums in the German day-ahead electricity market. *Energy Policy*, 2011, 39(1), 386–394.

Working, H., Price relations between July and September wheat futures at Chicago since 1885. *Wheat Studies of the Food Research Institute*, 1933, 9(6), 187–238.

Working, H., The theory of price of storage. *American Economic Review*, 1949, 39(6), 1254–1262.

Appendix A
Proofs

A.1. Proposition on convergence

Proof of Proposition 4. Assume that $\mathbb{P}(F_T \neq S_T) > 0$ and let $A = \{F_T > S_T\}$ and $B = \{F_T < S_T\}$. Consider the following sequence of trading-production strategies: for $n \geq 1$,

$$q = u = 0, \quad \theta_t^n := \left(\alpha \mathbb{P}\left(A \mid \mathcal{F}_{T-\frac{1}{n}} \right) - \beta \mathbb{P}\left(B \mid \mathcal{F}_{T-\frac{1}{n}} \right) \right) \mathbf{1}_{\left(T-\frac{1}{n} \leq t \leq T \right)},$$

where α and β are arbitrary positive numbers. Since A and B are $\mathcal{F}_{T-}$-measurable (S_t and F_t are both continuous processes), each θ^n is a predictable and (F_t)-integrable trading strategy. Moreover the left-limit θ_{T-} exists for all $n \geq 1$. Pursuing such a sequence of strategies yields a limiting terminal wealth as $n \to \infty$ given by $r_0 + \alpha(F_T - S_T)\mathbf{1}_A + \beta(S_T - F_T)\mathbf{1}_B$.

Hence, letting $\alpha \to \infty$ and $\beta = 0$, if $\mathbb{P}(A) > 0$ or $\beta \to \infty$ and $\alpha = 0$ if $\mathbb{P}(B) > 0$ we get $v(x) = \infty$ (recall that $U(x) \to \infty$ when $x \to \infty$), which contradicts the well-posedness of our maximization problem. Thus, we can conclude that a.s. $F_T = S_T$.

For any family $\mathcal{X}$ of random variables, $\mathrm{conv}(\mathcal{X})$ will denote the set of all convex linear combinations of elements in $\mathcal{X}$.

A.2. Proposition on $v(r_0)$

Proof of Proposition 6. First notice that for all $r_0 > M$ we have

$$\infty > v(r_0) = \sup_{u,q,\theta} \mathbb{E}[U(R_T^{r_0,u,q,\theta})] \leq \sup_{\theta} \mathbb{E}[U(r_0 + V_T^{\theta})] \leq \sup_{\theta} \mathbb{E}[U(M + V_T^{\theta})]$$

$$=: v_I(M),$$

where v_I denotes the value function for the pure investment optimization problem. Now, suppose that NFLVR with simple trading strategies, production and storage is violated, so that we can find a sequence of terminal payoffs $R_T^n = \int_0^T \pi_t^n dt + \int_0^T \theta_t^n dF_t$ such that $R_T^n \to R_T^0$ for some nonnegative random variable R_T^0 with $\mathbb{P}(R_T^0 > 0) > 0$ and $\| (R_T^n)^- \|_\infty \to 0$ as $n \to \infty$. Here π^n denotes the instantaneous profit coming from a production q^n and a storage u^n. Hence, we have

$$R_T^n - M \leq V_T^n \leq R_T^n + M,$$

where we denote $V^n := V^{\theta^n}$. By Theorem 15.4.10 in [21] there exists a sequence $\tilde{V}_T^n \in \text{conv}(V_T^n, V_T^{n+1}, \ldots)$ which converges a.s. to some random variable $\tilde{V}_T^0$, which takes values in $[R_T^0 - M, R_T^0 + M]$ a.s. Therefore $\tilde{V}_T^0 \geq R_T^0 - M \geq -M$ and $\mathbb{P}(\tilde{V}_T^0 > -M) > 0$. Moreover, since $\| (\tilde{V}_T^n + M)^- \|_\infty \leq \| (R_T^n)^- \| \infty \to 0$ and the latter converges to zero as $n \to \infty$, we also have $\| (\tilde{V}_T^n + M)^- \| \to 0$. Hence, using Proposition 1.2 in [6], we obtain that $v_t(M) = \infty$ implying $v(r_0) = \infty$.

A.3. Proposition on the optimal production q^*

Proof of Proposition 7. It suffices to maximize ω-wise inside the integral in the term Y_T^q containing the production controls. Differentiating with respect to q_t for a fixed t gives $S_t - c'(q_t) = 0$ so that, taking into account the constraint $q_t \in [0, \bar{q}]$ and since c is strictly convex, we have (3.1).

A.4. Proposition on the optimal storage and trading portfolio (u^*, θ^*)

Proof of Proposition 8. First of all, if one admits the existence of a solution, its uniqueness follows at once from the strict concavity of the utility function U. Let (u^n, θ^n) be a maximizing admissible sequence for the problem (3.2), i.e., $\mathbb{E}(U(r_0 + Y_T^* + Z_T^n + V_T^n)) \to v(r_0)$ as $n \to \infty$, where we denoted

$$Z_T^n := - \int_0^T (u_t^n S_t + k(X_t^n)) dt, \quad X_t^n := u_0 + \int_0^t u_s^n ds, \quad V_T^n := \int_0^T \theta^n dF_t.$$

We prove the compactness property of the sequences u^n and θ^n separately.

For the sequence of storage strategies u^n, we use the Komlós theorem, stating that for any sequence of r.v.'s (ξ^n) bounded in L^1, one can extract a subsequence (ξ^{n_k}) converging a.s. in Cesaro sense to a random variable $\xi^0 \in L^1$ (see, e.g., Theorem 5.2 in Kabanov and Safarian, 2009 [26]). We apply this theorem to the sequence of processes u^n, that can be viewed as random variables defined on the product space $(\Omega \times [0, T], \mathcal{P}, d\mathbb{P}dt)$ where $\mathcal{P}$ is the predictable σ-field. The sequence u^n is clearly in L^1 since it takes values in the interval $[-\bar{u}, \bar{u}]$. Thus, there exists a predictable process u^0 taking values in the same interval, such that the Cesaro mean sequence $\tilde{u}^n := (1/n) \sum_{j=1}^n u^j$ converges a.e. towards u^0. Indeed it is immediate to check that the sequence $\tilde{u}^n$ takes values in $[-\bar{u}, \bar{u}]$ as well. Moreover, the cumulated storage process along the new sequence, $\tilde{X}_t^n := \int_0^t \tilde{u}_s^n ds$, is well-defined since each $\tilde{u}^n$ is bounded and it takes values in $[0, \bar{X}]$. By Lebesgue dominated convergence we have $\tilde{X}_t^n \to X_t^0 :=$

$\int_0^t u_s^0 ds$ a.s. for all $t \in [0, T]$. Since the function k is continuous, we have $k(\tilde{X}_t^n) \to k(X_t^0)$ a.s. for all t. Finally, thanks once more to the boundedness of the controls and to the continuity of k, we have $|\tilde{Z}_T^n| \leq C |\int_0^T S_t dt|$, which is bounded (since S_t is bounded uniformly in t). Therefore, applying the dominated convergence theorem again, we get $\tilde{Z}_T^n \to Z_T^0$ a.s. as $n \to \infty$.

As for the compactness of the sequence of trading strategies θ^n, we can work with the corresponding wealth process Cesaro mean sequence, that we denote by $\tilde{V}_T^n$. The admissibility property and the uniform boundedness of $\tilde{Z}_T^n$ yields that this sequence is uniformly bounded from below by some constant. Therefore, we can apply Theorem 15.4.10 in [21], implying that there exists a convex combination $\hat{V}_T^n \in \text{conv}(\tilde{V}_T^n, \tilde{V}_T^{n+1}, \ldots)$, which converges a.s. and whose limit is dominated by some $V_T^0 := \int_0^T \theta_t^0 dF_t$ for some admissible θ^0. Moreover, applying this procedure to the Cesaro means of storage strategies $\tilde{u}^n$ one gets another sequence of admissible storage strategies $\hat{u}^n$ converging a.s. to the same process u^0 as $\tilde{u}^n$ before.

To conclude the proof, we need to show that:

$$v(r_0) \leq \mathbb{E}[U(x + Y_T^* + V_T^0 + Z_T^0)]$$

To do so, it suffices to use the assumption that U satisfies RAE by proceeding as in the proof of, e.g., Theorem 7.3.4 in Pham (2000). Repeating his arguments gives us the inequality above getting that (u^0, θ^0) is the optimal storage control (u^*, θ^*). The proof of existence is now completed.

8 Compound Hawkes processes in limit order books

Anatoliy Swishchuk, Bruno Remillard,
Robert Elliott, and Jonathan Chavez-Casillas

1. Introduction

The Hawkes process (HP) is named after its creator Alan Hawkes (1971, 1974). The HP is a so-called "self-exciting point process" which means that it is a point process with a stochastic intensity which, through its dependence on the history of the process, captures the temporal and cross sectional dependence of the event arrival process as well as the 'self-exciting' property observed in empirical analysis. HPs have been used for many applications, such as modeling neural activity, genetics Cartensen (2010), occurrence of crime, bank defaults, and earthquakes.

The most recent application of HPs is in financial analysis, in particular, to model limit order books (e.g., high frequency data on price changes or arrival times of trades). In this paper we study two new Hawkes processes, namely, compound and regime-switching compound Hawkes processes to model the price processes in the limit order books. We prove a law of large numbers and functional central limit theorem (FCLT) for both processes. The latter two FCLTs are applied to limit order books where we use these asymptotic methods to study the link between price volatility and order flow in our two models by using the diffusion limits of these price processes. The volatilities of price changes are expressed in terms of parameters describing the arrival rates and price changes. The general compound Hawkes process was first introduced in Swishchuk (2017) to model a risk process in insurance.

Bowsher (2007) was the first who applied a HP to financial data modeling. Cartea et al. (2011) applied an HP to model market order arrivals. Fillimonov and Sornette (2012) and Fillimonov et al. (2013) apply a HP to estimate the percentage of price changes caused by endogenous self-generated activity, rather than the exogenous impact of news or novel information. Bauwens and Hautsch (2009) use a 5-D HP to estimate multivariate volatility, between five stocks, based on price intensities. We note, that Brémaud et al. (1996) generalized the HP to its nonlinear form. Also, a functional central limit theorem for the nonlinear Hawkes process was obtained in Zhu (2013). The 'Hawkes diffusion model' was introduced in Ait-Sahalia et al. (2010) in an attempt to extend previous models of stock prices and include financial contagion. Chavez-Demoulin et al. (2012) used Hawkes processes to model high-frequency financial data. Some applications of Hawkes processes to financial data are also given in Embrechts et al. (2011).

Cohen et al. (2014) derived an explicit filter for Markov-modulated Hawkes process. Vinkovskaya (2014) considered a regime-switching Hawkes process to model its dependency on the bid-ask spread in limit order books. Regime-switching models for the pricing of European and American options were considered in Buffington and Elliott (2000) and Buffington and Elliott (2002), respectively. A semi-Markov process was applied to limit order books in Swishchuk and Vadori (2017) to model the mid-price. We note, that a level-1 limit order books with time dependent arrival rates $\lambda(t)$ were studied in Chavez-Casillas et al. (2017), including the asymptotic distribution of the price process. General semi-Markovian models for limit order books were considered in Swishchuk et al. (2017).

The paper by Bacry et al. (2015) proposes an overview of the recent academic literature devoted to the applications of Hawkes processes in finance. The book by Cartea et al. (2015) develops models for algorithmic trading in contexts such as executing large orders, market making, trading pairs or collecting of assets, and executing in dark pool. That book also contains link to a website from which many datasets from several sources can be downloaded, and MATLAB code to assist in experimentation with the data. A detailed description of the mathematical theory of Hawkes processes is given in Liniger (2009). The paper by Laub et al. (2015) provides a background, introduces the field and historical developments, and touches upon all major aspects of Hawkes processes.

This paper is organized as follows. Section 2 gives the definitions of a Hawkes process (HP), definitions of compound Hawkes process (CHP) and regime-switching compound Hawkes process (RSCHP). These definitions are new ones from the following point of view: summands associated in a Markov chain but not are i.i.d.r.v. Section 3 contains Law of Large Numbers and diffusion limits for CHP and RSCHP. Numerical examples are presented in Section 4.

2. Definitions of a Hawkes process (HP), compound Hawkes process (CHP), and regime-switching compound Hawkes process (RSCHP)

In this section we give definitions of one-dimensional, compound and regime-switching compound Hawkes processes. Some properties of Hawkes process can be found in the existing literature (see, e.g., Hawkes 1971 and Hawkes and Oakes, 1974, Embrechts et al., 2011, Zheng et al., 2014, to name a few). However, the notions of compound and regime-switching compound Hawkes processes are new.

2.1. One-dimensional Hawkes process

Definition 1 (Counting Process). A counting process is a stochastic process $N(t)$, $t \geq 0$, taking positive integer values and satisfying: $N(0) = 0$. It is almost surely finite, and is a right-continuous step function with increments of size +1.

Denote by $\mathcal{F}^N(t), t \geq 0$, the history of the arrivals up to time t, that is, $\{\mathcal{F}^N(t), t \geq 0\}$, is a filtration, (an increasing sequence of σ-algebras).

A counting process $N(t)$ can be interpreted as a cumulative count of the number of arrivals into a system up to the current time t. The counting process can also be characterized by the sequence of random arrival times $(T_1, T_2, ...)$ at which the counting process $N(t)$ has jumped. The process defined by these arrival times is called a point process (see Daley and Vere-Jones 1988).

Definition 2 (Point Process). If a sequence of random variables $(T_1, T_2, ...)$, taking values in $[0, +\infty)$, has $P(0 \leq T_1 \leq T_2 \leq ...) = 1$, and the number of points in a bounded region is almost surely finite, then, $(T_1, T_2, ...)$ is called a point process.

Definition 3 (Conditional Intensity Function). Consider a counting process $N(t)$ with associated histories $\mathcal{F}^N(t), t \geq 0$. If a non-negative function $\lambda(t)$ exists such that

$$\lambda(t) = \lim_{h \to 0} \frac{E[N(t+h) - N(t)|\mathcal{F}^N(t)]}{h}, \tag{1}$$

then it is called the conditional intensity function of $N(t)$ (see Laub et al., 2015). We note, that sometimes this function is called the hazard function (see Cox, 1955).

Definition 4 (One-dimensional Hawkes Process). The one-dimensional Hawkes process (see Hawkes, 1971 and Hawkes and Oakes, 1974) is a point process $N(t)$ which is characterized by its intensity $\lambda(t)$ with respect to its natural filtration:

$$\lambda(t) = \lambda + \int_0^t \mu(t-s)dN(s), \tag{2}$$

where $\lambda > 0$, and the response function $\mu(t)$ is a positive function and satisfies $\int_0^{+\infty} \mu(s)ds < 1$.

The constant λ is called the background intensity and the function $\mu(t)$ is sometimes also called the excitation function. We suppose that $\mu(t) \neq 0$ to avoid the trivial case, which is, a homogeneous Poisson process. Thus, the Hawkes process is a non-Markovian extension of the Poisson process.

With respect to definitions of $\lambda(t)$ in (1) and $N(t)$ (2), it follows that

$$P(N(t+h) - N(t) = m|\mathcal{F}^N(t)) = \begin{cases} \lambda(t)h + o(h), & m = 1 \\ o(h), & m > 1 \\ 1 - \lambda(t)h + o(h), & m = 0. \end{cases}$$

The interpretation of equation (2) is that the events occur according to an intensity with a background intensity λ which increases by $\mu(0)$ at each new event then decays back to the background intensity value according to the function $\mu(t)$. Choosing $\mu(0) > 0$ leads to a jolt in the intensity at each new event, and this feature is often called a self-exciting feature, in other words, because an arrival causes the conditional intensity function $\lambda(t)$ in (1)–(2) to increase then the process is said to be self-exciting.

We should mention that the conditional intensity function $\lambda(t)$ in (1)–(2) can be associated with the compensator $\Lambda(t)$ of the counting process $N(t)$, that is:

$$\Lambda(t) = \int_0^t \lambda(s)ds. \tag{3}$$

Thus, $\Lambda(t)$ is the unique $\mathcal{F}^N(t), t \geq 0$, predictable function, with $\Lambda(0) = 0$, and is non-decreasing, such that

$$N(t) = M(t) + \Lambda(t) \quad a.s.,$$

where $M(t)$ is an $\mathcal{F}^N(t), t \geq 0$, local martingale. (This is the Doob-Meyer decomposition of N.)

A common choice for the function $\mu(t)$ in (2) is one of exponential decay (see Laub et al. (2015)):

$$\mu(t) = \alpha e^{-\beta t}, \tag{4}$$

with parameters $\alpha, \beta > 0$. In this case the Hawkes process is called the Hawkes process with exponentially decaying intensity.

Thus, the equation (2) becomes

$$\lambda(t) = \lambda + \int_0^t \alpha e^{-\beta(t-s)} dN(s), \tag{5}$$

We note, that in the case of (4), the process $(N(t), \lambda(t))$ is a continuous-time Markov process, which is not the case for the choice (2).

With some initial condition $\lambda(0) = \lambda_0$, the conditional density $\lambda(t)$ in (5) with the exponential decay in (4) satisfies the following stochastic differential equation (SDE):

$$d\lambda(t) = \beta(\lambda - \lambda(t))dt + \alpha dN(t), \quad t \geq 0,$$

which can be solved (using stochastic calculus) as

$$\lambda(t) = e^{-\beta t}(\lambda_0 - \lambda) + \lambda + \int_0^t \alpha e^{-\beta(t-s)} dN(s),$$

which is an extension of (5).

Another choice for $\mu(t)$ is a power law function:

$$\lambda(t) = \lambda + \int_0^t \frac{k}{(c + (t-s))^p} dN(s) \tag{6}$$

for some positive parameters c, k, p. This power law form for $\lambda(t)$ in (6) was applied in the geological model called Omori's law, and used to predict the rate of aftershocks caused by an earthquake.

Remark 1. Many generalizations of Hawkes processes have been proposed. They include, in particular, multi-dimensional Hawkes processes (Embrechts et al., 2011), non-linear Hawkes processes (Zheng et al., 2014), mixed diffusion-Hawkes models (Errais et al., 2010), Hawkes models with shot noise exogenous events (Dassios and Zhao, 2011), and Hawkes processes with generation dependent kernels (Mehdad and Zhu, 2011).

2.2. Compound Hawkes process (CHP)

In this section we give definitions of compound Hawkes process (CHP) and regime-switching compound Hawkes process (RSCHP). These definitions are new ones from the following point of view: summands are not i.i.d.r.v., as in classical compound Poisson process, but associated in a Markov chain.

Definition 5 (Compound Hawkes Process (CHP)). Let $N(t)$ be a one-dimensional Hawkes process defined as above. Let also X_t be ergodic continuous-time finite state Markov chain, independent of $N(t)$, with space state X. We write τ_k for jump times of $N(t)$ and $X_k := X_{\tau_k}$. The compound Hawkes process is defined as

$$S_t = S_0 + \sum_{k=1}^{N(t)} X_k.$$

(7)

Remark 2. If we take X_k as i.i.d.r.v. and $N(t)$ as a standard Poisson process in (10) ($\mu(t) = 0$), then S_t is a compound Poisson process. Thus, the name of S_t in (10)-*compound Hawkes process*.

Remark 3. (Limit Order Books: Fixed Tick, Two-values Price Change, Independent Orders). If Instead of Markov chain we take the sequence of i.i. d.r.v. X_k, then (10) becomes

$$S_t = S_0 + \sum_{i=1}^{N(t)} X_k.$$

(8)

In the case of Poisson process $N(t)$ ($\mu(t) = 0$) this model was used in Cont and Larrard (2013) to model the limit order books with $X_k = \{-\delta, +\delta\}$, where δ is the fixed tick size.

2.3. Regime-switching compound Hawkes process (RSCHP)

Let Y_t be an N-state Markov chain, with rate matrix A_t. We assume, without loss of generality, that Y_t takes values in the standard basis vectors in R^N. Then, Y_t has the representation

$$Y_t = Y_0 + \int_0^t A_s Y_s ds + M_t,$$

(9)

for M_t an R^N-valued P-martingale (see Buffington and Elliott, 2000 for more details).

Definition 6 (One-dimensional Regime-switching Hawkes Process). A one-dimensional regime-switching Hawkes Process N_t is a point process character-ized by its intensity $\lambda(t)$ in the following way:

$$\lambda_t = <\lambda, Y_t> + \int_0^t <\mu(t-s), Y_s> dN_s, \tag{10}$$

where $<\lambda, Y_t>$ is an inner product and Y_t is defined in (12).

Definition 7 (Regime-switching Compound Hawkes Process (RSHP)).

Let N_t be any one-dimensional regime-switching Hawkes process as defined in (13), Definition 6. Let also X_n be an ergodic continuous-time finite state Markov chain, independent of N_t, with space state X. The regime-switching compound Hawkes process is defined as

$$S_t = S_0 + \sum_{i=1}^{N_t} X_k, \tag{11}$$

where N_t is defined in (13).

Remark 3. In similar way, as in Definition 6, we can define regime-switching Hawkes processes with exponential kernel, (see (4)), or power law kernel (see (6)).

Remark 4. Regime-switching Hawkes processes were considered in Cohen and Elliott (2014) (with exponential kernel) and in Vinkovskaya (2014), (multi-dimensional Hawkes process). Cohen and Elliott (2014) discussed a self-exciting counting process whose parameters depend on a hidden finite-state Markov chain, and the optimal filter and smoother based on observations of the jump process are obtained. Vinkovskaya (2014) considers a regime-switching multi-dimensional Hawkes process with an exponential kernel which reflects changes in the bid-ask spread. The statistical properties, such as maximum likelihood estimations of its parameters, etc., of this model were studied.

3. Diffusion limits and LLNs for CHP and RSCHP in limit order books

In this section, we consider LLNs and diffusion limits for the CHP and RSCHP, defined above, as used in the limit order books. In the limit order books, high-frequency and algorithmic trading, order arrivals and cancellations are very fre-quent and occur at the millisecond time scale (see, e.g., Cont and Larrard 2013, Cartea et al., 2015). Meanwhile, in many applications, such as order exe-cution, one is interested in the dynamics of order flow over a large time scale, typically tens of seconds or minutes. It means that we can use asymptotic methods to study the link between price volatility and order flow in our model by studying the diffusion limit of the price process. Here, we prove functional central limit theorems for the price processes and express the volatilities of price changes in terms of parameters describing the arrival rates and price changes. In this section, we consider diffusion limits and LLNs for both CHP, sec. 3.1, and RSCHP, sec. 3.2, in the limit order books. We note, that level-1 limit order books with time dependent arrival rates $\lambda(t)$ were studied in Chavez-Casillas et al. (2017), including the asymptotic distribution of the price process.

3.1. Diffusion limits for CHP in limit order books

We consider here the mid-price process S_t (CHP) which was defined in (10) as,

$$S_t = S_0 + \sum_{k=1}^{N(t)} X_k. \tag{12}$$

Here, $X_k \in \{-\delta, +\delta\}$ is continuous-time two-state Markov chain, δ is the fixed tick size, and $N(t)$ is the number of price changes up to moment t, described by the one-dimensional Hawkes process defined in (2), Definition 4. It means that we have the case with a fixed tick, a two-valued price change and dependent orders.

Theorem 1 (Diffusion Limit for CHP). Let X_k be an ergodic Markov chain with two states $\{-\delta, +\delta\}$ and with ergodic probabilities $(\pi^*, 1-\pi^*)$. Let also S_t be defined in (15). Then

$$\frac{S_{nt} - N(nt)s^*}{\sqrt{n}} \to_{n \to +\infty} \sigma \sqrt{\lambda/(1-\hat{\mu})} W(t), \tag{13}$$

where $W(t)$ is a standard Wiener process, $\hat{\mu}$ is given by

$$0 < \hat{\mu} := \int_0^{+\infty} \mu(s)ds < 1 \quad and \quad \int_0^{+\infty} \mu(s)sds < +\infty, \tag{14}$$

$$s^* := \delta(2\pi^* - 1) \quad 1em \ and \ 1em \ \sigma^2:$$

$$= 4\delta^2 \left(\frac{1 - p' + \pi^*(p' - p)}{(p + p' - 2)^2} - \pi^*(1 - \pi^*) \right). \tag{15}$$

Here, (p, p') are the transition probabilities of the Markov chain X_k. We note that λ and $\mu(t)$ are defined in (2).

Proof. From (15) it follows that

$$S_{nt} = S_0 + \sum_{k=1}^{N(nt)} X_k, \tag{16}$$

and

$$S_{nt} = S_0 + \sum_{k=1}^{N(nt)} (X_k - s^*) + N(nt)s^*.$$

Therefore,

$$\frac{S_{nt} - N(nt)s^*}{\sqrt{n}} = \frac{S_0 + \sum_{k=1}^{N(nt)}(X_k - s^*)}{\sqrt{n}}. \tag{17}$$

Since $\frac{S_0}{\sqrt{n}} \to_{n \to +\infty} 0$, we have to find the limit for

$$\frac{\sum_{k=1}^{N(nt)}(X_k - s^*)}{\sqrt{n}}$$

when $n \to +\infty$.

Consider the following sums

$$R_n := \sum_{k=1}^{n}(X_k - s^*) \tag{18}$$

and

$$U_n(t) := n^{-1/2}[(1 - (nt - \lfloor nt \rfloor))R_{\lfloor nt \rfloor} + (nt - \lfloor nt \rfloor))R_{\lfloor nt \rfloor + 1}], \tag{19}$$

where $\lfloor \cdot \rfloor$ is the floor function.

Following the martingale method from Swishchuk and Vadori (2015), we have the following weak convergence in the Skorokhod topology (see Skorokhod, 1965):

$$U_n(t) \to_{n \to +\infty} \sigma \mathcal{W}_t, \tag{20}$$

where σ is defined in (18), and $\mathcal{W}_t$ is a standard Brownian motion.

We note that w.r.t LLN for Hawkes process $N(t)$ (see, e.g., Daley et al. (1988) we have:

$$\frac{N(t)}{t} \to_{t \to +\infty} \frac{\lambda}{1 - \hat{\mu}} := \bar{\lambda},$$

or

$$\frac{N(nt)}{n} \to_{n \to +\infty} \frac{t\lambda}{1 - \hat{\mu}} = \bar{\lambda}t, \tag{21}$$

where $\hat{\mu}$ is defined in (17).

Using a change of time in (23), $t \to N(nt)/n$, we can find from (23) and (24):

$$U_n(N(nt)/n) \to_{n \to +\infty} \sigma \mathcal{W}(t\lambda/(1 - \hat{\mu})),$$

or

$$U_n(N(nt)/n) \to_{n \to +\infty} \sigma \sqrt{\lambda/(1 - \hat{\mu})} W(t), \tag{22}$$

where $W_t = W_{\bar{\lambda}t}/\sqrt{\bar{\lambda}}$. The Brownian motion $W(t)$ in (25) is equivalent by distribution to Brownian motion W in (23) by scaling property. The result (16) now follows from (20)–(25).

Remark 5. In the case of exponential decay, $\mu(t) = \alpha e^{-\beta t}$ (see (4)), the limit in (16) is $[\sigma/\sqrt{\lambda/(1-\alpha/\beta)}]W(t)$, because $\hat{\mu} = \int_0^{+\infty} \alpha e^{-\beta s} ds = \alpha/\beta$.

3.2. LLN for CHP

Lemma 1 (LLN for CHP). The process S_{nt} in (19) satisfies the following weak convergence in the Skorokhod topology (see Skorokhod, 1965):

$$\frac{S_{nt}}{n} \to_{n\to+\infty} s^* \frac{\lambda}{1-\hat{\mu}} t, \tag{23}$$

where s^* and $\hat{\mu}$ are defined in (18) and (17), respectively.

Proof. From (19) we have

$$S_{nt}/n = S_0/n + \sum_{k=1}^{N(nt)} X_k/n. \tag{24}$$

The first term goes to zero when $n \to +\infty$. From the other side, using the strong LLN for Markov chains (see, e.g., Norris, 1997)

$$\frac{1}{n}\sum_{k=1}^{n} X_k \to_{n\to+\infty} s^*, \tag{25}$$

where s^* is defined in (18).

Finally, taking into account (24) and (28), we obtain:

$$\sum_{k=1}^{N(nt)} X_k/n = \frac{N(nt)}{n} \frac{1}{N(nt)} \sum_{k=1}^{N(nt)} X_k \to_{n\to+\infty} s^* \frac{\lambda}{1-\hat{\mu}} t,$$

and the result in (26) follows.

Remark 6. In the case of exponential decay, $\mu(t) = \alpha e^{-\beta t}$ (see (4)), the limit in (26) is $s^* t(\lambda/(1-\alpha/\beta))$, because $\hat{\mu} = \int_0^{+\infty} \alpha e^{-\beta s} ds = \alpha/\beta$.

3.3. Corollary: extension to a point process

The price process S is expressed as

$$S_t = S_0 + \sum_{i=1}^{N(t)} X_i, \qquad t \geq 0,$$

where N is a point process, and Markov chain X_i is defined in (10).

Assumption C1: As $n \to \infty$, $N(nt)/n \to^{Pr} \bar{\lambda}t$, where $\bar{\lambda} := \lambda/(1-\hat{\mu})$.

Note that if $N(t) = \max\{n : V_n \leq t\}$, then $N(nt)/n \to^{Pr} \bar{\lambda}t = 1\bar{\nu}$ iff $V_n/n \to^{Pr} \bar{\nu}$. This representation is useful in particular for renewal processes where $V_n = \sum_{k=1}^{n} \tau_k$, with the τ_k i.i.d. with mean $\bar{\nu}$.

Assumption C2: $U_n(t) \to W$, where W is a Brownian motion, and $U_n(t)$ is defined in (22).

It then follows from Assumptions C1 and C2 that

$$n^{-1/2}\{S_{nt} - S_0 - s^*N(nt)\}\} = \sigma U_n(N(nt)/n)$$

$$= n^{-1/2}\sum_{i=1}^{N(nt)}\{X_i - s^*\} \to \sigma\sqrt{\bar{\lambda}}\,W_t,$$

where W is a Brownian motion, and s^* is denied in (18). In fact, for any $t \geq 0$, $W_t = W_{\bar{\lambda}t}/\sqrt{\bar{\lambda}}$.

The limiting variance $\sigma^2\bar{\lambda}$ can probably be approximated by summing the square of the increments $S_{nt_i} - S_{nt_{i-1}} - s^*(N(nt_i) - N(nt_{i-1}))$. In any cases, $\bar{\lambda}$ cab be easily estimated by $N(T)/T$, and σ can be estimated from the distribution of the price increments.

Suppose now that there is also a CLT for the point process N. More precisely,

Assumption C3: $n^{1/2}\left(\dfrac{N(nt)}{n} - t\lambda\right) \to \bar{\sigma}\bar{W}_t$, where $\bar{W}$ is a Brownian motion

independent of W.

Then under Assumptions C1–C3,

$$n^{-/2}(S_{nt} - nt\bar{\lambda}s^*) \to \tilde{\sigma}\mathbb{W}_t,$$

where $\mathbb{W} = (\sigma\sqrt{\bar{\lambda}}W + s^*\bar{\sigma}\bar{W})/\tilde{\sigma}$ is a Brownian motion, and

$$\tilde{\sigma} = (\sigma^2\bar{\lambda} + \{s^*\}^2\bar{\sigma}^2)^{1/2}.$$

This follows from Assumptions and the fact that

$$n^{-1/2}(S_{nt} - S_0 - nt\bar{\lambda}s^*) = n^{-1/2}\sum_{i=1}^{N(nt)}\{X_i - s^*\} + s^*n^{1/2}\left(\frac{N(nt)}{n} - t\lambda\right).$$

Remark 7. Assumption C3 is true in many interesting cases. For renewal processes, if σ_τ is the standard deviation of τ_k, then $\bar{\sigma} = \sigma_\tau\bar{\lambda}^{3/2}$. This is also true for Hawkes processes (Bacry et al., 2013) with $\lambda(t) = \lambda_0 + \int_0^t \mu(t - s)dN_s$, provided $\hat{\mu} = \int_0^\infty \mu(s)ds < 1$. Then $\bar{\lambda} = \frac{\lambda_0}{1-\hat{\mu}}$ and $\bar{\sigma} = \sqrt{\bar{\lambda}}/(1 - \hat{\mu})$.

3.4. Diffusion limits for RSCHP in limit order books

Consider now the mid-price process S_t (RSCHP) in the form

$$S_t = S_0 + \sum_{k=1}^{N_t} X_k, \tag{26}$$

where $X_k \in \{-\delta, +\delta\}$ is continuous-time two-state Markov chain, δ is the fixed tick size, and N_t is the number of price changes up to the moment t, described by a one-dimensional regime-switching Hawkes process with intensity given by:

$$\lambda_t = <\lambda, Y_t> + \int_0^t \mu(t-s)dN_s, \tag{27}$$

(compare with (11), Definition 6).

Here we would like to relax the model for one-dimensional regime-switching Hawkes process, considering only the case of a switching the parameter λ, background intensity, in (20), which is reasonable from a limit order book's point of view. For example, we can consider a three-state Markov chain $Y_t \in \{e_1, e_2, e_3\}$ and interpret $<\lambda, Y_t>$ as the imbalance, where $\lambda_1, \lambda_2, \lambda_3$, represent high, normal and low imbalance, respectively (see Cartea et al., 2015) for imbalance notion and discussion). Of course, a more general case (13) can be considered as well, where the excitation function $<\mu(t), Y_t>$, can take three values, corresponding to high imbalance, normal imbalance, and low imbalance, respectively.

Theorem 2 (Diffusion Limit for RSCHP). Let X_k be an ergodic Markov chain with two states $\{-\delta, +\delta\}$ and with ergodic probabilities $(\pi^*, 1-\pi^*)$. Let also S_t be defined in (29) with λ_t as in (30). We also consider Y_t to be an ergodic Markov chain with ergodic probabilities $(p_1^*, p_2^*, ..., p_N^*)$. Then

$$\frac{S_{nt} - N_{nt}s^*}{\sqrt{n}} \to_{n \to +\infty} \sigma\sqrt{\hat{\lambda}/(1-\hat{\mu})}W(t), \tag{28}$$

where $W(t)$ is a standard Wiener process with s^* and σ defined in (18),

$$\hat{\lambda} := \sum_{i=1}^{N} p_i^* \lambda_i \neq 0, \quad \lambda_i := <\lambda, i>, \tag{29}$$

and $\hat{\mu}$ is defined in (17).

Proof. From (29) it follows that

$$S_{nt} = S_0 + \sum_{i=1}^{N_{nt}} X_k, \tag{30}$$

and

$$S_{nt} = S_0 + \sum_{i=1}^{N_{nt}} (X_k - s^*) + N_{nt} s^*,$$

where N_{nt} is an RGCHP with regime-switching intensity λ_t as in (30). Then,

$$\frac{S_{nt} - N_{nt} s^*}{\sqrt{n}} = \frac{S_0 + \sum_{i=1}^{N_{nt}} (X_k - s^*)}{\sqrt{n}}. \tag{31}$$

As long as $\frac{S_0}{\sqrt{n}} \to_{n \to +\infty} 0$, we wish to find the limit of

$$\frac{\sum_{i=1}^{N_{nt}} (X_k - s^*)}{\sqrt{n}}$$

when $n \to +\infty$.

Consider the following sums, similar to (21) and (22):

$$R_n := \sum_{k=1}^{n} (X_k - s^*) \tag{32}$$

and

$$U_n(t) := n^{-1/2}[(1 - (nt - \lfloor nt \rfloor))R_{\lfloor nt \rfloor} + (nt - \lfloor nt \rfloor))R_{\lfloor nt \rfloor + 1}], \tag{33}$$

where $\lfloor \cdot \rfloor$ is the floor function.

Following the martingale method from Swishchuk and Vadori (2015), we have the following weak convergence in the Skorokhod topology (see Skorokhod, 1965):

$$U_n(t) \to_{n \to +\infty} \sigma W(t), \tag{34}$$

where σ is defined in (18).

We note that with respect to the LLN for the Hawkes process N_t in (34) with regime-switching intensity λ_t as in (30) we have (see Korolyuk and Swishchuk, 1995 for more details):

$$\frac{N_t}{t} \to_{t \to +\infty} \frac{\hat{\lambda}}{1 - \hat{\mu}},$$

or

$$\frac{N_{nt}}{n} \to_{n \to +\infty} \frac{t\hat{\lambda}}{1 - \hat{\mu}}, \tag{35}$$

where $\hat{\mu}$ is defined in (17) and $\hat{\lambda}$ in (32).

Using a change of time in (37), $t \to N_{nt}/n$, we can find from (37) and (38):

$$U_n(N_{nt}/n) \to_{n \to +\infty} \sigma W(t\hat{\lambda}/(1-\hat{\mu})),$$

or

$$U_n(N_{nt}/n) \to_{n \to +\infty} \sigma \sqrt{\hat{\lambda}/(1-\hat{\mu})} W(t), \tag{36}$$

The result (31) now follows from (33)–(39).

Remark 8. In the case of exponential decay, $\mu(t) = \alpha e^{-\beta t}$ (see (4)), the limit in (31) is $[\sigma\sqrt{\hat{\lambda}/(1-\alpha/\beta)}]W(t)$, because $\hat{\mu} = \int_0^{+\infty} \alpha e^{-\beta s} ds = \alpha/\beta$.

3.5. LLN for RSCHP

Lemma 2 (LLN for RSCHP). The process S_{nt} in (33) satisfies the following weak convergence in the Skorokhod topology (see Skorokhod, 1965):

$$\frac{S_{nt}}{n} \to_{n \to +\infty} s^* \frac{\hat{\lambda}}{1-\hat{\mu}} t, \tag{37}$$

where s^*, $\hat{\lambda}$ and $\hat{\mu}$ are defined in (13), (27) and (12), respectively.

Proof. From (33) we have

$$S_{nt}/n = S_0/n + \sum_{i=1}^{N_{nt}} X_k/n, \tag{38}$$

where N_{nt} is a Hawkes process with regime-switching intensity λ_t in (30).

The first term goes to zero when $n \to +\infty$.

From the other side, with respect to the strong LLN for Markov chains (see, e.g., Norris, 1997)

$$\frac{1}{n}\sum_{k=1}^{n} X_k \to_{n \to +\infty} s^*, \tag{39}$$

where s^* is defined in (18).

Finally, taking into account (38) and (42), we obtain:

$$\sum_{i=1}^{N_{nt}} X_k/n = \frac{N_{nt}}{n} \frac{1}{N_{nt}} \sum_{i=1}^{N_{nt}} X_k \to_{n \to +\infty} s^* \frac{\hat{\lambda}}{1-\hat{\mu}} t.$$

The result in (40) follows.

Remark 9. In the case of exponential decay, $\mu(t) = \alpha e^{-\beta t}$ (see (4)), the limit in (40) is $s^* t(\hat{\lambda}/(1-\alpha/\beta))$, because $\hat{\mu} = \int_0^{+\infty} \alpha e^{-\beta s} ds = \alpha/\beta$.

4. Numerical examples and parameters estimations

Formula (16) in Theorem 1 (Diffusion Limit for CHP) relates the volatility of intraday returns at lower frequencies to the high-frequency arrival rates of orders. The typical time scale for order book events are milliseconds. Formula (16) states that, observed over a larger time scale, e.g., 5, 10, or 20 minutes, the price has a diffusive behavior with a diffusion coefficient given by the coefficient at $W(t)$ in (16):

$$\sigma\sqrt{\lambda/(1-\hat{\mu})}, \tag{40}$$

where all the parameters here are defined in (17)–(18). We mention, that this formula (43) for volatility contains all the initial parameters of the Hawkes process, Markov chain transition and stationary probabilities and the tick size. In this way, formula (43) links properties of the price to the properties of the order flow.

Also, the left hand side of (16) represents the variance of price changes, whereas the right hand side in (16) only involves the tick size and Hawkes process and Markov chain quantities. From here it follows that an estimator for price volatility may be computed without observing the price at all. As we shall see below, the error of estimation of comparison of the standard deviation of the LNS of (16) and the RHS of (16) multiplied by $\sqrt{n}$ is approximately 0.08, indicating that approximation in (16) for diffusion limit for CHP in Theorem 1, is pretty good.

Section 4.1 below presents parameters estimation for our model using CISCO Data (5 days, 3–7 November 2014 (see Cartea et al., 2015)). Section 4.2 contains the errors of estimation of comparison of of the standard deviation of the LNS of (16) and the RHS of (16) multiplied by $\sqrt{n}$. Section 4.3 depicts some graphs based on parameters estimation from Section 4.1. And Section 4.4 presents some ideas of how to implement the regime switching case from Section 3.4.

4.1. Parameters estimation for CISCO data (5 days, 3–7 November 2014 (see Cartea et al., 2015))

We have the following estimated parameters for 5 days, 3–7 November 2014, from Formula (16):

$s^* = 0.0001040723; 0.0002371220; 0.0002965143;$ $0.0001263690; 0.0001554404;$

$\sigma = 1.066708e - 04; 1.005524 - 04; 1.165201e - 04; 1.134621e - 04;$
$\qquad 9.954487e - 05;$

$\lambda = 0.0323888; 0.02643083; 0.02590728; 0.02530517; 0.02417804;$

$\alpha = 438.2557; 401.0505; 559.1927; 418.7816; 449.8632;$

$\beta = 865.9344; 718.0325; 1132.0741; 834.2553; 878.9675;$

$\hat{\lambda} := \lambda/(1 - \alpha/\beta) = 0.06560129; 0.059801686; 0.051181133; 0.050801432; 0.04957073.$

Volatility Coefficient $\sigma\sqrt{\lambda/(1-\alpha/\beta)}$ (volatility coefficient for the Brownian Motion in the right hand-side (RHS) of (16)):

0.04033114; 0.04098132; 0.04770726; 0.04725449; 0.04483260.

Transition Probabilities p:

Day 1:

	uu	ud
	0.5187097	0.4812903
	du	dd
	0.4914135	0.5085865

Day 2:

	0.4790503	0.5209497
	0.5462555	0.4537445

Day 3:

	0.6175041	0.3824959
	0.4058722	0.5941278

Day 4:

	0.5806988	0.4193012
	0.4300341	0.5699659

Day 5:

	0.4608844	0.5391156
	0.5561404	0.4438596

We note, that stationary probabilities $\pi_i^*, i = 1, ..., 5$, are, respectively: 0.5525; 0.6195; 0.6494; 0.5637; 0.5783. Here, we assume that the tick δ size is $\delta = 0.01$.

The following set of parameters are related to the the following expression

$$S_{nt} - N(nt)s^* = S_0 + \sum_{k=1}^{N(nt)}(X_k - s^*),$$

LHS of the expression in (16) multiplied by $\sqrt{n}$.

The first set of numbers are for the 10 minutes time horizon ($nt = 10$ minutes, for 5 days, the 7 sampled hours, total 35 numbers):

Series 1

[1]24.50981; [2]24.54490; [3]24.52375; [4]24.59209; [5]24.47209; [6]24.57042; [7]24.61063;

[8]24.76987; [9]24.68749; [10]24.81599; [11]24.77026; [12]24.79883; [13]24.80073; [14]24.90121;

[15]24.87772; [16]24.98492; [17]25.09788; [18]25.09441; [19]24.99085; [20]25.18195; [21]25.15721;

[22]25.04236; [23]25.18323; [24]25.15222; [25]25.20424; [26]25.14171; [27]25.18323; [28]25.25348;

[29]25.10225; [30]25.29003; [31]25.28282; [32]25.33267; [33]25.30313; [34]25.27407; [35]25.30438;

The standard deviation (SD) is: 0.2763377. The standard error (SE) for SD for the 10 minutes is: 0.01133634 (for standard error calculations see Casella and Berger, 2002, page 257).

The second set of numbers are for the 5-minute time horizon ($nt = 5$ minutes, for 5 days, the 7 sampled hours):

Series 2

[1]24.49896; [2]24.52906; [3]24.50417; [4]24.53417; [5]24.53500; [6]24.51458; [7]24.55479;

[8]24.93026; [9]24.66931; [10]24.74263; [11]24.79358; [12]24.80310; [13]24.84500; [14]24.88405;

[15]24.85729; [16]24.98907; [17]25.08085; [18]25.07500; [19]24.99322; [20]25.13381; [21]25.15144;

[22]25.15197; [23]25.12475; [24]25.15449; [25]25.18475; [26]25.20348; [27]25.20500; [28]25.25348;

[29]25.21251; [30]25.35376; [31]25.30407; [32]25.30469; [33]25.30469; [34]25.27500; [35]25.30469;

The standard deviation for those numbers is: 0.2863928. The SE for SD for the 5 minutes is: 0.01233352.

The third and last set of numbers are for the 20-minute time horizon ($nt = 20$ minutes, for 5 days, the 7 sampled hours):

Series 3

[1]24.48419; [2]24.53970; [3]24.56292; [4]24.57105; [5]24.48938; [6]24.52751; [7]24.50751;

[8]24.76465; [9]24.59753; [10]24.82935; [11]24.76552; [12]24.81741; [13]24.75409; [14]24.84077;

[15]24.92942; [16]24.99721; [17]25.05551; [18]25.04848; [19]25.08492; [20]25.09780; [21]25.09551;

[22]24.95124; [23]25.24222; [24]25.19096; [25]25.18273; [26]25.14070; [27]25.20171; [28]25.26785;

[29]25.23013; [30]25.38661; [31]25.32127; [32]25.34065; [33]25.30313; [34]25.25251; [35]25.24972;

The standard deviation is: 0.2912967. The SE for SD for the 20 minutes is: 0.01234808.

As we can see, the SE is approximately 0.01 for all three cases.

4.2. Error of estimation

Here, we would like to calculate the error of estimation comparing the standard deviation for

$$S_{nt} - N(nt)s^* = S_0 + \sum_{k=1}^{N(nt)}(X_k - s^*)$$

and standard deviation in the right-hand side of (16) multiplied by $\sqrt{n}$, namely,

$\sqrt{n}\sigma\sqrt{\lambda/(1-\alpha/\beta)}.$

We calculate the error of estimation with respect to the following formula:

$$ERROR = (1/m)\sum_{k=1}^{m}(sd - \hat{sd})^2,$$

where $\hat{sd} = \sqrt{n}Coef$, where $Coef$ is the volatility coefficient in the right-hand side of equation (16). In this case $n = 1000$, and $Coef = 0.3276$.

We take observations of $S_{nt} - N(tn)s^*$ every 10 min and we have 36 samples per day for 5 days.

Using the first approach with formula above we take $m = 5$ and for computing the standard deviation "sd" we take 36 samples of the first day. In that case, we have $ERROR = 0.07617229$.

Using the second approach with formula above, we take $m = 36$ and for computing "sd" we take samples of 5 elements (the same time across 5 days). In that case we have $ERROR = 0.07980041$.

As we can see, the error of estimation in both cases is approximately 0.08, indicating that approximation in (16) for diffusion limit for CHP, Theorem 1, is pretty good.

4.3. Graphs based on parameters estimation for CISCO data (5 days, 3–7 November 2014 (Cartea et al., 2015)) from Sec. 4.1

The following graphs, see Figure 8.2, contain the empirical intensity for the point process for those 5 days versus a simulated path using the above-estimated parameters.

In the next graphs we estimate the left hand-side (LHS) of (16). The time horizon is $nt = 10$ min. We took the time from which the start time measuring the 10 min. as the independent variable or x-axis. The dependent variable or y-axis is

$$F(t_0) = (S_{t_0} + S_{tn} - N(tn)s^*)/\sqrt{n}. \tag{41}$$

The following graphs are the same as above but just considering the median of the 1,000 simulations and zoomed in the range so that it is easy to compare. See Figure 8.3.

The next graphs contain information on the quantiles of simulations of the price process according to equation (16). That is, for a fixed big n and fixed t_0 and t. We use 1,000 simulations of the process (with the parameters estimated for $N(t)$). The time horizon is a trading day. The first top line is 99 percentile, the next second line is 3 quantile, the third line from the top is the median,

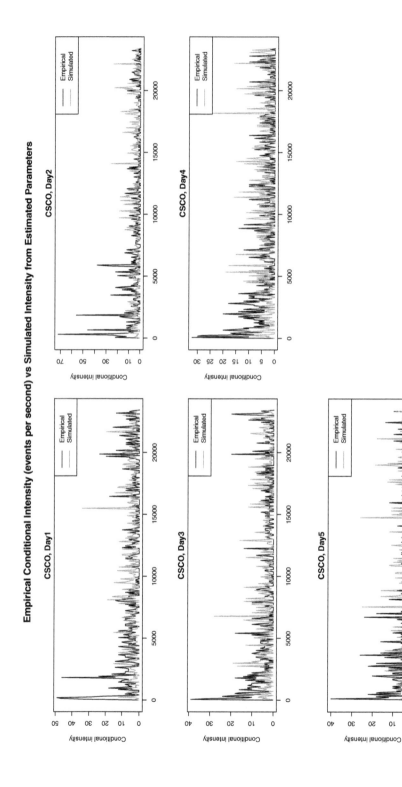

Figure 8.1 Empirical conditional intensity vs. simulated intensity from estimated parameters

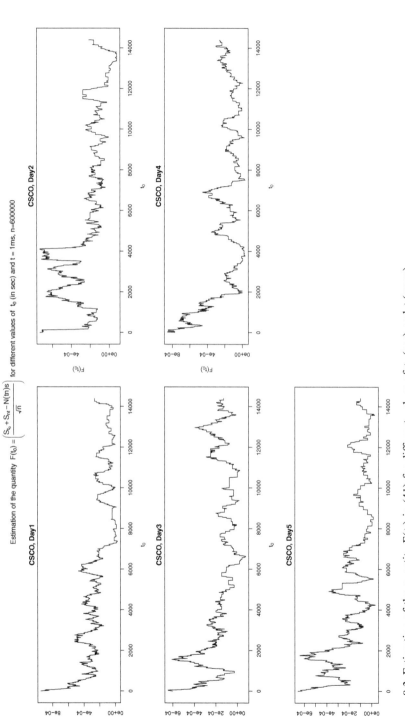

Figure 8.2 Estimation of the quantity $F(t_0)$ in (41) for different values of t_0 (sec) and t (msec)

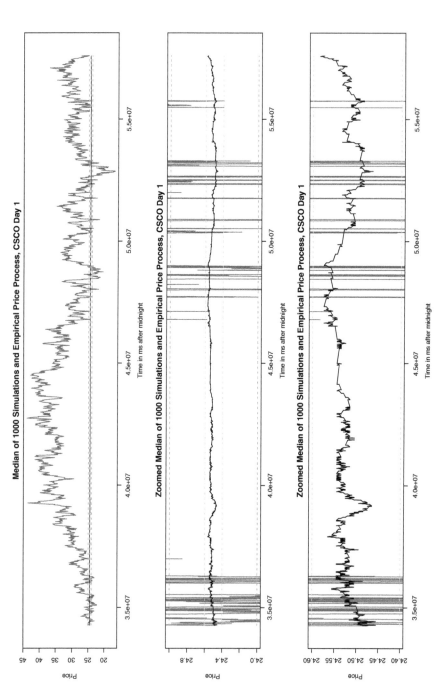

Figure 8.3 Median of 1000 simulations and empirical price process, CISCO, Day 1

the straight fourth line is empirical one, the fifth line from the top is the 1 quantile, and the last line is 1 percentile. See Figure 8.4.

The following graph, see Figure 8.5, is the same as above but the time horizon is 5 minutes (e.g., $nt = 5$ minutes now, n is the same).

The last graph, see Figure 8.6, is the same as above but the time horizon is 60 minutes (e.g., $nt = 60$ minutes now, n is the same).

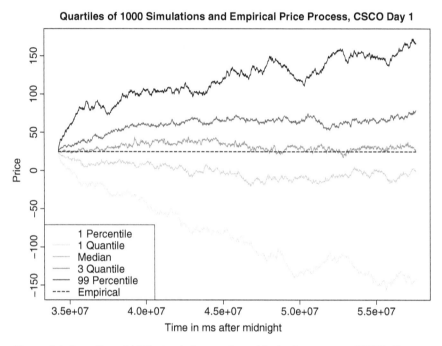

Figure 8.4 Quantiles of 1000 simulations and empirical price process, CISCO, Day 1

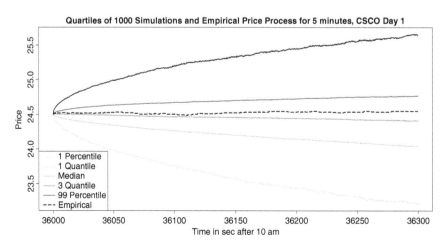

Figure 8.5 Quantiles of 1000 simulations and empirical price process for 5 minutes, CISCO, Day 1

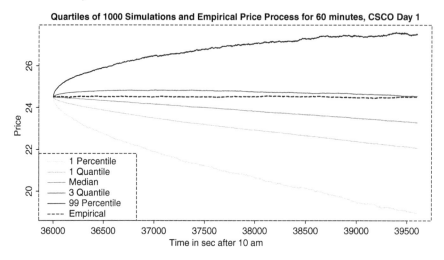

Figure 8.6 Quantiles of 1000 simulations and empirical price process for 60 minutes, CISCO, Day 1

4.4. Remark on regime-switching case (section 3.4)

We present here some ideas of how to implement the regime-switching case from Section 3.4. We take a look at the case of two states for intensity λ. The first state is constructed as the intensity that is above the intensities average, and the second state is constructed as the intensity that is below the intensities average. The transition probabilities matrix P are calculated using the relative frequencies of the intensities, and the stationary probabilities $\to p = (p_1, p_2)$ are calculated from the equation $\to pP = \to p$. Then $\hat{\lambda}$ can be calvculated from formula (32). For example, for the case of 5 days CISCO data we have $\lambda_1 = 0.03238898$, $\lambda_2 = 0.02545533$ and $(p_1, p_2) = (0.2, 0.8)$. In this way, the value for $\hat{\lambda}$ in (32) is $\hat{\lambda} = 0.02688$. As we could see from the data for λ in sec. 4.1 and the latter number, the error does not exceed 0.0055. It means that the errors of estimation for our standard deviations in section 4.2 is almost the same. This is the evidence that in the case of regime-switching CHP the diffusion limit gives a very good approximation as well.

5. Acknowledgemnts

The authors wish to thank IFSID (Institut de la Finance Structurée et des Instruments Dérivés), Montréal, Québec, Canada, for financial support of this project. Robert Elliott also wishes to thank the SSHRC and ARC for continuing support, and the rest of the the authors wish to thank NSERC for continuing support.

Bibliography

Ait-Sahalia, Y., Cacho-Diaz, J. and Laeven, R. (2010). Modelling of financial contagion using mutually exciting jump processes. *Tech. Rep.*, 15850, Nat. Bureau of Ec. Res., USA.

Bacry, E., Delattre, S., Hoffman, M. and Muzy, J.-F. (2013). Some limit theorems for hawkes processes and application to financial statistics. *Stochastic Processes and their Applications*, 123(7), pp. 2475–2499.

Bacry, E., Mastromatteo, I. and Muzy, J.-F. (2015). Hawkes processes in finance. arXiv:1502.04592v2 [q-fin.TR] 17, May.

Bauwens, L. and Hautsch, N. (2009). *Modelling Financial High Frequency Data Using Point Processes*. Springer.

Bowsher, C. (2007). Modelling security market events in continuous time: Intensity based, multivariate point process models. *J. Econometrica*, 141(2), pp. 876–912.

Brémaud, P. and Massoulié, L. (1996). Stability of nonlinear Hawkes processes. *The Annals of Probab.*, 24(3), 1563.

Buffington, J. and Elliott, R. J. (2000). Regime Switching and European Options. Lawrence, K. S. (ed.) *Stochastic Theory and Control*. Proceedings of a Workshop, 73–81. Berlin Heidelberg New York: Springer.

Buffington, J. and Elliott, R. J. (2002). American options with regime switching. *International Journal of Theoretical and Applied Finance*, 5, pp. 497–514.

Cartea, Á., Jaimungal, S. and Penalva, J. (2015). *Algorithmic and High-Frequency Trading*. Cambridge: Cambridge University Press.

Cartea, A., Jaimungal, S. and Ricci, J. (2011). Buy low, sell high: A high-frequency trading prospective. *Tech. Report*.

Cartensen, L. (2010). *Hawkes processes and combinatorial transcriptional regulation*. PhD Thesis, University of Copenhagen.

Casella, G. and Berger, R. (2002). *Statistical Inference*. Duxbury-Thompson Learning Inc.

Chavez-Demoulin, V. and McGill, J. (2012). High-frequency financial data modelling using hawkes processes. *J. Banking and Finance*, 36(12), pp. 3415–3426.

Chávez-Casillas, J. A., Elliott, R. J., Rémillard, B. et al. (2019). *Methodol Comput Appl Probab*. Also available on https://doi.org/10.1007/s11009-019-09715-7.

Chavez-Casillas, J., Elliott, R., Remillard, B. and Swishchuk, A. (2017). A level-1 limit order book with time dependent arrival rates. *Proceed. IWAP*, p. 1-21. Toronto, June-20–25. Also available on arXiv: https://arxiv.org/submit/1869858.

Cohen, S. and Elliott, R. (2014). Filters and smoothness for self-exciting Markov modulated counting process. *IEEE Trans. Aut. Control*.

Cont, R. and de Larrard, A. (2013). A Markovian modelling of limit order books. *SIAM J. Finan. Math.*, 4(1), pp. 1–25.

Cox, D. (1955). Some statistical methods connected with series of events. *J. R. Stat.Soc.*, ser. B, 17(2), pp. 129–164.

Daley, D. J. and Vere-Jones, D. (1988). *An Introduction to the Theory of Point Processes*, 1. Elementary Theory and Methods. Applied Probability Trust. Springer-Verlag, New York.

Dassios, A. and Zhao, H. (2011). A dynamic contagion process. *Advances in Applied Probab.*, 43(3), pp. 814–846.

Embrechts, P., Liniger, T. and Lin, L. (2011). Multivariate hawkes processes: An application to financial data. *J. Appl. Prob.*, 48, A, pp. 367–378.

Errais, E., Giesecke, K. and Goldberg, L. (2010). Affine point processes and portfolio credit risk. *SIAM J. Fin. Math.* 1, pp. 642–665.

Fillimonov, V. and Sornette, D. (2012). Quantifying reflexivity in financial markets: Toward a prediction of flash crashes. *Physical Review E*, 85(5), p. 056108.

Fillimonov, V., Sornette, D., Bichetti, D. and Maystre, N. (2013). Quantifying of the high level of endogeneity and of structural regime shifts in comodity markets, 2013.

Hawkes, A. (1971). Spectra of some self-exciting and mutually exciting point processes. *Biometrica*, 58, pp. 83–90.

Hawkes, A. and Oakes, D. (1974). A cluster process representation of a self-exciting process. *J. Applied Probab.*, 11(3), pp. 493–503.

Korolyuk, V. S. and Swishchuk, A. V. (1995). *Semi-Markov Random Evolutions*. Dordrecht, The Netherlands: Kluwer Academic Publishers.

Laub, P., Taimre, T. and Pollett, P. (2015). Hawkes processes.arXiv: 1507.02822v1[math. PR]10 Jul 2015.

Liniger, T. (2009). *Multivariate hawkes processes*. PhD thesis, Swiss Fed. Inst. Tech., Zurich.

McNeil, A., Frey, R. and Embrechts, P. (2015). *Quantitative Risk Management: Concepts, Techniques and Tools*. Princeton University Press.

Mehdad, B. and Zhu, L. (2014). On the Hawkes process with different exciting functions. *arXiv: 1403.0994*.

Norris, J. R. (1997). *Markov Chains*. In Cambridge Series in Statistical and Probabilistic Mathematics. UK: Cambridge University Press.

Skorokhod, A. (1965). *Studies in the Theory of Random Processes*. Reading, MA: Addison-Wesley (Reprinted by Dover Publications, NY).

Swishchuk, A. (2017). Risk model based on compound Hawkes process. Abstract, IME 2017, Vienna.

Swishchuk, A. and Vadori, N. (2015). Strong law of large numbers and central limit theorems for functionals of inhomogeneous Semi-Markov processes. *Stochastic Analysis and Applications*, 13(2), pp. 213–243.

Swishchuk, A. and Vadori, N. (2017). A semi-Markovian modelling of limit order markets. *SIAM J. Finan. Math.*, 8, pp. 240–273.

Swishchuk, A., Cera, K., Hofmeister, T. and Schmidt, J. (2017). General semi-Markov model for limit order books. *Intern. J. Theoret. Applied Finance*, 20, 1750019.

Vinkovskaya, E. (2014). *A point process model for the dynamics of LOB*. PhD thesis, Columbia University.

Zheng, B., Roueff, F. and Abergel, F. (2014). Ergodicity and scaling limit of a constrained multivariate hawkes process. *SIAM J. Finan. Math.*, 5.

Zhu, L. (2013). Central limit theorem for nonlinear Hawkes processes, *J. Appl. Prob.*, 50(3), pp. 760–771.

Part 3

Financial volatility and covariance modeling

9 Models with multiplicative decomposition of conditional variances and correlations

Cristina Amado, Annastiina Silvennoinen, and Timo Teräsvirta

1. Introduction

Many daily or weekly volatility series appear nonstationary. In the generalized autoregressive conditional heteroskedasticity (GARCH) framework this nonstationarity has been explicitly modeled by integrated GARCH models (Engle and Bollerslev, 1986) or using a more general version, the Fractionally Integrated GARCH model (Baillie, Bollerslev, and Mikkelsen, 1996). Another strand of literature, see for example Lamoureux and Lastrapes (1990) or Mikosch and Stărică (2004), builds on the assumption that nonstationarity is due to structural changes in the volatility process. One way of adjusting the GARCH model to the latter type of nonstationarity is to modify the observations (typically but not exclusively daily returns of financial assets) to fit a weakly stationary GARCH model. This is done by augmenting the GARCH model multiplicatively by a positive-valued component. Van Bellegem and von Sachs (2004) and Feng (2004) are the first examples of this approach.

A GARCH model may be multiplicatively augmented also because of the desire to explain and predict variations in volatility by economic variables. This variant of multiplicative volatility models allows the long-run component to be stochastic, where the random variables governing such component can be stationary or nonstationary. GARCH-MIDAS models, pioneered by Engle, Ghysels, and Sohn (2013), are an example of this. In this review models of both types of multiplicative decomposition are considered. The plan of the review is as follows. The decomposition is described in Section 2. Section 3 concerns models with a deterministic multiplicative component and in Section 4 this component is stochastic. Multivariate generalizations are discussed in Section 5. Section 6 contains final remarks.

2. Multiplicative decomposition of variance

Most univariate or single-equation models to be considered in this article are of the following form

$$y_t - \mu_t = \varepsilon_t = z_t h_t^{1/2} g_t^{1/2} \tag{1}$$

where z_t is iid$(0, 1)$. In this review it is assumed that μ_t is known so that ε_t is observable (y_t is assumed observable). The conditional variance component is assumed to have a GARCH representation (Bollerslev, 1986; Taylor, 1986). Thus, when $g_t \equiv 1$,

$$h_t = \alpha_0 + \sum_{j=1}^{q} \alpha_j \varepsilon_{t-j}^2 + \sum_{j=1}^{p} \beta_j h_{t-j} \tag{2}$$

where $\alpha_0 > 0$, $\alpha_j \geq 0, j = 1, \ldots, q - 1$, $\alpha_q > 0$, $\beta_j \geq 0, j = 1, \ldots, p$. The process is weakly stationary if and only if $\sum_{j=1}^{q} \alpha_j + \sum_{j=1}^{p} \beta_j < 1$.

The positive-valued function g_t is either deterministic or stochastic and represents the slowly moving component of ε_t^2. It follows that $\sigma_t^2 = \mathrm{E}h_t g_t$ is the total time-varying variance of ε_t at time t. The role of h_t is to chacterize clustering of volatility present for instance in asset or index return series of sufficiently high frequency, as already observed by Mandelbrot (1963) and originally parameterized by Engle (1982). When g_t is deterministic and nonconstant, ε_t is nonstationary. One of the important purposes of g_t is to render $\phi_t = \varepsilon_t / g_t^{1/2}$ weakly stationary in situations where the return series appears nonstationary. A standard GARCH model (2) fitted to the data would in that case be inadequate. From (1) it is seen that ϕ_t would then follow a GARCH process. There exist many variants of (2), but in this article the standard GARCH structure with $p = q = 1$ or its asymmetric counterpart, the GJR-GARCH by Glosten, Jagannathan, and Runkle (1993), is mostly sufficient for our purposes. When $p = q = 1$, the subscript will be omitted from α_1, β_1 and κ_1 (the coefficient of the asymmetry term in the GJR-GARCH model).

3. Models with a deterministic long-run component

3.1. Nonparametric deterministic component

One of the first examples of the use of a deterministic component in modeling returns is the time-modulated (tm) process proposed by Van Bellegem and von Sachs (2004) and further discussed in Van Bellegem (2012). The observable return (the conditional mean is abstracted away) equals $\varepsilon_t = \zeta_t g^{1/2}(t/T)$, where $g(t/T)$ is deterministic positive-valued function of rescaled time and T is the number of observations. The error term ζ_t is assumed to be either white noise with zero mean and unit variance, an autoregressive moving average (ARMA) process, or a GARCH process. In the latter case, $\zeta_t = z_t h_t^{1/2}$, where $z_t \sim$ iid$(0,1)$, so that ε_t is defined as in (1) and h_t by (2) with ε_{t-j}^2 replaced by $\varepsilon_{t-j}^2 / g(t/T)$. When $h_t \equiv 1$, the white noise assumption is sufficient for $\mathrm{E}\varepsilon_t \varepsilon_{t-j} = 0$ for $j \neq 0$, which is a property for many financial time series. The lack of a GARCH component is (partly) compensated by the assumption that the error ζ_t in $\varepsilon_t = \zeta_t g^{1/2}(t/T)$ has a leptokurtic density.

As already seen, in the tm-process time is rescaled between zero and one. It may be assumed that $g(t/T)$ is a smooth function of its argument. More specifically, $g(t/T)$ is assumed Lipschitz continuous: $|g(r_1) - g(r_0)| < C|r_1 - r_0|$ for all $0 < r_0, r_1 < 1$. The reason for rescaling time is that $g(t/T)$ is estimated nonparametrically. The observations $\varepsilon_t, t = 1, \ldots, T$, are squared, and the sequence $\{\varepsilon_t^2\}$ is smoothed using kernel estimation. The smoothed values are the estimated values of $g(t/T)$. Using the terminology of Dahlhaus (1997), the tm-variance process is locally stationary if z_t is weakly stationary.

Van Bellegem and von Sachs (2004) also consider the situation in which the process contains breaks but is piecewise Lipschitz continuous. The variance for the continuous segments is estimated by kernel estimation, but finding the break-points then becomes an essential part of the modeling process. To choose the segments or break-points, the authors suggest using two tests for detecting breaks in the unconditional variance based on the cumulative sum of squares. The first one is the post-sample prediction test which depends on knowing the time point where the time series is split. The second one is the CUSUM test which does not require splitting the returns into two subsamples but instead controls changes in the unconditional variance at each time point.

When $\zeta_t = z_t h_t^{1/2}$ (the GARCH case), Van Bellegem and von Sachs (2004) explain that the purpose of the deterministic component is to transform the potentially nonstationary sequence $\{\varepsilon_t\}$ into a weakly stationary one $\{\phi_t\}$ by the normalization $\phi_t = \varepsilon_t / g^{1/2}(t/T)$. They point out that once this has been done, 'standard econometric techniques' can be used to build models for ϕ_t.

Feng (2004) also considers the multiplicative decomposition of variance (1) such that h_t is a weakly stationary GARCH(p,q) process. The deterministic component $g(t/T)$ is assumed at least twice continuously differentiable on [0,1] and the errors are iid$\mathcal{N}(0,1)$. The ensuing model is called the Semiparametric GARCH (SEMIGARCH) model since $g(t/T)$ is estimated nonparametrically as in the tm-model of Van Bellegem and von Sachs. Even here, the observations ε_t are squared, and the estimates of $\hat{g}(t/T)$, $t = 1, \ldots, T$, are obtained as smoothed values of the sequence $\{\varepsilon_t^2\}$ by the Nadaraya-Watson kernel estimator. The GARCH model is fitted into the normalized observations $\hat{\phi}_t = \varepsilon_t / \hat{g}^{1/2}(t/T)$.

Feng (2004) derives the bias and variance of $\hat{g}(t/T)$ (or a transformation of it). Both are functions of the squared bandwidth, and the asymptotic bias is the same as in the nonparametric regression of iid variables. The results also include the asymptotic distribution of $\hat{g}(t/T)$. As expected, the rate of convergence is a function of the bandwidth.

To investigate consequences of two-step estimation, Feng uses the normal log-likelihood for ϕ_t when the model is GARCH(1,1), which he calls approximate because it is conditional on $\hat{g}(t/T)$. Under regularity conditions and denoting the GARCH parameter vector by $\boldsymbol{\theta}$, its maximum likelihood estimator by $\hat{\boldsymbol{\theta}}$ and the true parameter vector by $\boldsymbol{\theta}_0$, the following result emerges:

$$\sqrt{T}(\hat{\boldsymbol{\theta}} - \boldsymbol{\beta}_\theta - \boldsymbol{\theta}_0) \xrightarrow{d} \mathcal{N}(\mathbf{0}, \boldsymbol{\Sigma}_{\theta_0}^{-1})$$

where $\boldsymbol{\beta}_\theta$ is the asymptotic bias and $\boldsymbol{\Sigma}_{\theta_0}$ the expected Hessian evaluated at $\boldsymbol{\theta} = \boldsymbol{\theta}_0$. The bias term is of the order $O(b^2 + (Tb)^{-1})$ and negligible when the bandwidth b in the estimation of $g(t/T)$ is sufficiently small, that is, $O(T^{-1/2}) < b < O(T^{-1/4})$. In that case one can confidently base the statistical inference on the standard asymptotic theory for the weakly stationary GARCH(1,1) model.

Properties of the SEMIGARCH model are studied by simulation. The purpose of the experiments is twofold: study both the choice of bandwidth and the behavior of the GARCH parameter estimates. One of the simulation experiments is highlighted here, the focus being on GARCH parameter estimates. The GARCH component equals

$$h_t = 0.15 + 0.1\varepsilon_{t-1}^2 + 0.75h_{t-1}$$

so the total variance when $g(t/T) = 1$ equals one. The true $g(t/T)$ is a linear combination of a linear trend, a cosine function, and a hyperbolic tangent function which is close to a logistic function. The linear trend means that the amplitude of the clusters in the data increases over time. The other two components add extra movements to these changes.

The average estimated GARCH equation based on 2000 realizations and ignoring $g(t/T)$ becomes

$$\hat{h}_t = 0.0363 + 0.0540\varepsilon_{t-1}^2 + 0.9432\hat{h}_{t-1}$$

which yields the total variance of ε_t equal to 12.96. As can be expected, $\hat{\alpha} + \hat{\beta} = 0.9972$ is very close to one. When ε_t is rescaled and the GARCH model fitted to $\hat{\phi}_t$, the equation has the following average form

$$\hat{h}_t = 0.2052 + 0.0937\hat{\phi}_{t-1}^2 + 0.6965\hat{h}_{t-1}.$$

The coefficient of h_{t-1} is slightly underestimated while the average estimate of the total variance of ϕ_t equals 0.978, which is not far off the mark. It seems that rescaling is very important and that it works quite well. It is expected to do so even when there are several amplitude changes in the data at irregular intervals.

There are two empirical examples in Feng (2004). The SEMIGARCH model is fitted to daily returns of the New York S&P 500 index and to the Frankfurt DAX 100 index for the period from 3 January 1994 to 23 August 2000. It may be mentioned that the aforementioned simulation experiment was fashioned after the observed behavior of DAX 100. For S&P 500 returns, the estimated GARCH(1,1) model is

$$\hat{h}_t = 5.684 \times 10^{-7} + 0.0674\varepsilon_{t-1}^2 + 0.9302\hat{h}_{t-1} \tag{3}$$

so $\hat{\alpha} + \hat{\beta} = 0.9976$, and the estimated total variance equals 2.4×10^{-4}, which is unrealistically low. The SEMIGARCH model yields

$$\hat{h}_t = 0.0649 + 0.0686\hat{\phi}_{t-1}^2 + 0.8676\hat{h}_{t-1}. \tag{4}$$

In (4), $\hat{\alpha} + \hat{\beta} = 0.9362$ and the total variance estimate is 1.018. In comparing (3) and (4) it is seen that $\hat{\beta}$ decreases, whereas $\hat{\alpha}$ does not change much. This is in fact typical for many applications in which rescaling is employed. The weight of the lagged conditional variance in the GARCH model diminishes when the scale change is properly modeled. This is important in forecasting, because the decay rate of the conditional variance in the GARCH(1,1) model equals $\alpha + \beta$. A rate close to one leads to forecasts in which volatility remains too high for too long when the starting-value, the most recent estimated conditional variance, is high. Results for DAX 100 are quite similar to the ones for S&P500: $\hat{\alpha} + \hat{\beta} = 0.9849$ for GARCH corresponds to 0.9354 for SEMIGARCH. For details, see Feng (2004).

Zhang, Feng and Peitz (2017) suggest estimating the scale function from $|\varepsilon_t|^\lambda$ instead of ε_t^2. This is motivated by moment requirements on financial return series in choosing the bandwidth. The relationship between the resulting scale function $g_\lambda(t/T)$ and the one based on smoothing ε_t^2 is demonstrated. The resulting model is called the Box-Cox SEMIGARCH model. It may be mentioned that in the paper the rescaled observations are modeled using several GARCH models, including the Exponential GARCH model by Nelson (1991). The application is to daily S&P 500 and DAX index returns.

When high-frequency (intradaily) returns r_t are being modeled, one also has to consider diurnal variation patterns due to investors' average behavior over the day. Feng and McNeil (2008) extend SEMIGARCH to this situation. The decomposition (1) is augmented by a periodic component $s_{k(t)}$, $k = 1, \ldots, K$, where K is the length of the period. For instance, if ε_t is a five-minute return, K is the number of five-minute returns included in the 'day', a subset of the time the exchange is open for trading. The periodic SEMIGARCH has the form

$$r_t = z_t V_0^{1/2} h_t^{1/2} g^{1/2}(t/T) s_{k(t)} \tag{5}$$

where $t = 1, \ldots, T$, $z_t \sim \text{iid}\mathcal{N}(0,1)$, $V_0^{1/2} > 0$, $(1/K)\sum_{k=1}^K s_k = 1$, and $\int_0^1 g(u)du = 1$. The positive constant V_0 is a consequence of variance targeting: $\mathsf{E}h_t = 1$ because the intercept is defined as

$$\alpha_0 = 1 - \sum_{j=1}^q \alpha_j - \sum_{j=1}^p \beta_j \tag{6}$$

in (2). Rescaling leads to $\phi_t = r_t/(V_0^{1/2} g^{1/2}(t/T) s_{k(t)})$ such that ϕ_t has a weakly stationary GARCH representation with $\mathsf{E}\{\phi_t^2 | \mathcal{F}_{t-1}\} = 1$, where $\mathcal{F}_{t-1}$ contains the conditioning information. Feng and McNeil (2008) discuss nonparametric estimation and asymptotic properties of the estimators. The authors also suggest a test of the null hypothesis $g(t/T) = 1$, whose empirical null distribution is obtained by simulation. The model is fitted to 20-minute returns of four German stocks from 28 November 1997 to 30 December 1999.

Recently, another representation for modeling deterministic periodicity of electricity prices has been proposed by Escribano and Sucarrat (2018) using the log-GARCH class of models. In their representation, volatility is multiplicatively decomposed into a nonstationary component that captures periodicity effects and a stationary component specified by a log-GARCH dynamics. In its simplest form, the nonstationary function is a linear function of time dummy variables to capture the calendar effects. However, the authors do not restrict the nonstationary function to be of this type as it can assume any parametric or nonparametric form.

3.2. Deterministic splines

Engle and Rangel (2008) introduce another multiplicative decomposition which is based on exponential quadratic splines. The aim of the authors is to examine links between return volatility and macroeconomics. To do this they develop the spline-GARCH model 'to allow the high frequency financial data to be linked with the low-frequency macro data.' In this review these links are not considered, and the focus is instead on the model. The scaling function of the spline-GARCH model is defined as

$$g_t = c \exp \left[w_0 t + \sum_{i=1}^{k} w_i (t - t_i)^2 I(t - t_i > 0) + \gamma x_t \right] \qquad (7)$$

where $I(A)$ is the indicator variable, defined as $I(A) = 1$ when A is true, and zero otherwise, and x_t is a weakly exogenous random variable. The exponential form (7) is used to make sure that $g_t > 0$ for all t. Here the decomposition is classified as nonparametric because g_t is a spline function, but g_t also contains the parameter vector $\mathbf{w} = (c, w_0, w_1, \ldots, w_k, \gamma)'$. To facilitate estimation, the knots are assumed equidistant, and their number in the spline function, k, is determined by the data. This is done by estimating the spline-GARCH model with 1, 2, ..., K splines and choosing the final model as the one for which $k \in \{1, \ldots, K\}$ minimizes BIC of Rissanen (1978) and Schwarz (1978). Selecting another model selection criterion such as AIC (Akaike, 1974) which is more generous than BIC in selecting knots may sometimes lead to a substantially larger number of them, see, for example, Amado, Silvennoinen, and Teräsvirta (2017).

Using model selection criteria may cause identification problems. Let the true $k = k_0$, but suppose that the largest k to be considered exceeds k_0. When this is the case, the search leads to estimating unidentified models. Also, since variance forecasts from rescaled GARCH models depend on the end-point of the deterministic component (and also on how this component is extrapolated), the choice of the model selection criterion may have a large effect on forecasts. Furthermore, the larger the number of knots and splines, the smaller the sum $\hat{\alpha} + \hat{\beta}$ in the GARCH(1,1) equation. This has an effect on persistence of a shock, which in turn affects forecasts for several periods ahead.

Unlike the SEMIGARCH model, there is no asymptotic theory available for the maximum likelihood or other estimators of the parameters of the spline-GARCH model. Obviously, the reported standard deviation estimates are based on the assumption that the estimators are consistent and asymptotically normal. Engle and Rangel (2008) fit the spline-GARCH model to daily return series for 48 stock indexes from stock exchanges around the world. Variance targeting is used in estimation of spline-GARCH models, which means setting $\alpha_0 = 1 - \alpha - \beta$ in (2). The same appears not to be true for the estimated GARCH models because in some cases $\hat{\alpha} + \hat{\beta} > 1$. The spline-GARCH results show the same pattern as in the SEMIGARCH applications. First, the sum $\hat{\alpha} + \hat{\beta}$ from the spline-GARCH model is generally clearly lower than what is obtained with the GARCH model. Second, the estimate $\hat{\beta}$ decreases, sometimes quite strongly, when one moves from GARCH to spline-GARCH, whereas changes in $\hat{\alpha}$ remain relatively minor. The number of knots varies from one to 15. The extreme case is Russia with 14 knots, one knot for only 167 observations. The estimated models for this dataset do not contain macroeconomic or other weakly exogenous variables, i.e., $\gamma = 0$ in (7).

Brownlees and Gallo (2010) define g_t with a different spline function. They consider the Multiplicative Error Model (MEM) that is similar to GARCH but used for realized variances (a daily realized variance is denoted as RV_t; there are several definitions for it), but this function can also be used for GARCH specifications. A first-order MEM has the following form:

$$h_t = \alpha_0 + \alpha_1 RV_{t-1} + \beta_1 h_{t-1} \tag{8}$$

where $RV_{t-1} > 0$. Brownlees and Gallo (2010) include an asymmetry term as in the GJR-GARCH model, but for notational simplicity this extension is omitted here. The spline function is a modification of the so-called *B*-spline. In the exponential case

$$g_t = c \exp\left\{ \sum_{i=1}^{k} w_i B_i(t) \right\} \tag{9}$$

where $B_i(t)$ consists of pieces of polynomials. If $B_i(t)$ is of order q, it means that it consists of $q + 1$ polynomial pieces of degree q that join at inner knots. The total number of knots spanning $B_i(t)$ equals $q + 2$, and outside the outer knots the spline equals zero. The sum $\sum_{i=1}^{k} w_i B_i(t)$ is a *B*-spline. For more properties and information, see Eilers and Marx (1996). One of the advantages of *B*-splines is that they are easy to compute.

In practice, B-splines may not be used as such. An approach recommended by Eilers and Marx (1996) and followed by Brownlees and Gallo (2010) is to first select a large number of (equidistant) knots and reduce the dimension of the problem imposing a roughness penalty (Good and Gaskins, 1971) on the log-likelihood. There are many ways of doing that, one of them being to assume the penalty to be a function of the jth differences of the adjacent spline coefficients w_i. If the log-likelihood for T observations is denoted as $L_T(\boldsymbol{\theta})$ where $\boldsymbol{\theta} \in \Theta$ contains the parameters in (8) and (9), their estimates are obtained as

$$\hat{\boldsymbol{\theta}} = \arg \max_{\boldsymbol{\theta} \in \Theta} \left\{ L_T(\boldsymbol{\theta}) - \frac{\lambda}{2} \sum_{i=j+1}^{k} (\Delta^j w_i)^2 \right\}. \tag{10}$$

The resulting splines are called penalized B-splines, or P-splines for short. Useful properties of P-splines are listed in Eilers and Marx (1996). The idea is that while a B-spline with a large number of knots is not very smooth, the penalty of type (10) smooths the spline. Brownlees and Gallo (2010) point out, among other things, that quadratic splines have poor numerical properties compared to P-splines and that choosing the knots using a model selection criterion is not an appealing procedure. As already suggested, it may lead to numerical difficulties if a quadratic spline with 'too many' knots is estimated. But then λ, the size of the penalty in the P-spline, is determined by a model selection criterion. Eilers and Marx (1996) prefer AIC; note, however, the way they define the penalty.

The purpose of Brownlees and Gallo (2010) is to forecast the Value at Risk, and they are also interested in the performance of various estimators of realized variance. Since the main interest in this review lies in how well rescaling handles nonstationarity in the original return or realized variance series, their empirical results are bypassed here.

3.3. Flexible Fourier Form

Parameterizing the scaling function using the Flexible Fourier Form (FFF) by Gallant (1981, 1984) constitutes an alternative to splines. Mazur and Pipień (2012) introduce a model consisting of (1) and (2) in which ε_t is replaced by $\phi_t = \varepsilon_t / g^{1/2}(t/T)$ such that

$$g(t/T) = \exp \left\{ \sum_{i=1}^{k} \{ w_i^c \cos \left(\frac{2\pi i}{T} t \right) + w_i^s \sin \left(\frac{2\pi i}{T} t \right) \} \right\} \tag{11}$$

where w_i^c and w_i^s are parameters, k is in practice small and the terms in the exponent of $g(t/T)$ are the lowest frequencies of the Fourier decomposition of the unknown scaling function. This model is called an almost periodically correlated (APC-)GARCH model. The inference is Bayesian, and the authors consider both normal and t-distributed errors for z_t. The application is to the daily returns of the S&P500 returns from 18 January 1950 to 7 February 2012. First-order APC-GARCH models with $k = 0, 1, 2, 3, 4$ are fitted to the data. The results show that standard GARCH ($k = 0$) fits clearly less well than the APC-GARCH models, and this outcome does not depend on the error process. Interestingly, but not unexpectedly, when the error is assumed normal estimated posterior probabilities are largest for models with $k \geq 2$, whereas $k = 1$ or 2 is favored for models with t-distributed errors. This shows how an error distribution with thicker tails than the standard normal is able to absorb some of the movements in the series.

A look at the GARCH coefficients shows that the sum $\hat{\alpha} + \hat{\beta}$ or the corresponding sum for the GJR-GARCH model hardly changes when one moves from GARCH to APC-GARCH. This is different from both SEMIGARCH and spline-GARCH and somewhat surprising as the purpose of rescaling is to handle long-run movements so that the GARCH coefficients would only reflect short-run movements (volatility clustering) in the data. The joint prior distribution for the GARCH parameters α and β is uniform $[0, 1]^2$, which means that nonstationarity is not excluded even under scaling.

Multiplicative decomposition with FFF as the scaling function is also used in modeling realized variance. The purpose of the deterministic component is to describe the diurnal variation in high-frequency returns as in Feng and McNeil (2008). Andersen and Bollerslev (1998) apply this idea as follows. Let $R_{t,n}$ be an intradaily, in their case a 5-minute, return and $\mathsf{E}R_{t,n}$ the expected return, and set $r_{t,n} = R_{t,n} - \bar{R}$, where $\mathsf{E}R_{t,n}$ is approximated by the sample mean $\bar{R}$. The decomposition is

$$r_{t,n} = z_{t,n} h_{t,n}^{1/2} g_{t,n}^{1/2} \tag{12}$$

where $z_{t,n} \sim \mathrm{iid}(0, 1)$, $h_{t,n}$ has a GARCH or stochastic volatility structure, and $g_{t,n}$ represents diurnal variation and intradaily announcement ('news') effects. This is different from the approach of Feng and McNeil (2008) as the focus is solely on the periodic variation. The authors square (12) and take logarithms, so

$$x_{t,n} = \ln r_{t,n}^2 - \ln h_{t,n} = \mathsf{E} \ln z_{t,n}^2 + \ln g_{t,n} + u_{t,n}$$

where the iid error term $u_{t,n} = \ln z_{t,n}^2 - \mathsf{E} \ln z_{t,n}^2$. This is made operational by estimating $h_{t,n}$ from the data and assuming that while $\ln g_{t,n}$ is stochastic and mean-stationary, $\mathsf{E} \ln g_{t,n}$ has an FFF augmented by M news dummies $I_m(t, n)$:

$$\mathsf{E} \ln g_{t,n} = c_0 + \sum_{m=1}^{M} \lambda_m I_m(t, n) + \sum_{i=1}^{k} \left\{ w_i^c \cos\left(\frac{2\pi i}{N} n\right) + w_i^s \sin\left(\frac{2\pi i}{N} n\right) \right\} \tag{13}$$

where N is the number of intervals within a day. Apart from the news dummies, (11) is similar to (13).

Assume now that $\hat{h}_{t,n}$ is an appropriate estimator of $h_{t,n}$ and write

$$x_{t,n} = \ln r_{t,n}^2 - \ln \hat{h}_{t,n} = \hat{c} + \mathsf{E}\ln g_{t,n} + u_{t,n}^* \tag{14}$$

where $\hat{c}$ is an intercept and $u_{t,n}^*$ a stationary error ($u_{t,n}$ is iid). The model is fitted to 5-minute Deutsche mark–US dollar logarithmic bid-ask spot price quotes from 1 October 1992 to 29 September 1993. For details of (14) and empirical results, see Andersen and Bollerslev (1998).

It may be mentioned that multiplicative decomposition is also used in modeling diurnal variation in duration series when the idea is to model the dynamic behavior of the length of the interval between adjacent trades (duration). Since in this review is about volatility models and modeling, multiplicative decomposition of durations in models of autoregressive conditional duration, see Engle and Russell (1998), is not discussed here.

3.4. Parametric deterministic component

The models in which g_t is defined using splines or FFF already contain parameters, although they are in this review classified as nonparametric ones. In this section the focus is on models in which the decomposition is as in (1) but time is rescaled, and the smooth long-run component $g_t = g(t/T)$ is now fully parametric. The basic model of this kind is called the Multiplicative Time-Varying GARCH (MTV-GARCH) model. It is introduced in Amado and Teräsvirta (2008); see also Amado and Teräsvirta (2013, 2017). The purpose of the MTV-GARCH model is the same as before: jointly describe the short- and long-run movements in nonstationary return series. In (1), $\{z_t\} \sim$ iid$(0, 1)$ with $\mathsf{E}z_t^3 = 0$ and $\mathsf{E}|z_t^2|^{2+\phi} < \infty$, $\phi > 0$. The conditional variance component is a GARCH process, although the GJR-GARCH is also used, in particular when modeling stock returns and indexes. The positive-valued long-run component $g_t = g(t/T)$ is defined as follows:

$$g(t/T) = 1 + \sum_{l=1}^{r} \delta_l G_l(t/T; \gamma_l, \mathbf{c}_l) \tag{15}$$

where δ_l, $l = 1, \ldots, r$, are parameters and $G_l(t/T; \gamma_l, \mathbf{c}_l)$ is the generalized logistic transition function:

$$G_l(t/T; \gamma_l, \mathbf{c}_l) = \left(1 + \exp\left\{-\gamma_l \prod_{j=1}^{k_l}(t/T - c_{lj})\right\}\right)^{-1} \tag{16}$$

with $\gamma_l > 0$ and $c_{l1} \leq c_{l2} \leq \ldots \leq c_{lk_l}$. Positivity imposes restrictions on δ_l, $l = 1, \ldots, r$. The intercept in (15) is set to equal one for identification reasons: the multiplicative decomposition can only have one free intercept. When variance targeting is not used, the intercept in (15) has to be fixed to a known positive value. In parameter estimation some choices are for numerical reasons better than some others. Alternatively, one can use variance targeting, see (6), and have a free intercept in (15).

When $k = 1$, (16) is a monotonic function of rescaled time, whereas it is non-monotonic and symmetric around $(c_{l1} + c_{l2})/2$. When $k = 1$, the parameter γ_l controls the slope of the transition function, i.e., the speed of the transition. When $k = 1$ and $\gamma_l \to \infty$, (16) becomes a step function. Breaks in returns may not be straightforward to characterize by splines or FFF but are not difficult to model in the MTV-GARCH framework. In applications, almost invariably $k = 1$ or $k = 2$. Depending on the number of transitions, $g(t/T)$ can be a very flexible function of its argument.

In model specification there are issues similar to choosing the number of knots in spline-GARCH. If the number of transitions in (15) is too large, $g(t/T)$ is not identified. In order to avoid estimating unidentified models, r is determined by sequential testing. Constancy of (15) is tested first. If it is rejected, the TV-GARCH model is estimated and tested against a model with two transitions. Testing and estimation continues until the first non-rejection. The identification problem is circumvented by approximating the alternative model following Luukkonen, Saikkonen and Teräsvirta (1988). Details of the specification technique can be found in Amado and Teräsvirta (2017) and Amado et al. (2017).

In the SEMIGARCH model, the length of the series does not seem to affect modeling in any way. This is not quite the case in the MTV-GARCH framework. If the time series under consideration is very long and the number of transitions potentially large, the specification strategy outlined in Amado and Teräsvirta (2017) cannot be expected to work well. The solution is to split the series into subseries and identify the transitions in them before parameters of the model for the whole series are estimated. See Amado and Teräsvirta (2014b) and Amado et al. (2017) for examples of how this can be successfully done.

Maximum likelihood estimates of the parameters are obtained by dividing the maximization problem into two parts; see Song, Fan, and Kalbfleisch (2005). Amado and Teräsvirta (2013) show that under regularity conditions and using the results in Song et al. (2005), maximum likelihood estimators of the parameters of the MTV-GARCH (or MTV-GJR-GARCH) model are consistent and asymptotically normal. After the model has been estimated, its adequacy is examined using misspecification tests; see Amado and Teräsvirta (2017).

The MTV-GARCH model or its GJR version has been applied to several daily stock and stock index returns, exchange rate returns and commodity price returns. As an example, Amado and Teräsvirta (2017) describe the US dollar/Singapore dollar exchange rate returns using the model. The well-specified model has one transition with $k = 2$ in (16). The standard GARCH(1,1) model fitted to the series has the following form:

$$\hat{h}_t = \underset{(0.001)}{0.001} + \underset{(0.016)}{0.056}\,\varepsilon_{t-1}^2 + \underset{(0.019)}{0.938}\,\hat{h}_{t-1}$$

so $\hat{\alpha} + \hat{\beta} = 0.994$. The figures in parentheses are estimated standard errors. The corresponding component from the MTV-GARCH model is

$$\hat{h}_t = \underset{(0.005)}{0.011} + \underset{(0.020)}{0.065}\,\hat{\phi}_{t-1}^2 + \underset{(0.042)}{0.868}\,\hat{h}_{t-1}$$

where $\hat{\alpha} + \hat{\beta} = 0.933$. As expected from Feng (2004), $\hat{\beta}$ has changed much more than $\hat{\alpha}$. The total variance estimates are 0.167 for GARCH and 0.164 for MTV-GARCH.

The MTV-GARCH model may be modified by assuming that the argument of $g(\cdot)$ is a random variable. This is discussed in Section 4.1. Other models with a random long-run component are considered in Section 4.

4. Stochastic multiplicative decomposition

4.1. Nonparametric stochastic component

As discussed in Section 3.1, Feng (2004) constructs a semiparametric GARCH model with a deterministic nonparametric long-run component. He shows how this helps remove the 'IGARCH effect', that is, $\hat{\alpha} + \hat{\beta} \approx 1$, often found in the applications of the first-order GARCH. Han and Kristensen (2017) develop another semiparametric GARCH model which they call Semiparametric Multiplicative GARCH-X, or SEMIX for short. It differs from the SEMI-GARCH model in that in SEMIX the long-run component is stochastic. The stated goal of the authors is the same as that of Feng (2004): to develop a model in which the long-run component alleviates the IGARCH effect. The decomposition employed by Han and Kristensen (2017) can be written as $\varepsilon_t = z_t h_t^{1/2} g^{1/2}(x_{t-1})$, where the random variable x_t is quite persistent and strongly exogenous. It is defined as

$$x_t = \left(1 - \frac{c}{T}\right)x_{t-1} + v_t \tag{17}$$

where $c \geq 0$. The error term v_t has mean zero and is independent of the GARCH error term z_t.

Under the assumption that $\{v_t\}$ is an iid sequence and some moment conditions it is found that the autocorrelation function of ε_t^2 of the SEMIX model converges to a positive random variable. In other words, the autocorrelation function then displays the 'long memory property' in that the decay of the autocorrelations as a function of the lag is slower than exponential. Interestingly, Mikosch and Stărică (2004) have shown that if there is a break in the unconditional variance of the GARCH model, ignoring it when computing the autocorrelations of ε_t^2 the sequence of autocorrelations also converges to a positive value when the lag length approaches infinity. A break can be viewed as a nonsmooth version of change in the long-run component.

The asymptotic theory becomes nonstandard when x_t is nonstationary as in (17). For details, some of them still open at this moment, the reader is referred to Han and Kristensen (2017). For the case where x_t is weakly stationary, the limiting distribution of the (quasi) maximum likelihood estimator of the GARCH parameter vector is shown to be mixed normal.

Han and Kristensen (2017) fit the SEMIX model to three European daily index return series. The observation period stretches from 2 January 2004 to 30 December 2013. The indexes are FTSE (London), CAC (Paris) and DAX (Frankfurt). The random variable is the Chicago Board Options Exchange volatility index VIX. It represents implied volatility calculated from the options of the S&P 500 index. Given that the US stock market is likely to influence European markets, VIX may be used as the random variable for SEMIX. Furthermore, the index is close to being nonstationary and its dynamic behavior agrees with the definition (17). The GARCH model of the authors is GJR-GARCH(1,1), and in all three cases the sum $\hat{\alpha} + \hat{\kappa}/2 + \hat{\beta}$ is slightly below but very close to one. The corresponding sums for GJR-SEMIX are 0.931 (FTSE), 0.937 (CAC) and 0.947 (DAX), so the model works as intended. These results are quite similar to those of Feng (2004) who applies his SEMIGARCH model to S&P 500 and DAX returns, as discussed Section 3.1.

Han and Kristensen (2017) also consider the case where $g(\mathbf{x}'_{t-1}\boldsymbol{\delta})$, that is, the argument of $g(\cdot)$ is a linear combination of more than one random variable. In addition, $\|\boldsymbol{\delta}\| = 1$, which makes it possible to compare coefficient estimates with each other. A GJR-SEMIX model with three variables, VIX, the country's industrial production index, and the price of crude oil is fitted to the three return series. The industrial production index is interpolated from a monthly to the daily level. The results show that VIX dominates the linear combination, and the oil price appears to be the least important variable as it always has the smallest coefficient estimate.

4.2. Time-varying ambiguity GARCH

Amado and Laakkonen (2013) introduce another model with a stochastic decomposition called the Time-Varying Ambiguity (TVA-)GARCH model. The word 'ambiguity' derives from Knight (1921) and is motivated by the application. In the financial literature, ambiguity or Knightian uncertainty refers to uncertainty with unknown probabilities; for a detailed explanation see Amado and Laakkonen (2013). The decomposition is the same as in Han and Kristensen (2017), but the model is a stochastic variant of the TV-GARCH model studied in Section 3.4. It is obtained simply by replacing t/T in (15) and (16) by an exogenous random variable x_{t-1}. The authors discuss the modeling strategy consisting of specification, estimation and evaluation of the TVA model. At the specification stage GARCH is tested against TVA-GARCH. Performing the test described in the paper requires x_t to be weakly stationary and possess a sufficient amount of higher moments. As is the case with the TV-GARCH model, maximum likelihood estimation of parameters in TVA is carried out by estimating the parameters jointly but splitting each iteration into two parts. Note, however, that the asymptotic theory for maximum likelihood estimators derived for TV-GARCH has not yet been extended to TVA-GARCH. The estimated model is evaluated by misspecification tests.

The TVA model is applied to three daily bond return series. The bonds are US, German and French 10-year bonds, and the time series cover the period from 3 January 2000 to 30 December 2011. VIX and some of its transformations ($\Delta VIX_t, \Delta|VIX_t|$ and $(\Delta VIX_t)^2$) are used as the stochastic variable in the model. The null hypothesis of GARCH is rejected for all transformations, and the strongest rejections (the p-values being really minimal) are obtained for the last two of them. The TVA model with $x_t = \Delta|VIX_t|$ is fitted to the three series. The estimated transition functions of type (16) are quite smooth, so the effect of the transformed VIX on volatility is gradual. Compared to Han and Kristensen (2017), an interesting observation is that the sum of the GARCH parameters remains very close to one even after accounting for the effect of VIX. A possible reason for this is there may be other factors which influence the conditional variance and which Amado and Laakkonen (2013) have not been able to consider because their model only allows a single stochastic variable in $g(x_{t-1})$.

4.3. Stochastic splines

Audrino and Bühlmann (2009) consider a model with stochastic B-splines. In fact, their model can be more general than a GARCH model, but the version discussed in the paper has the GARCH(1,1) model as the starting-point of iterations. The general task is to fit a nonparametric model of conditional heteroskedasticity to the data. The authors also include a conditional mean in their model, but for simplicity it is ignored here. This means that ε_t is observable, has mean zero, and $\varepsilon_t = z_t \sigma_t$, where $z_t \sim \text{iid}\mathcal{N}(0, 1)$. The conditional variance σ_t^2 has the following form:

$$\sigma_t^2 = \mathsf{E}\{\varepsilon_t^2|\mathcal{F}_{t-1}\} = f(\varepsilon_{t-1}^2, \sigma_{t-1}^2)$$

where the unknown $f(\varepsilon_{t-1}^2, \sigma_{t-1}^2)$ can be quite general and does not have to be smooth. To indicate that σ_t^2 contains parameters, denote $\sigma_t^2 = \sigma_t^2(\boldsymbol{\theta})$. The model equals

$$\ln \sigma_t^2(\boldsymbol{\theta}) = \ln f(\varepsilon_{t-1}^2, \sigma_{t-1}^2) = u_0(\varepsilon_{t-1}^2, \sigma_{t-1}^2)$$
$$+ \sum_{k_1=1}^{K_1}\sum_{k_2=1}^{K_2}\beta_{k_1,k_2} B_{k_1,k_2}(\varepsilon_{t-1}^2, \sigma_{t-1}^2) \tag{18}$$

where $B_{k_1,k_2}(\varepsilon_{t-1}^2, \sigma_{t-1}^2)$ is a two-dimensional B-spline, and β_{k_1,k_2} its weight. The spline function $B_{k_1,k_2}(\varepsilon_{t-1}^2, \sigma_{t-1}^2)$ is defined as follows:

$$B_{k_1,k_2}(\varepsilon_{t-1}^2, \sigma_{t-1}^2) = \sum_{k_1=1}^{K_1} \sum_{k_2=1}^{K_2} B_{k_1}(\varepsilon_{t-1}^2) B_{k_2}(\sigma_{t-1}^2). \tag{19}$$

Furthermore,

$$u_0(\varepsilon_{t-1}^2, \sigma_{t-1}^2) = \ln(\alpha_0 + \alpha\varepsilon_{t-1}^2 + \beta h_{t-1}) = \ln h_t \tag{20}$$

that is, the logarithm of the (weakly stationary) GARCH(1,1) process, and $\theta = (\alpha_0, \alpha, \beta, \beta_{k_1,k_2}, k_1 = 1, \ldots, K_1; k_2 = 1, \ldots, K_2)'$. It is assumed that the polynomials in $B_{k_1}(\varepsilon_{t-1}^2)$ are quadratic, and in $B_{k_2}(\sigma_{t-1}^2)$ they are linear. For illustration, graphs of B-splines of these dimensions can be found in Eilers and Marx (1996, p. 91). Before taking logarithms, (18) is a multiplicative decomposition (1) with h_t defined in (20) and the positive-valued g_t equalling

$$g_t = \exp\left\{ \sum_{k_1=1}^{K_1} \sum_{k_2=1}^{K_2} \beta_{k_1,k_2} B_{k_1,k_2}(\varepsilon_{t-1}^2, \sigma_{t-1}^2) \right\}.$$

The knots in (19) are determined as quantiles of the arguments ε_{t-1}^2 and σ_{t-1}^2.

The final model is obtained by iteratively updating (18). After the mth iteration,

$$u_{mt}(\varepsilon_{t-1}^2, \sigma_{t-1}^2) = u_{m,t-1}(\varepsilon_{t-1}^2, \sigma_{t-1}^2) + \beta_m B_m(\varepsilon_{t-1}^2, \exp\{u_{m,t-1}(\varepsilon_{t-1}^2, \sigma_{t-1}^2)\})$$

where β_m is a scalar weight function (note the change of notation from (k_1, k_2) to m), and $B_m(\varepsilon_{t-1}^2, \exp\{u_{m,t-1}(\varepsilon_{t-1}^2, \sigma_{t-1}^2)\})$ is the spline determined for this iteration. For space reasons is not possible to describe details of how the spline is constructed and the weight β_m obtained. They can be found in the paper. Assuming the estimation is terminated after M iterations, the final model can be expressed as a function of the starting-value as follows:

$$u_{Mt}(\varepsilon_{t-1}^2, \sigma_{t-1}^2) = u_0(\varepsilon_{t-1}^2, \sigma_{t-1}^2) + \sum_{m=1}^{M} \beta_m B_m(\varepsilon_{t-1}^2, \exp\{u_{m-1,t-1}(\varepsilon_{t-1}^2, \sigma_{t-1}^2)\}).$$

The stopping rule is determined by out-of-sample considerations. The time series is divided into two parts. The first 70% of observations are used to estimate the model and the remaining 30% are for determining M. The fit of the estimated model in the out-of-sample part determines M. In the multiplicative form (1), the final model has h_t defined as GARCH(1,1), and

$$g_t = \exp\left\{\sum_{m=1}^{M} \beta_m B_m(\varepsilon_{t-1}^2, \exp\{u_{m-1,t-1}(\varepsilon_{t-1}^2, \sigma_{t-1}^2)\})\right\}.$$

Audrino and Bühlmann (2009) remark that in practice it would be desirable to shrink β_m towards zero for every iteration. This would mean using $\beta_m(\kappa) = \kappa\beta_m$, $0 < \kappa < 1$, instead of β_m. The authors report that $0.1 < \kappa < 0.2$ works well in practice.

The paper contains two empirical examples. The first series is the daily annualized log-return series of the S&P 500 index and the second is the similarly defined returns of the 30-year US Treasury bill. Both series run from January 1990 to October 2003, 3,376 observations in total. The first 2,212 observations are used for estimation and the remaining 1,164 for out-of-sample forecasting. The performance of the spline-GARCH model is compared with that of GARCH(1,1) and an earlier nonparametric model the authors have developed (Audrino and Bühlmann, 2003). In order to make comparisons possible, the true volatility is proxied by realized volatility. The results indicate that the spline-GARCH model performs better in terms of the mean square errors and mean absolute deviations both in-sample and out of sample than its two competitors. The Diebold and Mariano (1995) test shows that many but not all of the out-of-sample improvements are significant at the 0.1 level.

4.4. GARCH-MIDAS

The SEMIX model in Section 4.1 and the TVA-GARCH model in Section 4.2 are designed to allow random variables in the long-run component of the model. Engle et al. (2013) introduce another way of incorporating macroeconomic variables into GARCH equations. Their aim is to find out how well these variables explain stock market volatility. The model they develop can be seen as another variant of multiplicative decomposition such that the 'long-run component' is stochastic. To emphasize the different time scales (after abstracting away the conditional mean) the decomposition of the return ε_t is written, analogously to (1), as $\varepsilon_{i,t} = z_{i,t} h_{i,t}^{1/2} g_t^{1/2}$. Now i is the short scale (for example, $\varepsilon_{i,t}$ is a daily return), and t is the long or aggregated scale (the unit is one month or one quarter). The short-run component $h_{i,t}$ is measured in days, whereas the long-run g_t is available on a monthly or maybe a quarterly basis. The short-run component (conditional variance) is defined as before:

$$h_{i,t} = (1 - \alpha - \beta) + \alpha \frac{\varepsilon_{i-1,t}^2}{g_{t-1}} + \beta h_{i-1,t} \tag{21}$$

where $\alpha + \beta < 1$. This implies that $\mathsf{E}h_{i,t} = 1$. As already discussed, fixing this expectation (to one) is necessary for identification reasons, but in fact any *known* positive value would do.

The first example of a model based on this decomposition is one in which g_t is defined as follows:

$$g_t = m + \theta \sum_{k=1}^{K} \varphi_k(\omega_1, \omega_2) RV_{t-k}. \tag{22}$$

The realized variance RV_t is the sum of daily squared returns,

$$RV_t = \sum_{i=1}^{M_t} \varepsilon_{i,t}^2 \tag{23}$$

In (23), M_t is the number of days in the month t of trading days. The purpose of the nonnegative function $\varphi_k(\omega_1, \omega_2)$ is to provide a parsimonious representation of a lag structure when K may be large. The beta-function

$$\varphi_k(\omega_1, \omega_2) = \frac{\left(\frac{k}{K}\right)^{\omega_1 - 1}\left(1 - \frac{k}{K}\right)^{\omega_2 - 1}}{\sum_{j=1}^{K} \left(\frac{j}{K}\right)^{\omega_1 - 1}\left(1 - \frac{j}{K}\right)^{\omega_2 - 1}} \tag{24}$$

is a popular choice. Engle et al. (2013) also consider the case in which the realized variance is defined by a rolling window:

$$RV_i = \sum_{j=1}^{M'} \varepsilon_{i-j}^2 \tag{25}$$

where the realized measure consists of M' terms from period i backwards in time.

The purpose of the lag structure is to smooth out erratic fluctuations in RV_t, meaning that (22) is preferred to $g_t = m' + \theta' RV_{t-1}$. Equations (21), (22) and (23) jointly with the definition of $\varepsilon_{i,t}$ form the GARCH-MIDAS-RV model.

If a (monthly) macroeconomic variable x_t replaces RV_t, to guarantee positivity g_t appears in the exponential form:

$$g_t = c \exp\left\{\theta \sum_{k=1}^{K} \varphi_k(\omega_1, \omega_2) x_{t-k}\right\} \tag{26}$$

where $E\varepsilon_t x_{t-k} = 0$, $k \geq 1$. The resulting model may be called the GARCH-MIDAS-X model. Engle et al. (2013) present (26) in the logarithmic form, but to stress similarity between (7) and (26) the exponential form is preferred here. Parameters of h_t and g_t are estimated jointly after the number of equidistant knots has been determined. Asymptotic properties of the maximum likelihood estimators of these parameters are not discussed in the paper. However, Wang and Ghysels (2015) prove consistency and asymptotic normality of maximum likelihood estimators of parameters in the GARCH-MIDAS-RV model in the rolling window (25) case.

In the application of Engle et al. (2013), the MIDAS function is exponential:

$$\varphi_k(\omega) = \frac{\omega^k}{\sum_{j=1}^{K} \omega^j}.$$

Furthermore, x_t is a quarterly series, and the variables are the growth rates of industrial production and the production price index, respectively. These are called 'level' series, and their error variance is named 'volatility'. The latter is computed by fitting an autoregressive model to the level series, taking the residuals, squaring them, and forming a sum of the squared residuals as in (23). One can of course consider a model in which only one of the four macro variables is present, but it is also possible to build more complicated models in which two or all four of them appear simultaneously. The authors also consider a spline-GARCH model in which g_t is defined by (7) but the longer time scale is retained.

The series to be modeled is long and consists of daily US stock returns over the period from 16 February 1885 to 31 December 2010. The two macroeconomic series also start in 1884. They are originally monthly but are temporally aggregated to the quarterly level. In addition to the complete period, GARCH-MIDAS models are also fitted to subperiods. The parameter estimates from the logarithmic g_t equation are strongly significant. Estimated GARCH equations are not reported, so it is not possible to assess the effect of g_t on the estimated sum of the GARCH(1,1) parameters α and β. The results indicate that for GARCH-MIDAS-RV models this sum is generally well below one, the only notable expectation being the subperiod 1953–1984. For the GARCH-MIDAS-X models this sum is well below one for the subperiod 1890–1919 and close to one, generally greater than 0.98 for all models independent of the level/volatility and the variable or variables included in the model. Results of fitting spline-GARCH models show that this sum is slightly lower than in corresponding MIDAS models. One may conclude that including macro variables in the GARCH model does not affect the amplitude of the volatility clusters in the way it does when g_t is deterministic. This outcome is quite different from what Han and Kristensen (2017) obtain with their SEMIX model, but the economic variable (VIX) in SEMIX is different from the four variables used by Engle et al. (2013).

As to the contribution of the macro variables, the authors find that quite a significant fraction of variation in expected volatility can be ascribed to economic sources. Variables with the strongest contribution are not the same throughout the whole period, but in general terms they seem useful in explaining stock market volatility. It is not possible here to describe forecasting experiments Engle et al. (2013) conduct with GARCH-MIDAS-X models but they seem to support this conclusion.

The work of Engle et al. (2013) has generated plenty of interest and applications. Girardin and Joyeux (2013) employ the GARCH-MIDAS-RV model to estimate the long-run component g_t for daily returns of indexes of A and B stocks in the Shanghai Stock Exchange. They then study connections between g_t and economic fundamentals as in Engle and Rangel (2008). The long-run time scale is monthly. Ashgarian, Hou and Javed (2013) combine the realized variance, the 'level' and the 'volatility' into a single model. A noteworthy detail is that they do not use the exponential form but rather extend the RV specification (22). Their long-run component has the form

$$
\begin{aligned}
g_t = {}& m + \theta_{RV}\sum_{k=1}^{K}\varphi_k(\omega_1,\omega_2)RV_{t-k} + \theta_L\sum_{k=1}^{K}\varphi_k(\omega_1,\omega_2)x_{L,t-k} \\
& + \theta_V\sum_{k=1}^{K}\varphi_k(\omega_1,\omega_2)x_{V,t-k}
\end{aligned}
\tag{27}
$$

where $x_{L,t}$ is a 'level' economic variable and $x_{V,t}$ is the corresponding 'volatility' variable. Principal components of economic variables are also used as an economic variable. This approach requires the level variable to remain positive during the observation period. In the application the long time scale t is monthly. Unlike Engle et al. (2013), these authors use squared first differences of economic variables as the measure of their volatility.

The series to be modeled and forecast is the S&P 500 daily return series from January 1991 to June 2008. The out-of-sample forecasting period begins in January 2004. Results show that adding the first principal component as the economic variable to the GARCH-MIDAS-RV model as in (27) improves forecasting performance compared to that of the GARCH-MIDAS-RV model.

Conrad and Loch (2015) employ both one- and two-sided MIDAS filters. The latter are employed to study lead and lag relationships between stock market volatility and macroeconomic variables and were already considered by Engle et al. (2013). The difference between these two is that the two-sided filter of Engle et al. (2013) contains future values that by definition are not available at $t-1$. Conrad and Loch (2015) replace these unknown observations by forecasts available at $t-1$, so their two-sided MIDAS filter can be used for forecasting. The returns are again continuously compounded daily returns of the S&P 500 index, and the observation period extends from 2 January 1969 to 30 December 2011. The long-run time scale is quarterly. Furthermore, the short-term GARCH component is a GJR-GARCH one. GJR-GARCH-MIDAS-X equations are estimated for 11 economic variables. The authors also fit a GJR-GARCH-MIDAS-RV model with a quarterly RV component to the data and finally, combine these two into a GJR-GARCH-MIDAS-RV-X model, in which, denoting the relevant macro variable by x_t,

$$
g_t = \exp\left\{ m + \theta_{RV}\sum_{k=1}^{K}\varphi_k(1,\omega_2^{RV})RV_{t-k} + \theta_x\sum_{k=1}^{K}\varphi_k(\omega_1^x,\omega_2^x)x_{t-k} \right\}.
\tag{28}
$$

The exponential form is used to make sure that g_t remains positive. Forecasting with GARCH-MIDAS is discussed, and forecasting with models with two-sided filters receives special attention. The reader is referred to the paper for a rich set of results concerning both fitted one and two-sided filter models and forecasts from them.

4.5. Misspecification testing

When a volatility model such as a GARCH model (2) has been estimated, its adequacy should be tested before using it for forecasting or other purposes. Multiplicative decomposition may be used for constructing alternative hypotheses to the estimated specification. As an example, Lundbergh and Teräsvirta (2002) derive a test statistic for testing the adequacy of the GARCH model. Under H_0, the parametric model collapses into $\varepsilon_t = z_t h_t^{1/2}$ where $z_t \sim iid\mathcal{N}(0,1)$ and h_t follows a GARCH process, whereas under the alternative $z_t = \zeta_t g_t^{1/2}$, where $\zeta_t \sim iid\mathcal{N}(0,1)$ and

$$g_t = 1 + \sum_{j=1}^{r} \delta_j z_{t-j}^2. \tag{29}$$

The null hypothesis is $\delta_i = 0$, $i = 1, \dots, r$, or, equivalently, there is no remaining ARCH in the standardized errors. Under regularity conditions, the resulting statistic follows a χ^2-distribution with r degrees of freedom.

As already indicated, another variant of (29) is one in which GARCH is tested against (15) with (16). The testing situation is, however, nonstandard because the alternative model is not identified when the null hypothesis is valid. More discussion about deriving a test statistic in that situation can be found in Amado and Laakkonen (2013) and Amado and Teräsvirta (2017).

Conrad and Schienle (2017) construct a Lagrange multiplier misspecification test for testing GARCH against GARCH-MIDAS, see (26). The null hypothesis is that the long-run component is constant. This implies $\theta \sum_{k=1}^{K} \varphi_k(\omega_1, \omega_2) = 0$. The authors show that their test statistic has an asymptotic χ^2-distribution with K degrees of freedom. They discuss the choice of K and find in simulations that $K = 1$ often already suffices to reject the null hypothesis when the alternative holds.

The multiplicative decomposition may also be used for improving a misspecified model or, in other words, dividing estimation of the true (unknown) model into two parts. Following Mishra, Su, and Ullah (2010), one first fits a GARCH model to the series (or residuals if a conditional mean has already been estimated) under consideration to parametrically remove some of the variation in ε_t^2. Then one makes use of the identity

$$\mathsf{E}\{\varepsilon_t^2 | \mathcal{F}_{t-1}\} = h_t \mathsf{E}\{\frac{\varepsilon_t^2}{h_t} | \mathcal{F}_{t-1}\} = h_t g_t. \tag{30}$$

If h_t is correctly specified, $\mathsf{E}\{(\varepsilon_t^2/h_t) | \mathcal{F}_{t-1}\} = 1$. If it is not, there may be structure left in g_t, and it is assumed that it can be estimated nonparametrically. The resulting model is called the Semiparametric GARCH (SPGARCH) model. Mishra et al. (2010) assume that g_t is locally linear, describe the subsequent estimation problem in detail and under regularity conditions prove consistency and asymptotic normality of the resulting maximum likelihood estimator.

To demonstrate the modeling strategy, the authors use the S&P500 daily returns from 3 January 2002 through 3 January 2007, a total of 1,258 observations. They fit an ARCH(1), the GARCH(1,1) and the GJR-GARCH(1,1) model to this series. They report the ARCH or GARCH parameter estimates and the amount of variation explained by the corresponding parametric model. The results are surprising in that this ratio is largest in ARCH (88.2%) and lowest in the GJR-GARCH model (81.1%). The likely explanation is, however, that g_t is a function of the variables in h_t. Since GARCH and GJR-GARCH have one variable more than ARCH, this gives the latter model better possibilities to improve the fit than it does to the former two. Misspecification checks suggest that the SPARCH model is misspecified, whereas the two GARCH models seem adequate. The persistence for h_t in the GARCH model is high: $\hat{\alpha}_1 + \hat{\beta}_1 = 0.982$, and the corresponding number for GJR-GARCH equals 0.983. It is very low for ARCH: $\hat{\alpha}_1 = 0.27$. From the plots in the paper Mishra et al. (2010) conclude that the nonparametric component is higher for negative than for positive shocks, so it contributes to explaining the asymmetry in the series.

5. Multivariate models

5.1. Stochastic discount factor model

Multiplicative decomposition of variance can be generalized to decomposing the covariance matrix. Section 5 is in its entirety devoted to this generalization. In this case, correlations between the return variables or functions of them come into play. To fix notation, let ε_t be an $N \times 1$ log-return vector, $\mathsf{E}\{\varepsilon_t|\mathcal{F}_{t-1}\} = \mathbf{0}$, and $\mathsf{E}\{\varepsilon_t\varepsilon_t'|\mathcal{F}_{t-1}\} = \mathbf{\Sigma}_t$, where $\mathcal{F}_{t-1}$ contains the historical information available at time $t-1$. There are several models in which $\mathbf{\Sigma}_t$ is multiplicatively decomposed to short and long run components. To begin with, Osiewalski (2009) and Osiewalski and Pajor (2009) consider the following simple multiplicative decomposition:

$$\varepsilon_t = \mathbf{z}_t g_t^{1/2} \tag{31}$$

where $\mathbf{z}_t \sim \text{iid}\mathcal{N}(\mathbf{0}, \mathbf{C})$, and $\mathbf{C}$ is positive definite covariance matrix. Furthermore, the latent process g_t is a positive-valued stochastic random variable such that

$$\ln g_t = \phi \ln g_{t-1} + \sigma_g \eta_t \tag{32}$$

where $\sigma_g > 0$, $\eta_t \sim \text{iid}\mathcal{N}(0,1)$ and η_t and z_t are mutually independent. The ensuing model is called the Stochastic Discount Factor (SDF) model. The conditional covariance matrix of ε_t equals

$$\Sigma_t = \mathsf{E}\{\varepsilon_t\varepsilon_t'|\mathcal{F}_{t-1}\} = g_t\mathbf{C} = g_t[c_{ij}] \tag{33}$$

where $\mathbf{C}$ is a positive definite matrix. Since $\mathbf{C}$ is not a correlation matrix, it has to be transformed into one. This is done by defining $\boldsymbol{P} = (\boldsymbol{I}_N \odot \mathbf{C})^{-1/2}\mathbf{C}(\boldsymbol{I}_N \odot \mathbf{C})^{-1/2}$ where $\odot$ is the Hadamard matrix product operator and $\mathbf{P}$ is now the constant conditional correlation matrix. Time-variation in (33) is due to a scalar stochastic component g_t. It follows that the SDF model has two independent sources of noise, which makes estimation numerically demanding. The authors therefore adopt a Bayesian approach with priors on ϕ, $\mathbf{C}^{-1}$, and σ_g^{-2}. The model (even one with a vector autoregressive of order one as the conditional mean) can be analyzed using the Gibbs sampler. Osiewalski (2009), however, points out that the SDF model is too simple for practical purposes because the time-variation in covariances is controlled by a single stochastic variable.

Consequently, Osiewalski (2009) and Osiewalski and Pajor (2009) study a generalization of the SDF model. It consists of making $\mathbf{C}$ in (33) time-varying. The ensuing models are called Hybrid SDF-Scalar BEKK (SDF-SBEKK) models because the time-varying covariance matrix has a BEKK structure; for the BEKK-GARCH model, see Engle and Kroner (1995). The first-order scalar BEKK with covariance targeting has the following form:

$$\mathbf{H}_t = (1 - \alpha - \beta)\mathbf{C} + \alpha\varepsilon_{t-1}\varepsilon_{t-1}' + \beta\mathbf{H}_{t-1} \tag{34}$$

where α and β are positive scalars, $\alpha + \beta < 1$, $\mathbf{H}_t$ is a conditional covariance matrix, and $\mathbf{C}$ is a symmetric positive definite matrix. The hybrid model combines scalar BEKK and stochastic volatility. The multiplicative decomposition of ε_t has the following form:

$$\varepsilon_t = \Omega_t^{1/2}z_t g_t^{1/2} \tag{34}$$

where g_t is defined as in (32), $\Omega_t^{1/2} \in \mathcal{F}_{t-1}$ is a time-varying positive definite matrix, $\eta_t \sim \text{iid}\mathcal{N}(0,1)$, $z_t \sim \text{iid}\mathcal{N}(\mathbf{0}, \mathbf{I}_N)$, and z_t and η_t are mutually independent. The decomposition (35) implies $\mathsf{E}\{\varepsilon_t\varepsilon_t'|\mathcal{F}_{t-1}\} = g_t\Omega_t$. Two hybrid models emerge. The first one, called the type I hybrid, has $\Omega_t = \mathbf{H}_t$, which means that Ω_t is defined by (34) and does not depend on g_t. In type II model it is assumed that ε_t is rescaled: $\phi_t = \varepsilon_t/g_t^{1/2}$, and that ϕ_t has the scalar BEKK structure. This is analogous to the rescaling of ε_t in the univariate GARCH case in Section 2, where the rescaled returns are assumed to follow a GARCH process. In the type II model, $\Omega_t = \mathbf{H}_t^*$, where

$$\mathbf{H}_t^* = (1 - \alpha - \beta)\mathbf{C} + \alpha\phi_{t-1}\phi_{t-1}' + \beta\mathbf{H}_{t-1}^*. \tag{36}$$

When $N = 1$, the rescaled BEKK (36) collapses into the rescaled GARCH in (1), where now g_t is stochastic and follows a stochastic volatility process (32). Up to now, this 'hybrid SDF-GARCH' may not have been used in applied work.

The Bayesian analysis (estimation) of these two hybrid models by Gibbs sampling is described in detail in Osiewalski (2009). To alleviate numerical problems, C is estimated by the sample covariance matrix of ϕ_t. This is analogous to how the 'intercept matrix' is estimated in the DCC-GARCH model of Engle (2002). As discussed in Osiewalski and Pajor (2009), Ω_t in (35) need not be of BEKK type. The DCC-GARCH is deemed as a promising alternative, although it would be computationally more complicated to handle than the relatively simple scalar BEKK parameterization. More information about this can be found in Osiewalski and Pajor (2007).

Osiewalski and Pajor (2009) apply the SDF-GARCH and a few other models to two bivariate datasets, of which the first one consists of two daily exchange rate log-returns for the period 1 February 1996 – 31 December 2001 and the second one of daily log-returns of WIG, the Warsaw stock exchange index, and the S&P 500 from 8 January 1999 to 1 December 2006. The estimated models are ranked according to their Bayes factors. In both cases, the SDF-BEKK fares better than the alternatives that include, among other things, BEKK, scalar BEKK, and DCC, all with t-distributed errors. Interestingly, type I SDF-BEKK is ranked above the computationally more demanding type II. SDF-DCC is also ranked ahead of the models without the SDF component. It may be noted from Tables 5 and 6 in the paper that the persistence calculated from the posterior means is very high in both bivariate SDF-BEKK models, so the SDF extension to BEKK does not have much impact on the standard BEKK in this respect.

The authors also present a high-dimensional application in which the dataset consists of daily log-returns of 23 stocks from the mWIG40 index and another 11 from WIG20. The period runs from 30 January 2003 to 29 August 2007. (Amado et al. (2017) have recently modeled daily log-retuns of the latter index using the MTV-GARCH model discussed in Section 3.4.) In this case the persistence, estimated from both the type I and type II model, remains below 0.9. Whether or not the persistence generally decreases when the dimension of the return vector increases is an open (empirical) question, but further study of this possibility could be interesting. Besides, the estimate (posterior mean) of ϕ in (32) is also fairly small, about 0.5 for both the type I and type II model. Anyway, the analysis shows that is quite possible to describe large (or medium-sized) return vectors with the SDF-BEKK model.

5.2. *Local dynamic conditional correlation model*

Feng (2006) presents a multivariate GARCH model in which both the variance and the correlation component are deterministically time-varying. He calls the model the Local Dynamic Conditional Correlation (LDCC-)GARCH model. It is a generalization of the SEMIGARCH model considered in Section 3.1. In this review, the fact that Feng even estimates the conditional mean (nonparametrically) as a part of the modeling process is ignored, and only modeling and estimating the variance and correlations are considered. The return or error vector ε_t is multiplicatively decomposed as follows: $\varepsilon_t = S(t/T)D_t z_t$, where $D_t = \text{diag}(h_{1t}^{1/2}, ..., h_{Nt}^{1/2})$ contains the short-run GARCH components and $S(t/T) = \text{diag}(g_1^{1/2}(t/T), ..., g_N^{1/2}(t/T))$ the deterministic elements. Furthermore, z_t is a vector of independent random variables with $Ez_t = 0$ and $Ez_t z_t' = P(t/T)$, where $P(t/T)$ contains the deterministically time-varying correlations. This implies the following decomposition for the covariance matrix $\Sigma(t/T) = E\{\varepsilon_t \varepsilon_t' | \mathcal{F}_{t-1}\}$:

$$\Sigma(t/T) = S(t/T)D_t P(t/T)D_t S(t/T) \tag{37}$$

The covariance matrix (37) is estimated as follows. First estimate the deterministic components $g_i(t/T)$, $i = 1, ..., N$, nonparametrically as in Feng (2004). This yields the residuals $\hat{\phi}_t = \hat{S}^{-1}(t/T)\varepsilon_t$. The elements of $\hat{\phi}_t$ are assumed to follow a GARCH process, so α_i and β_i are estimated from

$$h_{it} = (1 - \alpha_i - \beta_i) + \alpha_i \hat{\phi}_{i,t-1}^2 + \beta_i h_{i,t-1}$$

$i = 1, ..., N$, where $\alpha_i + \beta_i < 1$ when the standard first-order GARCH process is used. For identification reasons, $Eh_{it} = 1$, $i = 1, ..., N$. This operation gives the residuals $\hat{z}_t = D_t^{-1}\hat{\phi}_t$. The correlations will be functions of $z_{t-j}, j = 1, ..., p$, where the lag length p is determined by the user. The correlation matrix is estimated nonparametrically. Curse of dimensionality when N is large is dealt with in the following way. Consider the random vector $y_t = (y_{1t}, ..., y_{pt})'$, where $y_{jt} = (1'z_{t-j})^2$. Define two kernels, a univariate one, K_0, for t/T and a multivariate spheric kernel K for y_t. The estimator for the correlation matrix becomes

$$\hat{Q}(\tau, y) = \sum_{t=n_1}^{n_2} w_t \hat{z}_t \hat{z}_t' \tag{38}$$

where

$$w_t = \frac{K_0\left(\frac{t/T - \tau}{b_0}\right)K\left(\frac{y_{1t} - y_1}{b}, ..., \frac{y_{pt} - y_p}{b}\right)}{\sum_{t=n_1}^{n_2} K_0\left(\frac{t/T - \tau}{b_0}\right)K\left(\frac{y_{1t} - y_1}{b}, ..., \frac{y_{pt} - y_p}{b}\right)}.$$

The two bandwidths b_0 and b are different from each other because t/T and y_{jt} are of different magnitude. How to select the bandwidths and n_1 and n_2 in (38) is discussed in the paper. Theoretical results obtained for biases and variances of the elements of $\hat{Q}(\tau, y)$ are derived under the assumption that even a nonparametric mean is estimated. Note that $Q(\tau, y)$ does not automatically become a correlation matrix, so the by now familiar adjustment

$$\hat{\mathbf{P}}(\tau, \mathbf{y}) = (\mathbf{I}_N \odot \hat{\mathbf{Q}}(\tau, \mathbf{y}))^{-1/2} \hat{\mathbf{Q}}(\tau, \mathbf{y})(\mathbf{I}_N \odot \hat{\mathbf{Q}}(\tau, \mathbf{y}))^{-1/2} \tag{39}$$

is required. Results on optimal bandwidths are building on the same premises. As already mentioned, the mean has been ignored in this exposition.

Feng (2006) fits the LDCC-GARCH model to the daily foreign exchange rate series of the British pound, euro, Japanese yen and Canadian dollar vis-à-vis the US dollar from 4 January 1999 to 30 December 2005. It may be noted that conditional variance of the euro returns is modeled as a GARCH(2,2) process, whereas for the other three series GARCH(1,1) is deemed adequate. The six estimated correlations show a tendency to increase towards the end of the period. The deterministic component is clearly useful, and the short-run fluctuations around it are relatively minor in comparison. The short-run component in correlations is due to $\mathbf{D}(t/T)$. $\mathbf{Q}(\tau, \mathbf{y})$ itself does not contain a short-run component, but Feng (2006) mentions that having one could be worth investigating. His suggestion has been followed up later; see Section 5.7.

5.3. Local BEKK model

Hafner and Linton (2010) use the following multiplicative decomposition for ε_t:

$$\varepsilon_t = \mathbf{\Sigma}^{1/2}(t/T)\mathbf{H}_t^{1/2}\mathbf{z}_t \tag{40}$$

where $\mathbf{z}_t$ is a strictly stationary martingale difference sequence with $\mathsf{E}\{\mathbf{z}_t|\mathcal{F}_{t-1}\} = \mathbf{0}$ and $\mathsf{E}\{\mathbf{z}_t\mathbf{z}_t'|\mathcal{F}_{t-1}\} = \mathbf{I}_N$. The matrix $\mathbf{\Sigma}(t/T)$ is a deterministic nonparametric function of rescaled time, positive definite and at least twice continuously differentiable. The stochastic $\mathbf{H}_t$ is also a positive definite matrix but with a parametric representation. Decomposition (40) is another generalization of SEMIGARCH to the multivariate case. Writing $\boldsymbol{\phi}_t = \mathbf{\Sigma}^{-1/2}(t/T)\varepsilon_t$, one obtains $\boldsymbol{\phi}_t = \mathbf{H}_t^{1/2}\mathbf{z}_t$. As an example of $\mathbf{H}_t$ the authors use the 'full' first-order BEKK-GARCH:

$$\mathbf{H}_t = \mathbf{I}_N - \mathbf{A}\mathbf{A}' - \mathbf{B}\mathbf{B}' + \mathbf{A}\boldsymbol{\phi}_{t-1}\boldsymbol{\phi}_{t-1}'\mathbf{A}' + \mathbf{B}\mathbf{H}_{t-1}\mathbf{B}'$$

where $\mathsf{E}\mathbf{H}_t = \mathbf{I}_N$. This condition is needed for identification of the model. The model of Hafner and Linton (2010) could then, following Feng (2006), be called the Local-BEKK (LBEKK) model.

Estimation of LBEKK can be carried out in stages by first estimating $\mathbf{\Sigma}(t/T)$ nonparametrically from $\varepsilon_t = \mathbf{\Sigma}^{1/2}(t/T)\mathbf{z}_t$, using kernel estimation as in Feng (2004). How this is done when $\mathbf{\Sigma}(t/T)$ is a matrix is discussed in Rodríguez-Poo and Linton (2001). Analogously to Feng (2006), one then forms rescaled returns $\tilde{\boldsymbol{\phi}}_t = \tilde{\mathbf{\Sigma}}^{-1/2}(t/T)\varepsilon_t$, where $\tilde{\mathbf{\Sigma}}(t/T)$ is a nonparametric estimate of $\mathbf{\Sigma}(t/T)$ and estimates the BEKK parameters from

$$\mathbf{H}_t^* = \mathbf{I}_N - \mathbf{A}\mathbf{A}' - \mathbf{B}\mathbf{B}' + \mathbf{A}\tilde{\boldsymbol{\phi}}_{t-1}\tilde{\boldsymbol{\phi}}_{t-1}'\mathbf{A}' + \mathbf{B}\mathbf{H}_{t-1}^*\mathbf{B}'. \tag{41}$$

For a scalar BEKK variant of this, see (36). Since $\tilde{\boldsymbol{\Sigma}}(t/T)$ is not a function of any of the BEKK parameters, after assuming $\mathbf{z}_t \sim \text{iid}\mathcal{N}(\mathbf{0}, \mathbf{I}_N)$ maximum likelihood estimation of $\mathbf{A}$ and $\mathbf{B}$ in (41) proceeds as in the standard BEKK case. Hafner and Linton (2010) write that the estimator $\tilde{\boldsymbol{\gamma}}$ of $\boldsymbol{\gamma} = (\text{vec}(\mathbf{A})', \text{vec}(\mathbf{B})')'$ is 'expected to be consistent and asymptotically normal but not efficient.' In the univariate case Feng (2004) found an asymptotic bias which, however, was negligible in large samples. Whether or not the situation is similar here is not known. Efficiency may nevertheless be improved by re-estimating $\boldsymbol{\Sigma}(t/T)$ from $\boldsymbol{\varepsilon}_t = \boldsymbol{\Sigma}^{1/2}(t/T)\tilde{\mathbf{u}}_t$, where $\tilde{\mathbf{u}}_t = (\tilde{\mathbf{H}}_t^*)^{1/2}\mathbf{z}_t$ and then re-estimating the BEKK parameters. Computational details of the estimation procedure can be found in Hafner and Linton (2010).

The LBEKK model is fitted to the bivariate series of daily Dow Jones and NASDAQ index returns decomposition from 2 January 1990 to 7 January 2009, a total of 4795 observations. The autocorrelation of returns is first removed by fitting a VAR(1) model to the returns. In order to model the residuals from this model when the returns are stock index returns the BEKK model is augmented by an asymmetry term analogous to that in the univariate GJR-GARCH model. The results of modeling the residuals show that persistence of the BEKK-GARCH component declines when the time-varying component $\boldsymbol{\Sigma}(t/T)$ is included in the model. They also strongly support inclusion of the asymmetry component. The time-varying unconditional correlation between the two return series generally exceeds 0.5 and lies close to unity at the end of the sample. As expected, the conditional correlations fluctuate around the unconditional 'trend'. The paper does not contain higher-dimensional examples, so comparisons with the work of Osiewalski and Pajor (2009) are not possible.

5.4. Multiplicative DCC model

In modeling dynamics of electricity futures, Bauwens, Hafner, and Pierret (2013) apply the decomposition (37). They call their model a multiplicative DCC (mDCC) model. The difference between mDCC and LDCC is that the correlation matrix is estimated nonparametrically in LDCC and parametrically in mDCC. (Incidentally, 'DCC' means different things in these two abbreviations.) Estimation of parameters proceeds as in Feng (2006) and Hafner and Linton (2010). First, estimate the deterministic structure $\boldsymbol{\Sigma}(t/T)$ nonparametrically from $\boldsymbol{\varepsilon}_t = \boldsymbol{\Sigma}^{1/2}(t/T)\boldsymbol{\phi}_t$, assuming that the unconditional expectation $\mathsf{E}\boldsymbol{\phi}_t\boldsymbol{\phi}_t' = \mathbf{I}_N$. The vector $\boldsymbol{\phi}_t = \boldsymbol{\Sigma}^{-1/2}(t/T)\boldsymbol{\varepsilon}_t$ is now free of slowly moving variation in the variance of $\boldsymbol{\varepsilon}_t$ characterized by the deterministic component $\boldsymbol{\Sigma}(t/T)$. Next, estimate the conditional variances in $\mathbf{h}_t = (h_{1t}, \ldots, h_{Nt})'$, represented by the diagonal matrix $\mathbf{D}_t$ in (37). Bauwens et al. (2013) assume that they follow the GJR-GARCH model:

$$h_{it} = \alpha_{i0} + \alpha_{i1}\phi_{i,t-1}^2 + \kappa_i I(\phi_{i,t-1} < 0)\phi_{i,t-1}^2 + h_{i,t-1}$$

This yields the (estimated) error vector $\hat{\mathbf{z}}_t = \mathbf{D}_t^{-1}\hat{\boldsymbol{\phi}}_t$. Since $\mathsf{E}\boldsymbol{\phi}_t\boldsymbol{\phi}_t' = \mathbf{I}_N$, the unconditional variance $\mathsf{E}\mathbf{z}_t\mathbf{z}_t' = \mathbf{I}_N$ as well, while $\mathsf{E}\{\mathbf{z}_t\mathbf{z}_t'|\mathcal{F}_{t-1}\} = \mathbf{P}_t$, where $\mathbf{P}_t$ follows a DCC process. Estimating its parameters completes the estimation of the model. A noteworthy detail of the DCC equation

$$\mathbf{Q}_t = (1 - a - b)\mathbf{I}_N + a\hat{\mathbf{z}}_{t-1}\hat{\mathbf{z}}_{t-1}' + b\mathbf{Q}_{t-1}$$

is that the intercept matrix is an identity matrix. This is the case because, as already noted, $\mathsf{E}\mathbf{z}_t\mathbf{z}_t' = \mathbf{I}_N$.

The application consists of jointly modeling dynamics of volatilities and correlations of three electricity futures contracts written on the index of the European Energy Exchange (EEX). They correspond to monthly, quarterly, and yearly maturities. In this case ε_t is not a daily return vector but a residual vector from an estimated vector error correction model, see Bauwens et al. (2013) for details. The GJR-GARCH equations for the conditional variances of ϕ_{it} are in fact GJR-GARCH-X equations because the GJR-GARCH component is additively completed by a number of exogenous variables. The sum of the DCC coefficient estimates $\hat{a}$ and $\hat{b}$ is remarkably low compared to typical results, only 0.879. (In many applications this sum exceeds 0.99.) This demonstrates the importance of the deterministic component $\boldsymbol{\Sigma}(t/T)$ in this application. Other, slightly more general, DCC specifications are considered as well, but discussing them would be outside the scope of this review.

5.5. *Multivariate spline-GARCH models*

In the multivariate GARCH model by Rangel and Engle (2012) the spline-GARCH equations have a central role. The paper differs from the previous ones in that the starting point is the CAPM model by Sharpe (1964), and the interest lies in deriving correlations between excess returns of assets. Let r_{it} denote the excess return of asset i, and let r_{mt} be the market excess return. Then for asset i,

$$r_{it} = \alpha_i + \beta_i r_{mt} + \varepsilon_{it} \tag{42}$$

In order to work out the correlation between r_{it} and r_{jt} it is assumed that $\varepsilon_{it} = z_{it}h_{it}^{1/2}g_{it}^{1/2}$, where $z_{it} \sim \text{iid}(0,1)$. Furthermore, $r_{mt} = \alpha_m + \varepsilon_{mt}$ where $\varepsilon_{mt} = z_{mt}h_{mt}^{1/2}g_{mt}^{1/2}$. The GJR-GARCH type conditional variance of ε_{it} has the following representation:

$$h_{it} = 1 - \alpha_i - \kappa_i/2 - \beta_i + \alpha_i\frac{\varepsilon_{i,t-1}^2}{g_{i,t-1}} + \kappa_i\frac{\varepsilon_{i,t-1}^2}{g_{i,t-1}}I(r_{i,t-1} < 0) + \beta_i h_{it-1} \tag{43}$$

$i = 1, \ldots, N$, where it is assumed that $\alpha_i + \kappa_i/2 + \beta_i < 1$ and that g_{it} is as in (7) but with $\gamma = 0$ (the exogenous variable x_t is excluded). Also note that the argument in the indicator variable is $r_{i,t-1}$ and not $\varepsilon_{i,t-1}$ as would be the case in the standard GJR-GARCH model. This implies that $\mathsf{E}h_{it} \neq 1$. The conditional variance for r_{mt} equals

$$h_{mt} = 1 - \alpha_m - \kappa_m/2 - \beta_m + \alpha_m \frac{\varepsilon_{m,t-1}^2}{g_{m,t-1}} + \kappa_m \frac{\varepsilon_{m,t-1}^2}{g_{m,t-1}} I(r_{m,t-1} < 0) + \beta_m h_{m,t-1}.$$

Analogously to (43), the argument of $I(\cdot)$ is $r_{m,t-1} < 0$, not $\varepsilon_{t,m-1} < 0$, so $\mathsf{E}h_{mt} \neq 1$, unless $\alpha_m = 0$. The error vector $\mathbf{z}_t = (z_{mt}, z_{1t}, \ldots, z_{Nt})'$ has a DCC structure. Consequently, the (conditional) correlation between z_{it} and z_{jt} has a time-varying structure that involves the market long-run component g_{mt} as well as g_{it} and g_{jt}. The conditional correlation between the two excess returns r_{it} and r_{jt} has the following form:

$$\begin{aligned}
\rho_{ijt} &= \{\beta_i \beta_j h_{it} g_{it} + \beta_i h_{mt}^{1/2} g_{mt}^{1/2} h_{jt}^{1/2} g_{jt}^{1/2} \rho_{mjt} + \beta_j h_{mt}^{1/2} g_{mt}^{1/2} h_{it}^{1/2} g_{it}^{1/2} \rho_{mit} \\
&\quad + h_{it}^{1/2} g_{it}^{1/2} h_{jt}^{1/2} g_{jt}^{1/2} \rho_{ijt}\} \\
&\quad \times \{\beta_i^2 h_{mt} g_{mt} + h_{it} g_{it} + 2\beta_i h_{mt}^{1/2} g_{mt}^{1/2} h_{it}^{1/2} g_{it}^{1/2} \rho_{mit}\}^{-1/2} \\
&\quad \times \{\beta_j^2 h_{mt} g_{mt} + h_{jt} g_{jt} + 2\beta_j h_{mt}^{1/2} g_{mt}^{1/2} h_{jt}^{1/2} g_{jt}^{1/2} \rho_{mjt}\}^{-1/2}
\end{aligned}$$

where ρ_{mit} is the correlation between the market error $z_{mt} = \varepsilon_{mt}/(h_{mt}^{1/2} g_{mt}^{1/2})$ and $z_{it} = \varepsilon_{it}/(h_{it}^{1/2} g_{it}^{1/2})$, and ρ_{ijt} is the conditional correlation between z_{it} and $z_{jt} = \varepsilon_{jt}/(h_{jt}^{1/2} g_{jt}^{1/2})$. The deterministic components g_{it} and g_{jt} contribute to z_{it} and z_{jt}, respectively, and this way, together with g_{mt}, to ρ_{ijt}.

Rangel and Engle (2012) write that, assuming multivariate normality, the quasi-maximum likelihood estimators of the parameters in (42) lead to consistent GJR-GARCH type equations under mild regularity conditions for a model with correctly specified conditional mean and covariance; see Bollerslev and Wooldridge (1992). Estimating these parameters forms the first stage of estimation. The second stage consists of estimating the correlation parameters conditionally on the first stage parameter estimates. The authors point out that misspecification of the number of knots may lead to inconsistent estimates in stage one. They suggest minimizing the consequences of this by using t-distributed errors instead of the normally distributed ones. They also draw attention to biases in the estimates of the correlation (DCC) component when N is large and suggest alternatives to maximum likelihood.

The authors consider daily returns on Dow Jones Industrial Average (DJIA) stocks from December 1988 to December 2006 and have a sample of 33 stocks. Daily returns on the S&P 500 are used as a market factor, and the one-month T-bill rate functions as the time-varying risk-free rate. The market excess return r_m is the difference between these two returns. A set of models with various degrees of complexity are estimated. It is found that the models with the spline-GARCH deterministic component dominate models in which this component is constant (GARCH).

The performance of the SFG-DCC model is compared with that of a selection of competing approaches including a pure DCC-GARCH model and alternatives based on estimating large covariance matrices without any GARCH structure. The forecasts are generated by first estimating the models from December 1988 to June 1995 and forecasting from 1 to 126 days ahead. These 126 days are then added to the sample, the models are re-estimated and another set of forecasts up to 126 days are generated. This produces 22 sets of non-overlapping forecasts. Describing the whole experiment here would take too much space, but the main conclusion, based on long-run forecasts (from 87 to 126 days) and various measures is that the SFG-DCC model on the average performs better than the alternatives.

The research problem of Opschoor, van Dijk, and van der Wel (2014) is to assess the impact of financial conditions on volatility and correlations of returns of bank equities. They study it in the spline-GARCH framework. In their multivariate model, the decomposition (51) is defined such that $\mathbf{S}_t$ has a spline-GARCH formulation: $\mathbf{S}_t = \mathrm{diag}(g_{1t}^{1/2}, ..., g_{N,t}^{1/2})$ with $g_{it} = \exp\{\kappa_{i0} + \kappa_{i1}x_{t-1}\}$, $i = 1, ..., N$, where x_t is a stochastic random variable. In the application it is a financial conditions index. In $\mathbf{D}_t = \mathrm{diag}(h_{1t}^{1/2}, ..., h_{Nt}^{1/2})$, the diagonal elements h_{it} have a GJR-GARCH representation. Following Connor and Suurlaht (2013), the authors define

$$\mathbf{P}_t = \bar{\mathbf{P}} + m_{t-1}(\mathbf{11}' - \bar{\mathbf{P}}) = (1 - m_{t-1})\bar{\mathbf{P}} + m_{t-1}\mathbf{11}' \qquad (44)$$

where the N-vector $\mathbf{1} = (1, ...,1)'$, $\bar{\mathbf{P}}$ is the (sample) correlation matrix of $\mathbf{z}_t$, and

$$m_t = \frac{\exp\{x_t\beta\} - 1}{\exp\{x_t\beta\} + 1}.$$

This is called the DC-X correlation model. The expression (44) resembles the one in the STCC-GARCH model, see Section 5.7, but the resemblance is superficial. The time-varying correlation matrix $\mathbf{P}_t$ is not a convex combination of $\bar{\mathbf{P}}$ and $\mathbf{11}'$ because m_t fluctuates between -1 and 1, not between 0 and 1. Besides, $\bar{\mathbf{P}}$ and $\mathbf{11}'$ are known matrices, the former after the spline-GARCH equations have been estimated. When $m_t \to -1$, $\mathbf{P}_t \to 2\bar{\mathbf{P}} - \mathbf{11}'$, and when $m_t \to +1$, $\mathbf{P}_t \to \mathbf{11}'$. The latter limit may appear a bit strange because $\mathbf{11}'$ is no longer a positive definite correlation matrix but rather a matrix of rank one, suggesting that all errors z_{it} are perfectly linearly correlated with each other. Some conditions on the elements of $\bar{\mathbf{P}}$ are required for $\mathbf{P}_t$ to remain positive definite for $m_t < 1$.

This situation will change if the matrix $\mathbf{11}'$ in (44) is replaced by a positive definite correlation matrix $\mathbf{P}$ and m_t by a function bounded between zero and one. Setting

$$\mathbf{P}_t = (1 - G_t)\bar{\mathbf{P}} + G_t\mathbf{P} \tag{45}$$

where G_t is defined as in (16) with x_{t-1} as the transition variable, $\mathbf{P}_t$ is, as a convex combination of two positive definite correlation matrices, itself a positive definite correlation matrix. Compared to (44), definition (45) implies $N(N-1)/2$ additional parameters to be estimated. If, however, one wants both to save the 'spirit' of converging to $\mathbf{11}'$ and to save parameters, one could assume that $\mathbf{P}$ is an equicorrelation matrix, see Engle and Kelly (2012). But then, in this parameterization the correlations would no longer fluctuate around $\bar{\mathbf{P}}$.

The results for Morgan Stanley and Citigroup (for space reasons results for other pairs are not reported) show that the estimated coefficient of x_{t-1} is significantly different from zero in both spline-GARCH models. Figure 3 in Opschoor et al. (2014) indicates, however, that nonstationarity visible in both return series does not diminish by the introduction of g_t in the GARCH equations. The correlations estimated by DC-X and DCC, respectively, look different. The former are more stable than the latter. The paper also contains a portfolio Value at Risk analysis, but discussing it here would be beyond the scope of this review.

5.6. Multivariate GARCH-MIDAS

The MIDAS approach discussed in Section 4.4 can be generalized into multivariate GARCH models. Colacito, Engle and Ghysels (2011) consider this possibility. The GARCH equations contain a multiplicative decomposition as in the GARCH-MIDAS-RV model of Engle et al. (2013), see (22). Following the notation in (24), the weight function is defined as $\varphi_k(1, \omega_2)$, $k = 1, \ldots, K$. In Engle and Rangel (2008), the correlations follow a DCC structure, but Colacito et al. (2011) define them as having a MIDAS-type representation. This implies modifying the intercept (or sample correlation) matrix in the DCC-GARCH model. This is done in two ways. First, the matrix is estimated only through a rolling window. Let $v_{it} = (\sum_{j=t-n_c}^{t} z_{ij}^2)$, $i = 1, \ldots, N$, $\mathbf{V}_t = \text{diag}(v_{1t}, \ldots, v_{Nt})$ and $\mathbf{Z}_t = \sum_{j=t-n_c}^{t} \mathbf{z}_j \mathbf{z}_j'$. Then the rolling matrix $\mathbf{C}_t = \mathbf{V}_t^{-1/2} \mathbf{Z}_t \mathbf{V}_t^{-1/2}$. Second, the matrices are smoothed using a MIDAS type smoother. In the simplest case the beta function is the same for all elements of $\mathbf{C}_t$, and the correlation matrix becomes

$$\mathbf{P}_t(\omega) = \sum_{k=1}^{K} \varphi_k(1, \omega)\mathbf{C}_{t-k}. \tag{46}$$

but more complicated situations are possible as well. Incorporating (46) into the standard DCC model yields the following short-run dynamic structure:

$$\mathbf{Q}_t = (1 - a - b)\mathbf{P}_t(\omega) + a\mathbf{z}_{t-1}\mathbf{z}_{t-1}' + b\mathbf{Q}_{t-1}.$$

Colacito et al. (2011) consider more general DCC structures in which a and b are no longer scalars, but they are not discussed here.

Parameters are estimated in two stages as is the case with DCC models. The GARCH equations are estimated first, which gives the estimates of z_t. From these one obtains the rolling matrices C_t, which allows one to compute an estimate of $P_t(\omega)$. Given $\hat{P}_t(\omega)$, Q_t, a and b can be estimated. Asymptotic properties of the maximum likelihood estimators of these parameters are not known.

The paper contains several examples, of which only one is touched upon here. The main object of interest is correlations between industry portfolios and a 10-year bond. The observation period runs from 15 July 1971 to 30 June 2006. As an example, consider the combination of energy and hi-tech portfolios and the bond. The inclusion of the MIDAS-RV component in the GARCH has a strong impact on the GARCH(1,1) coefficient estimates. The sum $\hat{\alpha} + \hat{\beta}$ is now low, for the energy equation even below 0.9. As to DCC, adding the MIDAS component has a negligible impact on estimates of a and b. The sum $\hat{a} + \hat{b}$ exceeds 0.995 in both cases. The situation does not change when the DCC-MIDAS component is more richly parameterized, see Table 2 in Colacito et al. (2011) for details.

There exist variants of the DCC-MIDAS model. Conrad, Loch and Rittler (2014) construct a bivariate DCC-MIDAS-X model ('X' will be explained later) for investigating the oil–US stock market relationship. Their purpose is to consider macroeconomic determinants of the long-term correlation between the daily US stock market and crude oil price returns. The spline-GARCH daily short-run component (conditional variance) is defined as before:

$$h_{ji,t} = 1 - \alpha_j - \beta_j + \alpha_j \frac{\varepsilon_{j,i-1,t}^2}{g_{jt}} + \beta_j h_{j,i-1,t}$$

where i indicates the day, t the month, and $\alpha_j + \beta_j < 1$, $j = 1, 2$. The positive-valued monthly macroeconomic component g_{jt} is defined as follows:

$$g_{jt} = \exp\left\{m_j + \theta_j \sum_{k=1}^{K_j} \varphi_k(1, \omega) x_{t-k}\right\}$$

where x_t is a macro variable.

Correlations are defined as follows. Analogously to LDCC and other models, the conditional covariance matrix has the decomposition $\Sigma_{jt} = S_t D_{jt} P_t D_{jt} S_t$ where $D_{jt} = \text{diag}(h_{1j,t}^{1/2}, h_{2j,t}^{1/2})$ and $S_t = \text{diag}(g_{1t}^{1/2}, g_{2t}^{1/2})$. The correlation matrix P_t is a two-dimensional long-term or macroeconomic matrix, and its only time-varying correlation is defined as

$$\rho_{12t} = \frac{\exp\{2u_{12t}\} - 1}{\exp\{2u_{12t}\} + 1} \tag{47}$$

where u_{12t} has a spline-GARCH-X structure (hence 'X' in DCC-MIDAS-X)

$$u_{12t} = m_{12} + \theta_{12} \sum_{k=1}^{K_{12}} \varphi_k(1, \omega) x_{t-k}.$$

The expression (47) guarantees that ρ_{12t} qualifies as a correlation coefficient because it fluctuates between -1 and $+1$. As a result, the short-run DCC correlation fluctuates around the long-run one driven by lags of x_t. Unlike g_{jt}, u_{12t} does not have to be positive. The parameters of the model are estimated by (quasi) maximum likelihood. Asymptotic properties of the estimators are still unknown.

The stock market is represented through daily returns on the CRSP value-weighted portfolio. The oil price returns are constructed from the daily spot price for West Texas Intermediate (WTI) crude oil for delivery in Cushing, Oklahoma. The observation period extends from January 1993 to November 2011. Five candidate variables are considered in the empirical part of the model, and a DCC-MIDAS-X model is estimated for each of them. Estimates of the pure GARCH model suggest nonstationarity or near-nonstationarity in stock returns, as $\hat{\alpha} + \hat{\beta} = 0.992$. Adding the MIDAS component does have some effect on this sum for the five equations, and the MIDAS parameter estimates are significant. The estimated GARCH equation for the oil returns has $\hat{\alpha} + \hat{\beta} = 1.004$, and in this case rescaling by MIDAS pulls this sum safely below one.

A large number of models with macro variables and correlations are estimated. If the best model for variances is selected by BIC, it is GARCH(1,1) for the stock returns and GARCH-MIDAS-X based on the 'Leading Index' (LI) in for the oil. For the definition of LI, see Conrad et al. (2014). As to conditional correlations, there is little difference between DCC and DCC-MIDAS for each type of GARCH residuals. It appears that it is more important to specify GARCH equations correctly than to extend the DCC model. At least in the case of oil returns this is understandable, because there the GARCH equation is mildly explosive. Measured by AIC and BIC, the best models have GARCH-MIDAS-X residuals with LI, but after that there is little to choose between DCC and DCC-MIDAS-X. As to $\hat{a} + \hat{b}$, the sum of the estimated DCC coefficients, it equals 0.997 in the former and is marginally lower, equal to 0.989 in the latter.

Connor and Suurlaht (2013) apply the GARCH-MIDAS-RV model (21), (22) and (23) to analyzing correlations between daily returns of 11 European stock market indices. They are calculated from daily closing prices from 31 December 1991 to 31 December 2010. In the GARCH-MIDAS equations the choice of MIDAS weights is $\varphi(\omega_i, 1), i = 1, \ldots, 11$, and the correlations are defined using (44). In the application, the sum of the GARCH parameters is close to one for the 11 GARCH models, and including the MIDAS component does not change this outcome. There is a discussion of how to define the variable

m_t in (44), given a number of economic variables deemed useful for the purpose, but for space reasons details cannot be considered here.

Chen, Choudhry, and Wu (2013) build their analysis on the MEM model of the observed range of returns $r_{it} = \mu_i + \varepsilon_{it}$, with $E\varepsilon_{it} = 0$, where the range is the difference between the maximum and minimum logarithmic price within a time interval t. This range, OR_{it} for asset i, is decomposed as

$$OR_{it} = z_{it} h_{it} g_{it} \tag{48}$$

where $z_{it} \sim iidGamma(\varphi_i, 1/\varphi_i)$,

$$
\begin{aligned}
h_{it} &= 1 - \alpha_i - \kappa_i/2 - \beta_i \\
&+ \alpha_i \frac{OR_{i,t-1}}{g_{i,t-1}} + \kappa_i I(r_{i,t-1} < 0) \frac{OR_{i,t-1}}{g_{i,t-1}} + \beta_i h_{i,t-1}
\end{aligned}
\tag{49}
$$

and the MIDAS component g_{it} equals

$$g_{it} = m + \theta \sum_{k=1}^{K} \varphi_k(\omega_{i1}, \omega_{i2}) RVM_{i,t-k} \tag{50}$$

with the Rolling Window Volatility Measure $RVM_{i,t} = \sum_{j=0}^{N'-1} OR_{i,t-j}$. Note that $Eh_{it} \neq 1$, because the indicator variable in (49) is $r_{i,t-1}$ and not $\varepsilon_{i,t-1} = r_{i,t-1} - \mu_i$. The equations (48), (49) and (50) define the Conditional Autoregressive Range MIDAS (CARR-MIDAS) model.

The application concerns the relationship between the oil price and US dollar returns as those series are expected to move together. The original series are US dollar index futures and West Texas Intermediate oil futures prices. As the CARR model indicates, the observed range of returns is the variable of interest. The dependence between returns of them is modeled by a copula. For details, see Chen et al. (2013).

5.7. Multivariate time-varying GARCH model

The MTV-GARCH model discussed in Section 3.4 can also be generalized to the multivariate case. The resulting model, the multivariate MTV-GARCH model, is proposed and studied by Amado and Teräsvirta (2014a). It is a Conditional Correlation GARCH model with the difference that the GARCH equations are augmented by a multiplicative component as in the TV-GARCH model. More formally, set $\varepsilon_t = S(t/T)D_t z_t$, where $z_t \sim indep(0, P_t)$, so the time-varying $N \times N$ conditional covariance matrix of ε_t becomes, as in (37),

$$E\{\varepsilon_t \varepsilon_t' | \mathcal{F}_{t-1}\} = \Sigma_t = S(t/T)D_t P_t D_t S(t/T) \tag{51}$$

where $D_t = diag(h_{1t}^{1/2}, ..., h_{Nt}^{1/2})$, $S(t/T) = diag(g_1^{1/2}(t/T), ..., g_N^{1/2}(t/T))$ and P_t is a positive definite time-varying correlation matrix. The positive-valued functions

$g_i(t/T)$, $i = 1, \ldots, N$, are defined as in (15) and (16). Analogously to the univariate case, $\boldsymbol{\phi}_t = \mathbf{S}(t/T)^{-1}\boldsymbol{\varepsilon}_t$ follows a standard conditional correlation GARCH model. Setting $\mathbf{P}_t \equiv \mathbf{P}$ yields the Constant Conditional Correlation (CCC-) GARCH model by Bollerslev (1990). If $\mathbf{P}_t \equiv \mathbf{P}$, $\mathbf{D}_t = \mathbf{I}_N$ and $\mathbf{S}(t/T) = g(t/T)\mathbf{I}_N$, one obtains an analogue to the model (33) that Osiewalski and Pajor (2009) considered but discarded as too simple.

Defining the recursion

$$\mathbf{Q}_t = (1 - a - b)\bar{\mathbf{P}} + a\sum_{j=1}^{n}\mathbf{z}_{t-j}\mathbf{z}'_{t-j} + b\mathbf{Q}_{t-1} \tag{52}$$

where $n \geq N$, $a + b < 1$, and $\bar{\mathbf{P}}$ is the sample correlation matrix of $\mathbf{z}_t$, gives the Varying-Correlation (VC-)GARCH model by Tse and Tsui (2002). Setting $n = 1$ in (52) leads to the Dynamic Conditional Correlation (DCC-)GARCH model of Engle (2002). As in LDCC, since recursions in $\mathbf{Q}_t$ do not automatically generate correlation matrices, the adjustment (39) has to be made to obtain a proper correlation matrix for time t.

The multivariate MTV-GARCH or MTV-CC-GARCH model thus consists of N univariate TV-GARCH components and a (possibly) time-varying correlation matrix $\mathbf{P}_t$. Maximum likelihood estimation of parameters can be carried out in two stages: by first jointly estimating $\mathbf{S}(t/T)$ and $\mathbf{D}_t$ and then, given the estimates $\hat{\mathbf{z}}_t$, the correlations. From Amado and Teräsvirta (2013) it follows that maximum likelihood estimators of the parameters $\mathbf{S}(t/T)$ and $\mathbf{D}_t$ are consistent and asymptotically normal under the assumption $\mathbf{P}_t = \mathbf{I}_N$. No asymptotic theory is available for the model when $\mathbf{P}_t$ (or $\mathbf{Q}_t$) is time-varying as in (52).

The conditional correlations are defined as the ones in $\mathbf{P}_t$, so they are correlations between the elements of $\mathbf{z}_t = \mathbf{S}^{-1}(t/T)\mathbf{D}_t^{-1}\boldsymbol{\varepsilon}_t$. Similarly to the LDCC, it follows that the deterministic components (diagonal elements of $\mathbf{S}(t/T)$) affect the correlations. This may be useful in cases where the correlations are changing systematically over time and do not fluctuate around a constant level as in, say, the VC- or DCC-GARCH models.

The functions $g_i(t/T)$, $i = 1, \ldots, N$, may also be defined using other than TV-GARCH specifications. Asymptotic properties of maximum likelihood estimators of GARCH parameters in SEMIGARCH are known from Feng (2004), whereas for the exponential quadratic spline- or P-spline GARCH models they are unknown.

Amado and Teräsvirta (2014a) apply the MTV-CC-GARCH model to daily returns of seven frequently traded stocks belonging to the S&P 500 index. The modeling period extends from 29 September 1998 to 7 October 2008. The observations from 8 October 2008 to 31 December 2009 are saved for forecasting. Because the returns are stock returns, GJR-GARCH equations are used instead of standard GARCH. The aforementioned asymptotic results obtained for the GARCH equations remain valid in the GJR-GARCH case; see Amado and Teräsvirta (2013) for discussion.

Persistence estimates from the seven TV-GJR-GARCH models vary from 0.97 to 0.78. The estimated $g_i(t/T)$ have a rather similar shape: values of the function decrease around 2002–2004 and increase again around 2008. The authors fit a model with a CCC, VC and DCC structure to the estimated residuals $\hat{z}_t$. Judging from the maximized log-likelihood, MTV-GJR-VC-GARCH fits the data best and, as may be expected, CCC-GARCH has the lowest maximum. For comparison, the performance of CC-spline-GJR-GARCH is studied as well. It has the best fit overall, whereas, again as expected, GJR-CCC-GARCH with $\mathbf{S}(t/T) = \mathbf{I}_N$ is worst in this respect.

The covariance matrix $\mathbf{\Sigma}_t$ is being forecast one day ahead. Since the true $\mathbf{\Sigma}_t$ is unknown, following Andersen, Bollerslev, Diebold, and Labys (2003) it was proxied by the realized covariance matrix based on 5-minute returns. The main forecast error loss function is the Frobenius distance

$$L_{F,T+i} = (1/N^2)\mathrm{vec}(\mathbf{\Sigma}_{T+i} - \hat{\mathbf{\Sigma}}_{T+i})'\mathrm{vec}(\mathbf{\Sigma}_{T+i} - \hat{\mathbf{\Sigma}}_{T+i}) \tag{53}$$

where $\hat{\mathbf{\Sigma}}_{T+i}$ is the one-step-ahead forecast of $\mathbf{\Sigma}_{T+i}$. The Root Mean Square Error (RMSE) over the forecasting period is computed from (53). The mean Absolute Deviation and Median Squared Error were also used but not discussed here. Since the estimated splines of the spline-GARCH model by Engle and Rangel (2008) all point strongly upwards at the end of the estimation period, there is the question of how to extrapolate them when forecasting. This is not an important issue if one is only forecasting one day ahead but becomes one when the forecast horizon is long. Amado and Teräsvirta (2014a) assume that when the starting-point for forecasting is T, $g_i(1 + 1/T) = g_i(1)$ for $i = 1, \ldots, N$.

The results indicate that the models with MTV-GJR-GARCH equations generate better forecasts than the ones with Spline-GJR-GARCH or GJR-GARCH. This is true for both CCC, VC and DCC specifications. The best model overall is the MTV-GJR-VC-GARCH model. The Model Confidence Set obtained from this set of models, see Hansen, Lunde and Nason (2011), consists of the three models (CCC, VC and DCC) in which the GARCH equations are MTV-GJR-GARCH equations of Amado and Teräsvirta (2013). It seems that at least in this seven-dimensional example getting the levels, i.e., g_{iT}, $i = 1, \ldots, 7$, 'right' is more important than choosing between the three correlation structures.

Due to the correlation structure (52) of VC and DCC, the correlations are restricted to fluctuate around $\bar{\mathbf{P}}$. Besides, the structure is aimed at capturing 'correlation clustering'. If the correlations in reality for example move monotonically in one direction over time, this translates into $\hat{a} + \hat{b}$ being very close to one (because of correlation targeting, the restriction $a + b < 1$ has to be maintained). This problem is avoided by applying the multiplicative Time-Varying Smooth Transition Conditional Correlation GARCH (TVC) model by Silvennoinen and Teräsvirta (2017). In this model, the correlation matrix $\mathbf{P}_t = \mathbf{P}(t/T)$ is changing deterministically:

$$\mathbf{P}(t/T) = G_{\text{corr}}(t/T, \gamma, c)\mathbf{P}_{(1)} + \{1 - G_{\text{corr}}(t/T, \gamma, c)\}\mathbf{P}_{(2)} \tag{54}$$

where $\mathbf{P}_{(1)}$ and $\mathbf{P}_{(2)}$, $\mathbf{P}_{(1)} \neq \mathbf{P}_{(2)}$, are positive definite correlation matrices, and

$$G_{\text{corr}}(t/T, \gamma, \mathbf{c}) = (1 + \exp\{-\gamma \prod_{k=1}^{K}(t/T - c_k)\})^{-1}, \; \gamma > 0 \tag{55}$$

and $c_1 \leq \ldots \leq c_K$. As a convex combination of $\mathbf{P}_{(1)}$ and $\mathbf{P}_{(2)}$, $\mathbf{P}(t/T)$ is positive definite. The definition of $\mathbf{P}(t/T)$ in (54) is analogous to that in the Smooth Transition Conditional Correlation (STCC-)GARCH, see Silvennoinen and Teräsvirta (2005, 2015). The difference is that the transition variable in (54) is deterministic, not stochastic.

Silvennoinen and Teräsvirta (2017) show that maximum likelihood estimators of the parameters of the TVC model, parameters in the correlation component included, are consistent and asymptotically normal. This paves way for misspecification testing which should be an essential part of any model building exercise.

With the exception of Silvennoinen and Teräsvirta (2017), correlations become deterministically time-varying through deterministic components in GARCH equations, see (51). Preceding these developments Silvennoinen and Teräsvirta (2009a), assuming that $\mathbf{S}(t/T) = \mathbf{I}_N$ in (51), have proposed the following correlation matrix:

$$\begin{aligned}
\mathbf{P}_t &= (1 - G_{2t})\{(1 - G_{1t})\mathbf{P}_{(11)} + G_{1t}\mathbf{P}_{(21)}\} \\
&\quad + G_{2t}\{(1 - G_{1t})\mathbf{P}_{(21)} + G_{1t}\mathbf{P}_{(22)}\}
\end{aligned} \tag{56}$$

where G_{1t} and G_{2t} are logistic transition functions defined in (16) for $k_i = 1$, $i = 1$, 2, and $\mathbf{P}_{(ij)}$, $i, j = 1, 2$, are positive definite correlation matrices. The ensuing model is called the Double Smooth Transition Conditional Correlation (DSTCC-)GARCH model. Suppose that the argument of G_{2t} is rescaled time t/T whereas G_{1t} controls rapid movements in correlations. Then (56) allows for long-run changes in the dynamics of correlations. The correlations may gradually as a function of time move to fluctuate around a new level. In the standard Smooth Transition Conditional Correlation model (Silvennoinen and Teräsvirta 2005, 2015) where $G_{2t} = 0$, the correlations fluctuate between two positive definite correlation matrices and do not experience systematic changes unless of course G_{1t} is a function of t/T. This special case has been first studied in the bivariate setting by Berben and Jansen (2005).

As already mentioned, Silvennoinen and Teräsvirta (2017) reintroduce $\mathbf{S}(t/T)$ with $\mathbf{P}_t = \mathbf{P}(t/T)$ in $\mathbf{\Sigma}(t/T)$ and prove consistency and asymptotic normality of maximum likelihood estimators for all parameters of the model, provided G_{1t} is a function of t/T, while still assuming $G_{2t} = 0$. The TVC model can be generalized to the DSTCC case, but the asymptotic properties of maximum likelihood estimators for parameters of that model are not known. (The parameters are estimated jointly, unless G_{2t} is a function of lagged z_{it}.) However, given the available asymptotic theory, TVC can be tested against DSTCC. Silvennoinen and Teräsvirta (2009a) have developed an LM test for this purpose with just assuming that the maximum likelihood estimators of the parameters of the null model are consistent. Despite the lack of asymptotic theory, it may be argued that DSTCC offers an alternative to the LDCC model by Feng (2006) and the FSG-DCC model by Rangel and Engle (2012) when the number of assets in the model remains reasonably small.

The paper contains a bivariate application to daily log-returns of the S&P 500 index and the 30-year US Treasury bill from 3 January 2000 to 6 July 2015, 4,046 observations. The amplitude of clusters in both return series varies strongly over time, and after testing and rejecting constancy of $g_i(t/T)$, $i = 1$, 2, TV-GARCH equations are specified for both series. Constancy of the correlation between z_t^S (S for stock) and z_t^B (B for bond) is also tested and rejected. (The relevant test will be discussed in a forthcoming working paper.) Joint modeling of GARCH parameters and time-varying correlations, that is, a complete TVC model, gives a correlation function with two sharp changes, one from about -0.3 to close to zero around 2004 and another back to -0.3 around 2007.

5.8. Misspecification testing

There do not seem to be many misspecification tests available for testing the adequacy of multivariate GARCH models with multiplicative decomposition of the (conditional) covariance matrix. Catani, Teräsvirta and Yin (2017) develop a Lagrange multiplier test of the model

$$\varepsilon_t = \mathbf{D}_t \mathbf{z}_t$$

where $\mathbf{D}_t = \text{diag}(h_{1t}^{1/2}, ..., h_{Nt}^{1/2})$ contains the GARCH equations, so $\mathbf{z}_t = \mathbf{D}_t^{-1} \varepsilon_t$. Under the alternative it is assumed that $\mathbf{z}_t$ is not iid but contains dynamic structure such that $\mathbf{z}_t = \mathbf{G}_t \zeta_t$, where $\zeta_t \sim \text{iid} \mathcal{N}(\mathbf{0}, \mathbf{P})$. Under H_0, $\mathbf{G}_t = \mathbf{I}_N$, so the null model is the CCC-GARCH model. The diagonal matrix $\mathbf{G}_t = \text{diag}(g_{1t}^{1/2}, ..., g_{Nt}^{1/2})$ is a multivariate generalization of (29) in that $g_{it} = 1 + \sum_{j=1}^{r} \delta_{ij} z_{i,t-j}^2$, $i = 1, ..., N$. Letting $\boldsymbol{\delta} = (\boldsymbol{\delta}_1', ..., \boldsymbol{\delta}_N')'$ be an Nr-vector whose $r \times 1$ vector blocks are $\boldsymbol{\delta}_i = (\delta_{i1}, ..., \delta_{ir})'$, the null hypothesis can be expressed as $\boldsymbol{\delta} = \mathbf{0}$. The authors develop a Lagrange multiplier test for testing this hypothesis and show that the resulting test statistic has an asymptotic χ^2-distribution with Nr degrees of freedom. The Lagrange multiplier statistic by Lin and Li (1997) turns out to be a parsimonious special case of the statistic by Catani et al. (2017).

Generalizing the test to the situation in which the null model is a DCC or VC model, say, is hindered by the fact that the asymptotic properties of the maximum likelihood estimators of parameters in these models are not known. For an illuminating discussion, see Engle and Kelly (2012). For the same reason, testing for example DCC against DCC-MIDAS does not seem possible.

6. Final remarks

This survey only concerns a small subset of GARCH models. It consists of models in which the usual conditional variance component is multiplicatively augmented by another time-varying component that can be either deterministic or stochastic. For readers who want more background information about GARCH there is a modern overview by Francq and Zakoïan (2010) that also covers the statistical inference, and a more compact exposition by Gouriéroux (1997). Many econometrics or financial econometrics texbooks contain chapters on ARCH and GARCH; see for example Tsay (2010), Teräsvirta, Tjøstheim, and Granger (2010), or Box, Jenkins, Reinsel, and Ljung (2015). Engle (1995) contains the most important early contributions reprinted in a single volume. Surveys of univariate GARCH models published over the years include Bollerslev, Chou and Kroner (1992), Bollerslev, Engle, and Nelson (1994), Palm (1996), Teräsvirta (2009), and Zivot (2009). Li, Zhang, Zhu, and Ling (2018) develop a nonstationary GARCH model (Zero-Drift GARCH). It describes volatility series that contain clusters with varying amplitudes but does it without multiplicative decomposition. Multivariate GARCH models are surveyed by Bauwens, Laurent, and Rombouts (2006) and Silvennoinen and Teräsvirta (2009b). De Almeida, Hotta, and Ruiz (2018) provide a useful discussion of popular BEKK- and DCC-GARCH type of models and compare their performance in forecasting in cases where the data are generated by a more general model than either of the two. Finally, in addition to articles already mentioned, the two volumes, Andersen, Davis, Kreiss, and Mikosch (2009) and Bauwens, Hafner, and Laurent (2012), contain several useful contributions on various aspects of GARCH models.

Acknowledgments

This research has been supported by Center for Research in Econometric Analysis of Time Series (CREATES), funded by the Danish National Research Foundation, Grant No. DNRF 78. The first author also acknowledges funding from the Portuguese Foundation for Science and Technology under the sabbatical fellowship SFRH/BSAB/143058/2018 and from COMPETE (Ref. No. POCI-01-0145-FEDER-028234), with the FCT/MEC's (Fundação para a Ciência e a Tecnologia, I.P.) financial support through national funding and by the ERDF through the Operational Programme on "Competitiveness and Internationalization" – COMPETE 2020 under the PT2020 Partnership Agreement. We wish to thank Christian Conrad and an anonymous referee for useful remarks. Any errors and shortcomings in this work are the authors' responsibility.

Bibliography

Akaike, H.: 1974, A new look at statistical model identification, *IEEE Transactions on Automatic Control* 19, 716–723.

Amado, C. and Laakkonen, H.: 2013, Modeling time-varying volatility in financial returns: Evidence from the bond markets, *in* N. Haldrup, M. Meitz and P. Saikkonen (eds), *Essays in Nonlinear Time Series Econometrics*, Oxford University Press, Oxford, pp. 139–160.

Amado, C., Silvennoinen, A. and Teräsvirta, T.: 2017, Modelling and forecasting WIG20 daily returns, *Central European Journal of Economic Modelling and Econometrics* 9, 173–200.

Amado, C. and Teräsvirta, T.: 2008, Modelling conditional and unconditional heteroskedasticity with smoothly time-varying structure, *SSE/EFI Working Paper Series in Economics and Finance 691*, Stockholm School of Economics.

Amado, C. and Teräsvirta, T.: 2013, Modelling volatility by variance decomposition, *Journal of Econometrics* 175, 153–165.

Amado, C. and Teräsvirta, T.: 2014a, Conditional correlation models of autoregressive conditional heteroscedasticity with nonstationary GARCH equations, *Journal of Business & Economic Statistics* 32, 69–87.

Amado, C. and Teräsvirta, T.: 2014b, Modelling changes in the unconditional variance of long stock return series, *Journal of Empirical Finance* 25, 15–35.

Amado, C. and Teräsvirta, T.: 2017, Specification and testing of multiplicative time-varying GARCH models with applications, *Econometric Reviews* 36, 421–446.

Andersen, T. G. and Bollerslev, T.: 1998, Deutsche Mark-Dollar volatility intraday activity patters, macroeconomic announcements, and longer run dependencies, *Journal of Finance* 53, 219–265.

Andersen, T. G., Bollerslev, T., Diebold, F. X. and Labys, P.: 2003, Modeling and forecasting realized volatility, *Econometrica* 71, 579–625.

Andersen, T. G., Davis, R. A., Kreiss, J.-P. and Mikosch, T. (eds): 2009, *Handbook of Financial Time Series*, Springer, Berlin.

Ashgarian, H., Hou, A. J. and Javed, F.: 2013, The importance of the macroeconomic variables in forecasting stock return variance: A GARCH-MIDAS approach, *Journal of Forecasting* 32, 600–612.

Audrino, F. and Bühlmann, P.: 2003, Volatility estimation with functional gradient descent for very high-dimensional financial time series, *Journal of Computational Finance* 6, 65–89.

Audrino, F. and Bühlmann, P.: 2009, Splines for financial volatility, *Journal of the Royal Statistical Society, Series B* 71, 655–670.

Baillie, R. T., Bollerslev, T. and Mikkelsen, H. O.: 1996, Fractionally integrated generalized autoregressive conditional heteroskedasticity, *Journal of Econometrics* 74, 3–30.

Bauwens, L., Hafner, C. and Laurent, S. (eds): 2012, *Handbook of Volatility Models and Their Applications*, Wiley, New York.

Bauwens, L., Hafner, C. M. and Pierret, D.: 2013, Multivariate volatility modeling of electricity futures, *Journal of Applied Econometrics* 28, 743–761.

Bauwens, L., Laurent, S. and Rombouts, J. V. K.: 2006, Multivariate GARCH models: A survey, *Journal of Applied Econometrics* 21, 79–109.

Berben, R.-P. and Jansen, W. J.: 2005, Comovement in international equity markets: A sectoral view, *Journal of International Money and Finance* 24, 832–857.

Bollerslev, T.: 1986, Generalized autoregressive conditional heteroskedasticity, *Journal of Econometrics* 31, 307–327.

Bollerslev, T.: 1990, Modelling the coherence in short-run nominal exchange rates: A multivariate generalized ARCH model, *Review of Economics and Statistics* 72, 498–505.

Bollerslev, T., Chou, R. Y. and Kroner, K. F.: 1992, ARCH modeling in finance: A review of the theory and empirical evidence, *Journal of Econometrics* 52, 5–59.

Bollerslev, T., Engle, R. F. and Nelson, D. B.: 1994, ARCH models, *in* R. F. Engle and D. L. McFadden (eds), *Handbook of Econometrics*, Vol. 4, North-Holland, Amsterdam, pp. 2959–3038.

Bollerslev, T. and Wooldridge, J.: 1992, Quasi-maximum likelihood estimation and inference in dynamic models with time-varying covariances, *Econometric Reviews* 11, 143–172.

Box, G. E. P., Jenkins, G. M., Reinsel, G. C. and Ljung, G. M.: 2015, *Time Series Analysis: Forecasting and Control*, fifth edn, Wiley, New York.

Brownlees, C. T. and Gallo, G. M.: 2010, Comparison of volatility measures: A risk management perspective, *Journal of Financial Econometrics* 8, 29–56.

Catani, P., Teräsvirta, T. and Yin, M.: 2017, A Lagrange multiplier test for testing the adequacy of constant conditional correlation GARCH model, *Econometric Reviews* 36, 599–621.

Chen, W.-P., Choudhry, T. and Wu, C.-C.: 2013, The extreme value in crude oil and US dollar markets, *Journal of International Money and Finance* 36, 191–210.

Colacito, R., Engle, R. F. and Ghysels, E.: 2011, A component model for dynamic correlations, *Journal of Econometrics* 164, 45–59.

Connor, G. and Suurlaht, A.: 2013, Dynamic stock market covariances in the Eurozone, *Journal of International Money and Finance* 37, 353–370.

Conrad, C. and Loch, K.: 2015, Anticipating long-term stock market volatility, *Journal of Applied Econometrics* 30, 1090–1114.

Conrad, C., Loch, K. and Rittler, D.: 2014, On the macroeconomic determinants of long-term volatilities and correlations in U.S. stock and crude oil markets, *Jounal of Empirical Finance* 29, 26–40.

Conrad, C. and Schienle, M.: 2017, Testing for an omitted multiplicative long-term component in GARCH models, *Working Paper*, Heidelberg University, Available at SSRN: http://dx.doi.org/10.2139/ssrn.2631976.

Dahlhaus, R.: 1997, Fitting time series models to nonstationary processes, *Annals of Statistics* 25, 1–37.

de Almeida, D., Hotta, L. K. and Ruiz, E.: 2018, MGARCH models: Trade-off between feasibility and flexibility, *International Journal of Forecasting* 34, 45–63.

Diebold, F. X. and Mariano, R. S.: 1995, Comparing predictive accuracy, *Journal of Business & Economic Statistics* 13, 253–263.

Eilers, P. H. C. and Marx, B. D.: 1996, Flexible smoothing with B-splines, *Statistical Science* 11, 89–121.

Engle, R. F.: 1982, Autoregressive conditional heteroscedasticity with estimates of the variance of United Kingdom inflation, *Econometrica* 50, 987–1007.

Engle, R. F.: 2002, Dynamic conditional correlation: A simple class of multivariate generalized autoregressive conditional heteroscedasticity models, *Journal of Business & Economic Statistics* 20, 339–350.

Engle, R. F. and Bollerslev, T.: 1986, Modelling the persistence of conditional variances, *Econometric Reviews* 5, 1–50.

Engle, R. F. (ed.): 1995, *ARCH Selected Readings*, Advanced Texts in Econometrics, Oxford University Press, Oxford.

Engle, R. F., Ghysels, E. and Sohn, B.: 2013, Stock market volatility and macroeconomic fundamentals, *Review of Economics and Statistics* 95, 776–797.

Engle, R. F. and Kelly, B.: 2012, Dynamic equicorrelation, *Journal of Business & Economic Statistics* 30, 212–228.

Engle, R. F. and Kroner, K. F.: 1995, Multivariate simultaneous generalized ARCH, *Econometric Theory* 11, 122–150.

Engle, R. F. and Rangel, J. G.: 2008, The spline-GARCH model for low-frequency volatility and its global macroeconomic causes, *Review of Financial Studies* 21, 1187–1222.

Engle, R. F. and Russell, J. R.: 1998, Autoregressive Conditional Duration: A new model for irregularly spaced transaction data, *Econometrica* 66, 1127–1162.

Escribano, Á. and Sucarrat, G.: 2018, Equation-by-equation estimation of multivariate periodic electricity price volatility, *Energy Economics* 74, 287–298.

Feng, Y.: 2004, Simultaneously modeling conditional heteroskedasticity and scale change, *Econometric Theory* 20, 563–596.

Feng, Y.: 2006, A local dynamic conditional correlation model, *MPRA Paper 1592*, http://mpra.ub.uni-muenchen.de/1592.

Feng, Y. and McNeil, A. J.: 2008, Modelling of scale change, periodicity and conditional heteroskedasticity in return volatility, *Economic Modelling* 25, 850–867.

Francq, C. and Zakoïan, J.-M.: 2010, *GARCH Models: Structure, Statistical Inference and Financial Applications*, Wiley, Chichester.

Gallant, A. R.: 1981, On the bias in flexible functional forms and an essentially unbiased form: The Fourier flexible form, *Jounal of Econometrics* 15, 211–245.

Gallant, A. R.: 1984, The Fourier flexible form, *American Journal of Agricultural Economics* 66, 204–208.

Girardin, E. and Joyeux, R.: 2013, Macro fundamentals as a source of stock market volatility in China: A GARCH-MIDAS approach, *Economic Modelling* 34, 59–68.

Glosten, L. W., Jagannathan, R. and Runkle, D. E.: 1993, On the relation between the expected value and the volatility of the nominal excess return on stocks, *Journal of Finance* 48, 1779–1801.

Good, I. J. and Gaskins, R. A.: 1971, Nonparametric roughness penalties for probability densities, *Biometrika* 58, 255–277.

Gouriéroux, C.: 1997, *ARCH Models and Financial Applications*, Springer, Berlin.

Hafner, C. M. and Linton, O.: 2010, Efficient estimation of a multivariate multiplicative volatility model, *Journal of Econometrics* 159, 55–73.

Han, H. and Kristensen, D.: 2017, Semiparametric multiplicative GARCH-X model: Adopting economic variables to explain volatility, *Unpublished paper.*

Hansen, P. R., Lunde, A. and Nason, J. M.: 2011, The model confidence set, *Econometrica* 79, 453–497.

Knight, F.: 1921, *Risk, Uncertainty, and Profit*, Houghton Mifflin, Boston.

Lamoureux, C. G. and Lastrapes, W. G.: 1990, Persistence in variance, structural change and the GARCH model, *Journal of Business & Economic Statistics* 8, 225–234.

Li, D., Zhang, X., Zhu, K. and Ling, S.: 2018, The ZD-GARCH model: A new way to study heteroscedasticity, *Journal of Econometrics* 202, 1–17.

Lin, S. and Li, W. K.: 1997, Diagnostic checking of multivariate nonlinear time series with multivariate ARCH errors, *Journal of Time Series Analysis* 18, 447–464.

Lundbergh, S. and Teräsvirta, T.: 2002, Evaluating GARCH models, *Journal of Econometrics* 110, 417–435.

Luukkonen, R., Saikkonen, P. and Teräsvirta, T.: 1988, Testing linearity against smooth transition autoregressive models, *Biometrika* 75, 491–499.

Mandelbrot, B.: 1963, The variation of certain speculative prices, *Journal of Business* 36, 394–419.

Mazur, B. and Pipień, M.: 2012, On the empirical importance of periodicity in the volatility of financial returns – time varying GARCH as a second order APC(2) process, *Central European Journal of Economic Modelling and Econometrics* 4, 95–116.

Mikosch, T. and Stărică, C.: 2004, Nonstationarities in financial time series, the long-range dependence, and the IGARCH effects, *Review of Economics and Statistics* 86, 378–390.

Mishra, S., Su, L. and Ullah, A.: 2010, Semiparametric estimator of time series conditional variance, *Journal of Business & Economic Statistics* 28, 256–274.

Nelson, D. B.: 1991, Conditional heteroskedasticity in asset returns: A new approach, *Econometrica* 59, 347–370.

Opschoor, A., van Dijk, D. and van der Wel, M.: 2014, Predicting volatility and correlations with financial conditions indexes, *Jounal of Empirical Finance* 29, 435–447.

Osiewalski, J.: 2009, New hybrid models of multivariate volatility (a Bayesian perspective), *Przeglad Statystycny* 56, 15–22.

Osiewalski, J. and Pajor, A.: 2007, Flexibility and parsimony in multivariate financial modelling: A hybrid bivariate DCC-SV model, *in* W. Milo and

P. Wdowiński (eds), *Financial Markets: Principles of Modeling, Forecasting and Decision-Making*, Vol. 3 of *FindEcon Monograph Series*, Lódz University Press, Lódz, pp. 11–26.

Osiewalski, J. and Pajor, A.: 2009, Bayesian analysis for Hybrid MSF-SBEKK models of multivariate volatility, *Central European Journal of Economic Modelling and Econometrics* 1, 179–202.

Palm, F. C.: 1996, GARCH models of volatility, *in* G. Maddala and C. Rao (eds), *Statistical Methods in Finance*, Vol. 14 of *Handbook of Statistics*, Elsevier, Amsterdam, pp. 209–240.

Rangel, J. G. and Engle, R. F.: 2012, The Factor-Spline-GARCH model for high and low frequency correlations, *Journal of Business & Economic Statistics* 30, 109–124.

Rissanen, J.: 1978, Modeling by shortest data description, *Automatica* 14, 465–471.

Rodríguez-Poo, J. M. and Linton, O.: 2001, Nonparametric factor analysis of residual time series, *TEST* 10, 161–182.

Schwarz, G.: 1978, Estimating the dimension of a model, *Annals of Statistics* 6, 461–464.

Sharpe, W. F.: 1964, Capital asset prices: A theory of market equilibrium under conditions of risk, *Journal of Finance* 19, 425–442.

Silvennoinen, A. and Teräsvirta, T.: 2005, Multivariate autoregressive conditional heteroskedasticity with smooth transitions in conditional correlations, *SSE/EFI Working Papers in Economics and Finance 577*, Stockholm School of Economics.

Silvennoinen, A. and Teräsvirta, T.: 2009a, Modelling multivariate autoregressive conditional heteroskedasticity with the double smooth transition conditional correlation GARCH model, *Journal of Financial Econometrics* 7, 373–411.

Silvennoinen, A. and Teräsvirta, T.: 2009b, Multivariate GARCH models, *in* T. G. Andersen, R. A. Davis, J.-P. Kreiss and T. Mikosch (eds), *Handbook of Financial Time Series*, Springer, New York, pp. 201–229.

Silvennoinen, A. and Teräsvirta, T.: 2015, Modeling conditional correlations of asset returns: A smooth transition approach, *Econometric Reviews* 34, 174–197.

Silvennoinen, A. and Teräsvirta, T.: 2017, Consistency and asymptotic normality of maximum likelihood estimators of a multiplicative time-varying smooth transition correlation GARCH model, *Research Paper 2017–28*, CREATES, Aarhus University, Aarhus.

Song, P. X., Fan, Y. and Kalbfleisch, J. D.: 2005, Maximization by parts in likelihood inference, *Journal of the American Statistical Association* 100, 1145–1158.

Taylor, S. J.: 1986, *Modelling Financial Time Series*, Wiley, Chichester.

Teräsvirta, T.: 2009, An introduction to univariate GARCH models, *in* T. G. Andersen, R. A. Davis, J.-P. Kreiss and T. Mikosch (eds), *Handbook of Financial Time Series*, Springer, New York, pp. 17–42.

Teräsvirta, T., Tjøstheim, D. and Granger, C. W. J.: 2010, *Modelling Nonlinear Economic Time Series*, Oxford University Press, Oxford.

Tsay, R.: 2010, *Analysis of Financial Time Series*, third edn, Wiley, Hoboken, NJ.

Tse, Y. K. and Tsui, K. C.: 2002, A multivariate generalized autoregressive conditional heteroscedasticity model with time-varying correlations, *Journal of Business and Economic Statistics* 20, 351–362.

Van Bellegem, S.: 2012, Locally stationary volatility models, *in* L. Bauwens, C. Hafner and S. Laurent (eds), *Wiley Handbook in Financial Engineering and Econometrics: Volatility Models and Their Applications*, Wiley, New York, pp. 249–268.

Van Bellegem, S. and von Sachs, R.: 2004, Forecasting economic time series with unconditional time-varying variance, *International Journal of Forecasting* 20, 611–627.

Wang, F. and Ghysels, E.: 2015, Econometric analysis of volatility component models, *Econometric Theory* 31, 362–393.

Zhang, X., Feng, Y. and Peitz, C.: 2017, A general class of SemiGARCH models based on the Box-Cox transformation, *Working Paper 2017–06*, Center for International Economics, Paderborn University.

Zivot, E.: 2009, Practical issues in the analysis of univariate GARCH models, *in* T. G. Andersen, R. A. Davis, J.-P. Kreiss and T. Mikosch (eds), *Handbook of Financial Time Series*, Springer, New York, pp. 113–155.

10 Do high-frequency-based measures improve conditional covariance forecasts?

Denisa Banulescu-Radu
and Elena Dumitrescu

1. Introduction

In this paper we investigate conditional volatility and covariance forecasting by making use of ex-post high-frequency-based measures of volatility and correlation.

Although volatility is unobservable, it is a particularly relevant element in financial market analyses such as option pricing and risk management. To construct precise ex-post proxies of volatility econometricians exploit high-frequency financial data. This method has been popularized as the realized volatility approach, and it provides *realized measures* of volatility that are more informative about the current level of volatility than the squared returns, and are hence expected to improve volatility modeling and the accuracy of its forecasts. This part of the literature is devoted to volatility *measurement* and it can be distinguished from volatility *prediction* that is basically a reduced-form or model-based approach. The main idea is to use high-frequency data to compute ex-post realized measures of volatility at a lower frequency. The econometrics of realized volatility was first explored in Andersen and Bollerslev (1998), Andersen et al. (2001, 2003), Barndorff-Nielsen and Shephard (2002), and Dacorogna et al. (2001), inter alia. The first realized measure of volatility was introduced by Andersen and Bollerslev (1998) and it is known as the realized variance (RV). The properties of this estimator are studied by Andersen et al. (2001, 2003) and Barndorff-Nielsen and Shephard (2002), who show that it is a conditionally unbiased estimator of the true daily conditional variance of the equity returns.

However, very high-frequency data may be polluted by jumps and market microstructure noise that induces autocorrelation in the intraday returns and makes the realized variance prone to a well-known bias problem. This issue was investigated in greater details by Andreou and Ghysels (2002), Bai et al. (2004), Aït-Sahalia et al. (2005), and Griffin and Oomen (2011). In the meanwhile, this sensitivity of the realized variance has motivated the development of a large number of improved proxies of volatility. We can mention the power and bipower variation introduced by Barndorff-Nielsen and Shephard (2004), the two-scale and multi-scale estimator by Zhang (2006), the median realized variance introduced by Andersen et al. (2012), the realized kernel by Barndorff-Nielsen et al. (2008), and the intraday range- and quantile-based estimators by Christensen and Podolskij (2007) and Christensen et al. (2010).[1]

The research on volatility *prediction* has also massively evolved during the last decades and its particularity consists mainly in proposing volatility forecasting models that make extensive use of realized measures. A first approach includes the Heterogeneous Autoregressive (HAR) family of models, that produce realized volatility forecasts by using only information from the realized measures dynamics see Corsi (2009) among others. Second, model-based approaches consist in augmented GARCH models, i.e., that combine asset return information with realized measures so as to output conditional volatility forecasts. The GARCH-X model of Engle (2002) was the first one to be proposed, but it is an "incomplete" model in the sense that it does not model the dynamics of the realized volatility and hence it cannot produce multi-period ahead forecasts. A complete framework that jointly models returns and realized measures, i.e., Multiplicative Error Model – MEM, was introduced by Engle and Gallo (2006) and its structure was simplified by Shephard and Sheppard (2010) in their HEAVY models. However, these models operate with multiple latent volatility processes. In contrast, the Realized GARCH (henceforth RGARCH) framework by Hansen et al. (2012) relies on a so-called measurement equation to relate the realized measure to the underlying conditional variance. Hansen and Huang (2016) and Lunde and Olesen (2013) find that RGARCH models significantly improve volatility forecasts. Extensions to a multivariate setup including financial assets or exchange rates are also found to provide good empirical fit for the data under analysis (see Hansen et al., 2014; Dumitrescu and Hansen, 2018).

Nevertheless, when a large set of assets is to be analyzed, all volatility forecasting approaches with or without realized measures suffer from the curse of dimensionality. Various hypotheses have been made in the literature so as to be able to model large financial systems (see, e.g., Engle (2002); Engle and Kroner (1995) in the GARCH framework and Chiriac and Voev (2011); Callot et al. (2017); Hansen et al. (2014)) in frameworks using realized measures.

A simpler, flexible and more parsimonious way to model high-dimensional systems is through the use of copula-based models. Indeed, copulas can be used to construct high-dimension distributions with specified dependence and arbitrary marginal distributions (see Patton (2012) for a review). Based on Sklar's (1959) theorem extended to conditional distributions by Patton (2006), the researcher can model the marginal distributions separately from the conditional one (here a conditional copula). The major advantages of this approach are its flexibility beyond existing multivariate distributions and the simplicity of implementation of two-stage estimation that reduces computational burden.

In this paper we investigate the possible benefits from using realized measures in conditional covariance forecasting. For this, on the one hand we propose to model large systems of financial assets by combining the advantages of the RGARCH framework, that will be used to model the conditional marginal distributions of the assets, and those of time varying conditional copulas so as to form a dynamic conditional joint distribution. We henceafter label this approach the Realized GARCH copula model (i.e., RGARCH copula). On the other hand, we estimate multivariate realized GARCH models similar to those proposed by Dumitrescu and Hansen (2018). The forecasting abilities of these two types of models relatively to those of traditional models, that do not exploit the information included in high-frequency financial data, are assessed by relying on the Model Confidence Set (MCS) approach of Hansen et al. (2011) with robust loss functions à la Patton (2011).

We illustrate the usefulness of the realized measures for conditional covariance forecasting in an empirical application on three pairs of SP500 companies exhibiting different levels of daily return correlation and covering different sectors: Citigroup–JP Morgan, Boeing–Procter and Gamble, and Pepsi–Coca-Cola.

We analyze the one-period ahead forecasting abilities of the RGARCH copula and the bivariate RGARCH models relatively to those of well-established competing models from the literature: the GJR-GARCH copula of Patton (2013) and the corrected-DCC model by Aielli (2013). We also include in this horse race the Robust-RGARCH version of the proposed model by drawing on Banulescu-Radu et al. (2018). We find that significant gains in conditional covariance forecasting emerge from the use of ex-post high-frequency-based measures of volatility and correlation. The role that realized measures of volatility and correlation play in conditional covariance forecasting should therefore receive more attention in larger-scale empirical forecasting analyses.

The rest of the paper is organized as follows. Section 2 introduces the copula-based models and the multivariate RGARCH ones, while Section 3 presents the conditional covariance forecasting approach. The results of the empirical analysis are revealed in Section 4, and Section 5 concludes.

2. Methodology

In this section we first introduce briefly the main realized measures of variance and correlation. Then, we detail the multivariate models compared that include realized measures of variance and/or correlation: (1) the RGARCH Copula models, and (2) the bivariate RGARCH models.[2]

2.1. Realized measures of variance and correlation

The realized measures of volatility rely on the continuous-time volatility process or the evolution of the spot volatility (i.e., instantaneous volatility). Nevertheless, volatility measurements are generally restricted to discrete-time intervals. By integrating the spot volatility over a daily horizon, for instance, one obtains the ex-post daily integrated variance (IV). In presence of jumps, the natural target for realized volatility measurement is the quadratic variation (QV), which extends the definition of the integrated volatility by including also the cumulative squared jumps.

To set notations, let p_t denote the logarithmic price for a financial asset sampled at daily frequency t, and the corresponding daily return be defined by $r_{t,t-1} \equiv \log(p_t) - \log(p_{t-1})$. Equally spaced series of continuously compounded returns are assumed to be observed m times per day (or to have an intraday sampling frequency $\tau = 1/m$), and be computed as $r_{t,i}^{(\tau)} = p_{t,i/m} - p_{t,(i-1)/m}$.

In the following, we limit our attention to three commonly used realized measures of volatility, and introduce first the so-called realized variance estimator (RV) proposed by Andersen and Bollerslev (1998). This estimator is simply obtained by summing up the squared intraday returns over a day t. More formally, it is defined as follows:

$$RV_t^{(\tau)} = \sum_{j=1}^{m} r_{t,j}^{(\tau)2}. \tag{1}$$

Under suitable conditions (such as the absence of serial correlation in the intraday returns) it can be shown that $RV_t^{(\tau)}$ converges to the so-called integrated variance as $m \to \infty$. However, in the presence of jumps, the realized volatility is not a consistent estimator of the integrated volatility anymore. Several estimators of IV robust to jumps have been developed. One such consistent measure of the integrated variance is the bipower variation (BPV) pioneered by Barndorff-Nielsen and Shephard (2004) and defined as:

$$BPV_t^{(\tau)} = \mu_1^{-2} \frac{m}{m-1} \sum_{j=2}^{m} |r_{t,j}^{(\tau)}| |r_{t,j-1}^{(\tau)}|, \tag{2}$$

where $\mu_1 \equiv \sqrt{2/\pi} \approx 0.79788$. Unlike the RV, BPV is designed to be robust to jumps by construction, i.e., it is obtained by summing up the product of two consecutive returns instead of the squared return, which means that a jump occurring at time t will be multiplied by a very small return observed at time $t + 1$.[3]

However, in practice, at very high-frequencies, returns are polluted by microstructure noise (e.g., bid-ask bounce, unevenly spaced observations, discreteness, etc.), which induces autocorrelation in the high-frequency returns. To counteract the adverse effects of microstructure noise, the price process is often sampled at 1, 5, or 30 minutes, the 5-minute frequency arising as the optimal one in many empirical applications (see, e.g., Liu et al. (2015); Banulescu-Radu et al. (2016)). At the same time, motivated by the specificities of the intraday financial time series (namely the presence of microstructure noise), researchers have proposed improved estimators of the quadratic variation. A benchmark class of estimators is given by the so-called realized kernel estimators, who provide a simple solution to the problem of estimating the long-run variance of a process observed at discrete times. In particular, a consistent measure of QV in the presence of second-order stationary noise is the realized kernel (RK) estimator by

Barndorff-Nielsen et al. (2008):[4]

$$RK_t^{(\tau)} = \sum_{h=-H}^{H} k\left(\frac{h}{H+1}\right)\gamma_{h,t}, \tag{3}$$

where $\gamma_{h,t} = \sum_{j=|h|+1}^{m} r_{t,j}^{(\tau)} r_{t,j-|h|}^{(\tau)}$, $\gamma_{h,\ t} = \gamma_{-h,\ t}$, $k(.)$ is the Parzen kernel function and H is a bandwidth determined by following the recommendations of Barndorff-Nielsen et al. (2009).

In the sequel of this chapter we rely on the multivariate versions of the realized variance and the realized kernel estimators. The realized quadratic covariation (hereinafter realized covariance estimator, RCov) by Andersen et al. (2003) is an immediate extension of the RV measure:

$$RCov_t^{(\tau)} = \sum_{j=1}^{m} \mathbf{r}_{t,j}^{(\tau)} \mathbf{r}_{t,j}^{(\tau)\prime}, \tag{4}$$

where $\mathbf{r}_t(\tau)$ is an n-dimensional return vector observed at time τ on day t. At the same time, the multivariate extension of the realized kernel approach ($MRK_t^{(\tau)}$) arises by feeding the n-dimensional return vector $\mathbf{r}_t^{(\tau)} = [r_{1,t}^{(\tau)}, r_{2,t}^{(\tau)}, \dots, r_{n,t}^{(\tau)}]^\prime$ to $\gamma_{h,\ t}$ in (3).

The corresponding realized measures of correlation can be subsequently derived from the realized covariance matrices:

$$RCorr_{ij,t} = \frac{RCov_{ij,t}^{(\tau)}}{\sqrt{RV_{i,t}^{(\tau)} RV_{j,t}^{(\tau)}}} \quad \text{or} \quad RKCorr_{ij,t} = \frac{MRK_{ij,t}^{(\tau)}}{\sqrt{RK_{i,t}^{(\tau)} RK_{j,t}^{(\tau)}}}. \tag{5}$$

2.2. Multivariate models with copula dependence

Let $\mathbf{r}_t = [r_{1,\ t}, r_{2,\ t}, \dots, r_{n,\ t}]^\prime$, $t = 1, \dots, T$, denote the vector of asset returns under analysis at time t. Its conditional distribution with respect to the information set, $\mathbf{G}(\cdot|\mathcal{F}_{t-1})$, is given by $\mathbf{r}_t|\mathcal{F}_{t-1} \sim \mathbf{G}(\cdot|\mathcal{F}_{t-1})$, where $\mathcal{F}_{t-1}$ denotes the information set generated by $(\mathbf{r}_{t-1}, \mathbf{r}_{t-2}, \dots)$. As usual, the DGP for each asset returns allows for time-varying conditional mean and variance,

$$r_{i,t} = \mu_{i,t} + \sqrt{h_{i,t}} z_{i,t}, \quad i = 1, \dots, n, \tag{6}$$

with the conditional mean, $\mu_{i,t} = \mathbb{E}(r_{i,t}|\mathcal{F}_{t-1})$, often considered to be constant or zero, $h_{i,t}$ the conditional standard deviation, and where the studentized innovations, $z_{i,t}$, follow a parametric distribution of mean zero and variance one, $z_{i,t}|\mathcal{F}_{t-1} \sim G_i(\cdot|\mathcal{F}_{t-1})$.

2.2.1. Copula dependence

Using Sklar's theorem extended to conditional joint distributions in Patton (2006), the conditional distribution of $\mathbf{r}_t$ given $\mathcal{F}_{t-1}$ is decomposed into the conditional marginal distributions of returns and the conditional copula that accounts for the dependence structure:

$$\mathbf{G}(\mathbf{r}_t|\mathcal{F}_{t-1}) = \mathbf{C}\big(G_1(r_{1,t}|\mathcal{F}_{t-1}), \ldots, G_n(r_{n,t}|\mathcal{F}_{t-1})\big), \tag{7}$$

where $\mathbf{C}: [0, 1]^n \to [0, 1]$ is a n-copula function and $G_1(.), \ldots, G_n(.)$ are the marginal distribution functions.

This decomposition allows one to draw on the vast literature on modeling and forecasting conditional covariance matrices by relying either on low or on high-frequency data. At the same time, one can avoid the curse of dimensionality and computational burden by estimating the model in stages (see Subsection 2.2.3 for more details). Consequently, a major advantage of this decomposition is that the proposed model can be easily extended to high dimensions and the estimation is feasible and fast.

A variety of copula functions have been proposed to date in the statistical literature, but we recall here only the most commonly used ones in financial applications, that belong to (1) the elliptical family of distributions, i.e., Gaussian and Student-t, or to (2) the Archimedian family, i.e., Gumbel and Clayton.

Also called implicit copulas, the Gaussian and Student-t copulas do not have a simple closed form, but are implied by well-known multivariate distribution functions. Indeed, the probability density functions of these copulas are easy to compute. The underlying distributions imply symmetry and different degrees of heavy-tailness for the copulas according to the degrees of the freedom parameter v. If one believes in the asymmetries of financial return dependence, such copulas could appear as too restrictive to provide a reasonable fit.

Asymmetric copula, exhibiting larger dependence in one tail than in the other, might be a better choice. This is the case of Archimedean copulas. If the Clayton puts dependence in the negative tail, the Gumbel has only positive tail dependence. A rotated version of the Gumbel is hence preferred in financial analyses where negative events tend to cluster together more than positive ones. Archimedean copulas are explicit copulas, that although are not derived from multivariate distribution functions, do have simple closed forms. They play an important role in finance because they present several desired properties: they are asymmetric, easily derived, associative and easy to estimate. Archimedean copulas are capable of capturing wide ranges of dependence for different choices of the generator function and they are related to multivariate distributions generated by mixtures. All these copulas and extensions thereof will be compared in the empirical application in Section 4.

Various extensions of the aforementioned copulas have been proposed in the literature so as to account for the specificities of financial data. In particular, time varying copulas, that allow the dependence parameter to vary through time, have gained a lot of attention. A nice way to specify the dynamics of the dependence parameter is by relying on realized measures of correlation. For this reason, the mechanism of these extended copulas will be detailed in Section 2.2.2, where we introduce the proposed multivariate models that mix realized measures and copula dependence.

2.2.2. Multivariate models with realized measures and copula dependence

The forecasting abilities of the model in (6) will depend upon the choices made for the marginal distributions as well as for the conditional copula.

The benchmark multivariate copula model in the financial literature is a constant GJR-GARCH copula one, i.e., based on the traditional GJR-GARCH for modeling the marginal distribution of each asset and constant correlation parameter, which belongs to the general class of copula-MGARCH models. By analogy with the traditional multivariate GJR-GARCH models, e.g., DCC GJR-GARCH, this specification is designed to account for leverage, i.e., stronger impact of negative shocks on volatility than that of positive shocks while specifying the joint dynamics of the return series. In the empirical illustration, in Section 4, the copula-MGARCH models obtained by combining these GJR-GARCH marginals with the various copulas described in the previous section will be compared in terms of forecasting abilities.

To this comparison we add a new class of multivariate copula models, called Realized GARCH copula, that account for the benefits from using both realized measures and copula dependence in conditional covariance forecasting. There are basically two ways to include realized measures in a multivariate copula model. The first one consists in modeling the marginal distributions of returns jointly with realized measures of volatility, as in the Realized GARCH framework (see, e.g., Hansen et al., 2012). The second approach derives from the multivariate character of the model and it consists of linking the dynamics of the copula correlation parameter to a realized measure of correlation. In the latter case the model belongs to the time-varying class of copulas.

In the Realized GARCH copula we hence propose to account for realized measures in both components of the model by drawing on the works on RGARCH on the one hand and on Generalized Autoregressive Score (GAS) models by Harvey (2013) and Creal et al. (2013) on the other hand. In particular, we specify the time-varying conditional marginal distribution of each asset as a RGARCH model. Indeed, modeling the dynamics of the realized measures in relation with the conditional measures of volatility through measurement equations has been shown to improve conditional volatility estimation and forecasting relatively to traditional GARCH models (see, for instance, Hansen et al., 2012; Lunde and Olesen, 2013; Dumitrescu and Hansen, 2018). To make the RGARCH model complete, besides the returns equation in (6) we specify the GARCH and measurement equations, for which we choose a log-linear form that easily guarantees the positivity of the variance:

$$\log h_{i,t} = \alpha_i + \beta_i \log h_{i,t-1} + \tau_i(z_{t-1}) + \gamma_i u_{i,t-1} \tag{8}$$

$$\log x_{i,t} = \xi_i + \varphi_i \log h_{i,t} + \delta_i(z_t) + u_{i,t}, \tag{9}$$

where $\tau_i(z_{t-1}) = \tau_{i,1} z_{i,t-1} + \tau_{i,2} z_{i,t-1}^{(2)}$ is called the leverage function. Here we adopt a quadratic specification with $z_{i,t-1}^{(2)} = z_{i,t-1}^2 - 1$ for $i = 1, \ldots, n$ by following Hansen et al. (2012), with $z_{i,t} = r_{i,t}/\sqrt{h_{i,t}}$. Similarly, $\delta_i(z) = \delta_{i,1} z_{i,t} + \delta_{i,2} z_{i,t}^{(2)}$. Besides, the measurement errors, $z_{i,\ t} \sim iid(0,\ 1)$ and $u_{i,t} \sim iid(0, \sigma_u^2)$, are assumed to be mutually independent, in the sense that the dependence of realized measures of volatility on returns is fully captured by $\delta_i(z)$.

To account for unusually large shocks to returns and volatility, we also consider the robustified version of the RGARCH model proposed by Banulescu-Radu et al. (2018), hereinafter RRGARCH model, as a specification for the marginals. For this extension, the authors adopted some insights from Harvey (2013) by introducing parameters that serve to dampen the impact of outliers in returns and volatility. To implement the model, one substitutes $z_{i,\ t}$ by $\tilde{z}_{i,t} = z_{i,t}/\sqrt{1 + z_{i,t}^2/d_{z_i}}$, and $u_{i,\ t}$ by $\tilde{u}_{i,t} = u_{i,t}/\sqrt{1 + \left(u_{i,t}/\sigma_{u_i}\right)^2/d_{u_i}}$ in the GARCH equation, where d_{z_i} and d_{u_i} are robustness parameters to be estimated. The standard RGARCH model emerges in the limit as $d_{z_i}, d_{u_i} \to \infty$.

To construct each of the parsimonious multivariate models we map returns' univariate marginal distribution, G_i, to the joint distribution, $\mathbf{G}$, through a constant or time-varying copula function such as those discussed in Section 2.2. Anticipating on the empirical results, the time varying Student-t copula, with constant degrees of freedom and time varying correlation parameter ζ_t, appears to perform best:

$$\mathbf{G}(\mathbf{r}_t|\mathcal{F}_{t-1}) = \mathbf{C}(U_{1,t}, \ldots, U_{n,t}; \zeta_t) \tag{10}$$

where $U_{i,t} \equiv G_i(r_{i,t}|\mathcal{F}_{t-1})$ are conditional probability integral transform variables of the return data. Indeed, Patton (2013) also finds it to perform well in financial applications. The evolution of the copula parameter ζ_t is assumed to be governed by the "GRAS" specification (Realized Generalized Autoregressive Score) inspired by the GAS models proposed by Harvey (2013) and Creal et al. (2013), and augmented with realized measures as discussed in Salvatierra and Patton (2015). Since correlation has restricted support, we model the dynamics of a strictly increasing transformation of ζ_t, $F(\zeta_t) = \frac{1}{2} \log \left(\frac{1+\zeta_t}{1-\zeta_t}\right)$, i.e., its Fisher transform, as:

$$F(\zeta_t) = \omega + BF(\zeta_{t-1}) + As_{t-1} + \vartheta F(y_{t-1}), \tag{11}$$

where $F(y_t)$ is the Fisher transform of a generic realized measure of correlation, y_t, and s_t the score of the copula likelihood given by $s_t = S_t \nabla_t$, with $\nabla_t = \frac{\partial \log \mathbf{c}(U_{1,t},...,U_{n,t};\zeta_t)}{\partial \zeta_t}$. $\mathbf{c}$ is the copula density function and $S_t = \mathbf{I}^{-1/2}$ the (Cholesky) square root of the inverse Hessian matrix. Note also that the "GRAS" specification comes down to the "GAS" one if the dependence of the copula parameter on the realized measure of correlation is dropped, i.e., the last term in (11) vanishes.

2.2.3. Likelihood function

The (R)RGARCH-GRAS-copula models are simple to estimate by multi-stage quasi-maximum likelihood (MSQML). Although this approach is less efficient than one-stage MLE, according to Patton (2006) the loss is not great in many cases, while the estimation problem in high dimensional systems is greatly simplified. Denote by $\boldsymbol{\theta} = [\psi, \theta_c]'$ the parameters for the entire model, with $\psi' = [\psi_1, ..., \psi_n]$ containing the parameters related to all the marginal distributions, i.e., ψ_i includes the parameters of the (R)RGARCH model for asset i, $i = 1, ..., n$, and θ_c the parameters of the copula.

The conditional joint distribution of the returns can be decomposed into the conditional marginal return distribution for each asset and the conditional copula by applying the extended version of the Sklar's theorem Patton (2006):

$$\mathbf{f}(\mathbf{r}_t|\mathcal{F}_{t-1}) = \prod_{i=1}^{n} f_{i,t}(r_{i,t}|\mathcal{F}_{t-1}; \psi_i)$$
$$\times \mathbf{c}\big(G_1(r_{1,t}|\mathcal{F}_{t-1}; \psi_1), \dots, G_n(r_{n,t}|\mathcal{F}_{t-1}; \psi_n); \theta_c\big),$$

where $\mathbf{c}$ denotes the copula density function. The associated log-likelihood function is:

$$\log \mathcal{L}(\theta) = \sum_{t=1}^{T} [\sum_{i=1}^{n} \log f_{i,t}(r_{i,t}|\mathcal{F}_{t-1}; \psi_i) \tag{12}$$
$$+ \log \mathbf{c}(G_1(r_{1,t}|\mathcal{F}_{t-1}; \psi_1), \dots, G_n(r_{n,t}|\mathcal{F}_{t-1}; \psi_n); \theta_c)].$$

The model is hence specified in such a way that the parameters can be estimated in two stages. In the first stage, the parameters of each margin are estimated independently of the other margins (assets) as

$$\hat{\psi}_i = \arg\max_{\psi_i} \sum_{t=1}^{T} f_{i,t}(r_{i,t}, x_{i,t}|\mathcal{F}_{t-1}; \psi_i), \quad i = 1, \dots, n, \ t = 1, \dots, T,$$

where the joint density of the RGARCH model can be rewritten as

$$f_{i,t}(r_{i,t}, x_{i,t} | \mathcal{F}_{t-1}; \psi_i) = f_{i,t}(r_{i,t} | \mathcal{F}_{t-1}; \psi_i^{(1)}) \times f_{i,t}(x_{i,t} | r_{i,t}, \mathcal{F}_{t-1}; \psi_i)$$

$$= -\frac{1}{2} \sum_{t=1}^{T} [\log (h_{i,t}) + r_{i,t}^2 / h_{i,t} + \log (\sigma_{u_i}^2) + u_{i,t}^2 / \sigma_{u_i}^2],$$

with $\psi_i^{(1)}$ the vector of RGARCH parameters except for $\sigma_{u_i}^2$, and the first term in the decomposition being precisely the conditional marginal return density function. The density of the RRGARGH model takes a similar form, where we account for the two transformations of the innovations and their corresponding parameters.

In the second stage, the parameters of the time-varying copula are estimated by

$$\hat{\theta}_c = \arg\max_{\theta_c} \sum_{t=1}^{T} \log c \left(G_1(r_{1,t} | \mathcal{F}_{t-1}; \hat{\psi}_1), \dots, G_n, (r_{n,t} | \mathcal{F}_{t-1}; \hat{\psi}_n), ; \theta_c \right).$$

Following Patton (2013), we choose for G_i Hansen's (1994) skewed-t distribution. Combining parametric marginal distributions for the standardized residuals with parametric models for the conditional means and variances simplifies the inference procedure for the copula parameters. Under standard regularity conditions it can be shown that $\sqrt{T}(\hat{\theta}_T - \theta^*) \xrightarrow{d} N(0, V_{MSML})$, *as* $T \to \infty$.[5] A consistent estimator of the asymptotic covariance matrix V_{MSML} can be obtained in the form of a "sandwich" estimator so as to capture the effect of first-step estimation error on the estimation of the copula parameter.[6]

2.3. Multivariate realized GARCH

In this section we introduce a second category of multivariate models for conditional covariance that make use of realized measures. Multivariate Realized GARCH models are simple extensions of univariate RGARCH models (see Hansen et al., 2012; Hansen and Huang, 2016). They have been shown to exhibit good forecasting abilities in the particular case of exchange rates by Dumitrescu and Hansen (2018). Similar to the univariate model, the multivariate model is structured in three sets of equations: (1) equations for returns, (2) equations constituting the multivariate GARCH system, and (3) measurement equations. If the n return equations are given in (6) and hence supposed common across all multivariate models under analysis, the multivariate GARCH system jointly models the dynamics of the log-conditional variances as well as the dynamics of the Fisher transformed conditional correlations:

$$H_t := \alpha + \beta H_{t-1} + \tau(z_t) + \gamma w_t, \tag{13}$$

with

$$H_t = \begin{pmatrix} \log(h_t) \\ F(\rho_t) \end{pmatrix}, \quad z_t = \begin{pmatrix} z_{1,t-1} \\ \cdots \\ z_{n,t-1} \end{pmatrix}, \quad w_t = \begin{pmatrix} u_{1,t-1} \\ \cdots \\ u_{n,t-1} \\ v_{t-1} \end{pmatrix},$$

and where $\tau(z_t) = \tau_1 z_{t-1} + \tau_2 z_{t-1}^{(2)}$ as discussed in the univariate setup. Denote by $q = n(n + 1)/2$ the number of elements in H_t. Then scalar parameters in (8) and (9) are replaced here by vectors or matrices, but they preserve their interpretation. In particular, α is a $q \times 1$ vector, β and γ are $q \times q$ matrices, while τ_1 and τ_2 are $q \times n$ matrices. $F(\rho_t)$ is the Fisher transform of the conditional correlation and the set of measurement equations accounts for the dynamics of both realized measures of variance $x_t = \{x_{1,\ t},..., x_{N,\ t}\}$ and correlation $y_t = \{y_{ij,\ t}\}$, $i \neq j$, $i > j$, $i, j \in \{1, ..., N\}$:

$$\log(x_t) = \xi + \varphi \log(h_t) + \delta(z_t) + u_t, \tag{14}$$

$$F(y_t) = \zeta + \psi F(\rho_t) + v_t. \tag{15}$$

Note that for parsimony reasons the measurement equations do not account for cross-assets dependence, i.e., they are designed exactly as in the univariate case. For simplicity, we further assume that the vector of measurement errors $u_{t-1} = (u_{1,t-1}, u_{2,t-1}, v_{t-1})' \sim \mathcal{N}_{n(n+1)/2}(0, \Omega)$, i.e., it follows a multivariate normal distribution with zero-mean and covariance matrix Ω:

$$\Omega = \begin{pmatrix} \Omega_{11} & \Omega_{12} \\ \cdot & \Omega_{22} \end{pmatrix},$$

where the three submatrices correspond to the covariances of the innovations in (14), (15) and cross covariances of all these innovations, respectively.

The conditional measures in (13) follow a vector autoregressive process of order one, VAR(1) with multiple sources of dynamics. First, the β matrix accounts for traditional interdependence between the conditional covariance elements in the form of persistence (on the main diagonal) and spillovers (off-diagonal). Its diagonal elements are subject to standard stationarity constraints. Second, through the leverage function, $\tau(.)$, the lagged studentized returns can impact conditional covariance elements in an asymmetric way. Besides, the lagged measurement errors can drive the conditional covariance dynamics up and down through the γ matrix.

The multivariate Realized GARCH model can be easily estimated by QMLE by following the same steps as for the univariate RGARCH (see Dumitrescu and Hansen, 2018, for more details). However, this model suffers from the curse of dimensionality when n increases. To make it more parsimonious, constraints such as diagonalizing the matrix β and / or γ in (13) can be imposed to the full model. This suggestion, that we will refer to as the diagonal bivariate RGARCH model, will be taken into account in the empirical analysis.

3. Forecasting

The fully parametric structure of the various models compared makes it easy to forecast the covariance matrix one-period ahead.

In the case of the copula-dependence models, the variance and covariance terms are forecasted separately based on the specifications chosen for the marginals (GJR-GARCH, RGARCH or RRGARCH) and for the time-varying copula (with "GAS" or "GRAS" correlation dynamics), respectively. On the one hand, by iterating forward on (8) for each asset and using the exponential transform, one immediately computes the one-step-ahead variances.[7] On the other hand, the computation of the correlation and implicitly that of the covariance has to be done in two steps. First, iterating on (11) in a similar way as for the marginals, followed by the inverse Fisher transform of the outcome, reveals the one-period ahead time-varying correlation parameter of the Student copula. To extract the level of linear correlation from the copula, we then rely on the simulation approximation proposed by Patton (2013) with 20 nodes and 50,000 repetitions. At the same time, one can use the bivariate RGARCH model for forecasting. In this case one obtains one-period-ahead forecasts of the full covariance matrix by iterating forward on (13).

If one is interested instead in multi-period forecasts, some adjustments are necessary. Within the "GRAS" copula specification, one would need to model the dynamics of the realized measure of correlation, for example with a heterogeneous autoregressive model à la Audrino and Corsi (2010), in order to construct multi-period forecasts of it. The time-varying correlation coefficient of the Student copula results then immediately from (11) with the realized measure replaced by its forecast and by the nullity of the multi-period score of the copula likelihood. Second, to predict the variances instead of the log-variances, one should proceed by residual bootstrap based on (8) and (9), as indicated for example in Lunde and Olesen (2013), see also Hansen et al. (2014). The variance forecasts will be given by the average of the exponential of all the possible log-variance forecasts obtained in S simulations. A similar bootstrap procedure, but involving (13), (14) and (15), easily produces covariance forecasts as for the bivariate model in Dumitrescu and Hansen (2018).

Once the forecast sequences on the covariance matrix are obtained, they are compared based on the robust loss function proposed by Patton (2011) and the Model Confidence Set (MCS) test introduced by Hansen et al. (2011). More specifically, in order to compare the covariance matrix forecasts, one is supposed to use a loss function defined as a general function of the covariance forecasts and the true covariances. But the true volatilities and correlations are unobserved and forecast evaluation has to rely on an ex-post covariance estimator generally called "proxy". To this aim, both the realized covariance and the multivariate realized kernel estimators are used as proxies.

However, it is well known that, because of its randomness, the use of a proxy may distort the ranking of models based on loss functions. Andersen et al. (2005) show that the comparison of losses – even based on a conditionally unbiased proxy – may lead to a different ranking than the one obtained if the true latent variable had been used. More recently, Hansen and Lunde (2006), Patton and Sheppard (2009a), Patton (2011), Laurent et al. (2013) have also focused on the possible distortions induced by the use of a noisy proxy in the ranking of variance/volatility forecasts. In the context of univariate models, Hansen and Lunde (2006) provided conditions for both the loss function and the volatility proxy under which the approximated ranking (based on the proxy) is consistent with the true ranking (based on the unobserved volatility).[8] Going further, Patton (2011) derives necessary and sufficient conditions on the functional form of the loss function for the models to be consistently ordered. Laurent et al. (2013) extended the previous results to the evaluation of multivariate volatility models, the comparison and the ordering relying on the sequences of covariance matrices. The authors provide (1) the theoretical conditions that a loss function should satisfy in order to deliver the same ranking regardless whether the true conditional variance matrix or an unbiased proxy of it is used, and (2) the necessary and sufficient conditions on the functional form of the loss function to order the models consistently in matrix and vector spaces.

Following these studies, we consider as loss functions the quasi-likelihood loss function (*QLike*), the squared Frobenius distance and the EntryWise norm:

$$QLike(\Sigma_t, H_t) = \text{tr}(H_t^{-1}\hat{\Sigma}_t) - \log|H_t^{-1}\hat{\Sigma}_t| - K,$$

$$L_F(\Sigma_t, H_t) = \text{tr}[(\hat{\Sigma}_t - H_t)^2] = \sum_N \lambda_i,$$

$$L_{1M}(\Sigma_t, H_t) = \text{tr}[|\hat{\Sigma}_t - H_t|],$$

where $\hat{\Sigma}_t$ is a realized proxy of the true but latent conditional covariance matrix, H_t is a candidate model for the conditional covariance matrix and λ_i are the positive eigenvalues of the matrix $(\hat{\Sigma}_t - H_t)^2$.

Knowing that in the empirical application we have to compare six competing models in terms of their predictive abilities, we decide to implement the Model Confidence Set approach, which is a multiple comparison-based test proposed by Hansen et al. (2011). This test aims at identifying, among the set of competing models, M_0, the subset of models $\hat{M}_{1-\alpha}$, which are equivalent in terms of forecasting ability and which outperform all the other models for a given confidence level $(1 - \alpha)$.[9] We set the significance level for the MCS to $\alpha = \{10\%, 25\%\}$ and use 10,000 bootstrap resamples (with a block length of 12 daily observations) to obtain the distribution under the null of equal predictive accuracy.

4. Empirical application

In this section we implement the two types of multivariate models including realized measures that were discussed in Section 2.2.2, and analyze their forecasting abilities relative to those of a selection of benchmark models.

4.1. Dataset

We use an extensive sample of high-frequency 1-minute data on S&P 500 companies from January 5, 2009 to June 30, 2016. The data are quotations prices taken from QuantQuote. All high-frequency prices are cleaned using the procedure outlined in Barndorff-Nielsen et al. (2009), and public holidays (e.g., Christmas, New Year, Good Friday, Easter Monday, Memorial Day, Independence day, Labor Day, Thanksgiving) are deleted. The daily returns are constructed as the log-difference of close prices, i.e., the last intraday price observed before or at 4PM precisely. The realized measures of volatility and correlation are computed from 390 one-minute intra-day returns using the multivariate realized kernel estimator by Barndorff-Nielsen et al. (2011). This estimator is widely used nowadays, since it is robust to microstructure noise and it insures the positive definiteness of the estimated covariance matrix. We hence rely on it for both the estimation of the model and the evaluation of its forecasting abilities. The Realized Covariance estimator of Andersen et al. (2003) is also used as a covariance matrix proxy in the spirit of a robustness check, see Section 2.1 for a short description of both realized measures.

   We consider three pairs of stocks in this analysis: Citigroup–JP Morgan (C–JPM), Boeing–Procter & Gamble (Boeing–PG), and Pepsi–Coca-Cola (PEP–KO). This selection covers assets from different sectors and different levels of sample linear correlation: around 0.66, 0.38, and 0.60, respectively. Such an analysis is expected to provide empirical evidence on the models' forecasting abilities according to the level of dependence between the companies and their sector of activity. Table 10.1 presents a summary of descriptive statistics for the daily log-return series, the Realized Kernel measure and the Realized Correlation estimator used in our analysis. The daily returns exhibit very small means for all assets and quite large overdispersion (i.e., the standard deviation is greater than the mean). They also display a high kurtosis, which indicates much heavier tails than a normal distribution. The skewness of the return series of the couple Citigroup–JP Morgan is positive, while the other return series have a left-skewed shape. Citigroup appears as the most volatile asset (having a standard deviation of 5.049 and a Realized Kernel average of 6.192), followed by Boeing. As expected, the realized kernel series present very strong positive skew and kurtosis. At the same time, the realized correlations have a positive mean and they are negatively skewed.

   One-period ahead forecasts are obtained for the period July 2014 to June 2016 through the rolling windows strategy with daily re-estimation of the competing models on 5 years and 6 months of data each time. This amounts to an in-sample

Table 10.1 Descriptive statistics

C-JPM

		Min	Q25%	Median	Mean	Q75%	Std Dev	Skewness	Kurtosis
Returns	C	-40.23	-1.586	0.000	-0.030	1.410	5.049	0.026	10.10
	JPM	-4.549	-0.360	0.000	0.009	0.361	0.759	0.111	8.131
RK	C	0.101	0.908	2.034	6.192	4.638	25.04	18.90	538.4
	JPM	0.060	0.873	1.869	4.493	4.273	10.55	10.74	184.6
RCorr		-0.341	0.453	0.597	0.573	0.721	0.197	-0.688	3.438

Boeing-PG

		Min	Q25%	Median	Mean	Q75%	Std Dev	Skewness	Kurtosis
Returns	Boeing	-11.23	-0.502	0.024	0.021	0.554	1.079	-0.433	10.35
	PG	-8.954	-0.260	0.016	0.013	0.301	0.571	-1.018	21.00
RK	Boeing	0.073	0.865	1.559	2.680	3.042	3.788	5.829	56.95
	PG	0.027	0.436	0.758	1.544	1.594	3.017	11.49	229.0
RCorr		-0.608	0.112	0.264	0.261	0.419	0.221	-0.168	2.765

PEP-CO

		Min	Q25%	Median	Mean	Q75%	Std Dev	Skewness	Kurtosis
Returns	PEP	-6.071	-0.293	0.008	0.018	0.325	0.584	-0.186	9.072
	CO	-2.432	-0.142	0.004	0.005	0.156	0.312	-0.229	8.053
RK	PEP	0.034	0.427	0.799	1.662	1.775	3.567	22.38	884.5
	CO	0.047	0.453	0.817	1.566	1.709	2.420	6.848	90.83
RCorr		-0.478	0.305	0.478	0.455	0.629	0.227	-0.464	2.821

Note: The table displays the summary statistics on daily log-returns (Returns), Realized Kernel (RK) and Realized Correlation (RCorr) for the six US companies under analysis. Min stands for the minimum value, Qa% for the a quantile of the distribution and StdDev for the standard deviation.

size of 1,341 observations and 499 out-of sample observations on which we base the performance evaluation tests.

4.2. Preliminary results

This analysis is designed to select the best copula functional form and to check whether simplifying the specification of the multivariate RGARCH model could be useful. It is based on likelihood comparisons, where the out-of-sample likelihood is obtained simply by plugging the in-sample estimates into the out-of-sample log-likelihood function. Note that in both analyses we report the likelihood and not the likelihood ratios for two reasons: (1) in the QMLE framework, the likelihood-ratio statistic does not have a standard χ^2 limit distribution, and (2) the asymptotic distribution of the out-of-sample likelihood-ratio statistic is non-standard (see Hansen et al., 2012, for a more thorough discussion on this topic).

Table 10.2 reports the in-sample and pseudo-out-of-sample likelihood for a large number of constant and time-varying copulas conditional on the three types of marginal models selected, i.e., GJR-GARCH, RGARCH, and RRGARCH. The results generally reveal the improved fit provided by the time-varying Student's t-GRAS copula, both in-sample and out-of-sample, regardless of the asset-pair under analysis. This finding indicates that allowing for joint fat tails in multivariate models of asset returns is important and more relevant than accounting for asymmetry for example with a Rotated Gumbel-GAS copula. The superior likelihood of the GRAS specification of this copula observed in most of the cases analyzed also shows that high-frequency data on correlations seems to improve the fit of dynamic copula models both in-sample and out-of-sample.

At the same time, Table 10.3 presents full and partial likelihood results for two specifications of our bivariate RGARCH model, i.e., the full and the diagonal specifications described in Section 2.3. Recall that the diagonal model assumes that β is a diagonal matrix, i.e., there are no direct spillovers between the elements of the assets' conditional covariance matrix. The results provide evidence of possible out-of-sample gains from simplifying the structure of the model and support the use of the diagonal specification in the subsequent forecasting analysis.

Nevertheless, this preliminary analysis is just indicative and it does not distinguish between the performance of the selected (R)RGARCH t-GRAS copula models, that of the diagonal bivariate RGARCH model and the performance of the traditional benchmarks. Therefore, in the following, we specifically check the relative out-of-sample forecasting performance of the selected multivariate models.

4.3. Forecast evaluation

As discussed previously, the empirical application illustrates the results for one-period-ahead forecasts on the conditional covariance matrix obtained from six

Table 10.2 Copula likelihood

In-sample likelihood

Copula	C-JPM			Boeing-PG			PEP-KO		
	GJR	RG	RRG	GJR	RG	RRG	GJR	RG	RRG
Normal	489.36	492.45	492.45	94.61	87.03	87.03	284.86	276.00	276.00
Clayton	427.22	424.12	424.12	85.24	77.93	77.93	229.66	220.65	220.65
Rot Gumbel	514.39	509.13	509.13	99.82	94.52	94.52	281.42	275.56	275.56
Student	546.23	533.88	533.88	106.62	104.16	104.16	304.25	297.07	297.07
RotGumbel-GAS	551.11	542.79	542.79	110.35	111.94	111.94	295.55	290.32	290.32
t-GAS	579.98	564.68	564.68	119.42	121.67	121.67	321.58	316.80	316.80
t-GRAS	**591.74**	**576.59**	**576.59**	**130.00**	**129.40**	**129.40**	**332.46**	**329.71**	**329.71**

Out-of-sample pseudo-likelihood

Copula	C-JPM			Boeing-PG			PEP-KO		
	GJR	RG	RRG	GJR	RG	RRG	GJR	RG	RRG
Normal	296.29	328.29	325.78	54.74	71.21	70.61	179.27	211.10	211.12
Clayton	258.57	250.62	245.68	54.09	67.88	67.02	161.16	193.06	192.41
Rot Gumbel	310.31	313.48	308.86	59.31	77.54	76.56	185.97	224.54	224.01
Student	327.08	333.79	329.98	60.67	86.18	85.39	189.44	226.79	226.46
RotGumbel-GAS	339.97	312.51	307.24	58.30	74.78	73.89	190.53	223.69	222.86
t-GAS	356.83	**339.03**	**334.81**	62.22	85.57	84.78	196.32	**228.13**	**227.58**
t-GRAS	**362.60**	313.61	307.97	**66.52**	**87.73**	**86.96**	**202.15**	227.34	226.25

Notes: The table displays the in-sample likelihood and out-of-sample pseudo-likelihood, respectively, for seven types of copula models: the first four are traditional copulas with constant correlation parameter, the next two specify a GAS dynamics for the time-varying correlation parameter and the last one augments the dynamics of the correlation parameter with realized measures of correlation. The results are based on three types of marginal models for each asset return: the GJR, the realized GARCH (RG), and the robust realized GARCH (RRG). The out-of-sample values are obtained simply by plugging the in-sample parameter estimates into the out-of-sample likelihood formula. Bold values indicate the largest likelihood.

Table 10.3 Bivariate realized GARCH likelihood

In-sample likelihood

	C-JPM	Boeing-PG	PEP-KO
Diagonal Bivariate	−5236.71	−6266.45	−3513.21
Full Bivariate	**−4669.36**	**−5055.62**	**−2742.99**

Out-of-sample likelihood

	C-JPM	Boeing-PG	PEP-KO
Diagonal Bivariate	**−916.10**	**−1737.81**	**−1048.89**
Full Bivariate	−2004.80	−2745.44	−1629.99

Note: The table displays the in-sample likelihood and out-of-sample pseudo-likelihood, respectively, for the full and diagonal bivariate RGARCH models. The out-of-sample values are obtained by plugging the in-sample parameter estimates into the out-of-sample likelihood formula. Bold values indicate the largest likelihood, i.e., the preferred specification.

competing models. Their forecasting abilities are compared based on the MCS test of Hansen et al. (2011) with three robust loss functions proposed by Patton (2011), i.e., the quasi-likelihood loss function, the squared Frobenius distance and the EntryWise matrix norm. Indeed, simulation results in Patton and Sheppard (2009a), and empirical results in Hansen and Lunde (2005), Patton and Sheppard (2009b) and Patton and Sheppard (2015) all suggest that using such loss functions leads to good power to reject inferior estimators when the true variance (covariance matrix) is unobserved and hence replaced by an unbiased proxy.

The results are synthesized in Tables 10.4 and 10.5. They display the average loss over the evaluation period and the MCS p-value for each competing model under analysis. The three aforementioned robust loss functions are considered for each couple of stocks, i.e., Citigroup–JP Morgan, Boeing–Procter & Gamble, and Pepsi–Coca-Cola. The best models, as identified by the MCS test, are signaled by one (significance level of 10%) and two (significance level of 25%) asterisks, respectively. The main difference between these two tables is that they rely on different covariance matrix proxies for the true unobserved covariance matrix when evaluating the forecasting abilities of the six models. Table 10.4 uses the multivariate realized kernel of Barndorff-Nielsen et al. (2011), while the results in Table 10.5 rely on the classic realized covariance of Andersen et al. (2003).

Taking as example the couple Citigroup–JP Morgan (Table 10.4), we observe that the smallest average QLIKE losses are recorded by the bivariate RGARCH model, followed by the RRGARCH-GRAS copula and the RGARCH-GRAS copula specifications. Only the first specification is selected as the best model by the MCS test. The two other specifications are in the subset of superior forecasting models when the MCS test is based on the losses given by the squared Frobenius distance. When considering the EntryWise norm, the MCS test identifies RRGARCH-GRAS copula as the best model. This change in the composition of the subset of best models according to the MCS is not surprising since the

Table 10.4 Out-of-sample forecast evaluation using Realized Kernel covariance proxy (MCS test)

QLIKE

	C-JPM		Boeing-PG		PEP-KO	
	Loss	P_{MCS}	Loss	P_{MCS}	Loss	P_{MCS}
Bivariate-RG	0.82	1.00**	3.77	0.00	5.82	0.00
cDCC	1.11	0.00	35.38	0.00	4.74	0.86**
RRG-GRAS-Copula	0.88	0.03	3.49	0.00	6.46	0.00
RG-GRAS-Copula	0.90	0.00	3.47	0.00	6.47	0.00
GJR-GRAS-Copula	1.09	0.00	2.43	0.00	5.38	0.00
GJR-GAS-Copula	1.09	0.00	1.95	1.00**	4.70	1.00**

Squared Frobenius distance

	C-JPM		Boeing-PG		PEP-KO	
	Loss	P_{MCS}	Loss	P_{MCS}	Loss	P_{MCS}
Bivariate-RG	7.430	0.32**	20.13	0.02	2.80	0.42**
cDCC	14.47	0.01	21.18	0.01	2.81	0.55**
RRG-GRAS-Copula	7.310	1.00**	20.58	0.01	2.85	0.11*
RG-GRAS-Copula	7.330	0.32**	20.56	0.01	2.83	0.10*
GJR-GRAS-Copula	15.94	0.02	19.80	1.00**	2.78	0.55**
GJR-GAS-Copula	15.94	0.02	19.80	0.14*	2.78	1.00**

EntryWise norm

	C-JPM		Boeing-PG		PEP-KO	
	Loss	P_{MCS}	Loss	P_{MCS}	Loss	P_{MCS}
Bivariate-RG	1.93	0.04	3.65	0.00	1.46	0.00
cDCC	3.53	0.00	4.31	0.00	1.40	0.52**
RRG-GRAS-Copula	1.84	1.00**	3.69	0.00	1.47	0.00
RG-GRAS-Copula	1.85	0.04	3.69	0.00	1.46	0.00
GJR-GRAS-Copula	3.58	0.00	3.26	1.00**	1.39	1.00**
GJR-GAS-Copula	3.60	0.00	3.30	0.00	1.41	0.01

Note: The tables displays the MCS average loss over the evaluation sample and the p-value for each of the six competing models under analysis. The conditional covariance forecasts in the 90% ($\hat{M}_{90\%}$) and 75% ($\hat{M}_{75\%}$) confidence sets are identified by one and two asterisks, respectively. Three loss functions are used, i.e., quasi-likelihood, the squared Frobenius distance and the EntryWise matrix norm. The multivariate realized kernel is used as a proxy for the true unobserved covariance matrix at each point in time.

consistency of the ranking is defined with respect to a given loss function. Thus, the ranking may change when a different loss function is used in MCS. Identical results are obtained when changing the proxy used for the covariance matrix (see Table 10.5).

For the Boeing–Procter & Gamble pair, the MCS test selects the GJR-GRAS copula and/or the GJR-GAS copula specifications as the subset of best models, whatever the loss function considered. Pepsi–Coca-Cola is the only couple including the traditional cDCC model in the subset of superior forecasting models among some other models.

Table 10.5 Out-of-sample forecast evaluation using realized covariance proxy (MCS test)

QLIKE

	C-JPM		Boeing-PG		PEP-KO	
	Loss	Pmcs	Loss	Pmcs	Loss	Pmcs
Bivariate-RG	0.82	1.00**	4.43	0.00	7.15	0.00
cDCC	1.05	0.00	36.66	0.00	5.80	0.90**
RRG-GRAS-Copula	0.88	0.02	3.95	0.00	7.95	0.00
RG-GRAS-Copula	0.91	0.00	3.94	0.00	7.97	0.00
GJR-GRAS-Copula	1.04	0.00	2.95	0.00	6.59	0.00
GJR-GAS-Copula	1.03	0.00	2.28	1.00**	5.76	1.00**

Squared Frobenius distance

	C-JPM		Boeing-PG		PEP-KO	
	Loss	Pmcs	Loss	Pmcs	Loss	Pmcs
Bivariate-RG	8.100	0.30**	7.35	0.10*	3.24	0.08
cDCC	14.37	0.01	8.440	0.00	3.24	0.59**
RRG-GRAS-Copula	8.050	1.00**	7.86	0.01	3.31	0.04
RG-GRAS-Copula	8.070	0.30**	7.84	0.01	3.28	0.04
GJR-GRAS-Copula	15.73	0.02	7.08	0.18*	3.17	0.59**
GJR-GAS-Copula	15.73	0.02	7.08	1.00**	3.17	1.00**

EntryWise norm

	C-JPM		Boeing-PG		PEP-KO	
	Loss	Pmcs	Loss	Pmcs	Loss	Pmcs
Bivariate-RG	1.78	0.04	3.68	0.00	1.64	0.00
cDCC	3.35	0.00	4.33	0.00	1.54	0.52**
RRG-GRAS-Copula	1.74	1.00**	3.71	0.00	1.64	0.00
RG-GRAS-Copula	1.75	0.04	3.70	0.00	1.64	0.00
GJR-GRAS-Copula	3.39	0.00	3.23	1.00**	1.53	1.00**
GJR-GAS-Copula	3.43	0.00	3.28	0.00	1.55	0.01

Note: The tables displays the MCS average loss over the evaluation sample and the p-value for each of the six competing models under analysis. The conditional covariance forecasts in the 90% ($\hat{M}_{90\%}$) and 75% ($\hat{M}_{90\%}$) confidence sets are identified by one and two asterisks, respectively. Three loss functions are used, i.e., quasi-likelihood, the squared Frobenius distance and the EntryWise matrix norm. The realized covariance is used as a proxy for the true unobserved covariance matrix at each point in time.

All in all, these findings indicate that the new specifications making use of ex-post information contained in realized correlation data (either taking the form of multivariate realized models or copula-type approaches) lead to significant improvement in the quality of the conditional covariance (and implicitly, of the correlation) matrix forecasts. Most of the time, the use of realized measures of volatility also proves to be useful in the context of covariance forecasting, suggesting that both high-frequency-based measures of volatility and of correlation should be exploited to improve conditional covariance forecasts in larger-scale empirical analyses.

5. Conclusion

In this paper we tackle the usefulness of ex-post high-frequency-based measures of volatility and correlation in forecasting the conditional covariance matrix. For this, we propose various model specifications that rely on the multivariate RGARCH framework, or on univariate (R)RGARCH/GJR-GARCH models augmented with copula dependence functions. These models hence include either realized measures of variance or realized measures of correlation, or both or none. A horse-race of their out-of-sample forecasting abilities is organized in an empirical analysis on three pairs of assets, i.e., Citigroup–JP Morgan, Boeing–Procter & Gamble, and Pepsi–Coca-Cola, that exhibit different levels of unconditional correlation and cover different sectors. The one-period-ahead forecasting abilities of the six models in competition are scrutinized through the MCS test by relying on robust loss functions. Our main finding is that the specifications proposed contain useful information in covariance forecasting that goes beyond that of traditional multivariate GARCH models. Still, none of the models proposed outperforms all the other specifications in all cases. We thus show that the role the realized measures of volatility and correlation play in conditional covariance forecasting seems to deserve more attention in larger-scale empirical forecasting analyses. Besides, the possible connection between the results of the forecast evaluation and the level of correlation between the assets, as indicated by Pearson's coefficient, is still to be investigated, as no clear pattern emerges from our analysis.

Notes

1 See also Andersen et al. (2009), Hansen and Horel (2009), and references therein.
2 The traditional DCC-type models are not detailed here. For a review of them, see Bauwens et al. (2012), and Aielli (2013) for the specificities of the cDCC model.
3 Other well-known alternatives to the BPV include the median realized variance (medRV) proposed by Andersen et al. (2012) and computed as the sum of the squared median of three consecutive intraday returns, the quantile-based realized variance (QRV) of Christensen et al. (2010), the "nearest neighbor truncation" estimators of Andersen et al. (2012), i.e., the "MinRV" and "MedRV" estimators, and the truncated or threshold realized variance of Mancini (2001, 2009).
4 Several other estimators of QV based on high-frequency data that correct for microstructure noise, and which under certain conditions on the market microstructure noise are consistent at the optimal rate, have been proposed in the literature, e.g., the two-scale realized variance (TSRV) of Zhang et al. (2005), the multi-scale realized variance (MSRV) of Zhang (2006), the pre-averaged realized variances estimator by Podolskij and Vetter (2009) and Jacod et al. (2009), the "realized range-based variance" (RRV) of Christensen and Podolskij (2007) and Martens and Van Dijk (2007), the maximum likelihood realized variance of Aït-Sahalia et al. (2005), etc., but their analysis is out of the scope of this paper.
5 For more details, see White (1996), as well as the discussion in Patton (2013).
6 An alternative method is to use a block bootstrap for inference, see Gonçalves and White (2004).
7 A similar iteration is performed in the case of the GJR-GARCH model.

8 At this stage, a confusion between the consistency of the ranking and the invariance of the ordering may appear and it has to be avoided. As stated by Laurent et al (2013), consistency is understood as the accuracy of the proxy and this for a given loss function, i.e., we talk about consistency between the true and the approximated ranking. On the other hand, the invariance of the ranking means that the ordering does not change with respect to the choice of the loss function.

9 The main advantages of the MCS test are that we do not have to specify a benchmark model and that it relies on simple hypotheses that lead to standard asymptotics. However, when the number of competing models is large, the test statistic has a non-standard distribution, reason for which a bootstrap scheme is employed to obtain the distribution under the null hypothesis.

Bibliography

Aielli, G. P. Dynamic conditional correlation: On properties and estimation. *Journal of Business & Economic Statistics*, 31(3):282–299, 2013.

Aït-Sahalia, Y., P. A. Mykland, and L. Zhang. How often to sample a continuous-time process in the presence of market microstructure noise. *The Review of Financial Studies*, 18(2):351–416, 2005.

Andersen, T. G., and T. Bollerslev. Answering the skeptics: Yes, standard volatility models do provide accurate forecasts. *International Economic Review*, 39(4):885–905, 1998.

Andersen, T. G., T. Bollerslev, F. X. Diebold, and P. Labys. The distribution of exchange rate volatility. *Journal of the American Statistical Association*, 96(453):42–55, 2001. Correction published in 2003, volume 98, page 501.

Andersen, T. G., T. Bollerslev, F. X. Diebold, and P. Labys. Modeling and forecasting realized volatility. *Econometrica*, 71(2):579–625, 2003.

Andersen, T. G., T. Bollerslev, and N. Meddahi. Correcting the errors: Volatility forecast evaluation using high-frequency data and realized volatilities. *Econometrica*, 73(1):279–296, 2005.

Andersen, T. G., D. Dobrev, and E. Schaumburg. Duration-based volatility estimation. *Working paper*, 2009.

Andersen, T. G., D. Dobrev, and E. Schaumburg. Jump-robust volatility estimation using nearest neighbor truncation. *Journal of Econometrics*, 169(1): 75–93, 2012.

Andreou, E., and E. Ghysels. Rolling-sample volatility estimators: Some new theoretical, simulation, and empirical results. *Journal of Business & Economic Statistics*, 20(3):363–376, 2002.

Audrino, F., and F. Corsi. Modeling tick-by-tick realized correlations. *Computational Statistics & Data Analysis*, 54(11):2372–2382, 2010.

Bai, X., J. R. Russell, and G. C. Tiao. Effects of non-normality and dependence on the precision of variance estimates using high-frequency financial data. *Working paper*, University of Chicago, GSB, 2004.

Banulescu-Radu, D., P. R. Hansen, Z. Huang, and M. Matei. Volatility during the financial crisis through the lens of high frequency data: A realized GARCH approach. *Working paper*, SSRN, 2018.

Banulescu-Radu, D., C. Hurlin, B. Candelon, and S. Laurent. Do we need high frequency data to forecast variances? *Annals of Economics and Statistics/ Annales d'Économie et de Statistique*, (123/124):135–174, 2016.

Barndorff-Nielsen, O. E., P. R. Hansen, A. Lunde, and N. Shephard. Designing realized kernels to measure the ex post variation of equity prices in the presence of noise. *Econometrica*, 76(6):1481–1536, 2008.

Barndorff-Nielsen, O. E., P. R. Hansen, A. Lunde, and N. Shephard. Multivariate realised kernels: Consistent positive semi-definite estimators of the covariation of equity prices with noise and non-synchronous trading. *Journal of Econometrics*, 162(2):149–169, 2011.

Barndorff-Nielsen, O. E., P. R. Hansen, A. Lunde, and N. Shephard. Realized kernels in practice: Trades and quotes. *The Econometrics Journal*, 12(3): C1–C32, 2009.

Barndorff-Nielsen, O. E., and N. Shephard. Econometric analysis of realised volatility and its use in estimating stochastic volatility models. *Journal of the Royal Statistical Society B*, 64(2):253–280, 2002.

Barndorff-Nielsen, O. E., and N. Shephard. Power and bipower variation with stochastic volatility and jumps (with discussion). *Journal of Financial Econometrics*, 2(1):1–48, 2004.

Bauwens, L., C. M. Hafner, and S. Laurent. *Handbook of volatility models and their applications*, volume 3. John Wiley & Sons, 2012.

Callot, L. A., A. B. Kock, and M. C. Medeiros. Modeling and forecasting large realized covariance matrices and portfolio choice. *Journal of Applied Econometrics*, 32(1):140–158, 2017.

Chiriac, R., and V. Voev. Modelling and forecasting multivariate realized volatility. *Journal of Applied Econometrics*, 26(6):922–947, 2011.

Christensen, K., R. Oomen, and M. Podolskij. Realised quantile-based estimation of the integrated variance. *Journal of Econometrics*, 159(1):74–98, 2010.

Christensen, K., and M. Podolskij. Realized range-based estimation of Integrated Variance. *Journal of Econometrics*, 141(2):323–349, 2007.

Corsi, F. A simple approximate long-memory model of realized volatility. *Journal of Financial Econometrics*, 7(2):174–196, 2009.

Creal, D. D., S. J. Koopman, and A. Lucas. Generalized autoregressive score models with applications. *Journal of Applied Econometrics*, 28(5):777–795, 2013.

Dacorogna, M. M., R. Gencay, U. Müller, R. B. Olsen, and O. V. Pictet. *An introduction to high-frequency finance*. Academic Press, London, 2001.

Dumitrescu, E.-I., and P. R. Hansen. Exchange rate volatility forecasting: a multivariate realized-GARCH approach. *Working Paper*, 2018.

Engle, R. F. New frontiers for ARCH models. *Journal of Applied Econometrics*, 17(5):425–446, 2002.

Engle, R. F., and G. M. Gallo. A multiple indicators model for volatility using intra-daily data. *Journal of Econometrics*, 131(1–2):3–27, 2006.

Engle, R. F., and K. F. Kroner. Multivariate simultaneous generalized ARCH. *Econometric Theory*, 11(1):122–150, 1995.

Gonçalves, S., and H. White. Maximum likelihood and the bootstrap for nonlinear dynamic models. *Journal of Econometrics*, 119(1):199–219, 2004.

Griffn, J. E., and R. C. Oomen. Covariance measurement in the presence of non-synchronous trading and market microstructure noise. *Journal of Econometrics*, 160(1):58–68, 2011.

Hansen, B. E.. Autoregressive Conditional Density Estimation. International Economic Review 35, 705-730, 1994.

Hansen, P. R., and G. Horel. Quadratic variation by markov chains. *Working paper*, 2009.

Hansen, P. R., and Z. Huang. Exponential GARCH modeling with realized measures of volatility. *Journal of Business & Economic Statistics*, 34(2):269–287, 2016.

Hansen, P. R., Z. Huang, and H. H. Shek. Realized GARCH: A joint model for returns and realized measures of volatility. *Journal of Applied Econometrics*, 27(6):877–906, 2012.

Hansen, P. R., and A. Lunde. Consistent ranking of volatility models. *Journal of Econometrics*, 131(1–2):97–121, 2006.

Hansen, P. R., and A. Lunde. A forecast comparison of volatility models: Does anything beat a GARCH (1,1)? *Journal of Applied Econometrics*, 20(7):873–889, 2005.

Hansen, P. R., A. Lunde, and J. M. Nason. The model confidence set. *Econometrica*, 79(2):456–497, 2011.

Hansen, P. R., A. Lunde, and V. Voev. Realized beta GARCH: A multivariate GARCH model with realized measures of volatility. *Journal of Applied Econometrics*, 29(5):774–799, 2014.

Harvey, A. C.,. *Dynamic models for volatility and heavy tails: With applications to financial and economic time series*. Cambridge University Press, Cambridge, 2013.

Jacod, J., Y. Li, P. A. Mykland, M. Podolskij, and M. Vetter. Microstructure noise in the continuous case: The pre-averaging approach. *Stochastic Processes and their Applications*, 119(7):2249–2276, 2009.

Laurent, S., J. V. Rombouts, and F. Violante. On loss functions and ranking forecasting performances of multivariate volatility models. *Journal of Econometrics*, 173(1):1–10, 2013.

Liu, L. Y., A. J. Patton, and K. Sheppard. Does anything beat 5-minute rv? A comparison of realized measures across multiple asset classes. *Journal of Econometrics*, 187(1):293–311, 2015.

Lunde, A., and K. V. Olesen. Modeling and forecasting the volatility of energy forward returns. *Working Paper*, 2013.

Mancini, C. Disentangling the jumps of the di usion in a geometric jumping brownian motion. *Giornale dell'Istituto Italiano degli Attuari*, 64(19–47):44, 2001.

Mancini, C. Non-parametric threshold estimation for models with stochastic di usion coe cient and jumps. *Scandinavian Journal of Statistics*, 36(2):270–296, 2009.

Martens, M., and D. Van Dijk. Measuring volatility with the realized range. *Journal of Econometrics*, 138(1):181–207, 2007.

Patton, A. J. Copula methods for forecasting multivariate time series. In *Handbook of economic forecasting*, volume 2, pages 899–960. Elsevier, 2013.

Patton, A. J. Estimation of multivariate models for time series of possibly different lengths. *Journal of Applied Econometrics*, 21(2):147–173, 2006.

Patton, A. J. A review of copula models for economic time series. *Journal of Multivariate Analysis*, 110:4–18, 2012.

Patton, A. J. Volatility forecast comparison using imperfect volatility proxies. *Journal of Econometrics*, 160(1):246–256, 2011.

Patton, A. J. and K. Sheppard. Evaluating volatility and correlation forecasts. In *Handbook of financial time series*, pages 801–838. Springer, 2009a.

Patton, A. J., and K. Sheppard. Good volatility, bad volatility: Signed jumps and the persistence of volatility. *Review of Economics and Statistics*, 97(3):683–697, 2015.

Patton, A. J., and K. Sheppard. Optimal combinations of realised volatility estimators. *International Journal of Forecasting*, 25(2):218–238, 2009b.

Podolskij, M. and M. Vetter. Bipower-type estimation in a noisy di usion setting. *Stochastic Processes and Their Applications*, 119(9):2803–2831, 2009.

Salvatierra, I. D. L., and A. J. Patton. Dynamic copula models and high-frequency data. *Journal of Empirical Finance*, 30:120–135, 2015.

Shephard, N., and K. Sheppard. Realising the future: Forecasting with high-frequency-based volatility (HEAVY) models. *Journal of Applied Econometrics*, 25(2):197–231, 2010.

Sklar, M. *Fonctions de répartition à n dimensions et leurs marges*. Université Paris 8, 1959.

White, H. *Estimation, Inference and Specification Analysis*. Number 22. Cambridge University Press, Cambridge, 1996.

Zhang, L. Efficient estimation of stochastic volatility using noisy observations: A multi-scale approach. *Bernoulli*, 12(6):1019–1043, 2006.

Zhang, L., P. Mykland, and Y. Ait-Sahalia. A tale of two time scales. *Journal of the American Statistical Association*, 100(472):1394–1411, 2005.

11 Forecasting realized volatility measures with multivariate and univariate models

The case of the US banking sector

*Gianluca Cubadda, Alain Hecq,
and Antonio Riccardo*

1. Introduction

Realized volatility measures, such as the realized variance (RV) or the bipower variation, are estimates of asset volatilities within a short period, for instance one day, using intra-day returns. The 5-minute Realized Variance (RV5), a benchmark often considered in empirical finance (see Liu et al., 2015), is obtained as $RV5_t \equiv \sum_{j=1}^{M} r_{t,j}^2$, where $r_{t,j}$ are the high frequency returns, observed for M intra-day 5-min periods. Both computational simplicity and theoretical foundations make realized volatility measures very attractive among practitioners and academics for modeling time varying volatilities and monitoring financial risk. When co-volatilities are involved as well, realized volatility measures are alternatives to multivariate GARCH models for building portfolios. Andersen and Benzoni (2009) or McAleer and Medeiros (2008) are frequently cited papers introducing this subject. Since high frequency returns are difficult to obtain and tedious to manipulate and clean, several institutions, including the Oxford-Man Institute of Quantitative Finance, preprocess the data and provide various volatility measures for aggregate stock price indexes. In this paper, we instead analyze and forecast the realized volatilities of the asset prices of 13 major US banks. We build both RV5 and median RV5 using raw intra-day data from the Thomson Reuters database. We focus on these assets since it is commonly believed that the banking sector is highly exposed to contagion, in particular since the financial crisis (Billio et al., 2012; Ahelegbey et al., 2016). Working instead with country or sector indices might lead to confusing results as those aggregate series merge different behaviors in individual asset volatilities.

A common empirical characteristic of realized volatility measures is the presence of long-memory dependence, as suggested by the typical slow decay pattern of the empirical autocorrelation function. This feature has been documented by many authors, including Andersen et al. (2001) for exchange rates, and Corsi et al. (2008) as well as Hillebrand and Meideiros (2016) for stock prices. Although long-memory processes are also observed in other fields than financial econometrics (see Baillie, 1996 and references therein) and that several models of long range dependence have been proposed in the literature (Haldrup and Vera-Valdés, 2017), the fractional integration process of order d, denoted I(d), has been extensively studied in econometrics and statistics since, at least, Granger (1980) and Granger and Joyeux (1980). An example of an I(d) process is the fractional white noise (FWN)

$$(1 - L)^d y_t = \varepsilon_t \Leftrightarrow y_t = (1 - L)^{-d} \varepsilon_t, \tag{1}$$

with

$$(1 - L)^d = 1 - dL + \frac{d(d - 1)}{2!} L^2 - \ldots \tag{2}$$

where L denotes the lag operator, $-0.5 < d < 0.5$ and ε_t is a white noise sequence. For $0 < d < 0.5$, the process is long-memory with positive autocorrelation decaying at a hyperbolic rate. For $-0.5 < d < 0$ the sum of absolute values of the auto-correlations tends to a constant and the process is said to be antipersistent. The class of fractionally integrated processes extends to the autoregressive fraction-ally integrated moving average (ARFIMA) processes of orders (p, d, q), where ε_t admits a covariance stationary and invertible ARMA representation. Corsi (2009) proposed the univariate Heterogeneous Autoregressive model (HAR) as an alternative way to approximate the long range dependence observed in vola-tility series. For daily series, HAR is a parsimonious restricted autoregressive model of lag order 22 with daily, weekly and monthly effects. The HAR model can easily be estimated by ordinary least squares (OLS) and it has been illustrated to perform well in forecasting exercises (see, e.g., Santos and Ziegel-mann, 2014, and the references therein).

The literature on the sources of long-memory is quite large, among which the aggregation across heterogeneous series argument raised by Granger (1980), the impact of structural changes that spuriously lead to the detection of a fractional integrated process (Diebold and Inoue, 2001), the linear approximation of an underlying nonlinear process (Miller and Park, 2010) or the learning by eco-nomic agents in forward looking models of expectations (Chevillon and Mav-roeidis, 2017).

In this paper we focus on the alternative explanation developed in Chevillon et al. (2018, CHL18). Indeed, CHL18 investigate the mechanisms underlying the long-memory feature generated from a vector autoregressive model (VAR). They start by assuming that the dynamic interactions between n daily realized volatility measures is generated by a VAR(1). Then for $n \rightarrow \infty$, namely when the number of series increases without bounds, and under some regularity con-ditions that are commonly satisfied by real data, CHL18 prove that the marginal model of each individual time series (i.e., the final equation representation) is a FWN processes with the same d parameter. Having the same d parameter for dif-ferent assets is in accordance for instance with Andersen et al., (2001) who found $d = 0.4$ for most exchange rate realized volatilities. CHL18 provide two specific examples of those conditions among which the VAR(1) coefficient matrix has diagonal elements converging to 1/2 as $n \to \infty$, and vanishing off-diagonal elements. This means in practice that there exist contagion effects, that individually are tiny but jointly potentially important.

However, many papers have also documented the presence of co-movements in the volatility of asset returns. In integrated markets, common factors in volatility are the result of a common reaction of investors, policy makers or central banks to news/shocks in some macroeconomic and financial variables (see, inter alia, Engle et al., 1990; Diebold and Nerlove, 1989). Nevertheless, an important assumption underlying the results by CHL18 is the existence of non-zero diagonal elements in the VAR coefficient matrix along with small but not null off-diagonal ones. This would contradict the presence of a reduced-rank structure in the VAR, and hence of a particular form of commonalities, named common features in volatility, observed, inter alia, by Engle and Marcucci (2006), Engle and Susmel (1993), Hecq et al. (2016), and Anderson and Vahid (2007). Discriminating between these two views on the cause of the contagion in a potentially high dimensional setting is challenging and it might well be unfeasible using conventional testing approaches. Indeed, we would face an obvious curse of dimensionality issue when modeling a large system. One may argue that shrinkage techniques leading to sparse regression models could be an attractive option for the problem at hand. However, the two alternative views that we want to evaluate generally imply the use of models that are non-nested each other. Moreover, the 13 series that we consider might be seen as a subset of a very large dimensional multivariate process that we do not observe nor estimate. For instance a very large VAR with all the NYSE asset volatilities might in principle have generated the 13 series considered here. Hence, estimating a marginal VAR model for the considered series only and testing for the presence of contagion effects would not provide a convincing answer to the question that we wish to address in this paper, namely the origin of the contagion in volatility.

Consequently, this paper compares the forecasting performances of two different modeling strategies: on the one hand, we consider a set of univariate models potentially derived from a huge system with hidden correlations as proposed in CHL18; on the other hand, we rely on medium-scale multivariate models, possibly with common factors. For the former framework, we model the long-memory feature of the individual series using both the maximum likelihood (ML) estimation of the FWN process, i.e., the ARFIMA(0, d, 0) model, as well as the OLS estimates of HAR models. For the second multivariate strategy, we must be able to capture the long-memory features observed in the series as a VAR(1), with or without a reduced rank structure, does not have such a feature. Consequently, we first look at a multivariate version of the HAR model called the Vector HAR (VHAR), introduced by Bubak et al. (2011), in order to incorporate the possibility to have long memory features. Then, we look at the presence of co-movements in volatilities and we study the performance of the VHAR Index model (VHARI) proposed by Cubadda et al. (2017), in which the VHAR is restricted by imposing a common index structure. Note that we use these multivariate models and not, for instance, generic factor models based on principal component analysis. There are two reasons for that. First the VHARI is nested within the unrestricted VHAR, which is in turn restricted versions of a VAR with 22 daily lags. Hence, the restrictions underlying the VHAR and the VHARI could, in principle, be tested for, whereas the factor structure is typically postulated in dynamic factor models. Second, at the representation theory level, the common factors obtained from the VHARI preserve the same temporal cascade structure as in the univariate HAR with the weekly (monthly) index being equal to the weekly (monthly) moving average of the daily index. This is an important property that is not shared by most of the alternative factor methods (e.g., principal components, canonical correlations, etc.) and makes the forecasts from a set of univariate models and a multivariate system easily comparable. To some extent, our paper is close to the recent work of Bauwens et al. (2018). However, the authors of this paper examine a set of 50 realized volatilities by means of both univariate models and high dimensional VARs under the constraints that are derived from CHL18. They consequently compare the forecasting performances of the different models in a nested perspective with the aim to empirically corroborate the theoretical results of CHL18. Instead, we do not impose any theoretically based constraint to the time series models that we use in our forecasting exercise.

The rest of the paper is as follows. Section 2 sketches the results on the final equation representation as well as the main conclusions of CHL18 for the explanation of the origins of the long-memory. Section 3 reviews and discusses the VHAR and the VHARI models. Section 4 motivates our study by first looking at the presence of long-memory features in the volatility in the return series of the 13 major US banks. We further examine the properties of our series by estimating univariate HAR and ARFIMA models as well as a VAR on the whole sample size. Section 5 compares the forecasting performances of the different models using a rolling sample scheme. Section 6 draws conclusions.

2. The univariate implications of a multivariate structure

In this section we briefly review the main results on the marginal model of each element of a VAR process, and those of CHL18 regarding the relation between the dimension of the VAR and the presence of long-memory in the individual time series.

2.1. The final equation representation

CHL18 investigate the mechanisms underlying the long-memory feature generated from a VAR model based on the final equation representation of a multivariate $n-$dimensional time series $Y_t \equiv (Y_{1t}, \ldots, Y_{nt})'$. In order to brush up some of the basic tools needed for the understanding of the paper, let us consider a

VAR(1) model

$$(I_n - A_n L)Y_t = \epsilon_t. \tag{3}$$

where the innovations ε_t are i.i.d. with $E(\epsilon_t) = 0$, and $E(\epsilon_t \epsilon_t') = \Sigma$ (positive definite).

The final equation representation (FER) is obtained by premultiplying both sides of (3) by the adjoint matrix of the matrix polynomial $(I_n - A_n L)$:

$$\mathrm{adj}(I_n - A_n L) = \det(I_n - A_n L)(I_n - A_n L)^{-1},$$

which leads to

$$\det(I_n - A_n L)Y_t = \mathrm{adj}(I_n - A_n L)\epsilon_t. \tag{4}$$

It is observed in (4) that each elements of $Y_t \equiv (Y_{1t}, \ldots, Y_{nt})'$ follows an ARMA $(n, n-1)$ process with a common autoregressive polynomial for each series. More generally, one would obtain ARMA$(np, (n-1)p)$ processes for a VAR (p). Additional details about the FER can be found in Zellner and Palm (1974, 1975, 2004), Palm (1977), Cubadda et al. (2009), and Hecq et al. (2012), among others.

As a numerical example, consider the following trivariate VAR(1) model

$$\begin{bmatrix} Y_{1t} \\ Y_{2t} \\ Y_{3t} \end{bmatrix} = \begin{bmatrix} a_{11} & a_{12} & a_{13} \\ a_{21} & a_{22} & a_{23} \\ a_{31} & a_{32} & a_{33} \end{bmatrix} \begin{bmatrix} Y_{1t-1} \\ Y_{2t-1} \\ Y_{3t-1} \end{bmatrix} + \begin{bmatrix} \epsilon_{1t} \\ \epsilon_{2t} \\ \epsilon_{3t} \end{bmatrix}. \tag{5}$$

Computing both $\det(I_3 - A_3 L)$ and $\mathrm{adj}(I_3 - A_3 L)$ leads to the observation that all univariate elements of Y_t follow and ARMA(3, 2) processes.

Note that the orders derived from the FER are maximal orders. There are cases, in which orders do not depend on n, with smaller numbers. The first important one is when A_n is exactly diagonal, i.e., when

$$A_3 = \begin{bmatrix} a_{11} & a_{12} & a_{13} \\ a_{21} & a_{22} & a_{23} \\ a_{31} & a_{32} & a_{33} \end{bmatrix} = \begin{bmatrix} a_{11} & 0 & 0 \\ 0 & a_{22} & 0 \\ 0 & 0 & a_{33} \end{bmatrix} \tag{6}$$

leading to ARMA(1,0) processes for every series.

Another interesting case is when A_n is of reduced rank. For instance each series is an ARMA(1,1) whatever the dimension n when rank$(A_n) = 1$ such as in the example

$$A_3 = \begin{bmatrix} a_{11} & a_{12} & a_{13} \\ a_{21} & a_{22} & a_{23} \\ a_{31} & a_{32} & a_{33} \end{bmatrix} = \begin{bmatrix} a_{11} \\ a_{21} \\ a_{31} \end{bmatrix} \begin{bmatrix} 1 & 1 & 1 \end{bmatrix} \tag{7}$$

(see Cubadda et al. (2009) for details).

2.2. High dimensional VARs and long-memory

The approach of CHL18 (2018) builds on the previous FER. They start from the same VAR(1) as in (3) but they look at the behavior of (4) when more and more data are collected. From the previous results and without root cancellation between the determinant and the adjoint, we know that when $n \to \infty$, each series is an ARMA(∞, ∞). Obviously a smaller number of significant lags are found in practice. This process with an infinite number of lags is still of short memory however, with the usual exponential decrease of the coefficient parameters.

Then for $n \to \infty$, namely when the number of series increases without bounds, and under some regularity conditions on A_n that are commonly satisfied by real data, CHL18 show that the marginal model of each individual time series is a FWN process $(1 - L)^d Y_{it} = \epsilon_{it}$ with the same d parameter. Having the same d parameter for different assets is in accordance with Andersen et al. (2001) who found $d = 0.4$ for most exchange rate realized volatilities. Contrarily to the exactly diagonal case illustrated in the previous subsection, CHL18 consider an n-variate autoregressive matrix that is near diagonal such as

$$A_n = \begin{bmatrix} a & o(1) \\ o(1) & A_{n-1} + o(1) \end{bmatrix}. \tag{8}$$

Indeed, it is frequently observed when estimating multivariate volatility models, for instance a multivariate GARCH (see, e.g., Bauwens et al., 2006, and the references therein) or a BEKK (Baba et al., 1989), that the most important contribution for the volatility comes from their own lags Although individually small, the off-diagonal elements are usually jointly significantly different from zero. This is intuitively what the structure of the matrix (8) captures. Note that a sparse modeling approach such as Lasso would likely force many of those small off-diagonal elements to be exactly equal to zero.[1]

With this particular framework, the FER for the first row (Y_{1t}) is

$$\det (I_n - A_n L) Y_{1t} = \det (I_{n-1} - A_{n-1} L) \epsilon_{1t} + o_p(1) \tag{9}$$

then the moving average lag polynomial associated with Y_{1t} is asymptotically

$$Y_{1t} \approx \frac{\det\left(I_{n-1} - A_{n-1}L\right)}{\det\left(I_n - A_n L\right)} \epsilon_{1t}. \tag{10}$$

CHL18 further parameterize A_n by defining a scalar sequence (δ_n) with $\delta_n \in (0, 1)$ such that $\lim_{n \to \infty} \delta_n = \delta \in (0, 1)$, and a circulant matrix C_n such that the polynomials $\det(I_n - A_n z) \sim \det(I_n - C_n z)$ as $n \to \infty$. C_n is assumed to possess close to a fraction $n\delta$ of unit eigenvalues. The first Szegö theorem is then used to prove that, under some high level assumptions, $\det(I_{n-1} - A_{n-1}z)/\det(I_n - A_n z) \to (1 - z)^{-\delta}$ as $n \to \infty$. From this result, it follows the weak convergence of the process Y_{1t} to the fractional white noise $(1 - L)^{-\delta}\epsilon_{1t}$. This is also the case for each of the n series in Y_t.

Those high level assumptions needed by CHL18 are satisfied for at least two specific examples of VAR(1) models. In the first example of parameterization of interest for this paper, A_n denotes a Toeplitz matrix with diagonal elements converging to $\delta = 1/2$ as $n \to \infty$, and with vanishing off-diagonal elements. Importantly, the off-diagonal elements decrease at an $O(n^{-1})$ rate and the sum of each row equals 1 at all n. Then as $n \to \infty$, each series of the system behaves as an ARFIMA(0, 1/2, 0). Note that this result cannot hold when A_n is exactly diagonal since A_{n-1} contains $\lfloor n\delta \rfloor$ or $\lfloor n\delta \rfloor - 1$ unit eigenvalues, not $\lfloor (n - 1)\delta \rfloor$. From a practical view point (see also the simulation study in CHL18) this implies having a near diagonal matrix with some contagion effects, that individually are tiny but jointly potentially important. For instance with $n = 500$ series, there is a large value close to 0.5 (say $0.5 - \varepsilon$) on the diagonal and in each rows of A_n, the sum of the 499 contagion parameters are $0.5 + \varepsilon$.

For each series, univariate ARFIMA models can be estimated. Several estimators of the long-memory parameters of series have been proposed in the literature, including the log periodogram regression of Geweke and Porter-Hudak (1983), the Local Whittle Likelihood Estimator of Robinson (1995), as well as the usual Gaussian ML estimator of the ARFIMA(p, d, q) model.

3. The vector heterogeneous autoregressive model and its index extension

Corsi (2009) proposed the HAR as an alternative way to approximate the long-memory feature. Let us start with considering the univariate HAR specification. For daily series, HAR is a parsimonious restricted autoregressive model of lag order 22 with daily, weekly, and monthly effects. For a daily volatility measure $Y_{it}^{(day)}$ one can run by OLS for $i = 1, \ldots, n$ volatility returns the following regressions

$$Y_{it}^{(day)} = \beta_{i0} + \varphi_i^{(day)} Y_{i,t-1day}^{(day)} + \varphi_i^{(w)} Y_{i,t-1day}^{(w)} + \varphi_i^{(m)} Y_{i,t-1day}^{(m)}$$

$$+ \varepsilon_{it}, \quad t = 1, 2, \ldots, T, \tag{11}$$

where (day) (w), and (m) respectively denote time horizons of one day, one week (5 days a week), and one month (assuming 22 days within a month) such that

$$Y_{it}^{(w)} = \frac{1}{5} \sum_{j=0}^{4} Y_{i,t-jday}^{(day)}, \qquad Y_{it}^{(m)} = \frac{1}{22} \sum_{j=0}^{21} Y_{i,t-jday}^{(day)}. \tag{12}$$

and where β_{i0}, $\phi_i^{(day)}$, $\phi_i^{(w)}$, $\phi_i^{(m)}$ are scalar parameters; ε_{it} is i.i.d. with mean 0 and variance σ_i^2.[2] Note that this can be extended to time varying GARCH type errors (see the HAR-GARCH in Corsi et al., 2012).

The Vector Heterogeneous Autoregressive model (VHAR), proposed by Bubák et al. (2011) and Soucek and Todorova (2013), is a multivariate generalization of the previous univariate process (11). The VHAR reads as follows for the levels of the n volatility daily series $Y_t^{(day)} \equiv (Y_{1t}^{(day)}, \ldots, Y_{nt}^{(day)})'$:

$$Y_t^{(day)} = \beta_0 + \Phi^{(day)} Y_{t-1day}^{(day)} + \Phi^{(w)} Y_{t-1day}^{(w)} + \Phi^{(m)} Y_{t-1day}^{(m)} + \epsilon_t,$$
$$t = 1, 2, ..., T, \tag{13}$$

with

$$Y_t^{(w)} = \frac{1}{5} \sum_{j=0}^{4} Y_{t-jday}^{(day)}, \qquad Y_t^{(m)} = \frac{1}{22} \sum_{j=0}^{21} Y_{t-jday}^{(day)}. \tag{14}$$

and where β_0 is an $n \times 1$ vector of intercepts, and $\Phi^{(day)}$, $\Phi^{(w)}$, $\Phi^{(m)}$ are $n \times n$ coefficient matrices.

Clearly the VHAR in (13) involves $(n^2 \times 3)$ parameters in addition to the vector of intercepts and is therefore much more parsimonious than a VAR with 22 unrestricted daily lags. Moreover, a VHAR is an interesting model to consider, as it is able to generate long-memory features and to introduce contagion effects between volatilities. System (13) can easily be estimated by multivariate least square regressions, which means using OLS equation by equation if no cross equation restrictions are present.

Let us further assume that (13) can be rewritten as follows

$$Y_t^{(day)} = \beta_0 + \beta^{(day)} \omega' Y_{t-1day}^{(day)} + \beta^{(w)} \omega' Y_{t-1day}^{(w)} + \beta^{(m)} \omega' Y_{t-1day}^{(m)} + \epsilon_t, \tag{15}$$

where ω is a full-rank $n \times q$ matrix, and $\beta^{(day)}$, $\beta^{(w)}$, $\beta^{(m)}$ are $n \times q$ coefficient matrices. Since we can always normalize ω such as $\omega' = (I_q, \varpi')$, where ϖ is a $(n - q) \times q$ matrix, model (15) needs $4(n \times q) - q^2$ parameters instead of $n^2 \times 3$ of them as in (13). Following Reinsel (1983), we label (15) as the VHAR-index (VHARI) model.

Beyond the important aspect in terms of parsimony that is shared with many factor models, there are two further motivations for using (15). First, the indexes

$f_t^{(day)} = \omega' Y_{t-1day}^{(day)}$ obtained from (15) satisfy the property

$$f_t^{(w)} = \frac{1}{5} \sum_{j=0}^{4} f_{t-jday}^{(day)}, \quad f_t^{(m)} = \frac{1}{22} \sum_{j=0}^{21} f_{t-jday}^{(day)}. \tag{16}$$

as for the observed univariate realized volatilities. Hence, the temporal cascade structure of the HAR model is preserved meaning that the weekly (monthly) index is equal to the weekly (monthly) moving average of the daily index. This would not be generally the case with either traditional reduced-rank regression models as in Engle and Marcucci (2006) or principal component methods.

Second, premultiplying both sides of (15) by ω' yields

$$f_t^{(day)} = \omega' \beta_0 + \omega' \beta^{(day)} f_{t-1day}^{(day)} + \omega' \beta^{(w)} f_{t-1day}^{(w)} + \omega' \beta^{(m)} f_{t-1day}^{(m)} + \omega' \epsilon_t, \tag{17}$$

which shows that the indexes themselves follow a VHAR model. Moreover, when $q = 1$, the unique index is generated by an univariate HAR model. This property is not shared by alternative methods to aggregate time series (e.g., averages, principal components, canonical correlations, etc.) since the resulting linear combination would generally follow a rather complicated ARMA structure (see Cubadda et al., 2009; Hecq et al., 2016, and the references related to the final equation representation of multivariate models therein).

To some extent, the VHARI model is related to the pure variance model of Engle and Marcucci (2006), in the sense that a reduced-rank restriction is imposed to the mean parameters of a multivariate volatility model. However, a fundamental difference between (15) and the common volatility model (see also Hecq et al., 2016) stems from the fact that the former has in general a different left null space for the loading matrices of the factors $\beta = (\beta^{(day)}, \beta^{(w)}, \beta^{(m)})$. Obviously, common volatility is allowed in the VHARI model as well in the case that the loading matrix β has reduced column rank.

In order to better appreciate the differences between the VHARI and a VHAR with a reduced-rank structure, let us write the latter as

$$Y_t^{(day)} = \beta_0 + \alpha \psi^{(day)\prime} Y_{t-1day}^{(day)} + \alpha \psi^{(w)\prime} Y_{t-1day}^{(w)} + \alpha \psi^{(m)\prime} Y_{t-1day}^{(m)}$$
$$+ \epsilon_t, \quad t = 1, 2, ..., T, \tag{18}$$

where α is full-rank $n \times q$ matrix, and $\psi^{(day)}$, $\psi^{(w)}$, $\psi^{(m)}$ are $n \times q$ coefficient matrices.

Reduced-rank VAR models are popular in economics and finance because of their interpretation in terms of common features and their ease in estimation (see, e.g., Centoni and Cubadda, 2015, and the references therein). However, although Equations (15) and (18) look similar, the interpretation of the latter is less intuitive since the coefficients of the common components, namely ($\psi^{(day)}$, $\psi^{(w)}$, $\psi^{(m)}$), are specific for each frequency. Hence, Model (18) is less easily justified on the grounds of the existence of common factors in such VHAR type volatility models.

In order to estimate the parameters of model (15), we resort to a switching algorithm (see details about the estimation technique and its Monte Carlo evaluation in Cubadda et al., 2017) that is widely applied in cointegration analysis (see Boswijk and Doornik, 2004, and their references). The strategy consists in alternating between estimating ω for a given value of β and Σ, and estimating β and Σ for a given value of ω. In details, the procedure goes as follows:

1   Conditional to an (initial) estimate of the ω, estimate β and Σ by OLS on (15).
2   Premultiplying both the sides of (15) by $\Sigma^{-1/2}$ one obtains

$$\Sigma^{-1/2}(Y_t^{(day)} - \beta_0) = \Sigma^{-1/2}\beta^{(day)}\omega' Y_{t-1day}^{(day)} + \Sigma^{-1/2}\beta^{(w)}\omega' Y_{t-1day}^{(w)}$$
$$+ \Sigma^{-1/2}\beta^{(m)}\omega' Y_{t-1day}^{(m)} + \Sigma^{-1/2}\epsilon_t. \tag{19}$$

Applying the Vec operator to both sides of the above equation, using the property $\text{Vec}(ABC) = (C'\otimes A)\text{Vec}(B)$, and keeping in mind that the Vec of a column vector is itself, one gets

$$\Sigma^{-1/2}(Y_t^{(day)} - \beta_0) = (Y_{t-1day}^{(day)'} \otimes \Sigma^{-1/2}\beta^{(day)})\text{Vec}(\omega')$$
$$+ (Y_{t-1day}^{(w)'} \otimes \Sigma^{-1/2}\beta^{(w)})\text{Vec}(\omega') \tag{20}$$
$$+ (Y_{t-1day}^{(m)'} \otimes \Sigma^{-1/2}\beta^{(m)})\text{Vec}(\omega') + \Sigma^{-1/2}\epsilon_t,$$

from which we can finally estimate by OLS the ω coefficients conditional to the previously obtained estimates of the parameters β and Σ.
3   Switch between steps 1 and 2 till numerical convergence occurs.

As shown by Boswijk (1995), the proposed switching algorithm has the property to increase the Gaussian likelihood in each step.

Note that a numerical stability problem may arise when the number of series is large. As suggested by Cubadda and Guardabascio (2018), a possible solution to this problem is to resort to ridge regression in place of OLS in each of the steps 2–3 above. In particular, ridge estimation can be directly applied to model (20) and to model (15) after having applied the Vec operator to both sides of the related equation, which leads to

$$Y_t^{(day)} = \beta_0 + (f_{t-1day}^{(day)'} \otimes I_n)\text{Vec}(\beta^{(day)}) + (f_{t-1day}^{(w)'} \otimes I_n)\text{Vec}(\beta^{(w)})$$
$$+ (f_{t-1day}^{(m)'} \otimes I_n)\text{Vec}(\beta^{(m)}) + \epsilon_t, \tag{21}$$

Clearly, each of the two ridge regressions above requires to fix its own tuning parameter. This can be done following Hoerl et al. (1975), namely using the ML estimates to compute the optimal values of the tuning parameters (see Cubadda and Guardabascio, 2018, for further details).

4. Data description

We have considered intra-day data extracted from the NYSE "trade and quote" (TAQ) dataset downloaded from Thomson Reuters. It contains the 250 most liquid assets quoted on New York Stocks Exchange covering the period from 03/01/2006 to 31/12/2014 not including weekends and holidays, for a sample of 2,265 trading days. From the dataset, we focus in this study on the asset prices of 13 major banks. These are, in alphabetical order of the acronyms, (1) BAC: Bank of America Corporation, (2) BBT: BB&T Corporation, (3) BK: Bank Of New York Mellon Corporation (The), (4) C: Citigroup Inc., (5) COF: Capital One Financial Corporation, (6) JPM: JP Morgan Chase & Co., (7) KEY: KeyCorp, (8) PNC: PNC Financial Services Group, Inc. (The), (9) RF: Regions Financial Corporation, (10) STI: SunTrust Banks, Inc., (11) STT: State Street Corporation, (12) USB: US Bancorp and (13) WFC: Wells Fargo & Company. We focus on the these assets since it is commonly believed that the banking sector is highly exposed to contagion effects.

Data have been cleaned following the procedure proposed by Barndorff-Nielsen et al. (2009). It consists of the following different steps:

Steps applied to all data

P1. Delete entries with a time stamp outside the 9:30 a.m. to 4 p.m. window when the exchange is open.
P2. Delete entries with a bid, ask or transaction price equal to zero.

Steps applied only to quote data

Q1. When multiple quotes have the same timestamp, replace all these with a single entry with the median bid and median ask price.
Q2. Delete entries for which the spread is negative.
Q3. Delete entries for which the spread is more than 50 times the median spread on that day.
Q4. Delete entries for which the mid-quote deviated by more than 10 mean absolute deviations from a rolling centered median (excluding the observation under consideration) of 50 observations (25 observations before and 25 after).

Steps applied only to trade data

T1. If multiple transactions have the same time stamp: use the median price.
T2. Delete entries with prices that are above the ask plus the bid-ask spread. Similar for entries with prices below the bid minus the bid-ask spread.
T3. Delete entries for which the price deviated by more than 10 mean absolute deviations from a rolling centered median (excluding the observation under consideration) of 50 observations (25 observations before and 25 after).[3]

At the end of the procedure, the number of trades has been reduced from around 225 millions to slightly more than 105 millions. Notice that, although only trade prices are considered in the analysis, the above cleaning procedure also involves quote data. The reason of this choice is to obtain the more coherent trade prices as possible.

Then, prices have been sampled at 5-minute frequency using the previous point interpolation method and two different realized volatility measures have been computed from the correspondent returns, namely the 5-minute Realized Variance (RV5) already defined in the introduction section and the 5-minute Median Truncated Realized Variance (MedRV5), such as

$$RV5_t \equiv \sum_{j=1}^{M} r_{t,j}^2, \tag{22}$$

$$MedRV5_t \equiv \frac{\pi}{6 - 4\sqrt{3} + \pi} \left(\frac{M}{M-2} \right) \sum_{j=2}^{M-1} \text{med}(|r_{t,j}||r_{t,j-1}||r_{t,j+1}|)^2, \tag{23}$$

where $r_{t,j}$ are the high frequency intra-day returns, observed for M intra-day 5-min periods we have considered each day.

Figures 11.1 and 11.2 display the levels as well as the log levels of the 13 realized variance series, over the period of 03/01/2006 to 31/12/2014.[4] We can see later that this distinction has an impact on the interpretation of the factors that we extract from those variables. Indeed, although taking the logs seems natural to get variables with properties closer to the Gaussian distribution, the aggregation of the levels is easier when the goal is to obtain an index from the (weighted) sum of individual volatilities. In Figures 11.1 and 11.2, "whole sample" denotes the period 03/01/2006 to 31/12/2014. In the forecasting exercise of Section 4, we will only report forecasting performances for the post-crisis period 03/01/2008 to 31/12/2014 as results might have changed since the financial crisis (Billio et al., 2012; Ahelegbey et al., 2016). While our study stays valid for highly volatile periods, a model confidence set approach was not able to statistically distinguish the different clusters when such a huge crisis period is included in the sample. This issue, that we can summarize by, all models are bad and cannot be distinguished, has also been noticed by Hecq et al. (2012) for instance. Finally, even though not reported here, ACFs for each series for both the 03/01/2006 to 31/12/2014 and the 03/01/2008 to 31/12/2014 periods show slow decay patterns. Consequently we really have a long-memory feature present in our series and not a spurious phenomenon due to structural breaks (before and after the financial crisis) as in Diebold and Inoue (2001) or Haldrup and Kruse (2014) for instance.

Table 11.1 illustrates that for the log of the 13 realized volatility series, both the HAR and the FWN models fit pretty well the long-memory feature.[5] We provide OLS estimates of HAR equations (11). We also report the adjusted determination coefficient $\bar{R}^2$ as well as the p-value of the Ljung-Box χ^2 test for the null hypothesis that the first 10 error lags are zero. The goodness of fit, above

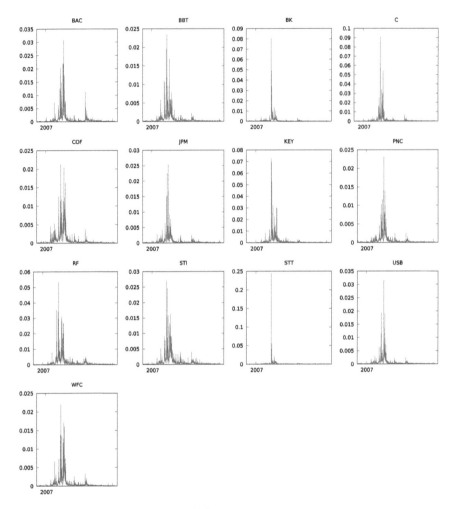

Figure 11.1 Levels of realized volatilities

0.82 for both the fractional white noise and the HAR is very similar for each asset volatilities. Note that the maximum likelihood estimates of d of the ARFIMA(0, d, 0) are rather close to 0.5, one of the example considered by CHL18. Whereas ML bounds the parameter estimate at that value, we have also considered the estimation for the series in first differences before we obtain "unbounded" estimates of $d + 1$. In every case we obtain estimated values for $d + 1$ between 0.5 and 0.54 with a significant difference to 0.5 in only one case at 1% level.

Finally, let us have a look at VAR coefficient matrices in a VAR(1) in order to figure out how close we are to the CHL18 setup. Estimating VARs for the log of the 13 RV5 series as well as for the log of MedRV5 we obtain VAR(5), VAR(1) and VAR(2) with respect to AIC, BIC and HQIC using $p$max = 22 days. Table 11.2

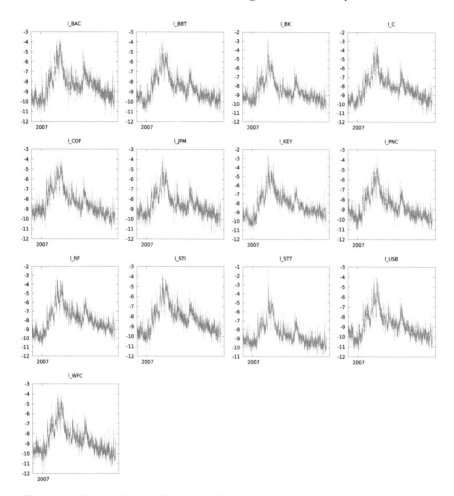

Figure 11.2 Log-levels of realized volatilities

provides results for the VAR(1) coefficient matrix chosen by the BIC for the logs of the realized variances. We denote $\hat{A}_{13}$ that estimated matrix for a 13-dimensional VAR(1) model. We indeed observe as in the model proposed by CHL18 a large value for the diagonal elements and relatively small and often non significant off-diagonal elements.

The hypothesis that the VAR model has a diagonal structure is strongly rejected. Indeed, the null hypothesis that the only non-zero coefficients are those of the lags of the dependent variable is overwhelmingly rejected in each equation. These findings suggest that these data may accord with the modeling framework of CHL18. However note that, as discussed in Section 1, the 13 series might have been generated from a larger VAR, in which the off-diagonal elements are likely to be even smaller. It might well be that some coefficients that are small but not insignificant would have been closer to zero if we had estimated

Table 11.1 Univariate models for log of realized volatility

Series	Model	d	α_1	α_2	α_3	$\bar{R}^2$	Q(10)
BAC	ARFIMA(0,d,0)	0.497*	–	–	–	0.83	0.306
	HAR	–	0.491*	0.263*	0.219*	0.83	0.594
BBT	ARFIMA(0,d,0)	0.496*	–	–	–	0.85	0.049
	HAR	–	0.416*	0.347*	0.215*	0.85	0.108
BK	ARFIMA(0,d,0)	0.496*	–	–	–	0.82	0.109
	HAR	–	0.449*	0.307*	0.214*	0.82	0.103
C	ARFIMA(0,d,0)	0.497*	–	–	–	0.85	0.054
	HAR	–	0.441*	0.339*	0.195*	0.84	0.000
COF	ARFIMA(0,d,0)	0.497*	–	–	–	0.86	0.003
	HAR	–	0.421*	0.367*	0.190*	0.86	0.037
JPM	ARFIMA(0,d,0)	0.497*	–	–	–	0.82	0.135
	HAR	–	0.498*	0.266*	0.205*	0.82	0.782
KEY	ARFIMA(0,d,0)	0.497*	–	–	–	0.85	0.107
	HAR	–	0.444*	0.305*	0.230*	0.86	0.252
PNC	ARFIMA(0,d,0)	0.496*	–	–	–	0.84	0.058
	HAR	–	0.432*	0.342*	0.201*	0.84	0.028
RF	ARFIMA(0,d,0)	0.497*	–	–	–	0.86	0.000
	HAR	–	0.418*	0.356*	0.203*	0.86	0.000
STI	ARFIMA(0,d,0)	0.496*	–	–	–	0.85	0.005
	HAR	–	0.415*	0.353*	0.209*	0.85	0.011
STT	ARFIMA(0,d,0)	0.490*	–	–	–	0.82	0.015
	HAR	–	0.371*	0.384*	0.216*	0.82	0.049
USB	ARFIMA(0,d,0)	0.497*	–	–	–	0.85	0.014
	HAR	–	0.452*	0.343*	0.179*	0.85	0.347
WFC	ARFIMA(0,d,0)	0.498*	–	–	–	0.85	0.006
	HAR	–	0.481*	0.286*	0.209*	0.85	0.294

Note: d is the estimated integration order, α_i, for $i = 1, 2, 3$, are the estimated HAR coefficients, $\bar{R}^2$ is the determination coefficient, *p*-value refers to the Ljung-Box test for the null hypothesis that the first 10 lags are zero, * denotes significance (HCSE) at the 1% significance level.

a VAR model with a larger number of volatilities than 13. This would be the case if there is a positive omitted variable bias if one estimates such a smaller system.

5. Forecasting

We compare the forecasting performances of the VHAR and the VHARI with those of univariate models such as the FWN and the HAR. The forecasting exercises are performed using a rolling window of 500 days. Table 11.3 refers to the levels of MedRV5, whereas Table 11.4 refers to their logarithmic transformation. In each rolling sample, the FWN is estimated by Gaussian ML, the HAR by OLS, whereas the VHAR and the VHARI have been estimated by the switching algorithm using either OLS or ridge regression. In the latter case, they are denoted respectively as VHAR (R) and VHARI (R) in Tables 11.3 and 11.4. For both the VHARI and VHARI (R), the number of indexes q has been determined using the usual information criteria proposed by Schwarz (BIC), Hannan-Quinn (HQIC) and Akaike (AIC). Forecasts are

Table 11.2 VAR(1) estimated matrix for logs of realized volatilities

$$\hat{A}_{13}=$$

0.52	−0.04	−0.02	0.01	−0.06	0.02	−0.01	−0.07	0.12	0.06	−0.04	−0.01	−0.05
−0.08	0.31	0.07	−0.07	0.06	0.03	0.03	−0.01	0.00	0.02	0.05	−0.01	−0.01
0.03	0.07	0.39	−0.03	0.03	0.11	−0.01	−0.01	−0.04	0.00	0.12	0.00	0.00
0.11	0.01	0.01	0.54	0.06	0.07	0.10	0.04	0.07	0.11	0.04	0.07	0.10
0.04	0.18	0.09	0.13	0.49	0.14	0.04	0.16	0.07	0.15	0.13	0.10	0.21
0.05	0.01	0.18	−0.00	0.01	0.38	−0.10	0.00	−0.10	−0.07	0.06	0.00	0.02
0.03	0.10	0.03	0.09	0.03	0.02	0.45	0.12	0.17	0.12	0.07	0.09	0.04
−0.05	0.00	−0.04	−0.04	0.08	−0.06	0.02	0.30	−0.05	−0.02	0.05	0.07	0.00
0.17	0.09	0.013	0.11	−0.02	0.02	0.18	0.05	0.48	0.15	0.00	0.08	0.06
0.06	−0.03	−0.02	0.07	−0.02	−0.04	0.05	−0.01	0.15	0.30	−0.06	−0.02	0.01
0.00	0.03	0.14	0.02	0.04	0.03	0.05	0.08	−0.03	−0.03	0.34	0.06	0.06
0.03	0.09	0.01	−0.03	0.03	0.03	0.08	0.12	0.04	0.07	0.05	0.35	0.04
0.000	0.08	0.02	0.11	0.18	0.09	0.04	0.12	0.00	0.04	0.08	0.12	0.43

Table 11.3 Forecast comparison for levels of MedRV – post crisis period

Method/Criterion	ARMSFE			$\hat{q}$			
	h = 1	h = 5	h = 22	[Q1	Q2	Q3]	Mode
VHARI/BIC	137,9*	108,3	110,5*	[1	2	3]	3
VHARI/HQIC	136,3*	112,0	106,6*	[3	4	6]	3
VHARI/AIC	134,6*	111,0	109,9*	[7	8	9]	8
VHAR	135,5*	118,0	111,9*				
VHARI (R)/BIC	135,0*	102,4	107,7*	[1	2	2]	2
VHARI (R)/HQIC	131,1*	104,0	105,5*	[1	3	3]	3
VHARI (R)/AIC	130,3*	110,9	105,3*	[13	13	13]	13
VHAR (R)	130,3*	110,9	105,3*				
FWN	97,3*	100,1*	95,6*				
HAR	100*	100*	100*				

Note: h is the forecasting horizon. ARMSFE is the average of the mean square forecast errors relative to the HAR univariate forecasts. Q_i indicates the *i*-th quartile of the number of factors distribution. The methods within the superior set of models, as identified by the MCS test, are denote by *.

Table 11.4 Forecast comparison for logs of MedRV – post crisis period

Method/Criterion	ARMSFE			$\hat{q}$			
	h = 1	h = 5	h = 22	[Q1	Q2	Q3]	Mode
VHARI/BIC	121,6	108,4	111,5*	[1	2	2]	2
VHARI/HQIC	117,9	110,1	120,6	[3	3	4]	3
VHARI/AIC	117,7	110,8	118,3*	[6	6	7]	6
VHAR	118,8	117,2	114,2*				
VHARI (R)/BIC	137,6	115,1	106,9*	[1	1	2]	1
VHARI (R)/HQIC	122,7	111,7	112,8*	[2	3	4]	2
VHARI (R)/AIC	115,2	111,2	111,4*	[5	8	9]	8
VHAR (R)	115,3	111,3	111,5*				
FWN	99 8*	99 2*	101,3*				
HAR	100*	100*	100*				

See the notes of Table 11.3.

obtained for each sample of 500 observations using the empirical number of factors $\hat{q}$ for that specific sample. What the last four columns of Tables 11.3 and 11.4 denote are summary statistics (quartiles and mode) over all rolling windows of 500 days. This gives an overall indication about the parsimony of the different information criteria in choosing q.

For all the methods, direct h–step ahead forecast for $h = 1, 5, 22$ are produced. As in Cubadda et al. (2017), the goodness of the forecasts has been evaluated trough the average relative mean squared forecast errors (ARMSFE). It is defined as

$$ARMSFE_{m,h} = \frac{1}{n}\sum_{i=1}^{n}\left(\frac{MSFE_{m,h,i}}{MSFE_{HAR,h,i}}\right) \times 100 \tag{23}$$

where m denotes the model (e.g., VHARI or VHAR) and n represents the number of assets, which is equal to 13 in our application. In order to find the set of models which forecast equally well, we rely of the model confidence set analysis by Hansen et al. (2011). In particular, the test for the null hypothesis of equal predictive ability at the 20% level is implemented using a block bootstrap scheme with 5,000 resamples.

Looking first at the results regarding the levels of MedRV5 in Table 11.3, it emerges that univariate models have smaller ARMSFEs than those of the multivariate ones at any time horizons, sometimes by 30%. The good approximation of the FWN model by the HAR is also illustrated in our results since they exhibit similar forecasting performances. However, the differences among the various methods are not always significant. Indeed, for $h = 1, 22$, the set of superior models includes all the models. In the case of the logs, the picture is more clear cut. Table 11.4 shows that, for $h = 1$, the subset of the best models includes only the univariate ones. There are no significant differences for $h = 22$.

These empirical findings are in sharp contrast with those obtained by Cubadda et al. (2017), which indicate that the VHARI often outperforms the HAR specification in forecasting. However, these authors used a rather different kind of data from those considered here, namely several realized volatility measures of the same equity index for three different markets. Hence, it might well be possible that a common index structure is more appropriate for modeling various measures of the same underlying volatility rather than the realized volatilities of different assets.

Remarkably, the VHAR and the three specifications of the VHARI have similar forecasting performances, thus suggesting that imposing a common index structure is not of particular help for modeling the considered volatilities. Indeed, the best forecasting results for the VHARI are obtained when the number of indexes is selected by the AIC, which of course provides the less parsimonious specification of the model (with the estimated q ranging in median from 6 to 13). Finally, ridge regularization in estimation slightly improves in forecasting when the model is either the VHAR or the VHARI with q selected by the AIC.

Overall, the empirical results seem to indicate that the contagion effect among the various volatilities is to some extent limited or, at least, is not well captured by the two multivariate versions of the HAR model that we have considered here. A scheme, à la CHL18, in which there exists at the multivariate level a large dimensional system with large diagonal autoregressive coefficients in the volatility of the series and tiny but jointly significant off-diagonal elements is not rejected by the data. FWN models as well as HAR, although estimated independently on each variables, seem to keep a footprint of what is referred to as the cross-sectional hidden dependence issue in CHL18.

6. Conclusions

In this paper we have evaluated the performances of various models in forecasting the volatilities of 13 asset returns. Our empirical findings indicate that univariate methods outdo the multivariate ones, although the differences in the associated ARMSFEs are often insignificant according to the model confidence set analysis. Moreover, imposing common components in the VHAR does not significantly improve forecast accuracy.

Overall, this evidence is line with the view that a large dimensional VAR with small contagion effects is the underlying generating mechanism of the considered realized volatilities (Chevillon et al., 2018).

An interesting option is to develop a multivariate model for realized volatilizes that, differently from the VHARI, allows for both idiosyncratic and common components. This issue is currently on our research agenda.

Acknowledgments

The authors thank Sébastien Laurent and Bilel Sanhaji as well as an anonymous referee. A previous version of this paper has been presented at the CFE 2017 meeting, London and the QFFE 2018 meeting, Marseille. The usual disclaimers apply

Notes

1 See, for instance, Chapter 3 in Hastie et al. (2011) for an introduction to Lasso and other regularization schemes in linear regression.
2 We use the notation *day* to avoid the confusion with the long-memory parameter d.
3 Both Q4 and T3 are very closely related to the procedure by Brownlees and Gallo (2006). Indeed, the median is used in place of the trimmed sample mean, $\bar{p}_i(k)$, and the mean absolute deviation from the median in place of $s_i(k)$.
4 Similar patterns emerge for the MedRV.
5 Similar results are obtained on MedRV. Also we only report the results for the logs of the series while we compare forecasting performances of both levels and log levels in the forecasting section.

Bibliography

Ahelegbey, D., Billio, M. and R. Casarin (2016), Sparse graphical vector autoregression: A Bayesian approach, *Annals of Economics and Statistics*, GENES, issue 123–124, 333–361.
Andersen, T. and L. Benzoni (2009), Realized volatility, in Andersen, T. G., Davis, Richard A., Kreiss, J. P. and Thomas Mikosch (eds.), *Handbook of Financial Time Series*, Springer-Verlag, 555–575.
Andersen, T., Bollerslev, T., Diebold, F. X. and P. Labys (2001), The distribution of realized exchange rate volatility, *Journal of the American Statistical Association*, 96, 42–55.
Anderson, H. and F. Vahid (2007), Forecasting the volatility of Australian stock returns: Do common factors help?, *Journal of Business and Economic Statistics*, 25, 76–90.

Baba, Y., Engle, R. F., Kraft, R. F., and K. F. Kroner (1989), Multivariate simultaneous generalized ARCH, in *Department of Economics*, University of California, San Diego Discussion Paper, 89/57.

Baillie, R. T. (1996), Long memory processes and fractional integration in econometrics, *Journal of Econometrics*, 73, 5–59.

Barndorff-Nielsen, O. E., Hansen, P. R., Lunde, A. and N. Shephard (2009), Realized kernels in practice: Trades and quotes, *The Econometrics Journal*, 12, C1–C32.

Barndorff-Nielsen, O. E. and N. Shephard (2002), Econometric analysis of realized volatility and its use in estimating stochastic volatility models, *J. R. Statist. Soc. B*, 64, 253–280.

Barndorff-Nielsen, O. E. and N. Shephard (2004), Power and bipower variation with stochastic volatility and jumps (with discussion), *Journal of Financial Econometrics*, 2, 1–37.

Bauwens, L., Chevillon, G. and S. Laurent (2018), Forecast Comparisons for Long Memory, mimeo.

Bauwens, L., Hafner, Ch. and S. Laurent (2012), Volatility models, in Bauwens, L., Hafner, Ch. and S. Laurent (eds.), *Handbook of Volatility Models and Their Applications*, Wiley, Ch. 1.

Bauwens, L., Laurent, S. and J. V. K. Rombouts (2006), Multivariate GARCH models: A survey, *Journal of Applied Econometrics*, 21, 79–109.

Billio, M., Getmansky, M., Lo, A. and L. Pelizzona (2012), Econometric measures of connectedness and systemic risk in the finance and insurance sectors, *Journal of Financial Economics*, 104(3), 535–559.

Boswijk, H. P. (1995), Identifiability of cointegrated systems, *Tinbergen Institute Working Paper*, 95/78.

Boswijk, H. P. and J. A. Doornik (2004), Identifying, estimating and testing restricted cointegrated systems: An overview, *Statistica Neerlandica*, 58, 440–465.

Bubák, V., Kočenda, E. and F. Žikeš (2011), Volatility transmission in emerging European exchange markets, *Journal of Banking & Finance*, 35, 2829–2841.

Centoni M., and G. Cubadda (2015), Common feature analysis of economic time series: An overview and recent developments, *Communications for Statistical Applications and Methods*, 22, 1–20.

Chevillon, G., Hecq, A. and S. Laurent (2018), Generating univariate fractional integration within a large VAR(1), *Journal of Econometrics*, 204, 54–65.

Chevillon, G. and S. Mavroeidis (2017), Learning can generate long memory, *Journal of Econometrics*, 198, 1–9.

Corsi, F. (2009), A simple approximate long-memory model of realized volatility, *Journal of Financial Econometrics*, 7, 174–196.

Corsi, F., Audrino, F. and R. Renò (2012), HAR modeling for realized volatility forecasting, in Bauwens, L., Hafner, Ch. and S. Laurent (eds), *Handbook of Volatility Models and Their Applications*, Wiley, Ch. 15.

Corsi, F., Mittnik, S., Pigorsch, C. and U. Pigorsch (2008), The volatility of realized volatility, *Econometric Reviews*, 27, 46–78.

Cubadda, G. and B. Guardabascio (2019), Representation, estimation and forecasting of the multivariate index-augmented autoregressive model, *International Journal of Forecasting*, 35, 67–79.

Cubadda, G., Guardabascio, B., and A. Hecq (2017), A vector heterogeneous autoregressive index model for realized volatility measures, *International Journal of Forecasting*, 33, 337–344.

Cubadda, G., Hecq, A. and F. C. Palm (2009), Studying co-movements in large multivariate models prior to modeling, *Journal of Econometrics*, 148, 25–35.

Diebold, F. and A. Inoue (2001), Long memory and regime switching, *Journal of Econometrics*, 105, 131–159.

Diebold, F. and M. Nerlove (1989), The dynamics of exchange rate volatility: A multivariate latent-factor ARCH model, *Journal of Applied Econometrics*, 4, 1–22.

Engle, R. F. and J. Marcucci (2006), A long-run pure variance common features model for the common volatilities of the Dow Jones, *Journal of Econometrics*, 132, 7–42.

Engle, R. F, Ng, V. K. and M. Rothshild (1990), Asset pricing using the FACTOR-ARCH model, *Journal of Econometrics*, 45, 213–237.

Engle, R. F. and R. Susmel (1993), Common volatility in international equity markets, *Journal of Business and Economic Statistics*, 11, 167–176.

Fengler, M. and K. Gisler (2015), A variance spillover analysis without covariances: What do we miss?, *Journal of International Money and Finance*, 51, 174–195.

Geweke, J. and S. Porter-Hudak (1983), The estimation and application of long memory time series models, *Journal of Time Series Analysis*, 4, 221–238.

Granger, C. W. J. (1980), Long memory relationships and the aggregation of dynamic models, *Journal of Econometrics*, 14, 227–238.

Granger, C. W. J. and R. Joyeux (1980), An introduction to long-memory time series models and fractional di erencing, *Journal of Time Series Analysis*, 1, 15–29.

Haldrup, N. and R. Kruse (2014), Discriminating between fractional integration and spurious longmemory, CREATES Research Paper 2014-19.

Haldrup, N. and E. Vera-Valdés (2017), Long memory, fractional integration, and cross sectional aggregation, *Journal of Econometrics*, 199, 1–11.

Hansen, P. R., Lunde, A. and J. Nason (2011), The model confidence set, *Econometrica*, 79, 453–497.

Hastie T., Tibshirani, R. and J. Friedman (2011), *The Elements of Statistical Learning: Data Mining, Inference, and Prediction*, 2nd ed., Springer, New York.

Heber, G., Lunde, A., Shephard, N. and K. Sheppard (2009), Oxford-Mann institute's realized library version 0.1. Oxford-Man Institute, University of Oxford.

Hecq, A., Laurent, S. and F. Palm (2012), Common intraday periodicity, *Journal of Financial Econometrics*, 10, 325–335.

Hecq, A., Laurent, S. and F. Palm (2016), On the univariate representation of BEKK models with common factors, *Journal of Time Series Econometrics*, 8, 91–113.

Hillebrand, E. and Marcelo C. Meideiros (2016), Nonlinearity, breaks and long-range dependence in time-series models, *Journal of Business & Economic Statistics*, 34, 23–42.

Hoerl, A. E., Kennard, R. W. and K. F. Baldwin (1975), Ridge regression: Some simulations, *Communications in Statistics: Theory and Methods*, 4, 105–123.

Liu, L., Patton, A. and K. Sheppard (2015), Does anything beat 5-minute RV? A comparison of realized measures across multiple asset classes, *Journal of Econometrics*, 187, 293–311.

McAleer, M. and M. C. Medeiros (2008), Realized volatility: A review, *Econometric Reviews*, 27, 10–45.

Miller, J. and J. Park (2010), Nonlinearity, nonstationarity, and thick tails: How they interact to generate persistence in memory, *Journal of Econometrics*, 155, 83–89.

Palm, F. C. (1977), On univariate time series methods and simultaneous equation econometric models, *Journal of Econometrics*, 5, 379–388.

Patton, A. (2011), Data-based ranking of realised volatility estimators, *Journal of Econometrics*, 161, 284–303.

Patton, A. and K. Sheppard (2009), Optimal combinations of realised volatility estimators, *International Journal of Forecasting*, 25, 218–238.

Reinsel, G. (1983), Some results on multivariate autoregressive index models, *Biometrika*, 70, 145–156.

Robinson, P. M., (1995), Gaussian semiparametric estimation of long range dependence, *Annals of Statistics*, 23, 1630–1661.

Santos, D. G. and F. A. Ziegelmann (2014), Volatility forecasting via MIDAS, HAR and their combination: An empirical comparative study for IBOVESPA, *Journal of Forecasting*, 33, 284–299.

Souček, M. and N. Todorova (2013), Realized volatilities transmission between crude oil and equity futures markets: A multivariate HAR approach, *Energy Economics*, 40, 586–597.

Zellner, A. and F. C. Palm (1974), Time series analysis and simultaneaous equation econometric models, *Journal of Econometrics*, 2, 17–54.

Zellner, A. and F. C. Palm (1975), Time series and structural analysis of monetary models of the US economy, *Sanhya: The Indian Journal of Statistics, Series C*, 37, 12–56.

Zellner, A. and F. C. Palm (2004), *The Structural Econometric Time Series Analysis Approach*, Cambridge University Press, Cambridge.

12 Covariance estimation and quasi-likelihood analysis

Yuta Koike and Nakahiro Yoshida

1. Nonparametric covariance estimation from high-frequency data

For a semi-martingale, the quadratic covariation is a natural quantity to measure its covariance structure. This motivates researchers to develop statistical inference for the quadratic covariation of a semi-martingale based on high-frequency observation data. Starting with the pioneering work in financial econometrics of Foster and Nelson[34], Andersen and Bollerslev [6] and Barndorff-Nielsen and Shephard [11], a number of articles have been devoted to this subject in the past two decades. In this section we give a brief review on this topic.

1.1. Realized covariance

Let $X = (X_t)_{t \in [0,T]}$, $X_t = (X_t^1, \cdots, X_t^d)^*$ be a d-dimensional semi-martingale that is left-continuous at T and defined on a stochastic basis $\mathcal{B} = (\Omega, \mathcal{F}, \mathbf{F} = (\mathcal{F}_t)_{t \in [0,T]}, P)$ ($*$ stands for the transpose of a matrix). Suppose that we observe these processes at some discrete time points on the interval $[0, T]$, say $0 \leq t_0 < t_1 < \cdots < t_N \leq T$. It is well-known in stochastic calculus that the quantity

$$\widehat{[X,X]}_T := \sum_{i=1}^N (X_{t_i} - X_{t_{i-1}})(X_{t_i} - X_{t_{i-1}})^*$$

converges in probability to the quadratic covariation matrix $[X, X]_T = ([X^p, X^q]_T)_{1 \leq p, q \leq d}$ of X as long as t_i's are $\mathbf{F}$-stopping times for every i and $r_N := t_0 \vee \max_{1 \leq i \leq N}(t_i - t_{i-1}) \vee (T - t_N)$ converges in probability to 0 (see, e.g., Theorem I-4.47 of [52]). The condition that r_N tends to 0 is naturally linked with situations of high-frequency observations, hence it is very natural to use the (observable) quantity $\widehat{[X,X]}_T$ as a measurement of the quadratic covariation matrix $[X, X]_T$. In this context, the "estimator" $\widehat{[X,X]}_T$ is usually referred to as the *realized covariance matrix* of X. The above fact immediately yields the consistency of the realized covariance under the high-frequency asymptotics such that r_N tends to 0 (in probability).

Given the consistency of the estimator, the next step we should develop is the asymptotic distribution theory. In the context of financial econometrics, this is extensively studied in [12] when X is a continuous Itô semi-martingale and observation times are equidistant. Specifically, we assume that the observation times are of the form $t_i = i\Delta_n$, $i = 0, 1, \ldots, N := \lfloor T/\Delta_n \rfloor$ with some sequence $(\Delta_n)_{n=1}^{\infty}$ of (deterministic) positive numbers such that $\Delta_n \to 0$ as $n \to \infty$. We also suppose that X is of the form

$$X_t = X_0 + \int_0^t b_s ds + \int_0^t \sigma_s dW_s, \qquad t \in [0, T], \tag{1.1}$$

where $b = (b_s)_{s \in [0, T]}$ is a d-dimensional $\mathbf{F}$-progressively measurable process, $\sigma = (\sigma_s)_{s \in [0, T]}$ is an $\mathbb{R}^d \otimes \mathbb{R}^r$-valued $\mathbf{F}$-progressively measurable process and $W = (W_s)_{s \in [0, T]}$ is an r-dimensional standard $\mathbf{F}$-Wiener process. Additionally, we suppose that

$$\int_0^T (|b_s|^2 + |\Sigma_s|^2) ds < \infty \qquad \text{a.s.,} \tag{1.2}$$

where $\Sigma_s = \sigma_s \sigma_s^{\star}$ and $|\cdot|$ denotes the Euclidean norm. In particular, expression (1.1) makes sense. Assumption (1.2) is slightly stronger than the one to make expression (1.1) well-defined, but it is still very weak. However, as we will see below, this condition is sufficient to prove a (stable) central limit theorem for $\widehat{[X,X]}_T$. We shall remark that, if X is of the form (1.1), the quadratic covariation matrix can be written as

$$[X, X]_T = \int_0^T \Sigma_t dt.$$

In this sense, $[X, X]_T$ is often called the *integrated covariance matrix* when X is a continuous Itô semi-martingale.

Before stating the asymptotic distribution theory for $\widehat{[X,X]}_T$, we need to introduce the notion of *stable convergence in law*, which is a (slightly) stronger mode of convergence than convergence in law.

Definition 1.1 (Stable convergence in law) Let S be a Polish space. S-valued random variables Z_n, $n = 1, 2, \ldots$, are said to *converge stably in law* to an S-valued variable Z defined on an extension $(\tilde{\Omega}, \tilde{\mathcal{F}}, \tilde{P})$ of $(\Omega, \mathcal{F}, P)$ if $E[Yf(Z_n)] \to \tilde{E}[Yf(Z)]$ as $n \to \infty$ for any bounded continuous function f on S and any bounded $\mathcal{F}$-measurable variable Y, where $\tilde{E}$ denotes the expectation with respect to $\tilde{P}$. We then write $Z_n \to^{d_s} Z$.

We refer to Section 2.2.1 of [51] for a short exposition of this concept and references therein for more details. An important consequence of this definition is the following (the notation $\to^P$ stands for convergence in probability):

Proposition 1.2 *In the setting of Definition 1.1, let* (V_n) *be a sequence of random variables, and suppose that* $Z_n \to^{d_s} Z$ *and* $V_n \to^p V$ *as* $n \to \infty$ *for some variable* V *on* $(\Omega, \mathcal{F}, P)$. *Then* $(Z_n, V_n) \to^{d_s} (Z, V)$ *as* $n \to \infty$.

In our problem, the asymptotic distribution of an estimator is typically mixed-normal whose covariance matrix is dependent on $\mathcal{F}$ due to the non-ergodic nature of the problem. For statistical applications we need to studentize the estimator by its asymptotic variance, but convergence in law alone does not ensure the validity of such an operation, while stable convergence in law does thanks to the above proposition (and the continuous mapping theorem).

Now we are ready to state the asymptotic distribution of the realized covariance matrix $[\widehat{X,X}]_T$. For a $d{\times}d$ matrix $A = (A^{ij})_{1 \le i, j \le d}$, we denote the vectorization of A by vec(A):

$$\mathrm{vec}\,(A) := (A^{11}, A^{21}, \cdots, A^{d1}, A^{12}, A^{22}, \cdots, A^{d2}, \cdots, A^{1d}, A^{2d}, \cdots, A^{dd})^\star \in \mathbb{R}^{d^2}.$$

Theorem 1.3 (Asymptotic distribution of the realized covariance matrix). *Suppose that X is of the form (1.1) and the coefficient processes b and σ satisfy (1.2). Then we have*

$$\frac{1}{\sqrt{\Delta_n}} \left\{ \mathrm{vec}\left([\widehat{X,X}]_T \right) - \mathrm{vec}\left([X,X]_T \right) \right\} \to^{d_s} \mathfrak{C}_T^{1/2} \zeta$$

as $n \to \infty$, where ζ is a d^2-dimensional standard normal variable independent of $\mathcal{F}$, and $\mathfrak{C}_T = (\mathfrak{C}_T^{pq})_{1 \le p, q \le d^2}$ is a $d^2 \times d^2$ random matrix whose elements are given as follows:

$$\mathfrak{C}_T^{d(p-1)+q, d(p'-1)+q'} = \int_0^T (\Sigma_t^{pp'} \Sigma_t^{qq'} + \Sigma_t^{pq'} \Sigma_t^{p'q})dt, \qquad p, q, p', q' = 1, \cdots, d.$$

Remark 1 The above result is taken from Theorem 5.4.2 of [51]. The original result of [12] assumes additional regularity conditions, especially the independence between the processes σ and W. This assumption enables us to apply a standard central limit theorem for martingales with deterministic asymptotic covariance matrix via conditioning. Such an assumption was removed later by an application of Jacod's stable central limit theorem from [47] (see also Chapter IX, Section 7 of [52] and Theorem 2.2.15 of [51]), which is now a standard tool to derive the asymptotic distribution of an estimator in this area. We refer to [84] for a concise exposition on how to apply Jacod's theorem to typical problems in this area.

Remark 2 Apart from application to high-frequency financial data, central limit theorems of the type of Theorem 1.3 were already studied in 1980s. For example, [30] derived such a type of CLT in the context of estimating the diffusion coefficient of an Itô process. Moreover, given that Itô's formula yields

$$
\begin{aligned}
&[\widehat{X^p, X^q}]_T - [X^p, X^q]_{\lfloor T/\Delta_n\rfloor\Delta_n} \\
&= \sum_{i=1}^{\lfloor T/\Delta_n\rfloor} \left\{ \int_{(i-1)\Delta_n}^{i\Delta_n} (X_{t-}^p - X_{(i-1)\Delta_n}^p)dX_t^q + \int_{(i-1)\Delta_n}^{i\Delta_n} (X_{t-}^q - X_{(i-1)\Delta_n}^q)dX_t^p \right\}
\end{aligned}
\tag{1.3}
$$

for $p, q = 1, \ldots, d$, Theorem 1.3 connects with evaluation of the error distribution of approximating a stochastic integral. In this context research would go back to [91].

Focusing on the marginal distributions, we obtain the following corollary:

Corollary 1.4. *Under the assumptions of Theorem 1.3, we have*

$$
\frac{1}{\sqrt{\Delta_n}} \left([\widehat{X^p, X^q}]_T - [X^p, X^q]_T \right) \to^{d_s} \sqrt{\int_0^T \{\Sigma_t^{pp}\Sigma_t^{qq} + (\Sigma_t^{pq})^2\} dt} \cdot \zeta
$$

as $n \to \infty$ for any $p, q = 1, \ldots, d$, where ζ is a standard normal variable independent of $\mathcal{F}$.

By an application of the (generalized) delta method, we can also derive the asymptotic distributions of the *realized correlation* and *realized beta* given by

$$
\frac{[\widehat{X^p, X^q}]_T}{\sqrt{[\widehat{X^p, X^p}]_T [\widehat{X^q, X^q}]_T}} \qquad \text{and} \qquad \frac{[\widehat{X^p, X^q}]_T}{[\widehat{X^p, X^p}]_T}
$$

for $p, q = 1, \ldots, d$, respectively; see, e.g., section 3 of [12] for details.

The next question would be asking what happens when we drop the continuity of X and/or consider non-equidistant sampling schemes, thus we briefly review these topics in the subsequent sections.

1.2. Jumps

It is interesting from both theoretical and practical points of view to incorporate jumps into the model. This is especially important in financial applications because continuous semi-martingale models are often too restrictive to capture several empirical properties of asset returns and option prices quoted on markets, as illustrated in chapter 1 of Cont and Tankov [25]. Fortunately, the realized covariance matrix $[\widehat{X, X}]_T$ converges in probability to the quadratic covariation matrix $[X, X]_T$ for *any* semi-martingale X as r_N converges in probability to 0 (as long as the observation times are stopping times), so it does not matter whether X has jumps or not for the consistency of the estimator $[\widehat{X, X}]_T$ under the current asymptotic regime.

The situation completely changes once we focus on the asymptotic distribution of $[\widehat{X,X}]_T$. In the presence of jumps, it is known that the asymptotic distribution of $[\widehat{X,X}]_T$ is generally no longer $\mathcal{F}$-conditional Gaussian. Keeping expression (1.3) in mind, one can find this type of result in Theorem 6.1 of Jacod and Protter [50], where the result was proven in the case of Lévy processes; a general Itô semi-martingale case is treated in Jacod [48] (see also Theorem 5.4.2 of [51]). We remark that all of these results give non-degenerate asymptotic distributions only when the continuous martingale part of X does not vanish. If X is a pure jump Itô semi-martingale, the scaling factor $1/\sqrt{\Delta_n}$ is no longer appropriate and we need to distinguish various types of jump process to derive central limit theorems for $[\widehat{X,X}]_T$; see Diop et al. [29] for details.

Meanwhile, when jumps do matter, econometricians are often interested in separating effects of jumps from the diffusive part. Taking account of the decomposition of the quadratic covariation matrix given by

$$[X,X]_T = [X^c,X^c]_T + \sum_{0<t\leq T}(\Delta X_t)(\Delta X_t)^*,$$

where X^c is the continuous martingale part of X and $\Delta X_t := X_t - X_{t-}$ is the jump of X at the time t (see, e.g., Theorem 4.52 from chapter I of [52]), they interpret this problem as estimating the quantity $[X^c, X^c]_T$ from discrete observations of X. In this context, $[X^c, X^c]_T$ is often referred to as the *integrated covariance matrix* of X due to the following reason: If X is of the form

$$X_t = X_0 + \int_0^t b_s ds + \int_0^t \sigma_s dW_s + M_t, \qquad t \in [0, T],$$

where $M = (M_t)_{t \in [0, T]}$ is a d-dimensional purely discontinuous local martingale (see Definition I-4.11 of [52] for the definition of a purely discontinuous local martingale), $[X^c, X^c]_T$ is given by

$$[X^c,X^c]_T = \int_0^T \Sigma_t dt.$$

In high-frequency financial econometrics, this kind of study was pioneered by Barndorff-Nielsen and Shephard [14] with the introduction of *bipower variation* for the univariate case. A multivariate extension of this work has been considered in Barndorff-Nielsen and Shephard [13], where the polarization identity

$$[X^p,X^q]_T = \frac{1}{4}([X^p + X^q, X^p + X^q]_T \qquad (1.4)$$
$$- [X^p - X^q, X^p - X^q]_T), \qquad p,q = 1,\cdots,d$$

makes the problem amount to the univariate case. Another prominent approach to separate diffusive parts and jumps is the so-called *thresholding method*, the idea of which goes back to studies of limit theorems for Lévy processes and semi-martingales and was used in this problem by Mancini [68] and Shimizu and Yoshida [95]. Application of the thresholding method to estimating integrated covariance matrices has been studied in Mancini and Gobbi [70] and Mancini [69].

1.3. *Irregular sampling schemes and non-synchronous observations*

In the previous sections we have assumed that the observation times of each asset are regularly spaced. More importantly, we have supposed that all assets share common observation times. Namely, they have been observed in a *synchronous* manner. However, these assumptions are unrealistic in raw high-frequency financial data because they are usually recorded at time points where some events (typically transactions or order arrivals) occur. In particular, this makes it more common to sample high-frequency financial data *non-synchronously*. Such a non-synchronous nature of observation times are quite serious for measuring the covariance structure because conventional construction of covariance estimators depends heavily on the synchronicity of observation times.

Specifically, for each $p = 1, \ldots, d$, let us assume that the p-th asset X^p is observed at the time points $0 \le t_0^p < t_1^p < \cdots < t_{n_p}^p \le T$. Then it is no longer evident how to construct the realized covariance matrix $\widehat{[X, X]}_T$ from this data. A naïve approach to resolve this issue is synchronizing the data by interpolation or imputation. That is, for each $p = 1, \ldots, d$, we construct pseudo observation data $\hat{X}_t^p$ for all $t \in [0, T]$ by interpolating the observation data $X_{t_0^p}^p, X_{t_1^p}^p, \cdots, X_{t_{n_p}^p}^p$ in some way. Then, taking a positive number L, we consider $\{\hat{X}_{Ti/L}\}_{i=0}^{L}$ as if they are really observed and construct the realized covariance matrix as

$$\widehat{[X, X]}_T^{(L)} := \sum_{i=0}^{L} (\hat{X}_{Ti/L} - \hat{X}_{T(i-1)/L})(\hat{X}_{Ti/L} - \hat{X}_{T(i-1)/L})^\star.$$

The most standard interpolation method used in high-frequency financial econometrics would be the *previous-tick method* where we set $\hat{X}_t^p := X_{t_i^p}^p$ if $t_i^p \le t < t_{i+1}^p$ for some $i = 0, 1, \ldots, n_p-1$ and $\hat{X}_t^p := X_{t_{n_p}^p}^p$ if $t_{n_p}^p \le t$.

An apparent issue of the above approach is how to select the positive integer L. We should take L as large as possible to avoid throwing away available data. However, as shown in Hayashi and Yoshida [40] Zhang [110], under some mild regularity conditions the estimator $\widehat{[X^p, X^q]}_T^{(L)}$ typically underestimates the quadratic covariation $[X^p, X^q]_T$ in the absolute value for $p \ne q$, and the bias becomes more serious as the degree of non-synchronicity increases and one takes the number L larger. This result can be seen as a theoretical explanation for the phenomenon found in Epps [33], which is known as the *Epps effect*.

To avoid such a bias and obtain a reasonable estimate, the number L must be sufficiently small, which results in much loss of efficiency.

Therefore, one will gravitate towards seeking estimation methods requiring no synchronization procedure. In the present context, there are two prominent approaches in this direction: One is the frequency-domain approach initiated in Malliavin and Mancino [67], and the other is the time-domain approach proposed in Hayashi and Yoshida [40]. Since the former approach is well-documented in the monograph [71], we focus on the latter one in the following. Hayashi and Yoshida [40] have proposed the following estimator for the quadratic covariation $[X^p, X^q]_T$ $(p, q = 1, \ldots, d)$:

$$\widehat{[X^p, X^q]}_T^{HY} := \sum_{i=1}^{n_p} \sum_{j=1}^{n_q} (X_{t_i^p}^p - X_{t_{i-1}^p}^p)(X_{t_i^p}^p - X_{t_{i-1}^p}^p) 1_{\{(t_{i-1}^p, t_i^p] \cap (t_{j-1}^q, t_j^q] \neq \emptyset\}}.$$

This estimator is now called the *cumulative covariance estimator* or the *Hayashi-Yoshida estimator*. In the synchronous observation case (i.e., $n_p = n_q$ and $t_i^p = t_i^q$ for all i), this estimator coincides with the realized covariance, hence it can be considered as a generalization of the realized covariance to the non-synchronous observation case. When X is a continuous Itô semi-martingale, the consistency of the Hayashi-Yoshida estimator has been shown in Hayashi and Yoshida [40] for a simplified setting and in Hayashi and Kusuoka [39] for a fully general setting; the asymptotic mixed normality has been shown in Hayashi and Yoshida [41] for a deterministic volatility setting and in Hayashi and Yoshida [42] for a stochastic volatility setting. In addition, Dalalyan and Yoshida [27] have derived the second-order asymptotic expansions for a deterministic volatility setting. Meanwhile, Bibinger and Vetter [20] have established the consistency and asymptotic distribution of the Hayashi-Yoshida estimator in the presence of jumps (Theorem 3 of [20]), where the asymptotic distribution is typically non-standard. Besides, applying the thresholding method to the Hayashi-Yoshida estimator, Mancini and Gobbi [70] have constructed a consistent estimator for the integrated covariance matrix of X when X is observed in a non-synchronous manner. The asymptotic mixed normality of their estimator has been established in Koike [55].

Except for [39], all the above papers impose a kind of predictability condition on observation times to avoid the technical difficulty caused by the dependence between observed processes and observation times, which is known as endogenous observations. Endogenous observations naturally occur in high-frequency financial data, and they lead to non-standard asymptotic distributions even in the univariate (so the problem of non-synchronous observations is absent) and continuous case, as shown in Fukasawa [35] and Li et al. [64] (see also the recent result of Vetter and Zwingmann [103] in the presence of jumps). For the Hayashi-Yoshida estimator this problem has been studied in Potiron and Mykland [85] when X is continuous; see also Robert and Rosenbaum [89] for related work.

1.4. Microstructure noise

When we deal with raw (or ultra) high-frequency financial data, it is well-known that we should take account of measurement errors of the data in addition to the sampling problem discussed in the previous section. Although no-arbitrage based asset pricing theories imply that market price processes should usually follow a semi-martingale (see, e.g., [28,31]), empirical evidence suggests the existence of additional noise in the prices; see [38] for example. This leads researchers to the view that semi-martingale models for asset prices are latent rather than observable at high-frequencies. Then, as the first step, it would be natural to consider an additive noise (or regression-type) model. Namely, we shall assume that observation data $Y^p_{t^p_0}, Y^p_{t^p_1}, \cdots$ of the p-th asset can be written as follows:

$$Y^p_{t^p_i} = X^p_{t^p_i} + \epsilon^p_i, \qquad i = 0, 1, \cdots, n_p, \tag{1.5}$$

where X^p is the "latent" semi-martingale and $\epsilon^p_0, \epsilon^p_1, \cdots$ are centered i.i.d. random variables independent of X. In fact, this model can explain some well-documented empirical evidence for the presence of noise in high frequency financial data, e.g., unit roots and first order negative autocorrelation of returns [37] as well as shapes of volatility signature plots [7].

In the univariate case $d = 1$, Zhou [112] adopted model (1.5) to estimate the volatility from high frequency data, and proposed an unbiased estimator for the quadratic variation of X, provided that X is a time-changed Brownian motion. A similar model to (1.5) has already appeared in Roll [90] where the observation noise is originated by bid-ask bounces. However, Zhou [112] found that effects of noise arose even in bid price data, and concluded that the source of the noise is a combination of various market microstructure effects such as bid-ask bounce, screen-fighting effect, misprints and so on. For this reason one refers to observation noise as *microstructure noise* in this area. Since this work, many authors have proposed methods to estimate the quadratic variation of X from the above model in the univariate case. Thus far the most prominent ones are the subsampling (or multi-scale) approach [109, 111], the realized kernel estimation [9], the pre-averaging method [49, 83], the quasi-maximum likelihood (QML) approach [105], the Separating Information Maximum Likelihood (SIML) method [61] and the spectral approach [88]. We refer to chapter 7 of Aït-Sahalia and Jacod [4] for more details on this topic.

Since our objective is the quadratic covariation matrix, we need to include the problem of non-synchronous observations in consideration as well. That is, the simultaneous treatment of non-synchronous observations and microstructure noise is necessary. In the following we give a short review on this topic.

In the remainder of this section, we assume that X is continuous Itô semi-martingale unless otherwise stated.

1.4.1. Synchronization and de-noising

As seen in the previous section, synchronization procedures typically cause serious biases in the obtained realized covariance matrices. However, if they are combined with de-noising procedures used in volatility estimation in the presence of microstructure noise (e.g., the ones described in the above), we usually obtain correct estimates, at least asymptotically. This is mainly because such a de-noising procedure often removes synchronization errors as well since they are typically less serious than microstructure noise. This fact was first found in Barndorff-Nielsen et al. [10], and they have proposed the *multivariate realized kernel with refresh time based synchronization* as an estimator for the quadratic covariation matrix, which we describe in the following.

We first introduce the concept of refresh time:

Definition 1.5 (Refresh time). The refresh times T_0, T_1, ..., T_N of the sampling times $(t_i^p)_{i=0}^{n_p}$ ($i = 0$, 1, ..., n_p) are defined inductively by $T_0 := \max\{t_0^1, \cdots, t_0^d\}$ and

$$T_k := \max_{1 \le p \le d} \min\{t_i^p : t_i^p > T_{k-1}\} \qquad (k = 1, \cdots, N),$$

where N is the integer such that there is no t_i^p such that $t_i^p > T_N$ for some p.

Barndorff-Nielsen et al. [10] have proposed constructing synchronized observation data $(\hat{Y}_{T_k})_{k=0}^N$ by previous-tick interpolation. Namely, for every $p = 1$, ..., d, we set $\hat{Y}_{T_k}^p := Y_{t_i^p}^p$ if $t_i^p \le T_k < t_{i+1}^p$ for some $i = 0$, 1, ..., n_p-1 and $\hat{Y}_{T_k}^p := Y_{t_{n_p}^p}^p$ if $t_{n_p}^p \le T_k$. After that, we construct a multivariate realized kernel based on the data $(\hat{Y}_{T_k})_{k=0}^N$ as if they are right observation data. Barndorff-Nielsen et al. [10] have shown the consistency and asymptotic mixed normality of such a multivariate realized kernel. The multivariate realized kernel proposed in Barndorff-Nielsen et al. [10] is a consistent estimator for the quadratic covariation matrix under a broad class of noise specification and always ensures the positive semi-definiteness of the estimate, but the convergence rate is suboptimal.

This type of approach has been studied in many subsequent articles for different de-noising methods, sometimes under different (or more general) synchronization procedures. Zhang [110] has studied the asymptotic property of the two scales realized covariance (TSCV) under general previous-tick based synchronization. Bibinger [15] has proposed a novel synchronization procedure inspired by the Hayashi-Yoshida estimator and constructed the multi-scale realized covariance based on this synchronization, which is called the *generalized multi-scale estimator* (see [109] for the original multi-scale estimator). Bibinger [15] has also derived the optimal convergence rate for this problem and shown that the generalized multi-scale estimator achieves this optimal rate. The asymptotic mixed normality has been established in [16] and [19].

Using the polarization identity (1.4), one can always construct an estimator for $[X^p, X^q]_T$ by constructing estimators for $[X^p + X^q, X^p + X^q]_T$ and $[X^p - X^q,$

$X^p - X^q]_T$, hence we can always return the problem of constructing a consistent estimator for $[X^p, X^q]_T$ to the univariate case as long as the observation times are synchronous. Using this fact, Aït-Sahalia et al. [3] have constructed a rate-optimal estimator for the quadratic covariation matrix from noisy and non-synchronous observations using the realized QML estimator from [105]. Their results also allow more general synchronization methods than the one based on refresh times. The class of such synchronization methods is called the *Generalized Synchronization method* in [3]. In the meantime, Liu and Tang [65] have considered a direct multivariate generalization of the QML approach from [105] with the Generalized Synchronization method and obtained a rate-optimal estimator for $[X, X]_T$.

For the pre-averaging method, Christensen et al. [22] have studied the finite sample performance of the pre-averaged version of the realized covariance (called *modulated realized covariance*) with refresh time based synchronization by numerical experiments. A formal asymptotic theory has been studied in [59] for a continuous Itô semi-martingale setting and in [58] for a general Itô semi-martingale setting with the Generalized Synchronization method.

Kunitomo et al. [60] have proposed the SIML estimator with refresh time based synchronization and established the asymptotic mixed normality.

Rate-optimal modifications of the original multivariate realized kernel have been proposed by some authors as well. Based on synchronized data, Ikeda [45] has constructed a multivariate version of the *two-scale realized kernel* from Ikeda [44] and Varneskov [101] has constructed a multivariate version of the *generalized flat-top realized kernel* of Varneskov [102]. Both the authors have shown the asymptotic mixed normality of the proposed estimators and allowed very general structures on microstructure noise.

1.4.2. Pre-averaged Hayashi-Yoshida estimator

Although synchronization does not matter asymptotically when it is combined with a de-noising method, simulation studies reported in [10] and [22] show the existence of downward biases (in absolute values) in the estimates of synchronization plus de-noising type covariance estimators presented above. In addition, if the observation frequencies are quite different between multiple assets, the synchronization amounts to throwing away a lot of available data, which is uncomfortable from a statistical point of view. These motivate us to seek an estimation method for quadratic covariation matrices without synchronization. One natural idea would be construct a Hayashi-Yoshida type estimator after de-noising the data. The pre-averaging method is perfectly suitable to this purpose because it is originally introduced in [83] to systematically make functionals of semi-martingale increments robust against microstructure noise. This idea is implemented in [22] by introducing the *pre-averaged Hayashi-Yoshida estimator* as follows. We choose a positive number k_n as the window size of pre-averaging. We also choose a continuous function $g : [0, 1] \to \mathbb{R}$ which is piecewise C^1 with a piecewise Lipschitz derivative g' and satisfies

$g(0) = g(1) = 0$ and $\psi_{HY} := \int_0^1 g(x)dx \neq 0$. The function g is used as the weight function in pre-averaging. Then we define the pre-averaged returns of the p-th asset by

$$\bar{Y}_i^p = \sum_{k=1}^{k_n-1} g\left(\frac{k}{k_n}\right)\left(Y_{t_{i+k}^p}^p - Y_{t_{i+k-1}^p}^p\right), \qquad i = 0, 1, \cdots, n_p - k_n + 1.$$

Now summation by parts yields

$$\bar{Y}_i^p = -\sum_{k=0}^{k_n-1}\left(g\left(\frac{k+1}{k_n}\right) - g\left(\frac{k}{k_n}\right)\right)Y_{t_{i+k}^p}^p \approx -\frac{1}{k_n}\sum_{k=0}^{k_n-1}g'\left(\frac{k}{k_n}\right)Y_{t_{i+k}^p}^p,$$

hence if the noise is centered and i.i.d., one may expect that the pre-averaged returns are close to the returns of the latent process X up to multiplicative constants due to the law of large numbers. This leads us to the following construction of a Hayashi-Yoshida type estimator:

$$[\widehat{Y^p, Y^q}]_T^{PHY} := \frac{1}{(\psi_{HY}k_n)^2}\sum_{i=0}^{n_p-k_n+1}\sum_{j=0}^{n_q-k_n+1}\bar{Y}_i^p\bar{Y}_j^q\mathbb{1}_{\{(t_i^p,t_{i+k_n}^p]\cap(t_j^q,t_{j+k_n}^q]\neq\emptyset\}}.$$

The consistency of the pre-averaged Hayashi-Yoshida estimator has been established in [22], while the asymptotic mixed normality has been shown in [23] when the observation times are deterministic transformations of equidistant sampling schemes. The form of the asymptotic covariance matrix given in [23] depends strongly on this assumption, hence it is difficult to generalize their result to the case of other sampling schemes such as Poisson sampling schemes. For this reason, Koike [56] has proposed constructing the pre-averaged Hayashi-Yoshida estimator based on partially synchronized data using refresh times in the same spirit as that discussed in Section 6.3 of [16]. For this modified pre-averaged Hayashi-Yoshida estimator, [56] have shown the asymptotic mixed normality in a more general sampling setting containing Poisson sampling schemes.

It is worth mentioning that, unlike the standard pre-averaged counterpart of the realized covariance (i.e., the modulated realized covariance, see [22]), the pre-averaged Hayashi-Yoshida estimator has consistency without explicit bias correction caused by noise. This is a (probably unexpected) byproduct of the Hayashi-Yoshida type construction, which turns out to perform an additional averaging (see Remark 3.2 of [23] and Remark 2.5 of [57] for details). This feature leads to the robustness of the pre-averaged Hayashi-Yoshida estimator against serially correlated noise; see Remark 3.3 of [23] and Section 4.2 of [57]. However, this additional averaging has a drawback that it typically increases the asymptotic variance of the estimator than the usual one and thus lessens the efficiency; see Remark 3.5 of [23] for a discussion on this point.

One can naturally apply the thresholding method to the pre-averaged Hayashi-Yoshida estimator in order to construct a consistent estimator for integrated covariance matrices when jumps may exist. Asymptotic properties of such an estimator have been studied in Wang et al. [104], Koike [57] and Hounyo [43], where the last paper has also developed a general bootstrap method for high-frequency data.

1.4.3. Local generalized method of moments in the spectral domain

Apart from the idea of synthesizing a method to handle non-synchronous observations and a de-noising technique, Bibinger et al. [17] have proposed a rather different approach than what we have discussed in the previous sections. Their idea is inspired by the asymptotic equivalence result (in the Le Cam sense) between high-frequency (but *discrete*) observations of the form (1.5) and *continuous* observations of a certain Gaussian white noise model in the univariate case from [88]. To be precise, let $T = 1$ for simplicity and suppose that the latent d-dimensional semi-martingale X is written as follows:

$$X_t = X_0 + \int_0^t \Sigma_s^{1/2} dB_s, \qquad t \in [0, 1],$$

where $B = (B_s)_{s \in [0, 1]}$ is a d-dimensional standard Wiener process and $\Sigma = (\Sigma_s)_{s \in [0, 1]}$ is a $d \times d$ p.s.d. symmetric matrix valued process independent of X which satisfies some regularity conditions (see Assumption 3.2 of [17]). Suppose also that the measurement errors $(\epsilon_i^p)_{i=0}^{n_p}$ for the p-th asset are i.i.d. Gaussian variables with mean 0 and variance $\eta_p^2 > 0$ as well as independent across different assets. Suppose further that the observation times $(t_i^p)_{i=0}^{n_p}$ of the p-th asset are written as $t_i^p = F_p^{-1}(i/n_p)$, $i = 0, 1, \ldots, n_p$ with some differentiable distribution function $F_p \colon [0, 1] \to [0, 1]$ satisfying some regularity conditions (see Assumption 3.1(α) of [17]). In this situation Bibinger et al. [17] have shown that, under some regularity conditions, observing model (1.5) is asymptotically equivalent (in the Le Cam sense) to observing the continuous-time signal-in-white noise model

$$Y_t = \int_0^t X_s ds + \int_0^t H_n(s) dW_s, \qquad t \in [0, 1] \tag{1.6}$$

as $n_{\min} := \min_{1 \le p \le d} n_p \to \infty$, where $H_n(s) := \operatorname{diag}\left(\eta_p / \sqrt{n_p F_p'(s)}\right)_{1 \le p \le d}$ and $W = (W_s)_{s \in [0, 1]}$ is a d-dimensional standard Wiener process independent of B (see Theorem 3.4 of [17] for the precise description). Their proof of this result especially enables us to transfer any statistical procedure developed in model (1.6) to a counterpart in model (1.5) with the same asymptotic properties as the original one in a constructive way, hence we may work with model (1.6) to construct an estimator for the quadratic covariation matrix of X without loss of information. In model (1.6) the information of the observation times is embedded to the noise part and the non-synchronicity of the original model (1.5) causes no trouble: In fact, the above asymptotic equivalence implies that the non-synchronicity in model (1.5) does not affect the asymptotically efficient procedure.

Now we describe the concrete construction of their estimator in the following. First, we split the interval into small blocks $[kh_n, (k + 1)h_n)$ $(k = 0, 1, \cdots, h_n^{-1} - 1)$. The width h_n of the blocks is chosen so that $h_n^{-1} \in \mathbb{N}$ and the spot covariance matrix Σ_t are approximately constant on each block. Then, following [88], we define localized Fourier sine coefficients of the returns by

$$
S_{jk} = \left(\sum_{i=1}^{n_p} \left(Y_{t_i^p}^p - Y_{t_{i-1}^p}^p \right) \Phi_{jk} \left(\frac{t_{i-1}^p + t_i^p}{2} \right) \right)^*_{1 \le p \le d},
$$

$$
k = 0, 1, \cdots, h_n^{-1} - 1; \; j = 1, 2, \cdots,
$$

where $\Phi_{jk}(t) := \sqrt{2/h_n} \sin(j\pi h_n^{-1}(t - kh_n)) 1_{[kh_n, (k+1)h_n)}(t)$ denotes the sine function of frequency j on the block $[kh_n, (k+1)h_n)$. They are referred to as the *spectral statistics*. By construction the spectral statistics are independent (conditionally on Σ) and each S_{jk} approximately follows the d-dimensional centered normal distribution with covariance matrix $C_{jk} := \Sigma_{kh_n} + \pi^2 j^2 h_n^{-2} H_n(kh_n)^2$. This suggests that we could estimate each Σ_{kh_n} by the generalized method of moments for the statistics $(S_{jk})_{j=1}^\infty$, which yields (the oracle version of) the *local method of moments estimator* for $\mathrm{vec}([X, X]_T)$ as follows:

$$
\mathrm{LMM}_{\mathrm{or}}^n := \sum_{k=0}^{h_n^{-1}-1} h_n \sum_{j=1}^\infty W_{jk} \, \mathrm{vec} \left(S_{jk} S_{jk}^* - \frac{\pi^2 j^2}{h_n^2} H_n(kh_n)^2 \right),
$$

where $I_{jk} := C_{jk}^{-1} \otimes C_{jk}^{-1}$, $I_k := \sum_{j=1}^\infty I_{jk}$, and $W_{jk} := I_k^{-1} I_{jk}$ ($\otimes$ denotes the Kronecker product of matrices). In practice this estimator is infeasible because it contains unknown parameters Σ_{kh_n} and $H_n(kh_n)^2$ (the former is indeed what we would like to estimate). To obtain a feasible estimator, we need to construct appropriate pilot estimators for those parameters and plug them into the above estimator, which is discussed in pp. 93–94 of [17] (see also sections 3.3–3.4 of [5]). The resulting adaptive version of the local method of moments estimator is indeed a consistent estimator for $\mathrm{vec}([X, X]_T)$ and asymptotically centered mixed normal under appropriate regularity conditions (see Theorem 4.4 of [17]). Moreover, its asymptotic covariance matrix attains a semiparametric Cramér-Rao type lower bound, hence it is asymptotically efficient in a semiparametric Cramér-Rao sense (see Theorem 5.2 of [17]).

The asymptotic mixed normality of the local method of moments estimator in a general continuous Itô semi-martingale setting has been established in

Altmeyer and Bibinger [5]. Application of the local method of moments to spot covariance estimation is studied in Bibinger et al. [18]. Bibinger and Winkelmann [21] have developed asymptotic theories for related estimators in the presence of jumps.

1.4.4. Multivariate realized QML approach

Yet another approach for quadratic covariance matrix estimation from model (1.5) has been proposed in Shephard and Xiu [92], which is also free from synchronization of data. Their approach is a multivariate generalization of the QML approach of [105] as in [3] and [65], but unlike those studies, they have explicitly handled non-synchronous observations within the quasi-likelihood function, so no synchronization is necessary. More precisely, given that $X_t = \Sigma W_t$ ($t \in [0, T]$) with a $d \times d$ symmetric p.s.d. matrix Σ and a d-dimensional Wiener process W, ϵ_i^p's are i.i.d. centered Gaussian variables with variance $\eta_p^2 > 0$ for every p as well as independent across different assets, and t_i^p's are deterministic, we can explicitly write down the likelihood function of model (1.5) as $\Sigma, \eta_1^2, \cdots, \eta_d^2$ being unknown parameters. The maximizer of this likelihood function, which is called the *multivariate realized QML estimator*, turns out to work well as an estimator for $[X, X]_T$ even when X is a general Itô semi-martingale and microstructure noise is non-Gaussian.

From a computational point of view, the quasi-likelihood function corresponds to the likelihood function of a Gaussian state space model and the non-synchronous observations can be seen as observations missing as illustrated in Lo and MacKinlay [66], hence the maximization of the quasi-likelihood function is effectively implemented by Kalman filtering and an EM algorithm. This point is discussed in section 3 of [92] as well as in section 3.1 of [26]. The asymptotic mixed normality of the estimator has been established in Shephard and Xiu [92] for the equidistant and synchronous sampling setting. Due to the complexity of the quasi-likelihood function, the asymptotic distribution in a general non-synchronous setting has not been developed so far.[1]

In terms of asymptotic efficiency, the local method of moments estimator is the best possible one at least within a submodel of (1.5) discussed in the previous section. Although the multivariate realized QML estimator is asymptotically efficient in the simplified setting stated above by construction (under an appropriate regularity condition on the observation times), it is not asymptotically efficient if the spot covariance matrix is time-varying. This is already true in the univariate case as discussed in view of the results from [105] and [88]. However, the realized QML approach has several advantages over the competitors. First, it contains no tuning parameter for implementation. Second, it always ensure the positive semi-definiteness of the estimated quadratic covariation matrix. Third, it can be accommodated to incorporate a factor structure into the model (see [92] for details). These features are especially important for empirical applications.

2. Quasi-likelihood analysis and parametric inference for stochastic processes

2.1. Quasi-likelihood analysis

In this section, we will discuss parametric inference for stochastic differential equations. The approach is based on the so-called quasi-likelihood analysis (QLA), that emerged in a modification and facilitation of the Ibragimov-Has'minsikii theory or the Ibragimov-Has'minsikii-Kutoyants program in asymptotic decision theory for stochastic processes, by a systematically derived polynomial type large deviation inequality.

Let $\mathbb{T}$ be a subset of $\mathbb{R}_+$ such that $\sup \mathbb{T} = \infty$. Let Θ be a bounded open set in $\mathbb{R}^{\mathsf{p}}$ and let $\theta^* \in \Theta$. We will consider a sequence of random fields $\mathbb{H}_T : \Omega \times \Theta \to \mathbb{R}$, $T \in \mathbb{T}$, given a probability space $(\Omega, \mathcal{F}, P)$. Let $\mathbb{U}_T = \{u \in \mathbb{R}^{\mathsf{p}}; \theta^* + a_T u \in \Theta\}$ for a fixed $\theta^* \in \Theta$ and a sequence $(a_T)_{T \in \mathbb{T}} \subset \mathrm{GL}(\mathsf{p})$ satisfying the norm $|a_T| \to 0$ as $T \to \infty$. For simplicity of exposition, we will assume that the mapping $\theta \mapsto \mathbb{H}_T(\omega, \theta)$ is continuously extended to $\bar{\Theta}$ for every $\omega \in \Omega$.

The QLA theory uses the random field

$$\mathbb{Z}_T(u) = \exp\{\mathbb{H}_T(\theta_T(u)) - \mathbb{H}_T(\theta^*)\} \quad (u \in \mathbb{U}_T)$$

where $\theta_T(u) = \theta^* + a_T u$. In most cases where the statistical random field $\mathbb{H}_T$ is differentiable with respect to θ, the random field $\mathbb{Z}_T$ is asymptotically quadratic in that

$$\mathbb{Z}_T(u) = \exp\left(\Delta_T[u] - \frac{1}{2}\Gamma[u^{\otimes 2}] + r_T(u)\right) \tag{2.1}$$

with $r_T(u) \to^P 0$ as $T \to \infty$ for every $u \in \mathbb{R}^{\mathsf{p}}$. Here Δ_T is a p-dimensional random vector, Γ is a $\mathsf{p} \times \mathsf{p}$ random matrix, and the brackets [] stand for linear and multi-linear functions. Suppose that

$$(\Delta_T, \Gamma) \to^d (\Delta, \Gamma) \tag{2.2}$$

as $T \to \infty$, where the p-dimensional random variable Δ is defined on an extension $(\bar{\Omega}, \bar{\mathcal{F}}, \bar{P})$ of $(\Omega, \mathcal{F}, P)$. Then, under certain weak conditions, the convergence

$$\mathbb{Z}_T|_{\overline{B(R)}} \to^d \mathbb{Z}|_{\overline{B(R)}} \quad \text{in} \quad C(\overline{B(R)}) \quad (T \to \infty) \tag{2.3}$$

holds for every $R > 0$, where $B(R) = \{u \in \mathbb{R}^{\mathsf{p}}; |u| < R\}$, $C(\overline{B(R)})$ is the space of continuous functions on $B(R)$ equipped with the supremum norm, and

$$\mathbb{Z}(u) = \exp\left(\Delta[u] - \frac{1}{2}\Gamma[u^{\otimes 2}]\right) \quad (u \in \mathbb{R}^{\mathsf{p}}).$$

An essential role is played by the polynomial type large deviation inequality

$$\limsup_{T \in \mathbb{T}} \sup_{r > 0} r^L P \left[\sup_{u \in \mathbb{V}_T(r)} \mathbb{Z}_T(u) \geq e^{-2^{-1} r^{c_0}} \right] < \infty \qquad (2.4)$$

for every $L > 0$, where $c_0 \in (0, 2)$ is a constant and $\mathbb{V}_T(r) = \{u \in \mathbb{U}_T; |u| \geq r\}$. The supremum over the empty set should read as $-\infty$.

Denote by $\hat{C}(\mathbb{R}^p)$ the space of continuous functions f on $\mathbb{R}^p$ such that $\lim_{|u| \to \infty} |f(u)| = 0$. Equipped the supremum norm, $\hat{C}(\mathbb{R}^p)$ becomes a separable Banach space. The random field $\mathbb{Z}_T$ can be extended to $\mathbb{R}^p$ as an element of $\hat{C}(\mathbb{R}^p)$ so that $\sup_{u \in \mathbb{R}^p \backslash \mathbb{U}_T} \mathbb{Z}_T(u) \leq \sup_{u \in \partial \mathbb{U}_T} \mathbb{Z}_T(u)$. This extension will be denoted by $\mathbb{Z}_T$. Then we obtain

$$\mathbb{Z}_T \to^d \mathbb{Z} \text{ in } \hat{C}(\mathbb{R}^p) \ (T \to \infty) \qquad (2.5)$$

from (2.3) and (2.4).

The quasi-maximum likelihood estimator (QMLE) $\hat{\theta}_T^M$ is a measurable map from Ω to $\bar{\Theta}$ satisfying

$$\mathbb{H}_T(\hat{\theta}_T^M) = \max_{\theta \in \bar{\Theta}} \mathbb{H}_T(\theta).$$

The quasi-Bayesian estimator (QBE) $\hat{\theta}_T^B$ is a mapping from Ω to the convex hull of Θ defined by

$$\hat{\theta}_T^B = \left[\int_\Theta \exp\left(\mathbb{H}_T(\theta)\right) \varpi(\theta) d\theta \right]^{-1} \int_\Theta \theta \exp\left(\mathbb{H}_T(\theta)\right) \varpi(\theta) d\theta$$

with a continuous prior density ϖ such that $0 < \inf_{\theta \in \Theta} \varpi(\theta) \leq \sup_{\theta \in \Theta} \varpi(\theta) < \infty$. Then it follows from (2.4) and (2.5), if Γ is appropriately nondegenerate, that

$$\hat{u}_T^A \to^d \Gamma^{-1/2} \Delta \qquad (2.6)$$

and

$$E[f(\hat{u}_T^A)] \to \bar{E}[f(\hat{u}^A)] \qquad (2.7)$$

for $A \in \{M, B\}$ and any continuous function f on $\mathbb{R}^p$ that is of at most polynomial growth. The convergence (2.6) is stable if so is (2.2).

The strong mode of convergence (2.7) is thanks to the polynomial type large deviation inequality (2.4). Convergence of moments is backing asymptotic theory in the arguments about asymptotic optimality, prediction, model selection and information criterion, asymptotic expansion, higher-order optimal estimation, bootstrap and resampling methods, information geometry, and so on.

As seen above, the polynomial type large deviation inequality (2.4) is the bottleneck of the theory. However, it can be derived in an abstract setting only by assuming easily tractable moment conditions; see [107] for details. Thus the applications of the QLA have spread to various stochastic processes, even non-linear or time-discretely sampled, such as diffusion processes, jump-diffusion processes, point processes, and so on.

2.2. Ergodic diffusion process

Given a filtration $\mathbf{F} = (\mathcal{F}_t)_{t \in \mathbb{R}_+}$ on $(\Omega, \mathcal{F}, P)$, let us consider a stationary $\mathbf{F}$-adapted diffusion process $X = (X_t)_{t \in \mathbb{R}_+}$ satisfying the stochastic differential equation

$$dX_t = a(X_t, \theta_2)dt + b(X_t, \theta_1)dw_t,$$

where $w = (w_t)_{t \in \mathbb{R}_+}$ is an r-dimensional $\mathbf{F}$-Wiener process. The parameter θ_i is in Θ_i, a bounded open set in $\mathbb{R}^{\mathsf{p}_i}$, $i = 1, 2$, and we assume each Θ_i has a good boundary. We will assume that $X_0 \in L^{\infty-} = \cap_{p > 1} L^p$ and that the functions $a : \mathbb{R}^d \times \bar{\Theta}_2 \to \mathbb{R}^d$ and $b : \mathbb{R}^d \times \bar{\Theta}_1 \to \mathbb{R}^d$ are sufficiently smooth and their derivatives are of at most polynomial growth uniformly in $\theta = (\theta_1, \theta_2) \in \bar{\Theta}_1 \times \bar{\Theta}_2$.[2] Moreover, uniform non-degeneracy of $S(x, \theta_1) = (bb^*)(x, \theta_1)$ will be assumed. For estimation of θ from the sampled data $(X_{t_j})_{j=0,1,\dots,n}$ with an increasing sequence t_j in $\mathbb{R}_+$, a standard random field is

$$
\mathbb{H}_n(\theta_1, \theta_2) = -\frac{1}{2} \sum_{j=1}^{n} \Bigg\{ \log \det S(X_{t_{j-1}}, \theta_1) + S(X_{t_{j-1}}, \theta_1)^{-1} \\
[(\Delta_j X - ha(X_{t_{j-1}}, \theta_2))^{\otimes 2}] \Bigg\}
\tag{2.8}
$$

where $\Delta_j X = X_{t_j} - X_{t_{j-1}}$. Suppose that X is geometrically mixing. A simple sampling scheme is such that $t_j = jh$, $h \to 0$, $nh \to \infty$ and $nh^2 \to 0$ as $n \to \infty$. In this situation, applying the general QLA theory for $T = n$, we obtain asymptotic normality and moment convergence of the QMLE $\hat{\theta}_n^M = (\hat{\theta}_{1,n}^M, \hat{\theta}_{2,n}^M)$, i.e., for $\hat{u}_n^M = (\sqrt{n}(\hat{\theta}_{1,n}^M - \theta_1^*), \sqrt{nh}(\hat{\theta}_{2,n}^M - \theta_2^*))$, $\theta^* = (\theta_1^*, \theta_2^*)$, the convergence

$$E(f(\hat{u}_n^M)) \to \bar{E}(f(\hat{u})) \quad (n \to \infty) \tag{2.9}$$

holds for any $f \in C(\mathbb{R}^{\mathsf{p}_1 + \mathsf{p}_2})$ of at most polynomial growth, where $\hat{u} \sim N_{\mathsf{p}_1 + \mathsf{p}_2}(0, \Gamma^{-1})$ and the matrix $\Gamma = \text{diag}[\Gamma_1, \Gamma_2]$ is written by

$$\Gamma_1[u_1^{\otimes 2}] = \frac{1}{2} \int_{\mathbb{R}^d} \text{Tr}\left(S^{-1}(\partial_{\theta_1} S) S^{-1}(\partial_{\theta_1} S)(x, \theta_1^*)[u_1^{\otimes 2}] \right) v(dx) \quad (u_1 \in \mathbb{R}^{\mathsf{p}_1})$$

and

$$\Gamma_2[u_2^{\otimes 2}] = \int_{\mathbb{R}^d} S(x, \theta_1^*)^{-1} \Big[(\partial_{\theta_2} a(x, \theta_2^*)[u_2])^{\otimes 2} \Big] v(dx) \quad (u_2 \in \mathbb{R}^{p_2})$$

with the invariant probability measure v of X (Yoshida [107]).

The QBE $\hat{\theta}_n^B = (\hat{\theta}_{1,n}^B, \hat{\theta}_{2,n}^B)$ can be treated in the QLA based on $\mathbb{H}_n$. On the other hand, the adaptive Bayesian estimator $\hat{\theta}_n^{aB} = (\hat{\theta}_{1,n}^{aB}, \hat{\theta}_{2,n}^{aB})$ has an advantage from computational aspects since it involves only p_1 and p_2 dimensional integrals, not the $(p_1 + p_2)$-dimensional one. The adaptive Bayesian estimator $\hat{\theta}_{1,n}^{aB}$ for θ_1 is defined by

$$\hat{\theta}_{1,n}^{aB} = \left[\int_{\Theta_1} \exp\left(\mathbb{H}_n(\theta_1, \theta_2^0) \right) \varpi_1(\theta_1) d\theta_2 \right]^{-1} \int_{\Theta_1} \theta_1 \exp\left(\mathbb{H}_n(\theta_1, \theta_2^0) \right) \varpi_1(\theta_1) d\theta_2$$

where θ_2^0 is a value in Θ_2 arbitrarily chosen by the observer, and ϖ_1 is a continuous prior density bounded from 0 and above. Then the adaptive Bayesian estimator $\hat{\theta}_{2,n}^{aB}$ for θ_2 is inductively defined as

$$\hat{\theta}_{2,n}^{aB} = \left[\int_{\Theta_2} \exp\left(\mathbb{H}_n(\hat{\theta}_{1,n}^{aB}, \theta_2) \right) \varpi_2(\theta_2) d\theta_1 \right]^{-1} \int_{\Theta_2} \theta_2 \exp\left(\mathbb{H}_n(\hat{\theta}_{1,n}^{aB}, \theta_2) \right) \varpi_2(\theta_2) d\theta_2$$

with a continuous prior density ϖ_2 bounded from 0 and above. Yoshida [107] showed the same asymptotic property as (2.9) for $\hat{\theta}_n^{aB}$.

The joint asymptotic normality (2.9) for bounded functions f was given in Yoshida [106] and generalized in Kessler [54]. Certain asymptotic properties of estimators for sampled diffusion processes are found in Prakasa Rao [86, 87], where the condition $nh^2 \to 0$ was called a condition of rapidly increasing experimental design. Relaxation of this condition to $nh^p \to 0$ for $p > 2$ is a practical issue. Yoshida [106] gave an adaptive scheme for $p = 3$, and Kessler [54] generalized it to arbitrary p. Though a more sophisticated construction of $\mathbb{H}_n$ than (2.8) is necessary but this problem has been pursued, within the framework of the QLA theory, by Uchida and Yoshida [96, 98] for adaptive estimators, and Kamatani and Uchida [53] for hybrid multi-step estimators.

Finally we should remark that statistical inference for ergodic diffusion processes has a long history especially for estimation of drift parameters under continuous observations. See Kutoyants [62, 63] and the references therein. The series of his work motivated one of the authors to extend the scheme to sampled nonlinear processes.

2.3. Jump-diffusion process

The QLA theory can apply to diffusion processes with jumps. Consider a d-dimensional process $X = (X_t)_{t \in \mathbb{R}_+}$ satisfying the following stochastic integral equation

$$X_t = X_0 + \int_0^t a(X_s, \theta_2)ds + \int_0^t b(X_s, \theta_1)dw_s$$

$$+ \int_0^t \int c(X_{s-}, z, \theta_2)(p - q)(ds, dz) \tag{2.10}$$

where $w = (w_t)_{t \in \mathbb{R}_+}$ is an r-dimensional Wiener process and p is a Poisson random measure on $(0, \infty) \times \mathbb{R}^m \backslash \{0\}$ with (deterministic) intensity measure q. We will assume suitable regularity conditions for the functions $a : \mathbb{R}^d \times \Theta_2 \to \mathbb{R}^d$, $b : \mathbb{R}^d \times \Theta_1 \to \mathbb{R}^d \otimes \mathbb{R}^r$ and $c : \mathbb{R}^d \times \mathbb{R}^m \times \Theta_2 \to \mathbb{R}^d$. Suppose that the jump part of X is finitely active, i.e., $\sum_{s \in [0, t]} |\Delta X_s| < \infty$ a.s for every $t > 0$. The drift term and the jump term of (2.10) share the same parameter θ_2 but this expression includes the case where those parts have individual parameters.

Under ergodicity, Ogihara and Yoshida [80] showed asymptotic normality of the QMLE and QBE, besides, moment convergence of their errors. The convergence rates of those estimators are the same as the ergodic diffusion case of Section 2.2 and they are asymptotically optimal. Construction of a jump filter is essential to split intervals with/without jumps, that are unobservable, to achieve optimal estimation; otherwise, obviously, many ad hoc approaches would be possible even in infinitely active jump cases. Shimizu and Yoshida [95] proposed a construction of jump filter by threshold method for stochastic differential equations with jumps. Shimizu [94] applied QLA to threshold estimation for stochastic processes with small noise.

Recently Inatsugu and Yoshida [46] proposed a global filter that enhances the correct identification rate of jump intervals. Their filter depends on the whole data and more involved treatment is necessary since it could destroy adaptivity and the martingale structure in the semi-martingale.

Parametric estimation of processes driven by pure jump processes was studied within the QLA theory by Masuda [72] for approximate self-weighted LAD estimation of discretely observed ergodic Ornstein-Uhlenbeck processes, and by Masuda [73] for convergence of Gaussian quasi-likelihood random fields for ergodic Lévy-driven SDE observed at high frequency. The latter result has recently been extended to the misspecified case by Uehara [99]. See also Masuda [74] for parametric estimation of Lévy processes.

2.4. Parametric estimation of volatility

As seen in the previous sections, estimation of the volatility yields the non-ergodic statistics. Typically, estimators become asymptotically mixed normal, differently from ergodic statistics. Let us consider a stochastic regression model

$$Y_t = Y_0 + \int_0^t b_s ds + \int_0^t \sigma(X_s, \theta)dw_s \qquad (t \in \mathbb{I})$$

defined on a stochastic basis $(\Omega, \mathcal{F}, \mathbf{F}, P)$ with a filtration $\mathbf{F} = (\mathcal{F}_t)_{t \in \mathbb{I}}$, where $\mathbb{I} = [0, T]$ and T is a fixed positive value, namely, finite time horizon. Y_0 is $\mathcal{F}_0$-measurable. The process $w = (w_t)_{t \in \mathbb{I}}$ is an r-dimensional $\mathbf{F}$-Wiener process, and $\sigma : \mathbb{R}^m \times \Theta \to \mathbb{R}^m$ a function for which certain regularity conditions are assumed. The process $b = (b_t)_{t \in \mathbb{I}}$ is an m-dimensional progressively measurable process. We want to estimate the true value θ^* of $\theta \in \Theta$, an open set in $\mathbb{R}^p$ having a good boundary, based on the data $(X_{t_j}, Y_{t_j})_{j=0,1,\dots,n}$ with $t_j = jT/n$.

The quasi-log-likelihood function is

$$\mathbb{H}_n(\theta) = -\frac{1}{2} \sum_{j=1}^{n} \left\{ \log \det S(X_{t_{j-1}}, \theta) + h^{-1} S(X_{t_{j-1}}, \theta)^{-1} \left((\Delta_j Y)^{\otimes 2} \right) \right\}$$

where $\Delta_j Y = Y_{t_j} - Y_{t_{j-1}}$ and $S = \sigma^{\otimes 2}$. Uchida and Yoshida [97] proved the stable convergence of the QMLE and QBE and convergence of moments as follows. Let $\hat{u}_n^{\mathsf{A}} = \sqrt{n}(\hat{\theta}_n^{\mathsf{A}} - \theta^*)$ for the QMLE $\mathsf{A} = M$ and for the QBE $\mathsf{A} = B$. Then

$$E(f(\hat{u}_n^{\mathsf{A}})\Phi) \to \bar{E}(f(\Gamma^{-1/2}\zeta)\Phi) \tag{2.11}$$

for $\mathsf{A} \in \{M, B\}$, where f is any continuous function with at most polynomial growth, ζ is a p-dimensional random vector independent of $\mathcal{F}$, Φ is any bounded $\mathcal{F}$-measurable random variable, and the random matrix Γ is defined by

$$\Gamma[u^{\otimes 2}] = \frac{1}{2T} \int_0^T \operatorname{Tr}(S^{-1}(\partial_\theta S[u]) S^{-1}(\partial_\theta S[u])(X_t, \theta^*)) dt$$

for $u \in \mathbb{R}^p$.

Let

$$\mathbb{Y}(\theta) = -\frac{1}{2T} \int_0^T \left\{ \log \frac{\det S(X_t, \theta)}{\det S(X_t, \theta^*)} + \operatorname{Tr}\left(S(X_t, \theta)^{-1} S(X_t, \theta^*) - I_m\right) \right\} dt.$$

Index χ_0 is defined by

$$\chi_0 = \inf_{\theta \neq \theta^*} \frac{-\mathbb{Y}(\theta)}{|\theta - \theta^*|^2},$$

which measures how models are separated from the true one when the parameters are different from the true ones (note that the process $\mathbb{Y}(\theta)$ is appeared as the limit of $\mathbb{Y}_n(\theta) := n^{-1}\{\mathbb{H}_n(\theta) - \mathbb{H}_n(\theta^*)\}$; see Uchida and Yoshida [97] for details). It is a key index because if

$$P(\chi_0 \leq r^{-1}) \leq C_L r^{-L} \quad (r > 0) \tag{2.12}$$

then the polynomial type large deviation inequality (2.4) for $T = n$ holds under mild additional conditions. The non-degeneracy (2.12) of χ_0 is not easy to prove but Uchida and Yoshida [97] provided an analytic criterion and a geometric criterion for it.

Related to this result, the convergence (2.11) for $A = M$ and bounded f was given by Genon-Catalot and Jacod [36]. Non-synchronous case was solved by Ogihara and Yoshida [81] with construction of the QLA. The local asymptotic mixed normality was proved by Ogihara [78].

2.5. Other topics in the quasi-likelihood analysis

Since it is universal, the QLA theory is widely applicable to various problems. Recently applications of the QLA spread to point processes and other stochastic processes, and as a methodology to regularization methods for sparse estimation.

By ultra high frequency data, the latest quantitative finance is demanded to model mechanisms in a more and more precise time-scale where aggregation Gaussianity does not occur and Brownian motions can no longer serve as the sources of randomness. Instead, point processes give a promising approach. Limit order book (LOB) is the case. Abergel and Judidi [2], Muni Toke [76] and Bacry et al. [8] proposed approaches with Hawkes processes. Abergel et al. [1] gives an excellent exposition of modeling LOB. Muni Toke and Yoshida [77] presented intensities models of order flows in a limit order book. As for QLA, Clinet and Yoshida [24] constructed QLA for ergodic point processes and applied it to LOB. Ogihara and Yoshida [82] gave QLA for point processes for ultra high frequency data observed in finite time horizon. They considered the situation where the intensity goes to infinity and proved asymptotic mixed normality of the QLA estimators.

LOB models often have many parameters. Then sparse estimation is an issue. Recently it was found that properties of sparse estimators by regularization methods can be deduced with the aid of the QLA. Once QLA incorporating regularization methods is established, because of its universality, we will be able to apply regularization methods to various stochastic processes. Masuda and Shimizu [75] applied QLA to regularized M-estimators, while Shimizu [93] discussed the case of regularized least-squares estimation in details. Umezu et al. [100] studied AIC for non-concave penalized likelihood method by using QLA. Kinoshita, Suzuki and Yoshida recently showed generally the error probability in selection consistency of non-concave penalized estimators is of $O(n^{-L})$ for any positive number L. Eguchi and Masuda [32] proposed BIC type information criteria within the QLA framework and showed their asymptotic properties.

As we have discussed in Section 1.4, in financial econometrics ultra high-frequency data are often modeled as a discretely observed semi-martingale contaminated by noise. QLA for this type of model has recently been developed in Ogihara [79].

The original QLA theory [107] requires existence of certain order of moments. In analysis of stochastic models under finite time horizon, it is straightforward to relax such assumption by localization. That is, we can apply the present QLA directly after suitable localization. Localization causes no damage in asymptotic arguments. On the other hand, if a stochastic process is observed in long-run and if some component in the system has long memory, then localization may not enable the QLA to apply. Even in such a case, there is a possibility that the partial quasi-likelihood analysis works, as shown in a recent paper [108].

Acknowledgments

This work was in part supported by CREST Japan Science and Technology Agency; Japan Society for the Promotion of Science Grants-in-Aid for Scientific Research Nos. 17H01100, 16K17105 and 17H01702 (Scientific Research); and by a Cooperative Research Program of the Institute of Statistical Mathematics.

Notes

1 In a parametric setting, however, the recent work of Ogihara [79] has established the asymptotic distribution theory for quasi-maximum likelihood estimators based on more sophisticated quasi-likelihood functions. The paper has indeed developed stronger results known as the *quasi-likelihood analysis*, which we detail in the next section. See also Ogihara and Yoshida [81] for relevant analysis in the absence of noise.
2 Indeed, the smoothness depends on the situation. Detailed conditions are given in the papers we list at the end of this subsection.

Bibliography

[1] Abergel, F., Anane, M., Chakraborti, A., Jedidi, A. and Toke, I. M. (2016). *Limit order books*. Cambridge University Press.

[2] Abergel, F. and Jedidi, A. (2015). Long-time behavior of a Hawkes process-based limit order book. *SIAM J. Financial Math.* 6, 1026–1043.

[3] Aït-Sahalia, Y., Fan, J. and Xiu, D. (2010). High-frequency covariance estimates with noisy and asynchronous financial data. *J. Amer. Statist. Assoc.* 105, 1504–1517.

[4] Aït-Sahalia, Y. and Jacod, J. (2014). *High-frequency financial econometrics*. Princeton University Press, Princeton.

[5] Altmeyer, R. and Bibinger, M. (2015). Functional stable limit theorems for quasi-efficient spectral covolatility estimators. *Stochastic Process. Appl.* 125, 4556–4600.

[6] Andersen, T. G. and Bollerslev, T. (1998). Answering the skeptics: Yes, standard volatility models do provide accurate forecasts. *Internat. Econom. Rev.* 4, 885–905.

[7] Andersen, T. G., Bollerslev, T., Diebold, F. X. and Labys, P. (2000). Great realizations. *Risk* 13, 105–108.

[8] Bacry, E., Jaisson, T. and Muzy, J.-F. (2016). Estimation of slowly decreasing Hawkes kernels: Application to high-frequency order book dynamics. *Quant. Finance* 16, 1179–1201.

[9] Barndorff-Nielsen, O. E., Hansen, P. R., Lunde, A. and Shephard, N. (2008). Designing realised kernels to measure the ex-post variation of equity prices in the presence of noise. *Econometrica* 76, 1481–1536.

[10] Barndorff-Nielsen, O. E., Hansen, P. R., Lunde, A. and Shephard, N. (2011). Multivariate realised kernels: Consistent positive semi-definite estimators of the covariation of equity prices with noise and non-synchronous trading. *J. Econometrics* 162, 149–169.

[11] Barndorff-Nielsen, O. E. and Shephard, N. (2002). Econometric analysis of realized volatility and its use in estimating stochastic volatility. *J. R. Stat. Soc. Ser. B Stat. Methodol.* 64, 253–280.

[12] Barndorff-Nielsen, O. E. and Shephard, N. (2004a). Econometric analysis of realized covariation: High frequency based covariance, regression, and correlation in financial economics. *Econometrica* 72, 885–925.

[13] Barndorff-Nielsen, O. E. and Shephard, N. (2004b). Measuring the impact of jumps in multivariate price processes using bipower covariation. Discussion paper, Nuffield College, Oxford University.

[14] Barndorff-Nielsen, O. E. and Shephard, N. (2004c). Power and bipower variation with stochastic volatility and jumps. *Journal of Financial Econometrics* 2, 1–37.

[15] Bibinger, M. (2011). Efficient covariance estimation for asynchronous noisy high-frequency data. *Scand. J. Stat.* 38, 23–45.

[16] Bibinger, M. (2012). An estimator for the quadratic covariation of asynchronously observed Itô processes with noise: Asymptotic distribution theory. *Stochastic Process. Appl.* 122, 2411–2453.

[17] Bibinger, M., Hautsch, N., Malec, P. and Reiss, M. (2014). Estimating the quadratic covariation matrix from noisy observations: local method of moments and efficiency. *Ann. Statist.* 42, 80–114.

[18] Bibinger, M., Hautsch, N., Malec, P. and Reiss, M. (2017). Estimating the spot covariation of asset prices—statistical theory and empirical evidence. *J. Bus. Econom. Statist.* (forthcoming).

[19] Bibinger, M. and Mykland, P. A. (2016). Inference for multi-dimensional high-frequency data with an application to conditional independence testing. *Scand. J. Stat.* 43, 1078–1102.

[20] Bibinger, M. and Vetter, M. (2015). Estimating the quadratic covariation of an asynchronously observed semimartingale with jumps. *Ann. Inst. Statist. Math.* 67, 707–743.

[21] Bibinger, M. and Winkelmann, L. (2015). Econometrics of co-jumps in high-frequency data with noise. *J. Econometrics* 184, 361–378.

[22] Christensen, K., Kinnebrock, S. and Podolskij, M. (2010). Pre-averaging estimators of the ex-post covariance matrix in noisy diffusion models with non-synchronous data. *J. Econometrics* 159, 116–133.

[23] Christensen, K., Podolskij, M. and Vetter, M. (2013). On covariation estimation for multivariate continuous Itô semi-martingales with noise in non-synchronous observation schemes. *J. Multivariate Anal.* 120, 59–84.

[24] Clinet, S. and Yoshida, N. (2017). Statistical inference for ergodic point processes and application to limit order book. *Stochastic Process. Appl.* 127, 1800–1839.

[25] Cont, R. and Tankov, P. (2004). *Financial modeling with jump processes.* Financial Mathematics Series. Chapman & Hall/CRC.

[26] Corsi, F., Peluso, S. and Audrino, F. (2015). Missing in asynchronicity: A Kalman-EM approach for multivariate realized covariance estimation. *J. Appl. Econometrics* 30, 377–397.

[27] Dalalyan, A. and Yoshida, N. (2011). Second-order asymptotic expansion for a non-synchronous covariation estimator. *Ann. Inst. Henri Poincaré Probab. Stat.* 47, 748–789.

[28] Delbaen, F. and Schachermayer, W. (1994). A general version of the fundamental theorem of asset pricing. *Math. Ann.* 300, 463–520.

[29] Diop, A., Jacod, J. and Todorov, V. (2013). Central limit theorems for approximate quadratic variations of pure jump Itô semimartingales. *Stochastic Process. Appl.* 123, 839–886.

[30] Dohnal, G. (1987). On estimating the diffusion coefficient. *J. Appl. Probab.* 24, 105–114.

[31] Duffie, D. (1991). The theory of value in security markets. In W. Hildenbrand and H. Sonnenschein, eds., *Handbook of mathematical economics*, vol. 4, chap. 31. Elsevier Science Publishers B.V., pp. 1615–1682.

[32] Eguchi, S. and Masuda, H. (2018). Schwarz type model comparison for LAQ models. *Bernoulli* 24, 2278–2327.

[33] Epps, T. W. (1979). Comovements in stock prices in the very short run. *J. Amer. Statist. Assoc.* 74, 291–298.

[34] Foster, D. P. and Nelson, D. B. (1996). Continuous record asymptotics for rolling sample variance estimators. *Econo metrica* 64, 139–174.

[35] Fukasawa, M. (2010). Realized volatility with stochastic sampling. *Stochastic Process. Appl.* 120, 829–852.

[36] Genon-Catalot, V. and Jacod, J. (1993). On the estimation of the diffusion coefficient for multi-dimensional diffusion processes. *Ann. Inst. H. Poincaré Probab. Statist.* 29, 119–151.

[37] Goodhart, C. A. E. and Figliuoli, L. (1991). Every minute counts in financial markets. *Journal of International Money and Finance* 10, 23–52.

[38] Hansen, P. R. and Lunde, A. (2006). Realized variance and market microstructure noise. *J. Bus. Econom. Statist.* 24, 127–161.

[39] Hayashi, T. and Kusuoka, S. (2008). Consistent estimation of covariation under nonsynchronicity. *Stat. Inference Stoch. Process.* 11, 93–106.

[40] Hayashi, T. and Yoshida, N. (2005). On covariance estimation of nonsynchronously observed diffusion processes. *Bernoulli* 11, 359–379.

[41] Hayashi, T. and Yoshida, N. (2008). Asymptotic normality of a covariance estimator for nonsynchronously observed diffusion processes. *Ann. Inst. Statist. Math.* 60, 357–396.

[42] Hayashi, T. and Yoshida, N. (2011). Nonsynchronous covariation process and limit theorems. *Stochastic Process. Appl. 121*, 2416–2454.

[43] Hounyo, U. (2017). Bootstrapping integrated covariance matrix estimators in noisy jump-diffusion models with non synchronous trading. *J. Econometrics* 197, 130–152.

[44] Ikeda, S. S. (2015). Two-scale realized kernels: A univariate case. *Journal of Financial Econometrics* 13, 126–165.

[45] Ikeda, S. S. (2016). A bias-corrected estimator of the covariation matrix of multiple security prices when both mi crostructure effects and sampling durations are persistent and endogenous. *J. Econometrics* 193, 203–214.

[46] Inatsugu, H. and Yoshida, N. (2018). Global jump filters and quasi likelihood analysis for volatility. *arXiv preprint arXiv: 1806.10706.*

[47] Jacod, J. (1997). On continuous conditional Gaussian martingales and stable convergence in law. In *Séminaire de probabilitiés xxxi*, vol. 1655 of *Lecture Notes in Math.* Springer, Berlin, New York, pp. 232–246.

[48] Jacod, J. (2008). Asymptotic properties of realized power variations and related functionals of semimartingales. *Stochas tic Process. Appl.* 118, 517–559.

[49] Jacod, J., Li, Y., Mykland, P. A., Podolskij, M. and Vetter, M. (2009). Microstructure noise in the continuous case: The pre-averaging approach. *Stochastic Process. Appl.* 119, 2249–2276.

[50] Jacod, J. and Protter, P. (1998). Asymptotic error distributions for the Euler method for stochastic differential equations. *Ann. Probab.* 26, 267–307.

[51] Jacod, J. and Protter, P. (2012). *Discretization of processes.* Springer.

[52] Jacod, J. and Shiryaev, A. N. (2003). *Limit theorems for stochastic processes.* Springer, 2nd edn.

[53] Kamatani, K. and Uchida, M. (2014). Hybrid multi-step estimators for stochastic differential equations based on sampled data. *Stat. Inference Stoch. Process.* 18, 177–204.

[54] Kessler, M. (1997). Estimation of an ergodic diffusion from discrete observations. *Scand. J. Statist.* 24, 211–229.

[55] Koike, Y. (2014a). An estimator for the cumulative co-volatility of asynchronously observed semimartingales with jumps. *Scand. J. Stat.* 41, 460–481.

[56] Koike, Y. (2014b). Limit theorems for the pre-averaged Hayashi-Yoshida estimator with random sampling. *Stochastic Process. Appl.* 124, 2699–2753.

[57] Koike, Y. (2016a). Estimation of integrated covariances in the simultaneous presence of nonsynchronicity, microstructure noise and jumps. *Econometric Theory* 32, 533–611.

[58] Koike, Y. (2016b). Quadratic covariation estimation of an irregularly observed semimartingale with jumps and noise. *Bernoulli* 22, 1894–1936.

[59] Koike, Y. (2017). Time endogeneity and an optimal weight function in pre-averaging covariance estimation. *Stat. Inference Stoch. Process.* 20, 15–56.

[60] Kunitomo, N., Misaki, H. and Sato, S. (2015). The SIML estimation of integrated covariance and hedging coefficient under round-off errors, micro-market price adjustments and random sampling. *Asia-Pacific Financial Markets* 22, 333–368.

[61] Kunitomo, N. and Sato, S. (2013). Separating information maximum likelihood estimation of the integrated volatility and covariance with micro-market noise. *The North American Journal of Economics and Finance* 26, 282–309.

[62] Kutoyants, Y. A. (1984). *Parameter estimation for stochastic processes*, vol. 6. Heldermann. Translated from the Russian and edited by B. L. S. Prakasa Rao.

[63] Kutoyants, Y. A. (2004). *Statistical inference for ergodic diffusion processes.* Springer Series in Statistics. Springer-Verlag London Ltd., London.

[64] Li, Y., Mykland, P. A., Renault, E., Zhang, L. and Zheng, X. (2014). Realized volatility when sampling times are possibly endogenous. *Econometric Theory* 30, 580–605.

[65] Liu, C. and Tang, C. Y. (2014). A quasi-maximum likelihood approach for integrated covariance matrix estimation with high frequency data. *J. Econometrics* 180, 217–232.

[66] Lo, A. W. and MacKinlay, A. C. (1990). An econometric analysis of non-synchronous trading. *J. Econometrics* 45, 181–211.

[67] Malliavin, P. and Mancino, M. E. (2002). Fourier series method for measurement of multivariate volatilities. *Finance Stoch.* 6, 49–61.

[68] Mancini, C. (2001). Disentangling the jumps of the diffusion in a geometric jumping Brownian motion. *Giornale dell'Istituto Italiano degli Attuari* 64, 19–47.

[69] Mancini, C. (2017). Truncated Realized Covariance when prices have infinite variation jumps. *Stochastic Process. Appl.* 127, 1998–2035.

[70] Mancini, C. and Gobbi, F. (2012). Identifying the Brownian covariation from the co-jumps given discrete observations. *Econometric Theory* 28, 249–273.

[71] Mancino, M. E., Recchioni, M. C. and Sanfelici, S. (2017). *Fourier-Malliavin volatility estimation: Theory and practice.* Springer.

[72] Masuda, H. (2010). Approximate self-weighted LAD estimation of discretely observed ergodic Ornstein-Uhlenbeck processes. *Electron. J. Stat.* 4, 525–565.

[73] Masuda, H. (2013). Convergence of Gaussian quasi-likelihood random fields for ergodic Lévy driven SDE observed at high frequency. *Ann. Statist.* 41, 1593–1641.

[74] Masuda, H. (2015). Parametric estimation of Lévy processes. In *Lévy matters IV.* Springer, pp. 179–286.

[75] Masuda, H. and Shimizu, Y. (2017). Moment convergence in regularized estimation under multiple and mixed-rates asymptotics. *Math. Methods Statist.* 26, 81–110.

[76] Muni Toke, I. and Pomponio, F. (2011). Modelling trades-through in a limited order book using hawkes processes. *Economics discussion paper.*

[77] Muni Toke, I. and Yoshida, N. (2017). Modelling intensities of order flows in a limit order book. *Quant. Finance* 17, 683–701.

[78] Ogihara, T. (2015). Local asymptotic mixed normality property for nonsynchronously observed diffusion processes. *Bernoulli* 21, 2024–2072.

[79] Ogihara, T. (2018). Parametric inference for nonsynchronously observed diffusion processes in the presence of market microstructure noise. *Bernoulli* 24, 3318–3383.

[80] Ogihara, T. and Yoshida, N. (2011). Quasi-likelihood analysis for the stochastic differential equation with jumps. *Stat. Inference Stoch. Process.* 14, 189–229.

[81] Ogihara, T. and Yoshida, N. (2014). Quasi-likelihood analysis for nonsynchronously observed diffusion processes. *Stochastic Process. Appl.* 124, 2954–3008.

[82] Ogihara, T. and Yoshida, N. (2015). Quasi likelihood analysis of point processes for ultra high frequency data. *arXiv preprint arXiv:1512.01619*.

[83] Podolskij, M. and Vetter, M. (2009). Estimation of volatility functionals in the simultaneous presence of microstructure noise and jumps. *Bernoulli* 15, 634–658.

[84] Podolskij, M. and Vetter, M. (2010). Understanding limit theorems for semimartingales: A short survey. *Stat. Neerl.* 64, 329–351.

[85] Potiron, Y. and Mykland, P. A. (2017). Estimation of integrated quadratic covariation with endogenous sampling times. *J. Econometrics* 197, 20–41.

[86] Prakasa Rao, B. L. S. (1983). Asymptotic theory for non-linear least squares estimator for diffusion processes. *Math. Operationsforsch. Statist. Ser. Statist.* 14, 195–209.

[87] Prakasa Rao, B. L. S. (1988). Statistical inference from sampled data for stochastic processes. In N. U. Prabhu, ed., *Statistical inference from stochastic processes*, vol. 80 of *Contemporary Mathematics*. American Mathematical Society, pp. 249–287.

[88] Reiss, M. (2011). Asymptotic equivalence for inference on the volatility from noisy observations. *Ann. Statist.* 39, 772–802.

[89] Robert, C. Y. and Rosenbaum, M. (2012). Volatility and covariation estimation when microstructure noise and trading times are endogenous. *Math. Finance* 22, 133–164.

[90] Roll, R. (1984). A simple implicit measure of the effective bid-ask spread in an efficient market. *Journal of Finance* 39, 1127–1139.

[91] Rootzén, H. (1980). Limit distributions for the error in approximations of stochastic integrals. *Ann. Probab.* 8, 241–251.

[92] Shephard, N. and Xiu, D. (2017). Econometric analysis of multivariate realised QML: Estimation of the covariation of equity prices under asynchronous trading. *J. Econometrics* 201, 19–42.

[93] Shimizu, Y. (2017a). Moment convergence of regularized least-squares estimator for linear regression model. *Ann. Inst. Statist. Math.* 69, 1141–1154.

[94] Shimizu, Y. (2017b). Threshold estimation for stochastic processes with small noise. *Scand. J. Stat.* 44, 951–988.

[95] Shimizu, Y. and Yoshida, N. (2006). Estimation of parameters for diffusion processes with jumps from discrete obser vations. *Stat. Inference Stoch. Process.* 9, 227–277.

[96] Uchida, M. and Yoshida, N. (2012). Adaptive estimation of an ergodic diffusion process based on sampled data. *Stochas tic Process. Appl.* 122, 2885–2924.

[97] Uchida, M. and Yoshida, N. (2013). Quasi likelihood analysis of volatility and nondegeneracy of statistical random field. *Stochastic Process. Appl.* 123, 2851–2876.

[98] Uchida, M. and Yoshida, N. (2014). Adaptive Bayes type estimators of ergodic diffusion processes from discrete obser vations. *Stat. Inference Stoch. Process.* 17, 181–219.

[99] Uehara, Y. (2017). Statistical inference for misspecified ergodic Lévy driven stochastic differential equation models. *arXiv preprint arXiv:1702.00908*.

[100] Umezu, Y., Shimizu, Y., Masuda, H. and Ninomiya, Y. (2015). AIC for non-concave penalized likelihood method. *arXiv preprint arXiv:1509.01688. Ann. Inst. Statist. Math.* (forthcoming).

[101] Varneskov, R. T. (2016). Flat-top realized kernel estimation of quadratic covariation with nonsynchronous and noisy asset prices. *J. Bus. Econom. Statist.* 34, 1–22.

[102] Varneskov, R. T. (2017). Estimating the quadratic variation spectrum of noisy asset prices using generalized flat-top realized kernels. *Econometric Theory* 33, 1457–1501.

[103] Vetter, M. and Zwingmann, T. (2017). A note on central limit theorems for quadratic variation in case of endogenous observation times. *Electron. J. Stat.* 11, 963–980.

[104] Wang, K., Liu, J. and Liu, Z. (2013). Disentangling the effect of jumps on systematic risk using a new estimator of integrated co-volatility. *Journal of Banking & Finance* 37, 1777–1786.

[105] Xiu, D. (2010). Quasi-maximum likelihood estimation of volatility with high frequency data. *J. Econometrics* 159, 235–250.

[106] Yoshida, N. (1992). Estimation for diffusion processes from discrete observation. *J. Multivariate Anal.* 41, 220–242.

[107] Yoshida, N. (2011). Polynomial type large deviation inequalities and quasi-likelihood analysis for stochastic differential equations. *Ann. Inst. Statist. Math.* 63, 431–479.

[108] Yoshida, N. (2017). Partial quasi likelihood analysis. *arXiv preprint arXiv:1801.00279.*

[109] Zhang, L. (2006). Efficient estimation of stochastic volatility using noisy observations: A multi-scale approach. *Bernoulli* 12, 1019–1043.

[110] Zhang, L. (2011). Estimating covariation: Epps effect, microstructure noise. *J. Econometrics* 160, 33–47.

[111] Zhang, L., Mykland, P. A. and Ait-Sahalia, Y. (2005). A tale of two time scales: determining integrated volatility with noisy high-frequency data. *J. Amer. Statist. Assoc.* 100, 1394–1411.

[112] Zhou, B. (1996). High-frequency data and volatility in foreign-exchange rates. *J. Bus. Econom. Statist.* 14, 45–52.

13 The log-GARCH model via ARMA representations

Genaro Sucarrat

1. Introduction

The starting point of Engle's (1982) Autoregressive Conditional Heteroskedasticity (ARCH) class of models is

$$y_t = \mu_t + \epsilon_t, \qquad \epsilon_t = \sigma_t \eta_t, \qquad \sigma_t > 0, \qquad \eta_t \sim iid(0,1),$$

where y_t denotes the variable of interest (e.g., financial return), μ_t is the mean specification (e.g., an AR-X model) or simply zero, ϵ_t is the error term or mean-corrected variable of interest, σ_t is the conditional standard deviation or volatility, and η_t is an innovation with mean zero and unit variance. Arguably, the most common specification of σ_t is the first-order Generalized ARCH (GARCH) model of Bollerslev (1986):

$$\sigma_t^2 = \omega + \alpha_1 \epsilon_{t-1}^2 + \beta_1 \sigma_{t-1}^2, \qquad \omega > 0, \quad \alpha_1, \beta_1 \geq 0. \tag{1}$$

Usually, this model is referred to as the GARCH(1,1) model. The log-ARCH class of models was, independently, first proposed by Geweke (1986), Pantula (1986) and Milhøj (1987). However, the idea of modeling the log-variance goes at least back to Park (1966). The logarithmic counterpart of the GARCH (1,1) is the log-GARCH(1,1) model, which is given by

$$\ln \sigma_t^2 = \omega + \alpha_1 \ln \epsilon_{t-1}^2 + \beta_1 \ln \sigma_{t-1}^2, \qquad \omega, \alpha_1, \beta_1 \in \mathbb{R}. \tag{2}$$

Just as in the GARCH model, the ω is the volatility intercept, α_1 is the ARCH-parameter and β_1 is the GARCH-parameter: ω controls the level of volatility (but in a multiplicative way), α_1 controls the impact of shocks or news η_{t-1}^2, whereas $\alpha_1 + \beta_1$ controls the degree to which volatility σ_t^2 is persistent. If ϵ_t is a (mean-corrected) daily financial return, then typical estimates of α_1 and β_1 lie around 0.05 and 0.9, respectively, both in the GARCH(1,1) and log-GARCH(1,1) cases. See Section 2.5 for an illustration of the latter. Let $\ln^+ x = \max\{x, 0\}$. If $Pr(\eta_t = 0) = 0$, $E|\ln \eta_t^2| < \infty$ and $E(\ln^+ |\ln \eta_t^2|) < \infty$, then a sufficient condition for strict stationarity and ergodicity of (2) is

$$|\alpha_1 + \beta_1| < 1, \tag{3}$$

see Francq et al. (2013, Theorem 2.1 on p. 36).

From a user-perspective, the log-GARCH model has many attractive features:

- *Fitted volatility is guaranteed to be positive due to the exponential specification.* This is particularly important in higher order specifications, which may be needed in daily data with weekly periodicity (e.g., electricity prices), and in quarterly and monthly data. For example, when Engle (1982) proposed his ARCH model, he had to substantially restrict his ARCH(4) specification of quarterly UK inflation uncertainty to ensure positivity of his conditional variance estimates: The specification was assumed to follow $\sigma_t^2 = \omega + \alpha_1(0.4\epsilon_{t-1}^2 + 0.3\epsilon_{t-2}^2 + 0.2\epsilon_{t-3}^2 + 0.1\epsilon_{t-4}^2)$ so that only ω and α_1 were estimated, see Engle (1982, p. 1002).

- *No non-negativity constraints on parameters.* In the GARCH model, parameters must satisfy non-negativity constraints. In the GARCH(1,1), for example, the constraints are $\omega > 0$ and $\alpha_1, \beta_1 \geq 0$. The first means σ_t^2 is bounded from below and hence cannot be smaller than ω. The second, i.e., α_1, $\beta_1 \geq 0$, implies that autocorrelations of ϵ_t^2 are non-negative. The log-GARCH, by contrast, does not impose non-negativity constraints on the parameters. This means its volatility is bounded from below by 0 (and not ω as in the GARCH), and that it admits negative autocorrelations on ϵ_t^2. This latter is useful in regular data (e.g., daily data with a weekly 5-day or 7-day cycle, and monthly and quarterly data), since there it is likely that one or more autocorrelations of ϵ_t^2 are negative, see, e.g., Pretis et al. (2018, Section 5.4).

- *Standard inference valid under nullity of parameters.* Often it is of interest to formulate a test in which one or more parameters are 0 under the null, say, $H_0: \beta_1 = 0$. A test with this null can be carried out in a standard way (e.g., with a t-test) in the log-GARCH model, since the value of β_1 lies in the interior of the admissible parameter space under the null. In the GARCH model, by contrast, $\beta_1 = 0$ lies on the boundary of the admissible parameter space because of the non-negativity constraints. This means standard inference procedures are not valid. The practical implication of this is that it is usually easier to carry out hypothesis tests in the log-GARCH model when parameters are 0 under the null. Indeed, such tests can readily be carried out in standard software via the estimated ARMA representations.

- *No non-negativity constraints on covariates.* Often it is of interest to include covariates in the σ_t^2 specification. For example, does a large return yesterday in a different market (say, x_{t-1}^2) increase volatility σ_t^2 today? Numerous studies have been undertaken with covariates of this or a similar kind. For brevity, the inclusion of covariates is sometimes indicated by "X". In the log-GARCH-X model the covariates are not restricted to be non-negative. In the GARCH-X model, by contrast, the covariates must be non-negative to ensure that σ_t^2 is positive, see, e.g., Francq and Thieu (2018). This limits the type of questions that can be answered within a GARCH-X model, and compounds the problem described above of inference under nullity of parameters. These restrictions and challenges do not characterize the log-GARCH.

- *Invariance to power-transformations.* Consider the δth. power log-GARCH (1,1) specification

$$\ln \sigma_t^\delta = \omega_\delta + \alpha_1 \ln |\epsilon_{t-1}|^\delta + \beta_1 \ln \sigma_{t-1}^\delta, \qquad \delta > 0. \tag{4}$$

This specification is of interest if the objective is to forecast, say, the conditional standard deviation σ_t (or any σ_t^δ with $\delta > 0$) rather than σ_t^2. In contrast to the power GARCH counterpart, (4) can be re-written in terms of its second power as

$$\ln \sigma_t^2 = \omega + \alpha_1 \ln \epsilon_{t-1}^2 + \beta_1 \ln \sigma_{t-1}^2 \text{ with } \omega = \frac{\omega_\delta}{\delta}. \tag{5}$$

In other words, an estimate of (4) for any power $\delta > 0$ is straightforwardly obtained via the estimate of (5). The power GARCH model, by contrast, is not characterized by this invariance to power transformations.

- *Robustness to outliers.* It is well-known that the GARCH model is fragile when outliers or large jumps in ϵ_t are present, see, e.g., Carnero et al. (2007) and the references therein. Similarly, the unconditional variance in Nelson's (1991) EGARCH may not exist if η_t is too fat-tailed, e.g., student's t, see Nelson's own discussion in the Appendix (same place). In the log-GARCH, by contrast, the effect of η_t^2 is dampened due to the log-transformation. This means the log-GARCH is much more robust to outliers or jumps and fat-tailedness of η_t. This can be illustrated by revisiting the daily Apple log-return series used by Harvey and Sucarrat (2014, pp. 320-321) to illustrate a similar robustness for the Beta-t-EGARCH model. On Thursday 28 September 2000 the firm Apple issued a profit warning after closing hours, which led its stock-value to fall from USD 26.75 to USD 12.88. Volatility, however, was not affected on the subsequent days. Figure 13.1 contains a snapshot of the event and the surrounding days. The figure plots absolute returns, the fitted conditional standard deviations of a GARCH(1,1) specification, and the fitted conditional standard deviations of a log-GARCH(1,1). The GARCH forecasts (one-step-ahead) of standard deviations exceed absolute returns for almost two months after the event, a clear-cut example of forecast failure. The forecasts of the log-GARCH, by contrast, remain in the same range of variation as the absolute returns due to the log-transformation.[1] This provides an empirical example of the GARCH model being prone to forecast failure in the presence of large outliers or jumps.

- *Generality of specification.* Two common alternatives to the log-GARCH are the Stochastic Volatility (SV) class of models, and the EGARCH of Nelson

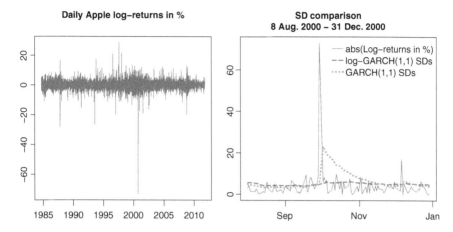

Figure 13.1 Daily Apple log-return in % (left graph) and a snapshot (right graph) of the period before and after a profit warning 28 September 2000, see section 1.

Source: Yahoo Finance.

(1991). In a sense, the log-GARCH is more general than these model-classes, since both admit a log-GARCH representation (but not necessarily vice-versa), see Asai (1998), and Francq et al. (2017).

• *Log-GARCH models admit ARMA representations.* This was already noted by Pantula (1986), and has been exploited in numerous subsequent works, see, e.g., Psaradakis and Tzavalis (1999). The usefulness of this is that a vast number of results, methods and techniques from the time-series literature is available. In particular, widely available software provide routines for the estimation of ARMA and/or VARMA models can be applied, which means univariate and multivariate log-GARCH models can readily be estimated in practice via their (V)ARMA representation(s).

The focus of this chapter is the last of these features. In the next part, Section 2, we provide an overview of univariate models. We start by outlining an asymmetric specification, before we turn to its ARMA representation. Next we add stochastic conditioning covariates ("X"), and then sketch how estimates of the coefficient-covariances can be obtained in numerical software. We complete the Section by empirical illustrations of the log-GARCH(1,1) model. Section 3 provides an overview of multivariate models. Again, we start by outlining the asymmetric specification and its corresponding VARMA and VARMA-X representations. Next, we turn to specifications that are amenable to equation-by-equation estimation, both stationary and non-stationary versions, even in the presence of Dynamic Conditional Correlations (DCCs) of unknown form. The focus on multivariate specifications that can be estimated equation by equation is motivated by the fact that estimation becomes infeasible in practice as the dimension grows too large. We end the section with a short note on how models of Dynamic Conditional Correlations (DCCs) can be estimated subsequently. Section 4 provides some suggestions on how to handle zeros in practice, whereas Section 5 outlines how log-GARCH models can be used to model positively valued variables. Finally, Section 6 concludes and provides suggestions for further research.

2. Univariate log-GARCH models

2.1. The asymmetric log-GARCH

Financial returns are often more volatile after a fall in price compared to a rise. This is usually referred to as asymmetry or leverage. To accommodate this commonly found feature, Francq et al. (2013) proposed the asymmetric log-GARCH. If $Pr(\eta_t = 0) = 0$ for all t, then their asymmetric log-GARCH can be re-parametrized as

$$\ln \sigma_t^2 = \omega + \sum_{i=1}^{p} \alpha_i \ln \epsilon_{t-i}^2 + \sum_{j=1}^{q} \beta_j \ln \sigma_{t-j}^2 + \sum_{k=1}^{r} \gamma_k 1_{\{\epsilon_{t-k}<0\}} \ln \epsilon_{t-k}^2, \tag{6}$$

where

$$1_{\{\epsilon_t<0\}} \ln \epsilon_t^2 = \begin{cases} \ln \epsilon_t^2 & \text{if } \epsilon_t < 0 \\ 0 & \text{if } \epsilon_t > 0 \end{cases}$$

is the asymmetry or leverage term. The advantages of the re-parametrization in (6) are that it is more straightforward to test for the presence of asymmetry in practice, and that it closely resembles the most common asymmetric non-exponential GARCH-counterpart of Glosten et al. (1993). In the log-GARCH(1,1), for example, asymmetry can be tested by means of a simple t-test. The re-parametrization implies, however, that the sufficient conditions for strict stationarity and ergodicity (i.e., Theorem 2.1 in Francq et al. (2013, p. 36)) also needs to be re-parametrized. For example, in the first order case (i.e., $p = q = r = 1$), the sufficient condition becomes

$$|\alpha_1 + \beta_1|^{Pr(\eta_t>0)} \cdot |\alpha_1 + \beta_1 + \gamma_1|^{1-Pr(\eta_t>0)} < 1.$$

In the absence of asymmetry we obtain the usual condition in (3), i.e., $|\alpha_1 + \beta_1| < 1$.

2.2. The ARMA representation

If $Pr(\eta_t = 0) = 0$ and $E|\ln \eta_t^2| < \infty$, then (6) admits, almost surely, a (nonlinear in variables) ARMA(p, q) representation. It is obtained in two steps. First, $\ln \eta_t^2$ is added to each side of (6). Second, $\sum_{j=1}^{q} \beta_j(\ln \eta_t^2 - E(\ln \eta_t^2)) - \sum_{j=1}^{q} \beta_j(\ln \eta_t^2 - E(\ln \eta_t^2))$ is added to the right-hand side. Re-organizing gives the nonlinear

ARMA representation

$$\ln \epsilon_t^2 = \omega^* + \sum_{i=1}^{p} \phi_i \ln \epsilon_{t-i}^2 + \sum_{j=1}^{q} \theta_j u_{t-j}^2 + \sum_{k=1}^{r} \gamma_k 1_{\{\epsilon_{t-k}<0\}} \ln \epsilon_{t-k}^2 + u_t, \tag{7}$$

$$u_t \sim iid(0, \sigma_u^2),$$

where

$$\omega^* = \omega + (1 - \sum_{j=1}^{q} \beta_j) \cdot E(\ln \eta_t^2), \quad \phi_i = \alpha_i + \beta_i, \quad \theta_j = -\beta_j, \tag{8}$$

$$u_t = \ln \eta_t^2 - E(\ln \eta_t^2).$$

If, in addition, $E[(\ln \eta_t^2)^2] < \infty$, then $\sigma_u^2 < \infty$ with $\sigma_u^2 = E[(\ln \eta_t^2)^2] - E(\ln \eta_t^2)^2$. Note that the specification is a nonlinear (in variables) ARMA due to the asymmetry terms. The stationarity conditions of Francq et al. (2013) still apply, since $\ln \epsilon_t^2$ is simply a sum of the stationary variables $\ln \sigma_t^2$ and $\ln \eta_t^2$. The model is therefore amenable to estimation by well-known ARMA-methods and widely available software. All the ARCH and GARCH parameters are identified via the relations in (8), and inference – even under the null of zero parameters – is readily carried out via a suitable transformation of the estimated coefficient covariance matrix, see Section 2.4. However, to identify the volatility intercept ω an estimate of $E(\ln \eta_t^2)$ is needed, and $E(\ln \eta_t^2)$ depends on the distribution of η_t^2. Sucarrat et al. (2016) show that, under mild and general assumptions,

$$-\ln \left[\frac{1}{T} \sum_{t=1}^{T} \exp (\hat{u}_t) \right] \xrightarrow{p} E(\ln \eta_t^2), \tag{9}$$

where T is the sample size and $\hat{u}_t$ is the residual from the estimated ARMA representation. Note that the expression inside the square brackets of (9) is the smearing estimator of Duan (1983). The motivation behind this estimator is that, if $E(\eta_t^2) = 1$ and $E(\ln \eta_t^2) < \infty$, then the population counterpart is equal to $E(\ln \eta_t^2)$:

$$-\ln E(e^{u_t}) = -\ln E \left[e^{\ln \eta_t^2 - E(\ln \eta_t^2)} \right] = -\ln \left[\frac{1}{e^{E(\ln \eta_t^2)}} \cdot E(\eta_t^2) \right] = E(\ln \eta_t^2).$$

Subject to suitable assumptions, therefore, consistent estimation of the ARMA representation (7) and the log-moment $E(\ln \eta_t^2)$, leads to consistent estimation of all the log-GARCH parameters in (6).

Another notable property of the estimator in (9) is that it ensures the sample variance of the standardized residuals $\{\hat{\eta}_t\} = \{\epsilon_t/\hat{\sigma}_t\}$, where $\hat{\sigma}_t^2$ is the fitted value of σ_t^2, is approximately equal to 1 in empirical applications. This is required for

$\hat{\sigma}_t^2$ to be a valid estimate of the conditional variance σ_t^2. To see that the estimator in (9) ensures that the sample variance of $\{\hat{\eta}_t\}$ is approximately equal to 1, let $\hat{\eta}_t^* = \epsilon_t/\hat{\sigma}_t^*$ denote the residual scaled by the square root of the fitted value of the exponentiated ARMA-representation: $\hat{\sigma}_t^{*2} = \exp(\widehat{\ln \epsilon_t^2})$, where $\widehat{\ln \epsilon_t^2}$ is the fitted value of the ARMA-representation. Noting that we also have $\hat{\eta}_t^* = \exp(\hat{u}_t/2)$, it follows that

$$\frac{\hat{\eta}_t^*}{\sqrt{T^{-1}\sum_{t=1}^{T}\exp(\hat{u}_t)}} = \frac{\hat{\eta}_t^*}{\exp(\ln T^{-1}\sum_{t=1}^{T}\exp(\hat{u}_t)/2)}$$

$$= \frac{\epsilon_t}{\exp(\widehat{\ln \epsilon_t^2}/2 - \hat{E}(\ln \eta_t^2)/2)} = \hat{\eta}_t,$$

where $\hat{E}(\ln \eta_t^2)$ is the estimator in (9). In other words, the smearing estimate $T^{-1}\sum_{t=1}^{T}\exp(\hat{u}_t)$ is approximately equal to the sample variance of $\{\hat{\eta}_t^*\}$, thus ensuring the sample variance of $\{\hat{\eta}_t\}$ is always approximately equal to 1 in empirical applications.

2.3. Adding stationary covariates ("X")

Let $x_t = (x_{1t}, ..., x_{st})'$ denote a vector of strictly stationary and ergodic covariates. The (asymmetric) log-GARCH-X model is given by

$$\ln \sigma_t^2 = \omega + \sum_{i=1}^{p}\alpha_i \ln \epsilon_{t-i}^2 + \sum_{j=1}^{q}\beta_j \ln \sigma_{t-j}^2 + \sum_{k=1}^{r}\gamma_k 1_{\{\epsilon_{t-k}<0\}} \ln \epsilon_{t-k}^2$$
$$+ \sum_{l=1}^{s}\lambda_l x_{l,t-1}. \tag{10}$$

A common example of a covariate is realized volatility, i.e., a volatility proxy, but another example is *extended* asymmetry. In other words, the extended asymmetric log-GARCH model of Francq et al. (2017) is nested in (10). The (nonlinear) ARMA-X representation is obtained in the same way as earlier (see above), and it is given by

$$\ln \epsilon_t^2 = \omega^* + \sum_{i=1}^{p}\phi_i \ln \epsilon_{t-i}^2 + \sum_{j=1}^{q}\theta_j u_{t-j}^2 + \sum_{k=1}^{r}\gamma_k 1_{\{\epsilon_{t-k}<0\}} \ln \epsilon_{t-k}^2$$
$$+ \sum_{l=1}^{s}\lambda_l x_{l,t-1} + u_t, \tag{11}$$

where the relations between the log-GARCH and ARMA parameters are exactly as before, i.e., they are given by (8). Also, as noted earlier, no non-negativity constraints on the parameters $(\lambda_1, ..., \lambda_s)'$ nor on the covariates x_t are needed. Accordingly, standard inference methods are available under the null of 0s on one or more of the $\lambda_1, \ldots, \lambda_s$, i.e., that one or more covariate has no impact on volatility. To estimate $E(\ln \eta_t^2)$, the same formula as earlier, i.e., (9), can be used. Estimation of (10), therefore, can straightforwardly be undertaken in widely available software.

2.4. Estimation of the coefficient covariance matrix

For inference on the parameters an estimate of the coefficient covariance matrix is needed, and this expression depends on the estimator. The two most common estimators of ARMA-models are Least Squares (LS) and Gaussian Maximum Likelihood (ML). Both provide consistent and asymptotically normal estimates under mild assumptions – even when the error u_t is non-Gaussian, and most of the asymptotic properties of the two estimators are identical, see, e.g., Brockwell and Davis (2006). The LS and Gaussian ML estimators are asymptotically efficient when η_t is sufficiently fat-tailed or skewed (or both). If, however, η_t is Gaussian or nearly Gaussian, then improved efficiency can be achieved with the exponential Chi-squared (Quasi) ML estimator proposed by Francq and Sucarrat (2018). Here, we outline the details of the LS estimator, but the approach is similar for both the Gaussian and Chi-squared ML estimators.

Let $\varphi = (\omega^*, \phi_1, \ldots, \phi_p, \theta_1, \ldots, \theta_q, \gamma_1, \ldots, \gamma_r, \lambda_1, \ldots, \lambda_s)'$ denote the parameter of the ARMA representation given by (11), and let

$$\hat{\varphi} = \arg \min_{\varphi} \frac{1}{T} \sum_{t=1}^{T} u_t^2 \tag{12}$$

denote its Least Squares (LS) estimate. Often, numerical software provide utility functions for the computation of the Hessian at the optimum. Francq and Sucarrat (2017, pp. 27-28) show that this can be used to build an estimate of the coefficient covariance matrix. Specifically, they show that an estimate of the asymptotic coefficient matrix is obtained as

$$\left(\frac{1}{T} \sum_{t=1}^{T} \hat{u}_t^2 \right) \cdot 2 \cdot \hat{S}^{-1},$$

where $\hat{u}_t$ is the residual of the estimated ARMA-representation and $\hat{S}$ is the Hessian at $\hat{\varphi}$ based on (12). If LS estimation is implemented by minimizing the sum instead of the average, i.e.,

$$\hat{\varphi} = \arg \min_{\varphi} \sum_{t=1}^{T} u_t^2, \tag{13}$$

then the estimate of the asymptotic coefficient matrix is modified to

$$\left(\frac{1}{T}\sum_{t=1}^{T}\hat{u}_t^2\right) \cdot 2T \cdot \hat{S}^{-1},$$

where $\hat{S}$ is now the Hessian at $\hat{\varphi}$ based on (13).

Let $\zeta = (\omega, \alpha_1, ..., \alpha_p, \beta_1, ..., \beta_q, \gamma_1, ..., \gamma_r, \lambda_1, ..., \lambda_s)'$ denote the parameter of the log-GARCH specification (10), and let $\hat{\zeta}$ denote its estimate. An estimate of its asymptotic coefficient matrix is available by using the relationships between the log-GARCH and ARMA-parameters given by (8). For example, if $\widehat{Var}(\hat{x})$ and $\widehat{Cov}(\hat{x}, \hat{y})$ denote the variance of the estimate $\hat{x}$ and the covariance of the estimates $\hat{x}$ and $\hat{y}$, respectively, then the variance of the ARCH-parameter $\hat{\alpha}_i$ is obtained as $\widehat{Var}(\hat{\alpha}_i) = \widehat{Var}(\hat{\phi}_i) + \widehat{Var}(\hat{\theta}_i) + 2\widehat{Cov}(\hat{\phi}_i, \hat{\theta}_i)$. Similarly, the variance of the GARCH-parameter $\hat{\beta}_i$ is obtained as $\widehat{Var}(\hat{\beta}_i) = \widehat{Var}(-\hat{\theta}_i) = \widehat{Var}(\hat{\theta}_i)$. All the variances and covariances are readily available in this way, apart from those associated with the estimate of the log-GARCH intercept $\hat{\omega}$. These computations are more involved and requires the use of the delta-method, see Francq and Sucarrat (2017, pp. 21–22).

2.5. Empirical examples

To provide an empirical illustration of the log-GARCH model, we re-visit six daily financial return series: The FTSE100 and SP100 indices (source: Bloomberg), the Apple stock price (source: Yahoo Finance, https://yahoo.finance.com), the USD/EUR exchange rate (source: The European Central Bank, http://www.ecb.int/), the Brent blend oil price (source: The US Energy Information Agency, http://www.eia.gov/) and the gold price (source: Kitco, http://www.kitco.com/). The first two return series were studied in Francq and Sucarrat (2017, Section 5.1), whereas the latter four return series were studied in Harvey and Sucarrat (2014, Section 6). Note that the Apple series is the same as the one used to illustrate the robustness to outliers of log-GARCH models in the introduction (Section 1).

Let P_t denote the index-value or price of the asset in question in day t. The return $y_t = \epsilon_t$ is computed as the log-return in percent, i.e., $\epsilon_t = (\ln P_t - \ln P_{t-1}) \cdot 100$. The sample periods and descriptive statistics of the returns are contained in the upper part of Table 13.1, whereas Figure 13.2 contains graphs of the return series. As commonly found, the returns exhibit excess kurtosis relative to the normal distribution, and first-order ARCH at 5% and higher significance levels according to a Ljung and Box (1979) test for first-order autocorrelation in ϵ_t^2. Also, the plots in Figure 13.2 confirm that volatility is persistent in the sense that the returns are characterized by volatility clustering.

Arguably, the most common volatility model is the plain GARCH(1,1). The plain log-GARCH(1,1) counterpart is given by

$$\ln \sigma_t^2 = \omega + \alpha_1 \ln \epsilon_{t-1}^2 + \beta_1 \ln \sigma_{t-1}^2,$$

Table 13.1 Empirical examples of log-GARCH models (see Section 2.5)

Descriptive statistics:

	Sample	T	s^2	s^4	ARCH [p-val]
FTSE100	5/1/1998-2/6/2015	4397	1.51	8.59	97.9 [0.00]
SP100	5/1/1998-1/6/2015	4379	1.60	10.10	220.1 [0.00]
Apple	10/9/1984-12/10/2011	6835	9.63	53.85	5.90 [0.02]
USD/EUR	5/1/1999-12/10/2011	3274	0.45	5.45	205.9 [0.00]
Oilprice	21/5/1987-4/10/2011	6190	5.59	17.47	78.6 [0.00]
Gold	4/1/2006-12/10/2011	1448	1.96	6.18	6.76 [0.01]

Plain log-GARCH(1,1) models:

	$\hat{\omega}$	$\hat{\alpha}_1$ (s.e.)	$\hat{\beta}_2$ (s.e.)	$\hat{E}(ln\,\eta_t^2)$
FTSE100	0.067	0.047 (0.006)	0.942 (0.008)	−1.415
SP100	0.072	0.047 (0.006)	0.945 (0.008)	−1.513
Apple	0.055	0.032 (0.005)	0.963 (0.007)	−1.375
USD/EUR	0.025	0.022 (0.005)	0.971 (0.007)	−1.380
Oilprice	0.069	0.037 (0.005)	0.952 (0.007)	−1.401
Gold	0.054	0.032 (0.007)	0.958 (0.010)	−1.522

Asymmetric log-GARCH(1,1) models:

	$\hat{\omega}$	$\hat{\alpha}_1$ (s.e.)	$\hat{\beta}_2$ (s.e.)	$\hat{\gamma}_1$ (s.e.)	$\hat{\lambda}_2$ (s.e.)	$\hat{E}(ln\,\eta_t^2)$
FTSE100	−0.126	0.003 (0.006)	0.945 (0.006)	0.069 (0.010)	0.362 (0.035)	−1.365
SP100	−0.112	0.011 (0.007)	0.934 (0.008)	0.070 (0.012)	0.374 (0.040)	−1.453
Apple	0.046	0.028 (0.007)	0.954 (0.009)	0.016 (0.007)	0.053 (0.019)	−1.361
USD/EUR	0.013	0.024 (0.007)	0.970 (0.007)	−0.003 (0.010)	0.021 (0.027)	−1.374
Oilprice	0.058	0.030 (0.006)	0.952 (0.007)	0.014 (0.008)	0.024 (0.016)	−1.396
Gold	0.063	0.036 (0.009)	0.961 (0.011)	−0.012 (0.014)	−0.025 (0.049)	−1.517

T, number of non-missing returns. s^2, sample variance. s^4, sample kurtosis. ARCH, Ljung and Box (1979) test statistic of first-order serial correlation in the squared return. $p-val$, the p-value of the test-statistic. s.e., approximate standard errors (obtained via the numerically estimated Hessian) of estimate. All computations in R (R Core Team (2018)), estimation with the lgarch function (Sucarrat (2015)).

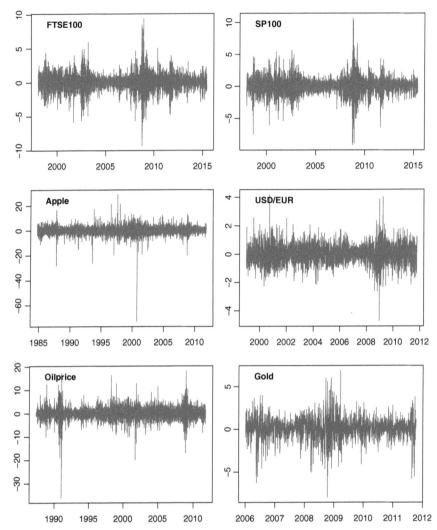

Figure 13.2 Daily financial log-returns in %, see Section 2.5 and Table 13.1

Sources: Bloomberg, Yahoo Finance, European Central Bank, US Energy Information Agency and Kitco

and estimates of this model are contained in the middle part of Table 13.1. Estimation is undertaken via the ARMA(1,1) representation with the lgarch function from the *R* package lgarch, see Sucarrat (2015). Usually, in ordinary GARCH (1,1) models, the estimate of the ARCH parameter α_1 lies around 0.05, and the estimate of the GARCH parameter β_1 lies around 0.95. The results show that this is also the case for the log-GARCH(1,1) models. When estimation is via the ARMA-representation, then an estimate of $E(\ln \eta_t^2)$ is needed in order to estimate ω. If $\eta_t \sim N(0, 1)$, then $E(\ln \eta_t^2) = -1.27$. In other words, the discrepancy from -1.27 can be viewed as a measure of departure from normality. For example, if η_t is a standardized t with 10 degrees of freedom (a "moderate" departure from normality), then $E(\ln \eta_t^2) = -1.39$. The estimates of $E(\ln \eta_t^2)$ range from -1.375 to -1.522, which suggests η_t is non-normal, albeit not dramatically so.

Often daily financial return series exhibit volatility asymmetry, i.e., a negative return tends to increase the volatility on the subsequent day. For stocks, this is typically referred to as a leverage effect, since leverage is often cited as the reason for the effect. For other return series, the more generic label "asymmetry" may be more appropriate, since the effect can be positive instead of negative, and since the reason for asymmetry may not be leverage. For exchange rates, for example, the presence and sign of asymmetry will usually depend on the relative strength of the two currencies in question. In other words, asymmetry is unlikely to be present in the USD/EUR exchange rate, since both the USD and euro currencies are considered as strong currencies in international money markets. To explore the presence of volatility asymmetry in the six return series we fit a log-GARCH(1,1) model with extended asymmetry, i.e.,

$$\ln \sigma_t^2 = \omega + \alpha_1 \ln \epsilon_{t-1}^2 + \beta_1 \ln \sigma_{t-1}^2 + \gamma_1 1_{\{\epsilon_{t-1} < 0\}} \ln \epsilon_{t-1}^2 + \lambda_1 1_{\{\epsilon_{t-1} < 0\}}.$$

The $1_{\{\epsilon_{t-1}<0\}} \ln \epsilon_{t-1}^2$ is the ordinary asymmetry term, and $1_{\{\epsilon_{t-1} < 0\}}$ is the extended asymmetry term. As noted by Francq et al. (2017), to ensure invariance to scale-transformations the extended asymmetry term is needed when the ordinary asymmetry term is present. If we use ± 2 as critical values in a two-sided t-test with zero as null, then both the ordinary and extended asymmetry terms are significant for the stock returns (i.e., FTSE100, SP100, and Apple). For the remaining returns, however, neither the ordinary nor the extended term is significant. In other words, the results suggest the stock returns tend to be more volatile on days subsequent to a negative return, but not the exchange rate, oil price, or the gold return.

3. Multivariate log-GARCH models

Let $\boldsymbol{y}_t = (y_{1t}, \ldots, y_{Mt})'$ denote an M-dimensional vector of variables (e.g., financial returns) at t. A generic model of $\boldsymbol{y}_t$ can be written as (see, e.g., Engle (2002))

$$\boldsymbol{y}_t = \boldsymbol{\mu}_t + \boldsymbol{\epsilon}_t,$$

$$\boldsymbol{\epsilon}_t = (\epsilon_{1t}, \cdots, \epsilon_{Mt})', \qquad \boldsymbol{H}_t = E_{t-1}(\boldsymbol{\epsilon}_t \boldsymbol{\epsilon}_t'), \qquad \boldsymbol{D}_t^2 = \mathrm{diag}(\boldsymbol{H}_t),$$

$$\boldsymbol{\eta}_t = \boldsymbol{D}_t^{-1} \boldsymbol{\epsilon}_t, \qquad \boldsymbol{R}_t = E_{t-1}(\boldsymbol{\eta}_t \boldsymbol{\eta}_t'),$$

where $\boldsymbol{\mu}_t = (\mu_{1t}, \ldots, \mu_{Mt})'$ is the conditional mean specification of, say, a VARMA-X model, $\boldsymbol{\epsilon}_t = (\epsilon_{1t}, \ldots, \epsilon_{Mt})'$ is the error term, $\boldsymbol{H}_t$ is an $M \times M$ covariance matrix conditional on the past information $\mathcal{F}_{t-1}$, $E_{t-1}(\cdot)$ is shorthand notation for $E(\cdot|\mathcal{F}_{t-1})$, $\boldsymbol{D}_t^2$ is a diagonal $M \times M$ matrix with the conditional variance or volatility $\boldsymbol{\sigma}_t^2 = (\sigma_{1t}^2, \ldots, \sigma_{Mt}^2)'$ on the diagonal, $\boldsymbol{\eta}_t = (\eta_{1t}, \ldots, \eta_{Mt})'$ is the standardized error, i.e., $E(\boldsymbol{\eta}_t) = \boldsymbol{0}$ and $Var(\boldsymbol{\eta}_t) = \boldsymbol{1}$ where $\boldsymbol{0}$ and $\boldsymbol{1}$ are $M \times 1$ vectors, $\boldsymbol{D}_t^{-1}$ is a diagonal $M \times M$ matrix with $(1/\sigma_{1t}, \ldots, 1/\sigma_{Mt})'$ on the diagonal and $\boldsymbol{R}_t$ is the correlation matrix conditional on the past. The relationships between $\boldsymbol{H}_t$ and $\boldsymbol{R}_t$ are given by $\boldsymbol{H}_t = \boldsymbol{D}_t\boldsymbol{R}_t\boldsymbol{D}_t$ and $\boldsymbol{R}_t = \boldsymbol{D}_t^{-1}\boldsymbol{H}_t\boldsymbol{D}_t^{-1}$.

3.1. A multivariate asymmetric log-GARCH-X model

The multivariate asymmetric log-GARCH-X model is given by

$$\ln \boldsymbol{\sigma}_t^2 = \boldsymbol{\omega} + \sum_{i=1}^{p} \boldsymbol{\alpha}_i \ln \boldsymbol{\epsilon}_{t-i}^2 + \sum_{j=1}^{q} \boldsymbol{\beta}_j \ln \boldsymbol{\sigma}_{t-j}^2 + \sum_{k=1}^{r} \boldsymbol{\gamma}_k \boldsymbol{1}_{\{\epsilon_{t-k}<0\}} \ln \boldsymbol{\epsilon}_{t-k}^2 + \boldsymbol{\lambda}\boldsymbol{x}_{t-1}, \qquad (14)$$

where $\ln \boldsymbol{\sigma}_t^2 = (\ln \sigma_{1t}^2, \ldots, \ln \sigma_{Mt}^2)'$, $\boldsymbol{\omega} = (\omega_1, \ldots, \omega_M)'$, $\ln \boldsymbol{\epsilon}_{t-i}^2 = (\ln \epsilon_{1,t-i}^2, \ldots, \ln \epsilon_{M,t-i}^2)'$, $\boldsymbol{1}_{\{\epsilon_{t-k}<0\}} \ln \boldsymbol{\epsilon}_{t-k}^2 = (\boldsymbol{1}_{\{\epsilon_{1,t-k}<0\}} \ln \epsilon_{1,t-k}^2, \ldots, \boldsymbol{1}_{\{\epsilon_{M,t-k}<0\}} \ln \epsilon_{M,t-k}^2)'$ and $\boldsymbol{x}_{t-1} = (x_{1,\,t-1}, \ldots, x_{M,\,t-1})'$ are all $M \times 1$ vectors, and where

$$\boldsymbol{\alpha}_i = \begin{pmatrix} \alpha_{11.i} & \cdots & \alpha_{1M.i} \\ \vdots & \ddots & \vdots \\ \alpha_{M1.i} & \cdots & \alpha_{MM.i} \end{pmatrix}, \quad \boldsymbol{\beta}_j = \begin{pmatrix} \beta_{11.j} & \cdots & \beta_{1M.j} \\ \vdots & \ddots & \vdots \\ \beta_{M1.j} & \cdots & \beta_{MM.j} \end{pmatrix}, \qquad (15)$$

$$\boldsymbol{\gamma}_k = \begin{pmatrix} \gamma_{11.k} & \cdots & \gamma_{1M.k} \\ \vdots & \ddots & \vdots \\ \gamma_{M1.k} & \cdots & \gamma_{MM.k} \end{pmatrix}, \quad \boldsymbol{\lambda}_l = \begin{pmatrix} \lambda_{11.l} & \cdots & \lambda_{1M.l} \\ \vdots & \ddots & \vdots \\ \lambda_{M1.l} & \cdots & \lambda_{MM.l} \end{pmatrix} \qquad (16)$$

are all $M \times M$ matrices. The (nonlinear) VARMA-X representation is obtained in the same way as in the univariate case, and it is given by

$$\ln \boldsymbol{\epsilon}_t^2 = \boldsymbol{\omega}^* + \sum_{i=1}^{p} \boldsymbol{\phi}_i \ln \boldsymbol{\epsilon}_{t-i}^2 + \sum_{j=1}^{q} \boldsymbol{\theta}_j \boldsymbol{u}_{t-j}^2 + \sum_{k=1}^{r} \boldsymbol{\gamma}_k \boldsymbol{1}_{\{\epsilon_{t-k}<0\}} \ln \boldsymbol{\epsilon}_{t-k}^2 + \boldsymbol{\lambda}\boldsymbol{x}_{t-1} + \boldsymbol{u}_t, \qquad (17)$$

where

$$\boldsymbol{\omega}^* = \boldsymbol{\omega} + \left(\boldsymbol{I} - \sum_{j=1}^{q} \boldsymbol{\beta}_j\right) E(\ln \boldsymbol{\eta}_t^2), \quad \boldsymbol{\phi}_i = \boldsymbol{\alpha}_i + \boldsymbol{\beta}_i, \qquad (18)$$

$$\boldsymbol{\theta}_j = -\boldsymbol{\beta}_j, \quad \boldsymbol{u}_t = \ln \boldsymbol{\eta}_t^2 - E(\ln \boldsymbol{\eta}_t^2).$$

Without asymmetry (i.e., $\gamma_1 = \cdots = \gamma_r = 0$), (17) is simply a VARMA-X model. Accordingly, the model is stable if all eigenvalues of $\sum_{i=1}^{p}(\boldsymbol{\alpha}_i + \boldsymbol{\beta}_i)$ are strictly less than 1 in modulus, and it is invertible if all the eigenvalues of $\sum_{j=1}^{q}\boldsymbol{\beta}_j$ are strictly less than 1 in modulus. To conduct inference on the log-GARCH parameters, an approach similar to the one outlined in Section 2.4 can be used.

If $\boldsymbol{\eta}_t$ is *iid*, then the conditional correlation matrix $\boldsymbol{R}_t$ is constant, so that (14) is a Constant Conditional Correlation (CCC) model. Under suitable stationarity and regularity conditions, the (nonlinear) VARMA-X representation (17) can then be estimated by common methods, e.g., multivariate Gaussian Quasi ML (QML). If $\boldsymbol{R}_t$ is time-varying (and stationary), then a reasonable conjecture is that estimates will still be consistent subject to suitable assumptions. However, the asymptotic properties of such an estimator are currently unknown.

3.2. Equation-by-equation estimation

Multivariate volatility models are plagued by the "curse of dimensionality": As the dimension grows, estimation becomes infeasible due to the large amount of parameters that are estimated. One solution, if available, is equation-by-equation estimation. For this to be possible the GARCH-matrices (i.e., $\beta_1, \ldots, \beta_q$) must be diagonal, and

$$\text{each } \eta_{mt}, \; m = 1, \ldots, M, \text{ must be independent of the past} \atop \text{information } \mathcal{F}_{t-1}, \tag{19}$$

see Francq and Zakoïan (2016). Francq and Sucarrat (2017) propose a first order version (i.e., $p = q = 1$) of the multivariate log-GARCH-X that satisfies these properties, and which allows for certain types of Dynamic Conditional Correlations (DCCs) of unknown form. A generalization of their model allows for higher orders and asymmetry, and the mth equation in such a generalized model is given by

$$\ln \sigma_{mt}^2 = \omega_m + \sum_{i=1}^{p} \boldsymbol{\alpha}_{m.i} \ln \boldsymbol{\epsilon}_{t-i}^2 + \sum_{j=1}^{q} \beta_{mm.j} \ln \sigma_{m,t-j}^2$$
$$+ \sum_{k=1}^{r} \gamma_{m.k} \mathbf{1}_{\{\epsilon_{t-k}<0\}} \ln \boldsymbol{\epsilon}_{t-k}^2 + \lambda_m \boldsymbol{x}_{t-1}, \tag{20}$$

where $\boldsymbol{\alpha}_{m.i}$, $\gamma_{m.k}$ and λ_m are $1 \times M$ vectors made up of the mth row in the matrices α_i, γ_k and λ, respectively. The $\beta_{mm.j}$ is the mth element of the mth column in the diagonal matrix β_j.

The univariate ARMA-X representation of the mth equation is

$$\ln \epsilon_{mt}^2 = \omega_m^* + \sum_{i=1}^{p} \boldsymbol{\phi}_{m.i} \ln \boldsymbol{\epsilon}_{t-i}^2 + \sum_{j=1}^{q} \theta_{mm.j} u_{m,t-j}$$
$$+ \sum_{k=1}^{r} \gamma_{m.k} \mathbf{1}_{\{\epsilon_{t-k}<0\}} \ln \boldsymbol{\epsilon}_{t-k}^2 + \lambda_m \boldsymbol{x}_{t-1} + u_{mt}, \tag{21}$$

where

$$
\left.\begin{array}{l}
\omega_m^* = \omega_m + \left(1 - \sum_{j=1}^{q} \beta_{mm.j}\right) E(\ln \eta_{mt}^2), \qquad \phi_{m.i} = \alpha_{m.i} + \beta_{m.i}, \\
\theta_{mm.j} = -\beta_{mm.j} \quad \text{and} \quad u_{mt} = \ln \eta_{mt}^2 - E(\ln \eta_{mt}^2).
\end{array}\right\} \tag{22}
$$

Under stationarity and suitable regularity conditions, (21) can be estimated consistently with standard software. Subsequently, the log-GARCH parameters can be identified via the relations in (22). To identify ω_m, the formula in (9) can be applied to the residuals of equation m to estimate $E(\ln \eta_{mt}^2)$. For inference on the log-GARCH parameters in equation m, an approach similar to the one outlined in Section 2.4 can be used. For inference that involves parameters from more than one equation, then the joint coefficient covariance is needed, see Francq and Sucarrat (2017).

For equation-by-equation estimation to be available the GARCH-matrices $\beta_1, \ldots, \beta_q$ must all be diagonal. To test whether this is indeed the case, a Lagrange-Multiplier (LM) test of equation m can be devised: Under the null all the elements of $\{\beta_{mi.j}: i \neq m, j = 1, \ldots, q\}$ are equal to zero, whereas under the alternative one or more elements are non-zero. Formally, this has not been pursued yet in the theoretical log-GARCH literature.

3.3. Non-stationary models

A common approach to non-stationary volatility is to decompose σ_t^2 multiplicatively, see (among others) Val Bellegem and Von Sachs (2004), Engle and Rangel (2008), Mazur and Pipien (2012), and Amado and Terasvirta (2014a, 2014b). This means

$$
\sigma_t^2 = g_t \odot h_t = (g_{1t} h_{1t}, \ldots, g_{Mt} h_{Mt})',
$$

where g_t is the non-stationary component, h_t is the stationary component (e.g., a GARCH-like process), and $\odot$ is the elementwise (Hadamard) matrix product.[2] Escribano and Sucarrat (2018) propose a non-stationary multivariate log-GARCH-X specification that can be estimated equation by equation. Their motivation was the presence of non-stochastic periodicity in the intraday electricity price market. However, their idea applies more generally. The non-stationary component in their model is given by

$$
\ln g_t = \left(\ln g_1(\lambda_1^f, x_{1t}^f), \ldots, \ln g_M(\lambda_M^f, x_{Mt}^f)\right)',
$$

where $\ln g_1, \ldots, \ln g_M$ are known functions (linear or nonlinear), $x_{1t}^f, \ldots, x_{Mt}^f$ are known, non-stochastic or fixed (hence the superscript f) regressors, and $\lambda_1^f, \ldots, \lambda_M^f$ are unknown parameters to be estimated. Neither the x_{mt}^f's nor the $\ln g_m$'s are restricted to be equal across equations, and the $\ln g_m$'s can assume a variety of shapes. In the simplest case the ln g_m's are linear functions made up of time dummies (e.g., calendar effects), but it can also take the shape of an exponential spline as in Engle and Rangel (2008), and Hafner and Linton (2010), the Fourier Flexible Form (FFF) as in Mazur and Pipien (2012), or smooth threshold models as in Amado and Terasvirta (2014a, 2014b). The functions may also be estimated non-parametrically, as in Van Bellegem and Von Sachs (2004).

If we for notational simplicity exclude asymmetry and covariates, then the stationary component is given by

$$\ln \boldsymbol{h}_t = \boldsymbol{\omega} + \sum_{i=1}^{p} \boldsymbol{\alpha}_i \ln \tilde{\boldsymbol{\epsilon}}_{t-i}^2 + \sum_{j=1}^{q} \boldsymbol{\beta}_j \ln \boldsymbol{h}_{t-j}, \qquad (23)$$

where $\ln \boldsymbol{h}_t = \ln \boldsymbol{\sigma}_t^2 - \ln \boldsymbol{g}_t = (\ln h_{1,t}, \dots, \ln h_{M,t})'$, $\boldsymbol{\omega} = (\omega_1, \dots, \omega_M)'$, $\ln \tilde{\boldsymbol{\epsilon}}_t^2 = (\ln \boldsymbol{\epsilon}_t^2 - \ln \boldsymbol{g}_t) = (\ln h_{1t} \eta_{1t}^2, \dots, \ln h_{Mt} \eta_{Mt}^2)'$, and $\boldsymbol{\alpha}_i$ and $\boldsymbol{\beta}_j$ are both $M \times M$ matrices as in (15). The matrices $\boldsymbol{\beta}_j$ need not be diagonal. However, we will impose this restriction to enable an equation-by-equation estimation scheme. The mth log-volatility equation thus becomes

$$\ln \sigma_{mt}^2 = \ln g_{mt} + \ln h_{mt}, \qquad (24)$$

$$\ln g_{mt} = \ln g_m(\boldsymbol{\lambda}_m^f, \boldsymbol{x}_{mt}^f), \qquad (25)$$

$$\ln h_{mt} = \omega_m + \sum_{i=1}^{p} \boldsymbol{\alpha}_{m.i} \ln \tilde{\boldsymbol{\epsilon}}_{t-i}^2 + \sum_{j=1}^{q} \beta_{mm.j} \ln h_{m,t-j}^2, \qquad (26)$$

where $\boldsymbol{\alpha}_{m.i}$ is the mth row of $\boldsymbol{\alpha}_i$, i.e., $\boldsymbol{\alpha}_{m.i} = (\alpha_{m1.i}, \dots, \alpha_{mM.i})$. Let λ_{m0}^f denote the unconditional mean of $\ln \tilde{\epsilon}_{mt}^2$, i.e., $\lambda_{m0}^f = E(\ln \tilde{\epsilon}_{mt}^2)$ with $E|\ln \tilde{\epsilon}_{mt}^2| < \infty$. If we add $\ln \eta_{mt}^2$ to each side of (24), and then $\lambda_{m0}^f - \lambda_{m0}^f$ to the right-hand side, we obtain

$$\ln \epsilon_{mt}^2 = \lambda_{m0}^f + \ln g_m(\boldsymbol{\lambda}_m^f, \boldsymbol{x}_{mt}^f) + w_{mt}, \qquad w_{mt} = (\ln \tilde{\epsilon}_{mt}^2 - \lambda_{m0}^f).$$

This is simply a regression with a fixed or non-stochastic part, i.e., $\lambda_{m0}^f + \ln g_m(\boldsymbol{\lambda}_m^f, \boldsymbol{x}_{mt}^f)$, and a zero-mean stationary error w_{mt} governed by the mean-corrected ARMA model

$$w_{mt} = \sum_{i=1}^{p} \phi_{m.i} w_{t-i} + \sum_{j=1}^{q} \theta_{mm.j} u_{m,t-j} + u_{mt}, \qquad (27)$$

where $\phi_{m.i}$ is the mth row of $\phi_i = \alpha_i + \beta_i$, $w_{mt} = \ln \tilde{\epsilon}_{mt}^2 - E(\ln \tilde{\epsilon}_{mt}^2)$ and $\boldsymbol{w}_t = (w_{1t}, \dots, w_{Mt})'$. This means the mth equation can be estimated in three steps:

1   Estimate λ_{m0}^f and $\boldsymbol{\lambda}_m^f$ via the auxiliary regression

$$\ln \epsilon_{mt}^2 = \lambda_{m0}^f + \ln g_m(\boldsymbol{\lambda}_m^f, \boldsymbol{x}_{mt}^f) + w_{mt},$$

where λ_{m0}^f is the intercept and w_{mt} is a zero-mean stationary error-term governed by (27). If λ_m^f enters linearly in $\ln g_m$, then the parameters can simply be estimated by OLS.

2 Fit an ARMA model to the residuals $\hat{w}_{mt}$ from the first step. The relation between the parameters of the log-GARCH model and the parameters of the mean-corrected ARMA-representation are the same as in the case where the ARMA-representation is not mean-corrected, i.e., (22). So Step 2 provides an estimate of all the log-GARCH parameters apart from the intercept ω_m. An estimate of ω_m, however, is not needed if the aim is to estimate σ_{mt}^2. The reason for this is that the fitted values from the first two steps provide estimates of $E(\ln \tilde{\epsilon}_{mt}^2) + \ln g_{mt}$ and $E_{t-1}(w_{mt})$, respectively. Adding these gives

$$
\begin{aligned}
E(\ln \tilde{\epsilon}_{mt}^2) + \ln g_{mt} + E_{t-1}(w_{mt}) &= \ln g_{mt} + E_{t-1}(\ln \tilde{\epsilon}_{mt}^2) \\
&= \ln g_{mt} + \ln h_{mt} + E(\ln \eta_{mt}^2),
\end{aligned}
$$

since $\ln \tilde{\epsilon}_{mt}^2 = \ln h_{mt} + \ln \eta_{mt}^2$. So only an estimate of $E(\ln \eta_{mt}^2)$ is needed to complete the estimate of σ_{mt}^2.

3 Estimate the log-moment $E(\ln \eta_{mt}^2)$ to complete the estimate of σ_{mt}^2. Again, we can use the residuals from Step 2 in combination with (9).

Summarized, then, the estimate of σ_{mt}^2 is given by

$$
\hat{\sigma}_{mt}^2 = \exp\left(\underbrace{\hat{E}(\ln \tilde{\epsilon}_{mt}^2) + \ln \hat{g}_{mt}}_{\text{Step 1}} + \underbrace{\hat{E}_{t-1}(w_{mt})}_{\text{Step 2}} - \underbrace{\hat{E}(\ln \eta_{mt}^2)}_{\text{Step 3}} \right),
$$

where $\hat{E}(\ln \tilde{\epsilon}_{mt}^2) + \ln \hat{g}_{mt}$ is the fitted value of the auxiliary regression in Step 1, $\hat{E}_{t-1}(y_{mt})$ is the fitted value of the mean-corrected ARMA representation in Step 2, and $\hat{E}(\ln \eta_{mt}^2)$ is the estimate of $E(\ln \eta_{mt}^2)$ in Step 3. Note that the three-step procedure can in fact be reduced to two steps if the centered exponential Chi-squared QMLE of Francq and Sucarrat (2018) is used in the Step 2, since $E(\ln \eta_{mt}^2)$ enters explicitly as a parameter to be estimated in the centered exponential Chi-squared density. This will also be more efficient if η_{mt} is Gaussian or close to Gaussian.

An estimate of ω_m requires estimation of the other equations, in addition to equation m. This is because the expression for $E(\ln \tilde{\epsilon}_{mt}^2)$, which can be written as $E(\ln \tilde{\epsilon}_{mt}^2) = \omega_m^* + \sum_{i=1}^p \phi_{m.i} E(\ln \tilde{\epsilon}_t^2)$, depends on the unconditional expectations of the other equations. Recalling, from (22), that $\omega_m^* = \omega_m + (1 - \sum_{j=1}^q \beta_{mm.j}) E(\ln \eta_{mt}^2)$ when the GARCH-matrices are diagonal, solving for ω_m

in the expression for $E(\ln\tilde{\epsilon}_{mt}^2)$ gives

$$\omega_m = (1 - \sum_{j=1}^{q}\beta_{mm,j})E(\ln\tilde{\epsilon}_{mt}^2) - \sum_{i=1}^{p}\alpha_{m,i}E(\ln\tilde{\boldsymbol{\epsilon}}_t^2) - (1 - \sum_{j=1}^{q}\beta_{mm,j})E(\ln\eta_{mt}^2),$$

(28)

where we have used that $\sum_{i=1}^{p}\boldsymbol{\phi}_{m,i}E(\ln\tilde{\boldsymbol{\epsilon}}_t^2) = \sum_{i=1}^{p}\boldsymbol{\alpha}_{m,i}E(\ln\tilde{\boldsymbol{\epsilon}}_t^2) + \sum_{j=1}^{q}\beta_{mm,j}$ $E(\ln\tilde{\epsilon}_{mt}^2)$. It should be noted that only the elements in $E(\ln\tilde{\boldsymbol{\epsilon}}_t^2)$, apart from the mth entry, comes from the other equations. In other words, if there is no feedback effets (i.e., all entries in the $\boldsymbol{\alpha}_{m,i}$'s apart from the mth entry are zero), then there is no need to estimate the other equations in order to estimate ω_m.

Asymmetry terms and stochastic covariates ("X") can be added without affecting the estimation procedure just sketched. The only caveat is that they need to be mean corrected. Specifically, if $\boldsymbol{x}_{t-1}$ is a $(r + s) \times 1$ vector that collects all the asymmetry terms and conditioning covariates of the stationary part, then they need to enter as $(\boldsymbol{x}_{t-1} - \bar{\boldsymbol{x}})$ in the ARMA representation, where $\bar{\boldsymbol{x}} = (\bar{x}_1,\ldots,\bar{x}_M)'$ are the sample means of the stationary covariates. The stationary component is thus

$$\ln\boldsymbol{h}_t^2 = \boldsymbol{\omega} + \sum_{i=1}^{p}\boldsymbol{\alpha}_i\ln\tilde{\boldsymbol{\epsilon}}_{t-i}^2 + \sum_{j=1}^{q}\boldsymbol{\beta}_j\ln\boldsymbol{h}_{t-j}^2 + \boldsymbol{\delta}(\boldsymbol{x}_{t-1} - \bar{\boldsymbol{x}}),$$

where $\boldsymbol{\delta}$ is a parameter-matrix of appropriate size, and the mean-corrected ARMA representation of equation m is

$$w_{mt} = \sum_{i=1}^{p}\boldsymbol{\phi}_{m,i}\boldsymbol{w}_{t-i} + \sum_{j=1}^{q}\theta_{mm,j}u_{m,t-j} + \boldsymbol{\delta}_m(\boldsymbol{x}_{t-1} - \bar{\boldsymbol{x}}) + u_{mt},$$

(29)

where w_{mt}, $\boldsymbol{\phi}_{m,i}$, $\boldsymbol{w}_t$ and u_{mt} are defined as earlier, and $\boldsymbol{\delta}_m$ is the mth. row of $\boldsymbol{\delta}$. The practical consequence of this is that the three step estimation procedure described above only requires one minor modification: Estimate (29) instead of (27) in Step 2. The other steps are unchanged, and if an estimate of ω_m is needed, then formula (28) can still be used.

The asymptotic theory of non-stationary log-GARCH models has not been formally developed yet. Nevertheless, approximate inference procedures are readily available. For the stationary ARMA-representation a procedure similar to the one outlined in Section 2.4 can be used for inference within a single equation. The unknown is whether, or to what extent, this procedure is affected by the prior estimation of the non-stationary part. For inference that involves parameters from more than one equation, then an approximate joint coefficient covariance can be obtained along the lines of Francq and Sucarrat (2017). For inference regarding the parameters in the non-stationary part, then an approximate coefficient covariance can be computed by classical methods. For example, if the parameters of the non-stationary part in equation m are estimated by OLS, and if X_m denotes the $T \times k$ regressor matrix of the OLS estimator, then an approximate expression is obtained as

$$(X_m' X_m)^{-1} X_m' \hat{\Omega}_m X_m (X_m' X_m)^{-1},$$

where $\hat{\Omega}_m$ is an estimate of the autocovariance matrix of $w_{m1}, \ldots, w_{mT}$. The estimation results of the stationary part can be used to compute $\hat{\Omega}_m$. Indeed, if the stationary part is an ARMA, then this procedure is already available in a number of softwares.

3.4. Dynamic conditional correlations (DCCs)

Assumption (19) is compatible with certain types of DCCs when a multivariate log-GARCH is estimated equation-by-equation. The estimation procedures described above, however, do not provide estimates of the DCCs. Nevertheless, they can – if needed – be estimated in a subsequent step. The estimates $\hat{\sigma}_{1t}^2, \ldots, \hat{\sigma}_{Mt}^2$ lead to the standardized residuals $\hat{\eta}_t = (\hat{\eta}_{1t}, \ldots, \hat{\eta}_{Mt})'$, where $\hat{\eta}_{mt} = \epsilon_{mt}/\hat{\sigma}_{mt}$. These residuals can be used to estimate a DCC specification of $R_t = E(\eta_t \eta_t' | \mathcal{F}_{t-1})$. An example is the DCC of Engle (2002), or alternatively the corrected version of Aielli (2013), see, e.g., the empirical section of Francq and Sucarrat (2017). Other options include the robust (to spikes) DCC model proposed for electricity prices by Dupuis (2017), and the stochastic correlation model of Pelletier (2006).

4. Handling zeros in practice

Throughout we have relied on the theoretical assumption $Pr(\eta_t = 0) = 0$. In practice, however, if no conditional mean equation is fitted (i.e., we set $\mu_t = 0$ so that $y_t = \epsilon_t$ for all t), we may experience that $\epsilon_t = 0$ for some t. The most straightforward solution to this is to fit a specification μ_t, e.g., an intercept. This is not only justifiable in most contexts, it is also recommendable in order to ensure that the fitted values of ϵ_t are centered about zero.

A second solution consists of replacing zeros with some non-zero value c. One such value is a number very close to zero, say, the machine epsilon (e.g., $2.22e - 16$) of the software used. This is probably the worst possible choice! The reason for this is that $\ln c^2$ will usually be much smaller than any empirical non-zero value of $\ln \epsilon_t^2$. Accordingly, this will induce a large ARCH shock, an inlier, at each zero location. A more sensible solution is to set c equal to a value informed by the economic application in question. If there is no (obvious) economic motivation to inform the choice of c, then one may choose a certain quantile of the non-zero values of ϵ_t^2 (e.g., 10%), or the sample average of $\ln \epsilon_t^2$ (zeros excluded), or simply the value 1. The latter is very neat and justified in the log-GARCH(1,1) when the estimates of α_1 and β_1 are typical, i.e., about 0.05 and 0.9, respectively. Setting $c = 1$ thus means $\ln c^2 = 0$, so that all the weight (in predicting $\ln \sigma_t^2$) is shifted on to the GARCH term, i.e., $\ln \sigma_{t-1}^2$. If β_1 is large (e.g., about 0.9), then setting $c = 1$ is a very sensible solution.

A third solution consists of estimating the replacement value. This is the solution proposed by Sucarrat and Escribano (2018). Specifically, they propose to treat zeros as missing values, and to impute the missing values by the estimate of $E_{t-1}(\ln \epsilon_t^2)$ at each missing location. This means an optimal replacement value is inserted at each missing location in the ARMA representation, where "optimal" means the conditional (squared) forecast error is minimized, and/or that the likelihood is maximized. Arguably, treating zeros as missing values is the most appealing solution if no conditional mean is fitted. However, implementing the solution usually requires more of the user, and consistent parameter estimates are not guaranteed – in particular if the proportion of zeros is large. The freely available *R* package lgarch (Sucarrat 2015) implements the missing value approach.

A fourth solution consists of adding a non-zero value c to *all* the squared observations $\epsilon_1^2, \ldots, \epsilon_T^2$. This leads to a new series $\{\epsilon_t^{*2}\}$ with $\epsilon_t^{*2} = \epsilon_t^2 + c$ and $\epsilon_t^* = \sigma_t^* \eta_t^*$, such that σ_t^{*2} is approximately equal to $\sigma_t^2 + c$. In other words, approximate forecasts of σ_t^2 can be obtained by using the estimates of σ_t^{*2}, and noting that $\sigma_t^2 \approx \sigma_t^{*2} - c$. If the values of ϵ_t^2 are sufficiently large compared with c, then adding c will not alter the dynamics of ϵ_t^2 in a notable manner. An example is the case where ϵ_t^2 is the traded volume of a financial asset, i.e., a positively valued variable (see Section 5). In this case ϵ_t^2 will usually be much larger than, say, $c = 1$.

5. Modeling positively valued variables

Engle and Russell (1998) noted that ϵ_t^2 could be interpreted as positively valued variable, and hence showed that σ_t^2 can be interpreted as the conditional expectation of the positively valued variable. Put differently, Engle and Russell (1998) showed that the ARCH-class of models can be used to model positively valued variables like duration, volume, price-spread, realized volatility, and so on. This spurred the Multiplicative Error Model (MEM) literature, see Brownlees et al. (2012) for an overview. A particularly useful characteristic of the MEM interpretation is that, in practice, an ARCH estimation routine can be used to estimate a MEM. For example, suppose y_t denotes the positively valued variable in question. By providing the software in question with $\sqrt{y_t}$, then the software will return estimates of the MEM.

Formally, the MEM class is given by

$$y_t = \psi_t \zeta_t, \qquad \zeta_t \sim iid(1, \sigma_\zeta^2), \qquad \psi_t, \sigma_\zeta^2 > 0, \qquad \zeta_t \geq 0,$$

where $\psi_t = E_{t-1}(y_t)$ is interpreted as the expectation of y_t conditional on past information. In other words, the relationships between the ARCH and MEM interpretations are given by $\psi_t = \sigma_t^2$ and $\zeta_t = \eta_t^2$, respectively. Bauwens and

Giot (2000) were the first to propose a logarithmic version of the MEM, i.e., a log-MEM. They noted that the MEM interpretation associated with ordinary GARCH models was restricted by the non-negativity constraints on the parameters, and by the non-negativity constraints on the conditioning variables. Instead, they proposed a first order log-MEM with a single (stochastic) conditioning covariate. More generally, however, the univariate log-MEM(p, q) with stochastic conditioning variables can be written as

$$\ln \psi_t = \omega + \sum_{i=1}^{p} \alpha_i \ln y_{t-i} + \sum_{j=1}^{q} \beta_j \ln \psi_{t-j} + \sum_{l=1}^{s} \lambda_l x_{l,t-1}.$$

That is, a univariate log-GARCH-X without asymmetry (ordinary and extended asymmetry terms are not meaningful in MEMs). If $Pr(\zeta_t = 0) = 0$ and $E|\ln \zeta_t| < \infty$, then the model admits – as earlier—an ARMA representation almost surely given by

$$\ln y_t = \omega^* + \sum_{i=1}^{p} \phi_i \ln y_{t-i} + \sum_{j=1}^{q} \theta_j u_{t-j} + \sum_{l=1}^{s} \lambda_l x_{l,t-1} + u_t,$$

and the relations between the log-MEM and ARMA parameters are exactly the same as before, i.e., they are given by (22). The existence of an ARMA representation of the log-MEM was, to the best of my knowledge, first pointed out by Allen et al. (2008). Similarly, the model can be extended to the multivariate case as in Section 3, and non-stationarities can be introduced in the same way as in Section 3.3. Finally, fractionally integrated extensions of the log-MEM are considered in Beran et al. (2015), and in Feng and Zhou (2015).

6. Conclusions

The log-GARCH model provides a very flexible framework for the modeling of economic uncertainty, financial volatility, and a range of other positively valued variables. In this chapter we have outlined how univariate and multivariate log-GARCH models can be represented by (V)ARMA-like representations, and – as a consequence – how well-known (V)ARMA results can be used to estimate univariate and multivariate log-GARCH models. Nevertheless, there is still a large, unexploited potential. There exists a wide range of well-known results on time-varying coefficients, non-stationarities, missing data, and efficient estimation, among others, that can potentially be used to shed light on and further extend the log-GARCH class of models via its (V)ARMA-like representations.

Acknowledgment

I am grateful to Bilel Sanhaji, a reviewer, and Hamdi Raissi for useful comments, suggestions, and questions. All errors are mine.

Notes

1 Estimation in R (R Core Team 2018). The GARCH model is estimated with the garch function from the tseries package of Trapletti and Hornik (2016). The log-GARCH model is estimated via its ARMA representation with the lgarch function from the lgarch package of Sucarrat (2015).
2 For example, if a and b are two equally sized $M \times 1$ vectors, say, $a = (a_1, ..., a_M)'$ and $b = (b_1, ..., b_M)'$, then $a \odot b = (a_1 b_1, ..., a_M b_M)'$.

Bibliography

Aielli, G. P. (2013). Dynamic conditional correlations: On properties and estimation. *Journal of Business and Economic Statistics 31*, 282–299. http://dx.doi. org/10.1080/07350015.2013.771027.

Allen, D., F. Chan, M. McAleer, and S. Peiris (2008). Finite sample properties of the QMLE for the log-ACD model: Application to australian stocks. *Journal of Econometrics 147*, 163–185.

Amado, C. and T. Terasvirta (2014a). Modelling changes in the unconditional variance of long stock return series. *Journal of Empirical Finance 25*, 15–35.

Amado, C. and T. Terasvirta (2014b). Modelling volatility by variance decomposition. *Journal of Econometrics 175*, 142–153.

Asai, M. (1998). A new method to estimate stochastic volatility models: A log-GARCH approach. *Journal of the Japanese Statistical Society 28*, 101–114.

Bauwens, L., and P. Giot (2000). The logarithmic ACD model: An application to the bid-ask quote process of three NYSE stocks. *Annales d'Economie et de Statistique 60*, 117–149.

Beran, J., Y. Feng, and S. Gosh (2015). Modelling long-range dependence and trends in duration series: An approach based on EFARIMA and ESEMIFAR models. *Statistical Papers 56*, 431–451.

Bollerslev, T. (1986). Generalized autoregressive conditional heteroscedasticity. *Journal of Econometrics 31*, 307–327.

Brockwell, P. J., and R. A. Davis (2006). *Time Series: Theory and Methods*. New York: Springer. 2nd. Edition, first published in 1991.

Brownlees, C., F. Cipollini, and G. Gallo (2012). Multiplicative error models. In L. Bauwens, C. Hafner, and S. Laurent (Eds.), *Handbook of Volatility Models and Their Applications*, pp. 223–247. NJ: Wiley.

Carnero, M. A., D. Pena, and E. Ruiz (2007). Effects of outliers on the identification and estimation of GARCH models. *Journal of Time Series Analysis 28*, 471–497.

Duan, N. (1983). Smearing estimate: A nonparametric retransformation method. *Journal of the American Statistical Association 78*, 605–610.

Dupuis, D. J. (2017). Electricity price dependence in new york state zones: A robust detrended correlation approach. *Annals of Applied Statistics 11*, 248–273.

Engle, R. (1982). Autoregressive conditional heteroscedasticity with estimates of the variance of United Kingdom inflations. *Econometrica 50*, 987–1008.

Engle, R. (2002). Dynamic conditional correlation: A simple class of multivariate generalized autoregressive conditional heteroskedasticity models. *Journal of Business and Economic Statistics 20*, 339–350.

Engle, R. F., and J. G. Rangel (2008). The spline GARCH model for low frequency volatility and its global macroeconomic causes. *Review of Financial Studies 21*, 1187–1222.

Engle, R. F., and J. R. Russell (1998). Autoregressive conditional duration: A new model of irregularly spaced transaction data. *Econometrica 66*, 1127–1162.

Escribano, Á., and G. Sucarrat (2018). Equation-by-equation estimation of multivariate periodic electricity price volatility. *Energy Economics 74*, pp. 287–298. DOI: http://doi.org/10.1016/j.eneco.2018.05.017

Feng, Y., and C. Zhou (2015). Forecasting financial market activity using a semiparametric fractionally integrated Log-ACD. *International Journal of Forecasting 31*, 349–363.

Francq, C., and G. Sucarrat (2017). An Equation-by-equation estimator of a multivariate Log-GARCH-X model of financial returns. *Journal of Multivariate Analysis 153*, 16–32.

Francq, C., and G. Sucarrat (2018). An exponential Chi-Squared QMLE for Log-GARCH models via the ARMA representation. *Journal of Financial Econometrics 16*, 129–154. Working Paper Version. http://mpra.ub.uni-muenchen.de/51783/.

Francq, C., and L. Q. Thieu (2018). Qml inference for volatility models with covariates. *Econometric Theory.* https://doi.org/10.1017/S0266466617000512.

Francq, C., O. Wintenberger, and J.-M. Zakoïan (2013). GARCH models without positivity constraints: Exponential or Log-GARCH? *Journal of Econometrics 177*, 34–36.

Francq, C., O. Wintenberger, and J.-M. Zakoïan (2017). Goodness-of-fit tests for log and exponential GARCH models. *TEST.* http://dx.doi.org/10.1007/s11749-016-0506-2.

Francq, C., and J.-M. Zakoïan (2016). Estimating multivariate volatility models equation by equation. *The Journal of the Royal Statistical Society: Series B 78*, 613–635. Working Paper Version. MPRA Paper No. 54250. http://mpra.ub.uni-muenchen.de/54250/.

Geweke, J. (1986). Modelling the persistence of conditional variance: A comment. *Econometric Reviews 5*, 57–61.

Glosten, L. R., R. Jagannathan, and D. E. Runkle (1993). On the relation between the expected value and the volatility of the nominal excess return on stocks. *Journal of Finance 48*, 1779–1801.

Hafner, C., and O. Linton (2010). Efficient estimation of a multivariate multiplicative volatility model. *Journal of Econometrics 159*, 55–73.

Harvey, A. C., and G. Sucarrat (2014). EGARCH models with fat tails, skewness and leverage. *Computational Statistics and Data Analysis 76*, 320–338.

Ljung, G., and G. Box (1979). On a measure of lack of fit in time series models. *Biometrika 66*, 265–270.

Mazur, B., and M. Pipien (2012). On the empirical importance of periodicity in the volatility of financial returns: Time varying GARCH as a second order APC(2) Process. *Central European Journal of Economic Modelling and Econometrics 4*, 95–116.

Milhøj, A. (1987). *A Multiplicative Parametrization of ARCH Models*. Research Report 101. University of Copenhagen: Institute of Statistics.

Nelson, D. B. (1991). Conditional heteroskedasticity in asset returns: A new approach. *Econometrica 59*, 347–370.

Pantula, S. (1986). Modelling the persistence of conditional variance: A comment. *Econometric Reviews 5*, 71–73.

Park, R. (1966). Estimation with heteroscedastic error terms. *Econometrica 34*, 888–888.

Pelletier, D. (2006). Regime switching for dynamic correlations. *Journal of Econometrics 131*, 445–473.

Pretis, F., J. Reade, and G. Sucarrat (2018). Automated General-to-Specific (GETS) Regression modeling and indicator saturation for outliers and structural breaks. *Journal of Statistical Software 86*, 1–44.

Psaradakis, Z., and E. Tzavalis (1999). On regression-based tests for persistence in logarithmic volatility models. *Econometric Reviews 18*, 441–448.

R Core Team (2018). *R: A Language and Environment for Statistical Computing*. Vienna, Austria: R Foundation for Statistical Computing.

Sucarrat, G. (2015). *lgarch: Simulation and Estimation of Log-GARCH Models*. R package version 0.6-2.

Sucarrat, G. and Á. Escribano (2018). Estimation of Log-GARCH Models in the Presence of Zero Returns. *European Journal of Finance 24*, 809–827. http://dx.doi.org/10.1080/1351847X.2017.1336452.

Sucarrat, G., S. Grønneberg, and Á. Escribano (2016). Estimation and Inference in Univariate and Multivariate Log-GARCH-X Models When the Conditional Density is Unknown. *Computational Statistics and Data Analysis 100*, 582–594.

Trapletti, A. and K. Hornik (2016). *Tseries: Time Series Analysis and Computational Finance*. R package version 0.10-35.

Van Bellegem, S., and R. Von Sachs (2004). Forecasting economic time-series with unconditional time-varying variance. *International Journal of Forecasting 20*, 611–627.

Index

Note: numbers in italic indicate figures and numbers in bold indicate tables on the corresponding page.

For Product Safety Concerns and Information please contact our EU
representative GPSR@taylorandfrancis.com
Taylor & Francis Verlag GmbH, Kaufingerstraße 24, 80331 München, Germany

www.ingramcontent.com/pod-product-compliance
Ingram Content Group UK Ltd.
Pitfield, Milton Keynes, MK11 3LW, UK
UKHW021021180425
457613UK00020B/1013